THE OTHER
DIMENSION

THE OTHER DIMENSION

A Search for the Meaning
of Religious Attitudes

LOUIS DUPRÉ

Doubleday & Company, Inc., Garden City, New York   1972

Contents

THE OTHER
DIMENSION

Introduction

What is faith to religious man? This is the question which the present study attempts to answer. It was conceived some years ago when its author became deeply concerned over the principle, apparently accepted by most religious people, that faith must be *the* meaning-giving factor of human existence. Such a claim, it seemed to him, could not be upheld without seriously distorting the orientation of life as we experience it today. Modern life has many facets which develop autonomously. It was no longer obvious what religious faith could contribute to this development. To believe in God does not enhance one's scientific integrity, sharpen one's business sense, or heighten one's perception of reality, contrary to what we often hear on Sunday morning radio programs. Yet it is equally obvious that religion cannot survive as a *particular* aspect of life. The moment it ceases to transform all of existence, it withers away and becomes, as we now say, irrelevant. I saw no way out of this dilemma and, since I considered religious faith in some obscure way important, it became increasingly hard for me to accept it or reject it. Was faith *everything* or merely *something* to religious man? If it was everything it seemed totally incompatible with the modern world view. Gradually it dawned upon me that the answer to that question was perhaps no longer what it used to be. Religion itself had shifted its function and emphasis.

This realization forced me to revise my original concept.

Religion was a much more flexible thing than I had recognized. It constantly changes faces and shifts ground. It does not consist in the mere acceptance of a given reality determined as sacred, and even less in a purely subjective state of consciousness.[1] Eventually I came to regard it as a complex dialectical relation of the mind to reality. I call it dialectical because it is both active and passive, but primarily because it continues to negate its acquired positions. In the process it opens up a new dimension in human existence. But it is never an *a priori* definable reality. To test this new insight on all the major aspects of religion was the single purpose of this book.

The reader will be disenchanted if on the basis of this somewhat relativist definition he expects another "radical" book on religion. The task of the philosopher is to understand *what is,* not to instruct about *what ought to be* or to predict *what will be.* He may understand it in a new way but his understanding should not produce a new thing. This is particularly true in a field which by its very nature excludes creative competence on the part of the philosopher. A general reflection upon the real such as he is used to making in metaphysics or ontology may lead to a transcendent horizon, but it does not penetrate into the transcendent reality itself. Religion, on the other hand, appears to have access to this reality both in an active and passive way. The philosopher, then, must be satisfied with critical reflection upon a religious *given* which he should primordially try to understand. Yet his understanding is by no means docile, for he retains the full autonomous right to reject what is logically incoherent or what conflicts in any way with established principles of his science. Obviously, this is not the method which most philosophically inclined writers have followed in the past two centuries. As a rule they present their subject as if they had invented it, decreeing what ought to be said and done to make religion conform to their ideal. Religious man has followed those various, often elaborate constructions with a mixture

[1] In the second chapter we shall have occasion to criticize some of those purely objective or subjective concepts of religion.

of utter amazement and benevolent skepticism. They have seldom disturbed his thought or changed his conduct. After he closes the book he goes about his business in the usual unphilosophical way—intellectually enriched but religiously unreformed. Basically he is right. Philosophical reflection upon religion must never become a substitute for faith—or even for theology. Only epochs which no longer believe in the true greatness of theology, Heidegger writes, arrive at the disastrous notion that philosophy can help to provide a refurbished theology which will satisfy the taste of the time.[2] I therefore hope to resist the temptation of building my own religious construction at the roadside or to preach reforms which will never be implemented. In this book I am only the critic, not the actor. Religious man is the sole virtuoso on the stage. In that sense my work is basically a conservative enterprise from which no pastor will learn how to radicalize his sermons. At the same time I consider it my privilege to interpret religious phenomena until they make some sense to me and, if they refuse to do so, to reject them as ill conceived. Without critical independence serious reflection becomes impossible.

From the preceding remarks it already appears that few predictions will be made about the "religion of the future." The author prefers not to follow the prophetic trend of most current books and articles on religion. Indeed, he confesses himself to be almost totally devoid of well-founded opinions on the future of religion and his ignorance has increased as he has become more aware of the complexity of the matter. Those interested in the future will have no difficulty finding the predictions which best suit their own inclinations. Religious publishers have in this respect amply served the public over the last years. Unfortunately, they have not always realized that the high tolerance of religious readers is directly proportionate to their low interest level. If the latter goes up, the former goes down. This explains

[2] *Einführung in die Metaphysik,* Tübingen, 1958, p. 5. *An Introduction to Metaphysics,* tr. by Ralph Manheim (Garden City, N.Y.: Doubleday, 1961) p. 6.

perhaps why the great religious publishing tide is now being swept back into nonexistence. To those who want to study religion *as it is*, this reversal ought to be a source of comfort: I can think of no single act that would be more beneficial to the understanding of religious phenomena than to withdraw most religious publications of recent years. My judgment on futuristic literature by no means implies that things will not change over the coming years. I also expect most of the conceptual and institutional framework to be drastically altered. For religious concepts and institutions so obviously need to be overhauled that few people still accept them unreservedly. Yet such shifts follow from the moving nature of religion itself. The basic attitude and vision remain remarkably identical. In writing this I am not forecasting the future but merely interpreting the past and the present. Since conceptual constructions are usually interpretive of religion rather than foundational, the philosopher can be unrestrainedly critical of them while adopting a respectful attitude toward the underlying symbols and attitudes. Only in that way can the philosopher contribute to free the permanent core of religion from the shell which it has cast off. The very turmoil of the present has made us aware that there is considerably more shell than even students of religion had believed.

A great deal has been written about the secularization of our own age. I am not in a position to define the extent of this phenomenon, but it obviously is a fundamental factor in the changes of the present. Yet two current interpretations of this factor are based upon misunderstandings. One is that religious symbols also should be given a secular interpretation and translated into moral commitments. To say this is to misread the meaning of religion altogether. For a moral commitment needs no religious dimension. Perhaps the most morally committed man I ever knew was a judge who had no need for transcendence and saw no purpose in religious attitudes. A number of well-intentioned people nowadays believe that the sagging cause of religion can be lifted up only by giving social interpretations to religious messages. Faith has everything to lose

and society nothing to gain by such a change. For I do not
see how religious considerations can do anything to social planning
but muddle the issue, *unless* they express a transcendent dimension beyond social issues. A second error would be to interpret
the increased autonomy of the secular as the end of religious
concerns. That religious institutions, practices, ideas of the past
are deeply in trouble is obvious. That the religious dimension
itself has ceased to hold man's interest is false.

Revolutionary change seems a driving factor in all developments of human culture—also in religion. At certain points the
old gods die and new ones appear. After the cults of the mother
in Greece arose the religion of the Olympian gods; after the
Olympian mythology broke down, monotheism entered. All signs
indicate that once again we are passing through a revolution.
Traditional monotheistic interpretations seem to have become inadequate. But that does not mean that the faiths which adopted
them are on their way out, much less that religion itself is
vanishing. Concepts in religion are essential but they remain
subordinate to the basic intentionality of a faith: if the intentionality loses its appeal, the religion itself dies. As for religious
concern in general, I doubt whether it has been more alive at
any time since the sixteenth century. A weekly news magazine,
in a recent issue on religious developments in America today,
concluded (correctly in my opinion) that the most significant
trend of the '70s may well be a religious revival.[3] As the achievements of nuclear physics, biochemistry, and cybernetics marked
previous decades, religious developments have already started
to shape the present age. Times of religious awakening and
upheaval tend to be times of social and cultural unrest. The
Hellenistic epoch, the end of the Roman Empire, the culmination of the barbaric age in the seventh century, the break-through
of the cities in the thirteenth century, the epoch of the Reformation, all were periods of crisis and, at the same time, of intense
religious life.

In the past this was no mere coincidence, for religion was

[3] *Time,* December 19, 1969, p. 23.

the cement of society. Quite naturally, religious reforms followed or set off cultural and social changes. But the presence
of religious factors in today's crisis must be explained in a
different way. For in the West religion has ceased to be the
binding force of our culture. After a prolonged conflict between
a culture emancipating itself toward full autonomy and religious
institutions refusing to loosen their grip on it, society ended up
banning religion from its public life altogether. This tension, I
suppose, was inevitable in the development of Western history.
Yet now we find ourselves with a different problem. Our society
is growing increasingly uncomfortable within the pragmatic world-
oriented culture to which it has committed itself so wholeheartedly.
Its members feel that depth and quality have been sacrificed
to technical achievement and material abundance. The utopia
of a scientific paradise which kept our hopes glowing has abruptly
vanished after the brilliant technical performances of the last
world war: the scientific liquidation of people in concentration
camps, the total destruction of atomic explosions, the unbridled
exploitation of the human environment. Once more men feel
that a culture cannot be truly human without another dimension.
We crave for a number of things which are missing in our
world. Religion, at least in the most primitive sense of the term,
seems to occupy a central place in those desires. Once more
the search for the mystical experience, the retreat to the desert,
the communal sharing of earthly possessions in Arcadian simplicity, have become respectable and even fashionable. Even
the strange urge toward primitivism, the cult of nudity, and the
desire to overcome sexual differentiation in dress and in orgies
express a need for union which has its hidden springs in the
religious drive. To be sure, the established religious institutions
are not likely to reap much profit from these irrational tendencies.
Nor will their fulfillment solve our social problems, relax our
racial tensions, rehumanize our cities. The romantic confidence
of the new prophets as well as the enthusiastic hopes with which
believers of the old faith welcome their arrival are a source of
profound amazement to me.

Yet one thing the new trend does reveal: man is not ready to forego the dimension of reality which religious faith opened up in the past. His inadequacy in coping with it plays a large part in his present feeling of alienation. A correct understanding of the meaning of the religious attitude, then, would seem to be an essential requirement for solving our cultural crisis. This conclusion made me decide to direct my study to the intellectual community at large rather than to a few specialists in the field of philosophy. Religion has become too important a matter to be left to theologians or philosophers. I therefore avoided as much as possible technical language and esoteric discussions. To some readers the discussion of Chapter 3, which deals with the problems of philosophical methodology in the study of religion, may still appear abstruse. It may be bypassed without interrupting the argument. Yet it contains the justification of the method followed in this study.

The problem of method is so important that something must be said about it in this introduction. Since philosophy in the final analysis is and has always been the ultimate reflection upon experience, it receives its subject matter from nonphilosophical sources. In the study of religion, as in most other cases, the philosopher's private experience is obviously insufficient. The philosopher of religion must therefore depend upon other disciplines such as theology, anthropology, and the positive science of religion, in order to enlarge his field of experience. On the other hand, since philosophy attempts to be the ultimate reflection, it can invoke no higher court of appeal, no other science to justify its principles: it must take care of itself, which is to say that it must be autonomous and can accept no extrinsic authority over its conclusions. As a result, theological statements used in a philosophical context change their meaning rather basically. The theologian reflects *within* his faith: he does not question his basic commitment. The philosopher, on the contrary, uses everything but takes nothing for granted. His professional commitment extends no further than his own conclusions. Such an attitude may result in un-

expected consequences. For instance, since one of my own conclusions is that philosophy cannot independently (that is, by
mere reflection upon the real as such, according to its own
method) arrive at the existence of God, this study can never
accept that existence as an established fact. It can only reflect
upon the *religious assertion* of this existence. The philosopher
may independently discover the transcendent horizon of reality,
but of the content of this horizon he knows nothing. My study,
then, can never lend support to religious assertions by supplying
them with a philosophical foundation. Beyond establishing the
possibility of meaningful religious assertions, the philosopher can
give no assistance. This means that all that follows can be read
on two levels: as a critical analysis of certain attitudes, feelings,
and concepts of man's relation to reality, or as an analysis of
a mutual relation established between man and a transcendent,
self-revealing reality. Even the concept of revelation, to which
an entire chapter is devoted, does not necessarily imply the
existence of a "supernatural" reality: it refers to religious man's
passive way of *experiencing* the transcendent. What causes the
passivity falls beyond the philosopher's competence. If adequately
performed, the analysis must appear as true to the believer as
to the unbeliever.

Of course, this does not mean that the author can be on
both sides of the fence at once. A careful reflection requires
that at one time or other, the philosopher has been personally
exposed to the experience upon which he reflects. Since this
experience is always limited, the reflection upon it tends to be
somewhat one-sided. Thus as a Christian I have no firsthand
knowledge of the other great religious traditions. This is true
even for Judaism, however much I have always felt it to be
part of my own spiritual patrimony; it is particularly true for
the Islam, and the various forms of Hinduism and Buddhism.
In spite of a long-standing interest I can claim no particular
expertise in those faiths.

My philosophical limitations will reveal themselves in the
process of this work. Having been exposed first to a critical,

Kantian-style philosophy, I gradually came more and more under the influence of Hegel and his unorthodox followers, Kierkegaard, Feuerbach, Marx, and Engels. Since all these thinkers can in some way be called "dialectical," and since I published studies on three of them, the reader may suspect my own dialectical theory of religion to be preconceived rather than discovered. Although the suspicion is without substance, there is little I can do to dispel it. Yet I welcome this opportunity to define my position with regard to dialectical philosophy. Kierkegaard's dialectical view of Christian existence undoubtedly had a direct impact upon my own thinking. Yet what for him was characteristic of the Christian faith, became for me, although in a different way, the hallmark of the religious attitude as such. Marx and Engels have primarily been negative stimuli. However much one may sympathize with their vision of man, their theories of religion are so obviously deficient that the student of religion automatically suspects any assertion they make on the subject. For Hegel the case is more complex. Although I had been a student of his philosophy for a long time, I could not bring myself to take seriously a definition of religion according to which philosophy must "go beyond" religion even while continuing to need it for its inspiration. It has always seemed to me that no religious person will ever accept that the best way of dealing with religion is to *understand* it so well that one can stop believing its message and practicing its precepts. Furthermore, I suspected that the dialectical nature of religion in Hegel's philosophy had its origin in the assumption that everything of the mind must be dialectical. At best, I thought, I would not gather much specific information from such a general principle. On this last point I changed my mind, but my conversion to a dialectical view of religion occurred entirely under the impact of positive and phenomenological studies, most notably the work of Mircea Eliade, not under the influence of Hegel. Indeed, it now seems to me that the dialectical nature of the religious vision is at the origin of dialectical philosophy, which, in Hegel's case, was conceived under the direct influence of the Christian religion. Hegelian philosophy is dialectical *because Christianity was*—not the other way round. At any rate, my conclusions on the dialectical nature of religion returned me to Hegel, particularly to his theory on religious negativity. But I have never been able to overcome my initial objections to his view of the relation between philosophy and religion and therefore continue to reject what is perhaps his most basic principle.

Finally, a word about the self-imposed limitations of this work. Despite its length it claims to be no more than an introduction. It maps out an area of studies, plants a few borderstones and warns the traveler about some dead-end streets. Above all it attempts to establish what is permanent and what is transitory in the religious phenomenon. But by no means can the author claim that he has fully explored the terrain. Over the next years he hopes to venture into some of the passages discovered along the way. Yet a comprehensive survey of the entire domain, with its major hills and valleys, was most urgently needed. For the main problem in the exploration of the religious phenomenon has been that we do not know where to locate it in the entirety of human experience. Neither theology nor philosophy are lacking in brilliant analyses. But they often fail to achieve their effect upon today's reader because he is unable to assign their subjects a place in existence.

To situate religious faith and its essential aspects in human life has been the main objective of this study. Its basic message may be summarized in a few phrases. The religious act is not a simple experience, but a complex movement by which the mind discovers a new reality which, although lying beyond the phenomenal and contrasting with it, ultimately integrates all reality in a higher synthesis. This other dimension of consciousness is the same today as it was in the past. Yet on the whole the sacred is no longer directly experienced. Modern man has access to it in the more reflective and deliberate attitude of faith. Yet, in faith, however unemotional, he achieves the same all-comprehensive unity. Any attempt to reduce the religious phenomenon to a purely subjective experience or a scientifically analyzable "object" is as misdirected in the present as it was in the past. It is essential to the religious experience to overcome the opposition between subject and object. The religious symbol and its mythical explication bring this subjective-objective unity to expression. To understand the distinct nature of this expression is necessary if one is to attain any insight into the uniquely religious category of revelation. Revelation is neither objective information nor subjective expression: its symbols unveil the transcendent dimension in which the real reaches its unification. Only after having fully understood the nature of religious expression and the concept of revelation can one attack the problem of God. For the concept of God originates exclusively in, and is developed solely by, the religious act. It never is a philosophical discovery and no philosophical argument can prove it to be true or false. Yet philosophy provides this key religious concept with a logical structure enabling it to justify the central position which faith claims for it. No past philosophy of God is entirely satisfactory, for none does justice to the religious intuition at its origin. The traditional theist position may be less deficient than the atheist and the pantheist ones. But it is too one-sided and polemical to support fully the religious idea of God.

This brings us to the final part of the study—the concrete development of the religious dialectic as it is presented to the believer in three fundamental themes: the dependence upon an *absolute reality* (in the Western tradition symbolized in the notion of creation), the *estrangement* of all that is not yet accepted in this reality (in Christianity and Judaism mainly represented in the concept of sinfulness), and the *integration* with the absolute and, through it, with all other beings (almost universally proposed as salvation). Salvation is symbolized on several levels: in the sacred community, in the development of history, in the moral conversion, in the mystical union, and, at least in some faiths, in the beatific vision of an afterlife. The sacred community and the afterlife will not be discussed in this work, for the simple reason that at the present I feel unable to treat them adequately. I intend to return to them in future publications.

A study of this nature is likely to draw a good amount of justified criticism. Its span is so wide that inaccuracies both of fact and of interpretation are almost inevitable. To eliminate this possibility entirely and to achieve completeness in all essential matters would have required another decade of work. But, *vita brevis.* So I decided that I would rather spend my remaining years filling the gaps and correcting possible errors in future writings than continuing work on a book that might no longer be needed when and if it would ever be ready. Faced with a choice between immaturity and senility I opted for the former, remembering a venerable rabbinic saying: If not now, then when? In lieu of an apology I shall only say with the great Professor Huizinga: "I had to write now, or not at all. And I wanted to write." Let the reader judge for himself whether my decision was presumptuous.

The usual words of thanks are omitted from this introduction, for I am heavily indebted to too many persons. I must mention the American Council of Learned Societies for awarding me a fellowship and Georgetown University for a summer grant. To all the others I can orally express my feelings of gratitude. Yet I cannot close without thanking those great masters of the past who during the years of preparation of this study were my principal instructors and constant companions. Through their works they spoke to me. I could never speak to them. Now at least I am able to recognize my debt publicly. Hoping that I did not betray the ideas of their silent conversation, I want this long meditation on their words to appear under the motto of my Flemish countryman, the painter Jan Van Eyck: *Als ich can,* which, roughly translated, means: I did the best I could.

Chapter 1
Religious Experience Past and Present

1. THE DIALECTIC OF THE SACRED

Any object or event can become sacred to religious man. This first, striking characteristic excludes pure objectivity. Objects and events are *constituted* as sacred symbols by a religious attitude. Independently of this attitude nothing is either sacred or profane. As Mircea Eliade once pointed out, we must get used to the idea of finding the sacred in every area of life. "Indeed, we cannot be sure that there is *anything*—object, movement, psychological function, being or even game—that has not at some-time in human history been somewhat transformed into a hierophany."[1] Yet, to conclude therefrom that religion is a subjective experience, as was customary in the nineteenth century, is unwarranted. For the religious attitude is always directed beyond the self. Religious man does not create his "object"; it is revealed to him in a disposition to perceive a deeper reality under the appearance of objects and events. Rudolf Otto would say that he "divines" it. What does he see? An overwhelming depth of being, a reality of such ontic richness that only the most comprehensive concepts approximate it. Van der Leeuw defined it

[1] *Patterns in Comparative Religion,* tr. by Rosemary Sheed (New York: Sheed & Ward, 1958), p. 11.

as power that possesses form and will.[2] But power and will are not ultimates, for they are religious only to the extent that they reveal a deeper form of *being.* Whatever *is* supremely possesses *mana:* it is dynamic and creative because it is transcendently *real.*[3] Religious man discovers an "ultimate reality," an absolute in which all things are founded[4] and on which even the self depends in its being.[5] Yet the distinction between absolute and relative being is not *per se* religious: it also appears in nonreligious metaphysical speculation. A further specification is needed.

The religious perception of absolute reality is unique only insofar as it is *symbolical* and *dialectical.* Sacred reality is grasped directly *in* the appearance of relative being—not as the conclusion of a logical process. The absolute shines directly through the relative. Yet the two never coincide as in the aesthetic intuition.[6] If idolatry implies a *total* identity of image and divinity, it has never existed, for even the most primitive religious perception experiences its symbols as inadequate. We therefore may add to our initial statement that every object is potentially religious, the negative counterpart that no object is sacred *in itself.*[7]

---

[2] He thereby synthesized the early animist and dynamist theories by transforming successive stages into permanent structures of the sacred. "Animism and dynamism designate not areas, but structures and are as such eternal." *Religion in Essence and Manifestation* (New York: Harper & Row, 1963), p. 88.

[3] "The *real* in archaic ontology is primarily identified with a 'force,' a 'life,' a fertility, an abundance, but also with what is strange or singular—in other words with everything that exists most fully or displays an exceptional mode of existence. Sacredness is above all *real.*" Mircea Eliade, *Patterns in Comparative Religon,* p. 459.

[4] Mircea Eliade, "Methodological Remarks on the Study of Religious Symbolism" in *The History of Religions,* ed. by Mircea Eliade and Joseph M. Kitagawa (Chicago: University of Chicago Press, 1959), p. 88.

[5] "This unconditional self-inclusion in the sphere of relative being—to the last jot of selfhood—is the foremost characteristic in the religious conception of this first attribute of divinity." Max Scheler, *The Eternal in Man* (New York: Harper & Brothers, 1960), p. 163.

[6] On the distinction between religious and aesthetic symbolism, see Louis Dupré, "Toward a Revaluation of Schleiermacher's Philosophy of Religion" in *The Journal of Religion* XLIV (1964), pp. 109–11.

[7] Eliade shows how this ambiguity adheres to even the most primitive

What singles out the sacred is the absolute appearing *through* the finite object. Scheler aptly compares the relation between the sacred and its symbol to a window that becomes conspicuous in the row only when someone looks out of it: not the window but what appears through it is different.[8]

The religious attitude is *dialectical* insofar as it is a relation (and therefore an opposition) to a transcendent term. Sacred reality can maintain itself only by means of an opposition to nonsacred, profane reality. Religion presents not just reality but *different* reality. The segregational aspect of the sacred appears over the entire range of its existence: in primitive taboos and Hindu asceticism, in Israel's wandering in the desert and in the Christian monk's retreat to the monastery. The sacred is separated from the ordinary: it manifests itself first as that which is forbidden to ordinary usage. Thus in the view of archaic man the criminal is sacred: he is set apart from other people until he is punished or absolved and thereby becomes *desecrated*. So is a woman after childbirth: she must formally be restored to the ordinary world. In Israel the segregation consisted in a divine election by which the entire people attained a sacred status. "You must be holy to me; for I the Lord am holy and have separated you from other peoples to be mine." (Lev. 20:26) Among Christians the same idea appears in a different form: they are separated from others not by race but by individual election and baptism. In the Fourth Gospel, Jesus says about his disciples: "They are strangers in the world, as I am." (Jn. 17:16) The world here is what is opposed to the sacred. Since the positive determination of the sacred is such an all-comprehensive, abundant reality, it can be described only in terms of this dialectical

---

religious symbols: "The sacred tree, the sacred stone are not adored as stone or tree; they are worshipped precisely because they are *hierophanies*, because they show something that is no longer stone or tree but the *sacred*, the *ganz andere* . . . By manifesting the sacred, any object becomes *something else*, yet it continues to remain itself, for it continues to participate in its surrounding cosmic milieu." *The Sacred and the Profane*, tr. Willard R. Trask (New York: Harper & Row, 1961), p. 12.

[8] Max Scheler, *op. cit.*, p. 164.

opposition to the profane.[9] Yet dialectical opposition does not imply withdrawal from reality or from life. For religious man the sacred appears eminently positive and the nonsacred reality is considered to be "as poor and bereft of existence as nothingness is to being."[10] Those aspects of existence are profane which can be taken at face value because they fail to reveal a deeper reality. The profane, then, is ultimately a negative religious term, created by religious man to distinguish his search for ultimate reality from the shallowness of ordinary life. It has no content in itself: what is profane to one group is sacred to another and can be accepted as such even by those who consider it profane for themselves.[11] What counts is the opposition itself, not the content which it adopts. The important thing to remember from this is that the term *transcendent,* so essential for religion, develops dialectically and takes various meanings in different contexts. It is always transcendent *in relation to* what surrounds it. Any attempt to give it a definitive, positive content in ordinary language is bound to fail because ordinary language can deal only with ordinary life, while the transcendent is precisely what stands out of the ordinary.[12]

Now the dialectical opposition of the sacred to the profane

[9] Durkheim was, I believe, the first to use the opposition to the profane in defining the sacred. (*The Elementary Forms of the Religious Life,* tr. by Joseph Ward Swain, New York: Macmillan, 1915: The Free Press, 1965, pp. 52ff.) But Robertson Smith in *The Religion of the Semites* had used a similar opposition between the sacred and the "common." Most authors today follow this dialectical definition. Thus for Caillois all we can say about the sacred is that it is the opposite of the profane. Otto describes the sacred entirely as *das ganz Andere.* Van der Leeuw claims that in primitive religion the sacred has hardly any content other than "something foreign and highly unusual." *Op. cit.,* p. 24.

[10] Roger Caillois, *L'homme et le sacré* (Paris, 1963), p. 20. *Man and the Sacred,* tr. by Meyer Barash (New York: The Free Press of Glencoe, 1959), p. 21.

[11] Roger Caillois, *op. cit.,* p. 91; *Man and the Sacred,* p. 73.

[12] A failure to realize this led to the fruitless discussions of the beginning of the century on the nature of the miracle in which theologians attempted to show that a miracle "transcends" objectively the entire series of natural events while scientists replied that no event taking place in nature could possibly transcend the "natural" order of events.

should lead naturally to the suppression of the profane. The ultimate reality tends to absorb the relative one and to transform man's entire activity into a religious ritual. In primitive societies and even in most civilized ones no aspect of life escapes the religious determination altogether. In the sacred are the sources of life: the profane must therefore stay in close subordination to what holds the very conditions of its existence.[13] The *secular,* that is, the profane conceived as a sphere of existence entirely independent of the sacred, seems to be of recent Western vintage. But how can a profane sphere of existence which remains subordinate to the sacred (although distinct from it) survive before the all-consuming energy of the sacred? What prevents the sacred from taking over altogether? Probably its own ambiguity. Religion beckons man away from his familiar world into a dangerously unknown region. Ordinary reality may contain little meaning for him but neither does it make excessive demands. Sacred reality requires purification and separates man from the ordinary. Man is as much repelled as attracted by this *mysterium tremendum.*

Yet even the ambivalence which man feels in face of the sacred cannot altogether protect the profane sphere of life from being absorbed. For the ambiguity of the sacred is only an expression of a transcendence which enables it to encompass its own opposite. The sacred assimilates by negation what it cannot conquer by attraction: it determines the profane not as *another* form of being, but as a hostile power of destruction—an "active nothingness."[14] Thus external opposition is transformed into internal negation, and the profane becomes the impure,[15] the unholy, even the diabolical. The sacred tends to extend its hold over all spheres of life. It usually maintains its totalitarian power until man finds

13 H. Hubert and M. Mauss, *Mélanges d'histoire des religions* (Paris, 1909), p. 125.
14 Roger Caillois, *op. cit.,* p. 20.
15 Originally the impure is often identified with the holy, from which W. Robertson Smith concludes that the concept of the holy is much more archaic than that of the personal deity. *Lectures on the Religion of the Semites* (1890), republished after the third edition by KTAV Publishing House, 1969, pp. 446–51.

its yoke too cumbersome in the exploration of new realms of experience, as in the upsurge of science in the modern age. The emancipation of the profane which inevitably follows may lead to a secularist reversal in which religion becomes a mere negation of the secular, as in Feuerbach's philosophy.

In its tendency to absorb everything the sacred manifests its unique power of integration. The ability to reconcile opposites (including its own opposite) under an ultimate unity—the *coincidentia oppositorum*—is as essential to religion as its dialectical opposition to the profane. The sacred embraces all oppositions because it transcends all distinctions. It is precisely this quality which enables religion to be the ultimate, integrating force of life and society. The religious activity is never limited to a specific value or a single point of view. It is the total value of life as well as its ultimate meaning. On its own ultimate level it tolerates no equals.[16] In a rare outburst of lyrical exaltation Hegel describes the integrating mood of religious man:

> All that has worth and dignity for man, all wherein he seeks his happiness, his glory, and his pride, finds its ultimate centre in religion, in the thought, the consciousness and the feeling of God. Thus God is the beginning of all things and the end of all things. As all things proceed from this point so all return back to it again. He is the centre which gives life and quickening to all things and which animates and preserves in existence all the various forms of being. In religion man places himself in a relation to this centre in which all other relations concentrate themselves, and in so doing he rises up to the highest level of consciousness and to the region which is free from relation to what is other than itself to something which is absolutely self-sufficient, the unconditioned, what is free and its own object and end.[17]

Religion can change all its conceptual expressions but it must die when it can no longer integrate. Even a partial loss of this

[16] Edward Spranger, *Lebensformen* (Halle, 1926), pp. 236–39.
[17] G. W. F. Hegel, *Vorlesungen über die Philosophie der Religion,* ed. by Georg Lasson (Hamburg, 1966), Vol. I, pp. 1–2. *Lectures on the Philosophy of Religion,* tr. by E. B. Speirs and J. Burdon Sanderson (London: Kegan Paul, 1962), p. 2.

ability as the one that resulted from the emancipation of science and philosophy in modern times or from the radical secularization of society in the communist world, causes a profound crisis. Yet it is in its integrating function that religion is most apt to degenerate into a power structure. Always tempted to take a short cut, religious man tends to destroy opposition rather than to integrate it under a more comprehensive absolute.[18] But by wiping out the profane, religion becomes itself "ordinary" and loses its entire *raison d'être.*

Through the discovery of original unity and his participation in it through myth and ritual, man transforms the sadness and tension of existence—*la grande tristezza*—into peace and joy. This is what religious man calls *salvation,* a term so exclusively sacred that it cannot be translated into the language of ordinary life. It combines two essential traits of the religious attitude: dissatisfaction with empirical reality and unlimited hope of ultimate liberation. "Religion is always directed towards salvation, never towards life itself as it is given; and in this respect all religion, with no exception, is the religion of deliverance."[19] The process of salvation never comes to a close. Man never attains the absolute unity itself, for ever new oppositions separate him from the divine reality. Salvation, then, rather than being the final term of religion is the dialectical movement itself which proposes a transcendent reality, opposes it to ordinary existence and composes the opposites in a participation of the divine.

The dialectical negation prevents the religious journey from reaching the end of its quest for transcendent reality. Precisely because the terminus of the quest is transcendent, religious language is always dialectical, that is, its terms have no fixed denotation but are *relative* to other terms. For the same reason religion

---

[18] Looking at religion's past record one would think that this is *the* religious temptation. Without it there would have been no religious wars, no Inquisition, and none of all the crafty schemes by which religious people so often "outwit the devil."

[19] Gerardus Van der Leeuw, *op. cit.,* p. 682. This statement is certainly correct for cultural religion. Whether the term "salvation" would be appropriate for primitive religion is a matter of dispute.

has no definable "essence," for religion never *is*—it always becomes.[20] Undoubtedly each type of religion displays a number of *objective* characteristics which may be described and classified, but they can never be deduced from an *a priori* form nor can they be reduced to a common denominator. A universal determination which confines religion to certain particular forms says too much. One which defines religion by its one universal objective trait, namely, a relation to some sort of transcendent reality, says too little, for such a relation is not exclusively religious. Nor is it possible to define religion by a subjective *a priori* as Rudolf Otto did, for a Kantian *a priori* formally determines all experience in an identical way and is therefore equally incompatible with a genuine religious pluralism.

2. SECULAR MAN AND HIS FAITH

The preceding description of the religious attitude has made no distinctions between the total experience of primitive man, the "religious" element in civilizations of the past (including our own), and the attitude of the modern believer. Such distinctions are essential, but they should not be drawn too rigidly. Much of the archaic mentality is present in the contemporary believer. Yet, by and large, the term "religious" today denotes a *specific* attitude or a reality distinct from the undivided life experience of the primitive. At the archaic stage a dance is no more cult than play or aesthetic expression, while myth is not merely a "religious" story but also a piece of philosophical reflection, a justification of social and cultural structures, a literary expression. The word *religion* nowhere appears at this stage. Yet we must not exclude it from our analysis since the religious dialectic is already present in one form or another, and religion will develop out of

[20] Even Van der Leeuw's masterly work, which displays such acute awareness of the varieties of religious expression, assumes that religion has a definable essence. For a most convincing refutation of this position, see Wilfred Cantwell Smith, *The Meaning and End of Religion* (New York: New American Library, 1964), pp. 55, 109–38.

this original attitude. More will be said about this in the chapter on symbol and myth.

In a second stage, religion still permeates all of existence. The concept of "secularity" does not exist yet, because the various spheres of life are not considered to be autonomous, even though they have become distinct spheres of existence. This entire sphere results from a further reflection upon the distinction between the sacred and the profane—a distinction which existed already in an initial state on the archaic level. All activities here are strictly subordinate to the religious realm without being identical with it. To most men living today this is probably what religion means.

Finally, a third stage is characterized by the distinction between the religious and the secular. It is a uniquely Western phenomenon. Although it was initiated when religion ceased to coincide with social life, it did not reach completion until the so-called *profane* areas of a previous age grew *entirely* independent of the religious sphere. Science, art, philosophy, and morality have emancipated themselves from their religious origins to the extent that apparently they can exist as well without religion as with it. The scientist is no longer puzzled by the parallelism between the laws of nature and the laws of the mind, since he knows that all laws are laws only for the mind. Economic goods are not considered any more a gift of divine largesse, but man's own response to self-created needs. What artists dimly felt in the past, they now bluntly assert, namely, that the work of art is not an imitation of nature, subject to an extrinsic code, but that it creates its own norms and reality. In his moral behavior also man has assumed full responsibility over himself: he has no more use for a divinely imposed, unchangeable code of conduct. Even religion can be accommodated in this man-centered universe as a symbolic expression of the human mind, structured according to immanent schemas.

Secularization in our society is the direct result of man's growing awareness of autonomy.[21] Having brought ever more spheres

[21] As I have pointed out elsewhere, autonomy is no more intrinsically secular than any idea is intrinsically religious. It may be interpreted in a

of existence under his control man has come to consider himself
as his own creator of values and no longer feels the need to
subordinate them to a transcendent source. In the past religion
was *the* integrating factor of human existence, relating all values
to a supreme principle. A general feeling of dependence in a
universe that dominated man more than he dominated it made
such a reference indispensable. But once he discovered that the
power to control the world was within himself, that all institutions
were man-made, this need ceased to exist. It is often said that
the desacralization of the world results directly from the view of
a totally transcendent Creator. The increasing awareness of God's
unity and transcendence reduces the religious status of the finite.
As the representation of God becomes more correct, Guardini
writes, the world grows more profane.[22] In the long range even
the Christian incarnation which resacralized the world may have
contributed to man's feeling of autonomy by its radical union
of the worldly and the divine. Some theologians therefore defend
the process of secularization as an authentically religious or at
least an authentically Christian development.[23] Yet the question

---

religious way, for instance when we see it as the image and likeness of God
in man. But the fact remains that it is the notion of autonomy which in the
West has been most instrumental in promoting secularization. Cf. my
article, "Divine Transcendence in Secular Theology" in *The Spirit and Power
of Christian Secularity*, ed. by A. Schlitzer (Notre Dame, Ind.: University
of Notre Dame Press, 1969), esp. p. 122.
[22] Romano Guardini, *Unterscheidung des Christlichen* (Mainz, 1963),
p. 321.
[23] The distinction between "religious" and "Christian" refers to the position
defended by Van Buren and Altizer, that Christianity itself should be
secularized to the point where it ceases to be religion. See: Paul van Buren,
The Secular Meaning of the Gospel (New York: Macmillan, 1966);
Thomas J. J. Altizer, *The Gospel of Christian Atheism* (Philadelphia: Westminster Press, 1966). Others defend secularity as a religious concept but
distinguish it from *secularism*. See: Paul Tillich, *Systematic Theology*,
Vol. I (Chicago: University of Chicago Press, 1951), *passim,* esp. p. 208;
Gabriel Vahanian, *The Death of God* (New York: George Braziller,
1966), pp. 60–78; Henry Duméry, *Foi et Interrogation* (Paris, 1953), pp.
29–56; Friedrich Gogarten, *Verhängnis und Hoffnung der Neuzeit* (München, 1966), pp. 134–48; Harvey Cox, *The Secular City* (New York: Macmillan, 1965), pp. 18–26. Of course, the thesis that Christianity leads to
a secular world view has existed since Hegel, who clearly states it in his

is not what caused secularity but whether it is compatible with a religious attitude.

Before answering it let us have a closer look at the phenomenon itself. Its most striking characteristic is that for secular man no particular sphere of existence can still be called sacred. He no longer *directly* experiences the holy either in the world or in the mind. The outer world has become totally humanized. Nature is no longer perceived as filled with God's presence. It has become a field of operation in which function determines meaning. Nor does man discover the divine in the secret of his own heart. "Considering the development of the theory of knowledge from Plato and Augustine through the Middle Ages to the present time, one is faced with an ever growing secularization of that sacred sphere of the soul which one may call the *intimum mentis.*"[24] Modern man is not given to contemplation and has little patience with those who are. To an unusual degree he has developed the active powers of his mind, the ability to grasp, to comprehend, to do, and to make. This has allowed him to attain an unprecedented control over his physical environment. But the unconditional commitment to the technical and the pragmatic has dulled the sensitivity of his interior life. Even modern art seldom forces him to move outside his technical world: instead it gives that world an aesthetic glow and clarity. Or, as Guardini expressed it: "The thing retains an aesthetic background but it no longer surpasses its immediate context in life."[25] With the

---

Philosophy of Religion. It has been constantly repeated by Marxists of every stripe. Cf. Ernst Bloch, *Subjekt-Objekt* (Berlin, 1949), pp. 295–325; Alexandre Kojève, *Introduction à la lecture de Hegel* (Paris, 1947), pp. 318–19; Roger Garaudy, *Dieu est mort* (Paris, 1962), pp. 279–84, 355–56, 399–415. Hegel's position is stated in *Vorlesungen über die Philosophie der Religion,* Vol. IV, pp. 218, 14–15, also relevant are III, pp. 67–68. For an intelligent commentary, cf. Emil Fackenheim, *The Religious Dimension in Hegel's Thought* (Bloomington: Indiana University Press, 1967), pp. 206–10.

[24] Peter Wust as quoted by Gabriel Marcel, *Être et avoir* (Paris, 1935), pp. 280–81.

[25] Romano Guardini, *Religion und Offenbarung,* Vol. I (Würzburg, 1958), p. 34. On modern man's loss of the ability to see the world and history as enlightening symbols the same author wrote a remarkable essay, "Die Situation des Menschen" in *Unterscheidung des Christlichen,* esp. pp. 230–34.

symbolic vision has disappeared the passive religious experience. Few if any experiences could be called unambiguously religious.

The feelings of most religious people about this change appear to be ambivalent. On the one hand, they feel liberated, as some secular theologians have strongly emphasized. Everything gets along without God as before and the religious angle is one complication less to cope with in an increasingly complicated world. On the other hand, even those who consider secularity a spiritual necessity find it a painful experience. A feeling of loneliness sets in when God no longer directly speaks in nature or in our hearts.

> Where religion once flowered like a blossoming meadow, there is nothing left now but dry clay. Perhaps it is better so; perhaps religion was like the Pontine Marshes that had to be drained. Nevertheless, the effect remains crushing.[26]

Of late, man also begins to have some afterthoughts about the one-sidedness with which he has pursued total "control" over his environment. Occasionally he wonders whether the achievement was worth its price. Western man's unconditional commitment to the technical and the pragmatic has banalized life for the sake of controlling it. Somehow he feels that he is leading a diminished existence. The original enthusiasm for a secular society has quickly waned in the light of our present crises. The lyrical prose written by secular theologians a decade ago on themes like *pragmatic* and *technical* has become as little comprehensible to us as the expectorations of eighteenth-century writers on progress.

Yet the important question from our point of view is whether religion can survive in a secular society. Of course, no historical precedents can answer this question. In the words of an American theologian: "Ours is the first attempt in recorded history to build a culture upon the premise that it is not important for the

[26] Hans Urs von Balthasar, *The God Question and Modern Man*, tr. by Hilda Graef (New York: The Seabury Press, 1967), p. 101.

workings of man and society whether or not God is present."[27] One thing appears certain to me: if religion loses its power to integrate other values it will cease to exist. Faith is either the all-integrating factor of life or nothing. A communist sociologist made this point very convincingly by showing how the regression of religious beliefs and practices in Czechoslovakia ran parallel with the loss of the integrating function of Christianity in postwar Czech society.[28] That religion has ceased to be the integrating factor of *public* life is simply a fact. The only question is whether values may be integrated in any other way. The Church can obviously no longer substitute for, or even compete with, secular society. It is not evident that religion in any form is needed to uphold the basic values of a society or to support social institutions which at one time were unable to support themselves.

Nor does faith offer unique solutions to the problems of our time. I do not believe that much would be gained in the battle against racial tension, city disintegration, and environment pollution if religious institutions or individuals were given a leading hand in solving these problems. The religious vision guarantees no mental subtlety in grasping the complexities of this world. In this respect I find the call to "secularize" theology puzzling, for the only secularization helpful in a practical situation is the particular expertise required by the nature of the problem. There is nothing in the secular sphere that man would not do as well without a secularized faith as with it. Nor is there any reason to believe that religious training improves the qualifications of the counselor, the educator, the city planner. The sort of integration by which faith provides the final answer to every problem is definitively lost. Religion may still be the ultimate integration for religious man. But for society and its survival it is no longer necessary that the ultimate integration be religious. There are

[27] Martin Marty, *Varieties of Unbelief* (Garden City, N.Y.: Doubleday, 1966), p. 58.
[28] Erika Kadlecova, "Kirche und Gesellschaft. Ergebnisse einer soziologischen Erhebung in der CSSR" in *Disputation zwischen Christen und Marxisten* (Münich, 1966), p. 252.

many meaningful patterns in which men synthesize their values, and not all of them require the acceptance of a transcendent principle in the religious sense. The Marxist world view is a good example of one that does not. Society can live with all of them as long as a certain balance among values is maintained.

Nevertheless I would assert without hesitation that to the believer faith remains the all-integrating force of life, although it fulfills this function from a new vantage point. The sources of modern man's faith lie in the individual and his conviction, not in the Church as social institution, and even less in a society determined by the Church. One might call such a faith private, but not if that term excludes very tangible public effects. For faith inspires the believer most powerfully to pursue certain values and to overcome obstacles along the way. However devoid religion may be of technical solutions, to the believer it remains a most effective motive of action and exploration. Prominent figures in the war protest, the migrant workers' strike, and the civil rights movement found both their inspiration and their strength in faith. Without it they would not have done what they did. Their faith, although nourished in religious communities, directed them in a private way. They took stands and braved dangers which a religiously established society would not have permitted and which were often frowned upon by their own Church. Nor do believers impair the autonomy of secular values by relating them to a transcendent principle. They merely prevent each value from separately becoming an absolute in its own right and thereby excluding others. To remain meaningful in a secular world, religion must continue to *relativize* values by placing them in a transcendent perspective.

Yet the mere fact that religious man today still finds his ultimate integration in faith does not mean that the secular mentality is *de jure* compatible with the religious attitude. Much of what he does and believes may be left over from a previous age. We must therefore probe deeper and find out if and how he is able to maintain a sense of religious reality within a secular world. Strangely enough, all signs seem to indicate that the very experiences which make him secular are also the ones which confront him with the religious choice. As a rule, the modern believer does not "undergo" the sacred any more. Instead he reflects upon certain ambiguous experiences and then interprets them—often hesitantly—in a religious way. This behavior obviously differs from the direct religious experiences which men at all times in the past seem to have felt. How the two are related to each other will be discussed in the next two sections. But first we must analyze some of the ambiguous experiences which modern man converts into religious ones.

One such experience appears mainly to result from the stupendous success of modern science. I would describe it as a new sense of the mysteriousness of the universe. The feeling is new insofar as it is not directly connected with any vision of a transcendent Creator as it was in the Middle Ages and still at the time of Newton and Pascal. Indeed, the experience is so far from being religious that one might consider it one of the main contributing factors to the secularization of the modern world view. Nevertheless, the astounding vistas on the nature of time, space, and matter opened up by modern science once again bring out the mysteriousness of the reality which man is and which surrounds him. The feeling that this universe surpasses even his powers of objectivation makes him pause, and this reflection is one of the avenues by which he frequently reaches the transcendent. The popular success of such religious writers as Teilhard de Chardin and Lecomte du Noüy seems to confirm this. Yet it is important for evaluating the situation correctly to be aware of the difference between this awe for the mystery of the universe and the theological speculations of the seventeenth century in which each part of the creation was thought to serve a particular purpose. What moves man today in the contemplation of the universe is more its mysterious incomprehensibility than whatever order he may find in it. Nor should one consider this new mystery experience intrinsically religious. Yet to those who interpret it religiously it conveys, upon reflection, a symbol of an *overwhelming,* transcendent *reality*—which, as we saw in the dialectic of the previous section, is an essential moment of the religious attitude.

Another experience is predominantly negative. It has been said that man today has a more radical awareness of contingency than his ancestors ever had. With respect to the meaning of life, he accepts situations as arbitrary effects of causes which in the final analysis must remain unintelligible. As he becomes more aware of the complexity of things, a search for ultimate intelligibility becomes a less and less promising project. So he abandons all hope of connecting the facts of life by a coherent intelligibility and stays mostly with the empirical and the functional. He no longer attempts to found the contingent in the necessary. This is one of the reasons why the proof for the existence of God based upon contingency provokes little interest today. Nonetheless, apart from the neo-positivist philosophers few people cease to be intrigued by the "facticity" of the real. Reality strikes man not just as a fact, but as a puzzling fact which fails to deliver its justification. Even what apparently happens necessarily since it always happens does not reveal its inner necessity. The concentration on this irrational gratuitousness has given rise to an entirely new *Weltanschauung* for which the unquestioning acceptance of contingency is the only authentically human attitude. It would be an abuse of language to call religious what is the very starting point of most contemporary atheist philosophies. Nonetheless, the same experience of contingency appears at the root of modern man's religious quest. Paradoxically, if he believes, it is not because he seeks ultimate intelligibility but because he no longer expects to find any. He accepts the universe and himself as a fact, but a frustrating fact the obtuseness of which fundamentally disturbs him. Frustration in the face of the totally unintelligible explains the high emotional quality which characterizes the existentialist philosophy of contingency. It also explains man's sudden detection of the transcendent, not as the "ultimately intelligible," but as the awesome presence of the totally unknown.[29]

The experience of contingency becomes most baffling when man concentrates upon his own condition. Here he is, without possessing any ground for his being today and his nonbeing tomorrow. He just happens to be, as all other things are—a mere fact. But the peculiar quality of this particular fact is that he never accepts it entirely. To be sure, the feeling of contingency does not have to be the gloomy experience which preachers and existentialist philosophers describe. The feeling of being alive at this moment without having to justify it may lead to joyous exaltation. Such was the mood expressed in Albert Camus' early Algerian sketches. To be alone with the sea, the sand, and my body, between the void of the past and the void of the future, is an intoxicating experience—and by no means sad. Nevertheless at the heart of contingency always lurks the anguished awareness that the void in which I live may at any moment overtake me. This awareness increases as man becomes more conscious of his unlimited creative powers. With the sense of freedom grows the feeling of precariousness. In the midst of his conquests man knows that in the end he himself will be conquered by his inherent contingency. His life and his creations carry the worm of death. He never fully comes to peace with this situation and continues to regard the void around existence as a threat. Since this threat envelops Being itself, it is unconditioned, transcendent. We all know Heidegger's descriptions of the existential anxiety caused by the awareness of nothingness.[30] Yet this same dread of

[29] Even Cox, the panegyrist of the factual, has recognized this phenomenon. "Thus we meet God at those places in life where we come up against that which is not pliable and disposable, at those hard edges where we were both stopped and challenged to move ahead. God meets us at the transcendent." *The Secular City*, p. 262.

[30] Martin Heidegger, *Was ist Metaphysik*, 7th ed. (Frankfurt, 1955), pp. 33–34; tr. by R. F. C. Hull and Alan Crick, "What Is Metaphysics" in *Existence and Being*, p. 336. Heidegger found the connection between freedom and nothingness in Kierkegaard. Cf. Søren Kierkegaard, *Begrebet Angest, Samlede Vaerker*, ed. by A. B. Drachmann, J. L. Heiberg, H. O. Lange (Copenhagen, 1964), Vol. 6, pp. 135–37; *The Concept of Dread*,

the void around his contingent existence is the experience in which modern man is most poignantly confronted with the mystery of transcendence. In a masterly essay on "The Dimension of Ultimacy in Secular Experience," Langdon Gilkey has shown the transcendent meaning of the feeling of contingency. This feeling, he concludes, "manifests itself as set within a dimension of ultimacy or of the unconditioned."[31] It points beyond itself to a transcendent horizon because its threat is all-comprehensive, unconditioned. Often man does not permit the experience of contingency to become explicit: anguish is repressed and man hides behind an appearance of confidence in the "normal course of events." Yet he seems to be unable to free himself of that vague feeling of not being quite at home to which Gabriel Marcel refers as *uneasiness*. Relentlessly it is prying at "the vise in which daily life squeezes us with the hundreds of cares that mask true reality."[32] Again, the experiences of anguish and uneasiness are not intrinsically religious. Frequently they are the very reason why religious people abandon the faith. Yet they bring man to a point where he must assert his contingency as an ultimate or profess a positive faith in a transcendent reality.

The connection between negativity and a religious attitude is by no means coincidental, as the previous section should make evident. Perhaps the most essential trait of the religious attitude is a dissatisfaction with existence as it is *given* and an attempt to overcome the present situation. Thus the consciousness of contingency and even of alienation is an essential part of the religious dialectic which requires the presence of the opposite of the wholesome and the self-sufficient. Obviously, the bold transition from

---

tr. by Walter Lowrie (Princeton: Princeton University Press, 1944), pp. 37–40. For comments, see Louis Dupré, *Kierkegaard as Theologian* (New York: Sheed & Ward, 1963), pp. 54–56.

[31] *Naming the Whirlwind* (Indianapolis: Bobbs-Merrill, 1969), p. 329. The entire essay is in my opinion the best reply to the thesis that the radical secularity of modern life excludes the transcendent dimension.

[32] Gabriel Marcel, *Problematic Man,* tr. by Brian Thomson (New York: Herder and Herder, 1967), p. 142. Slightly changed.

contingency to religious transcendence does not occur on a rational basis. All attempts to justify it rationally are futile. But, then, no positive relation to the transcendent can be "justified" in other than its own terms. Nor does this fact brand all religious interpretations as arbitrary. For once the vague and undirected experience has been transformed into a religious one it becomes integrated within a new totality and attains an intrinsic necessity of its own.

Finally, we must briefly consider another ambiguous experience which the believer converts into a specifically religious act of integration and reconciliation. Modern man, in spite of his increased aggressiveness, feels to some extent stronger ties with his fellow man. The idea that the plight of the suffering and the oppressed concerns each individual and the community as a whole, has begun to penetrate at least into the thinking patterns of our contemporaries. Not that man today cares more for his fellow man than his ancestors did, but the *idea* that members of the human race share a certain responsibility for each other has become more or less universally accepted in civilized thought. Obviously such an idea is not intrinsically religious nor does it need religious motivation to be converted into charitable practice. Nevertheless, it is in the responsibility for his fellow man that the believer in a secular age often discovers the transcendent dimension. His transition from one to the other cannot be justified by a logical deduction. In logical order it would appear as the following odd inference: The person is sacred, therefore the sacred *is*. To the believer the community of men comes to symbolize a community of all beings, integrated with and held together by a transcendent principle. The binding element is the sacred. Thus social movements, the joy of fellowship, even sexual liberty take on a sudden religious aspect for many young people that perplexes their elders. Illogical and undisciplined as the expression of this new awareness may be, its religious character is authentic. Yet again, it originated in an ambiguous rather than a religious experience. The brotherhood of revolutionary cells, resistance movements, and oppressed groups as often as not turns against a faith in the transcendent, particularly an institutionalized faith. Nevertheless for some the communion with others takes on the meaning of a religious integration. A personal encounter to them becomes a revelation of God; they interpret as a meeting with the transcendent what to the nonbeliever was merely a mysterious "depth experience."[33]

After this brief exploration of the rise of religious attitudes in secular man, we remain puzzled. Why does he feel the need to move into another realm on the basis of experiences which in themselves do not justify such a transition? I have no other answer than that some people are driven unexplainably beyond the purely empirical. Others are not. Objectively this may look like a matter of choice, but the choice depends so strongly on the nature of the subject that the fundamental option is perhaps not a choice at all.[34] At any rate, those who choose faith need, as Jaspers intimates, an unconditioned principle of meaning.[35] The dynamism of existence itself drives them toward transcendence. To others no step into the transcendent can be rationally justified. Religious attitudes today seem to be adopted as personal and reflective answers to experiences which present themselves in a questioning rather than in an assertive way. The experience preceding the religious act invites decision rather than passive submission. This is the precise point which distinguishes faith, that is, the active and reflective religious attitude, from the passive feeling which was predominant in the total religious experience of the past. In the following two sections we shall analyze both those religious attitudes, starting with the *predominantly* passive

[33] Donald D. Evans, "Differences Between Scientific and Religious Assertions" in *Science and Religion: New Perspectives on the Dialogue,* ed. by Ian G. Barbour (New York: Harper & Row, 1968), p. 103.

[34] Michael Novak suggests a similar explanation in presenting the alternatives: "The key lies in who one is and what one expects from life; by belief or by unbelief one defines oneself." *Belief and Unbelief* (New York: New American Library, 1965), p. 126.

[35] Karl Jaspers, *Philosophie* (Berlin, 1932), Vol. 2, pp. 270–81. Also, Bernard Welte, *Der philosophische Glaube* (Freiburg, 1954), Part 1, Section 6. Romano Guardini, *Unterscheidung des Christlichen,* p. 327.

one. I write "predominantly" because neither one ever appears *à l'état pur:* no wholly passive experience is religious, nor would a totally active faith (if that existed) be religious.

3. RELIGIOUS FEELING, THE MORE PASSIVE FORM OF EXPERIENCE

In the more elementary forms of religious life, the passive factor prevails. But even in the more reflective religious experience it played until recently an important role. Traditionally this aspect of the religious experience has been called religious feeling. Feeling is always some sort of totality experience in which the self is present more to itself than to external reality. It is a way of being with oneself in the world without precise object, although it is vaguely object-determined. This objectlessness is a universal characteristic of feelings, ranging from the mere sensation to the loftiest aesthetic, moral or religious emotions. When a sudden noise wakes me up out of a deep sleep, I do not at first perceive a noisemaking object (e.g., the alarm clock), but rather do I *feel myself* affected by noise. As Hegel said, in feeling, the double being of the self and its object disappears and the specific character of the object becomes my own.[36] Religious feelings are, of course, quite different from the transitional experience of a pure sensation which disappears as I become fully aware of it. Nevertheless, they reveal a striking similarity. Schleiermacher, who still remains our best source of information on this aspect of the religious experience, describes feeling as an identity experience with the All, "the holy wedlock of the universe with the incarnated reason," the rise of consciousness in which the mind listens to itself before it is fully awake.[37]

How can a feeling be called *religious,* when it has no "object" and is merely a vague affective state? The answer lies in the inevitable imbalance of feelings. Feeling, as an eminent Ameri-

[36] *Vorlesungen über die Philosophie der Religion,* Vol. I, p. 99.
[37] Friedrich Schleiermacher, *On Religion,* tr. by John Oman (New York: Harper & Brothers, 1958), pp. 43, 41.

can philosopher put it, reveals an instability in the conscious self, which pushes it outward without being objective.[38] If the harmony of a feeling were ever perfect, it would have no subject-object tension at all, but neither would it be conscious. Feelings can be specific only to the extent that they are impure. However, the specification never results in a fully constituted object (as it does in the reflective consciousness), but rather in a totality which *is on its way* to be this or that specific object. When I become conscious of a feeling, it has already taken on certain determinations. These determinations originate in the object orientation of feeling and account for the variety of feelings. The question then becomes: Which objective characteristics distinguish *religious* from other feelings? Schleiermacher described religion as a feeling of *absolute dependence.* Yet dependence presupposes the conscious presence of *another,* and this can exist only in the reflective, *objective* order in which the harmony of feeling has been broken. Schleiermacher admits that the feeling of dependence will inevitably result in a *search* for a definable absolute, but this search itself is a new state of consciousness, which is logically but not ontologically implied in the first one.[39] Consequently, the objective expression of religious feeling is nonreligious or postreligious and must remain subordinate to the objectless feeling which it attempts to symbolize.

But such an identification of religion and feeling leaves out an essential element of the religious act: its outward-directed intentionality. A religion of pure feeling would be an aesthetic experience. Although aesthetic experiences often take on a religious aspect, they lack the transcendence which the religious attitude requires. This appears clearly enough in the difference between religious symbols and aesthetic ones.[40] The aesthetic

[38] William E. Hocking, *The Meaning of God in Human Experience* (New Haven: Yale University Press, 1963), p. 66.
[39] *The Christian Faith* (New York: Harper & Row, 1963), Vol. I, p. 13.
[40] Obviously the distinction does not apply in the first of the three religious stages introduced at the beginning of the previous section. To archaic man art is as "religious" as the rest of his life. We shall treat the problem of religious symbolism explicitly in Chapter 4.

symbol adequately articulates the feeling which it expresses. The religious symbol, on the contrary, never fully symbolizes its transcendent content. It merely *points to* it in a loose connection between symbol and content, unintelligible to the uninitiated, whom it impresses as merely strange.[41]

This is not to say that there are no religious feelings, but only that the religious act is never exclusively a feeling. In fact, feelings can be called *religious* only to the extent that they are determined by a more outward-oriented act.[42] By themselves they remain self-centered and should not be called religious.[43] What Hocking says about all feelings is definitely true of the religious ones: they do no work apart from a guiding idea.[44] Yet feelings do play an important part in the religious experience. This is no coincidence, for the religious consciousness unites the self and the world in an absolute ground. To the extent that only feelings achieve a state of unity beyond the subject-object opposition, we may apply the term to the religious experience. Yet we must always keep in mind that no ordinary mood is at issue and that the religious "feeling" is directed beyond the self. Schleiermacher himself pointed out the self-transcending nature of religious feeling in his late *Dialektik:* "The transcendent determination of self-consciousness is its religious aspect, or the *religious feeling,* and in it the transcendent ground or the supreme being is itself presented."[45]

Since the religious act goes necessarily beyond the immediate

---

[41] Libert Vander Kerken, *Religious Gevoel en Aesthetisch Ervaren* (Antwerp, 1947), p. 52. I follow this remarkable study for the distinction between the aesthetic and the religious experience.

[42] Cf. Rudolf Otto, *The Idea of the Holy,* tr. by John F. Harvey (New York: Oxford University Press, 1958), pp. 10, 126. Otto's emphasis on the "intentional" nature of the religious act is all the more remarkable because he deals primarily with primitive and "pre-religious" experiences.

[43] Hegel, reacting against Schleiermacher, saw this very well: "What is rooted in my feeling only, is also only for me, not in and for itself but only mine . . . The old metaphysics therefore proved always first that there is a God, not merely a feeling of God." *Vorlesungen über die Philosophie der Religion,* I, p. 56. See also, I, pp. 96ff.

[44] *Op. cit.,* p. 69.

[45] *Dialektik* (Berlin, 1839), p. 430.

experience of the self, it is always reflective. In primary forms of religion this reflective element may be more potential than actual, and the word "feeling" here is more appropriate. But even on that elementary level the content of religious "feeling" urges on to reflection, while we detect no such dynamism in other feelings. The negativity inherent to the religious experience drives it to ever greater reflection until feeling recedes into the background.

However, the term "intentionality," by which I distinguished the religious experience from feeling, can be as misleading as the term "feeling." For the sacred is not a transcendent "object": it is the ground of objectivity as well as of subjectivity. It cannot be juxtaposed to "other" modes of reality, for it includes them all as their fount and origin. The religious experience, then, is not a different way of knowing by means of different categories. It reaches *beyond* all categories toward the source of all categorical differentiation in the mind itself.[46] It is a withdrawal into the self for the purpose of discovering the absolute which founds the self and all that is. Only the deepest experiences such as love and death reveal this absolute ground of the spirit.

Some Scholastics have attempted to relate this pre-categorical consciousness of the religious experience to the metaphysical experience of Being. Thus Johannes B. Lotz defines as religious the act in which man knows not a particular object but the transcendental horizon of the world of objects, that is, the background of transcendent Being which is not clearly perceived in the ordinary cognitive act but without which no thematic knowledge is possible.[47] For Lotz the religious experience *completes* the

[46] "All that can be grasped and distinguished as categorical modifications of the spirit is rooted in a transcategorical ground, in a space that comprehends all possibilities, in a light of the spirit that brings forth everything, even all differences. The ground, space, and light of the spirit are absolutely simple and precede all differences." Bernard Welte, "Zur geistesgeschichtlicher Lage der Fundamentaltheologie" in *Theologische Quartalschrift*, 130 (1950), p. 399.

[47] Johannes B. Lotz, "Zur Struktur der religiösen Erfahrung" in *Interpretation der Welt (Festschrift Guardini)*, ed. by Helmut Kuhn et alii (Würzburg, 1965), pp. 205–26. H. Ogiermann, "Die Problematik der

metaphysical experience. But obviously not every experience of Being becomes religious. What determines the difference? Lotz answers that the experience turns religious as soon as the transcendent horizon against which all beings are perceived is given the *positive* content of a self or of a person, when man experiences himself grounded in Being as in a transcendent. Although it is undoubtedly correct to distinguish the metaphysical from the religious by the positive content given to an otherwise unknown transcendent horizon, I nevertheless feel that to consider this distinction the essence of the religious act falsifies the perspective. Certainly, the metaphysical speculation of Being leaves further questions about the nature of its transcendence. And perhaps these questions are not fully answered until man combines the religious with the metaphysical experience.[48] But this still does not allow me to consider the religious experience *continuous* with the metaphysical experience. Few metaphysicians and even fewer students of religion will agree with a statement like this: "Immediate spiritual evidence leads to the point where through the experience of Being becomes transparent the God who is to be grasped spiritually; . . . the intuition of Being becomes religious intuition."[49] The religious experience resembles the metaphysical one insofar as the supreme reality somehow includes all beings. Metaphysical reflection, on the other side, can become religious if the notion of transcendence which it uses is further developed. But this does not actually occur until the transcendent is perceived *as self-revealing,* and at that moment it ceases to be metaphysical. It is possible that for some people, mainly metaphysicians I suppose, the Being of metaphysics attains a religious

---

religiösen Erfahrung" in *Scholastik,* 37 (1962), pp. 481–513; 38 (1963), pp. 481–518.

[48] "In the questions what it is that I am and that around me something is, lies a religious dimension. Only when this dimension is filled by an authentic religious experience does the question come to rest. Only in the religious experience does the intellectual concern towards the various realms of reality and experience of existence find its final depth dimension." Romano Guardini, "Religiöse Erfahrung und Glaube" in *Unterscheidung des Christlichen,* p. 313.

[49] H. Ogiermann, *art. cit., Scholastik,* 37 (1962), p. 496.

meaning if they are religiously disposed at the outset. But the transition from one to the other remains a μετάβασις εἰς ἄλλο γένος, a shift to a new experience. Nothing would be more misleading than to define the new through the old. In itself the metaphysical intuition of Being is no more religious than the religious approach to God is metaphysical. Neither the independence of Divine Being nor the dependence of contingent beings are reached as metaphysical conclusions. It is true that mystics like Sankara and Eckhart use metaphysical language. Yet their perspective is not metaphysical but religious. So is their purpose: the knowledge of Being and of the One is here proposed exclusively as a way of salvation, not as a means to satisfy intellectual curiosity.[50] The religious representation of Being is a symbol rather than a notion.[51]

4. FAITH, THE RELIGIOUS EXPERIENCE AS ATTITUDE

Earlier we saw that the religious experience of contemporary man is seldom direct and passive. He is incapable of "undergoing" the sacred, and if he does so at a rare occasion he distrusts the experience. If religion means blank wonder, irresistible attraction, overwhelming sense of reality, modern man no longer possesses it. Such passive sensations are too far removed from his usual vision of the world. Yet the religious experience is never *only* passive. Even at times when it totally overpowered man, it still remained primarily a call inviting a response. The sacred never allows man to remain neutral or detached in its presence. He is always asked to do something, to purify himself, to convert the profane or ambiguous aspects of life into religious ones. To ignore these unconditional demands is to destroy the

[50] The last chapter of this study will deal with this more in detail.
[51] That is why it is attained not by a discursive process but, as Lotz himself indicates, by an intuition. Johannes B. Lotz, "Il problema dell'esperienza religiosa" in *Atti del XV Convegno del Centro di Studi Filosofici tra Professori Universitari, Gallarate 1960* (Brescia, 1961), p. 273. The symbol will be analyzed in Chapter 4.

religious experience itself. The believer today remains aware of a divine calling, even though he seldom experiences it passively in his heart or in nature. He mostly seems to *hear about* the sacred reality through Scripture and education, but in spite of the indirectness of this approach he feels that he must actively respond. The appropriate name for this complex and reflective response is faith.

Now faith is obviously a good deal older than the contemporary world. In a very real sense one might say that it goes back as far as the conscious religious attitude itself. Yet a more narrow meaning seems to have entered the term with Christianity. In declaring that faith originates in hearing, Paul downgraded the element of "experience" which plays such an important role in most religious attitudes. In the Christian sense, faith is neither experience nor conviction based upon experience; it is primarily obedience and hope. "Faith gives substance to our hopes, and makes us certain of realities we do not see." (Hebr. 11:1) Of course, to some extent all religious experience, even the most direct one, goes beyond the actual experience, for the transcendent can never be given in the empirical. In that sense every religion contains at least implicitly a faith. Nevertheless most religious attitudes have been attempts to establish a direct contact with the divine via experience. Against them, Christianity stressed the need to surpass the empirical altogether in a reflective, free acceptance of the revealed.[52] As faith went up, religious experience went down. Not the intensity of the experience nor the depth of insight nor even the quality of the content are primary concerns of faith, but the attitude with which the revelation is being received. To the extent that a religion is reflective, faith is always present. But in past ages it hardly emerged out of the passive experience. Even in Christianity faith was still carried by religious feeling, a religious environment, and the strong support of worldly authority. This has largely ceased to be the case. Modern man's

[52] The same is largely true of Israel although the Hebrew faith was still directed toward the actual course of history while the Christian faith finds no support in history. The two views will be compared in the chapter on Salvation.

religion has become almost entirely reflective. The transcendent no longer "overwhelms" him, if he experiences it at all. He believes by sheer conviction, because he considers faith the correct attitude toward the transcendent. In the act of believing the content of faith becomes certain. But it rarely overpowers its believer. As a rule, the act remains shallow in intensity of experience.[53] Ours is a time of little experience and no religious immediacy.

Let us now analyze this strange attitude which connects the believer with the transcendent beyond experience. Since belief and faith share some basic characteristics, we shall not distinguish them until later. H. Richard Niebuhr defined it as that understanding of things which a person holds and uses without having direct relation to what he asserts to be true.[54] Essential in this definition is the indirectness of the relation between believer and believed. What I *believe* is never directly present to my mind. It thereby differs from what I *know,* which, to the extent that it is evident, is immediately present to the mind. On the basis of this absolute distinction between belief and knowledge H. H. Price concludes: "It follows that it is impossible to know and to believe the same thing at the same time. If I know that A is B I cannot at the same time believe that A is B, and if I believe it I cannot at the same time know it."[55] Belief, then, is not knowledge of a low degree of certainty which by improvement may yet become true knowledge. No, belief as such is not knowledge at all, even though it always involves knowledge. We never mistake one for the other: I always *know* that I believe and I never think that I know when I believe.[56]

Faith, then, is obviously not "knowledge." Yet it is equally certain that it fulfills a cognitive function. This appears in a

[53] Romano Guardini, "Der Glaube in der Reflexion" in *Unterscheidung des Christlichen,* p. 305.

[54] "On the Nature of Faith" in *Religious Experience and Truth,* ed. by Sidney Hook (London: Oliver & Boyd, 1962), pp. 94–95.

[55] H. H. Price, "Some Considerations About Belief" in *Knowledge and Belief,* ed. by Phillips Griffiths (New York: Oxford University Press, 1967), p. 42.

[56] H. A. Prichard, "Knowing and Believing" in *Knowledge and Belief,* ed. by Phillips Griffiths, p. 63.

number of ways. First, the believer must to some extent *understand* what is proposed to his belief and if he accepts it, it must *mean* something to him.[57] Christians have always considered their faith primarily an intellectual relation to God and Catholics would say that this is precisely what distinguishes it from charity. Paul speaks of faith as an imperfect *seeing,* to be replaced sometime by full vision. (1 Cor. 13:12) Both phases belong to the cognitive order. The Fourth Gospel is even more explicit: Christ is said to be bearing witness to the truth (Jn. 18:37). He is the truth himself (Jn. 14:6) and the one through whom the truth has come (Jn. 1:17). And eternal life is: *"to know you,* the only true God and Jesus Christ whom you have sent" (Jn. 17:3). Bultmann comments:

> There is a peculiar connection between believing and knowing . . . Faith is man's first step towards God, or the revelation of God; if it is maintained it will be rewarded with knowledge (Jn. 8:31f.; 10:30). Faith is that doing of God's will which leads to knowledge.[58]

The quoted texts reveal two cognitive aspects in faith: one which is present in the act of belief; the other, understanding, which this act requires as its own perfection. Full understanding is always regarded as a state superior to mere faith.[59] We shall consider it in a moment. But first the cognitive element *in* faith.

I already mentioned the understanding of meaning required for embracing a certain faith. In the case of Christianity—the prototype of a "faith" religion—this cognitive element increased in importance as creeds and theological structures developed to

[57] On the mind's need to "entertain" a position before accepting it, cf. R. B. Braithwaite, "The Nature of Belief" in *Knowledge and Belief,* p. 29, and H. H. Price, *art. cit.,* pp. 44–45. The cognitive activity discussed in these articles precedes the act of faith, but it must continue to exist within the act if the latter is to remain at all meaningful.

[58] "Gnosis" in *Bible Key Words,* II, tr. by J. R. Coates and H. P. Kingdon (New York: Harper & Brothers, 1948), p. 50.

[59] In the words of Augustine: "He who by true reason arrives at an understanding of what he had only believed is in a better state of advancement than he who still only desires to understand what he believes." *Epistulae,* 120, Ch. 2, 8, *Migne,* P. L., 33, 456.

which the faithful were expected to give their assent. Some of those may appear merely informative to the modern believer who fails to see their connection with his salvation. (For instance, the article that after his death Christ descended into hell.) But even those that refer directly to his personal situation carry a very specific meaning which requires understanding.[60] Yet these cognitive elements, as well as the propositions which correspond to them, are by no means independent intellectual processes. If we speak of truth here, as the believer thinks we must, we do so in a unique sense in which there is a maximum of existential involvement and a minimum of abstract objectivity. All religious assertions, to the extent that they are still meaningful to the believer, inform him about his own situation with regard to the transcendent, not about objective facts lying outside his existence. This holds true for the doctrine of the Trinity, the keystone of the fully developed Christian doctrine of salvation, as well as for the "events" of Jesus' life communicated in the gospels. When an article of a creed becomes purely informative, it is religiously dead and the next step will be its total disappearance.[61] All true religious propositions, however abstract and intellectual they appear, belong to the realm of symbolic knowledge, that is, of knowledge by existential participation, rather than to the realm of intellectual objectivity. The symbolic character of the cognition in faith does not exclude the presence of objectively established elements (for instance, certain facts of Jesus' life), but it precludes the object of faith from being fully known by purely theoretical insight. Neither purely empirical nor rational processes have access to the transcendent—which is to say that the cognitive element of faith is not knowledge in the ordinary sense at all. In interpreting the transcendent, faith opens up no speculative horizons but it places man in a different perspective. Even the more intellectualist interpreters of the Christian faith have been

[60] The thesis that they do not, is defended by R. M. Hare in "Theology and Falsification" in *New Essays in Philosophical Theology,* ed. by Antony Flew and Alasdair MacIntyre (New York: Macmillan, 1964), pp. 99–103.
[61] In Chapters 4 and 5 we shall learn more about the rise and decline of religious symbols.

aware of those distinctions. Thus Thomas in the *Summa Contra Gentiles,* I, 3–5, compares the "truths" of faith with man's knowledge of God. At first glance the former merely seem to add information to the latter. But in the same discussion, he writes: "Only then do we know God truly when we believe Him to be above everything that it is possible for man to think about Him."[62] Evidently "knowing" here carries a peculiar meaning. This is confirmed by St. Thomas' denial that the same thing can be an object of science and of belief at the same time.[63] Faith apparently gives a different assent than pure cognition. Even the "natural" knowledge of God differs from ordinary cognition, for Thomas writes: "The ultimate of man's cognition of God is to know that he does not know God."[64] Knowledge of God is never direct insight: it is an awareness of the insufficiency of the world.[65] The distinction between knowing and believing is made even more emphatically in less intellectualist theologians.

The second cognitive aspect in the act of faith is its tendency to become understanding. It is important, however, that it be no more than a tendency, essential to faith's need of self-understanding. If the believer is ever entirely successful in replacing faith by insight, he fundamentally changes his religious attitude and becomes a gnostic instead of a believer. The name *Gnosticism* covers such disparate religious movements that one may question whether a collective term is justified. Nevertheless all share the basic tenet that esoteric knowledge brings salvation, even that it *is* salvation.[66] To believers salvation is less immediately connected with the cognitive elements of faith. Still, *gnosis* is no ordinary knowledge since its object is inaccessible to the uninitiated. Like faith it must be revealed, but unlike

[62] *Summa Contra Gentiles,* Bk. I, Ch. 5, 3. *On the Truth of the Catholic Faith,* tr. by Anton C. Pegis (Garden City, N.Y.: Doubleday, 1955), p. 70.
[63] *Summa Theologiae,* II–II, 1, 5.
[64] *De Potentia,* Qu. 7, 5, ad. 14.
[65] Cf. Walter Brugge, "Gotteserkenntnis und Gottesglaube" in *Interpretation der Welt,* ed. by H. Kuhn, H. Kahlefeld, K. Forster (Würzburg, 1965), pp. 109–204.
[66] Hans Jonas, *The Gnostic Religion* (Boston: Beacon Press, 1963), p. 32.

faith the gnostic revelation is not passively received, yet actively acquired. Since all faith seeks understanding, Gnosticism is a more or less universal phenomenon, particularly visible in and around religions of faith. There have been Jewish, Christian, and anti-Christian forms of Gnosticism. They all disappeared, but after centuries of dormancy the gnosis emerged again during the Middle Ages, in the heart of Christianity. We also find it in the Islam.[67] Traits of it are visible in some of the Upanishads.[68]

Apart from the cognitive element within faith and the understanding toward which all faith strives, there still is a third form of knowledge connected with faith, although in a more extrinsic way. This is the knowledge of the so-called grounds of belief. I wrote "so-called" because in the strict sense they are not grounds at all, but extrinsic cognitive supports for what the believer accepts on an intrinsically religious basis. Yet these supports are necessary once man has reached a certain degree of reflection. The mature mind cannot believe that which has not the slightest basis in fact. The object of faith must possess at least a certain degree of probability. Of course, the believer does not require full evidence, for that would exclude faith itself. Nor is his assent ultimately determined by cognitive factors. The presence of a volitional element fundamentally distinguishes the assent of faith from a purely cognitive conclusion.

Yet, the precise impact of this volitional element has been a subject of discussion for a long time. In his *Grammar of Assent* Newman considers a decision of the will essential to any assent, even when the conclusions of the preceding ratiocinative process are logically convincing. "I could have withheld my assent, but I should have acted against my nature, had I done so when there was what I considered a proof."[69] This distinction between accepting a conclusion and giving one's assent has been severely attacked. How can one accept something as true and yet refuse to give his assent to it? How could one "decide" negatively with

[67] An example of Gnosticism would be the esoteric teachings of the Isma'iliya sect.
[68] Particularly the *Brihadaranyaka*.
[69] *A Grammar of Assent* (Garden City, N.Y.: Doubleday, 1958), p. 187.

respect to a content already accepted as true? If the conclusion is inevitable at the end of a process of reasoning, evidence and certitude coincide. Newman, perhaps under the influence of Hume, is overly cautious to consider anything as fully evident. To call all assent, even the cognitive one, a voluntary decision distorts the meaning of assent in the act of believing. For in belief I do not first "accept as true" and subsequently give or withhold my assent. The assent *itself* converts insufficient evidence into certain belief. There was no previous acceptance of truth, nor was there ever "a gap between accepting as true and assenting to it."[70] The truth in Newman's voluntaristic interpretation is that the assent surpasses the strictly cognitive order. But this should not allow him to call the noncognitive element in the act of cognition a voluntary decision. Something more basic than "willing" is at work here. It is, in Guardini's terms, the elementary act by which truth is impelled to assert itself against chaos and by which the person commits himself to the side of a truth which he sees as inevitable.[71]

Nonetheless, a volitional element definitely enters the act of belief, as appears in the fact that certainty results only from the decision to assent. It is the decision to believe which makes the partial evidence conclusive. The gap between evidence and believing assent can be bridged only by the will. Nor can one claim that the volitional element makes the assent irrational. Certainly the more rational man is, the less freedom he enjoys in deciding to what he will give his assent. Rational man does not "believe" where knowledge is readily available. But where it is not available—as often happens—man must *decide* what to believe. Whether such a decision is justified or not depends on the nature of the belief. To determine the issue in the present case we now must distinguish faith from belief.

So far we have simply identified both, because faith always

[70] See Bernard Mayo, "Belief and Constraint," in *Knowledge and Belief,* p. 148.
[71] Romano Guardini, "Der Glaube in der Reflexion" in *Unterscheidung des Christlichen,* p. 295.

includes belief and it is this belief which separates faith from knowledge. But belief belongs primarily to the intellectual order while faith is a more total commitment, formally determined by an intellectual act. It is a response of the whole nature which involves volitional and emotional elements as well as cognitive.[72] It is misleading, then, to present faith as if it were a particular belief, namely, a belief in certain doctrines expressly *because God has revealed them*.[73] Newman describes the content of faith as "a definite message from God to man . . . to be positively acknowledged, embraced and maintained as true, on the ground of its being divine, not as true on intrinsic grounds . . ."[74] But faith is not merely believing something. It is also, as Newman himself implies, believing *in someone*. Trust and confidence in the divine witness are so essential to the act of faith that the entire assent depends on it. I believe because I believe *in God*. Of course, one might argue that a certain trustfulness is part of every belief.[75] But trust in God differs from trust in a witness of belief, because I know no more about God than about the content of my faith. In fact, He is the content of that faith. So faith lacks the usual objective support which belief has when it knows its witness to be trustworthy. That is why the formula "because of my trust in God" fails to bring out the nature of the existential commitment of the act of faith. Catholics have traditionally been inclined to overstress the purely intellectual nature—the belief aspect—of faith.[76] But Protestants who rightly

[72] Dorothy M. Emmett, *The Nature of Metaphysical Thinking* (London: Macmillan, 1957), p. 139.

[73] John H. Newman, *A Grammar of Assent*, p. 94.

[74] *A Grammar of Assent*, p. 302.

[75] See Gail Kennedy, "Some Meanings of Faith" in *Religious Experience and Truth*, pp. 110, 115. Actually, this is not entirely true, for, as H. H. Price has proven, it is impossible to equate belief-*in* fully with belief-*that*. By conversion it follows that there are beliefs-*that* which are not beliefs-*in*. H. H. Price, "Belief 'in' and Belief 'that' " in *Religious Studies* (1965), pp. 5–27, esp. pp. 24–25.

[76] All too often faith is proposed as a mere intellectual belief where the will makes up what is lacking in rational evidence. "Faith implies an assent of the intellect to that which is believed . . . Now the intellect assents . . . through an act of choice, whereby it turns voluntarily to one side rather

object to the failure of Catholic theologians to distinguish adequately belief from faith have not improved matters very much by regarding the whole act as an act of trust. Trust in whom? To answer this question we must return to belief. Paul Tillich rightly rejected both characterizations as inadequate and proposed a more ontological definition.

> Faith is more than trust in even the most sacred authority. It is participation in the subject of one's ultimate concern with one's whole being. Therefore the term "faith" should not be used in connection with theoretical knowledge, whether it is a knowledge on the basis of immediate, prescientific or scientific evidence, or whether it is on the basis of trust in authorities who themselves are dependent on direct or indirect evidence.[77]

Faith as trust exists outside religion, but only religious faith has the total commitment which makes faith into a new way of existing, rather than a mere trust or belief.[78]

Even on purely cognitive grounds faith differs from belief. Belief is theoretically capable of verification or falsification. Of course, no man can ever verify all his beliefs and he may have to be contented with very few actual verifications. But at least he knows that sooner or later his beliefs will be tested by direct experience and thereby turn into knowledge. The religious believer holds no such hopes. Neither he nor his successors will ever be able to convert faith into knowledge, for its content does not belong in any way to the empirical world. Faith, therefore, must

---

than to the other; and if this be accompanied by doubt and fear of the opposite side, there will be opinion, while if there be certitude and no fear of the other side, there will be faith." *Summa Theologiae,* II–II, 1, 4. See also the *Exposition of Boethius on the Trinity,* III, 1c.

[77] Paul Tillich, *Dynamics of Faith* (New York: Harper & Brothers, 1958), p. 32. Perhaps Tillich plays down too much the cognitive aspect of accepting a positive content. In *The Courage to Be* (New Haven: Yale University Press, 1960), p. 172, he refers to faith as "accepting acceptance"—a beautiful but one-sided expression.

[78] See Gabriel Marcel, *Journal Métaphysique* (Paris, 1927), p. 152; *Être et avoir* (Paris, 1935), pp. 63, 308.

never be regarded as temporary information to be replaced some-
time by knowledge.[79] In fact, faith does not offer any information
about the empirical world at all. No empirical evidence, then,
can ever support the believer's interpretation of reality to the
point where the nonbeliever's becomes contradictory. Faith integrates the whole of empirical reality into a synthesis which itself
cannot be experienced. Of course, there are cognitive elements
present in the act of faith such as the understanding of the
meaning of a religious interpretation, the evaluation of the trustworthiness of the intermediary witnesses who present the message,
but unlike belief, faith is not "potentially" cognitive by being at
least in principle convertible through verification into an act of
knowledge.[80] The believer does not *know,* any more than the
nonbeliever, the ultimate foundation of the world of experience.
It is not even correct to say that the world makes "more" sense
to the believer, for "more" still implies that an "additional"
synthesis has been superimposed on man's rational synthesis of
the empirical world. The believer integrates the data of his
experience and the synthesis of his rational interpretations into
an ultimate nonrational synthesis, just as the nonbeliever integrates his into a set of ultimate beliefs. Both surpass the purely
rational order in their attempt to give some ultimate interpretation to experience. Faith interprets the same data which confront
the nonbeliever, but it interprets them differently by subordinat-
ing them to an ultimate principle which is neither the totality
nor an inherent part of the empirical order. Thus it gives a new
meaning to existence in relating it to the transcendent. But it
brings in no essentially new factors of information. Whatever
the believer asserts about the transcendent, he really asserts about
his own relation to the transcendent. Faith creates a new attitude;

[79] Eugene Fontinell, "Religious Truth in a Relational and Processive World"
in *Cross Currents,* XVII (1967), p. 304.
[80] The French philosopher Léon Ollé-Laprune considered the cognitive
elements merely preambulatory to the act of faith. *De la certitude morale*
(Paris, 1880), p. 85. I do not agree with this position, for although the
cognitive elements are not what ultimately determine the nature of the act,
they belong to the act itself.

it does not provide new knowledge, at least not in the usual sense of that term. In this respect one must agree with Bultmann that the believer does not adopt a new philosophy, but undergoes a reorientation of the self.

Is there nothing, then, to support the believer's view in the face of the nonbeliever's objections? Indeed, there is, and it is essential to the contemporary believer that he be able to justify his faith rationally. However, we should be aware of the limits of such a justification. What he justifies is not his faith but only, to some extent, his ability for giving an intellectual assent to the "object" of faith. Moreover, the evidence he introduces is never conclusive. In fact, he mainly shows that it is not irrational to believe even though he will never be able to "verify" his faith. Within these limits, however, modern man must in some way make his faith credible before he can accept it. Contemporary scholastic theologians have spent a great deal of acumen in attempting to define the precise nature of this credibility. Most of them distinguish a speculative from a practical credibility. The former includes all the reasons which make the claims of a particular creed plausible. Practical credibility, on the other side, provides the missing elements—moral attraction and religious impulse (the theologian calls this the impetus of divine grace)—to convert the deficient speculative credibility into an actual imperative toward belief.[81] How those two forms of credibility are connected remains a matter of dispute. According to some, the speculative credibility prepares a moral assent, while the concrete practical credibility induces the mind to believe independently of the external grounds. Others reject this independence but still accept a dual motivation.[82] Yet all maintain that neither

---

[81] Cf. Guy de Broglie, S.J., *Les signes de crédibilité de la révélation chrétienne* (Paris, 1964), pp. 40–43. Léopold Malevez, *Pour une théologie de la foi* (Paris, 1969), pp. 45–101.

[82] For the first opinion, cf. José de Wolf, S.J., *La justification de la foi chez St. Thomas* (Paris, 1946). Eduard Dhanis, S.J., "Le problème de l'acte de foi," *Nouvelle Revue Théologique* (1946), pp. 32–37. For the second opinion, cf. Guy de Broglie, S.J., "L'illumination des signes de crédibilité par la grâce," *Recherches de Science Religieuse*, 53 (1965), pp. 166ff.

speculative nor practical credibility compels the assent of faith which remains free.

Most arguments show only that faith is not altogether irrational. But that is not enough, for modern man demands *positive* reasons to believe. Without a positive need of faith, the reasonable thing to do in the face of doubt is to suspend judgment. Unless it can be proven to be indispensable or at least highly desirable to a full human life, faith remains unjustified. Philosophy may contribute to this justification by showing that the mind's dynamism tends toward an absolute, an ultimate, *unconditioned* principle of meaning and of Being. It is with this transcendent terminus that faith claims to establish a relation. In Chapter 3 we shall consider this approach more in detail.

5. FAITH AS TOTAL EXISTENCE

From the preceding section it should appear that faith is not objective in the sense in which knowledge or even belief is objective. This nonobjective character determines the nature of its assent in all respects. First let us turn toward the certitude of this assent. Certitude may be defined in two different ways: either as a firm assent or as a firm assent because of the full evidence of the matter.[83] We already know that there must be some evidence to support the belief which is an essential part of faith. Evidence is needed to embrace a religious faith or, once one has embraced it, to justify his decision to remain in it. Without some evidence faith loses its character of belief and becomes blind instinct.[84] But the supporting evidence is never complete. Nor is the certitude of belief sufficient for faith. Faith requires absolute certitude. All belief is certain, but its certainty is

[83] See Joseph Pieper, *Belief and Faith* (New York: Henry Regnery, 1966), p. 44.
[84] One cannot but agree with Paul Weiss: "Men can and do transfer to faith the certitude of true beliefs. Take away the certitude from the faith and the faith will become indistinguishable from longing, a hope deferred." *The God We Seek* (Carbondale: Southern Illinois University Press, 1964), pp. 203–4.

not without reservations. When I believe something, I always know that, although I am certain, it is theoretically possible that I am mistaken. It is precisely for not having distinguished faith sufficiently from belief in the *Grammar of Assent* that Newman fails to establish the particular certitude of faith. Newman's conditions for certitude distinguish certitude from blind conviction (which ignores the possibility of error): they do not distinguish the absolute certitude of faith from the relative one of belief.[85] The first condition, "that it follows on investigation and proof," is inconclusive by definition; for if the proofs were conclusive, faith would be replaced by knowledge. The second, "that it is accompanied by a specific sense of intellectual satisfaction and repose," provides no objective certainty whatever. The third, "that it is irreversible," merely proves that *thus far* I have had no reason to change my conviction. Faith needs more certitude than belief can ever provide. For belief never loses sight of the inconclusive nature of its evidence. The certitude of faith is based upon an entirely different sort of assent. Gabriel Marcel would say that an "existential index" is attached to belief.[86] In faith I totally commit myself to a person. This commitment transforms my *belief* that God exists into a *faith* in an existing God. Now unconditional surrender demands absolute certitude. As Kierkegaard remarked, a commitment to what is infinitely important to me excludes the possibility of doubt.[87] It has been objected that the exclusion of doubt implies the rejection of objectivity. Thus, Feuerbach:

> In faith the very principle of doubt is annulled; for to faith the subjective is in and by itself the objective—nay, the absolute. Faith is nothing else than belief in the absolute reality of subjectivity.[88]

[85] *A Grammar of Assent*, p. 207.
[86] *The Mystery of Being* (Chicago: Henry Regnery, 1954), Vol. II (*Faith and Reality*), p. 77.
[87] *Samlede Vaerker*, VI, p. 76; *Philosophical Fragments,* tr. by David Swenson (Princeton: Princeton University Press, 1944), p. 69.
[88] *Das Wesen oles Christentums* in *Sämtliche Werke* ed. by Wilhelm Bolin and Friedrich Jodl (Stuttgart, 1960) p. 151; *The Essence of Christianity,* tr. by George Eliot (New York: Harper & Brothers, 1957), p. 126.

It is false, as we shall see later, that total commitment excludes objectivity. But Feuerbach is right in assuming that the absoluteness of the certitude is due to the involvement of the subject. No objective data can ever provide the absolute certitude which faith requires. Catholics and "orthodox" Lutherans have frequently tried to provide this certitude by establishing the credibility of the Bible and Church. But far from being a source of absolute certitude, these objective realities require faith themselves to make their authority acceptable. As for historical facts, they may be sufficiently reliable to warrant *belief,* but they never justify the absolute certitude of faith. In a matter of infinite interest only a total commitment can generate an absolute certitude. This is what, according to Kierkegaard, Socrates did with respect to the immortality of the soul: he gained certitude only by staking his life on it. The risk itself provides a proof which objective data can never provide.[89]

Doubt, then, appears to be excluded by the very nature of the commitment of faith. But this conclusion is hardly confirmed by the struggle which our contemporaries fight for their faith. How do we account for that? Many authors, ancient and modern, have pointed out the objective uncertainty which remains in faith and causes "unrest," since belief always searches for more evidence.[90] According to St. Thomas, assent and unrest are equally strong in the act of faith.[91] Kierkegaard also defined faith as the tension between the passion of the individual's inwardness and objective uncertainty. "The more objective security the less inwardness, . . . and the less objective security the

[89] Søren Kierkegaard, *Papirer,* ed. by P. A. Heiberg, V. Kuhr, E. Torsting (Copenhagen, 1909–48), X², A406.
[90] See Joseph Pieper, *Belief and Faith,* pp. 45–46. Pieper comments on the text of St. Thomas: "Motus cogitationis in ipso remanet inquietus," *De Veritate,* 14, 1 ad. 5.
[91] "The movement of the mind is not yet stilled; rather there remains in it a searching and a pondering of that which it believes—although it nevertheless assents to what is believed with the utmost firmness." *De Veritate,* 14, 1.

more profound the possible inwardness."[92] Yet that is obviously not the whole answer, for if objective uncertainty is compatible with absolute certitude, doubt is not. And most believers at times suffer from genuine doubt. To me a distinction seems essential between faith as act (which *per se* excludes doubt) and faith as attitude (which is always close to doubt). Hardly anyone elicits the act of faith without having to overcome the fear that there may not be any reality at the other end.[93] It is normal enough to doubt before choosing what one does not know. The objective uncertainty of the terminus makes the believer hesitate before committing himself. In the act all doubt disappears.[94] But for most believers it returns. For the risk of faith is not overcome by a single decision made once in a lifetime. Faith remains a risk and the struggle between doubt and surrender never desists.

Modern man is in this respect at a serious disadvantage compared to his ancestors. Faith was, until recently, supposed to offer the final truth on virtually everything. Gradually the ties between faith and scientific knowledge have been severed. But many are no longer able to discern the proper sphere of faith. They feel that science is closing in on the content of their faith and may soon conquer its last foothold. Also, as man lives more reflectively, he doubts more and is less inclined to surrender. His commitments tend to be halfhearted and anemic. He has most of his experience derivatively, by thinking or reading about it or by watching it acted out in film or theater, rather than spontaneously, by being personally involved. The unsettled character of modern living has added to the problem. To believe, one must have learned to trust, for faith is trusting surrender. But to many of

[92] *Samlede Vaerker,* Vol. 9, p. 175; *Concluding Unscientific Postscript,* tr. by David Swenson and Walter Lowrie (Princeton: Princeton University Press, 1944), p. 69.

[93] See Erich Frank, *Philosophical Understanding and Religious Truth,* p. 43. Kierkegaard himself, who considered the act of faith incompatible with doubt, claims that faith is conditioned by doubt. *Papirer,* III, A36.

[94] I disagree with Tillich's *Dynamics of Faith,* pp. 17, 34, that the risk itself is accompanied by doubt. Objective uncertainty, yes; subjective doubt, no.

us who grew up in war, hatred, and social unrest, trust has
become impossible.[95] The German writer Ida Friederika Görres
caught the mood of lassitude and discouragement which besets
the contemporary believer, in a memorable description:

> What was important becomes indifferent; things which appeared
> necessary for life disappear without leaving a void. The circle of
> the absolute becomes smaller: the pressures of conditioned things
> circumscribing it are daily growing, and catching up with it . . .
> We are asked beyond our strength, that we believe, with rock-
> like firmness, that through these declines passes the road to salva-
> tion.[96]

We must not underestimate the potential destructiveness of the
present, all-pervasive climate of doubt. The language of theologians in the recent past mainly covered up those dark possibilities.
They continued to assure the believer that doubt had always
been an essential concomitant of faith—which is true—but they
failed to mention that doubt can take proportions which make
the act of commitment itself impossible. The point, then, is not
whether faith allows intermittent periods of doubt, but how much
doubt is possible before faith becomes paralyzed. It would seem
that for most contemporary believers the breaking point has
come close. It was a score for theological sincerity when a young
iconoclast recently charged:

> Let us continue to say that doubt is a necessary way for many
> of us to faith; that faith never overcomes doubt finally and
> completely; that lively faith can bear a good deal of doubt around
> the edges. But the depth of doubt is not the depth of faith; these
> are two places, not one, and a choice must finally be made
> between them. We cannot evade such a problem by a trick of
> redefinition.[97]

[95] On the genetic-psychological factors that make faith impossible, see the
study of the Dutch psychiatrist H. C. Rümke, *The Psychology of Unbelief*
(New York: Sheed & Ward, 1962).
[96] "The Believer's Unbelief" in *Cross Currents*, 1961, pp. 54, 58.
[97] William Hamilton, *The New Essence of Christianity* (New York: Association Press, 1961), p. 61.

The philosopher is obviously in no position to predict the outcome of this situation. If he is a believer he may take comfort
in the analyses of those sociologists who, on the basis of a new
sensitivity for the metempirical, foresee an easier future for the
believer.[98] Yet, his own task consists in the analysis of structures
of consciousness as they actually appear in and around the act
of faith. His conclusions must remain purely hypothetical: such
and such an attitude is incompatible or compatible with belief.
To what extent the present climate of doubt actually impairs the
attitude of faith, he is not competent to say. But he *knows* that
the mind's capacity of belief is not unlimited and neither is the
soul's potential of surrender in faith.

With the same logical necessity he can assert: if the act
occurs—and in many instances the amazing thing is that it still
does—then it remains as certain as it ever was. For the *act*
allows no doubt. In this certitude faith reveals its subjective
inwardness. Certitude refers to the subjective identity by which
the spirit possesses a content as its own.[99] Ordinary language
suggests the subjective nature of certitude in expressions such as,
I am as certain of something *as I am of myself*. By thus
interiorizing its content certitude resembles feeling. Yet unlike
feeling it has a *content,* which means that it exists "through the
medium of an object."[100] The act of faith reaches beyond
itself; it does not merely possess itself *at the occasion of an
object,* as feelings do. Nor does faith merely "long" for its content
as a sort of nostalgic aspiration of what remains forever out of
reach.[101] Faith is never *merely* a subjective believing *in,* but

[98] For instance, Peter Berger, *A Rumor of Angels* (Garden City, N.Y.:
Doubleday, 1969).
[99] Hegel, *Vorlesungen über die Philosophie der Religion,* I, p. 86. In
Vorlesungen über die Beweise vom Dasein Gottes (ed. by Georg Lasson,
Hamburg, 1966, p. 5). Hegel writes that faith expresses the inwardness of
certitude.
[100] *Vorlesungen über die Beweise vom Dasein Gottes,* p. 29.
[101] Hegel rejected this theory of faith which he attributed to Jacobi
already in his early *Glauben und Wissen* (Hamburg, 1962), pp. 45–46. In
the *Phenomenology* he compares Jacobi's "unhappy consciousness" to the
way in which true faith possesses its content, as a subjective yearning

always also a believing *that*. The believer is certain of *what* he believes. Yet, the content of faith is never a mere datum: it is a *connection* between consciousness and its datum, which the subject can grasp in *its awareness of itself*. In this respect the certitude of faith differs from the objective certainty of knowledge which grasps its object as independent of the subject.

The subjectivity of faith implies that it must *freely* accept its content. This distinguishes it clearly from a religion of nature in which the content is part of man's natural environment. In faith the individual takes a personal stand and accepts what he could have rejected. In a religion of nature a person is obviously not free to accept or reject his natural environment.[102] When faith enters, religion ceases to be the *substance* of everyday life. Even if its guidelines are imposed upon society, as was the case in the Middle Ages, its center still remains hidden in the inner *sanctum* of the heart. For faith must *be accepted* in order to be true. It is precisely this free acceptance which gives it its certitude and its personal character. "Faith is really conceived of as my personal faith, as an inmost certitude which is exclusively my own."[103]

Inwardness is not the final explanation of the subjective nature of faith, for the inward appropriation itself results from the transcendence of the appropriated content. The content of faith is not an *object*, that is, a cognitive terminus constituted by the

---

to the possession of an objective content. *Phänomenologie des Geistes,* ed. by Georg Lasson (Hamburg, 1952), p. 533, tr. J. B. Baillie (New York: Harper & Row, 1967), pp. 765–66 (slightly corrected). In Hegel's *Phenomenology* faith belongs to the order of reflection which "reflects" the real world into a *beyond* in order to *represent* this world. It is important to stress this, for, mainly due to Kierkegaard's attacks, Hegel has gained the reputation of considering faith as purely "immediate." Yet, for Hegel faith is neither feeling (Schleiermacher) nor longing (Jacobi), but *knowledge* and, as such, reflective. He denied the immediacy of faith from the beginning (*Phänomenologie,* pp. 392–94) to the end of his career (*Vorlesungen über die Beweise vom Dasein Gottes,* pp. 24–31). Faith is immediate only with respect to knowledge which can fully justify its form as well as its content.

[102] G. W. F. Hegel, *Vorlesungen über die Philosophie der Religion,* I, p. 261.

[103] *Vorlesungen über die Philosophie der Religion,* I, p. 263.

subject. The believer feels that he has no control over this content. Yet he is, by personal decision, deeply involved in it; he has nowhere to go but inward. In that sense Kierkegaard could write that faith is only *concern about faith,*[104] and Tillich that the concern about the unconditional is an unconditional concern.[105] This also explains why it is more important *how* one believes than *what* he believes, for to know God truly is not to know the true God, but to achieve a true relation to God.[106] Because of its transcendent nature the acceptance of the content of faith depends upon a voluntary *decision.* Earlier I mentioned this fact without justifying it. But why should man commit himself so totally to what he will never be able to understand? We are now in a better position to understand the answer. Precisely because the content of faith is transcendent, its appropriation requires a subjective commitment. The "truth" of faith then turns out to be no truth at all in the ordinary sense. The believer commits himself to a content which he can never "possess," but which becomes "true" for him in the commitment itself. Such a truth cannot be expressed in a set of universal propositions: personal acceptance plays an essential part. Since this acceptance cannot be determined by the nature of the content (which is transcendent), it must come entirely from the decision of the subject.

The need for a free decision where rational insight is insufficient has been emphasized most strongly in William James's theory of the "will to believe." According to James, the decision to believe is a moral decision which man cannot postpone until he possesses all the evidence. Once man has satisfied himself that the religious hypothesis is not patently untrue, faith must be treated as a good, rather than as a truth.

We see first that religion offers itself as a *momentous* option. We are supposed to gain, even now, by our belief, and to lose by our

104 *Papirer,* A32.
105 *Dynamics of Faith,* p. 9.
106 Kierkegaard, *Samlede Vaerker,* Vol. 9, p. 16. *Concluding Unscientific Postscript,* p. 178.

non-belief, a certain vital good. Secondly, religion is a *forced* option, so far as that good goes. We cannot escape the issue by remaining sceptical and waiting for more light, because, although we do avoid error in that way *if religion be untrue,* we lose the good, *if it be true,* just as certainly as we positively chose to disbelieve . . .[107]

James's conclusion seems similar to our own. Yet it is not, and James's position is unacceptable to the believer. No one could possibly decide to believe because he feels that there is more to lose by not believing, nor could he, after having embraced a faith, remain in it by James's argument. Certainly, faith is a decision, a choice, but it never is a choice between two positions of equal quality. The rational arguments may be equally strong on either side, but he who chooses to believe does so because of an inner attraction to one side rather than the other, not because of a moral choice between similar positions. To be sure, he could choose not to believe because evidence does not compel him, but he knows that in his case such a choice would be religiously *wrong.* For all the insufficiency of its evidence the act of faith presents itself to the believer as a *necessary* act. When this necessity is no longer perceived, faith itself is abandoned. Yet the necessity itself is religious in nature. The believer considers himself as much unable to *will* its content autonomously as he is incapable of *knowing* it objectively. To him man does not *choose* to enter into contact with the divine: he is being chosen. Consequently, a faith resulting from mere decision, as in James's voluntarist interpretation, is religiously inconceivable. If faith is a decision, the decision itself must be regarded as a gift. Rudolf Bultmann, who defines believing as a decision toward authentic existence, writes:

Faith is the work of God insofar as the grace which comes from him first makes possible the human decision, so that this decision

107 "The Will to Believe" in *Essays on Faith and Morals* (New York: World Publishing Company, 1962), p. 57.

itself can be understood only as God's gift, without on that account losing its character as decision.[108]

This description shows both the moral involvement and the intrinsically religious character of the act of faith. For faith unquestionably places moral demands on man once he hears its calling. Yet these demands can be discerned as genuine, and therefore binding in conscience, only *after* I have started to believe. As for the trust which enables the believer to accept the content of faith, one can only say with the French: *La confiance ne se commande pas.* The obligation to believe, then, must be quite different from other obligations. A British writer has cogently expressed the strange *petitio principii* of the imperative of the act of faith.

The difficulty is that "I ought to believe *p*" is something that I can never sincerely assert, unless I already do believe *p*. This makes it quite different from "I ought to be generous, tolerant, etc."; for I can perfectly well be aware of the value of certain character traits which I happen not to have, as well as the availability of certain exercises which might help me to acquire them. Yet, in the case of belief, although I do know what sort of exercises help me to acquire or part with beliefs—attending to the evidence for example—can I possibly be aware of the value of beliefs which I lack, or the faultiness of beliefs which I have? . . . Though belief may properly be said to be required of us, it is a requirement which we ourselves cannot endorse—until after we have complied with it if we do.[109]

The demands of faith, then, are demands *within* faith. Obedience and submission can be required only from him who already believes.

The "will to believe" is a will within belief: it affirms what already exists. Traditional Christian doctrine, while insisting on

[108] *Theologie des neuen Testaments* (Tübingen: 1958), pp. 325–26. Comments on this text in John MacQuarrie, *An Existentialist Theology,* p. 196. See also, Karl Jaspers, *Philosophie,* II, p. 281.
[109] Phillips Griffiths, "On Belief" in *Knowledge and Belief,* p. 140.

the obligation to believe, asserts that faith is "the beginning of human salvation" and "essentially a gift of God."[110] Faith must be a gift before being a demand or a virtue, because, for the believer, it participates in the transcendence which it intends, and self-transcendence in the religious sense can only be given. "The ultimate of the act of faith and the ultimate that is meant in the act of faith are one and the same."[111] In accepting the message of revelation, the religious mind believes he partakes of the divine life therein announced.[112] For the vision of faith can be seen only with divine eyes. This makes faith into an initial mystical awareness of union with God. As Eckhart wrote: "The eye by which I see God is the same as the eye by which God sees me. My eye and God's eye are one and the same—one in seeing, one in knowing and one in loving."[113] Faith, then, is not belief in a relation between God and man; to the believer it is that relation itself. But since the ground of the relation lies in what originates it, faith to the believer is participation in divine life.

Yet although faith initiates a total attitude, it does not complete it. Its inwardness is also its limitation. The total religious attitude requires outward expression in worship and social behavior, as much as inward commitment. No theologian, not even

[110] These assertions were made in the First Vatican Council *Enchiridion Symbolorum,* ed. by H. Denzinger, Cl. Bannwart, J. B. Umberg (Barcelona, 1948), ✳1793, 1789, 1791. The same was already affirmed in the Council of Orange (529). "He is an adversary of the apostolic teaching who says that the increase of faith as well as the beginning of faith and the very desire of faith . . . inheres in us naturally and not by a gift of grace." (Dz. ✳178)

[111] Paul Tillich, *Dynamics of Faith,* p. 11.

[112] Joseph Pieper, *Belief and Faith,* p. 90.

[113] Sermon 23, in *Meister Eckhart,* tr. by R. B. Blakney (New York: Harper & Brothers, 1957), p. 206. Hegel expressed the same: "Man knows God only insofar as God himself knows himself in man. This knowledge is God's self-consciousness, but it is at the same time a knowledge of man by God." *Vorlesungen über die Beweise vom Dasein Gottes,* p. 117, tr. in Hegel, *Lectures on the Philosophy of Religion,* by E. B. Speirs and J. Burdon Sanderson, Vol. 3, p. 303. Cf. also, Emil Fackenheim, *The Religious Dimension in Hegel's Thought,* pp. 124–25.

the prophets of religious inwardness of the Reformation, has
ever identified faith with the entire religious attitude. *Sola fide*
was a battle cry created for the purpose of de-emphasizing an
almost magical belief in external practices: it was never a total
religious program. Luther expects the believer to express his
faith in good deeds, even though the deeds as such have no redeeming quality. In worship and moral action, and for Christians particularly in brotherly love, faith is at once objectively
expressed and internally assimilated.[114] The Catholic tradition
indicates this dynamic aspect of faith by referring to it as *in-
choatio caritatis*. Love is initiated by faith. Yet Christians have
always been reluctant to say that faith is already the love in
which the consummation of their religion consists. Thomas clearly
distinguishes faith from love while fully admitting their relation.
"The beginning of faith consists in a certain affection insofar as
the will determines the mind to assent to what it believes. But
this element of the will is not the act of charity."[115] The believer is invited in his faith to achieve the surrender which the
act of faith only initiated.

114 Cf. the final paragraphs 565–71 on religion of Hegel's *Encyclopädie*,
1830 (Hamburg, 1959), pp. 447–49. Comments in André Léonard, *La
foi chez Hegel*, dissertation, Philosophical Institute, Louvain, 1968, pp.
410–18.
115 *De Veritate* 14, a. 2 ad. 10.

Chapter 2
How Not to Speak About Religion

1. THE OBJECTIVE FALLACY

There is a widespread belief that whatever exists as a fact can
be entirely understood as a fact, that is, objectively. A great
number of scientists and scientifically oriented philosophers would
agree with Julian Huxley that the gods are among the empirical
facts of cultural history, and can be investigated by the methods
of science like other empirical facts.[1] This belief is unfounded,
and in the case of religion, the surest way to misunderstand the
entire phenomenon. Religion produces cultural, social, and even
economic facts which must be studied according to the methods
of the respective disciplines in which they belong. But they are
not religion, and if identified with it, their interpretation will lead
to the strangest misconceptions. Religion may be explained as a
useful factor in the adaptation process "functionally analogous
with adjustive physical changes of biological evolution."[2] No one
can deny that religion fulfills a function in the adaptation process—what does not?—but to concentrate exclusively on this aspect is not a very promising method for exploring the nature of

[1] *Religion without Revelation* (New York: New American Library), p. 49.
[2] Credit for this curious explanation goes to Edward Norbeck, "Anthropological Views on Religion" in *Religion in Philosophical and Cultural Perspective*, ed. by Clayton Fever and William Horosz (Princeton: D. Van
Nostrand, 1967), pp. 418, 433.

the religious phenomenon. If religion serves no other purpose than preserving the group in which it originated, as Durkheim thought, the believer is sadly mistaken about its transcendent quality.

The entire factual, objectivist view of religion results not from science but from a scientist assumption that the approach of the positive sciences is the only valid one in all matters. This assumption has been given a semblance of truth by several philosophical theories. The oldest one is probably *materialism*. In the seventeenth century Thomas Hobbes decreed that philosophy was restricted to the science of bodies in motion.[3] He did not deny the existence of God but explicitly excluded it from any sort of valid cognition. Later materialist theories would rule out the possibility of a transcendent reality altogether. According to d'Holbach (1723) and Lamettrie (1709) nothing can be conceived beyond physical nature, nor is there any need for naming anything beyond it. The supernatural, d'Holbach explains in his *Système de la Nature,* was invoked to explain motion but nature provides its own motion, including the functioning of the brain. Its self-sufficiency would not admit interference from any outside factors. These theories were somewhat refined by the great materialists of the nineteenth century (Haeckel, Moleschott), but the basic principles have remained unchanged to the present day.

Related to the materialist position is that of *naturalism*. Yet while the former is essentially a static form of scientific monism, naturalism refuses to reduce nature to a single scientific system. Perhaps it is best understood as an attempt to rethink the dynamic process of Hegel's Spirit in terms of the natural sciences. Marx's early writings show in this respect a remarkable resemblance to the work of the twentieth-century naturalists, particularly John Dewey. Although a plurality of techniques is admitted, the unity of scientific method is strictly maintained.[4] Consistently naturalists reject the possibility of a reality which would transcend

[3] *Concerning Body*, I, 1, 8, *English Works of Thomas Hobbes,* ed. by W. Molesworth (London: Bohn and Longman, 1839–45).
[4] Cf. James Collins, *God in Modern Philosophy* (Chicago: Henry Regnery, 1959), p. 270.

the homogeneous world of the natural sciences and break up
the assumed unity of nature.

Most influential today is *positivism,* particularly the logical kind
which originated in the Vienna Circle of Moritz Schlick. Unlike
naturalism, logical positivism accepts no other method in philosophy than logical analysis. Not all logical analysis is positivist;
in fact, linguistic analysis is indispensable in the study of religious
language. But the positivist variety excludes the meaningfulness of
all religious statements. This appears clearly in the criterion of
truth as formulated by Schlick: "The meaning of a proposition
is the method of its verification."[5] This very narrow criterion
does not even cover the universal laws of the physical sciences.
It has some intrinsic flaws as well, for how can a proposition
be verified unless it already has a meaning?[6] Few if any logical
positivists still hold the original principle. As the theoretical framework of the sciences grew more abstract, the fraction of it open
to direct verification continued to decrease in proportion. The
question now is more which hypothesis gives the most consistent
and simplest explanation of the facts.[7] A. J. Ayer therefore proposed a modified version of the verification principle, requiring
only that some possible sense-experience should be relevant to
the determination of the truth or falsehood of an empirical
hypothesis. This may be more satisfactory to the physical sciences
but it hardly solves the problem of religious beliefs. As Professor
Ayer states, if a proposition fails to satisfy this principle (and is
not tautological) it is "metaphysical," that is, "neither true nor
false but literally senseless."[8] Such a "metaphysical" statement
would obviously be the proposition that there is a God. This
proposition is not even probable to Ayer, for if it were we would

[5] Moritz Schlick, "The Future of Philsophy" in *Gesammelte Aufsatze*
(Vienna, 1938), p. 181.
[6] Cf. J. Bochenski, *The Logic of Religion* (New York: New York University Press, 1965), p. 97.
[7] Ian Barbour, *Issues in Science and Religion* (Englewood Cliffs, N.J.:
Prentice-Hall, 1966), pp. 144–50.
[8] A. J. Ayer, *Language, Truth and Logic* (New York: Dover Publications,
1953), p. 31.

be able to deduce conclusions from it that would not follow from empirical hypotheses alone. But empirically the acceptance or rejection of the existence of God makes no difference whatever. The only phenomenon which in Ayer's mind could possibly require a transcendent being, would be the regularity in the processes of nature. Yet if this is the only instance, little is gained by a reference to a transcendent Being, for in that case to assert the existence of God is really no more than to assert the regularity of the phenomena themselves. Even if one were to widen the field of empirical relevance, the existence of God could never provide an answer to a *specific* question. Regardless of what the world was like, nothing would be more satisfactorily explained by the admission of an ultimate cause than by its rejection. Ayer therefore concludes that a sentence cannot be both meaningful and about God. He leaves open the possibility of a religious experience as long as no claims are made concerning the transcendent terminus of this experience.

Ayer's position came under severe attack and the criticism made him qualify his position considerably. In the introduction to the second edition of his *Language, Truth, and Logic* he modestly admits that, after all, a statement may be meaningful even though it is neither analytic nor empirically verifiable. Yet, he claims, there is at least one proper use of the word "meaning" which in that case would not apply, namely, the one of scientific hypotheses and most common sense statements.[9] But by his own admission, no "metaphysician" would claim this in the first place. The formidable principle of empirical verification has now been reduced to a harmless tautology: If a statement does not fulfill the requirements of the logic of science, it is not a scientific statement. It would be foolish not to agree with that principle, but one wonders what could possibly be gained by stating it.

The entire controversy turns around the universality of the verifiability principle. Why should the meaningful be restricted to the empirically verifiable? This has never been done in cultural history, including the present time. Nor is such a restrictive

[9] Ayer, *op. cit.,* p. 16.

principle ever likely to prevail. Verification in the positivist sense
is one possible meaning fulfillment. With the possible exception
of the physical sciences, it is not the only possible fulfillment. If
religion expresses its meanings in symbols, as we shall see it
does, a number of fulfillments are required, for symbols are
always polyvalent.[10] To be sure, religious assertions contribute
little to the explanation of the physical world. Neither the acceptance nor the rejection of Providence will increase our understanding of physical facts. But what does that mean? What
conclusions can be drawn from the fact that a religious belief
cannot be experimentally verified?[11] None at all. Nor can it be
said that we have broken the rule of scientific economy, for
religious assertions do not compete with the scientific hypotheses.
They deal with a different kind of question, where they prove
to be extremely useful.[12]

There is little purpose in belaboring this point since the main
challenge to religious assertions today comes from a different
scientific principle—*falsifiability*. Although the principle was first
posited (by Carl Popper) as a criterion for empirical meanings, it
appears to have expanded its rule over all meanings. In its most
general form we may formulate it as follows: an assertion which
no particular data could falsify in principle is meaningless. How it
applies to religious assertions is obvious. Antony Flew has attempted to show that no conceivable events or series of events
would ever be sufficient for the believer to concede: There is not
a God after all, or even: God does not love us. If no father
treats his children as the heavenly Father treats his, the believer
will always reply that God's love, unlike earthly love, is inscrutable. Nothing in his eyes can ever falsify the God hypothesis.[13]

Several philosophers took up the challenge, some by proving
that religious claims are indeed falsifiable, others by showing

[10] Cf. Paul Ricoeur, *De l'interprétation* (Paris, 1965), p. 39.
[11] The case is brought up in Morris Cohen, *Reason and Nature* (Chicago:
Free Press, 1953), p. 159.
[12] Cf. James Collins, *God in Modern Philosophy*, pp. 280–81.
[13] *New Essays in Philosophical Theology*, edited by Antony Flew and
Alasdair MacIntyre (New York: Macmillan, 1964), pp. 98–99.

that the principle does not apply since religious statements have no empirical content. Among the former, Basil Mitchell maintained that once a person has committed himself in faith, certain facts (such as evil and suffering) still count against his religious belief, but not decisively so.[14] Others pointed out quickly that the question was not whether the evidence counted, but whether it could ever count enough to render religious claims false.[15] Related to Mitchell's is the position of John Hick who sees the possibility of falsification in principle realized in the existence or nonexistence of an afterlife.[16] But how could eschatological statements constitute a falsifiability criterion for this life? Also, as William Blackstone points out, even if such a criterion were acceptable it would not cover most religious assertions, such as, God is love, etc.[17] Another British philosopher, I. M. Crombie, at first merely seems to combine the preceding two positions, but is in fact saying something entirely new. He accepts the need for a falsifiability principle in language, but rejects the possibility of an actual test in fact.[18] A statement is meaningless only when there exists a *rule of language* which precludes testing it. But this is not the case for religious utterances, for the very question: How can God be loving and allow pain? proves it most conceivable that one would exclude the other. Only when we turn to the facts do we become perplexed, because no amount of experience allows us to see the entire picture. This means: Although *outside the religious context* no man can devise an experiment that could make religious claims in principle falsifiable, within this context we know what a test of it would be like. If religious

14 *New Essays in Philosophical Theology*, pp. 103–5.
15 Cf. D. R. Duff-Forbes, "Theology and Falsification Again" in *The Australasian Journal of Philosophy*, 39 (1961), pp. 149–50, and W. T. Blackstone, *The Problem of Religious Knowledge* (Englewood Cliffs, N.J.: Prentice-Hall, 1963), pp. 110–11.
16 "Theology and Verification" in *Theology Today*, 17 (1960), No. 1, pp. 12–31.
17 Blackstone, *op cit.*, p. 115. Hick attempts to answer this criticism in his *Philosophy of Religion* (Englewood Cliffs, N.J.: Prentice-Hall, 1964), pp. 104–6.
18 *New Essays in Philosophical Theology*, pp. 109–30.

discourse deals with a segment of experience unaccounted for by ordinary or scientific language, then different tests must be adhibited than the ones which apply to those other realms of experience. Religious experience must be verified in terms of its own kind of experience, and this requires entirely different criteria. If religion is there, as Crombie thinks, "to fill in certain deficiencies in our experience that could not be filled in by further experience or scientific theory making,"[19] then it can make no straightforward statements about the world or about well-defined objects, but only about the new direction which certain experiences indicate. To these experiences the criterion of falsifiability cannot apply in the usual, empirical sense, since no object corresponds to them.[20] Instead of showing the actual falsifiability of religious statements, Crombie shows the internal coherence of religious language. Professor Crombie might have added that religious experiences are not only real but also are *intentional,* that is, they are states of consciousness which refer beyond the self. The aim of those experiences is not definable in object-terminology. But the possibility of an *objective* verification would jeopardize the specific nature of the religious experience. The different nature of the experience merely implies that it must be understood in its own terms.

I have analyzed Professor Crombie's discussion at some length not in order to criticize it but, on the contrary, because I believe it to be basically correct in exposing the limitations of what at first appeared to be a universal criterion of meaning. The question of falsifiability must definitely be raised for religious assertions, but it must be raised within a religious context. To say simply, as R. M. Hare does,[21] that the question should not be asked since faith gives us merely a general outlook on the world in which the terms "true" or "false" do not apply, is to rescue the religious position from possible criticism only to drown it in meaninglessness. Religious man is very much aware that his be-

[19] I. M. Crombie, "The Possibility of Theological Statements" in *Faith and Logic*, edited by Basil Mitchell (London: S.C.M. Press, 1957), p. 56.
[20] *New Essays in Philosophical Theology*, p. 124.
[21] *New Essays in Philosophical Theology*, pp. 99–102.

lief is in principle falsifiable. And his particular agony is that he never knows whether it will still be able to pass the test tomorrow. Job feels his faith wavering under the blows of God's trial. Yet he survives. However, the test must always be applied in terms of a particular religious faith and its specific promises. Thus a real crisis developed when the early Christians saw all the apostles and eyewitnesses dying while they all had expected to see Jesus returning soon. Similarly, the German concentration camps constituted a threat to the survival of Israel's faith as much as to its physical existence, since Yahweh is believed to be the God who saves *in* history.[22]

If the Christian faith would be wiped out altogether, it would have failed the falsifiability test, for Jesus clearly promised to stay with his followers. Also, if some incontrovertible evidence would suddenly prove that Jesus had not risen from the dead, a Christian faith in the strict sense would become impossible. More generally, if all religious beliefs could be adequately accounted for without reference to a transcendent reality, faith could justifiably be considered as falsified, since the presumption is that an explanation by purely intramundane factors is preferable to one which has recourse to an unknown transcendent cause. Of course, it is virtually impossible to submit an entire faith to this test. Yet there is a real possibility that empirical facts will close in on religious man and strongly decrease his grounds of belief. Although this can never be regarded as a decisive criterion and although those facts will be assessed differently by various people, it nevertheless introduces the principle of falsification.

To submit the Christian faith to such a test is precisely what Professor Broad must have had in mind when he presented the general impact of modern science as undermining the grounds of

---

[22] Two most moving accounts of religious Jews tortured by the falsifiability test are Richard Rubenstein, *After Auschwitz,* and Emil L. Fackenheim, "The People Israel Lives," in *The Christian Century,* 1970, pp. 563–68. The former reflects on Auschwitz and finds that his belief fails the test; the latter meditates on the new state of Israel in the light of Auschwitz and is still struggling in faith.

belief.[23] He mentions in particular the possibility of believing in miracles and in a life after death. Both, he alleges, have been rendered so improbable by modern science that "there is literally nothing but a few pinches of philosophical fluff to be put in the opposite scale to this vast coherent mass of ascertained facts."[24] One may disagree on Broad's evaluation of the impact of scientific conclusions, but the point has been made that religious beliefs can be falsified, if not absolutely, at least relatively by a study of empirical phenomena. However, in this case we notice how a subjective element enters the discussion which was absent from the previous suppositions. This is even more present in an assessment of moral evil and suffering such as the one with which Mr. Flew opened the debate. Here objective facts are relevant, they may even be decisive to the individual, but they cannot be so on a universal scale. The dying child in Camus' *The Plague* definitely excluded the idea of a merciful God for Rieux. *His* idea of God was evidently unable to accommodate the sight of children dying in great pain. But other people will reach a different conclusion. To them this is not a decisive criterion as the disappearance of Christianity obviously would be. Religious assertions, then, are in principle falsifiable, both on a universal and an individual scale. There may be no fact available that would *actually* falsify the Christian faith on a universal scale. But the principle does not demand that a hypothesis be actually false, only that we be able to state under what conditions it would become false. Nor do we need to wait for the possible application of a universal criterion to establish the actual falsifiability of faith: every day we observe people who lose their faith because they are unable to square its content with their view of the world. The believer does not refuse to submit his faith to the criterion of falsifiability, but only to *scientific* falsifiability. The test of faith must be administered in accordance with the nature of the religious experience itself, not with the standards of the scientific experience.

[23] C. D. Broad, *Religion, Philosophy and Psychical Research* (London: Routledge & Kegan Paul, 1953), pp. 231–41.
[24] *Op. cit.*, p. 235.

Admitting the particular nature of faith we might even find an acceptable version of the verifiability criterion. No objective facts can ever verify *by themselves* the truth or falsity of religious assertions. For faith allows no *a priori* criteria of its truth; it must provide its own justification. At the same time, some facts do contribute to the *religious* verification of religious claims. If historians were able to establish beyond the shade of a doubt the resurrection of Christ and all his major miracles, the truth of the Christian faith would still not be "proven" (from a purely empirical, scientific viewpoint a number of other interpretations are possible); nevertheless such a historical authentication of the original events would undoubtedly contribute to the verification of the Christian faith *for the believer*. They are pointers which, *when integrated within a religious context and only then,* become convincing. Facts are never full-fledged empirical proofs of faith, conclusive in any context, yet to the believer they are "starting points for references."[25] They take their place in a totality which *as a whole* is convincing mainly because of the intrinsic dynamism of the act of faith itself. Unfortunately, religious apologists usually show little awareness of the distinction and treat religious evidence as if it met the standards of scientific verification—which it never does and, by its very nature, never can do.

The neo-positivist, if he is religiously inclined, may grant us all this and still raise one final objection. If God is in no way an object, then human language, which is primarily object-language and indirectly subject-language, is not equipped to speak of God adequately. We do not *know* God objectively and consequently we cannot speak about him correctly. He may conclude with Wittgenstein at the end of the *Tractatus Logico-Philosophicus:* "Wovon man nicht sprechen kann, daruber musz man schweigen" —"What we cannot speak about we must pass over in silence."[26] A thorough discussion of religious language must be postponed to

25 William Christian, *Meaning and Truth in Religion* (Princeton: Princeton University Press, 1964), p. 211.
26 *Tractatus Logico-Philosophicus,* the German text with a translation by D. F. Pears and B. F. McGuinness (New York: Humanities Press, 1963), pp. 150–51.

a more appropriate place. Yet the objection can be taken care of immediately. For even though the transcendent cannot be expressed adequately in a language which is primarily object-oriented, such an expression is nevertheless justified by an intrinsic necessity of the religious act. By its very nature this act requires a commitment to the transcendent which does not allow the believer to remain silent. Because he must speak *to* God, he needs to talk *about* God. In doing so he does not hope to expand the field of empirical knowledge: he merely claims the right to name the transcendent. His naming is not a scientific description; it is a definition of the transcendent *as it is intended by the believer in the act of faith.*

2. THE ILLUSION OF THE BEGINNING

The great popularity of the evolutionary idea in the biology, sociology, and philosophy of the nineteenth century has had a strange side effect in the study of religion. For several decades it was assumed without question that the truth of a religion is to be found exclusively in its origin. Thus the search for a definition took the form of a quest for the beginning. Dubious as such a thesis may be, it would have remained relatively harmless had it not been accompanied by a perverted Darwinian belief that at the beginning of a religious species we find another genus. Thus it became widely accepted that faith is to be explained not through itself, but through something else. It is somewhat ungrateful to complain about this now, because most of what we know about the structure of primitive religion has been discovered or at least initiated by the pioneering missionaries of that creed of the beginning. Yet it is an illusion and must be exposed, all the more because many still secretly adhere to at least one of its articles. In religious matters, they feel, the origin must reveal the essence. There is some apparent foundation for this belief in the fact that the origin of a religion largely determines its direction and development. But this is true only if the origin is

the one *of the religion*—not something else. A glance at the conclusions of ethnologists and sociologists of the nineteenth and early
twentieth century will show how hazardous the assumptions were.

The animistic interpretation of Edward B. Tylor simply presupposes that religion originates in a primitive attempt to account
for the difference between living and dead bodies, and for the
detachment of the mind from the body in dreams and visions.
This would lead to a belief first in ghost-souls and eventually in
gods, Platonic Ideas, even a Hegelian Spirit.[27] The prime movers
of the evolutionary process were "an advancing intellectual condition" as well as a somewhat Victorian drive toward moral
progress.[28] Absent from the original condition was everything
that would make it in any way religious or even anticipating
religion. Instead Tylor described something with which he was
more familiar: a primitive interpretation of causality.

Although Tylor's thesis drew fire from all sides, his basic assumptions, that the first stage reveals the essence of religion and
that the origin basically differs from the development, went un-
challenged. What was questioned was the relatively unimportant
issue whether animism came first. To Tylor's thesis James Frazer
opposed his own: religion is not rooted in a primitive desire to
understand, but rather in the will to dominate. The original object of adoration is power, first conceived in an impersonal way,
later personified in spirits, ancestors, and gods.[29] A host of excellent scholars confirmed the power thesis by detailed mono-
graphs. Best known among them is Robert Henry Codrington's
study, *The Melanesians* (1891), in which he introduced the concept of *mana*. The accommodating vagueness of this concept
predisposed it for a most successful career. Codrington defines
it as a "power or influence, not physical and in a way super-

[27] *Religion in Primitive Culture* (new title of volume II of *Primitive
Culture*), New York: Harper & Brothers, 1958, pp. 17–18, 34, 82–85, 332.
[28] *Op. cit.,* pp. 443, 402, 408–10. Given his assumptions, Tylor is amazingly
objective. Thus he candidly states that the moral dualism between a good
and a bad god, postulated by his thesis of moral development, is seldom
found in primitive religion.
[29] James Frazer, *The Golden Bough* (Abridged ed. New York: Macmillan,
1922), Ch. IV.

natural" which may be displayed in any kind of excellence.[30]
Like Tylor in his concept of soul-ghosts, Frazer and Codrington
had discovered a permanent feature of the religious consciousness but had isolated and objectivated it to a point where it was
no longer religious at all. Part of the difficulty was, of course,
that religion cannot be "objectivated," and consequently that any
reduction of a total subjective-objective attitude to an objective
characteristic is bound to be erroneous. As Rudolf Otto remarked,
to notice power and to attempt its appropriation is not religion but
science.[31] Perhaps we might add: or magic. At any rate, power,
which is an important factor in the *manifestation* of the sacred,
is not its *origin*—no more than any other objective phenomenon
would be. The conceptions of the *dynamic* school, then, hardly
improve upon those of the *animist* one.

While the notion of power and its negative concomitant, the
taboo, were still being debated, another theory rose to prominence
and entered the competition for the position of "primitive" religion—totemism. The subject had been extensively explored by
W. Robertson Smith in *The Religion of the Semites* (1889) and
by James Frazer in his *Totemism and Exogamy* (1910), but
was not popularly accepted until Durkheim declared it to be the
simplest form and prototype of all religion.[32] Frazer had combined several elements which he believed to form an organic
unity, under the name totemism: (1) a belief on the part of
members of a clan that they are descended from the same totem-
animal; (2) the prohibition to kill this animal; (3) exogamy,
that is, the prohibition to marry a member of the same clan. To
Durkheim the totem center of the entire primitive cult symbolizes
the superhuman power of the group.[33] The original fact of religion, in this view, consists in the veneration which men feel for
the group to which they belong. Its social importance cannot be
exaggerated since religion alone provides the coherence which

[30] *The Melanesians* (Oxford: Clarendon Press, 1891), p. 118.
[31] *The Idea of the Holy*, pp. 120–21.
[32] Emile Durkheim, *The Elementary Forms of Religious Life*, tr. by Joseph
Ward Swain (New York: The Free Press, 1965), pp. 114–15, 194–95.
[33] *Op. cit.*, pp. 466, 472.

society needs to be stable. Negative reactions to this pan-totemism came soon enough. On the basis of his own research in the Trobriand Islands the anthropologist Bronislaw Malinowski retorted that society enacts the rules of the sacred, but it does not create them. In itself society is not what we would call sacred, for many of its functions belong to the profane side of life. Moreover, even in totemism (which Malinowski also regarded as religious) the social must remain subordinate to the magical—which is part of the sacred.[34]

In the meantime the totemist thesis had received support from an unexpected side. In 1913 Freud published *Totem and Taboo* and although he did not pretend to derive religion in its entirety from totemism, he nevertheless shared the belief of those anthropologists who were convinced that an exhaustive study of primitive man would lead to a complete understanding of religion. In it totemism would undoubtedly appear to have played a primary role. Yet on one essential point Freud differed from other "totemists": while for them the origin of religion was based upon an objective fact, for Freud the objective element primarily functioned as the carrier of subjective feeling—the feeling of guilt. Freud's basic theory therefore belongs in the next section which deals with the reduction of religion to a purely subjective feeling. What matters in Freud's totem hypothesis is not really what actually happened in the beginning, but how people feel about their desires, then and now. Totemism for Freud is not an ultimate; the primitive fact is the desire to kill the father and the

[34] Bronislaw Malinowski, *Magic, Science and Religion* (Garden City, N.Y.: Doubleday, 1954), p. 46. At this occasion Malinowski also brought to a temporary conclusion the long-standing dispute over the relation between religion and magic. Both share the domain of the sacred, but while magic always has an ulterior end, namely control over supernatural powers, religion which propitiates these powers is an end in itself. In both, man transcends the empirical: in magic he seeks access to hidden powers which would enable him to dominate the empirical world; in religion he constitutes a new reality which transcends the empirical altogether. *Op. cit.*, pp. 37–38; 87–88. For Claude Lévi-Strauss religion humanizes nature, while magic naturalizes human action. They appear together, because man ascribes superhuman powers to nature. (*The Savage Mind*, Chicago: University of Chicago Press, 1966, p. 221.)

feeling of guilt afterwards. Is the Darwinian hypothesis of the primal state of society, in which the jealous father of the clan kept all the females to himself, justified? Can the dramatic cohesion (partly supported by the ethnologist Atkinson) of the sons slaying the father and eating his flesh really be upheld? Does the yearly ritual slaying of the totem animal and its subsequent mourning express the guilty commemoration of an actual parricide? Freud feels that the answer to these questions is not decisive for his theory. For what touches off the entire totemic process is the *feeling of guilt* toward the father. And this feeling may result from the desire to kill as well as from the act. Moreover, the same feeling of guilt is still with us and drives us to similar ritualizations.

Nevertheless Freud remains within the illusion of the beginning insofar as he connects the primordial guilt with an event (actual or intentional) in the past. Not much has been gained from our point of view by changing the act into a desire. Quite the contrary, new problems arise which Freud's objectivist colleagues did not have to face. How does one generation transmit its psychic states to the next? By his own admission Freud had no answer. He assumed an "inheritance of psychic dispositions which, however, need incentives in the individual life in order to become effective,"[35] and stressed the necessity of further research. Even more basic is the question how social constraints can directly result from individual impulses. As Claude Lévi-Strauss pointed out in his own work on totemism: "Social behavior is not produced spontaneously by each individual, under the influence of emotions of the moment."[36] Freud's interpretation is historically important insofar as it constitutes an early attempt, from within those anthropological theories which had hitherto resulted in an objectivist concept of religion, to overcome objectivism. Yet because he still clung to the main dogma of the "beginning," the attempt could not be successful. In his later

[35] *Totem and Taboo, The Complete Psychological Works,* tr. under editorship of James Strachey, Vol. 13 (London: Hogarth Press), p. 158.
[36] *Totemism,* tr. by Rodney Needham (Boston: Beacon Press, 1963), p. 70.

work Freud abandons the search for the origin of psychic phenomena in historical developments. *Totem and Taboo* still hesitates between "the tradition of an historical sociology which . . .
searches in the distant past the justification of a present state of
affairs, and a scientifically sounder, modern attitude which expects its knowledge of the future and the past from an analysis
of the present."[37]

I quoted those last words from Claude Lévi-Strauss for a purpose. For with him the illusion of the beginning comes decisively
to an end and evolutionism is rejected in principle. To him the
various phenomena which Frazer had combined under the common name "totemism" to remove them as far as possible from
our own mentality, reveal in fact concerns remarkably similar to
our own. Contrary to Freud, Lévi-Strauss considers the ritual
celebrations of the totem not a commemoration of a past situation
in which things were different, but a symbolic expression of man's
ever present desire to shake off the restrictions of civilization.
Similarly, incest is taboo not because it was ever allowed in an
early state of civilization, but because it was never allowed, although often desired, in civilized life. Certainly a civilization in
which the pragmatic-scientific spirit has come to prevail, looks
upon the "savage mind" as primitive and different from our own.
But this evolutionary view is "the mind in its untamed state as
distinct from the mind cultivated or domesticated for the purpose
of yielding a return."[38] "Totemism," he claims, is a theory invented for the sole purpose of distinguishing the "primitive" from
ourselves, by attributing to him a coherent system of archaic beliefs. But Lévi-Strauss challenges the three basic facts which are
to support this attribution. (1) Some clans do not consider themselves descendants of the totem animal. (2) Some clans do eat the
totem animal and food prohibitions are not restricted to totemic
organizations. (3) There is no evidence of an intrinsic connection between exogamy and totem cult: exogamy merely rein-
forces the social kinship (symbolized in the totem) by an addi-

[37] Claude Lévi-Strauss, *Les structures fondamentales de la parenté* (Paris,
1949), p. 611.
[38] *The Savage Mind*, p. 219.

tional reference to the clan. Furthermore, the relation between totem and sacrifice, so important in Freud's theory, must be totally denied and interpreted as a projection upon primitive society of our embarrassment about the crudeness of our own sacrificial rites.

This last point illustrates Lévi-Strauss' entire attitude toward totemism. Far from being the origin of religion, "totemism" is itself the effect of modern man's religious beliefs. Its entire fantastic construction results from a hysterical exorcism of mental attitudes which Western man considers incompatible with the traditional Christian discontinuity between man and nature.[39] Thus he collects certain facts and arbitrarily places them under the common denominator of a "primitive religion" in order to set them off from his present moral and religious attitudes. In the conclusion of his book on *Totemism,* Lévi-Strauss writes:

> It is the obsession with religious matters which caused totemism to be placed in religion, though separating it as far as possible —by caricaturing it if need be—from so-called civilized religions, for fear that the latter might crumble at its touch.[40]

In reality, he thinks, the facts of "totemism" are of an intellectual kind. They manifest the more concrete way of thinking which we described as "savage." The relation between groups and totem animals is founded in a logical, objective analogy. The natural species furnish man with an intuitive picture of logical connections. Animals are sufficiently similar to man to provide him with symbols of his own social relations; at the same time they are sufficiently removed to serve as objective models.[41] As

[39] *Totemism,* p. 3.
[40] *Totemism,* p. 103.
[41] "The animals in totemism cease to be solely or principally creatures which are feared, admired, or envied: their perceptible reality permits the embodiment of ideas and relations conceived by speculative thought on the basis of empirical observations. We understand, too, that natural species are chosen not because they are "good to eat" (as Malinowski implied) but because they are "good to think." (*Totemism,* p. 89) The reason why animals are particularly apt to serve as concrete universals was first pointed

totems animals symbolize the relations of identity and opposition between one clan and another.

Assuming that Lévi-Strauss' interpretation of totemism as a logical instrument is correct (which has been repeatedly questioned), one may well wonder whether the separation between religion and totemism of his conclusion does not carry him beyond the premises of his argument. Repeatedly in the discussion Lévi-Strauss admits that totemic institutions have religious significance.[42] Totemism as an elaborate religious system may never have existed, but that does not mean that the totem animal has no religious significance. At any rate, Lévi-Strauss has brought an end to the evolutionary assumption which directed most past studies of primitive religion. Yet he has done it only for the primitive consciousness in general. When it comes to religion itself, Lévi-Strauss not only shares the evolutionary assumption but adds to it an intellectualism which none of his predecessors (including Tylor) ever displayed. In the conclusion of *Totemism* we read:

> If religious ideas are accorded the same value as any other conceptual system, as giving access to the mechanism of thought, the procedures of religious anthropology will acquire validity, but it will lose its autonomy and its specific character. This is what we have seen happen in the case of totemism, the reality of which is reduced to that of a particular illustration of certain modes of thought.[43]

Two things are stated in this text: one, religion is in the same position as totemism insofar as an objective study will take away

out by Bergson in *The Two Sources of Morality and Religion*. In the animal, individuality dissolves in class. "To recognize a man means to distinguish him from other men; but to recognize an animal is normally to decide what species it belongs to." (*Totemism*, p. 93)

[42] One example is the Tikopia region in which the clan is not descended from a totem animal but from an ancestor who had a relation to a god who entered into that animal. (*Totemism*, pp. 27, 29, 47)

[43] *Totemism*, p. 104.

its autonomous existence; two, the basic nature of religion as of totemism is intellectual—it is a system of thought. The first statement seems to depend on the second: religion cannot be autonomous *because* it is merely a particular illustration of certain modes of thinking. Now the second statement is such a sweeping, purely aprioristic declaration about an enormous and particularly complex field of experience that one wonders how an anthropologist can expect it to be taken seriously. Yet apparently Lévi-Strauss means just what he says, for in *The Savage Mind* he refers with approval to Auguste Comte who explained the transition from fetishism to polytheism by means of a purely intellectual operator, the species category.[44] Also, according to Lévi-Strauss, the distinctive trait of a "scientific" approach to religion is that it considers the area of religion a sphere of confused ideas which science must reduce to clarity and distinction.[45] I wonder how Lévi-Strauss would distinguish his own position adequately from Durkheim's whom he quotes as saying that the logic of religion is basically the same as that of scientific thought except for the greater subtlety of the latter,[46] or even from Comte's theory of the successive stages of culture. To me one form of evolutionary rationalism here seems to give way to another which reduces basically different forms of expression to a logic of thinking. Such reductionism remains faithful to nineteenth-century positivism and to the dogma that at the beginning of religion stands something else, the real thing.

3. THE SUBJECTIVIST REDUCTION

If religion consists in an attitude rather than in the mere acceptance of an object that is *a priori* determined as sacred, the religious consciousness is *constituted* by the subject rather than *given* in the object. This is no new discovery, for religious man has always been aware of his active involvement in the religious

[44] *The Savage Mind*, pp. 163–64.
[45] *Totemism*, pp. 103–4.
[46] *Totemism*, pp. 103–4.

experience. Yet, in recent times this awareness has been interpreted as if religion were nothing more than a subjective
experience. To empiricist philosophy and the psychology which
was derived from it, the religious consciousness remains entirely
enclosed within the self. Although such an interpretation obviously
conflicts with the nature of the religious experience, it is still
widely regarded as correct, especially in the Anglo-Saxon culture.
The empiricist view of religion was not entirely absent from
ancient philosophies—we find it clearly stated in Lucretius and,
to some extent, in Epicurus—but it is only in modern times
that it gained considerable acceptance. One of the first to make
it academically respectable was Thomas Hobbes who reduced
religion entirely to an effect of blind fear of invisible powers.
"This fear of things invisible, is the natural seed of that, which
everyone in himself calleth religion, and in them that worship
or fear that power otherwise than they do, superstition."[47] Hume
in the *Natural History of Religion* adopts the same thesis. The
gods personalize the various fears which beset human existence.[48]
Yet the subjectivist position did not become popular until it
acquired the support of the new science of psychology.

Psychology studies phenomena only as *experiences*. This restriction, imposed by the nature of the discipline, is totally justified. Neither should psychology be denied the right to consider
religion as an experience, for it obviously is one. But psychology
turns into psychologism when it *dogmatically assumes* that in
explaining the religious experience according to its own methods,
it explains religion *in its entirety*. An interpretation becomes
psychologistic by stretching psychology beyond its limits, not by
applying it. Not every theory which *results* in subjective conclusions is necessarily psychologistic. For Schleiermacher religion is
pure feeling, yet no one can accuse him of psychologism, for his
definition is a *conclusion*, not an initial assumption. Religion for
him must be subjective, because it is rooted in a primary aware-

---

[47] *Leviathan*, ed. by Michael Oakeshott (Oxford: Clarendon Press, 1946),
p. 35.
[48] *Natural History of Religion*, Section III, ed. by H. E. Root (London:
A. & C. Black, 1956), p. 29.

ness of existence which precedes the reflective distinction between subject and object.

The main error of psychologism, then, is not so much that it is
subjectivist (for in that respect other approaches may still prove
it right) but that it uncritically assumes the possibility of explaining the religious experience exhaustively through subjective characteristics, while *a priori* discarding the transsubjective meaning
of this experience. To consider Luther's compulsive personality
as the sole source of his religious inspiration (which was done
in a recent dramatic play) is subjective reductionism. The same
could be said about some studies on the obsessive disposition of
Kierkegaard or the hysterical temperament of St. Marguerite-
Marie Alacoque. Psychological studies of religious personalities
are useful to understand the various ways in which man acquires
religious attitudes. An admirable example of this genre is Erik-
son's monograph on Luther. But many psychoanalysts overstep
the boundaries of their territory. Even masters like Jung and
Freud did not altogether resist this temptation.

In *Psychology and Religion,* Jung correctly circumscribes the
limits of his method. His conclusions are to show the existence of
an archetypal image of God, not the existence of God himself.[49] Religious ideas are considered *formally* (that is, insofar
as they exist as ideas), not *intentionally* (that is, insofar as they
refer to a reality outside themselves).[50] Yet soon forgetting his
own cautious principles Jung recklessly ventures into defining religion as the impact of the collective unconscious upon consciousness, thereby declaring the collective unconscious the only source
of religious experience.[51] The highly rationalized creeds in which
modern man expresses his religion are downgraded to "substitutes" of the authentic experience. Jung's ultimate criterion for
religion is the adequacy of its symbols in expressing the relation
between consciousness and the subconscious. Conspicuously ab-

[49] *Psychology and Religion* (New Haven: Yale University Press, 1960),
p. 73.
[50] *Op. cit.,* p. 3.
[51] *Op. cit.,* p. 46.

sent is a distinction between the fulfillment of psychic needs and religion in itself.

Previously to *Psychology and Religion* Jung had simply considered religion as "true" *only* in a psychological sense.[52] Even after he had started distinguishing more adequately between the "psychological consideration of religion" and "its essential nature," he still continued to regard any study of the religious "object" as a reality in itself, at least superfluous. Thus in his *Two Essays on Analytical Psychology* (1926) we read:

> The concept of God is simply a necessary psychological function of an irrational character which has nothing to do with the question of the existence of God. The human intellect can never answer this question, and still less can it give any proof of God. Furthermore, such proof is altogether superfluous, for the idea of an allpowerful divine being is present everywhere, if not consciously recognized, then unconsciously accepted, because it is an archetype.[53]

Religion is valued exclusively for the psychic quality of the symbols which it produces from the collective unconscious, and the development of historical religion is entirely determined by psychic growth. This interpretation is psychologistic, not because it assumes a development determined by psychic factors, but because it leaves no room for other than psychic factors.[54]

How much of Jung's confusion of psychology with religion is due to his inability to deal with metaphysical subtleties is not clear. Nor does his lack of clarity diminish the value of his work for the understanding of religious myths and symbols. Jung's contribution to the study of religion is considerable, because in spite

[52] *The Psychology of the Unconscious* (1911), tr. by B. M. Hinkle (New York: Moffat, Yard, 1916), p. 41. On the entire evolution in Jung's attitude toward religion, see Raymond Hostie, S.J., *Religion and the Psychology of Jung* (Sheed & Ward, 1957).
[53] *Two Essays on Analytical Psychology*, tr. by C. F. Baynes (New York: Dodd, Mead, 1928), p. 72.
[54] *Answer to Job*, tr. by R. F. C. Hull (London: Routledge & Kegan Paul, 1954).

of his psychologizing he regarded the religious experience as unique, authentic, and irreducible to any nonreligious instinct. In this respect he differs from Freud, for whom religion is a transformed nonreligious drive.

Meanwhile, it is most difficult to assess Freud's theories on religion. To be sure, Freud is a professed atheist who considers religion to be an illusion. But this is not crucial to our discussion, since Freud himself clearly distinguishes between his analysis as a psychologist and his beliefs as a cultured man. His atheism belongs to the latter. After the publication of *The Future of an Illusion* Freud wrote to his friend Dr. Pfister, a Protestant pastor:

> Let us be quite clear on the point that the views expressed in my book form no part of analytic theory. They are my personal views, which coincide with those of non-analysts and pre-analysts, but there are certainly many excellent analysts who do not share them. If I drew on analysis for certain arguments—in reality only one argument—that need deter no-one from using the non-partisan method of analysis for arguing the opposite view.[55]

In *The Future of an Illusion* he argues that religious doctrines are most implausible and incompatible with what we know about the reality of the world, yet they can be neither proved nor disproved. It is only in their *psychological nature* that religious doctrines may be called "illusionary" by the psychoanalyst. This insight will undoubtedly influence man's judgment on their ultimate truth. Yet the psychoanalyst is not professionally qualified to make a final verdict.[56]

Freud's distinction shows a keen awareness of the danger of psychologism and a determined attempt to avoid it. The question is whether his attempt was successful. By interpreting the religious experience as a neurosis he seems to have excluded the

[55] *Psychoanalysis and Faith, The Letters of Sigmund Freud and Oskar Pfister,* tr. by Eric Mosbacher (New York: Basic Books, 1963), p. 117.
[56] *The Future of an Illusion,* in *The Complete Psychological Works,* tr. under direction of James Strachey, Vol. 21 (London: Hogarth Press, 1961), pp. 31–32.

need for a study of the religious "object" beyond the experience. Still, his indictment of the illusionary character of the religious experience follows as a *conclusion* upon genuine research; it is not an *a priori* assumption. One may criticize Freud's interpretation of the facts, but his method appears unimpeachable. Even after having established the neurotic character of the religious experience, Freud never transgresses upon the territory of objective reality. Scientifically he cannot disprove the possibility that neurotic inventions correspond exactly to a transcendent reality, although he does not believe that such a remote possibility deserves serious consideration.

> Just as no one can be forced to believe, so no one can be forced to disbelieve. But do not let us be satisfied with deceiving ourselves that arguments like these take us along the road of correct thinking. If ever there was a case of a lame excuse we have it here. Ignorance is ignorance; no right to believe anything can be derived from it.[57]

It is difficult to object to a scientific agnosticism which refuses to go into ontological hypotheses.

Nor must one hold against Freud his occasional lapses into psychologism, such as the statement in *The Future of an Illusion* that the truths contained in religious doctrines are so distorted "that the mass of humanity cannot recognize them as truth," although Freud here assumes that *the* truth of religion must be psychological. More serious is the statement in *The Psychopathology of Everyday Life:*

> I believe that a large portion of the mythological conception of the world which reaches far into the most modern religions, is nothing but *psychology projected to the outer world.* The dim perception (the endo-psychic perception, as it were) of psychic factors and relations of the unconscious was taken as a model in the construction of a *transcendental reality,* which is destined to be changed again by science into *psychology of the unconscious.* It is difficult to express it in other terms; the analogy of paranoia

[57] *The Future of an Illusion,* p. 32.

must here come to our aid. We venture to explain in this way the myths of paradise and the fall of man, of God, of good and evil, of immortality and the like—that is, to transform *metaphysics* into *metapsychology*.[58]

This sweeping conclusion is not justified by the premises and is a textbook example of psychologism. Yet, a single instance is no reason to discard the entirety of Freud's writings on religion.

Freud has devoted several works to religious problems. In the previous section I discussed the first, *Totem and Taboo* (1912–13), which deals with totemism and is still very much in the evolutionary tradition. *The Future of an Illusion,* on the contrary, deals directly with the faith of modern man. It is a genetic interpretation of religion in the psychological but not in the anthropological sense. Although Freud repeats the old interpretations of Lucretius and Hume, he gives them a new twist. Man feels constantly threatened by the superior forces of nature. In order to cope with them he attempts to humanize them. This allows him to manipulate them as he manipulates his fellow man, by prayer and by bribe. In his relation to the gods man relives the primeval relation to the father. The father provides protection —yet he also interferes with the child's close relation to the mother. The child fears him no less than it needs him. The same ambivalent attitude is carried over to man's relation to his gods.

> When the growing individual finds that he is destined to remain a child forever, that he can never do without protection against strange, superior powers, he lends those powers the features belonging to the figure of his father; he creates for himself the gods whom he dreads, whom he seeks to propitiate, and whom he nevertheless entrusts with his own protection.[59]

As man obtains more control over nature he extends the protective role of the gods to the functions of society. The gods then

---

[58] *The Basic Writings of Sigmund Freud,* tr. by Dr. A. Brill (New York: Random House, 1938), pp. 164–65.
[59] *The Future of an Illusion,* p. 24.

become the avengers of law and justice while society henceforth is secured of a divine foundation.

The content of religion has no roots in rational thoughts, but in wishdreams: that all events may be guided toward the good of man, that justice may prevail and that an eternal life may await us at the end of the present one. The term "illusions," by which Freud refers to these dreams, does not imply that religious ideas are false, but only that they have their origin in wishes rather than in experience.

The role of the father is further emphasized in *Civilization and Its Discontents* (1930). Civilization maintains itself by constantly controlling man's aggressive instincts. The discipline starts in the family with the father imposing restraint upon the child's un-limited desire for lust represented by the mother. The severance from the principle of lust, necessary for an active, autonomous existence, causes an ambivalent attitude toward the principle of discipline. The child is torn between love and fear, between *eros* and *thanatos*.[60] Love makes him accept and internalize the father's authority as his own. But it also causes a sense of guilt when the child directs his aggression against himself.

The aggressiveness is introjected, internalized; in fact, it is sent back where it came from, i.e. directed against the ego. It is taken over by a part of the ego that distinguishes itself from the rest as a super-ego, and now, in the form of *conscience*, exercises the same propensity to harsh aggressiveness against the ego that the ego would have liked to enjoy against others. The tension between the strict super-ego and the subordinate ego we call the *sense of guilt;* it manifests itself as the need for punishment.[61]

[60] *Civilization and Its Discontents*, in *The Complete Psychological Works*, Vol. 21, p. 132.

[61] *Civilization and Its Discontents*, p. 123. The relation between the father image and the feeling of guilt is confirmed by sociologists. See, for instance, John W. M. Whiting, "Sorcery, Sin and the Super-ego," in *Nebraska Symposium on Motivation*, 1959 (Lincoln: University of Nebraska Press, 1960). Whiting supports his thesis by several unpublished Harvard dissertations.

The sense of guilt, then, has two sources: dread of authority inducing the individual to renounce his instinctual gratifications, and internalized aggressiveness directed against the ego as a result of the renunciation. To those who object that love more than fear is at the origin of guilt feelings, Freud responds that the ultimate motive is still fear—fear of losing love.[62]

By ever more intensifying the repression of aggressive instincts civilization constantly heightens the sense of guilt. "The price we pay for our advance in civilization is a loss of happiness."[63] At this point religion is being introduced in order to teach man how to live with his sense of guilt (mainly by rationalizing and expressing it in the concept of sin), but above all in order to bring him relief from it in the promise of redemption. Freud's view of religion in *Civilization* completes the one of *Totem and Taboo* in which Christ takes the guilt of all upon himself. His sacrifice signifies the death of the totem animal which absolves man from the guilt incurred by the murder of the ancestral father.

Civilization and Its Discontents differs substantially from *The Future of an Illusion*. Yet the two views are not incompatible. The dread of losing love, which initiated the internalization process and caused the sense of guilt, is ultimately rooted in man's awareness of his dependence on others. Man cedes to authority because he knows that he is helpless. This helplessness is the very reason why he becomes religious according to *The Future of an Illusion*. In both cases religion is an expression of and an escape from frustration. In *The Future of an Illusion* the emphasis is on the *natural* frustration caused by a hostile environment; in *Civilization and Its Discontents* on *social* frustration resulting from the restrictions of civilized living.

Since Freud's theory deals with the unconscious, no empirical evidence can fully confirm or refute it. An analysis of the various motives leading to religious attitudes would have to include unconscious as well as conscious motives. To my knowledge such

[62] Since the fear that leads to guilt feelings is intimately connected with love, it is not necessary to accept Freud's controversial theory of the death wish (thanatos) as a separate instinct.

[63] *Civilization and Its Discontents*, p. 134.

an analysis has never been made. In the meantime Freud's position has been examined by means of traditional psychological methods (questionnaires, tests, etc.). The study of the Belgian psychologist Antoine Vergote which synthesizes several others has inspired the following critique.[64]

The threat of man's natural environment plays a certain role in religious attitudes. A man in need who sees no help coming may easily turn to the transcendent. Yet a "conversion" under those circumstances is usually short-lived. Skepticism and revolt follow if no help arrives. In general, distress or fear caused by natural events do not seem to play an important role in the religious attitude of modern man. Social frustration is a more important factor. Both Freud and Marx singled it out as a religious motive, but while Marx was convinced that in the society of the future frustration would disappear spontaneously, Freud became more and more convinced that it is inherent to the process of civilization as such. Freud may be right, but he definitely exaggerates the role played by the hope of an afterlife as compensation for the present one. Vergote points out how purely remunerative expectations are rather discouraged in the Gospel itself, when the workers of the eleventh hour receive as much as those who bore "the heat of the day." To modern man a remote heaven, difficult to imagine, offers but little consolation in the midst of deep and enduring frustration. Even people who have come to doubt personal immortality continue to be religious. Moreover, the hope in a personal immortality is almost entirely absent from some major religions (as Buddhism) and played virtually no role until late in the development of others (as Judaism). Nor are the socially frustrated groups the most religious. Precisely the opposite happened in Europe where the Christian Churches lost the entire workers class in the inhuman working conditions of the nineteenth century. On the other hand, it is undeniable that the formation of small religious sects has been promoted by social frustration or at least by isolation, as we

[64] Antoine Vergote, *The Religious Man*, tr. by Sister Marie-Bernard, O.S.B. (Dayton: Pflaum Press, 1969).

see in the rural South, the Appalachian Mountains, and in many Negro communities. Even so, the sect consoles more by what it offers *in this world* than by what it promises for the next one.[65]

The relation between guilt and religion, so direct according to *Totem and Taboo* and *Civilization and Its Discontents,* is in fact a very complex one. Most students of religion would admit that it plays an important role in the formation of the religious consciousness. Eliade thinks that modern man is justified in seeing in archaic man's adherence to religious archetypes

> a feeling of guilt on the part of man hardly emerged from the paradise of animality (i.e., from nature), a feeling that urges him to reidentify with nature's eternal repetition the few primordial, creative, and spontaneous gestures that had signalized the appearance of freedom.[66]

Whether modern man actually *experiences* guilt as a religious motivation depends on age, cultural development, and even nationality. Vergote suggests that confidence in a divine moral support decreases as the religious attitude matures.[67]

Yet, none of these objections refutes Freud's basic thesis that the frustration expressed in religion extends its roots to the Oedipal relation between father and child. Even if Freud were proven wrong on all previous accounts (which treat what is more or less conscious), his genetic theory could still stand. Of course, traditional methods alone can neither verify nor falsify the Freudian theory. All we can do is evaluate to what extent this theory helps us to understand the religious attitude.

Surveys indicate that paternal traits are indeed predominant in the Judeo-Christian image of God. But maternal elements such as patience, depth, interiority prove to be equally essential. Freud completely ignores them. His description of the religious attitude never transcends the conflict situation between father

[65] Vergote, *op. cit.,* pp. 108–13.
[66] *Cosmos and History* (New York: Harper & Brothers, 1959), p. 155.
[67] *Op. cit.,* pp. 116–18.

and child. God for him is primarily a lawgiver and religion concentrates mainly on man's feeling of guilt. But the father image itself is dialectical and refers to a maternal element: a restrictive God can be accepted only if he promises gratifications. Of this remuneration little is seen in Freud's image of God.

Moreover, in his analyses of the religious attitude Freud considers only paternal deities. According to a psychoanalytic study of attitudes in the cult of the Magna Mater, maternal religion is characterized by a unique ambivalence of attraction and fear which makes the image of the mother both "fascinans" and "tremendum."[68] The feeling of guilt which the author with Freud considers to be constitutive of paternal religion, is also present in forms of religion in which the mother-son relation predominates. But it takes on a different aspect. In the amoral cults of the mother, guilt is not moral guilt; it is primarily determined by a narcissistic fear of being deserted by the goddess. The religion of the mother, much more than that of the father, alternates fear with trust. The conclusion is that only religious attitudes which balance paternal with maternal elements harmoniously combine fear and trust.

Freud does not consider them. To him every religious attitude is directed toward the father and, consequently, is predominantly moral and repressive. In his austere monotheism all maternal elements are forcefully suppressed. The result is a moralistic religion obsessed by guilt.[69] Freud's one-sided description misrepresents even the religion of his own childhood. Judaism, despite its strong emphasis on the paternal element, also emphasizes the intimate union of the Covenant between God and his people.[70] In Christianity, which inherited from Judaism a paternal image of God, the feminine elements are even more abundant. Originally the Church regarded itself as the bride of Christ.

---

[68] Edith Weigert, "The Cult and Mythology of the Magna Mater from the Standpoint of Psychoanalysis" in *Psychiatry* (1939), pp. 347–78.

[69] Edith Weigert, *op. cit.*, p. 378.

[70] See Ewald Roellenbleck, *Magna Mater im Alten Testament* (Darmstadt, 1949).

Later the cult of the Virgin Mary almost came to equal that of the Redeemer. Protestantism discarded this element but compensated for it by strongly emphasizing the receptive, feminine attitude of the believer toward God's word.[71]

Jung, who had originally accepted Freud's idea that "the personal God is *psychologically* nothing other than a magnified father,"[72] was later forced to qualify this identity even for the "paternal" god and increasingly felt the need to introduce feminine elements into religion.[73] The importance of the mother in religion is not a recent discovery: students of religion have always stressed it. Gerardus Van der Leeuw in *Religion in Essence and Manifestation* devotes a chapter to the mother before he discusses the savior and the gods, because he considers it more basic than any other religious symbol. He prefaces his treatment with Bachofen's principle for the understanding of any religion: Search out the ancient mother.[74]

Finally we must briefly consider Freud's claim that religion is a communal *neurosis* in which the human race regresses to an earlier stage of development. The term *neurosis* here does not refer to a pathological condition, for religion may prevent many an individual from becoming neurotic. Yet it is a primitive attitude which must be replaced by a scientific one. The remedial function of religion should be taken over by psychoanalysis. With pastor Pfister we recognize in this scientific optimism "the idea of the eighteenth-century Enlightenment in proud modern

[71] Edith Weigert, *op. cit.*, pp. 352, 378.

[72] Ernest Jones, *The Life and Work of Sigmund Freud*, Vol. 3 (New York: Basic Books, 1957), p. 354.

[73] Compare "Die Bedeutung des Vaters für das Schicksal des Einzelnen," translated as "The Significance of the Father in the Destiny of the Individual," in *Collected Papers on Analytical Psychology*, tr. by C. E. Long (New York: Moffat, Yard, 1917), with writings such as "Die psychologischen Aspekten des Mutter-Archetypus" in *Von den Wurzeln des Bewusstseins*, Zurich, 1954, or even with a later edition (1949) of the same article.

[74] Gerardus Van der Leeuw, *Religion in Essence and Manifestation*, p. 91. On the importance of the mother, see also A. Dieterich, *Mutter Erde*, 1925; K. Leese, *Die Mutter als religiöses Symbol*, 1924; J. J. Bachofen, *Urreligion und antike Symbole*.

guise."[75] But this is accidental to the main question whether or not religion is a neurosis. Erich Fromm denies this and considers neurosis, on the contrary, a return to a more primitive form of religion.[76] Fromm is aware of the similarity between private, compulsive rituals and religious rites. But this similarity is not sufficient to reduce the latter to a socially organized form of the former. The compulsive ritual wards off repressed impulses, while religious ritual is a genuine, original expression. The compulsive ritual, then, is a degenerate form of the religious ritual rather than its origin.[77]

Unfortunately Fromm himself implies that religion has no other *raison d'être* than the fulfillment of psychological needs. This appears clearly in his discussion of the idea of God.

> That God is a symbol of man's need to love is simple enough to understand. But does it follow from the existence and intensity of this human need that there exists an outer being who corresponds to this need?[78]

Fromm answers negatively as logic demands. But no religious man would accept a viewpoint which envisages God primarily as a symbol of man's need to love. By such a psychological redefinition Fromm shifts the meaning of religion from a concern for transcendence to a concern for man. This concern for human development and union with one's fellow man may be expressed in theistic, nontheistic, or even atheistic terms (as was done in the writings of Marx and Rosa Luxemburg).[79]

> We must understand every ideal including those which appear in secular ideologies as expressions of the same human need and we must judge them with respect to their truth, to the extent to which

[75] *Psychoanalysis and Faith,* p. 115.
[76] *Psychoanalysis and Religion* (New Haven: Yale University Press, 1959), p. 27.
[77] *Ibid.,* pp. 107–8.
[78] *Ibid.,* p. 37.
[79] Erich Fromm, *Beyond the Chains of Illusion* (New York: Simon and Schuster, 1962), pp. 158–60.

they are conducive to the unfolding of man's powers and to the degree to which they are a real answer to man's need for equilibrium and harmony in this world.[80]

Now it may well be that religion is ultimately no more than concern for man, but such a radical reinterpretation of the beliefs of both the theist and the atheist needs to be proven rather than assumed. Fromm rejects as relativist any view of religion which limits its value to the feelings which it produces. But his own view of religious truth as the correspondence of a feeling or a doctrine to a need, not to a reality, is hardly less relativistic.

We must not conclude this discussion without saying a word about an early contemporary of Freud and Jung, whose approach to religion is in many respects more sophisticated. Because of his openmindedness and superior philosophical training, William James reveals the potential and the limitations of psychology of religion most clearly. Early in his classic *Varieties of Religious Experience,* James announces his intention to abstain from all final value judgment on the data of religious experience and to regard them "as if they were curious facts of individual history."[81] He never abandons his attitude of reserve while analyzing the complexities of conversion, saintliness, religious virtue. However, even a description must discriminate somewhat between a healthy religious attitude and a sick one. Yet such a distinction presupposes that one knows what is healthy from a religious point of view. James fully accepts this challenge to his method. But he decides to solve the problem pragmatically by applying the Gospel's advice to judge the tree by its fruits. Thus he infers the nature of the cause from its psychological effects and concludes that any form of religion which poses a threat to essential human values is *eo ipso* false. Whenever common sense and instinct make certain beliefs abhorrent, James

[80] Fromm, *Man for Himself* (New York: Rinehart, 1947), p. 50.
[81] *Varieties of Religious Experience* (New York: Collier Books, 1961), p. 35.

sides with the unbeliever. He feels religiously confident to do so, for religion itself has discredited its gods once they became contemptible or immoral.[82]

But the difficulty soon returns. For why do some forms of religion survive and flourish while others wither away? To say that they minister to specific psychological needs does not answer the question, since human needs may be fulfilled in a number of ways and mostly arise only as we are able to fulfill them. James himself is keenly aware of the variety of standards of success or failure which the protean nature of man admits.

How is success to be absolutely measured when there are so many environments and so many ways of looking at the adaptation? It cannot be measured absolutely; the verdict will vary according to the point of view adopted. From the biological point of view Saint Paul was a failure, because he was beheaded. Yet he was magnificently adapted to the larger environment of history; and so far as any saint's example is a leaven of righteousness in the world, and draws it in the direction of more prevalent habits of saintliness, he is a success no matter what his immediate bad fortune may be.[83]

How are we to evaluate in psychological terms the "magnificent adaptation" of a decapitated saint? The success or failure of such a religious commitment can obviously not be measured by another yardstick. An early disciple of Husserl, the French phenomenologist Jean Hering, pointed out long ago that to accept the satisfaction of human needs as an ultimate criterion of religion implies either that a false belief cannot render the same services or that a psychologically true belief must also be metaphysically true.[84] Both theses are obviously false. James proposes to leave out of consideration all nonpsychological reality. But this is extremely difficult in the case of religion, because religious reality by its very nature lifts man out of the immanent experience.

[82] *Op. cit.*, p. 264.
[83] *Op. cit.*, p. 297.
[84] Jean Hering, *Phénoménologie de la religion*, Strasbourg, 1925, p. 13.

James himself admits, "if religion is true, its fruits are good fruits, even though in this world they should prove uniformly ill adapted and full of naught but pathos."[85] An evaluation on the basis of man's psychological well-being remains ultimately foreign to what religious man considers to be the key to his experience and can therefore not be a final criterion of religious truth and falsity. James has avoided the initial temptation of religious psychology to describe the religious act as totally determined by its psychic antecedents. His psychology remains open to the possibility of a transcendent reality inspiring and motivating the immanent religious experience. But he must somehow come to grips with what lies within the province of experience, namely the qualitative difference between one experience and another. The difficulty with the religious act, however, is that the quality of the experience is determined by a terminus that lies entirely outside the experience itself.

Does this mean that the psychologist must be denied all competence in understanding the religious act? According to some phenomenologists that is exactly what it means. Hering, for instance, feels that a description which leaves out the terminus of the religious act misrepresents the entire experience. But since this terminus is exclusively an object of faith, it cannot be considered unless the describer adopts to some extent the attitude of the believer. Ironically, the objection affects the phenomenologist more than the psychologist. For reflection on the *intentional* aspect of the religious act (that is, its reference to a terminus outside the experience) will give the phenomenologist little insight in the act as long as he knows no more than the psychologist about the intended terminus. The alternative to this predicament is not phenomenology, but faith.[86] The psychologist at least makes no pretense of going beyond the mere experience in his interpretation of the religious act. The valid

---

[85] *Op. cit.,* p. 298.
[86] Scheler saw this when he considered active participation of the phenomenologist in the faith of the believer necessary for a correct description of the religious act. *The Eternal in Man,* tr. by Bernard Noble (New York: Harper & Brothers, 1960), p. 159.

part of the objection is that in view of its *intentional character* the religious experience cannot be understood by psychological methods *alone*. Yet in their reaction against the subjectivism of past psychologies of religion, phenomenologists have become overly critical of the psychological method itself. For Scheler even to ask whether religious acts are feelings, thoughts, or volitional acts is wrong. He considers the psychological states of the religious subject as irrelevant to understanding his attitude, as the health of a mathematician is to understanding his equations.

To this extreme position I object that psychology must not be excluded from the study of religion and for reasons which Scheler himself indicates. For Scheler correctly declares psychology competent to discriminate authentic religious acts from inauthentic ones.[87] Religion is a psychic phenomenon. But the unmasking of apparent religious behavior is an important, although negative, step toward the understanding of authentic religion, particularly today when many people who are not in the least religious deceive themselves by still professing a faith in ideals in which they have long ceased to believe. Religious ideals often camouflage motives which man does not want to admit to himself. I therefore believe that at a time when the real meaning of the sacred has become increasingly hidden, psychology can fulfill a real service by exposing sham religion.

However, not every religious attitude which has nonreligious elements admixed to it must be considered sham. There is no such thing as a *purely* religious attitude. An attitude is authentic when it has an irreducible intentionality of its own which distinguishes it from other attitudes. But no act is ever isolated from others since all are enmeshed in the same complex totality of man's psychic life. All psychic acts, including the religious ones, occur within a reality shaped by temperament, character, and early education. In that sense all acts arise out of a dark and mostly unconscious soil of which psychology can at least partially determine the nature. But, as James knew, insight into this nature does not explain the true originality of the act.

[87] *Op. cit.*, p. 157.

Only in pathological cases does a person's mental development exclude spontaneous activity from some psychic areas. When this is the case for man's religious activity, appearances of religious behavior must not be interpreted by religion alone: they no longer mean what they mean in the "healthy" individual. Yet a comparison between "spontaneous" and "determined" behavior is merely a matter of degree. No absolute statements should be made where no definite boundaries exist. The distinction between free and unfree acts may serve practical or juridical purposes, but it can claim no absolute support from philosophy or psychology for which both terms are abstractions. The psychologist, therefore, will seldom be able to conclude to a total absence of authentic religious activity underneath sham appearances. The attentive care which religious nurses in mental institutions lavish upon their most deprived patients may serve as an example of the infinite respect which man owes to the mystery of the clouded mind.

But psychology fulfills a positive function as well in analyzing the religious experience as it appears in the totality of the psychic structure. Provided such an analysis is not expected to yield the *entire* meaning of the act, the term "psychological meaning" is fully justified.

> The systematic exploration of religious facts in their human context must reveal us their content and meaning. But not their final meaning and truth. Psychology is competent to examine their human meaning and their relative truth with respect to their situation in the multiple vectors that compose the human.[88]

Even so, psychology of religion remains a difficult task which only certain types of psychology are able to achieve. I do not see how behaviorism, for instance, because of its inability to deal with meanings and motivational problems, could contribute much of value. The psychologist describes the religious experience in order to *understand* it, that is, to discover the psychological conditions

[88] Antoine Vergote, *Psychologie religieuse* (Brussels, 1966), p. 13. My translation.

which make it possible or impossible.[89] The difficulty here is that the psychologist must attempt to be as complete as possible without ever being allowed to consider his explanation exhaustive. His conclusions bear only upon the *experience* and its motivation, not upon the *act* as such, that is, the experience insofar as it is directed beyond itself *toward a transcendent terminus.*

The preceding part of this section may have left the impression that a subjectivist reduction is restricted to the field of psychology. Yet this is by no means the case. Ludwig Feuerbach's radically reductionist theory was the work of a philosopher, completed before psychology had emerged as an independent science. Nor does this theory reduce religion to a subjective experience. The religious act for Feuerbach is definitely intentional, but its terminus is man's own nature, not a transcendent deity. Its significance has been entirely positive, but what it has discovered about man must now be handed over to the new science of man, anthropology, which will establish these findings on firmer footing. At first Feuerbach's position may seem to be an instance of scientific reductionism. But it is not, for the new science is entirely the outcome of a religious development. Feuerbach merely brings to its logical conclusion the analytic religious principle that *to me God can be only what He appears to me.* He strongly defends this principle as the basis of true religion. Any attempt to go beyond an anthropocentric definition of God has its origin in irreligious skepticism or antireligious presumption. "To ask whether God is in himself what he is for me, is to ask whether God is God, is to lift oneself above one's God, to rise up against him."[90] A distinction between the object *as it is in itself* and *as it appears to me* is meaningful only when it can appear in another way than it actually appears. But all the attributes predicated of God are qualities of man, and they become increasingly

[89] A remarkable example of such an explanation is H. C. Rümke, *The Psychology of Unbelief,* tr. by M. H. C. Willems (New York: Sheed & Ward, 1962).

[90] *Das Wesen des Christentums, Sämtliche Werke,* ed. by Wilhelm Bolin and Friedrich Jodl (Stuttgart, 1960), Vol. 6, p. 21; *The Essence of Christianity,* tr. by George Eliot (New York: Harper & Brothers, 1957), p. 17.

human as man becomes more conscious of himself. Each new
insight in the nature of man abolishes all the gods of the previous
stage. Thus the gods graduate from natural forces to moral beings
as man detaches himself from physical nature. Whether God
differs from man depends entirely, then, upon the relationship
between those human predicates and their allegedly transcendent
subject. But, Feuerbach argues, a subject has no existence independent of its predicates. Its truth consists entirely in the sum
total of its predicates and their connection. If the predicates are
human, so must be the subject. God, then, is nothing more than
human nature taken in its totality.

The believer will object that the mode of attribution in the
case of God is not the same as in that of man. But Feuerbach
has no patience with a negative theology which places God above
his predicates. He considers it an offspring of modern unbelief.[91]
Nor does he admit that man can ever attain a truly transcendent
(that is, beyond-the-predicates) being. For the two mental functions through which man channels his relation to God—feeling
and reason—allow of no beyond. Feeling, as we know, has no
specific object at all and, consequently, is totally incapable of
having a transcendent terminus. The divine element of religious
feelings lies in the feelings themselves—not beyond them. If the
divine were truly transcendent, feelings with their self-enclosed
nature would be least qualified to reveal it. "Feeling is atheistic
in the sense of the orthodox belief which attaches religion to an
external object; it denies an objective God—it is itself God."[92]
The same holds true for reason although in a different way. In
the idea of God reason becomes aware of its own full potential.
It is the mind conceiving itself as overcoming the limits of individual embodiment. Reason is the content of the divine as well
as the power of abstraction which releases this content from its
empirical limits. God is "intelligence posited by itself."[93] The
element of estrangement by which reason views its own substance

[91] *Das Wesen des Christentums*, p. 18; *The Essence of Christianity*, p. 14.
[92] *Das Wesen des Christentums*, p. 13; *The Essence of Christianity*, p. 11.
[93] *Das Wesen des Christentums*, p. 44; *The Essence of Christianity*, p. 35.

as lying outside itself is due entirely to the imagination which Feuerbach, as Descartes and Spinoza, regards as the source of all confused thinking. "To the imagination, reason is the revelation of God; but to reason, God is the revelation of reason."[94] Feuerbach's thesis that it is the imagination which determines a representation into a religious one, is of great interest and, as we shall see in the discussion of religious symbolism, basically correct. The view of the imagination as the cause of error is a less desirable leftover from a rationalist past. Yet, even here, Feuerbach's judgment is not altogether negative. For without the "imaginary" thinking of the religious consciousness, man would never have reached reason at all. The separation between God and reason which Feuerbach calls "an involuntary, childlike, simple act of the mind"[95] results from man's initial inability to conceive of the object of thinking as identical with thought itself. The same inability induces him to project the supreme moral value of human nature outside the self onto a transcendent God. Incapable of viewing himself as a species-being rather than a mere individual, man in the earlier stages of his development forefeels nevertheless the unlimited perfection of his nature and ascribes to the gods what rightly belongs to himself. A full awareness of the human community will restore man into his rights. "Solitude is finiteness and limitation; community is freedom and infinity. Man for himself is man (in the ordinary sense); man with man—the unity of I and thou—is God."[96]

To the objection that human nature as a whole also has its limits, Feuerbach would reply that, if this be the case, man is

[94] *Das Wesen des Christentums*, p. 45; *The Essence of Christianity*, p. 36. Cf. also: "God as God . . . is nothing but the essence of reason itself. He is, however, conceived by ordinary theology or theism by means of the imagination as a being distinct from and independent of reason." *Grundsatze der Philosophie der Zukunft, Sämtliche Werke*, Vol. 2, p. 247; *Principles of the Philosophy of the Future*, tr. by Manfred Vogel (Indianapolis: Bobbs-Merrill, 1966), p. 6.

[95] *Das Wesen des Christentums*, p. 238; *The Essence of Christianity*, p. 197.

[96] *Grundsatze*, p. 318; *Principles of the Philosophy of the Future*, p. 71.

unable to know them. "If the nature is limited, so also is the feeling, so also is the understanding. But to a limited being its limited understanding is not felt to be a limitation."[97] We recognize Spinoza's definition of the finite as that which can be compared with other beings of the same nature.[98] Feuerbach interprets this to mean that each species is perfect and infinite in its own way. The so-called limits of man are not really limits of nature, but of the individual. Indeed, man would never be aware of his limitations if he did not perceive his finitude against the backdrop of his own infinity. The final question, then, is: Why does man make so basic an error in evaluating his own potential? Perhaps no answer to this question is needed for the early stage of mankind when, in Feuerbach's opinion, man is unable to identify himself with the species. But once he is able to do so his persistence in the religious attitude must be justified. Feuerbach offers two distinct explanations. According to one, mature man refuses to attribute the divine predicates to human nature, because he is reluctant to take the limitations upon himself as an individual. To ascribe them to the species is less humiliating.[99] But in another passage the religious inclination is explained through self-centered practical concerns which make the individual lose sight of his universal essence. The self, then, becomes the individual self, and the universal is placed outside the human sphere as a distinct being.[100]

The basic idea underlying these strange interpretations is that man refuses to face his full reality after he has grown up and therefore projects an internal relation outside the self. This attitude is not inappropriately referred to as an *alienation* of the self. In Feuerbach's concept of alienation we find the link between the psychological (Freud) and social (Marx, Marcuse)

[97] *Das Wesen des Christentums,* p. 10; *The Essence of Christianity,* p. 8.
[98] *Ethica more geometrica demonstrata,* Bk. I, Def. 2.
[99] *Das Wesen des Christentums,* pp. 9, 184; *The Essence of Christianity,* pp. 7, 153. The second text applies only to Christianity, which Feuerbach considered the religion *par excellence.*
[100] *Das Wesen des Christentums,* pp. 236–37; *The Essence of Christianity,* pp. 195–96.

forms of alienation which we shall discuss later. As in Marx, the religious attitude is man's alienation from his own existence in objective concepts. As in Freud, the religious projection which expresses this self-estrangement partially reconciles the believer with himself: it is a redeeming neurosis. For Feuerbach the redeeming element of religion is the concept of love. In religious love man is reunited with the species from which his initial disposition estranged him. Yet religious love never fully redeems—Freud would call it neurotic—insofar as faith backs away from its original affirmation that God is love. Love, it now adds, is only one attribute of a God who is *also* just, wise, etc. This places faith above love and prevents love from expanding beyond the limits of faith. Thus through faith, love becomes *Christian* love, that is, love which loves only what is Christian. "The Christian must therefore love only Christians—others only as possible Christians; he must only love what faith hallows and blesses."[101] Christ's teaching to love one's enemies includes only personal enemies, according to Feuerbach; it does not cover the enemies of the faith.

In later years Feuerbach's critique of the religious alienation would also include speculative philosophy which, with its notions of Spirit, Reason, etc., proceeds directly from theology. Modern philosophy negates theology, but negates it from a theological viewpoint.[102] Feuerbach instead proposes to return to man's concrete reality—"of flesh and blood"—in which there is no room for speculative abstractions. Gradually this would lead him to the materialism of his later years so strongly criticized in Marx's *Theses on Feuerbach*.[103] In the process his philosophy regressed from a philosophy of man to a philosophy of nature.[104]

101 *Das Wesen des Christentums*, p. 305; *The Essence of Christianity*, p. 254.
102 *Grundsatze*, p. 273; *Principles*, pp. 30–31. Also *Vorläufige Thesen zur Reform der Philosophie, Sämtliche Werke*, Vol. 2, pp. 222–44.
103 Feuerbach's materialism becomes outspoken in *Das Wesen des Religion* (1845).
104 On this change, cf. Henri Arvon, *Ludwig Feuerbach ou la transformation du sacré* (Paris, 1957), pp. 156–62.

At this point the real champion of the anthropological thesis of religion was no longer Feuerbach but Marx.[105]

4. THE IMMANENTISM OF PHENOMENOLOGY

The critical subtitles of this chapter must not obscure the positive contributions which scientific principles, anthropological research, and psychological analysis can make to the study of religion. If properly qualified the falsifiability principle does apply to religion, the quest for the beginning is an essential part of the study of any faith, and psychology is indispensable to the understanding of religious attitudes. Only when anthropological and psychological methods are used to reveal the full essence of religion do they become false. The same applies to phenomenology. Phenomenological analysis has directly and indirectly been used throughout this work. Still phenomenology *alone* cannot reveal the full meaning of the religious act.

The phenomenological approach differs from the psychological one in that it considers the religious experience not as a subjective state but as an intentional act, that is, an experience which points beyond itself toward a transcendent terminus. The terminus is considered only as *immanent in,* and *constituted by,* consciousness. This viewpoint opens up a double field of investigation: the experience to the extent that it intends its terminus (the *noesis*) and the terminus to the extent that it is intended by the experience (the *noema*).[106] In both cases only the variations in intending or being intended must be considered. Shifts in the

[105] On Marx's reductionist interpretation of religion, the reader may consult my article, "Marxism and Religion: An Impossible Marriage," first published in *The Commonweal,* 88, 6 (1968), 171–76, and later reprinted in *The New Theology,* 6, by Martin Marty and Dean Peerman (New York: Macmillan, 1969), pp. 151–64.

[106] The distinction between *noesis* and *noema* is defined in Husserl's *Ideen zu einer reinen Phänomenologie und phänomelogischen Philosophie, Husserliana,* III (The Hague, 1950), pp. 87–127. *Ideas, General Introduction to Pure Phenomenology.* Tr. by W. R. Boyce Gibson (New York: Macmillan, 1958), pp. 255–358.

subjective experience, as well as conditions under which this experience originates and develops, must be left entirely to the psychologist. The phenomenologist concentrates on the experience solely to the extent that it *is religious.* The advantages of the method are obvious: the religious "object" is never detached from the intentional "glance" of the subject—hence no objectivism. At the same time the intentional orientation prevents the religious act from being reduced to a mere experience—hence no subjectivism.

To phenomenology we owe the remarkable analyses of Van der Leeuw, Eliade, Scheler, and of the phenomenologist *avant la lettre,* Rudolf Otto. Since the first two restricted themselves to descriptive phenomenology without ever claiming a methodological ultimacy for their method, they remain exempt of the criticism of this section. Otto and Scheler are more ambitious in their use of phenomenology. Otto seems to have adopted the phenomenological method because it was suggested by his subject matter, not because he felt any doctrinal preference for it. In fact, he never called his method phenomenological (others did) and acknowledged no philosophical allegiance but to Kant. Intentionality entered his view of the religious experience mainly through dissatisfaction with Schleiermacher's definition of the religious experience—feeling of absolute dependence—for being insufficiently distinct from other experiences. Otto replaced it by *creature-consciousness,* which gives it an intentional orientation that was lacking in Schleiermacher. By emphasizing strongly the suprarational aspect of the holy as well as the deep involvement of the religious subject, he likewise avoided determining it as an object. The terms numinous, mysterious, fascinating, by which the sacred is described all have strongly subjective connotations, yet no one can call them subjectivist. If we must object to Otto's subjectivity it is for different reasons. The main one is his theory of an *a priori* in the religious subject which constitutes the religious "object." Faithful to Kant's agnosticism Otto claims that the transcendent itself remains totally unknown in the religious act. Whatever the subject knows in its relation to it, comes entirely from

its own immanent *a priori*. The *a priori* of the sacred differs
from all other cognitive structures by being nonrational. But it is
equally exhaustive in determining its subject matter. Some passages of *The Idea of the Holy* have an unmistakable Kantian
ring.[107] That the holy must be constituted by the subject is a
thesis which I wholeheartedly embrace. That it is entirely constituted by the subject is a Kantian position which in the final
analysis excludes any possibility of considering a content *as revealed*. If the transcendent remains totally unknown and the
content of the experience is entirely determined by a subjective
a priori, the religious experience is, once again, severed from its
intentional terminus. It would be unfair to brand as psychologistic
what has been defined in universal and intentional terms. Yet
for Otto the intentionality of the religious act is merely a reaching
toward, not an attaining *of,* the transcendent. His interpretation
remains psychological, not in the empirical but in the transcendental (Kantian) sense.

Phenomenologists may object that Otto's transcendental philosophy is ultimately not phenomenology. This is true enough,
but a phenomenology in the strict sense will have to face problems
of a similar nature. Phenomenology describes intentional acts,
that is, experiences insofar as they are directed toward a non-
immanent terminus. In the case of religion this terminus is defined as transcendent in the strict sense of the word: it cannot be
known except *in* and through the religious act. Religious man
attains the transcendent only *in faith*. But what can be grasped
in faith alone, appears to fall altogether beyond the scope of an
inquiry which is clearly limited to the intuition of the essences of
phenomena.

Of course, the phenomenologist will claim (and rightly so)
that his own attitude differs from the believer's in that he ab-

---

[107] We take one at random. "The proof that in the numinous we have to
deal with purely *a priori* cognitive elements is to be reached by introspection and a critical examination of reason such as Kant instituted. We
find, that is, involved in the numinous experience, beliefs and feelings
qualitatively different from anything that 'natural' sense perception is
capable of giving us." *The Idea of the Holy,* p. 113.

stains from all ontological value-judgment. He is concerned with what *appears* in consciousness: the transcendent object of the revelation interests him only to the extent that it is intended by an immanent experience. The notion of transcendence is phenomenologically relevant only insofar as it enters into the immanent experience. What the transcendent object is *in itself,* i.e., beyond its relation to the immanent being of consciousness, is unimportant. Has God *really* spoken to man? Does the transcendent really communicate with the immanent being of consciousness? Those questions do not interest phenomenology.

It would be a mistake, however, to interpret this bracketing of the transcendent as if phenomenology considered only the logical coherence of the affirmations made in faith and not the modality of faith itself which inspired them, for this modality enters into the very meaning of the religious assertion. It is all too obvious that the meaning of an affirmation made in faith is different from the same affirmation made without faith. To illustrate this point we could compare it with the differences of meaning which an identical statement can have within and outside a poetic context. In the first case we will encounter secondary meanings, emotive import, and certain connotations which are absent from the second, and which can be grasped only by someone who is in the right disposition. We must disagree, therefore, with Henry Duméry's thesis that the modality of faith belongs to the *credo* (the real experience) and not to the *creditum* (the ideal element of the experience, particularly the *noema*), which alone is being considered by the phenomenologist. The modality of faith is part of the ideal *noesis:* as such it profoundly influences the *noema* and may not be relegated to the existential part of the judgment which is bracketed in the phenomenological analysis. To abstract the terms from the modality of faith in which they are elicited is to take away the very element in which they make *religious* sense. To isolate the affirmation of the believer from his belief is to change the affirmation itself. Religious affirmations (and all religious acts are ultimately based upon affirmations) have only one meaning: the meaning which they have for the believer.

But to place the religious affirmation in its own modality is to take it as a response to a transcendent (and, therefore, trans-phenomenological) call. A full understanding of the religious act, then, is impossible without taking into account a transcendent intervention (be it as subjective attraction or as objective revelation), since it is precisely this transcendent terminus which in the believer's mind gives its specific meaning to the religious act. To bracket the transcendent entirely is to interpret this act in such a way that no religious person will recognize it.

The conclusion, therefore, seems unavoidable that phenomenology either must limit itself to a description of an immanent reaching toward a phenomenologically unknown transcendent terminus or that it must abandon its autonomous character and share the faith which alone recognizes the transcendent terminus. In both alternatives the problems are considerable. For the religious act does not "reach" toward an unknown transcendence. It attains it. To be correct a phenomenological description must include the transcendent *noema* of the act of faith. To do so it is not sufficient, as in the case of other acts, to reflect upon the act without "living" it. For other experiences bring their objects intentionally within the immanent realm of consciousness, whereas the religious act attains its terminus, but never possesses it: it makes its terminus immanent only by constituting it as entirely transcendent. The paradox of the act of faith is that it throws a bridge by declaring the gap unbridgeable. The religious experience, therefore, never becomes completely immanent; its immanent being retains an essential incompleteness, due to the elusive, transcendent nature of its *noema,* which is unique in human experience. We may conclude, then, that no purely phenomenological analysis can adequately describe the religious act, because its terminus never becomes sufficiently immanent in the experience to admit of an analysis in phenomenal terms.

This conclusion by no means denies phenomenology the right to deal with the religious experience, nor does it deny that religion and its object have an immanent aspect as well as a transcendent. If there is a religious *experience* at all, it must obviously be immanent and, consequently, describable in a purely phenomenological fashion. But the immanence of the religious experience is such that it constantly *transcends* itself in an intentionality which ultimately escapes the purely phenomenological analysis. One cannot simply bracket the transcendent aspect of the religious *noema* without losing the meaning of the act determined by this object. By its very nature, phenomenology is concerned with the immanent being of consciousness, but in the case of religion this immanent being itself can be understood only when seen in its essential connection with the transcendent. Consequently phenomenology alone cannot yield the entire meaning of the act, unless it somehow participates in the faith which establishes the actual connection with the transcendent. Unlike other thetic acts, the religious affirmation, because of its essential incompleteness, presents itself as *intrinsically* dependent upon a being other than the being of consciousness in which it takes place. To grasp the meaning of the act one must be able to share, at least ideally, in the believer's faith in a transconscious existence. How can this be done within the phenomenological *epochè?*

Scheler alone seems to have felt the full urgency of the question. He responded by declaring a minimal faith an essential condition for phenomenology of religion. According to him, the religious act cannot be understood at all without an *actual* acceptance of the real existence of its terminus. Intentional acts to which no finite object (nor a synthesis of finite objects) corresponds remain incomprehensible unless one accepts a transcendent realm of infinite being.

Only a real being with the essential character of divinity can be the cause of man's religious propensity, that is, propensity to execute in a real sense acts of that class whose acts, though finite experience cannot fulfill them, nevertheless demand fulfillment. The *object* of the religious acts is at the same time the *cause* of their existence. In other words, all knowledge of God is necessarily knowledge from God.[108]

108 *On the Eternal in Man,* p. 261.

If religious acts form an essential class of mental acts, irreducible to any others, then we are obliged to assume a separate domain of reality corresponding to those acts. Not to do so would be to reduce one intentionality to another, as in the psychological fallacy.

But thus to conclude from the fact that the religious act *intends* its terminus as *really* existent to the object's actual existence is to abandon all restrictions of the phenomenological *epochè*. Phenomenology deals with immanent being: it considers only the ideal being of consciousness. The intentional object is present only in its ideal aspect and the phenomenologist knows nothing of an existence beyond consciousness. To be sure, phenomenology uses the notion "transcendent being" in discussing consciousness' relation to the world, but this "transcendence" is no more than an indicator of immanent being: it refers to the sort of immanent being which is not manifest at once (as the object of introspection) but through an infinite series of perspective variations. Now, it may be possible on the basis of an analysis of the religious act or of consciousness itself to conclude to another sort of transcendence which—as opposed to that of the world which is not immanent because not given at once, hence defective—would be immanent *per excessum,* a ground of consciousness which could never be grasped in itself but only in its manifestations.[109] Yet, again, within the limits of his method, the phenomenologist cannot conclude to any *real* transcendence.

Although the phenomenologist must somehow follow the believer's movement of faith, I do not agree with Scheler that an actual affirmation of the transcendent reality (which would imply an abandonment of the phenomenological method) is required. Actual faith is not a necessary condition for phenomenological analysis. However, without at least some previous experience of faith the full meaning of the religious act must remain closed to the analyst. An adequate description undoubtedly requires more than an extrinsic acquaintance with the religious act.

[109] *Ideeen,* I, #58, p. 140; *Ideas,* p. 174. Cf. my article, "Husserl's Thought on God and Faith" in *Philosophy and Phenomenological Research,* 29 (1968) pp. 201–15.

Also, phenomenological analysis alone can never attain the understanding of the religious *noema* which religious man attains in the living experience. Professor Van der Leeuw, who himself so successfully applied the phenomenological method, understood this limitation and therefore proposed a distinction between religion-as-experience and religion-as-transcendent. Phenomenology may explain the former, not the latter, and in doing so "it implies an advance to the farthest boundary, where only one sole fact is understood—that all comprehension is 'beyond'; and thus the ultimate meaning is at the same moment the limit of meaning."[110] There is one further restriction which prevents the phenomenological method from giving an exhaustive interpretation of the meaning of religious acts. Religion deals with matters of existence and consequently it leads to ontological problems which phenomenology by itself (because of the existential *epochè*) is not equipped to handle. This particular limitation results not primarily from the unique nature of the religious *noema* (as Scheler implied), but is inherent to phenomenology in dealing with all existential problems. As Sartre showed in *Being and Nothingness* there is a *phenomenon* of existence.[111] But existence cannot be adequately dealt with unless phenomenology itself becomes ontology—which it first did in Heidegger. Since faith also is ultimately a matter of being and nonbeing, a phenomenology of religion must always be complemented by a philosophy in the older, metaphysical sense of the term.

[110] *Religion in Essence and Manifestation,* p. 680.
[111] *Being and Nothingness,* tr. by Hazel Barnes (New York: Philosophical Library, 1956), Introduction, esp. p. xlviii.

Chapter 3
Religious Faith and Philosophical Reflection

For many years metaphysicians have dealt with the object of the religious act as if they had invented it. Natural theology as a branch of philosophy was considered to be totally independent of man's religious activity. This view first appeared in Aristotle, survived to some extent in the Stoa, and disappeared in early Christian philosophy. It emerged again in late Scholasticism and reached new heights in the modern thinkers to whom we loosely refer as rationalists. Kant was at once one of its chief proponents and the main author of its decline in the recent philosophy. Unfortunately, to many the demise of natural theology implied the disappearance of the idea of God from philosophy altogether. Reacting against this trend but basically sharing the premise that there is no room in philosophy for an idea which philosophy itself has not invented, Whitehead returns to Aristotle's idea of God as a purely metaphysical conclusion, independent of all ethical and religious considerations.[1] Whitehead believes that the time has come to secularize once more the idea of God in philosophy.[2]

Against these positions my thesis is that philosophy alone never reaches the idea of God, yet that it can fully acknowledge its debt to religious faith while maintaining its own autonomy. I share this thesis with the French philosopher Henry Duméry who writes on the idea of God:

[1] *Science and the Modern World* (New York: New American Library, 1959), p. 156.
[2] *Process and Reality* (New York: Harper & Brothers, 1960), p. 315.

The philosopher *encounters* this idea; he is not the author of it. He must therefore seek to know what it signifies and what role in life can be assigned to it. But he is not to mold it as he pleases nor turn it to uses which do not answer to the fundamental aspiration of the subject. In these conditions, the God of philosophers is from the start a theft and a blunder. One pretends to believe that the idea of God is the property of philosophy, whereas it is borrowed from the religious life.[3]

First we shall see how myth and religion entered into philosophy, or rather how they are at the very roots of philosophy—roots which philosophy cannot cut off without basically changing itself. Then we shall show that all strictly philosophical claims on the idea of God are unfounded.

1. THE MYTHICO-RELIGIOUS ORIGINS OF PHILOSOPHY

For the philosopher there is no better way to initiate the study of religion than to recall the origins of his discipline. Even a brief survey shows them to be entirely mythico-religious. I shall contain the discussion within the limits of our own tradition. This choice, imposed by the restrictions of the author's competence, is not altogether arbitrary. For Western philosophy is an excellent test case, since, for the better or the worse, it developed far more autonomously than the philosophical systems of the Orient. If it appears that the roots of that radical and independent method of reflection which we in the West call philosophy are deeply buried in mythical soil, a case has been made for all philosophy. Greek philosophy arose mainly out of a rational reflection upon mythical etiology, that is, that particular aspect of the myth which satisfied archaic man's intellectual desire to know the cause and origin of things.[4] Until Aristotle attempted to work out a *purely* rational philosophy, many aspects of the myth were integrally

---

[3] *Le problème de Dieu* (Paris, 1957), p. 15.
[4] The distinction between the various aspects of the myth will be further explained in the next chapter which will also clarify the relation between myth and religion.

preserved in this reflection. What we now regard as the important contribution of the Milesian philosophers, the awareness that one principle had to explain both the variety and coherence of the universe, very likely had a mythical origin. At any rate the nature of this principle was conceived according to mythical patterns of thought rather than scientific method. Thales's view of the origin of things came close to that of the creation myths.[5] Undoubtedly, the concept of ψύσις competed with the existing myths, but not in the way rational philosophy is often believed to drive out the myth. It rather opposed one mythical view of the universe (which was *in one respect* more rationally developed) to another. When Thales declared everything to be full of gods,[6] he stated a theological position, although one which differed from the accepted ideas about the gods.

> This statement cannot refer to those gods with which the imaginative faith of the Greeks peopled mountain and stream, trees and spring, any more than to the inhabitants of Heaven or Olympus of whom we read in Homer. Thales' gods do not dwell apart in some sequestered and inaccessible region, but everything—that is, the whole familiar world about us, which our reason takes so soberly—is full of gods and the effects of their power.[7]

Thales's philosophy remained mythical with the particular connotation which that term possesses when the myth has already begun to fulfill a specifically religious function, but its mythology differed from the established one.[8]

The same applies even more directly to Anaximander whose "indefinite" has been frequently interpreted as an abstract philosophical principle. Like Thales, Anaximander sought the original

[5] Werner Jaeger, *The Theology of the Early Greek Philosophers* (New York: Oxford University Press, 1967), pp. 20–21.
[6] Aristotle, *De Anima*, I, 5. 411 a. 7.
[7] Werner Jaeger, *op. cit.*, p. 22.
[8] On the distinction between the mere myth as it exists among primitives who do not recognize a specifically "religious" level, and the already somewhat "specialized" religious myth as we find it in all the great civilizations of Assur, Babylon, Egypt, Persia, Greece, and Rome, see Chapter 6.

oneness which unites all things. Yet he balanced this principle by the equally mythical concept of harmony. None of the elements, he believed, could be primary, for if it were it would eliminate the others and the original "justice" would be broken. The ἄπειρον (indefinite) both gives birth to and integrates all oppositions. All definite elements are destroyed and return to their origin, the indefinite, "for they must pay the penalty and make atonement to one another for their injustice according to Time's decree."[9] May we read in these speculations on justice and injustice an early expression of the guilt which comes with individualization, as Jaspers suggests?[10] At any rate, the concept of justice in the balance of nature is clearly mythical. Noteworthy also is the entire conception of ἀρχή which, according to Simplicius, Anaximander was the first to employ.[11] Anaximander deduced from the indestructibility of the root principle that it must be divine.[12] Here *the divine* is defined as that which has neither beginning nor end.[13] The new idea of *the divine* (with the definite article), equated with the immortal and the limitless, constitutes an abstractive attempt to define the religious aspect of reality. Of course, the existing lore about the Greek gods was bound to lose some of its credibility because of this new theology. It created a gap between philosophical speculation and established mythology, which would grow ever wider. Yet the speculation itself was originally not an aggressive rationalism but a true "theology," that is, a thinking about the divine.

[9] Fragment taken from Simplicius, *Physics,* 6r, 24, 19. I follow mainly John Burnet, *Early Greek Philosophy* (New York: Meridian Books, 1958), p. 54.

[10] Karl Jaspers, *The Great Philosophers,* Vol. 2 (New York: Harcourt, Brace & World, 1966), p. 12.

[11] *Physics,* 32 r (150, 20); also 6 r (24, 26). Burnet questions this interpretation (*Early Greek Philosophy,* pp. 54–55). But Jaeger has, in my opinion, successfully refuted his skepticism (*The Theology of the Early Greek Philsophers,* pp. 26–28).

[12] Aristotle, *Physics,* III, 4. 203b 13–14.

[13] Perhaps the timeless nature of the ultimate principle was already perceived by Thales, if we may believe Diogenes Laërtius (*Lives and Opinions of Eminent Philosophers,* tr. by C. D. Yonge [London: H. G. Bohn, 1853], I, 36), but, as so often with him, it is doubtful whether we may.

Heraclitus, who according to legend deposited his writings in Artemis' temple, was moved by the same religious-mythical inspiration. He also established as ultimate principle a primeval, self-sufficient oneness: "This world that is the same for all, neither any god nor any man shaped it, but it ever was and is and shall be everliving fire that kindles by measures and goes out by measures."[14] As in Anaximander the One develops through harmony of oppositions. But giving more weight to the continuous changes in nature, Heraclitus postulated a constant movement and countermovement to maintain the original balance.[15] Divine fire, symbol of an ever-moving Logos, restores all the breaches in the original justice. "Fire advancing upon all things shall judge them and convict them."[16] The divine Logos fulfills the function of a law of nature which moves all things while preserving the initial energy, but its ultimate meaning is that of a divine justice which rules over the changing phenomena and holds them in balance. In it all oppositions are reconciled and so brought to unity.[17]

Even more mythical-religious in outlook than the Ionian philosophers were the Pythagoreans. This Orphic sect, held together by religious beliefs and practices, originally engaged in philosophy as an exercise in spiritual purification, a way of life. In the process its members discovered the essentially rational nature of the concept of number which could be indefinitely developed by the mind.[18] Yet the concept preserved its original religious meaning. *One* was the primal monad, referring as much to the

[14] Hermann Diels, *Fragmente der Vorsokratiker*, 7th ed., (Berlin, 1954), Fragment 30. Tr. by Richmond Lattimore in Matthew Thomson McClure, *The Early Philosophers of Greece* (New York: D. Appleton-Century, 1935), p. 120.

[15] "War is the father and king of all things; he has shown some to be gods and some mortals, he has made some slaves and others free." Diels, Fr. 53. "The harmony of the world is of tensions, like that of the bow and the lyre." Fr. 51.

[16] Diels, Fragment 66.

[17] ". . . all things are one" Fr. 1. "And good and evil are the same" Fr. 57. "All things are fair and good and right to God; but men think of some as wrong and others as right." Fr. 61.

[18] John Burnet, *Early Greek Philosophy*, pp. 82–84, 96.

mythical world egg as to a mathematical intuition, which inaugurated the entire process of reality. Some numbers were regarded as sacred. The distinction between the odd and the even reveals a primitive attempt to gain control over the world by ordering it. The later split of the sect into *akusmatikoi* who retained the entire religious part of the Pythagorean heritage, and *mathematikoi* who rejected what was not strictly mathematical, shows how deeply the religious spirit had continued to permeate a method and concepts which we would regard as strictly scientific.[19]

Equally arresting and somewhat in the same Orphic tradition is the case of Empedocles, who for historians of a later age became the chief naturalist philosopher, but who his contemporaries mainly knew as a wandering prophet and magician. Empedocles wrote a poem on *Purifications* which has been described as "the only surviving work of early Greek poetry in which we come face to face with the Orphic pietism."[20] But even his work *On Nature,* often regarded as the oldest textbook in mechanistic physics with its forces of attraction and repulsion, owes little to scientific thinking. The love and strife which join and separate the four elements are more than allegorical representations: they retain the mythical vision which appears in *Purifications.* The elements themselves bear the names of gods to denote their divine powers. All this takes more from cosmogony and even theogony than from philosophy of nature.

Even for the most rational minds of early Greek culture philosophy was a religious as well as an intellectual pursuit. Parmenides, the first authentic metaphysician, has often been presented as an ontologist devoid of religious interest.[21] Obviously, Parmenides' gigantic metaphysical achievement has overshadowed his religious significance. But Parmenides himself considered his

[19] See, W. K. C. Guthrie, *Orpheus and Greek Religion* (New York: W. W. Norton, 1966), pp. 219–21.
[20] Werner Jaeger, *The Theology of the Early Greek Philosophers,* p. 130.
[21] Such was roughly the thesis of Karl Reinhardt's important study *Parmenides und die Geschichte der griechischen Philosophie* (Frankfurt, 1959), particularly pp. 24, 67, 255–57.

truth divine and ascribed it to a revelation.[22] Yet his religious significance should not be measured by explicitly religious statements (the cultural mentality of his day was hardly ready for a full religious differentiation) but by his description of the absolute—*Being* (το ὄν). This is done almost exclusively in religious terms. Indeed, his *Being* has been compared with the Creator-God of the Bible who also is one, transcendent, perfect, eternal, and identical.[23] One trait which *Being* does not share with the later concept of God is infinity. Parmenides' Absolute, unlike that of his Ionian predecessors, but very like the Deity in Xenophanes, is finite. Gradually the aesthetic Greek mind had come to look upon the infinite as incomprehensible and formless, and therefore imperfect.

The religious orientation of Greek philosophy did not come to an end after the discovery of the subjective dimension. Socrates, who initiated this spiritual revolution, exemplified in his own person the close ties between philosophy and the religious aspect of existence. Although I do not believe that he was more a preacher, a prophet, or a missionary than a philosopher,[24] the events of his life leave us little doubt that to Socrates the new dimension of reality was essentially religious. The oracle of Delphi gave his teaching religious authority. Religious trust in immortality enabled him to fulfill his mission in the face of death and dishonor. His discovery of the divine within the self was to be the basis of all Christian theologies. What would religious life in the West have been without the "philosophies" of his disciples Plato and Plotinus?

There is no point in attempting to describe the religious implications of those philosophies, since they *are* thoroughly religious.

---

[22] Bruno Snell detects the religious currents of southern Italy at the basis of his thinking. *The Discovery of the Mind. The Greek Origins of European Thought.* Tr. by T. G. Rosenmeyer (New York: Harper & Brothers, 1960), p. 148.

[23] Richard Kroner, *Speculation in Pre-Christian Philosophy* (New York: Longmans, Green, 1956), p. 116.

[24] This thesis is stated explicitly by Richard Kroner, *op. cit.*, pp. 141–43; others have held similar views.

Plato's doctrine of Eros is fundamentally a doctrine of salvation.[25] Yet the Eros motive is the driving force of his entire philosophy. For this philosophy has no purpose but to liberate the soul from its earth-bound condition and to lead it up to the contemplation of its own spiritual essence. Eros leads us from a beautiful body to all physical beauty, then to the beauty of the soul and its various activities until it ultimately comes to rest in the contemplation of the supreme form, the Good. It would be futile to reopen here the discussion on the religious meaning of the Good. The issue has become confused mainly because modern readers attempted to impose their own idea of God upon Plato, while they should have realized that the notion of one, personal God was not adequately developed. Plato, more than any other Western philosopher, would contribute to its development. He never calls the Good or any other form a god, yet he attributes to them the adjective "divine." The gods themselves are "divine" only to the extent that they participate in the forms.[26] Nor is Plato's Absolute ever conceived as a person. Yet the real question is not whether Plato's ideas of Good or of god agree with what we call God, but whether the supreme principle of his philosophy possesses divine qualities. Of this there can be little doubt. The Good is the transcendent source of all reality and intelligibility. Moreover, as A. E. Taylor has pointed out, the distinction between essence and existence which characterizes all other forms, disappears in the supreme form of the Good.[27]

Important also is the fact that Plato uses mythical language to describe the upward journey of the soul. The general trend of his philosophy as well as the central theses of his thinking are stated in mythical form. The term Eros, which we used to characterize his philosophy, is mythical and so are the descriptions of its ultimate goal in the *Republic,* the *Symposium,* the *Phaedrus,* and the

25 Anders Nygren, *Agape and Eros,* tr. by Philip Watson (Philadelphia: Westminster Press, 1953), p. 163.
26 *Phaedrus,* 249c. Cf. Emiel de Strycker, *Beknopte Geschiedenis van de Antieke Filosofie* (Antwerp, 1967), pp. 112–13.
27 A. E. Taylor, *Plato: The Man and His Work* (New York: Meridian Books, 1956), p. 289.

Phaedo. Nothing could be more mistaken than to interpret these myths as mere allegorical devices in a logical system. They are rather the elements which determine the meaning and scope of the logical enterprise. Of course, the entire culture in which Plato grew up was still largely mythical in outlook. Rational thought was a new thing which had not fully proven itself. Plato often returns to the old and familiar world of the myth, not because he doubted the possibilities of logic and method, but because he was convinced that it remained the sole avenue to the deeper and darker sides of existence. How false, then, is the judgment of the French rationalist Léon Brunschvicg who complains that Plato in his written work recurs to the mythical tradition whenever scientific insight is lacking, and thereby jeopardizes the scrupulous honesty and methodical purity of his oral instruction.[28]

To be sure, Plato was aware of the limitations of the myth. After the mythical description of the kingdom of the dead at the end of the *Phaedo* he cautions the reader: "A man of sense ought not to say, nor will I be very confident, that the description which I have given of the soul and her mansions is exactly true. But I do say . . . that something of the kind is true." (114d) The *Republic* outright condemns a full trust in the myth. Plato knew that the myth, although irreplaceable, is uncritical. He was aware of the myth as myth, that is, of its relativity as a form of knowing. This is precisely why he did not hesitate to add and invent where the inherited myth fell short. But this is a long way from saying with Brunschvicg that he sinned against the spirit by taking epistemic short cuts which he himself condemned. In using the myth as a form of expression which is at once indispensable and insufficient, he used it exactly in the way religious man uses it.[29]

We shall not discuss the various other systems which sprang up

[28] *Héritage de mots, héritage d'idées* (Paris, 1945), p. 58. For a more sophisticated position, cf. John F. Callahan, "Some Aspects of Myth in Ancient Philosophy" in *Proceedings of the American Catholic Philosophical Association, 1971* (Washington: The Catholic University of America Press, 1972).

[29] The justification of this statement is to be found in Chapter 6.

in the wake of Socrates' thought. Their religious significance may
be less striking, but it is nevertheless very real. The British classi-
cist Gilbert Murray considers the combined impact of Cynics,
Epicureans, and Stoics one of the five "stages" in the development of Greek religion.[30] It takes little effort to see the mythical-
religious vision behind the world order of the Stoa which reconciles all oppositions of reality. Also, the later Stoic writers may well
have been the most expressive witnesses of the religious spirit of
Antiquity. Compared with them the theories of Antisthenes and
Epicurus may seem a-religious and even, in the case of the latter, atheistic. Yet in the final analysis they also are doctrines
of salvation and this is what gave them their appeal. That
Epicurus strongly attacked the prevailing views of the gods only
does him religious credit. Among the great religious thinkers of
Antiquity as of all times are the reformers, who, driven by an
increased awareness of divine transcendence, expurgate and even
destroy the inherited image of the gods. Epicurus, like Xenophanes and like Socrates, was one of those reformers. The reputation of self-indulgence and egotism which he acquired through
the ages is an ironical reversal of history upon a man who distinguished himself by courage, unselfishness, and an ascetically
frugal way of living. Epicurus venerated the gods but he did not
fear their anger.

Aristotle, whom Whitehead praised for having secularized the
idea of God, is perhaps the least religious, and undoubtedly the
least mythical of all Greek philosophers. Nevertheless, in attributing to the concept of God a crucial philosophical role, he
steered the religious consciousness into an entirely new direction
and provided the Hebrew idea of God with the philosophical
support it needed. Moreover, Aristotle rationalized a number of
mythical-religious ideas and tendencies of Plato. The very definition of God's action upon the world is closely related to the attraction which the form of the Good exercises upon all reality.
Justifiably he has been called Plato's faithful disciple with respect

[30] *Five Stages of Greek Religion* (Garden City, N.Y.: Doubleday, 1955),
pp. 76–118.

to the idea of Eros, the leading religious motive of his master's philosophy.[31] I therefore would agree with Gilbert Murray's unexpected encomium on the religious quality of the Stagirite's philosophy:

> Aristotle was not lacking in religious insight and imagination, as he certainly was not without profound influence on the future history of religion. His complete rejection of mythology and of anthropomorphism; his resolute attempt to combine religion and science, not by sacrificing one to the other but by building the highest spiritual aspirations on ascertained truth and the probable conclusions to which it pointed; his splendid imaginative conception of the Divine Being or First Cause as unmoved itself while moving all the universe "as the beloved moves the lover"; all these are high services to religious speculation, and justify the position he held, even when known only through a distorting Arabic translation, in medieval Christianity.[32]

Yet we must wait for Plotinus to bring out the full religious implications of Plato's philosophical vision. In Plotinus the upward flight of the Platonic Eros receives its ultimate justification from a downward process of emanation. The soul longs for the divine because it is itself of divine origin. Émile Bréhier has called Plotinus an Oriental mystic more than a Greek philosopher.[33] In the last chapter of this book we shall have occasion to compare Hindu mysticism with Neo-Platonic thought. I shall leave it to the reader to decide for himself how much they have in common. For the time being we may safely assume that some Oriental influence took place in the cultural melting pot of Alexandria. Nonetheless Plotinus was very much a Greek philosopher. To deny this is to strip all previous Greek philosophy from the mythical and mystical elements which gave it its main impulse and to regard the logical content alone as essential. Such a procedure was not uncommon in France at the beginning of the cen-

---

[31] Ulrich von Wilamowitz-Moellendorff, *Platon,* Vol. 1, (Berlin, 1919), p. 420. Cf. also, Nygren, *Agape and Eros,* p. 185.
[32] *Five Stages of Greek Religion,* p. 109.
[33] *La philosophie de Plotin* (Paris, 1928), pp. 106–33.

tury and in some philosophical circles of England and America at mid-century. But it is highly arbitrary.[34] Plotinus completed a line of thinking initiated by the Pythagoreans and culminating in Plato. More specifically, Plotinus brought out the full religious implications of this tradition. In emphasizing this aspect he may have modified the overall perspective, but not so as to inaugurate an entirely new tradition. In particular Plotinus did not discard reason for ecstacy. On the contrary, he showed how the process of reason attained its summit in mystical contemplation.[35] In accordance with the entire Greek tradition reason remains the primary power of the mind and Plotinus offers no substitute for it. He only adds to its impact by presenting the last step in the reasoning process as a higher stage of consciousness in which the opposition inherent to the reflective attitude ceases to exist. Nor is this final stage unrelated to the reasoning which precedes it. Once the ultimate object of the mind is defined as transcendent, the upward movement *must* eventually leave the intellectual order. A contemporary follower of Plotinus, Henry Duméry, has aptly described the transition from reasoning to contemplation as "the unique case of an intellectualism that requires a mystical flight."[36]

The early Christians, to the extent that they accepted Greek philosophy at all, reinforced its religious meaning by integrating it within their own religious world view. Some had Plato writing under the influence of Moses and thereby participating in the divine revelation. Others regarded the truth of the pagan philosophers as part of the whole truth which was revealed in Christ. Eventually they settled on two orders of truth, one containing

[34] Strongly reacting against Bréhier's thesis is P. V. Pistorius, *Plotinus and Neoplatonism* (Cambridge, Eng.: Bowes & Bowes, 1952), pp. 158–64.

[35] A distinguished writer on mysticism provides an interesting counterpart to the thesis of mystical irrationalism. According to Elmer O'Brien, S.J., Plotinus is a philosopher "of singular intellectual probity" and a most perceptive psychologist, but no mystic at all. *Varieties of Mystic Experience* (New York: Holt, Rinehart & Winston, 1964), pp. 16–17.

[36] *Phénoménologie et religion* (Paris, 1958), p. 91, in *Faith and Reflection*, ed. by Louis Dupré, tr. by M. Benedict Murphy and Stephen McNierney (New York: Herder and Herder, 1969), p. 99.

the principles to explain man's existence in the world, the other instructing him on the order of salvation.[37] Irenaeus developed this position, Augustine confirmed it, Thomas Aquinas gave it its classical expression. St. Thomas stands out for his daring attempt to adopt in its entirety a philosophy which already had a religious foundation of its own. Thus Aristotle's "theology" became the basis for the Christian theology of salvation. Thomas fully accepts the Greek term "theology" for metaphysics, and preserves its religious meaning, but at the same time he manages to distinguish it from the "theology" of Holy Scripture.

> There is one theology in which we treat of divine things not as the subject of the science but as the principles of the subject. Such is the theology pursued by the philosophers which is also called metaphysics. There is another theology, however, which studies divine things for their own sakes as the subject of the science; and this is the theology taught in Sacred Scripture.[88]

The theology which is metaphysics deals with those objects of speculation which do not depend upon matter for their existence, such as God and the angels or those principles which may or may not exist in matter. It fully deserves the name divine science, because "God is the principal thing known in it."[39] But it does not deal with the revealed as such. Some of the qualities and flaws of Thomas' synthesis will appear in the chapter on the problem of God. Here it may suffice to point out that the separation between the two orders prepared the chasm between religious experience and philosophical reflection which post-Reformation philosophy would complete. To be sure, Thomas or his contemporaries were not responsible for this split. But the analogy indicates that the separation so clearly visible in Descartes and

---

[37] On these early Christian positions, cf. A. M. Armstrong and R. A. Markus, *Christian Faith and Greek Philosophy* (New York: Sheed & Ward, 1964), pp. 135–58.

[88] *In Boethii De Trinitate*, 9.5, a. 4 c. Tr. by Armand Maurer, C.S.B. (Toronto: Pontifical Institute, 1953), p. 41.

[89] *Ibid.*, q. 5, a. 1 c.

his successors was not entirely due to factors active only at the beginning of modern times.[40] The process had a long prehistory. Even in Thomas, I believe, the separation between the two orders would ultimately have drained the religious element out of philosophy, if philosophy itself had not remained dependent upon theology. In the case of Thomas this dependence was so close that Gilson raises the question whether he ever was a philosopher at all. Be that as it may, at least the final authority of theology prevented speculation from being separated from the religious reality, as it is in most of modern philosophy.

A dependence of philosophy upon theology is no longer acceptable to us. If philosophy is to be at all, it must be autonomous; even in the study of religion it must remain its own supreme authority. We therefore must look elsewhere for a solution. Yet in their desire to make philosophy autonomous, modern thinkers have severed it from the religious aspect of existence altogether. Overreacting against past dependencies many came to equate the mere acceptance of a given experience with an intrusion upon the autonomy of their science. Ironically the disdain of the modern rationalist for the mythical and the religious resulted in a philosophy which itself was by no means "pure," but merely universalized the method of scientific thinking, namely, positivism. No one today believes in Auguste Comte's or John Stuart Mill's creed any more. Yet the aftereffect of their dogmas is all-pervasive. The theory that a truly scientific philosophy overcomes the myth (of which all religious beliefs were regarded as a subspecies) still held its full sway a few decades ago. The reaction which since has set in, has produced some remarkable conversions. Thus Lévy-Bruhl, educated in the old Comtean tradition, openly repudiated his former belief that the mythical mind is pre-logical. The mystical mentality, he claims in his later period, may be easier to detect in primitives but is present in every human

[40] The scrupulous adherence of modern philosophy to an autonomous method has often obscured its religious elements. The mystical background of the philosophies of Cusanus, Bruno, and Spinoza is obvious. But religious intuitions are present also in Leibniz, Schelling, and Hegel. The "separation" seems to be more one of method than of content.

spirit.[41] We know how Lévi-Strauss has strengthened this thesis in our time. In philosophy also we hear a new sound since Scheler, Jaspers, Heidegger, Bergson, and Blondel.

I wonder whether the time has not come for philosophy to recognize and accept its origins. Obviously we cannot return to mythical thinking nor abandon the autonomy (including total independence of theological principles) which it took Western thought so long to acquire. But autonomy does not entitle philosophy to turn its back to an entire realm of experience. When the philosopher stops reflecting *upon* a major field of experience, he starts inventing a surrogate experience. Instead of listening to those who have passed through the actual experience, he now prefers to tell them what they should feel, think, and do. Unsurprisingly they find his conclusions remote from reality. Remembering the apron strings of theology, the philosopher has become particularly reluctant to listen to religious talk. Moreover, his concern with keeping the rational air of philosophy pure from all contamination drives him away from anything as muddily irrational as mythical and religious thought. But the air of most contemporary philosophy is stale rather than pure, as those of its students know who have ventured out into other fields.

Perhaps philosophy ought to return to that radical empiricism which American philosophy so excitingly introduced at the beginning of this century. Most philosophical studies on religion of the recent past are totally outdated. In contrast with them the work of James, Royce, Hocking retains all its original freshness. The reason, I would guess, is that those authors, raised in the hard school of a pioneering country where a man had to find things out for himself, deemed it necessary to acquire experience before interpreting it. Nor did they, as the "empiricists" of the past, restrict experience to sense perception and its interpretation. Those men let no one tell them what was, and what was not "meaningful" as experience. Unfortunately, since then the "radical" American empiricism has again been replaced by the narrow variety of which it had discarded the sensationalist dog-

[41] *Les Carnets de Lucien Lévy-Bruhl* (Paris, 1949), p. 131.

matism. At a time when the new sciences of anthropology, ethnology, and comparative religion are tapping a wealth of information, the philosopher can no longer afford to stay closed up within his own little alchemy shop. He must open his doors and windows and welcome the fresh breezes of experience. He should become receptive once again to all dimensions of existence and willing to listen to those who have explored them. The shield above his door should bear the words of Thales: Enter, here too are gods. Our time is a period of change, in which painstakingly a new culture is being formed. It is already clear that the transcendent dimension will be increasingly explored. Present philosophy should forget its feuds of the past and attempt to contribute positively to the exploration.

2. METAPHYSICS AND THE RELIGIOUS IDEA OF GOD

That mythico-religious sources have determined the origin as well as most of the development of Western philosophy, is in itself no proof that metaphysics cannot independently attain the idea of God. This brings us to the second part of our thesis: philosophy alone is unable to reach the idea of God. This statement would be too sweeping to be capable of proof had not metaphysics itself staked out a well-defined compound within which all the decisive battles on this issue were fought: the arguments for the existence of God. To deflate the metaphysician's claims of self-sufficiency with respect to the idea of God it suffices to show that the arguments do not deliver what they promise. Since so many have been developed over the centuries, that may still appear to be an unmanageable task. Yet the basic error lies more in the general structure than in the particularities of each argument, and most arguments are reducible to a few basic types. The real difficulty of a critique consists in evaluating the original purport of what we now regard as "proofs." In many instances the idea of God was openly taken from religious sources and the author had no intention of construing an argument independently of

the religious experience. This is notably the case for the instigator
of the most controversial "argument," Anselm of Canterbury. It
holds true, I suspect, for most Medieval Scholastics. Their purpose with the argument differs substantially from that of modern
philosophers. They merely wanted to show how the existence of
the finite and the contingent requires the existence of an infinite,
necessary Being. This is difficult enough in itself and most attempts fail by serious flaws of reasoning. But at least Medieval
authors until Scotus did not claim to produce out of philosophy
an idea of God fully equipped like Athena stepping out of
Zeus's head. They merely attempted to find *some* rational justification for their religious beliefs. Once the finite's need of the infinite is established, they did not hesitate to identify this infinite
with their religious idea of God, since from theological reflection
they knew already that, among other things, the God in whom
they believed must be infinite and necessary. This procedure often
leads to sloppy thinking. Since the authors knew the outcome beforehand they were anxious to reach the goal and to have it all
over with. But in principle the method is unobjectionable.

What we reject are arguments which by a process of sheer
reasoning pretend to arrive at full-fledged religious conclusions.
All such arguments in some way fail to distinguish adequately
the transcendent from the phenomenal. They treat the phenomenal
as if it could give positive information about what transcends it,
and the transcendent as if it were part of the phenomenal. Both
errors are inherent in the structure of the purely philosophical
proof. The former was first denounced by Kant. An analysis of the
traditional arguments would show that a less agnostic philosophy
must remain equally critical of the positive transition from the
phenomenal to the transcendent.[42] The second error is less obvious. It consists in the fact that all attempts to "prove" God, reduce Him to an object and treat the finite and infinite as if they
were equal partners. To "prove" is to posit a content as objective,

[42] I have attempted such an analysis in a study on recent philosophy of
religion which will appear shortly.

as another reality. But an object can never be God, for the nature of transcendent Being is such that it cannot be separated from the immanent subject.[43]

More basically, all arguments misrepresent the relation between the finite and the infinite. The proof posits the finite first, as if it were the condition for the infinite's existence. The finite *is,* therefore the infinite must *also* be. Now, to some extent any affirmation of the transcendent ascends from the finite to the infinite. But an "argument" has no way of correcting this initial position.

What is equally noticeable here is that a finite form of being is accepted as the starting-point, and this finite being thus appears as that by means of which the infinite Being gets its foundation. A finite being thus appears as the foundation or basis. Mediation is given a position which implies that the consciousness of the infinite has its origin in the finite. To speak more accurately, what we have here is that the finite is expressed in terms which imply that it has only a positive relation between the two. The proposition thus means that the being of the finite is the being of the infinite.[44]

If the infinite is opposed to the finite, it is limited and thereby ceases to be infinite. Instead we must show that the finite is *in* the infinite. Which means that our initial affirmation of the finite must be followed by a negation of the finite's independent being. Such a negation cannot be provided by the argument which asserts the infinite as *also* existing and thereby juxtaposes it to the finite. A purely phenomenal starting-point does not allow a

---

[43] G. W. F. Hegel, *Vorlesungen über die Philosophie der Religion,* ed. by Georg Lasson (Hamburg, 1966), Vol. I, pp. 121, 44–45. Also, Emil Fackenheim, *The Religious Dimension in Hegel's Thought* (Bloomington: Indiana University Press, 1968), p. 121. Claude Bruaire, *Logique et religion chrétienne dans la philosophie de Hegel* (Paris, 1964), pp. 31–32.

[44] Hegel, *Vorlesungen über die Philosophie der Religion,* Vol. II, p. 54; *Lectures on the Philosophy of Religion,* tr. by E. B. Speirs and J. Burdon Sanderson (London: Routledge & Kegan Paul, 1962), Vol. I, p. 329. (Capitalization changed) This translation is to be used with caution not only because of its own inaccuracies but also because it is based upon the second, very uncritical edition of the *Vorlesungen.*

negation of the finite since the infinite is entirely based on it.[45] In the correct perspective the infinite negates the finite, because the finite itself considered from the infinite point of view, has only negative meaning. Not because the finite *is* is the infinite, but because it is *not*.[46] This is precisely the way religious man sees the relation between the infinite and the finite. For him the finite is what it is only through its limitation. In positing it, he pre-posits its negation. Of course, as we shall see later, the infinite negates the finite only insofar as the finite itself is negative. True infinity, therefore, preserves the finite within itself: it is its definitive affirmation. This in turn will require new negations to prevent the affirmation of the infinite from resulting in a Spinozistic monism.

Even if "purely rational" arguments for the existence of God could be made more successful than they are and were able to prove the existence of an infinite, perfect Being, they still would not reach the "object" of the religious act. Unless philosophy studies God from *within* the religious experience where his name was first heard, it will always fall into the error denounced by Scheler of identifying two differently intended objects without proving that they are identical. The absolute of philosophy solves an intellectual problem. The God of religion brings salvation. The latter is revealed in the religious experience, the former is a product of speculative thinking which borrows the name God from religious language for its own purposes. The metaphysical idea of God is never a subject, while the God of faith is. It is not merely that we speak differently *about* a person (object)

---

[45] "The metaphysical proofs of the existence of God are deficient interpretations and descriptions of the mind's elevation from the world to God, because they fail to express or, rather, to bring out the moment of negation which is implied in this elevation. For if the world is *contingent* (*zufällig*), it must be only *falling* (fallendes), only appearing, *nothing* in and for itself. The meaning of the elevation of the spirit is that the world possesses Being but Being which is only appearance, not true Being, absolute truth, and that the latter is beyond all appearances in God alone, that God alone is true Being." G. W. F. Hegel, *Encyclopädie der philosophischen Wissenschaften,* 1830, ed. by F. Nicolin and O. Pöggeler (Hamburg, 1959), 50, Zusatz.

[46] Hegel, *Vorlesungen,* II, p. 46.

than *to* a person. In the case of God we cannot talk *about* him except in a context of talking *to* him.

> God is the only one to whom we can speak only in the second person. When we speak about him, we do so only insofar as we stand in his presence. We therefore can speak of God while praying. When we speak in the third person, as is inevitable in human language, we speak inauthentically about him.[47]

For some, mostly contemporary religious philosophers, the arguments are rational articulations of the religious movement of the mind. To them the proposition that contingent being requires the existence of the necessary one, means: religious man cannot envision the beings of phenomenal experience without seeing them supported by divine necessity. Reflecting upon this vision he may retrace his steps and fix them in the successive phases of an argument. The procedure is rational insofar as each stage ideally contains its own justification, but the movement itself is driven by religious power rather than by logical necessity. This interpretation of the arguments has the advantage that it brings out their religious motivation, but it must abandon all claims of pure rationality. The arguments, then, cease to be proofs.

Although this approach is defensible, I feel that something more is needed to support the faith of modern man. For unless it can be proven that a transcendent horizon falls within man's vision of reality and that a positive urge drives him to explore this horizon, the foundation of the religious act remains dubious and the contemporary believer will not cease to question its meaningfulness. I shall therefore give some suggestions for such an "argument." But it must be clear from the beginning that this will be no proof *for the existence of God,* but for the transcendence of Being and, at most, also for the rational acceptability of a religious interpretation of this transcendence. One may accept its conclusion without admitting the idea of God as religious faiths have traditionally conceived it. To conclude to a transcendent

[47] Karl Heim, *Glauben und Denken* (Berlin, 1941), p. 316, quoted in Hessen, *op. cit.,* p. 181.

ground or to postulate such a ground in order to make the real intelligible, is not yet to attain the Divine. Is the absolutely intelligible which many philosophers require to found the intelligibility of the real, the perfect Being intended by the religious act? Karl Jaspers' philosophy of transcendence is there to prove that one does not necessarily imply the other.

The idea of transcendence is from a metaphysical point of view not further determinable, although it invites further investigation. Only from the kind of direct confrontation with the divine to which religious man gives such names as "revelation" and "grace" can transcendence acquire a positive content. An autonomous study of Being or consciousness can state the problem; it cannot provide the answer. The limits set by Kant are the limits of the *metaphysical* knowledge of God. Yet they are not the limits of the religious knowledge, nor are they the limits of philosophical language about God. To continue its investigation of the transcendent, philosophy must turn from metaphysics to critical reflection upon religious attitudes as they actually exist. In the remaining pages of this chapter, we shall consider how a pure metaphysics encounters the transcendent.

Varied as they are, those encounters may be reduced to two basic models depending on whether the metaphysics is one of being or of consciousness. Here a great deal of the work achieved since the end of the last century in the area of the so-called theodicy or natural theology, remains valuable, even though it never accomplished what its authors had hoped it would, namely, to prove the existence of God. The real objective of metaphysics ought to be to discover the *locus* in which a possible revelation could occur.[48] The term revelation in this context is meant to include also the *existence* of God.

Scholastic philosophers directly or indirectly influenced by Maréchal's theory of dynamism of the intellect regard the encounter with the transcendent as an apprehension of infinite Being which conditions every finite perception and which can be made reflectively conscious. Thus Karl Rahner discovers the existence

---

[48] Karl Rahner, *Hörer des Wörtes*, p. 138; *Hearers of the Word*, p. 112.

of transcendent reality in the *pre-apprehension* (*Vorgriff*) of Being which accompanies every assertion.

> The pre-apprehension of such Being is . . . no *a priori* knowledge of an object, but the *a priori* horizon of perception of a sensuous object presented *a posteriori*. It is the *a priori* condition of the knowledge of an *a posteriori* appearance.[49]

Being-as-such is grasped implicitly as the goal and horizon of all intellectual affirmation. To be sure, the notion of Being is not altogether transcendent. For the Being of all finite beings can be no more absolute than the totality of all possible determinations. Together they would yield no more than an intrinsically finite reality. Yet at the same time Being is affirmed as transcending all finite beings. As a horizon of affirmation, Being suggests a *beyond*. Moreover, since this horizon surpasses even the greatest conceivable totality of finite beings, Rahner feels justified in assuming that infinite Being is co-affirmed in every particular assertion. One might object that a purely negative infinity, that is, a horizon which is unlimited without containing anything, would do just as well. But Rahner answers: "The 'whither' does not itself have a private infinity with respect to what is to be apprehended. For otherwise the pre-apprehension would attain to 'nothing,' to the mere possibility of that which is to be apprehended as actuality."[50] The entire argument depends on the priority of the actual over the possible. This priority is supposed to exclude the possibility of a purely negative horizon. If the horizon is *pre*-apprehended it must be actual rather than possible.

If the preceding argument is supposed to be a proof for the existence of God, I remain unconvinced. Several things seem to be equated here which are by no means identical. I shall not challenge the pre-apprehension of Being, for the content of

---

[49] *Hörer des Wörtes*, p. 176; *Hearers of the Word*, p. 143. Cf. also *Spirit in the World*, tr. by William Dijch, S.J. (New York: Herder and Herder, 1968), p. 184.

[50] *Spirit in the World*, p. 184.

Being exceeds every possible actual affirmation. But I do not see why that which exceeds every conceivable finite being must be infinite in itself. A "surplus" of Being appears like a halo around the affirmation of each finite being, but there is no evidence that this halo must be conceived by itself as an infinite actuality. That the mind affirms Being infinitely does not imply that it affirms *an* infinite Being. Undoubtedly each affirmation of the finite as such implicitly asserts the possibility of a *more*. But must it therefore assert infinite actuality? Such an actuality is not proven by saying that "the esse of the pre-apprehension does not come of itself to a limit intrinsically."[51] It merely proves that the notion of Being is *de se* unlimited, not that its actual realization is unlimited.

This brings us to the notion of the infinite horizon. It is true that Being is the horizon of each affirmation and that this horizon is unlimited. But to bring both parts of this statement together and to conclude that an infinite Being is affirmed in the pre-apprehension of a limitless horizon seems unwarranted. Nor does the priority of the actual over the possible prove the point. For this priority does not require that an infinite actuality be asserted before a finite being can be affirmed as actual. To assume to the contrary, as Heidegger does, that Being itself is affirmed against a horizon of nothingness by no means implies that nothingness is *prior*. It simply means that Being is *co-affirmed* or *co-preapprehended* with nothingness. The notion of Being by itself is neither finite nor infinite—it is indefinite. How far it stretches depends on how far one's ontological affirmation reaches. The terms finite and infinite in this respect fulfill no other function than to reveal the scope of this affirmation. To call the totality of *what is,* finite means that one assumes the existence of an actuality which surpasses it. But the universe conceived as the totality of what is and what could be, offers no intrinsic grounds for being called finite. The term finite, as applied to the totality of the real and the possible, merely indicates that one gives a positive meaning to the notion of transcendence. Such a consideration may

[51] *Spirit in the World,* p. 184.

be justified on many grounds, but from a purely metaphysical point of view it is a *choice*.

Yet, my main purpose is not to criticize Rahner, but to express my agreement with his fundamental insight: that the metaphysical horizon of affirmation necessarily raises the *problem* of transcendence. What lies beyond the horizon? This question is so far from being meaningless, as positivists try to tell us, that I consider it inevitable. In going to the end I cannot avoid asking how much farther I could go. Insofar as the mind focuses on this *beyond* aspect of the horizon of Being it raises the question of transcendent Being. This, in my position, is as far as the mind can go in the metaphysical search. But it is far enough to make religious concerns meaningful and even sufficiently interesting for the metaphysician to allow himself to be drawn into the complex web of religious affirmations. His first question will, of course, be how religious man could speak about a reality which he himself describes as transcendent. The answer is: by means of negation. "Through the negation of the limit of any particular and immediately accessible 'having being' and through the removal of the upper limit in the direction of the absolute being of God, supra-mundane existents can be defined, at least negatively."[52] Religious affirmations of the transcendent, then, do not provide new philosophical knowledge *of* the transcendent. They describe new experiences in man's relation *to* the transcendent. As such, they fulfill a meaningful purpose and have an impact which, although stated in negative terms, is eminently positive.

Another major tradition encounters the problem of transcendence in the reflection upon consciousness. One of the great discoveries of Western philosophy, initiated by Socrates and completed by Augustine, Descartes, and Kant, is that the mind has a reality of its own which is irreducible to any other being.[53] Yet the mind cannot know itself unless it previously knows

[52] *Hörer des Wörtes*, p. 186; *Hearers of the Word*, p. 151.
[53] On the gradual discovery of the stages of Consciousness I wrote "The Philosophical Stages of Self-Discovery" in *Thought*, 39 (1964), pp. 17–28.

something else. As Husserl established, its nature is thoroughly intentional. It is then only by a process of bracketing what does not belong to the mind itself that we are able to discover its proper being. Eventually this gradual reduction will reveal some form of pure self, an act which itself is one but is at the origin of all conscious multiplicity. Can we go further? Ever since Plotinus philosophers have been found who said that we can and that we must go further. For in its basic dichotomy between subject and object, activity and passivity, the mind reveals itself as an already established order which refers to an ulterior, simple source. One contemporary writer who continues the Neo-Platonic tradition in the language of Husserl, concludes:

> Either one seeks to arrest the reductive effort at a given order (for example that of the I, or rather, the transcendental *We*) and is completely arbitrary, since the reducible remains. Or one pushes the purifying exigency the whole way, and establishes that it stops of itself only afer going beyond all the orders and even the notion of order.[54]

Duméry calls the One, God, as he well may in a philosophy of religion. Yet an analysis of consciousness alone would not justify this name. The reduction concludes only to a dynamic simplicity beyone order and intelligibility in which the dichotomy of the mind is overcome. In line with the Neo-Platonic tradition Duméry rejects even the name "Being" for the One and, consequently, rules out any possibility of participation.

> "It is sheer overflowing, without imperfection or ebb. If its aseity is at the beginning of the procession, we cannot tie it to the terms which proceed from it . . . The One-source is the triumphant

---

[54] Henry Duméry, *The Problem of God*, tr. by Charles Courtney (Evanston: Northwestern University Press, 1964), pp. 48–49. Cf. also *Philosophie de la religion*, Vol. I (Paris, 1957), pp. 47–54, 59–71. This passage has been translated by M. Benedict Murphy and Stephen McNierney in an anthology of Duméry's work, *Faith and Reflection*, ed. by Louis Dupré (New York: Herder and Herder, 1969), pp. 157–77.

irradiation, the fiery furnace in full blast. Once the rays are interpreted and reflected in various directions, finitude is introduced."[55]

Many philosophers may balk at such images and, for that matter, at the thought which produces them. If the phenomenological method is controversial, an "ultimate" reduction is even more so. But then the same could be said of the horizon of Being as developed by Rahner or Lonergan. A philosophical argument never moves in a vacuum; it is connected with a particular philosophical structure and ultimately originates in a personal vision of the universe. Without the vision and the structure it becomes incomprehensible.

Others have encountered the transcendent in the self-surpassing drive of consciousness. This was the road followed by Bergson, Blondel, and the entire school of Maréchal. Through scientific, moral, and aesthetic ideals the mind expresses its restless drive to go beyond itself. Their function is to draw the mind forever beyond its actual achievements. Thus, although ideals cannot be attained, they never cease to attract. Projecting the unattainable, ideals open up the mystery of transcendence. Why does man thus desire to transcend himself? This question intrigues the religious mind. It is not the existence of ideals that is mysterious, for they are man's own creation, but rather the force which drives man to create them, his urge toward transcendence. The religious mind merely concentrates upon an aspect of experience which presents itself to all. Reflective interpretations of this dimension vary from one philosophy to another. Nor are they all philosophical. A reflective awareness of the transcendent does not require methodic thought. It may occur in an existential situation, a moral decision, an aesthetic experience. The entire literature of our civilization bears witness to man's confrontation with transcendence. Philosophy can do no more than articulate the primal awareness of transcendence. Only the religious act can transform it into an awareness of God.

[55] *Philosophie de la religion*, Vol. I, p. 48; *Faith and Reflection*, p. 158.

3. FAITH'S NEED OF REFLECTION

The notion of transcendence may be established independently of the religious act. But whether or not it is to receive a positive content is a religious matter. In dealing with this content philosophy can only reflect on a *given* nonphilosophical experience of religious faith; it cannot *constitute* it by reflecting on the nature of the real as such. On the other hand, the content of faith must remain accessible to philosophical critique, for unless rational reflection be allowed on the sacred, the latter must remain meaningless. Moreover, since the believer holds certain views on the nature of the real which the philosopher explores in the light of reason alone, the believer must let that light in on his views. The mind cannot simultaneously embrace two positions on the same subject without being forced to harmonize them. Attempts to do so have resulted first in religious philosophies and, in the last two centuries, in philosophies of religion.

Here we face the fact that not all philosophies are fit to deal with the religious phenomenon. Any approach which rejects *a priori* all transcendent claims is obviously unable to evaluate the religious experience in terms acceptable to religious man. But equally unfit is a philosophy which feels too much at ease with religious statements and pretends to give them a full, rational support. Faith claims to create a transcendent world *within* the immanent and asks the philosopher to acknowledge this transcendence while abstaining from it.

Turning now to the particular modes in which philosophers have opened their metaphysics to the transcendent dimension, we notice an almost infinite variety. The approaches range from an idea of God which is the keystone of a system (a secularization after the fashion which we denounced in the previous section) to an open and benevolent agnosticism. Few today would still claim with Descartes that all certainties collapse unless there exists a transcendent, infinitely perfect Being. But all advocates of metaphysical arguments for the existence of God share, to some extent, Descartes' position insofar as their universe must become incoherent without God. For if this universe implies the necessary existence of God, the very thought of a world without God would conflict with the only possible conception of the present one. Some might say that the same argument applies to any philosopher who *accepts* the existence of God, insofar as the acceptance of a necessary being excludes a problematic attitude with respect to that idea: a necessary being once admitted, cannot be "bracketed" any more. Yet this conclusion does not follow, since there is a distinction between the thought of a necessary being and the necessary thought of a necessary being. The former is based upon a fluid concept of reality which can alternatively include and exclude the notion of a transcendent necessary being, while the latter, which is accepted by the adherents of the ontological argument, allows only one possible logical universe of which God is a necessary component. Nevertheless even those for whom God is such a philosophical necessity do not usually claim that philosophical discourse alone exhausts its riches. Whitehead, for instance, in the text referred to at the beginning of this chapter, praises Aristotle for having stayed within the confines of meta-physics: to him the poverty of the Aristotelian vision of God is the sign of its authenticity. Religious faith for Whitehead is by no means a mere extension of metaphysics, but rather an attempt to infuse "that non-temporal generality which primarily belongs to conceptual thought alone" into the particularity of emotion.[56] Whether religious faith needs philosophical reflection, as this statement implies, will be discussed shortly.

But first we must consider another position in which philosophy pretends neither to invent nor to prove the existence of God, but to remain "open" toward the transcendent. Such an open-ended philosophy confronts the various positions concerning the ultimate ground of the mind and the universe as so many

[56] *Process and Reality,* p. 23.

hypotheses. One of these deserves particular attention because it corresponds to an actually existing religious experience. Maurice Blondel, the main proponent of this theory, refers to it as a "necessary hypothesis," thus distinguishing it from a number of other hypotheses which the philosopher may prefer not to consider even though he does not regard them as logically contradictory.[57] Philosophy's task is to analyze the intrinsic coherence of the God-hypothesis as it is presented by religious man. In doing so metaphysics naturally develops into a philosophy of religion. The transition is smooth enough, but it is all the more important that the philosopher be fully aware of it. Otherwise he will conclude, as he has done so often in the past, to some "natural" theory of God which faith or theology merely "follows up and fills out more fully."[58]

The main objective of philosophy of religion is to determine the specific nature of the religious act in and through its various expressions. To achieve this purpose it must be above all a study of symbols, situating the symbolic activity within the totality of consciousness. This, I take it, is what Schelling in his philosophy of myth and of revelation and Hegel in his theory of representation attempted to accomplish. Obviously a philosophical reflection upon religious symbolism never recaptures the riches of the original symbols. Nor is it itself symbolic, as Jaspers implied. Philosophy of religion is purely rational. It analyzes the various noetic structures of religious representations without being symbolically creative. Nevertheless its critical work fills a basic religious need. For in having his expressions subjected to a critical analysis, religious man becomes aware of their relativity. This helps him to prevent faith from being taken over by the luxuriant undergrowth of its own creativity. Philosophical reflec-

---

[57] Blondel's thesis is found in *L'action* (1893) and *Lettre sur les exigences de la pensée contemporaine en matière d'apologétique* (1896). The method is further explained in Henry Duméry, *Blondel, et la religion* (Paris, 1960), and my own "Reflections on Blondel's Religious Philosophy," *The New Scholasticism*, 40 (1966), pp. 3–22.

[58] Karl Rahner, *Hörer des Wortes*, p. 27; *Hearers of the Word* (New York: Herder and Herder, 1969), p. 13.

tion also assists him in answering such critical questions as how a faith can maintain its identity throughout the various expressions which it adopts in the course of its development.

But most importantly from an intrinsically religious point of view, philosophy responds to faith's own need of reflection. The drive toward *gnosis* is part of the religious act itself. Faith seeks ever greater clarification. The adage *fides quaerens intellectum* is not an invention of philosophers but of theologians, and one which in the Christian tradition has been practiced ever since the Pauline and the Johannine writings. In an advanced culture faith naturally recurs to philosophical concepts to develop its ideas. The believer cannot avoid thinking about what a divine Creator, an immortal soul, and other tenets of this faith might possibly mean. But aside from particular beliefs, faith, as an overall integrating structure which assigns to all aspects of existence their ultimate meaning, must meet that rational interpretation of reality to which we refer as metaphysics. Windelband at one time went so far as to call religion "an intercourse with the inmost nature and foundation of all reality, a life in and with God, *a metaphysical life.*"[59] Far from threatening the religious act, philosophical reflection brings it to a heightened awareness of itself. It follows the self-transcending movement of faith in its restless desire to go beyond its present state and to approach closer to vision.

Yet, this affinity to reflection is fraught with danger both to metaphysics and faith. The believing metaphysician may be tempted to take the religious integration for an ultimate metaphysical answer. As Heidegger indicated, God is not the final answer to the question: Why is there something rather than nothing?[60] If anything he is part of the problem, for metaphysics must question his Being as much as that of all finite beings. Too eager a desire for philosophical insight may lead the religious man to substitute independent speculation for living experience. As

[59] "Das Heilige" in *Präludien* (1903), p. 357.
[60] *Einführung in die Metaphysik*, p. 5. *An Introduction to Metaphysics,* tr. by Ralph Manheim, pp. 6–7.

a result, the believer may pretend to understand what in another respect he declares to be beyond understanding.

But these dangers must be braved since religious man has no choice but to take the risk which is inherent in the nature of his experience. Whitehead forcefully expressed the need of reflection when he declared that faith, to maintain its religious status, must remain aware of its metaphysical implications. In this respect it differs from science.

> Science can leave its metaphysics implicit and retire behind our belief in the pragmatic value of its general descriptions. If religion does that, it admits that its dogmas are merely pleasing ideas for the purpose of stimulating its emotions. Science (at least as a temporary methodological device) can rest upon a naive faith; religion is the longing for justification. When religion ceases to seek for penetration, for clarity, it is sinking back into its lower forms.[61]

The degeneration to which Whitehead refers consists in a flight into the purely emotional and the wildly fantastic, denounced by all students of the religious experience. Tylor was not entirely wrong in presenting the development of religion as a rationalization process which gradually subdues the unruly forces of religious inspiration. Rudolf Otto, from a much better viewpoint, considered the interpenetration of the rational elements with the nonrational ones as axiomatic and as an intrinsically necessary process.[62] The category of the sacred is not fully realized until the nonrational numinous fact is "schematized" by rational elements.[63] Otto Karrer mentions the constant threat of a "Verwilderung" of the elements of imagination in religion.[64] We find the need for rationalization mentioned in Plato, in Locke, and in Hegel. Of course, the need for reflection in the religious act is not ex-

---

[61] *Religion in the Making* (New York: Meridian Books, 1961), p. 83.
[62] *The Idea of the Holy* (New York: Oxford University Press, 1958), p. 136.
[63] *Op. cit.*, p. 45.
[64] *Das Religiöse in der Menschheit und das Christentum* (Freiburg, 1934), p. 134. See also, Johannes Hessen, *op. cit.*, II, p. 36.

clusively being fulfilled by philosophy. Yet one inevitably leads to the other.

As I indicated previously, the philosophical reflection upon the religious act which is usually called philosophy of religion is to be distinguished from general metaphysics. While the latter must refrain from God talk in the strict, religious sense, the former must embrace the full content of the religious experience. But the desire for an intrinsically unified philosophical system may lead the philosopher to incorporate this reflection upon religious experience into general metaphysics. Something of that nature seems to have occurred in Hegel's philosophy. For Hegel the "system" of philosophy that begins with *Logic* and ends with the *Philosophy of Spirit* has no other content than religion.

> Philosophy has its own content, its need and interest common with religion; its object is the eternal truth, that is, nothing but God and his explication. Philosophy explicates itself only when it explicates religion and while it explicates itself, it explicates religion.[65]

But although its general object is the same as that of philosophy *as such,* philosophy of religion does not stay with pure thought: it descends to the religious representation in order to study thought in its external manifestation. At the same time, philosophy of religion does not consider the finite forms which the Spirit gives itself in nature and in the finite spirit and which general philosophy must also study. Instead it concentrates directly on the Idea as it appears in its infinite form, as absolute Spirit.[66] Obviously the unity between philosophy of religion and metaphysics here becomes uncomfortably close.

Related to this "religionization" of metaphysics is the position

[65] G. W. F. Hegel, *Vorlesungen über die Philosophie der Religion,* ed. by Georg Lasson (Hamburg, 1966), I, p. 29.

[66] *Vorlesungen,* I, pp. 31–33. See also, Albert Chapelle, *Hegel et la religion* (Paris, 1963), I, pp. 212–13. André Léonard, *La foi chez Hegel* (Louvain, pro manuscripto, 1968), pp. 216–17. Claude Bruaire, *Logique et religion chrétienne dans la philosophie de Hegel* (Paris, 1964), pp. 43–44.

held by some Catholic theologians in recent years. They simply subordinate philosophy to the theological reflection which occurs *in* the religious experience itself. Thus philosophical reflection is made dependent upon extraphilosophical norms and the autonomy of philosophical thought is jeopardized altogether. The nonbeliever is said to live an inauthentic existence and thereby to be at a definite disadvantage in philosophizing. The rejection of faith is thought to compromise the quality of his philosophical reflection. This position is a clear instance of an illegitimate intrusion of religion into the domain of metaphysics. We might even say: into the domain of philosophy, for when a thinker so widely extends the boundaries of theology, there is no proper domain for philosophy of religion left.[67]

A somewhat similar view, although more restrained, is defended by Étienne Gilson, who, on the basis of Thomas' *Summa Theologiae,* considers Christian philosophy an integral part of Christian theology. This position obviously tolls the death bell for an autonomous philosophy of the Christian experience. If this is Christian philosophy, there is no Christian *philosophy.*[68] If philosophy is an *autonomous* reflection upon living experience, it must be entitled to reflect upon the religious experience, in this case the Christian experience, without having to sacrifice its independence. Of course, all here depends on the meaning of "autonomy." If it means that philosophy must create or at least independently reconstitute basic religious concepts, then religious man will no longer recognize them as his own. But if "autonomy" is restricted to an independently critical interpretation of a

[67] We find this position in Henk van Luyk, S.J., *Philosophie du fait chrétien. L'analyse critique du christianisme de Henry Duméry* (Paris, 1964), pp. 190–280.

[68] See, for instance, "What Is Christian Philosophy?" in *A Gilson Reader,* ed. by Anton Pégis (Garden City, N.Y.: Hanover House, 1957), and *Elements of Christian Philosophy* (Garden City, N.Y.: Doubleday, 1959). For a critique see George P. Klubertanz, "Metaphysics and Theistic Convictions," in *Teaching Thomism Today,* ed. by George McLean (Washington: The Catholic University of America Press, 1963), pp. 271–306, and Germain Grisez, "Étienne Gilson: *Elements of Christian Philosophy*" in *The Thomist* (1960), pp. 448–76.

received experience, then there can be a philosophy of religion acceptable to religious man.

It is not always clear which one of the two positions an author adopts. In the case of Hegel this is a matter of dispute to the present day. Hegel accepts the unique authority of the Christian revelation. Yet he also argues that faith does not fully come into its own until it has philosophically *thought* the representational content of this revelation. Such a view may appear similar to the one proposed in the beginning of this section. But for Hegel philosophy is not merely a reflection upon faith: it is *faith itself* reaching its own truth. This does not mean, as has been argued so often in the past, that philosophy is a substitute for religion. (How could it be a substitute for what it presupposes?) But it does mean that religion cannot be fully true *in its own right* until it has become philosophy. Many will object to such a conclusion, because it places an exclusive emphasis upon the cognitive, the gnostic elements of the religious act. Certainly, a desire for clarification is essential to the act of faith, but it is not the whole act, nor can it ever change the act into a different one, an act of knowledge. Religious faith spontaneously tends toward philosophical reflection, but it never gives up its own identity in order to become philosophical reflection. To identify the two is to change the nature of the religious experience. It then becomes *primarily* an intellectual insight—which it was not before—claiming to understand its object *exhaustively*—which faith never does. To remain religious the gnostic drive of faith must be kept within the boundaries of faith. A religious act can never be transformed into one of reflection and still preserve its original identity. Hegel seems to set no limits to the gnostic drive. For him the act is its intellectual content. This appears even in the order of development of the *Philosophy of Religion*. How else could he claim that the Greek (indeed, the Roman) religion marked a higher stage of development than the Hebrew? Or that the Greek mysteries constituted a more "primitive" religious expression than the Greek mythology.[69] If "primitive" means "more crudely

[69] *Vorlesungen*, III, p. 138.

religious" and not merely "more archaic" this statement is patently false.

The exhaustive character of the (philosophical) religious insight is the other trait which makes Hegel's position suspect to the believer. The God of faith remains hidden, at the end of the clarification process as much as in the beginning. It is essential to faith *not* to understand. Hegel's philosophical religion has no such restrictions. The cognitive dynamism toward the absolute is pursued in the religious act until there remains nothing of the original darkness of faith. But is this still true *religious* insight? The question has given pause even to Hegel's most sympathetic commentators:

> Does speculative thought grasp the mystery as well as it thinks? Does the perfect knowledge, the spiritual gnosis, of the Trinitarian mystery not impose another negation, an abnegation, a passion of which the patient Idea does not seem to be overly aware? Perhaps it is not a mere figure of speech that a surplus of knowledge remains promised from the Spirit to the Spirit. But does the relentless idealist thought ever know a surplus?[70]

Hegel's case shows how difficult it is to keep the relations between philosophy and religion such that both preserve their full integrity. We are inclined to think that the impact of religion, via the philosophy of religion, upon general metaphysics is more modest. It consists mainly in the awareness of a new dimension in the Being which the metaphysician studies. This means not that all reality is to be interpreted with reference to theology, but that philosophy must adopt a consciously expectant attitude. Only a religious philosophy provides the necessary infrastructure for a philosophy of religion. Yet to be religious, philosophy must keep a precarious balance between admitting the experience of transcendence and making the most of it on the one hand, and abstaining from an independent, positive exploration of the transcendent on the other. To maintain this attitude the philosopher must be willing to listen, while retaining his full critical jurisdic-

[70] A. Chapelle, *Hegel et la religion*, II (Paris, 1967), p. 79.

tion. Past philosophies of religion have failed mainly by their unwillingness to expose the religious nature of their sources. By taking credit for doing independently what in fact they borrowed from religious sources, they jeopardized philosophy's autonomy and misinterpreted the nature of the religious experience.

Chapter 4
Of Holy Signs

1. SYMBOLS AND THE PROCESS OF REPRESENTATION

To write about symbols today is to invite controversy. I fully realize that in adopting for the general discussion of symbolism the basic principles of Kant, Cassirer, and Susanne K. Langer, I have taken a particular position which is at least in part rejected by other schools. Yet every position must of necessity be particular. Its qualities and defects may in the end not make too much difference. For religious symbols are quite unique, and the main purpose of the general discussion is merely to provide a background against which we may perceive their characteristic difference.

All symbols are signs and signs are forms which refer to something that is not directly given. Yet signs may merely *point* to the signified or they may *represent* it. In the former case we speak of signs in the strict sense (also called signals); in the latter, of symbols. Symbols are the exclusive property of man. They carry meaning in themselves (indeed, they are the sole bearers of meaning), which allows them to *articulate* the signified, rather than merely announcing it.[1] Symbols, then, do not refer the

[1] Susanne K. Langer's classic exposition on this difference between symbols and signs in *Philosophy in a New Key* (New York: New American Library, 1951) remains a model of clarity and accuracy in a field notorious for its confusion.

percipient directly to the signified object. Instead they *represent* it in the double sense of *making present* and *taking the place of*. Its mediating function grants the symbol an independence which signs do not possess. Instead of the rigidly univocal relation between sign and signified, we now perceive a wealth of meaning, revealing ever new aspects in the signified. This gives the symbol a certain ambiguity with respect to its object, which is missing in the sign. However, the univocity of the sign is not the result of greater mental accuracy, as Hegel thought,[2] but of cognitive poverty: a sign cannot afford to be ambiguous because it does not explain itself. The symbol *shows* the signified in its own structure. That is why, in spite of its independence, it stands in a more intimate relation to the signified. It truly presents what it represents and is therefore, unlike the sign, entitled to receive the respect due to the signified itself.[3]

Sign and symbol are then clearly distinct. Yet they are not entirely separated. A constant traffic in both directions takes place between them. While learning a new language, I first receive and use expressions as mere signs. I continue to think in my native tongue and employ the new words to signal simple meanings to a foreign speech partner. But as I begin to *structure* meaning in my expression, the linguistic signs gradually become symbols. This process is entirely different from that of children "learning" their own language in school; they use symbols from the start and attempt to expand their structuring function by means of grammar, extension of vocabulary, and use of metaphors.[4] The opposite of symbolization—gradual desymbolization —may be observed in instances such as numbers, where symbols have lost the religious or magical meaning which they originally possessed.

All symbols reveal a reality *beyond* their sensuous appearance. A common interpretation restricts the "reality" of this definition

---

[2] *Encyclopädie der philosophischen Wissenschaften* 1830, ⅍458.

[3] Hans-Georg Gadamer, *Wahrheit und Methode* (Tübingen, 1965), pp. 146–47.

[4] See the perceptive study of Anton van Leeuwen, "Aantekeningen over het symbool" in *Bijdragen*, 20 (1959), pp. 1–14.

to what precedes the symbolization process, the raw data to which the symbol gives form and structure. Such a view is far too simplistic. In fact, the symbol refers to that which it constitutes by its own articulation, not to the crude material which precedes it. A symbol never refers back to a pre-existing reality: it opens up a new one. Consequently, the common definition of signs which introduced this section, namely, an objective form referring to something else, is to be interpreted differently for a symbol than for an ordinary sign. A sign leaves the referent which precedes it unchanged. In a symbol, on the contrary, the original reality undergoes a fundamental transmutation. It is a dialectical movement in which the real is negated by the mind and elevated onto a higher level. The symbol points forward rather than backward. Yet even as an ordinary sign it also points beyond itself. What John of St. Thomas wrote in his celebrated treatise on signs is true for all symbols, although not in the same manner and degree.

> The essence of the sign does not consist only in the property of representing and manifesting something different from itself, but also in a particular way of manifestating, characterized by the inferiority of that which represents to that which is represented, the former being related to the latter as the less important to the more imporant.[5]

Somehow the content transcends the appearance even though it attains a new level of reality in and through the appearance.

But then one may well wonder what the exact function of the appearance is? Why can the mind not directly perceive what the appearance veils as much as it reveals? Why does the content need to be mediated by a symbol? Because of its embodied existence, the mind is intrinsically dependent upon sensuous forms. Symbols, then, are not arbitrary devices which the mind may

[5] *Cursus Philosophicus, Logica, Part II,* Qu. 21, a. 1. Tr. as *The Material Logic of John of St. Thomas. Basic Treatises* by Yves Simon, John Glanville, G. Donald Hollenhorst (Chicago: University of Chicago Press, 1955), p. 392.

either employ or forego. They are as essential to its expression as the body is to its existence. In its own dualism between appearance and content the symbol manifests the internal opposition of the mind which it expresses. To realize itself in and through the other is constitutive of the embodied mind.[6] The fundamental function of the symbol, then, is to enable this mind to express itself. The plurality of symbolic structures is due to the mind's protean nature which requires multiform expression. Nothing could be more mistaken than to reduce this variety of aspects to a common denominator.

Often the term "expression" is used to denote one particular aspect of the symbolic function, namely, the dynamic tension between the finite appearance and the infinite content which gives the symbol its suggestive power. The symbol always appears as containing a surplus of meaning beyond what it directly discloses. This is most visible in aesthetic symbols. Unfortunately aesthetic expression is often associated with a Romantic theory according to which the artist first feels emotions which he subsequently expresses. Such an interpretation of symbols is always wrong but is so particularly in the case of art, for nowhere is the connection between form and content more intimate than in the aesthetic image. Art means what it is and the expressed feelings are constituted *within* (not before) the expressive articulation. It is mistaken to regard a work of art as if it "expressed" the feelings of love or hatred which preceded and initiated it. The *aesthetic* feeling fully develops only in the expression itself. The term "expression," then, as it is used here, implies no separation between form and content, but rather suggests that the sensuous form of a symbol is by its very nature self-transcending.

The mind's road to symbolic expression is long and arduous. At the end we find scientific theories, philosophical systems, works of art, religious myths and rituals. But to reach this goal

[6] Karl Rahner, "The Theology of the Symbol" in *Theological Investigations* (Baltimore: Helicon Press, 1966), IV, p. 234. Also, Anton van Leeuwen, "Aantekeningen over het symbool" in *Bijdragen* (1959), p. 12.

the mind must slowly and painfully liberate itself from the oppression of an ever-flowing stream of sensations. A first condition is that the flux be halted and that certain data be given a representational function. Impressions must be made to last beyond their fleeting appearance and to represent a whole complex of impressions. Before the mind synthesizes impressions into units there is only an inexhaustible totality. Once the representational process is completed, there will be a network of relations in which each impression can stand for a number of others. Structuring the interminable flux of sense experience around a few primary data is not the result of a passive association process, as empiricists used to claim.[7] It is an active grasp by which the mind stabilizes and interrelates its sensations in order to be able to perceive representations rather than impressions.

The nature of this process was first analyzed in Kant's *Critique of Pure Reason*. Kant referred to it as the synthesis of the imagination.[8] Sensational appearances are synthesized into representations before the conditions are established which allow them to find their place in an objective world. To fulfill these conditions representations must be conceptualized—another symbolic function of the mind which will be briefly discussed afterward. Yet if the mind instead of delivering them to the objectifying process of the understanding, which inserts them into the coherent totality of the real world, lingers over its representations as independent units, the effect is what Kant would exclusively call a symbol (and which he opposes to a concept) and what certainly reveals the central function of the symbolic activity.[9]

[7] For a refutation see Carl Hamburg, *Symbol and Reality, Studies in the Philosophy of Ernst Cassirer* (The Hague, Martinus Nijhoff, 1956), p. 67.
[8] *Kritik der reinen Vernunft*, A101. *Critique of Pure Reason.* Tr. by Norman Kemp Smith (New York: St. Martin's Press, 1965), pp. 132–33.
[9] Kant's most important text is to be found in the *Kritik der Urteilskraft*, ※59, B 248–49, in which he opposes symbols to schemata. Symbols are indirect presentations of concepts; unlike schemata they cannot be directly converted into concepts but preserve an analogous relation to them.
    All intuitions which we supply to concepts *a priori* . . . are either *schemata* or *symbols* of which the former contain direct, the latter indi-

The synthesis of the imagination requires a reconstruction of the original succession of sensations into a new temporality. This, I take it, is what inspired Kant to define the role of the imagination as a synthesis *in accordance with time*. Only by means of a new temporal synthesis can percepts be detached from the continuous stream of sensation and made into independent representations. Kant's revolutionary theory of the imagination lay dormant until Hegel developed it in his theory of representation in the section on psychology (the final stage of the subjective Spirit) of the *Encyclopädie*. In the representation the mind detaches the content of the sensuous intuition from the restrictions of space and time. It interiorizes the content by re-presenting it in such a way that it is no longer tied to the here and now of the sensuous intuition. Representations are still essentially temporal, but their time is no longer the predetermined succession of sensations; it is the inner, free temporality of the subject. How this new temporality interiorizes the intuitive content appears clearly in the recollection (*Erinnerung*), the first form of representation which etymologically combines a temporal denotation with a connotation of interiority.

As first recollecting the intuition the intellect posits the content of feeling in its inwardness, in its own space and its own time. Thus it is an *image* freed from its first immediacy and its abstract isolation from others, assumed in the universality of the ego as such. The image is no longer completely determined as the intuition and it is, deliberately or accidentally, isolated from the external place, time and immediate connection in which the intuition oc-

---

rect, presentations of the concept. The former do this demonstrably; the latter by means of an analogy (for which we avail ourselves even of empirical intuitions) in which the judgment exercises a double function; first applying the concept to the object of a sensible intuition, and then applying the mere rule of the reflection made upon that intuition to a quite different object of which the first is only the symbol.

(Tr. by J. H. Bernard, New York, Hafner Publishing Co., 1951, pp. 197–98) Cf. François Marty, "La notion de symbole chez Kant" in *Le Langage. Actes du 13ieme Congrès des Sociétés de Philosophie de Langue Française* (Neuchâtel, 1966), pp. 153–56.

curred. The image taken for itself is transitional and the intellect is, in the form of attention, its time and space, its when and where.[10]

Time remembered differs from time perceived. By being re-temporalized the recollected representation becomes detached from its original setting. This enables it to stand for a number of similar experiences and to achieve a certain measure of universality. Yet recollection does not attain the logical structure of thought. Its coherence remains one of succession and juxtaposition.

> The coherence of the determinations appears to the representation as successive, not necessary (as only in the notion). The necessary interconnection of the determinations of the absolute content can be grasped only by the timeless, non-sensible notion. The representation retains these determinations as a succession in time.[11]

In the recollection the singular intuition is assumed into a representation with a universal content.[12] The form remains singular. Yet by omitting a number of particularities the recollection attains a meaning-potential which far surpasses that of any single intuition. The universality of the representation, then, consists in the transcendence of the content with respect to the singular form.

To reproduce a percept is to take it out of its original mode of givenness and to place it in a temporal setting which essentially transforms it. What results is not merely a reproduction but, as Kant knew, a novel production. Liberated from the actuality of perception the future is no longer tied to the past in rectilinear determination. As a result of the mind's escape from the immediate present, the future becomes a genuine possibility. This explains why the mind's awareness of freedom grows with the trust in its powers of imagination. Kant's emphasis on the *productive* (and not merely *re*productive) character of the synthesis of

[10] *Encyclopädie der Philosophischen Wissenschaften* 1830, pp. 452–53.
[11] *Vorlesungen über die Philosophie der Religion,* Vol. I, p. 297.
[12] *Encyclopädie,* ⸆454, p. 365.

the imagination led Fichte to conceive of the imagination as the moving power of the mind. According to Fichte, the productive imagination enables the mind to be totally autonomous, that is, at once determining (as productive imagination) and determined (as actual consciousness).[13] Fichte's productive imagination is not limited to the cognitive order, for the very ideals of freedom by which the mind constantly overcomes its finite determinations are as much its creation as the limiting determinations themselves.

Hegel identified the productive imagination with the *fantasy*. Fantasy abandons the order of actual perception in favor of a purely subjective succession of images. An overriding representation assembles a number of disparate perceptions into an entirely new structure. If the guiding representation endows the images with a power of meaning beyond the appearances, the effect is what Hegel calls a symbol (if the representation is concrete) or a sign (if it is abstract).[14] Strangely enough, Hegel rates signs higher than symbols. For him the symbol retains too much of its original image autonomy to be entirely clear in its meaning.[15] The sign enjoys no such autonomy. To posit a sign is to refer directly to the signified, since the sign has no other meaning.[16] What matters in the sign is that there is an intuitive form; *which one* is unimportant. "The sign retains nothing of itself; it sacrifices itself to its sense."[17]

[13] *Grundlage der gesammten Wissenschaftslehre,* in *Sammtliche Werke,* Vol. I, ed. by J. H. Fichte (Berlin, 1845), p. 227. See also *Grundriss des Eigentenlichen der Wissenschaftslehre* in *Sammtliche Werke I,* pp. 376–87, where Fichte posits the imagination at the origin of *all* the determinations of the real, including the complex articulations of the *object*-appearance which Kant ascribed to the categories of all the understanding.

[14] Hegel's use of the term "symbol" is more restrictive than our own; with Kant he opposes symbols to concepts.

[15] This explains why the "symbolic" art of Egypt and the Orient ranks lowest in the *Lectures on Aesthetics.*

[16] In the determination according to essence and notion of the intuition itself is more or less the content symbolically expressed. In the sign, on the contrary, the content of the intuition and the content of what is signified remain unrelated." *Encyclopädie,* ⁂458 Zusatz.

[17] Malcolm Clark, *Logic and System: A Study of the Transition from Vorstellung to Thought in the Philosophy of Hegel* (The Hague, 1971), p. 63.

For Hegel, symbolic representations prepare the objectivity of thought by raising the question of their own objectivity status. In *representing* something I am critically aware that a question about its objective reality may be raised, even though I choose not to raise it. This indicates that the representation already points beyond the merely accepted intuition toward the object *in itself*.[18] The representation knows itself to be only a representation. Hegel's representational consciousness has been described as "picture thinking in which the pictures are recognized as such."[19] But to know a representation to be *only* a representation is to relate it to objective, not purely representational, being and thus to initiate the problem of objectivity. *What* constitutes objectivity is not revealed in the representation, which remains too much caught in subjectivity to distinguish the real from the nonreal. It merely posits its content as objectively *problematic*. To do more would require that the mind be conscious of its own power to constitute the real as real. The representational consciousness merely raises a question and invites a deeper reflection which will eventually result in full objectivity. To *know* will consist in realizing that the representation represents *something*. The representation re- presents objective reality by letting a particular intuition take its place. Thought will *present* reality itself and thereby reveal the full meaning of the representation.

In his *Lectures on the Philosophy of Religion* Hegel strongly emphasizes the objective character of the representation. It is precisely the representation which prevents the subjectivity of religious feeling to degenerate into self-deification, fanaticism, and intolerance.[20]

Hegel's subordination of the symbol to the form of pure thought was a questionable philosophical decision. No genuine symbol can be adequately "translated" from representation into pure thought (although we consider the linguistic expression of pure thought

[18] See J. Hessing and J. G. Wattjes, *Bewustzÿn en Werkelijkheid* (Amsterdam, s.d.), p. 339.
[19] Clark, *op. cit.*, p. 22.
[20] *Vorlesungen über die Philosophie der Religion*, I, p. 286.

itself symbolic). Yet underneath these dubious formulations we detect the profound insight that symbols always lead to reflection. They invite thinking because they require interpretation. By pointing beyond their appearance, symbols draw attention to something that wants to be discovered but is at least partly concealed. Now it is typical of rationalism to understand this to mean that rational thought at a certain stage of reflection must take over and substitute for the symbol.[21] On the contrary, thought remains subordinate to the symbol: that is why we call it "interpretation."

2. LANGUAGE AND INTERPRETATION

Language is *the* symbol *par excellence*. Words can do much more than, for instance, pictures, which represent an object by giving an arrangement of parts analogous to that of the depicted object. Words *name* relations and by doing so they are able to "embody concepts not only of things, but of things in combination, or situations."[22] Of course, all this requires that words be used *in* a *context*. By themselves they would be merely indicative signs without intrinsic meaning.[23] Language thereby becomes an ideal symbol for the acquisition and communication of knowledge. Yet it would be mistaken to restrict all symbolism to a form of language. The mere articulation of visual or auditory experiences is also symbolic, although neither discursive nor linguistic. However, purely visual or auditory symbols do not *mean* in the way words do, even when used in nondiscursive language.

All symbolization aims at establishing relations between a number of impressions. But the conceptualizing symbols of language achieve this goal by transposing relations into a system of meanings where each unit is able to convey an independent content.

---

[21] The thought symbol (concept) is obviously excepted from this consideration: it always invites further rationalization.

[22] Susanne K. Langer, *op. cit.*, p. 73.

[23] Cf. Wilbur M. Urban, *Language and Reality* (London: George Allen & Unwin, 1939), p. 412.

The possibility of combining these units into enormously complex yet clearly defined meanings enables language to build structures of far greater variety than nonverbal symbols. In a memorable passage Ernst Cassirer has described this unique capacity of language to clarify relations.

> All the intellectual labor whereby the mind forms general concepts out of specific impressions is directed toward breaking the isolation of the datum, wresting it from the "here and now" of its actual occurrence, relating it to other things and gathering it and them into some inclusive order, into the unity of "a system." The logical form of conception, from the standpoint of theoretical knowledge, is nothing but a preparation for the logical form of judgment; all judgment, however, aims at overcoming the illusion of singularity which adheres to every particular content of consciousness.[24]

A linguistic term becomes a complete symbol only after it is interpreted in a proposition. In linguistic analysis this was first enunciated in the thesis that terms become concepts only if they can be formulated propositionally.[25]

Language is not restricted to the function of "depicting" the world, as images are. Nor is it limited to a rhythmic and melodious articulation of feelings and emotions as music mainly is and, until recently, exclusively was. It can do everything other symbols do, although in a different and often less perfect way. Verbal symbols *conceptualize* relations, that is, they symbolize them within a clearly defined system of meanings. It is the independent meaningfulness of the linguistic system which enables words to venture far away from all empirical footholds. This independence from the direct experience increases with the discursive quality. Thus scientific language gradually severs its ties with the experience-bound concepts of ordinary language and instead builds up

[24] Ernst Cassirer, *Language and Myth* (New York: Dover Publications, 1953), pp. 25–26.
[25] For the relation between Cassirer and Russell's theory of language, see Carl Hamburg, *Symbol and Reality. Studies in the Philosophy of Ernst Cassirer* (The Hague, 1956), p. 71.

a symbolic system over which it has total control. Ordinary language is but the first attempt to conceptualize relations. Science both completes and surpasses this attempt. Yet the confident self-sufficiency of scientific discourse is acquired at a considerable cost. The more self-sufficient it becomes, the more language loses the living contact with experience which is so richly present in non-discursive symbols. Discursive language schematizes and abstracts the real in order to extend its rational control over it.

> The forms of things as they are described in scientific concepts tend more and more to become mere formulae. These formulae are of a surprising simplicity. A singular formula, like the Newtonian Law of gravitation, seems to comprise and explain the whole structure of our material universe. It would seem as though reality were not only accessible to our scientific abstractions but exhaustible by them. But as soon as we approach the field of art this proves to be an illusion. For the aspects of things are innumerable, and they vary from one moment to another.[26]

Of course, not all language is discursive. Conceptual symbolization is predominant in scientific language. In poetry, prayer, child talk, etc., conceptualization remains subordinate to other functions. Instead of symbolizing by abstraction, nondiscursive language, as other symbols, *shows* its symbolic content and leads into it.[27] It opens up new ontological dimensions making what it represents more present, more authentic, more as it really is.[28]

Usually the term "symbol" is restricted to nonconceptual or, in the case of language, not primarily conceptual, symbols. Kant and Goethe, who are mainly responsible for our present interest

[26] Ernst Cassirer, *An Essay on Man* (New Haven: Yale University Press, 1968), p. 144. Also, Langer, *op. cit.*, p. 89.

[27] As Wilbur Urban puts it: "[Nonconceptual symbols] do not merely represent, through partial coincidence, characters and relations; they are, or at least are supposed to be, a vehicle or medium of insight." *Language and Reality* (London: George Allen & Unwin, 1939), p. 415.

[28] This is how Gadamer describes the role of the aesthetic image. I think the words apply to all nondiscursive symbols, particularly the aesthetic ones. *Wahrheit und Methode*, p. 147.

in the symbol, always oppose symbol to concept.[29] We shall follow the common usage, even though we must always be aware that conceptualization is an important function of the symbolization process and an essential one in all linguistic symbols. In doing so we assert our opposition to the view of the early linguistic analysts who restricted the field of *meaningful* verbal symbolization to discursive language. For Russell and Carnap the non-conceptual linguistic symbol is a mere "symptomatic" expression, an emotional cry. Miss Langer objects, much *à propos:*

> Why should we cry our feelings at such high levels that anyone would think we were talking? Clearly poetry means more than a cry: it has reason for being articulate.[30]

Narrow linguistic interpretations are inspired by a desire to reduce the various types of symbolization to one another. But a philosophy of symbolic forms must not sacrifice any set of symbols for the sake of simplicity. Rather should it distinguish symbols according to the various functions which they fulfill. The basic principle of hermeneutics is that the interpretation must respect the proper nature of the symbol and of the particular symbolic "language" to which it belongs. Positivist philosophers have been notoriously negligent in observing this principle. Their "interpretations" seem to consist mainly in tearing off the "masks" of all nonscientific symbols and replacing them by scientific expressions. Reality properly understood, thus goes the assumption, allows only one set of symbols.

Apart from philosophy (and recently also theology), reductionist theories are found primarily in psychology. An illustrious example is Freud's explanation of art and religion. The root of

[29] This is quite clear, for instance, in Goethe's description of the functioning of symbols: "Symbolism converts the appearance into idea, the idea into image, in such a way that the idea remains always infinitely operative and yet unattainable in the image; even when spoken in all languages, it remains unspeakable." (*Maximen und Reflexionen* in *Werke* [Weimar, 1887–1930], Vol. I, p. 4.)

[30] Susanne K. Langer, *Philosophy in a New Key,* p. 81. Also, *Problems of Art* (New York: Charles Scribner's Sons, 1957), p. 24.

the misunderstanding lies in Freud's interpretation of the symbolism of dreams which converts symbols into signs, that is, into forms which neither reveal nor transform their content. The relation between the symbolism of the dream and the psychic reality which it obscurely expresses is conceived as a rigidly fixed reference in which the sign adds no new meaning to the signified.[31] "The symbol intervenes in the dream after the fashion of a stenographic code sign that has once and for all acquired its precise meaning."[32] No genuine symbol can be condensed into a single concrete meaning. If a symbol intends reality in a unique way, it is clearly impossible to substitute other symbols for it. What Mircea Eliade writes about images is true for all symbols:

> Images by their very structure are *multivalent*. If the mind makes use of images to grasp the ultimate reality of things, it is just because reality manifests itself in contradictory ways and therefore cannot be expressed in concepts . . . It is therefore the image as such, as a whole bundle of meanings, that is *true,* and not any *one* of its meanings, nor one alone of its many frames of reference. To translate an image into a concrete terminology by restricting it to any one of its frames of reference is to do worse than mutilate it—it is to annihilate, to annul it as an instrument of cognition.[33]

Univocity of meaning in the interpretation of symbols is Freud's fundamental error. Yet it is not his only one. Even more serious perhaps is that Freud's basic symbols are dead. Instead of being creative of the future, as most symbols are, the ones he considers are remnants of a past that is not fully admitted. Yet symbols reveal the birth of a new meaning more often than the death of an old one. Some symbols—most dreams, legends, fairy tales—have indeed lost their creativity and set off no new

[31] Sigmund Freud, *Vorlesungen zur Einführung in die Psychoanalyse,* in *Gesammelte Werke* (London: Image Publishing Co., 1940), Vol. XI, p. 152. The entire tenth lecture deals with the symbolism of dreams.
[32] Paul Ricoeur, *De l'interprétation* (Paris, 1965), p. 480.
[33] *Images and Symbols,* tr. by Philip Mairet (New York: Sheed & Ward, 1961), p. 15.

symbolic processes any more. Paul Ricoeur in his important study on interpretation first drew attention to Freud's fundamental mistake in regarding these dead symbols as the basic forms of all others:

> The typical dreams around which Freud develops his theory of symbols, far from revealing the canonic form of symbols, reveal only the rejects on the level of sedimented expression. The real task would be to consider the symbol at its creative beginning, rather than at the end of the line where it shows up in stenographic signs "provided once and forever with a precise meaning."[34]

Even in symbols which are still alive and creative Freud selects only the element of the past as past. In the Oedipus myth he reads the violence of man's repressed incestual drives. No one will deny that this is part of the symbol. But is it all? Is it even the most important part? Only if one is willing to admit that Greek tragedy has missed the core of the symbol and relegated it to a secondary place. For Sophocles, not the "oedipal situation" constitutes the dramatic nucleus, but Oedipus' subsequent presumptuous claim of innocence, his reckless curse on the responsible "stranger," and his tragic self-recognition at the end. Far from being intrinsically added to the dark subconscious drives, as Freud thought, the second meaning reveals the truth of the first. Such an interpretation leads to a much more complex relation between the work of art, "the durable and memorable creation of the day," and the dream, "the fugitive and sterile product of the night": "The same content, the same object of desire, unites them, but the promotion of the figures of the spirit brings about what Freud himself calls a 'conversion of goal,' a 'sublimation.' "[35]

Yet, if a symbol cannot be translated, it still can be interpreted. It can be situated in a wider context which allows it to present itself. Karl Jaspers, who has given considerable attention to this task, describes it as "encircling" the symbol. Its effect is to

[34] *De l'interprétation*, p. 486.
[35] Ricoeur, *op. cit.*, p. 500. Jung's theory of symbols, which will be discussed immediately, is in this respect the opposite of Freud's. For him symbols are primarily projective: man's way of envisaging the future. Ernst Block shares this view despite his profound aversion to Jung's theories.

deepen and expand the symbol, not to eliminate it.[36] Since the symbol contains and structures the very reality to which it refers, no interpretation can ever be exhaustive. Each epoch finds new meaning in the great aesthetic, religious, and conceptual symbol structures of the past.

Even more important than the reality content of the symbol is its transcendent intentionality. The symbol is the mind's only way to surpass the purely empirical. The nature of the transcendence varies with the quality of the symbol: aesthetic symbols move beyond the appearances in a way which differs from religious and scientific symbols. But since the transcendence of each symbol is unique, a genuine interpretation cannot but participate in the symbol, that is, it must itself adopt a symbolic attitude. (This is yet another formulation of the slippery hermeneutic circle.) Of course, we may always attempt to repeat in ordinary discourse what we find expressed in other symbolic structures. But in doing so, we settle for a very limited aspect of the symbolic expression. A symbolic structure is by its very nature irreplaceable. Definitions of nondiscursive symbols are *per se* impossible, for the definition leaves out the unspeakable element by which a symbol transcends both itself and all other discourse. To define the cross as an expression of divine love through the passion of Christ is to convert its meaning into a much clearer concept than the original one but to lose in the process the proper transcendence of this particular symbol.[37]

[36] Karl Jaspers, *Von der Wahrheit*, München, 1947, p. 1039. The section on symbols has been translated under the title *Truth and Symbol* by Jean T. Wilde, William Kluback, and William Kimmel (New York: Twayne Publishers, 1959), p. 53.

[37] Carl Gustav Jung, from whom we borrowed this example, was very conscious of the unique transcendence of each symbol. He considered the recognition of this transcendence the mark that distinguishes a truly symbolic interpretation from a *semiotic* one (which reduces the symbol to a sign).

Every view which interprets the symbolic expression as an analogous or abbreviated expression of a known thing is *semiotic*. A conception which interprets the symbolic expression as the best possible formulation of a relatively unknown thing which cannot conceivably, therefore, be more clearly or characteristically represented is symbolic.

Psychological Types (New York: Harcourt, Brace, 1923), p. 601.

3. THE NEGATIVITY OF RELIGIOUS SYMBOLS

What distinguishes a religious symbol from all other symbols—
the experience which it articulates or the articulation itself? Most
people faced with this question would not hesitate to answer
that it is the experience. Yet in religion, as in aesthetics, only
the symbolization gives its specific character to the experience.
There is no religious experience prior to the religious symbolization. Certainly the immediate numinous feeling which Otto
describes does exist, but this feeling is not in itself a religious
experience, nor is it even indispensable to the religious experience,
as the faith of modern man shows. Faith is never an immediate
feeling or emotion. It is the awareness of a transcendent dimension
to all the experiences of life, the affirmation of a deeper *reality*
underlying the obvious appearances.

All symbols make us see a transcendent noema, but they do
not all make us see it in the same way. In the aesthetic symbol,
for instance, transcendence consists in the inexhaustible richness
of spiritual meaning articulated in the sensible form. But the
symbol fully *presents* its noema and emphasizes the unity between
what appears and what is signified. In the religious symbol, on the
contrary, the noema remains forever beyond our reach, and the
symbolizing act itself accentuates the discrepancy between form
and content. If religious symbols *present* their noema, they do so
primarily by showing what it is not and by concealing more than
they reveal. They maintain their religious intentionality only as
long as they convey, along with their meaning, an awareness of
their purely analogous character. By paradoxical phrasing, distorted forms, unusual settings, they warn us that we must entirely
surpass the empirical appearance in order to gain access to their
inexpressible content. The negative element, present in all symbols,
becomes predominant in the religious ones. Interpretation here
becomes necessary in a way in which it is not for the aesthetic
symbol, which is intrinsically self-revealing.

Genuine religious symbols are ontological in nature, and they
are so prior to any rational reflection. Indeed, what we now

call "religious" symbols grew out of man's first attempt to articulate reality. Originally all symbols belonged to the same sphere of existence. To most men even today religious symbols structure and distinguish not by juxtaposing two relatively unrelated spheres of the real—one religious, the other secular—as they seem to do for Western man, but by differentiating *within* the one sphere of the real that which is fully real, powerful, and meaningful—the *sacred,* from that which is not so real, immediate, and superficial—the *profane.* The transcendence of the sacred over the profane, its fundamental negation, does not relegate the two to different universes. The sacred is *in* the profane. It stands out but belongs to the same universe as its other dimension. Symbols, then, are born out of an initial, profound reflection upon the world-experience. Further reflection upon this experience will require rational concepts. But these will never become a substitute for the primary expression. Thinking about the original distinction between the sacred and the profane must remain forever reflection *upon* symbols. We might add that "religious" symbols also reintegrate the levels of reality which they oppose and in this task too they are unexcelled by rational concepts. Symbols reunite the world after they have first separated it into distinct levels. Lately psychology and sociology have given a great deal of attention to the unique power of symbols to integrate values and realities into existential units. Yet even more primitive than this integrating function is the negative power of separation. This aspect is clearly present in those particular symbols which we now call "religious" but which are in fact the direct descendants of primitive symbols.

Because of their negative nature, philosophers have traditionally connected religious symbols with the imagination, the function by which the mind is able to negate what is directly given.

The universal negative impulse in all active imagination is distrust of the "given," a stern doubt that the objects of jaded perception and arrested conception give what is there.[38]

[38] Ray Hart, *Unfinished Man and the Imagination* (New York: Herder and Herder, 1969), p. 247.

The words "arrested conception" in this quote from Ray Hart deserve further elaboration. For also in the conceptualizing process we negate the immediately given, but only to return to a more confident affirmation. Religious symbols, on the contrary, remain elusive. As all symbols, they are so *polyvalent* that no single rational interpretation can ever exhaust their meaning. In fact, the less specific a symbol is, the richer its symbolic meaning becomes. Eliade has noted that the various meanings of a symbol are not continuous with each other on the plane of immediate experience. Thus, the moon symbol reveals at once temporality, the female principle, death and resurrection.[39] Even the existence of archetypal structures in the infinite variety of symbolic meanings is dubious. Nature is infinite in its potential meanings and anything can symbolize.[40] Even after religious consciousness has brought some definite structure in the symbolization process its symbols remain polyvalent. An authentic symbol can never be pinned down to a one-to-one meaning as a discursive concept. Nor does the symbol ever relate to its referent by a single bond of purpose or causality. To define one event exhaustively as a clear anticipation of another arranged by God for that *purpose,* as seventeenth- and eighteenth-century exegesis often did with the typology of the Old Testament, impoverishes the symbol. By the polyvalence of its symbols the imagination is able to surpass not only what is directly given but even what can be rationally expressed.

Yet, however negative its function may be, the imagination contributes to the religious symbolization process positive images. They are the ones which cause us most of the problems. For if the "object" of the symbol is entirely beyond its reach, why should one representation be more appropriate than another? No satisfactory answer has yet been given to this difficult question. Yet Jung was undoubtedly right in ascribing a great deal of

[39] "Methodological Remarks on the Study of Symbolism" in *The History of Religions,* p. 99.
[40] See Antoine Vergote, "Les apories du symbolisme religieux" in *Cahiers Internationaux du Symbolisme,* 196, p. 73.

the religious creativity of the imagination to the subconscious. The inexpressible nature of transcendence perplexes the mind in its search for adequate symbols. At this point the subconscious opens up all its riches to an eager religious mind.

The symbols of the subconscious, as Jung sees them, serve a purpose remarkably similar to what the religious activity itself pursues. (Jung even identifies both activities.) The symbol harmonizes opposite drives of the unconscious and brings them into accord with the content of consciousness. It thus becomes the bridge between the conscious and the subconscious, providing the mind with a diagram of psychic unity, far more complex than could be attained by means of rational processes. Symbolic representation includes totally irrational elements which refuse to obey the laws of logical thinking. Yet its function is highly rational, for it sets up archetypal forms through which conscious conflicts may be interpreted and eventually resolved. Since this resolution is of primary importance in the actualization of the self, the symbol wields an enormous power in the psychic development of the individual. It draws this power from energy exceeding the maintenance needs of natural functions. Once they are constituted, symbols siphon ever more energy away toward transindividual objectives. The power of the symbol to transform *libido* reveals its *prospective* value. The symbol indicates for consciousness what ought to become. New and unique experiences of consciousness in a changing world require new and unique symbols. These symbols in turn point the way in which conscious action must be transformed. Symbolization anticipates the future; the symbol directs the individual to new activities, and points the way toward new cultural formulations for the group.[41]

The unconscious activity of the imagination fully deserves the intensive study which it receives at the present time. Yet it is an illusion to think, as Jung did, that it holds the key to the entire religious symbolization process. For subconscious images are *not*

---

[41] Carl Gustav Jung, *Symbols of Transformation* (Princeton University Press, 1967). See also *Psyche and Symbol: A Selection from the Writings of C. G. Jung,* ed. by Violet de Laszlo (Garden City, N.Y.: Doubleday, 1958).

fully constituted religious symbols. They are merely the material out of which the religious mind builds its symbols. They possess a symbolic meaning from the start insofar as they articulate and bring to expression complex mental structures. But this original symbolism is not religious. To become so it must be assumed by an explicit, fully conscious religious intentionality which is restricted neither to the subconscious nor to the imagination. An example found in Jung will illustrate this. The symbol of the cross exercises a singular appeal to the imagination. Yet this subconscious attraction does not explain its acceptance as central symbol of the Christian faith. For the *particular* meaning of the cross for Christians consists in its reference to Jesus' sacrificial death. A conscious religious "foundation" of the symbol is needed, and in historical faith this is to be found in a specific event that took place in the past. Of course, the conscious foundation does not explain the subconscious power of the symbol: it merely brings it into focus and allows it to exercise its full power.

This brings us to the further question whether religious symbols are constituted only by imagination. Here again the answer must be negative. It deserves to be stated explicitly, since the central role of images in the religious symbolization constantly tempt us to ascribe the entire process to the imagination. The religious act above all asserts a supereminent *reality,* a function which the imagination is least fit to fulfill. Images are as omnipresent in the religious symbolization as they are in the artistic expression. Yet they serve an entirely different purpose. For while in art the image *is* the aesthetic reality, in the religious experience it serves in a subordinate and largely negative function. Religious man has recourse to images because he cannot say *directly* what he wants to say and images allow him to escape the *given* reality. But he is reluctant to ascribe a definitive reality to the images themselves. Indeed, the same religious mind which creates images maintains an iconoclastic attitude toward them. Today it rejects as idols what yesterday it adored as icons. Hegel who relegated all religious symbols to the level of representation was nevertheless clearly aware of the negative drive which turns religion against its own images.

> Religion has a polemical aspect insofar as its content cannot be perceived immediately in the sensuous intuition or in the image, but only mediately by abstraction, that is, by elevating the imaginary and the sensible to a universal level. This elevation implies a rejection of the image.[42]

Nor must Hegel's religious representation even be identified with images. For images play only a subordinate (although necessary) role in the representation. Hegel considers fantasy the lowest function involved in the religious symbolization act. The innumerable crowd of bizarre deities who populate the world of the Vedas were the weakness of early Hinduism, not its strength.[43] Hegel also noticed that a too comfortable accommodation of a religion to its self-created images may result in its death. Greek mythological religion was satisfied with lifting the natural and moral powers of human life out of their ordinary context into aesthetically idealized forms: instead of negating ordinary existence it beautified it.

> In other forms of religion, sacrifice means to give up, to bring forward, to deprive oneself. But here . . . sacrifice consists in drinking the wine and eating the meat . . . Thus higher meaning and enjoyment is given to all activities of life. Here one finds no self-denial, no apology for eating and drinking. But every occupation and pleasure of daily existence is made into a sacrifice.[44]

Thus religion became caught in its own aesthetic *images*. The Greek gods, at least as we know them through Homer and Hesiod, were conceived as human ideals. The more perfect they grew, the more they lost their meaning as religious symbols, that is, as finite appearances which reveal an infinite *transcendence*.

[42] *Vorlesungen über die Philosophie der Religion,* I, p. 285.
[43] *Vorlesungen,* II, p. 144.
[44] *Vorlesungen,* III, p. 170.

Ultimately, their perfect containment within finite forms, their aesthetic potential, killed the Greek gods. Their very conception demanded an aesthetic treatment, long before poets and sculptors made them into actual works of art. Once they received it, they turned into sculpture and literature, and died to religion altogether.

4. RITES

The British anthropologist R. R. Marrett once wrote: "Savage religion is something not so much thought out as danced out."[45] I believe that the priority of deed over word is maintained long after religion has ceased to be savage. Even in our word-oriented Christian Churches moral action precedes theological change. First among religious symbols, then, are the ceremonial deeds of worship to which we refer by the general term of *rite*.

As all symbols, rites structure, articulate and support the life experience.[46] By being placed in symbolic relief, certain vital functions bestow a unique meaning upon life. They are conceived to *determine* ordinary experience and to interpret it. The Chinese, whose culture is perhaps more thoroughly ritualized than that of any other civilized nation, have long been acquainted with the normative quality of ritual behavior. One of their philosophers wrote in the third century before our era:

> Rites serve to shorten that which is too long and lengthen that which is too short, reduce that which is too much and augment that which is too little, express the beauty of love and reverence and cultivate the elegance of righteous conduct. Therefore, beautiful adornment and coarse sackcloth, music and weeping, rejoicing and sorrow, though pairs of opposites, are in the rites equally utilized and alternately brought into play.[47]

[45] *The Threshold of Religion* (London, 1914), p. xxxi.
[46] Roger Caillois, *L'homme et le sacré* (Paris, 1950), pp. 22–23; *Man and the Sacred*, pp. 23–24. G. Van der Leeuw, *Religion in Essence and Manifestation*, p. 341.
[47] *Hsun Tzu*, Ch. 19, in *Sources of Chinese Tradition*, ed. by W. Theodore de Bary, tr. by Y. P. Mei (New York: Columbia University Press, 1960), p. 123.

Rites *symbolize* joyful and sad occasions but never turn joyful or sad themselves. They express love without passion, austerity without hardship, sorrow without grief. Rites articulate real life, they mold it into their restrictive forms but they never fully merge with it.

It is a common error in the interpretation of rites to consider them identical with the functions which they symbolize. Thus in recent attempts at liturgical renewal in the Christian Churches one constantly hears the desire expressed to bring the cult "back to earth." In the mind of the more extreme reformers a Christian communion service should be an affair of coffee and doughnuts, spiced with warm feelings of love for one another and vaguely related to Christ as the "initiator" of such meals. However, the purpose of a ritual act is not to repeat the ordinary action which it symbolizes, but to bestow meaning upon it by placing it in a higher perspective.[48] A reduction of ritual gestures to common activity would defeat the entire purpose of ritualization, which is to transform life, not to imitate it.

Gerardus Van der Leeuw defined ritual as a game bound by rules.[49] Rites are indeed related to play acting. Yet rules do not provide the specific difference, for all games follow rules. However, before tackling the distinction we might do well to pursue the comparison with play. In his beautiful essay, *Man at Play,*

[48] Our presentation does not conflict with the fact, pointed out by Eliade, that the ritualizing drive tends to transform all activities into ritual acts. "The ideal of the religious man is, of course, that everything he does should be done ritually . . . On that account, every act is liable to become a religious act, just as every natural object is liable to become a hierophany." (*Patterns in Comparative Religion,* p. 460) Even today this tendency is clearly illustrated in the habits of monastic living: not only the liturgical, sacramental, and sacrificial acts are ritualized, but also all other communal activities, such as eating (in silence, preceded and followed by prayers, accompanied by *recto tono* readings), walking to and from the community meeting places, even the division and performance of household chores. Yet this drive is the exact opposite of the leveling tendency of secularists: it is an attempt to give ever more structure to existence. The ritual form is a constant reminder of the "different" nature of rites, even when they permeate all of life.

[49] *Religion in Essence and Manifestation,* p. 340.

Hugo Rahner obscurely hints at a deeper, religious meaning of play:

> There is a sacred secret at the root and in the flowering of all play: it is man's hope for another life taking visible form of gesture. To play is to yield oneself to a kind of magic, to enact to oneself the absolutely other, to preempt the future, to give the lie to the inconvenient world of fact.[50]

Huizinga went further and declared the form and function of play the first, highest, and holiest expression of man's consciousness of a sacred order of things.[51] Play acting, then, would be the simplest expression of a tendency which appears in man's need to ritualize life and even in what modern man regards as religious activity.

As rites, games move in an independent sphere, at a distance from everyday life. Opposite the hard world of facts they create a world of make-believe. However, the player takes his game-universe very seriously. To convince oneself of this, it suffices to watch how a monopoly game seduces the most even-tempered men into heated arguments. While a violation of rules due to inexperience generally meets with the indulgence of civilized society, it provokes irrepressible anger in the game-situation as I once found out upon joining a bridge club. The player remains fully aware of the different nature of play, yet he applies himself to its tasks with an energy seldom devoted to the demands of "real" life. The play universe tends to become so real that the player dismisses the ordinary world. Nor is such behavior restricted to pathological types. W. C. Fields' golf-playing dentist and Dostoevski's gamblers touch a chord in the heart of even the most duty-conscious man. The "pretending" of play acting, then, does not affect the seriousness of the involvement. In taking a temporary leave from the ordinary world the player does not

[50] *Man At Play*, tr. by Brian Battershaw and Edward Quinn (New York: Herder and Herder, 1967), p. 65.
[51] Johan Huizinga, *Homo Ludens*, tr. by R. F. C. Hull (London: Kegan Paul, 1949), p. 17.

dismiss the *real* as such. He affirms a different reality which cannot be reduced to the ordinary one. The resemblance with the affirmation and negation characteristic of the religious act is noticeable enough.

Yet there is more. The universe of play occupies a space and time of its own, removed from daily cares. The playground or the stage are as much "staked out" as the *locus sacer* of the temple (from τέμνειν: to stake out).

> A closed space is marked out for it, either materially or ideally, hedged off from the everyday surroundings. Inside this space the play proceeds, inside it the rules obtain. Now the marking out of some sacred spot is also the primary characteristic of every sacred act . . . Nearly all rites of consecration and initiation entail a certain artificial seclusion for the performers and those to be initiated.[52]

The similarity is even more striking between play time and religious celebration. The verb *to celebrate* which we apply to acts of worship is also the proper term for "having a good time." By their festive nature religious rites are related to the exuberant activity of playing.[53] The liturgy presents the same unique mixture of nonfunctional purposelessness and meticulous discipline as games. From a pragmatic viewpoint liturgical action is about the least efficient way to get things done or even to move from one point to another. In his *Spirit of the Liturgy* Guardini has shown convincingly how a certain playfulness is inherent to all ceremonial worship.[54] Play and ritual celebration have always belonged together. The Olympic games, as all Hellenic games, were part of a ritual celebration. Where I grew up in Flanders the yearly celebration of the patron saint's feast with Mass and procession (*kermis* from *kerk* [church]–*mis* [Mass]) introduced three

---

[52] Huizinga, *op. cit.*, pp. 19–20.
[53] On the close relation between feast and play, see Karl Kerényi, "Vom Wesen des Festes" in *Paideuma*, I, Heft 2 (1938), pp. 59–74.
[54] *The Spirit of the Liturgy*, tr. by Ada Lane (New York: Sheed & Ward, 1935), pp. 171–84.

days of revelry replete with all the earthly pleasures of Brueghel and often stretching its very tangible memories until nine months after the saint's birthday. The subdued religious expession of the established Churches in North America hardly warrants the term "celebration." Yet even here we begin to notice a desire to replace the preaching brand of moral religion by more abandoned forms of worship.[55] At any rate the divisions which the playing activity draws in space and time may have been instrumental in establishing the basic religious distinction between the sacred and the profane.

One other feature which seems to connect religious ceremonial with some forms of play acting is the dramatization which lifts seasonal and historical events out of the indifferent succession of time and conveys them a permanent structure. Huizinga's description of play applies equally well to ritual. "Into an imperfect world and into the confusion of life it brings a temporary, a limited perfection. Play demands order absolute and supreme."[56] In both cases this order is pursued for its own sake. It may result in practical effects, but as soon as they become the real end, the play becomes "professional" and ritual degenerates into magic.

What do we conclude from all this? Does the similarity between rite and play indicate a common origin? One would be inclined to say so. Yet anthropologists today, more cautious than their predecessors of a recent past, are reluctant to reduce the similar to the identical, and tend to interpret a basic distinction in the present as a sign of an original difference. Thus Claude Lévi-Strauss distinguishes even in archaic society rites and ritual games from ordinary games. The outcome of a ritual action must always be a state of equilibrium. In free games talent or chance separate the players and result in a disjunctive effect. In ritual, on the contrary, events are structured in a way which in the end conjoins the participants and obliterates the initial distinctions in a universal harmony.[57] This theory allows us to draw a clear distinction

[55] See Harvey Cox, *The Feast of Fools* (Cambridge: Harvard University Press, 1969).
[56] Huizinga, *op. cit.*, p. 10.
[57] *The Savage Mind*, pp. 31–32.

between ordinary playing and ritual games, such as the sacred ball game of the Mayas in Chichén Itzá or that of the bishop and the clergy in or around the cathdral of Auxerre on Easter Sunday. It raises the further question how ceremonial rites differ from ritual games. Lévi-Strauss does not answer this. But it would seem to me that all games, even the ritual ones, display a looser symbolic structure which may eventually allow the play element to go its own unpredictable way. Mere play is the play-rite deprived of its symbolic potential.[58]

However one conceives of the original relation between play and ritual, there is one way in which the distinction may not be stated. To call the rite "religious" and the play "not religious," is to attribute to the archaic mentality a distinction of which it is definitely unaware. If we understand by "religious" the quality which separates one sphere of existence from another (the secular), then neither play nor rite are originally religious, for primitive man knows only one sphere of existence which within itself admits the distinction between sacred and profane, but not the one between religious and secular. Consequently, to say that archaic dances are "religious" is as meaningless as to say that they are secular in the sense in which we call a modern ballet or a Japanese tea party secular. Neither term is appropriate. What we ask is: Is the original function of play in giving basic structure to existence different from that of ritual? That both are instrumental in the discovery of such elementary distinctions as the one between the sacred and the profane seems to me beyond

[58] The term "symbolic," we recall, must not be understood as if the original play-rite or, for that matter, any other rite had been created for the purpose of expressing some abstract, pre-existing truth. The meaning does not precede the symbol: it is discovered in and through the symbol itself.

My interpretation runs somewhat parallel with Émile Benveniste's claim that play results from the separation between myth and ritual: once the rite loses its mythic symbolism it becomes a "mere" play. But Benveniste posits myth before play. I believe the play impulse to be more archaic than the myth—at least the fully developed myth. Yet if we add to the word "myth" the qualifier "or the possibility of developing into myth," Benveniste's statement could hold universally true. "Le jeu comme structure" in *Deucalion* 2 (1947), pp. 165–66.

doubt. The only question is: Did they contribute to it in the same way or in a different way?

Whatever the answer may be, once man becomes reflectively conscious of the nature of the sacred, his attitude with respect to ritual (including ritual games) evidently differs from his play attitude. Man considers himself the inventor and creator of the game: he determines the rules and sets the stakes. In the religious universe, on the contrary, man feels at the mercy of powers which entirely surpass him. Nor can man ever completely relax in ritual as he can in play. Much as the sacred reality fascinates him, he experiences it nevertheless as a dangerous force which must be kept at bay. The dread of the sacred maintains in him an anguished tension that is absent from a genuine game.[59] Finally, the attitude with respect to ordinary reality differs. While the player is unconcerned about it to the point of oblivion, religious man remains constantly aware of its existence. It is present to him, not merely as that which he must leave but as that for which he is somehow held responsible and which he eventually must integrate with the sacred.

Rites dramatize the important moments of existence and thereby bring structure into life as a whole. Certain events are made to stand out and to function as symbols which arrange existence into a comprehensible, orderly complex. In a pure flux of temporal succession events would vanish as soon as they appear. In order to prevent this total separation of the past from the present man *re-presents* and re-enacts them in ritual behavior. All too often modern man interprets ritual celebrations of past events as memorial services. But their function is precisely the opposite, namely, to make the past *present,* not to commemorate it.[60] Thus the true meaning of the liturgical year is largely lost for Western

[59] Roger Caillois, "Jeu et sacré" in *L'homme et le sacré,* pp. 207–11; *Man and the Sacred,* pp. 158–61.

[60] Indeed, even the term "represents" is not without ambiguity, as Huizinga points out: "The word 'represents' does not cover the exact meaning of the act, at least not in its looser, modern connotation, for here 'representation' is really *identification,* the mystic repetition of re-presentation of the event." *Op. cit.,* p. 15.

Christians who consider Christmas, Easter, and Pentecost just so many memorial days.[61] A rite retains religious significance only as long as through it man is able to relive the past and to re-establish the beginning.

The other functions of ritual should be mentioned. One, its structuring activity is always for the group, never for the isolated individual. Whenever an individual starts developing strictly private rites we usually interpret his behavior as neurotic. The activity of the "ritualist" isolates rather than integrates, while rites are normally the cement of social life. Through participating in the same structuring activities men become aware of their essential togetherness. Moreover, the rites surrounding birth, adulthood, marriage, and death incorporate the individual into the group by giving the private events of his life a public character. The other function of ritual is to define man's relation to nature from which he emerged and upon which he continues to depend. Rites allow him to relive his union with nature while at the same time keeping the distance necessary for the building of culture. But the limits of this study force us to leave further investigation of these two functions entirely to sociologists and anthropologists, and to concentrate as much as possible on what we now call their "religious" function.

[61] In the nineteenth and the early part of the twentieth century a number of French and German monks forcefully reintroduced the idea into the Catholic Church that the liturgical celebration dealt with a *present* event. Dom Odo Casel, the most important of them, came under heavy criticism because his interpretation seemed to reactivate the historical acts of Christ in their physical reality. His critics rightly objected that time is irreversible and that the historical *as such* cannot be presentified. Yet the historical acts of the Godman are not *merely* historical and it is precisely their transcendent power which the ritual *re-presents* symbolically. See Louis Monden, S.J., *Het Misoffer als Mysterie. Een studie over de H.Mis als sacramenteel offer in hetlicht van de mysterieleer van Dom Odo Casel* (Roermond-Maaseik, 1948). Also, "Symbooloorzakelijkheid als eigen causaliteit van het sacrament" in *Bijdragen* 13 (1952), pp. 280–83; Edward Schillebeeckx, O.P., *De Sacramentele Heilseconomie* (Antwerp-Bilhoven, 1952), pp. 215–19. At any rate the rediscovery of the presence of historical events spawned the liturgical movement in the Catholic Church and with it such profoundly religious books as Dom Columba Marmion's *Christ in His Mysteries* (St. Louis: B. Herder Book Co., 1923).

The religious meaning of common rites has been aptly described by Mircea Eliade as a refounding of existence by reliving its initial acts. Thus the immersion in baptismal rites symbolizes a regression to the undifferentiated being from which all forms have emerged, while the emersion repeats the cosmogonic art of formal appearance.[62] However, we must avoid interpreting rites as if they dramatized a pre-existing myth, for, as we shall see, it usually is the symbolism of the rite itself which leads to the myth. "Historical" faiths such as Judaism, Christianity, and the Islamic are quite unique in that a historical event here clearly precedes the rite and predetermines its meaning. But even in them the rite is not a mere re-enactment of the historical event (as would be the case in a commemoration), for the rite re-creates it beyond its historical limits and gives it a permanent and universal significance.[63] The connection between rite and historical event varies in each case. Even Christianity and Judaism, in spite of their common historical orientation, differ considerably, since Christians as a rule were less reluctant to adopt the nature-oriented symbolism of classical antiquity.

Passage rites by which a person moves from one group to another (initiation, marriage, death) are of particular interest. For here we witness the sacralization of change as such.[64] They reveal perhaps most clearly the religious meaning of all rites: to establish the real by means of transformation. Kant's theory of the categories has made us aware of the close relation between

[62] *The Sacred and the Profane: The Nature of Religion,* Harper Torchbooks, (New York: Harper & Brothers, 1959), p. 130.

[63] Thus the relation of the rite to the original events in the Christian faith is described by Eliade: "For the Christian, baptism is a sacrament because it was instituted by Christ. But none the less for that, it repeats the initiatory ritual of the ordeal (i.e., the struggle against the monster), of death and of the symbolic resurrection (the birth of the new man) . . . The revelation conveyed by the faith did not dispel the primary meanings of the Images; it simply added a new value to them. For the believer, it is true, this new meaning eclipsed all others; it *alone* valorised the Image, transfiguring it into a Revelation." *Images and Symbols,* tr. by Philip Maigret (New York: Sheed & Ward, 1961), pp. 158–61.

[64] On passage rites the classical study is still Arnold Van Gennep, *Les rites de passage* (Paris, 1909).

conceptualization and the constitution of the real. But it has accustomed us to consider this constitution the outcome of a purely intellectual process, while the existential awareness of the real results from meaning-constituting acts which are by no means purely intellectual. Even modern man fully experiences the real only after he becomes totally involved. An important event does not become fully real until we have duly celebrated it. The festivities accompanying a wedding, an anniversary, or a birthday are not so much spontaneous expressions of joy (I fail to see what is so joyful about an aging marriage or about being a year closer to death) as well-planned rites which help us *realize* the temporality of existence. Even in its secularized version, the rite asserts an ultimate source of reality. Its constitution is at once a new event and a return to the foundations. Since the truly real is that which has existed from the beginning, rites give birth to, and are accompanied by, myths of the origin.[65]

5. SACRAMENTS

Let us now turn to those particular rites usually referred to as mysteries or sacraments. *Mysterion* in the Greek-speaking culture was a dedication to a god by means of a ritual initiation during which the secret meaning of certain symbols was revealed. In the mystery cults of Greece (Eleusis) or the ones of Egypt (Isis) and the Middle East (Attis, Mithra) which flourished in the Hellenistic and Roman worlds, the dedication centered around a ritual imitation of the god's suffering and death. Initiation established a direct contact with the godhead and assured participa-

---

[65] This unique combination of the new and the old is beautifully illustrated in the marriage rites of a tribe in South Borneo. The wedding ceremony is presented as a new event which allows man to rejoin his mythical beginning. The wedding is the re-enactment of the creation of the first human couple from the tree of life. By wedding each other bride and groom re-create the world in its primeval state and rejoin it with God. Hans Schärer, *Ngaju Religion: The Conception of God among a South Borneo People*, tr. by Rodney Needham (The Hague, 1963), pp. 84–85.

tion in his immortality. The German monk Odo Casel, who spent a lifetime studying the influence of ancient mysteries upon Christian worship, defines the former as "a sacred ritual action in which a saving deed is made present through the rite."[66] All mysteries temporarily abolished the distinction between the divine and the human.

Christianity borrowed some concepts from the mystery cults.[67] Yet it combined them with the Jewish idea of a salvific, eschatologically oriented design which God has revealed in history. While the emphasis of the ancient mysteries was all on secrecy, the Christian ones *manifested* what had previously been hidden. Thus for St. Paul who uses the term frequently, mystery means primarily the revelation of God's inner life and his plan of salvation in Christ Jesus, particularly the vocation of the Gentiles with the Jews.[68]

[66] *The Mystery of Christian Worship*, ed. by Burkhard Neuheuser (Westminster, Md.: Newman Press, 1963), p. 54. For a more elaborate description, see p. 98. On Eleusis, I consulted Karl Kerényi, *Eleusis*, tr. by Ralph Manheim (New York: Bollingen Series 65, Pantheon Books, 1967). Thassilo De Scheffer, *Mystères et oracles helleniques* (Paris, 1943), pp. 29–77. Ulrich von Willamowitz-Moellendorff, *Der Glaube der Hellenen* (Basel, 1956), Vol. II, pp. 42–49. Martin P. Nilsson, *A History of Greek Religion*, 2d ed., tr. by F. J. Fielden (New York: Oxford University Press, 1949), pp. 210–13. On the Hellenistic mysteries, Franz Cumont, *The Mysteries of Mithra*, tr. by Thomas J. McCormack (New York: Dover Publications, 1956). *Oriental Religions in Roman Paganism* (New York: Dover Publications, 1956), pp. 46–161.

[67] Whether St. Paul's use of *Mysterion* was directly influenced by the pagan mysteries is a debated question. Odo Casel affirmed it constantly and attempted to prove it in his posthumous *Zur Kultsprache des Heiligen Paulus* in *Archiv fur Liturgiewissenschaft*, I (1950), pp. 1–64. Others (Schillebeeckx, *De Sacramentele Heilseconomie*, pp. 38–39, K. Prümm, "Mystères" *Dictionnaire de la Bible, Supplement*, Vol. VI, pp. 2–225) deny any direct influence and claim that the word was taken from the common religious language of the Diaspora. At any rate, connotations of the Jewish faith prevail over the allusion to the mysteries.

[68] ". . . it was by a revelation that I was given the knowledge of the mystery. This mystery that has now been revealed through the Spirit to his holy apostles and prophets was unknown to any men in past generations; it means that pagans now share the same inheritance that they are parts of the same body and that the same promise has been made to them, in Christ Jesus,

Although in the New Testament concept of mystery the ritual element seems to have lost the primary position which it occupied in the ancient mysteries, the term *sacramentum,* by which the Vulgate usually translates it, would eventually acquire an exclusively ritual denotation. This development is not as illogical as it seems, for from the very beginning the mystery of redemption was to be fulfilled through participating actions.[69] The word *sacramentum* had originally a much more restricted meaning than mystery: it referred mainly to the military oath by which those who swore their allegiance consecrated themselves. It was probably through the concept of consecration that the term found its way into the language of salvation.[70] The original meaning was applied to baptism and would exert some influence on the development of sacramental theology in the West through Tertullian, Cyprian, Arnobius, *et alii.* Nevertheless for a long time the term would preserve all the richness of the Christian "mystery."[71]

Containing the discussion within the limits of the ritual mean-

---

through the Gospel." Eph. 3:2–6. Tr. Jerusalem Bible. The New English Bible translates mystery as "secret," but this is somewhat misleading since it must be revealed. See also 1 Cor. 2:7 and Col. 1:25–27.

[69] See Odo Casel, *The Mystery of Christian Worship,* p. 40.

[70] See Odo Casel, *op. cit.,* pp. 56ff. Edward Schillebeeckx, *De Sacramentele Heilseconomie,* pp. 89–91.

[71] Thus Paschasius Radbertus in the ninth century defines as sacrament any religious celebration in which a visible token of an invisible salvation is being given. The incarnation of Christ and the whole economy of salvation is "one great sacrament" or "mystery." *Liber de Corpore et Sanguine Domini,* Migne, *Patres Latini,* 120, 1275. Schillebeeckx in his fundamental study *De Sacramentele Heilseconomie* (pp. 158–60) shows how St. Thomas still uses the terms *sacramentum* and *mysterium* interchangeably in referring to the redemptive power of the acts of Christ. Nor does Thomas limit his usage of the term to these well-defined rites to which the Council of Trent was to restrict it. He calls "sacraments of nature" those rites which man, unaided by revelation, develops to establish contact with the Deity. See, for instance, *In IV Sent.,* q. 2 a. 6. For the impact of the meaning of a military oath upon the development of sacramentology in the Latin Fathers, cf. A. Michel, "Sacrements" in *Dictionnaire de Théologie Catholique* (Paris, 1939), 14/508–9.

ing of sacrament, we notice that not every rite is sacramental. A sacrament differs from other rites in that the ritual action itself is believed to yield a numinous influence. Although the present usage of the term sacrament is Christian, the idea of a rite which conveys a supernatural power is widespread even among primitives.[72] However the nature of this power be conceived, its effect is some form of salvation. This is clearly the case for the Christian sacrament. In the sacramental rite a common function of life obtains a salvific effect which it did not possess in an ordinary, nonsymbolic situation, and which is somehow directly connected to the action. Early scholastic theologians attempted to express this by the term *ex opere operato,* meaning that the effect depends exclusively upon the valid performance of the rite. The expression is misleading insofar as it seems to rule out altogether the intention of the minister and the disposition of the recipient—a theory which in spite of some unfortunate expressions in the early formulation of sacramental doctrine no theologian ever held.[73] It arouses the suspicion of magic in modern man. Yet sacraments have at all times been distinct from magic rites. For the salvific influence of the sacramental action does not originate in the nature of the rite *considered in itself,* as is the case in magic. Rather does the rite partake in a transcendent reality from which it derives an efficacy surpassing its ordinary power. Religious believers do not always keep this distinction in mind—that is why magic lurks always around the corner—but the religious consciousness as such has never confused the two.

Sacramental efficacy is not a univocal concept, even among Christians. Nevertheless most believers ascribe sufficient efficacy to the rite to make it more than a mere figurative sign of salvation.[74]

[72] See Jane Harrison, *Themis,* in *Epilegomena to the Study of Greek Religion* and *Themis* (New York: University Books, 1962), p. 138; G. Van der Leeuw, *Religion in Its Essence and Manifestation,* p. 365.
[73] On the history of the term, see Schillebeeckx, *Sacramentele Heilseconomie,* pp. 189–91; on the intention of the minister, *op. cit.,* pp. 457–79; of the recipient, *op. cit.,* pp. 481–84, 648–56.
[74] It is interesting to see how close early Lutheran theologians remain to Catholic doctrine in the interpretation of this efficacy. One of the shapers of

The fundamental principle in a discussion of this topic must be that *all* symbolic actions do more than signify: they also to some degree *realize* what they signify. The embrace, the handshake do not metaphorically "represent" or "express" my friendship, but, providing I do not feign nonexisting affection, they also "seal" it and effect its full realization. Terms as *express* and *sign* inadequately convey the full import of what happens in symbolic activity. For symbolic signs and expressions actually *produce* the signified and expressed reality. The epistemic function (the pure *sign*) to which we often reduce the entire symbolic activity is only one of its features. The symbol signifies, expresses, *and realizes*.[75] An exclusively concept-oriented way of thinking has accustomed us to conceive of a symbol as extrinsically connecting two things which are essentially different, in the manner of an allegory or a simile. But a true symbol intrinsically unifies the elements of which it is constituted. Its meaning must be grasped not by discursively adding one element to another, but by a synthetic insight which comprehends them all at once. This is particularly important for the understanding of sacraments. For they symbolize a reality which can in no way be directly approached. Its influence upon human existence, then, must be channeled through ordinary acts and functions of life, such as eating, drinking, washing.

To overlook the intrinsic unity of symbol and symbolized inevitably leads to an interpretation of sacramental efficacy as a mere *addition* to the ordinary one, resulting from some extrinsic

Lutheran Orthodoxy, Johann Gerhard (1582–1637) writes in his famous *Loci Theologici:* "Distinguendum est inter signum nude σημαντικόν et μεταδοτικόν sive προσφερόμενον. Quando patres symbola externa, panem et vinum, in sacra coena vocant signa corporis et sanguinis Christi, non intelligunt signa tantum σημαντικά sed μεταδοτικά και προσφερόμενα." *Opera,* ed. by Preuss (Berlin, 1867), Vol. 5, p. 112.

[75] Louis Monden, S.J., "Symbooloorzakelijkheid als eigen causaliteit van het sacrament" in *Bijdragen,* 13 (1952), p. 278. The intrinsic connection between sign and causality was to my knowledge, first pointed out in John of St. Thomas' remarkable treatise on sacraments. *Cursus Theologicus De Sacramentis.* Disputatio 22 a.1 dub. 1.

divine decree. Yet sacraments are symbolic *in their very essence* and, consequently, differ intrinsically from the acts which they ritualize. The exclusive emphasis on the institutional aspect of the sacraments (prompting mostly unconvincing proofs of Christ's "foundational" role) in much theology of the past clearly reveals an inadequate understanding of the *intrinsic* sacramentality of salvation symbols. The same misunderstanding appears in today's seemingly opposite attempts to restore the "natural" meaning of the sacraments. The only difference is that older theologians accepted the "supernatural" addition, while modern secularizers reject it. Both regard the sacramental character as superimposed upon the ordinary activity. However, sacraments must be recognized as intrinsically connected with the sacred before the specific nature of their symbolism of washing, eating, etc., can be understood.

> We must hold that the bodily washing in baptism, as the symbolic realization of Christ's own act, is more than bodily washing is on the merely human plane; it is indeed the gift of grace in tangible visibility, the outward sign of something inward.[76]

The sacrament is *first and primarily* a symbolic gesture of a transcendent reality. In the sacramental meaning this transcendent reality precedes rather than follows the visible, ordinary form. The latter results from the incarnated nature of man's entire existence, which includes his relation to the transcendent. The correct order of succession is indicated by Karl Rahner:

> *As* God's work of grace on man is accomplished (incarnate itself), it enters the spatio-temporal historicity of man as sacrament, and *as* it does so, it becomes active with regard to man, it constitutes itself . . . For at no stage can the sign be seen apart from what is signified, since it is understood *a priori* as a symbolic reality, which the signified itself brings about in order to be really present itself

[76] Edward Schillebeeckx, *Christ the Sacrament of the Encounter with God* (New York: Sheed & Ward, 1963), p. 75.

... In a word, the grace of God constitutes itself actively present in the sacraments by creating their expression, their historical tangibility in space and time, which is its own symbol.[77]

A clearer recognition of the intrinsic nature of religious symbolism could have constrained the bitter polemics among Christians over the number of sacraments. The positive, institutional element, peculiar to each faith, is undoubtedly more important than modernism and liberal protestantism allowed, yet it should not eclipse the primary truth that sacramentality is a universal form of symbolism. It must not be restricted, then, to those particular forms of which we know the historical institution. Christian tradition itself professed the all-pervasive nature of sacramental symbolism in its respect for "sacramentals," now all but abolished by the institutional legalism of the last centuries. Another instance of sacramental symbolization is the veneration of images, so important in the cult of the Eastern Christian Churches. Far from being idolatrous, as some Byzantine emperors thought, the sacramental character of the Christian cosmos is directly implied in the Incarnation.[78] If God communicates himself in Christ, the image of God, then he also communicates himself in the images of that image. An unsuspected witness, Ludwig Feuerbach upheld the logical consistency of Christian iconoduly:

[77] "The Theology of the Symbol" in *Theological Investigations* (Baltimore: Helicon Press, 1966), Vol. IV, p. 242. Rahner writes as a theologian; our method here is philosophical. Hence we must interpret the dogmatic parts of this statement ("God's work of grace on man is accomplished," "the grace of God constitutes itself as actively present") in a purely descriptive way and make abstraction of the existential commitment which underlies them.

[78] This last statement does not decide the debate between the Catholic Church and the Reformation on the sacraments. Our method of critical reflection is restricted to the discovery of logical structures in faith *as it actually exists*. It does not qualify us to make pronouncements about what *ought* to exist. Only where the religious manifestly degenerates into the nonreligious (as when sacraments are used as magic devices) or where theological interpretations of religious realities betray the original intuition can the critic reject *what is*. Some of the purely juridical theory of the sacraments in Catholic textbooks of the past two centuries would seem to require such a philosophical rejection.

The sanction of the archetype is the sanction of its semblance. If God has an Image of himself, why should not I have an image of God? If God loves his Image as himself, why should not I also love the image of God as I love God himself.[79]

Meanwhile, I fully admit that the peculiar nature of the sacrament invites a dualistic interpretation of its symbolism. Indeed, we may well wonder how religious man manages to unite the two elements in a single symbol: on the one hand, a transcendent "signified" which cannot be adequately expressed in tangible form; on the other, a human function which, outside the sacramental context, possesses a complete intentionality of its own. How can the former be integrated with the latter without seeming to be added? The answer lies entirely in the sacramental *word*. Only words can direct the intentionality of immanent acts toward a transcendent reality without first asserting their ordinary noema. The unique flexibility of language enables it to establish a symbolic meaning which directly (and not successively) subsumes the ordinary one. Without linguisitc interpretation an act is forever determined by its natural meaning. That is why "revelation," although it starts with the deed, cannot be completed but by the word. Language alone is equipped with the symbolic apparatus to say the unspeakable and to structure the invisible. Once the word is spoken, all human acts are able to participate in its transcendent meaning.

Of course, man is "religious" long before he is able to articulate his religious attitude linguistically. Nevertheless such an articulation soon becomes an inevitable requirement of the developing attitude. For the distinction between the sacred and the profane can be *adequately* expressed only in speech. We may therefore formulate as a law that all religious symbols are either verbal or require verbal interpretation. Scholastic theologians recognized this need of linguistic determination in the sacraments in referring,

[79] *Das Wesen des Christentums, Sämtliche Werke, VI*, p. 94. *The Essence of Christianity*, p. 77.

somewhat clumsily, to the word as the *form* of a sacrament (as opposed to the *matter* or element).[80] The transcendent intentionality of the word carries the deed and directly transforms its original "immanent" meaning. Once the word is spoken the entire action participates in the new intentionality and becomes "verbalized." Thus, according to Karl Rahner the sacramental deed itself becomes word.

> The sacramental action too has the character of a word. It designates something, it expresses something, it reveals something that is of itself hidden . . . (The sacramental signs) are all freely created signs, in the same sense that "words" are, which are not merely signs of the thing, but likewise always signs of the free personal self-disclosure of a person, in contrast to things, which have always automatically made themselves known and cannot be closed in on themselves. In other words: since grace is always free and personal self-communication of God, its divulgation is always free and personal and hence essentially word.[81]

The conclusion, then, of this section must be that the word is primary in religious symbolism even though the deed was first.

6. SACRIFICE: COMMUNION, GIFT AND EXPIATION

Before discussing the symbolism of the word, we must consider one more rite which is almost as common as the sacraments, of which some consider it to be a subspecies: the sacrifice. Sacrifices have always occupied a privileged place among ritual ceremonies. In the Chinese classic, Li Ki, we read:

> Of all the methods for the good ordering of men, there is none more urgent than the use of ceremonies. Ceremonies are of five kinds, and there is none of them more important than sacrifices.

---

[80] "*In sacramentis verba se habent per modum formae, res autem per modum materiae.*" St. Thomas, *Summa Theologiae*, III, q. 60, a. 7.
[81] Karl Rahner, *Theological Investigations*, Vol. IV, pp. 266–67.

Sacrifice is not a thing coming to a man from without; it issues from within him, and has its birth in his heart.[82]

The internal disposition in which according to the Chinese sage, sacrifice originates will eventually eliminate the actual deed itself, but not until the end of a long process. Meanwhile it is exceedingly difficult to define the nature of sacrifice. Apart from the idea of consecration suggested in the etymology—*sacrum facere* —hardly any general description would seem to fit all forms. Nevertheless it is possible, I believe, to collect enough common meaning from the variety of phenomena to justify a single name.

All ritual acts originate in man's feeling of dissatisfaction with his present status. Change to a different sphere of existence is the main objective of sacrifice. In their standard study, *Essai sur la nature et la fonction du sacrifice,* Henry Hubert and Marcel Mauss define sacrifice as "a religious act which, by the consecration of a victim, modifies the moral state of the sacrificer or of certain material objects with which he is concerned."[83] According to Hubert and Mauss the consecration is achieved by means of a destruction which severs the victim definitively from the profane sphere.[84] Although a true destruction does not always take place, the victim (and to some extent the participants) always loses its previous status.

A survey of the various theories indicates that sacrifices are basically considered either as gifts or as communion rites. Ed-

---

[82] Li Ki, *The Book of Rites,* tr. by James Legge, in *The Sacred Books of the East* (Oxford: 1885), 22, 13.

[83] "Essai sur la nature et la fonction du sacrifice" in *Mélanges d'histoire des religions* (Paris, 1909), p. 15. The essay was first published in *L'année sociologique,* II (1898). The neutral expression "modifies the moral state" is preferred over the more specific "sanctifies" because sacrifices are also brought to desacralize for profane usage what is originally sacred, as in the offering of the first fruits of the harvest. Yet I wonder whether the so-called desacralization rites are not really expiatory sacrifices, the effect of which is ultimately sanctifying. W. Robertson Smith regards the offering of the first fruits exclusively as a consecration. *Lectures on the Religion of the Semites* (1890). Republished after the third (1927) edition by KTAV Publishing House, 1969, in *The Library of Biblical Studies,* p. 241.

[84] *Op. cit.,* pp. 13, 50, 124.

ward B. Tylor first attempted a coherent interpretation of sacrifice as gift.[85] According to him, the original purpose of sacrificial gifts may have been to feed the spirits or gods. Gradually it was refined into the less primitive idea of pleasing the god by the fragrance of sacrificial smoke, perfume, or incense, until it became purely honorific. In a class by itself was the piacular sacrifice intended to restore the relation with the god after it had been broken by some defiling act. Like most of his theories, Tylor's interpretation of sacrifice came under strong attack because of its inherent anthropocentrism. Critics objected that sacrifices existed long before man had a "spiritual" concept of the sacred powers. Moreover, primitive man's desire to communicate with the mysterious and impersonal force which he found primarily present in his totem animal or plant, could not possibly be characterized as a *do-ut-des* relation.

Totemists explained the origins of sacrifice in relation to a group's awareness of unity with itself and with another nonhuman group. According to W. Robertson Smith, the most prominent advocate of the totemic theory of sacrifice, the original nucleus of the sacrifice was an act of communion.

The sacred function is the act of the whole community, which is conceived as a circle of brethren, united with one another and with their god by participation in one life or life-blood. The same blood is supposed to flow also in the veins of the victim, so that its death is at once a shedding of the tribal blood and a violation of the sanctity of the divine life that is transfused through every member, human or irrational, of the sacred circle. Nevertheless the slaughter of such a victim is permitted or required on solemn occasions, and all the tribesmen partake of its flesh, that they may thereby cement and seal their mystic unity with one another and with their God.[86]

[85] *Primitive Culture,* Chapter 18.
[86] *Op. cit.,* pp. 311–12. The existence of those sacrifices (specifically the propitiatory ones) in which the victim is entirely destroyed and no communion meal takes place is explained as the result of a social-economic development in which prolonged familiarity with domestic animals had dissipated the belief in the holiness of an animal, as such, while at the

Union, then, is considered to be the original objective of sacrifice. The notion of property would eventually be introduced in the relations with the gods and make the sacrifice into a gift. But this, according to Smith, was one of the most fatal aberrations in the development of ancient religion.[87] Even after the acceptance of the gift theory, however, the original idea of communion was preserved in sacrificial ceremonies.[88] Thus all piacular sacrifices were attempts to restore the power-giving current with the sacred after it had been interrupted by ritual or moral violations. It is here and not in the gift or substitution theories that we find the ultimate meaning of propitiatory sacrifices.

Jane Harrison, the classical scholar who became Smith's most fervent follower, modified the master's theory of sacrifice by emphasizing the primacy of the communal *deed* over the theory. Originally there is nothing but the eater and the eaten sacrificial victim: the mysterious *mana* resides in the act of communion itself, not in the nature of the communicants. No god presides over the banquet or is being eaten. The divinity of the victim results from the sacrificial deed. Primary is the eating ritual; the theology comes later.[89] That the sacrifice precedes the god of the sacrifice

---

same time respect for the *sacrifice* of the animal reserved to the gods had increased to a point where partaking in their flesh came to be considered sacrilegious. W. Robertson Smith, *op. cit.*, p. 353. Nevertheless, sacrificial meals continue to exist side by side with holocausts.

[87] How fatal appears in what Smith refers to as the revolting absurdity of human sacrifices. "Absurd since it does not follow that because a man's first-born son is dearer to himself than all his wealth, the life of that son is the most valuable gift that he can offer to his god; and revolting, when it came to be supposed that the sacrifice of children as fire-offerings was a gift of food to a deity who delighted in human flesh." *Op. cit.*, p. 394.

[88] *Op. cit.*, pp. 397–98.

[89] Jane Harrison, *Themis*, p. 136. Smith himself held similar views on the priority of the sacrificial deed, though less consistently. Thus he raises the question whether the Semitic concept of atonement did not arise out of a sacrificial communion with the sacred in which the destruction of the victim eventually led to mourning for a dead god. Similarly, he interprets the annual Hebrew *piacula* as being quite unrelated to the ideas of sin and redemption by which later generations attempted to justify their existence.

has been accepted by a number of students of archaic religion independently of the communion theory (particularly in its totemic form). The sacred nature of the sacrificial act consecrates and sometimes divinizes the victim.[90] All mythical references to the death of a god probably have their origin in a sacrificial ritual. Even in Christianity the "glorification" of Jesus, that is, the manifestation of his divinity, resulted from his sacrificial death and its acceptance by the Father.

Although the totemic theory shed new light upon several aspects of the sacrificial rite, as total explanation it proved insufficient. According to Malinowski, the ritual of a sacramental meal is well attested only in the few tribes of Australia and America in which the existence of a genuine totem has been established.[91] Recently some anthropologists have even denied all relationship between totem and sacrifice. For Lévi-Strauss, as we recall, the totem is exclusively a primitive means to establish some sort of rational homology between parallel series, while sacrifices, on the contrary, are performed to mediate between terms that have no previous homology at all, such as man and god.[92] Lévi-Strauss' purely logical interpretation of the totem may be unjustified, but his objections against a simple identification of the original sacrifice with a totemic meal are convincing enough. In spite of those flaws the totemic theory has substantially contributed to our understanding of sacrifice. It definitively established the attempt to be united with the sacred world by means of a ritual communion as an essential feature of sacrifice. Through

---

Only after the exile came the Day of Atonement, to be interpreted as a general atonement for the sins of Israel, an abstract concept entirely foreign to the original event. As long as the god and the animal were kinsmen, there was no ground for atonement. *Op. cit.*, p. 360.

[90] Philo of Byblos applies the expression ἀφιερώθη (he became sacred) to Oceanos after he had been mutilated by his son Chronos. Reports of this nature make Hubert and Mauss conclude that divinization is merely a superior form of sanctification and separation from the profane world. Hubert and Mauss, *op. cit.*, pp. 104–11.

[91] *Science, Magic and Religion* (Garden City, N.Y.: Doubleday, 1954), p. 43.

[92] *The Savage Mind*, pp. 225–28. See also his entire treatise on *Totemism*.

a participation in the victim's substance through consumption, physical contact, or blessing, the primeval power in which the universe is grounded returns to the communicants.[93] By participating in this common power the assistants to the sacrifice become united horizontally as well as vertically.[94]

Yet to accept some communion rite as essential to the nature of sacrifice is not to say that communion is the entire essence of sacrifice. The difficulty in discussing the "essence" of sacrifice in a universal way is that the essence itself has shifted from the archaic to the more recent types of sacrifice. Man's relation to the sacred underwent substantial changes which are reflected in his conceptions of sacrifice. Robertson Smith once wrote that the more primitive man is, the happier he is in the practice of his religion.[95] The statement may be overly simplistic, but it suggests correctly the ease with which archaic man communes with the beyond. A sacred meal never consisted in the simple act of taking food, but the further we regress toward the dawn of culture the closer each meal comes to being sacred and the more easily it can develop into a full-fledged religious event. The distinction between sacred and profane is constitutive of the sacred as such; yet in archaic culture the sacred is closest to what for us is most ordinary. Thus a ritualized act of eating strikes us as most significant because it differs so strongly from our own approach to the sacred. Yet is the significantly different the whole of what is significant? The idea of giving, although less conspicuous because less remote

[93] Hubert and Mauss, *op. cit.*, p. 57. See Mircea Eliade's remarks on the Brahman conception of sacrifice in *The Two and the One,* tr. by J. M. Cohen (New York: Harper & Row, 1969), p. 97.

[94] In the words of W. Robertson Smith: "The one thing directly expressed in the sacrificial meal is that the god and his worshippers are *commensals,* but every other point in their mutual relations is included in what this involves. Those who sit at meat together are united for all social affects." *Op. cit.*, p. 269. A similar idea was expressed by the seventeenth-century scholastic William of Paris in his remarkable treatise *De Legibus:* "There is nothing so conducive to make the whole household of children and family one as the partaking of food in common; so also the communion of spiritual food and drink more than any other thing makes for one spiritual household family." *Opera Omnia* (Paris, 1674), Vol. I, p. 30.

[95] *Op. cit.*, pp. 254–63.

from our own acts of worship, may be equally important to the meaning of sacrifice. To be sure, not in the anachronistic way in which Tylor understood sacrificial giving, but as a symbolic offering. It has been said that offering is the only characteristic which all sacrifices, bloody and bloodless, have in common.[96] Indeed, communion itself requires some notion of offering. In itself a meal is not sacred; to become so it must be *made sacred* (the original meaning of sacri-*ficium*) by a separation of the communicant from his ordinary self and what belongs to him.[97] The idea of giving is more basic than the well-defined property relations to which Smith seems to reduce it.[98] Exchanging gifts is as much a form of communion as eating. It is difficult for us to appreciate the full meaning of a gesture which we perform so frequently. Giving now consists mainly of purchasing what we hope will cause pleasure, at an expense which reflects both the wealth of the giver and his esteem of the beneficiary. Seldom does the giver give *himself* through his gifts.

But *dare* does not mean merely to dispose of some arbitrary object with a quite indefinite intention; the word *dare* means, rather, to place oneself in relation to, and then to participate in, a second person by means of an object, which however is not actually an "object" at all, but part of one's own self.[99]

[96] M. J. Lagrange, O.P., *Études sur les religions sémitiques* (Paris, 1905), pp. 266–70. We must not forget, however, that not every offering is sacrificial. A votive offering is not.

[97] This is beautifully illustrated in the Mass where the bread and wine are *converted* into the sacrifice of Christ in the very act of being *offered*. The consecration completes the offering act of the congregation by a rite of acceptance which transforms the gifts into divine substance. The transforming act allows the believer to say that there is only one offering in the Mass although there are clearly two acts of presentation: bread and wine in the offertory, the body and blood of Christ in the consecration.

[98] Malinowski, after having been exposed for years to the archaic culture of the Trobriand Islands, still considered it the leading notion of sacrifice. "That the idea of giving in all phases of social contact plays a great role in sacrifice seems—in spite of the unpopularity of this theory nowadays—unquestionable in view of the new knowledge of primitive economic psychology." *Op. cit.*, pp. 42–43.

[99] Gerardus Van der Leeuw, *Religion in Essence and Manifestation*, p. 351.

But in addition to communion, giving symbolizes *separation,* an aspect as essential to the religious act of *sacrum facere* as the unity which the communion theory emphasizes so strongly.[100] If fully understood, the communion and the gift theories are no longer mutually exclusive. A communion with the sacred implies a separation from one's ordinary self, an extraordinary form of giving, while giving is truly *sacri-ficial* only if it becomes a communion, that is, a sharing of the self with the sacred.

There is one further aspect to be considered in expiatory sacrifices: substitution. In a sense every sacrifice is substitutional. For except in the rare instance of a voluntary human victim, man can never give himself entirely to the sacred. The purer his concept of God becomes, the more will he be aware of the substitutional character of his offering. As he realizes that God has no need for gifts, he gains new insight in the symbolic character of his gesture. This is a critical moment, for the new awareness may easily lead to a token substitution in which the self is no longer personally involved. In such a view the gods lose their greed, but become tyrants insisting on legal formalities. Thus originated the notion that sin can be "redeemed" by the execution of another, preferably an innocent victim. But the expiatory sacrifice was offered not to pay a fine for ritual or moral transgressions, but to reintegrate man with the sphere of the sacred.[101] Expiation is not an evil that must be suffered because an evil has been committed. It symbolizes that I no longer want to assert my finitude as such and instead return my private existence to the sacred reality. As a token of this return I immolate or abandon some part of my profane existence. The purpose, then, of the expiatory

[100] The element of *separation* is wanting in the nineteenth-century theories of sacrifice as gift, another reason why they were so inadequate. It is remarkably present in William of Paris' definition: "For sacrifice is a gift which is made sacred in the offering, and to offer sacrifice is essentially this, to make the actual gift sacred by the offering." *Opera Omnia,* Vol. I, p. 72.
[101] See for instance the texts in Leviticus, Ch. 4–5. Commentary by A. R. S. Kennedy, "Sacrifice and Offering," revised by James Barr in *Dictionary of the Bible,* ed. by James Hastings, rev. by Frederick C. Grant and H. H. Rowley (New York: Charles Scribner's Sons, 1963), p. 875a.

sacrifice is, as Hegel put it, to give oneself "the consciousness of a separation that is overcome" (*das Bewusztsein der aufgehobenen Trennung*).[102]

I have reserved the critique of the juridical substitution theory for a later chapter. But even if I can show that this theory was a spurious interpretation of the idea of atonement and that blood is a symbol of life rather than of death, applying the notion of sacrifice to the death of Christ causes considerable difficulties. To slay a human being in order to present a gift of life may have been acceptable to a more archaic mentality. To us it is merely repulsive and the very crudeness of the rite destroys whatever symbolic value it may have had for the primitive. Nor does the rite become more acceptable by attributing the homicidal act to Jesus' enemies. For as long as ritual murder remained a condition of salvation it matters little who drew the knife. The ultimate responsibility rests with the faith which requires such sacrifices. Yet Jesus' passion and death must have had other grounds than a divine need for ritual murder. Otherwise they would long since have ceased to inspire his followers.[103]

Despite the sacrificial metonymies by means of which the authors of the New Testament stress the continuity with, and supersession of, the Old Covenant, Christ's sacrifice has little in common with the bloody sacrifices of the Old Testament.[104] There was neither a demand for blood nor an assigned sacrificial agent. Christ's sacrifice consisted in an attitude of unconditional obedience to God and a willingness to accept the suffering and death to which his uncompromising dedication might lead. The

[102] *Philosophie der Religion*, I, pp. 267–69.

[103] It is with considerable hesitation and methodological scruples that I briefly move into this discussion of theological interpretations of Christ's sacrifice. As always, however, I continue to restrict my investigation to an analysis of structures and abstain from any theological commitments.

[104] The distinguished theologian D. M. Baillie warns us not to take these expressions too literally. "However we translate those terms borrowed from the Jewish sacrificial system, it is quite plain that in the New Testament they undergo a transformation of meaning because of the really extraordinary setting which is now given to them." *God Was in Christ* (New York: Charles Scribner's Sons, 1948), p. 188.

prototype for this sort of sacrifice in the Old Testament is not Isaac on Mount Moriah, or the blood offerings of Leviticus, but the suffering servant of the Book of Isaiah.[105] The emphasis on the voluntary nature of his suffering excludes the idea of an impersonal justice which *demands* the death of the innocent for the sin of the wicked. Yahweh crushes his servant under the sins of all but, the sacred writer adds, "if he offers his life in atonement, he shall see his heirs, he shall have a long life and through him what Yahweh wishes will be done" (53, 10).[106]

The Gospel descriptions leave us little doubt that Jesus' death was voluntary. He predicted it, visited the places and did the deeds which would make it inevitable, and when his time had come, accepted it. He went to Jerusalem where he would die and left the cenacle to be arrested in the Cedron valley. Even after he had been captured, the passion stories imply, he could have made the authorities set him free, and he could have done so without outrightly denying his teaching. Still Jesus did not *intend* to die a violent death nor did he invite it. In the earlier stages of his public life he escaped several times from his enemies and even in the end he prayed for liberation. But he knew all along that his message would inexorably result in his death, and even that its meaning would not be fully revealed until he died. He

[105] The main passages are:

"We had all gone astray like sheep, each taking his own way, and Yahweh burdened him with the sins of all of us . . .

"By his sufferings shall my servant justify many taking their faults on himself.

"Hence I will grant whole hordes for his tribute, he shall divide the spoil with the mighty, for surrendering himself to death and letting himself be taken for a sinner, while he was bearing the faults of many and praying all the time for sinners." (Is. 53:6, 11–12.)

[106] St. Gregory of Nazianze put the matter very clearly in one of his Easter orations: "How is it, that the Father was well pleased with the death of the Only Begotten, and at the same time refused to accept the offering of Isaac by his father, providing the ram in place of the rational victim? It is clear that the Father did accept the sacrifice, but it was a sacrifice that he did not demand." *Oratio 45 in Pascha,* Migne, P.G. 36, 653. Text cited and translated in Maurice de la Taille, *The Mystery of Faith* (New York: Sheed & Ward, 1940), Vol. I, p. 126.

therefore considered his death the most essential part of his message.[107]

But did Jesus consider his death a sacrifice? Many religious men have died as witnesses for their message without regarding their death sacrificial. To the early Church, Jesus' death was unquestionably a sacrifice. Was it also one to Jesus himself? The Fourth Gospel ascribes to him the words: "for their sake I now consecrate myself" (Jn. 17:19). Also the story of the last supper, so well established by the Synoptics, contains words which clearly refer to a sacrificial immolation: "This is my blood, the blood of the covenant, shed for many" (Mt. 26, 28; Mk. 14, 24; Lk. 22, 20). The New Testament leaves no doubt about the primitive Church's interpretation of Christ's death. It alludes to sacrificial aspersions ("consecrated with the sprinkled blood of Jesus Christ," I Pet. 1:2); to the sacrificial lamb ("the Lamb that was slain" Rev. 5:12—also 5:6; 13:8; I Pet. 1:19); and to the entire sacrificial ritual of the Hebrews (Heb. 4:14–10:39). Yet the sacrifice of Christ is presented as unique and unprecedented. Christ is the priest as well as the victim. This meant that no sacrificer could perform the rites of immolation and that the offering was purely interior.

Only by taking full account of the interior and voluntary nature of Christ's immolation can one understand the notion of a human

[107] Nor can one claim that Jesus was not morally free, since the Father *required* the sacrifice of his life. Anselm based his entire satisfaction theory on the moral freedom of Christ's action. "For the Father did not compel him to suffer death, or even allow him to be slain, against his will, but of his own accord he endured death for the salvation of men . . . It seems to me that you do not rightly understand the difference between what he did and suffered at the demand of obedience, and what he suffered, not demanded by obedience, but inflicted on him, because he kept his obedience perfect . . . God did not, therefore, compel Christ to die; but he suffered death of his own will, not yielding up his life as an act of obedience in maintaining holiness; for he held out so firmly in this obedience that he met death on account of it." *Cur Deus Homo*, in *Opera Omnia*, ed. by G. S. Schmitt, Vol. III, pp. 60–62; tr. by S. N. Deane in *Basic Writings* (La Salle, Ill.: Open Court Publishing Co., 1965), pp. 191–94. On this whole problem see Maurice de la Taill, *The Mystery of Faith* (New York: Sheed & Ward, 1940), Vol. I, pp. 49–153; 27–33.

sacrifice in a strictly monotheistic tradition at a time when civilizing tendencies were in the ascendant. A return to primitive rites (of which there was no memory in the Hebrew culture) could not account for the lasting religious impact of the Christian faith. The ordinary believer's view is in this respect more intelligible than that of the later theology. Christ brought his death upon himself by a revelation of the nature of God which threatened the religious foundations of society as much as Socrates' philosophy had undermined the cultural traditions of Athens. The drama of Christ consists not in God's justice taking revenge, but in God's goodness revealing itself to a hostile world. His sacrificial death is reminiscent of the gigantic *agons* between a redeemer and the powers of darkness of the Near Eastern and Classical mythologies.[108] Originally, God's justice and God's mercy, then, are not successive stages in the drama. The crude notion of a revengeful God who demands satisfaction even if his own Son has to die for it was invented by theologians for the sole purpose of completing a logical construction.[109]

---

[108] Aulén opposes this "dramatic" view of the atonement which he finds not only in the New Testament but also in the Fathers (particularly in Irenaeus and Augustine) to the "Latin" view which was elaborated by Anselm and remained prevalent all through the Middle Ages. In the former, God himself acts as the sole effective agent of the redemptive work, by overcoming in Christ the hostile powers which held man in bondage. God is reconciled by his own act in reconciling the world to himself. No anti-thesis exists between Incarnation and atonement. The Latin view, on the contrary, assumes that *man* must make the satisfaction for his transgression. This is done by Christ, the only man without guilt. Incarnation and atonement are separated. *Christus Victor,* tr. by A. G. Herbert (London: S.P.C.K., 1937), pp. 50–51, 94, 102–3.

[109] In a few phrases D. M. Baillie disposes of whatever is left in today's theology of the satisfaction theory. "Throughout the whole of the New Testament material there is no trace of any contrast between the wrath of God and the love of Christ, or of the idea that God's attitude to sinners had to be changed by the sacrifice of Christ from wrath and justice to love and mercy . . . There is in the New Testament no uniformity of conception as to *how* this sacrifice brings about the reconciliation; and indeed some of its interpretations of the meaning of the Cross are in terms drawn from quite other realms than that of the sacrificial system. But in whatever way the process of salvation through the Cross is conceived, God's merciful attitude toward sinners is never regarded as the result of the process, but as its cause and source." *God Was in Christ,* pp. 186, 188.

The most puzzling fact about the notion of sacrifice is that it continues to occupy a central place in the thinking of most faiths, although the act itself is hardly ever performed outside primitive cults. Nor do I see very well how it could be performed in modern life. Human sacrifices went out of fashion at an early stage of civilization. Animal sacrifices have become equally repulsive. We would even frown upon the destruction of food and lifeless offerings for cultic purposes. Judaism illustrates the point most interestingly. Although sacrifice occupies a major place in the Law, Reform and Conservative Jews have eliminated it altogether. Now the question arises: Can an internal disposition alone substitute for the entire act?[110] Inevitably, once man becomes reflectively aware of the symbolic meaning of sacrifice, he internalizes his attitude toward it. But must he at that moment abandon the external act? To be sure, if the ritual act offends his sensibilities it is also experienced as an inadequate symbol and it loses its symbolic value. Nevertheless, the attitude itself would seem to require some external symbol.

Christianity solved this problem by means of a commemoration of Christ's sacrifice, a solution which created quite a few problems of its own. Furthermore, the Christian faith arrived at a time when the tendency was already to interiorize the sacrificial cult.[111] Christians had to decide to what extent the sacrifice of

[110] Richard L. Rubenstein questions this in "Atonement and Sacrifice in Contemporary Jewish Liturgy" in *After Auschwitz* (Indianapolis: Bobbs-Merrill, 1966), pp. 92–111. Rubenstein's reasons for reclaiming the sacrificial ritual are in no way "orthodox": for him sacrifice alone liberates man from dangerous feelings of guilt by allowing him to re-enact his psychic dilemmas.

[111] The new attitude is clearly described in the Epistle to the Hebrews:
"Sins can never be removed by the blood of bulls and goats.
That is why, at his coming into the world, he says:
Sacrifice and offering thou didst not desire,
But thou hast prepared a body for me.
Whole-offerings and sin-offerings thou didst not delight in.
Then I said, 'Here am I: as it is written of me in the scroll,
I have come, O God, to do thy will.'" (Heb. 10:4–7)
The interiorizing trend was continued by Church Fathers and Medieval theologians. Augustine writes: "A sacrifice is the visible sacrament or sacred sign of an invisible sacrifice . . . And so, when it is written, 'I desire mercy

Christ's death could be made present in a symbolic rite. It is well enough known how the answer has divided Christianity. All accepted a commemorative rite. But is this rite only a symbolic commemoration (even with a physical presence of the victim) or is it a true sacrifice itself? According to Catholic tradition it is. Its theologians quote texts from Augustine to the Council of Trent to support the thesis that the Mass is more than a non-sacrificial commemoration.[112] Usually, they justify the actuality of the sacrifice by distinguishing the sacrifice itself, which re-

---

rather than sacrifice,' nothing else is meant than that one sacrifice is preferred to another; for that which in common speech is called sacrifice is only the symbol of the true sacrifice. Now, mercy is the true sacrifice . . ." (*The City of God*, Bk. 10, Ch. 5. Tr. by Marcus Dods in *Great Books of the Western World*, Vol. 18, Chicago: University of Chicago Press, 1952, pp. 301–2. Yet precisely the awareness of this symbolic character requires a visible expression. *Op cit.*, Bk. 10, Ch. 19.) St. Thomas for whom a sacrifice is "a reminder of divine things even in the order of sensible things" (*Summa Contra Gentiles*, Bk. 3, Ch. 119, 1) also places all the emphasis of the passion of Christ on its internal aspect. (*Summa Theologiae*, III, 48, 3, ad. 3.) In his commentary on Thomas' *Summa*, Cajetan transforms this emphasis into an absolute distinction between external and internal sacrifices. "For in sacrifices which consist in action, the sacrificial rite is external, as in the sacrifices of animals and of the altar. But in the sacrifices which consist in suffering, the sacrificial rite is to be found in the interior action, wherein a person offers his suffering of his own free will. And thus Christ offered his sacrifice by an interior action, while the outward action of his executioners was not sacred, it was rather a dreadful sacrilege." Text cited and translated in Maurice de la Taille, *The Mystery of Faith*, I, p. 43. Taken literally Cajetan's words would abolish the external aspect altogether—the exact opposite of what Thomas had in mind.

[112] See Maurice de la Taille, *op. cit.*, pp. 96–122, 197–222. Meanwhile one should not exaggerate the "sacrificial" thesis. It is generally agreed among Catholics that no true immolation takes place on the altar and that all relation to the immolative act is purely symbolic. Also, those who defend the sacrificial nature of the rite do not claim that an entirely new sacrifice takes place each time, but rather that the original sacrifice is being *re-enacted*. A well-known passage of John Chrysostom stresses the identity of the Eucharistic sacrifice with the original event: "Do we not offer every day? Yes, indeed we do, but by making a memorial of his death: the victim is one, not many. How is it one and not many? Because it was offered once, like that other in the Holy of Holies. . . . We do not offer another sacrifice as the High Priest did, but we always offer the same; or rather we make a commemoration of the sacrifice." In *Hebraeos*, Hom. 17, 3. P.G. 63, 131.

mains identical with that of Calvary, from the mode of offering which is new in each Mass. Protestant Christians deny the sacrificial nature of the present commemoration of Jesus' supper and death: they accept a real communion but not a real sacrifice. Basic as the difference seems to be, the distinction ultimately depends only on an interpretation of symbolic re-enactment. Those who defend the actuality of the sacrifice are willing to go further in their interpretation of re-enactment than those for whom only the presence of the victim is re-created. Yet both unquestioningly accept the principle of re-presentation.[113] It is impossible for philosophy to take position on these issues since they are related to the very formation of religious symbols rather than to reflection upon this formation. Yet from the preceding theory of sacrifice it would seem to follow that *if one accepts the commemorative rite as a true sacrifice,* some sort of communion is essential to it.

[113] The extent to which they accept it is a matter which also separates Catholics from Catholics, and Protestants from Protestants. Among Protestants a great variety of interpretations exists on the "presence" of Christ in the communion, ranging from entirely "real" to purely "symbolic." Similarly, in the Catholic Church opinions differ about the mode in which the immolation is symbolically re-enacted and, above all, about the question whether the communion is an essential part of the sacrifice.

Chapter 5
The Symbolism of Words

1. RELIGIOUS LANGUAGES

The term religious language needs some justification. It is by no means obvious that the various religious usages of language can be reduced to a common denominator. Does the language of worship and sacrament have enough in common with the language of dogmatic theology or of the Biblical narratives to warrant a common name? A complete answer to this question requires a more intimate and comprehensive acquaintance with various types of religious literature of the past than I possess. But if I limit the argument to the various forms of religious speech used by modern man in the Judeo-Christian tradition I believe that the common term religious language may be justified on the basis of a common model of interpretation. All religious speech requires *faith* for its understanding, that is, it invites the listener to surpass the phenomenal world in a way which essentially differs from the demands of poetry, scientific language, philosophical discourse or the ordinary, functional speech we use going about our business in everyday living.[1]

Symbols can be religious in many ways but only words can name the sacred directly.[2] For language alone is sufficiently flexi-

[1] Cf. Joseph Bochenski, O.P., *The Logic of Religion* (New York: New York University Press, 1965), p. 94.
[2] "The Word and the Eucharist" in *Theological Investigations*, IV, pp. 266–67.

ble to mean explicitly reality other than the one to which its symbols refer in a nonreligious context. Two elements are important in this statement. (1) Language refers to *reality*. (2) Language alone can explicitly and directly refer to a *metempirical* reality. The first phrase requires little justification, I believe. Language alone can make us fully aware of the real as such, for language alone conceptualizes and only through concepts does the mind become aware of its own structuring activity and, thereby, of the real *as such*. Naming the real is not always the main purpose, for words may function in a number of roles: to express emotions, to symbolize feelings, to articulate aesthetic appearances. But even in those instances language implicitly refers to the real. Now in the religious act the affirmation of reality is primary. Earlier I have shown the ontic quality of every religious act: the discovery of a new reality is indeed the first and most basic characteristic of the religious experience. This reference to a transcendent reality makes religious symbols dependent upon language. Not all symbols are based upon language; nonverbal aesthetic symbols, for instance, need language only for further interpretation, not for basic understanding.[3] Religious symbols alone need language to be explicitly (that is, conscious of the sacred *as such*) religious.

Our second thesis, that language can directly refer to a metempirical reality, requires considerably more justification. Many people would reply that language is not fit to assert a reality beyond the empirical world. To do so it would have to use identical words with entirely different meanings. Moreover, what religious language refers to is not objectively verifiable; it can never compel the universal consent which ordinary and scientific language expects and achieves. What the believer considers to be eminently real, is to the nonbeliever a mere projection of a subjective experience. Neopositivist philosophers have therefore concluded that religious language is meaningless and, since it is also misleading in its reality claims, that its existence cannot be justified.

In the second chapter we saw that the criterion of empirical

[3] In this I disagree with Paul Ricoeur, *De l'interprétation* (Paris, 1965), pp. 23–24.

verifiability can obviously not apply to a language which pretends to go beyond the empirical. Success with that principle could only mean defeat for its transcendent claim. The basic linguistic thesis of neopositivism is that all language of reality must be structured upon the pattern of the physical sciences, that it must mean a *thing* if it is to mean the real.[4] But when religious man speaks of the transcendent he never speaks, or at least he should never speak, of a reality existing alongside the objects to which science and ordinary speech refer. Religious language never "intends" its referent as an object. This means that it never refers to it in the way science or common observation grasp an object. Instead of pointing outward, religious language must turn inward.

Despite their acceptance of the neopositivist restrictions, some analysts nevertheless attempt to justify religious language. A strange example of such an effort is Professor J. J. C. Smart's discussion of the existence of God. Smart begins with the assumption of Wittgenstein's *Tractatus* that all metaphysical questions are meaningless. Consequently, "Does God exist?" is not a proper question. Yet, in his effort to keep the religious position from being absurd, Smart makes the believer avoid posing the question:

> The question "Does God exist?" has no clear meaning for the unconverted. But for the converted the question no longer arises. The word "God" gets its meaning from the part it plays in religious speech and literature, and in religious speech and literature the question of existence does not arise.[5]

This statement is false both in fact and in principle. In fact faith is not a definitive acquisition and most believers intermittently face the question of God's existence. Nor do I see how the transition from unbelief to belief could be made without raising this question. Once the problem of God is eliminated, surely the

[4] Wilfred C. Smith, *The Meaning and End of Religion* (New York: New American Library, 1964), pp. 164–67.

[5] J. J. C. Smart, "The Existence of God" in Antony Flew and Alasdair MacIntyre, eds., *New Essays in Philosophical Theology* (New York: Macmillan, 1964), p. 41.

possibility of an existence in which the word of God makes sense must likewise disappear. The principle involved in Professor Smart's position raises even more serious problems. The purpose of religious language is to assert the transcendent as *real.* This is the main reason why religious man has recourse to language. Smart, however, seems to regard language as a purely formalistic game, deprived of any relation to the real and allowing no other questions than whether or not a particular concept fits into a particular language. Any reference to the extra-linguistic reality, including the very experience which language is attempting to articulate, must be treated as "metaphysical," that is, as meaningless.

Thomas McPherson's essay on "Religion as the Inexpressible" also combines a sympathetic appreciation of religious language with the position that statements not verifiable by sense experience are nonsense.

Nonsense is a pejorative word, and people do not like being told that they are talking nonsense. Theologians like it as little as anyone else. People who insult one are one's enemies. So the positivists are enemies of religion. I want to say that this opinion may be a mistaken one . . . Perhaps positivistic philosophy has done a service to religion. By showing in their own way, the absurdity of what theologians try to utter, positivists have helped to suggest that religion belongs to the sphere of the unutterable.[6]

Thus religious questions may be illegitimate, but the unutterable experience is a fact. It cannot be translated into rational language, although one can rationally write about it. I reply: If religious man insists upon using language, his reason for doing so is not the pleasure of indulging in rationalist, superfluous speculation, but the inability to be religious without it. Nor can the function of religious language be reduced to an expression of emotion without belying religious man's most basic belief, namely, to be speaking about what is. Faith may be suprarational but it is anything but "unutterable."

[6] In *New Essays in Philosophical Theology,* pp. 140–41.

The Oxford Professor R. M. Hare proposes that religious statements contain no information on the objective world but reveal the outlook of the speaker, his general attitude toward life. Hare calls this outlook a blik. Differences among bliks cannot be settled by observation of what happens in the world.[7] Since all truth must ultimately be verifiable by empirical observation, religious statements are neither true nor false. Nevertheless, Hare refers to certain bliks as sane and others as insane. The admission is significant, for religious man does not regard his "outlook" to be logically arbitrary. He adopts it because he considers it to be true and the opposite false. Similarly, religious statements to him contain not only meaning but truth.

Professor R. B. Braithwaite of Cambridge University reduces the intellectual content of religious language even further. He regards religious assertions as mere expressions of intent:

> Just as the meaning of a moral assertion is given by its use in expressing the asserter's intention to act, so far as in him lies, in accordance with the moral principle involved, so the meaning of a religious assertion is given by its use in expressing the asserter's intention to follow a specified policy of behavior.[8]

Braithwaite admits that a religious assertion, unlike a moral one, always refers to a "story." But, he explains, the connection between choosing a certain way of life and accepting these stories is purely accidental. People find it easier to overcome obstacles in following their fundamental option if the latter is symbolized in a story. The truth or falsity of the story is totally irrelevant to this basic purpose: fictional stories like *Pilgrim's Progress* are just as inspiring as the more or less factual reports of the Gospel. Religious statements thus become a subclass of moral assertion. Once again religious language is said to be meaningful without

[7] "Theology and Falsification" in *New Essays in Philosophical Theology*, p. 101.

[8] *An Empiricist's View of the Nature of Religion* (Cambridge: Cambridge University Press, 1955), p. 10.

possessing any claims to truth, or even making any such claims. Believers will take issue with Braithwaite's interpretation which so clearly inverts their scale of priorities. To them the "stories" (a poor term to describe the content of their faith) are true and determine their conduct which, by their own admission, often falls short of what faith requires.

The preceding and similar positions have their origin in the last pages of Wittgenstein's *Tractatus Logico-Philosophicus,* in which the limitations of language are described. Language can deal only with the question *how* the world works. But this does not encompass all reality. *"How* things are in the world is a matter of complete indifference for what is higher. God does not reveal himself *in* the world."[9] "The sense of the world must lie outside the world."[10] After all the *how* questions have been answered, man is still left to wonder about the world as a whole. This is the realm of the "mystical" which includes, at least potentially, the religious. "Feeling the world as a limited whole— it is this that is mystical."[11] "It is not *how* things are in the world that is mystical but *that* it exists."[12] Wittgenstein freely admits that all the problems of life would still remain after all scientific questions had been solved.[13] But these problems are meaningless as *questions:* "There are things that cannot be put into words: they make themselves manifest: they are what is mystical."[14] This is what McPherson called the "unutterable" reality.

It is, of course, well known that in his later *Philosophical Investigations* he changed his position considerably by allowing for a number of languages, each of which would follow its own rules which cannot be determined by another language. But, the less iconoclastic variety of linguistic analysis is not necessarily

---

[9] Wittgenstein, *Tractatus,* 6.432. Tr. by D. F. Pears and B. F. McGuinness (London: Routledge & Kegan Paul, 1961).
[10] *Tractatus,* 6.4.
[11] *Tractatus,* 6.45.
[12] *Tractatus,* 6.44.
[13] *Tractatus,* 6.52.
[14] *Tractatus,* 6.522.

more friendly toward the claims of religious language.[15] The ultimate problem is not whether a consistent religious language is possible, but whether such a language is able to deal with reality and, most importantly, with reality as it transcends the empirical world. Until such a possibility is fully recognized little will be gained by the admission of consistency. In the meantime, one of the most promising fields for linguistic analysis has remained largely unexplored as a result of metaphysical prejudices.

Neopositivists are not alone in questioning the meaningfulness of religious language. Naturalists, to the extent that they deal with linguistic problems, have held similar views. John Herman Randall, for instance, believes that religious language does not give us any information about the world which could not be discovered by empirical methods. Neither does it inform us of any "objects" other than those which fall under the empirical sciences. Nevertheless, religious language is more than an emotional response or an experience; to religious man at least, it reveals something. Randall calls this an "insight" or a "vision" because although it provides no information about any verifiable reality, it enlightens experience by symbolically anticipating future experience. Thus religious symbols become beacons for action, images of man's creative potential.

Religious symbols serve not as instruments of "knowledge" based on an experience of what the world has done, or how it has behaved and acted in the past, of the resources it has been found to provide for men, but rather as instruments of "insight" and "vision," of what it could do, of what it might offer, of what it might become and be. Religious symbols are thus like Platonic Ideas, which themselves developed from a refinement of the Pythagorean religious symbols: they do not tell us that anything is so, they rather make us see something. They enable us to discern possibilities beyond the actual, powers not yet fully realized; and in so doing they disclose what the nature of things "really is."[16]

[15] John Macquarrie, *God-Talk* (New York: Harper & Row, 1967), p. 61.
[16] John Herman Randall, *The Role of Knowledge in Western Religion* (Boston: Starr King Press, 1958), pp. 117–18.

Is this all? Does religious language only convey what we can hope for? It would seem to me that what religious man primordially affirms is what he cannot hope for in this world, what lies entirely beyond his potential. For Randall, God is merely "an intellectual symbol for the religious dimension of the world." Transcendence is not absolute but relative; man constantly overcomes it as he realizes his dreams. Randall's position is not primarily linguistic. Criticism should be directed not so much at his views on religious language as at a naturalistic interpretation of religion which he shares with many in North America and of which the British philosopher John Hick has exposed the implicit assumptions.

> Randall's theory of religion and of the function of religious language expresses with great clarity a way of thinking which in less clearly defined forms is widespread today and is, indeed, characteristic of our culture. This way of thinking is epitomized in the way in which the word "Religion" (or "faith" used virtually as a synonym) has largely come to replace the word "God." In contexts in which former generations objections were raised and debated concerning God, his existence, attributes, purpose and deeds, the corresponding objections today typically concern Religion, its nature, function, forms, and pragmatic value. A shift has taken place from the term "God" as the head of a certain group of words and locutions to the terms "Religion" as the new head of the same linguistic family.[17]

It is obvious that in such an interpretation, religious "truth" is not what the believer thinks it to be. God is a mere symbol for aspirations whose true nature religious man does not recognize.

This failure on the part of religious man to understand his own "truth" distinguishes Randall's position from that of Smart, and even more from that of Hare and Braithwaite. For them, religious discourse makes no truth claims at all, and the religious man has no need to be "straightened out" by the philosopher. He was right all along.

[17] *Philosophy of Religion* (Englewood Cliffs, N.J.: Prentice-Hall, 1963), pp. 87–88.

In contrast with the preceding interpretations I consider religious language to be basically *thetic,* that is, positing a reality beyond the subjective experience of the speaker and the objective reality of the world. Undoubtedly, religious language often takes the form of a poetic expression (as in the Psalms) or a value judgment (as in the Beatitudes) or an imperative (as in the Decalogue). But all such nonthetic statements retain their religious character only through the language in which the believer claims to express *what is.* This is particularly true for the religious language *par excellence,* prayer, which is always foremost a confession of God's reality, an exclamation of wonder that He is there. Now, to the extent that religious speech is *thetic,* the terms truth and falsity definitely apply to it. It may be a language of commitment, but this commitment itself presupposes an intellectual and intentional act which accepts as *true,* that is, as really existing, that to which one commits oneself.

2. CHARACTERISTICS OF RELIGIOUS LANGUAGE

One characteristic of religious language stands out immediately. Religious language reflects a more intimate connection between the speaker and the spoken than ordinary language. Unlike scientific and ordinary language, religious language does not refer to an object but to a more fundamental reality in which the subjective is united with the objective. Moreover it refers to this reality as transcendent and thereby differs from aesthetic language which asserts a similar unity *within* the subject. Unfortunately, religious people all too often attempt to assert transcendence by means of some sort of hyper-objectivity. They resist those who reduce all meaningful speech to object-languages. But their own God is described entirely in object terms, either far away or deep within.[18] Western religious man shares a great

[18] David Burrell, "God: Language and Transcendence" in *God, Jesus, Spirit,* ed. by Daniel Callahan (New York: Herder and Herder, 1969), p. 42.

deal of the prejudices of his objectivist critics, particularly the one that language can be meaningful only when it means an *object*. Yet as long as he continues to discourse about God "objectively," he exposes himself to all the criticism of his opponents, since there can be no object called God.

Ian Ramsey in his perceptive little study *Religious Language* was fully aware of the subjective nature of religious language. He ascribed it to the total commitment which, in his view, characterizes the religious attitude. The term is somewhat ambiguous. If commitment means that the subject is vitally involved with what he speaks about, religious language is unquestionably committed. But other meanings interfere which seem to make the term too restrictive and even, in some instances, wholly inadequate. For Ramsey, the phrase "God is love" is a tautology in that both terms reveal the same source of ultimate commitment. If the story of God's love were properly understood, we should respond: "Love so amazing, so divine, demands my soul, my life, my all."[19] Perhaps we should, but is that really what we mean when we say that God is love? Is Ramsey not mistaking a particular, ideal way of being religious for the involvement essential to the religious attitude? I would think it possible to make religious statements without any commitment whatever. Is this not what the sinner does? Or does he cease to be religious for being a sinner? Even the theologian while writing about religious matters is directly committed only to his work.[20] I therefore believe the subjective involvement of religious statements to be of a more general nature. Ideally this involvement would lead to a full commitment, but it may very well remain on that level to which the theologian refers as "faith without works." The language of "commitment" is one particular form of religious language; it is by no means the only one or even the most common. In Scripture, for instance, we encounter mostly a language of disclosure which

[19] *Religious Language An Empirical Placing of Theological Phrases* (New York: Macmillan, 1967), p. 52.
[20] Donald D. Evans considers the purely descriptive use of religious language secondary and dependent upon the primary "involved" use. Cf. *The Logic of Self-Involvement* (London: S.C.M. Press, 1963), pp. 50–51.

is primarily instructive (in parables, historical narratives, moral precepts, etc.).

A second pitfall to avoid is the opinion that a subjective involvement makes religious statements *purely* subjective. Such an interpretation would lead us right back to the position criticized in the preceding section. The religious act always asserts a reality *which cannot be identified with the self* even though the self must be included in it. The transcendent nature of the religious *noema* requires that it always be proposed as terminal of an *intentional* act—not as a mere experience.[21] This imposes some difficult conditions upon religious language, for the only thetic language man possesses is object-language. How can religious speech avoid being objective while doing full justice to God's transcendence?

The oldest way of coping with this problem is the analogy of predication. Scholastic authors applied this Aristotelean notion to God language in order to avoid, on the one hand, univocal talk about God which, however superlative, would never cease to be creature talk and, on the other, equivocal talk which, however earthbound in its origin, would be compelled to abandon any hope of saying anything meaningful. The main texts of Thomas Aquinas on analogy are found in *Summa Theologiae* I, 13, 5 and 6, and *Summa Contra Gentiles* I, 34. On the basis of these texts his commentator, Cajetan, made the classical distinction between analogy of attribution and analogy of proportionality in *De Nominum Analogia*.[22] The analogy of attribution predicates a quality properly and formally of one subject, and analogously of other subjects according to their relation to the first subject. The example, already found in Aristotle, of such an analogy is the quality of health, which can be ascribed to medicine (which may restore health), urine (which may be a sign of health), and a bodily organism (which properly possesses health). Thus Caje-

[21] I understand this distinction in the sense which Edmund Husserl gave it in his *Logische Untersuchungen*, particularly in the first critical part, the *Prolegomena* (5th ed. Tübingen, 1968).
[22] *Scripta Philosophica*, ed. by P. N. Zammit, O.P., revised by P. M. Hering, O.P. (Rome, 1952). To what extent Cajetan's distinction reflects Thomas' text, see Ralph McInerny, *The Logic of Analogy* (The Hague, 1961), pp. 1–23.

tan ascribes goodness to God in the formal sense, and to creatures by an "extrinsic nomination."[23]

The question is: Does this really enable us to say anything meaningful about God? Only if we first know how to speak meaningfully about God. But that was precisely the problem.[24] To learn something analogically about God you must first know something about him literally.[25] Moreover, the analogy of attribution still leaves us with the task of sorting out which qualities may be predicated of God, since God is the Creator of all finite beings and yet some perfections obviously do not apply to him.

Turning now to the analogy of proportionality, we find an analogy between two *relations* rather than two terms. The relation between divine goodness and God may be called analogous to the relation between human goodness and man.[26] But here again a statement of analogy, to be truly informative, must have at least three familiar terms. In the case of God, however, neither the attribute nor the essence nor the relation between them is known. Consequently, we do not really know whether equivocation can be avoided, and any attribution of a known term becomes meaningless. Neither do we know whether one term is more meaningful than any other.[27] An additional difficulty affects the analogy of proportionality: ignorance of two terms of the relation renders the relation itself problematic. In saying that the notion of goodness must be present in God in a way which resembles its presence in man because God is at the origin of

[23] *De Nominum Analogia,* a. 11.

[24] Frederick Ferré puts his finger on it. "The analogy of attribution allows us to remain in ignorance of the formal nature of one of the analogates; our aim, on the contrary, was to speak of these very formal characteristics of God and somehow to justify our language about them. The analogy of attribution tells us nothing we did not know before: it merely tells us that whatever is capable of producing an effect may have applied to it ("virtually") the term properly signifying that effect thanks solely to the fact that—it is able to produce that effect." (*Language, Logic and God,* New York: Harper & Row, 1969, pp. 73–74.)

[25] See William Christian, *The Problem of Religious Knowledge,* p. 66.

[26] For an excellent exposition and some of the problems, see E. L. Mascall, *Existence and Analogy,* pp. 102ff.

[27] Antony Flew, *God and Philosophy* (New York: Harcourt, Brace & World, 1966), p. 39.

all goodness, we must be aware that not only the goodness is analogous but also the *resemblance of the relation*. "This seems to leave one in a regress of analogical explanations."[28] Most philosophers prefer a less slippery principle of interpretation.

Yet the obvious nature of the objections should alert us to the possibility that the function of analogy is neither to provide new information about God nor to be a complete grammar and vocabulary for the production of meaningful religious language. Rather, analogy is a rule of logic which helps us define the limits of speech about God, *should such speech ever become possible from other sources*. A recent study makes precisely the point that the analogy of names in St. Thomas is not a metaphysical doctrine, but exclusively a logical one.[29] The author defines logical relations as "relations which are attributed to known things *precisely insofar as they are known*."[30] The analogy of names is not, then, a tool for invention; it is an instrument of discipline, a method of keeping order in one's thinking. In analogy we merely compare two sets of language: we do not compare God as he is in himself with the creatures.[31] Analogy does not teach anything new about God or about our way of speaking of him. Rather than being a method for speaking directly of God, it is the basis of religious speech. It merely reminds us that all expressions about God remain expressions about man.[32]

[28] William A. Christian, *The Problem of Religious Knowledge,* p. 67.
[29] Ralph McInerny, *The Logic of Analogy* (Notre Dame: University of Notre Dame Press, 1961), particularly Chapter II.
[30] *Logic of Analogy,* p. 41, italics mine.
[31] "If we allow ourselves to examine the logic of analogy as one means of providing criteria for the disciplined use of ordinary language in theological contexts, looking for its value on the 'formal' rather than the 'material' mode of speech, much that may be of interest to us remains." Frederick Ferré, *Language, Logic and God,* p. 76.
[32] This interpretation is not new. Étienne Gilson wrote long ago that to attribute to God the name of a perfection corresponding to a certain quality in his creatures is not to posit God as resembling his creature; it is to build upon the certainty that, since each effect resembles its cause, the creature from which we start must resemble God. *Le Thomisme* (Paris, 1948), p. 157. I would not describe the relation between Creator and creature as one of causality.

3. THE LANGUAGE OF PARADOX

Bishop Ramsey's theory of models and qualifiers is related to the concept of analogy, and yet entirely different in purpose. Here we have an attempt to understand how religious language is *created*, rather than how it can be logically *controlled*. God language takes as model a familiar situation but qualifies it in such a way that the religious event appears highly unfamiliar. Ramsey illustrates this by means of the proposition: God is the first cause. I consider the expression unfortunate because it has no roots in religious language as such, but in an independent philosophical reflection which is itself of a questionable nature, since the term "cause" does not strictly apply to God at all. Nevertheless, the illustration makes the point: the language of causality proceeds until it reaches a point where it becomes insufficient. The qualifier "first" is then used to indicate the element for which ordinary language is not adequate. But this "first cause" is not logically parallel to the others at all: it is so unique that the term "cause" here adopts a new meaning for the understanding of which ordinary causes can be only of indirect help. This holds true for all attributes of God. They are linguistic attempts to break out of ordinary speech.

Ramsey's theory of models and qualifiers is only an application of a far more general principle: that religious language is odd language. By describing a situation in words which disconcert his normal expectations, the reader or hearer is forced to perceive it as different from the empirical situation to which it is related. This appears most strikingly in the passage of Exodus 3 in which God reveals his name. The situation has certain familiar elements: the desert, the bush, a voice, a name revealed. Yet the familiar here is so profoundly mixed with the unfamiliar that no one could possibly mistake it for an ordinary event. The bush is burning but is not being consumed. The voice does not belong to a body. The name is no name at all but a statement by which the speaker declares himself to be above all names. Seemingly normal occurrences take a strange turn. When Jesus in John 4 asks the Samaritan woman to drink, he does a perfectly normal although slightly puzzling thing. But as he tells her about her own past, the situation takes on an oddness which climaxes in his revelation of himself as the Messiah. In events like the crucifixion, the resurrection, and the virgin birth, the nature of the *event* is so totally transformed that the term is hardly appropriate at all. Fact and religious interpretation here become so closely united as to exclude any ordinary or scientific explanation.

Hamann was the first philosopher to draw attention to the oddity of all God-talk. For him divine truth appears only through the "inner lies or contradictions of reason."[33] In a Christian perspective such a contrast is inevitable since God took on the lowly appearance of a servant. But Hamann saw the language of contrasts also used among the Greeks. His *Socratic Memorabilia* anticipates in the Greek myths the Jewish-Christian paradox that a man of sorrows should be the redeemer.

> Through the cleverly devised myths of their poets, the heathen were accustomed to such contradictions until their Sophists, like ours, condemned such things as a parricide which one commits against the first principles of human knowledge.[34]

Did not the oracle of Delphi proclaim the man who was most aware of his own ignorance the wisest man on earth?

---

[33] *Konxompax, Sämtliche Werke,* ed. by Josef Nadler (Vienna, 1950), Vol. 3, p. 227. It is worth noting that Hamann also uses a stylistic procedure, the *metaschematism,* which is related to the analogy of proportionality, except that it is a creative (not merely an interpretive) device. To a set of existential relations (not directly expressible in objective language), he substitutes an analogous set of objective ones. Thus the objective events of Socrates' life are used to cmmmunicate indirectly Hamann's personal involvement and to move the reader toward similar involvements.

[34] Johann Georg Hamann, *Sokratische Denkwürdigkeiten,* in *Sämtliche Werke,* Vol. 1, p. 68. *Socratic Memorabilia,* tr. by James O'Flaherty (Baltimore: Johns Hopkins Press, 1967), p. 157. See also in the excellent introduction, pp. 78–80.

Hamann's most famous follower, Søren Kierkegaard, developed the theory of the paradox into the basis of all religious expression. He refined it to a point where it would include even language which at first sight does not appear paradoxical. For Kierkegaard all existential truth is paradoxical: an eternal truth can never be directly assimilated by an "existing" individual, that is, a subject who lives *in time*. A matter of vital importance to a subject cannot be expressed adequately in objective language; yet all language is objective. A true confrontation, then, with existential truth requires that the expression be made repellent so as to turn the subject inward and to oblige him to assimilate the truth from within. Kierkegaard refers to this as the Socratic paradox. Socratically, truth is not paradoxical by its own nature —it becomes so because of the existence in time of the individual. "When subjectivity, inwardness, is the truth, the truth becomes objectively a paradox; and the fact that the truth is objectively a paradox shows in its turn that subjectivity is the truth."[35] With a religious revelation, the situation is different. Here the paradox no longer originates in the essential difficulty encountered by an existing subject in assimilating an eternal truth, but rather in the essential disproportion between the infinite and the finite subject. A transcendent noema can in no way be directly communicated by means of objective language. The whole purpose of language in this case is to turn the subject entirely away from the objective world in which language usually applies and to drive him inside

[35] *Samlede Vaerker*, ed. by A. B. Drachmann, J. L. Heiberg, H. O. Lange (Copenhagen, 1964), XII, p. 144. *Concluding Unscientific Postcript*, tr. by David Swenson and Walter Lowrie (Princeton: Princeton University Press, 1944), p. 183. On Kierkegaard's notion of paradox one may consult Per Lønning, "Kierkegaard's 'Paradox'" in *Symposium Kierkegaardianum* (Copenhagen, 1955), pp. 156–65; N. H. Søe, "Kierkegaard's Doctrine of the Paradox," in a *Kierkegaard Critique*, ed. by Howard Johnson and Niels Thulstrup (New York: Harper & Row, 1962), pp. 207–27; Kr. Olesen Larsen, "Zur Frage des Paradoxbegiffes in *Philosophische Brocken* und *Abschliessende unwissenschaftliche Nachschrift*," in *Symposium Kierke-gaardianum*, pp. 130–47; Hermann Diem, *Philosophie und Christen-tum bei Søren Kierkegaard* (München, 1929), pp. 176ff.; and Louis Dupré, *Kierkegaard as Theologian* (New York: Sheed & Ward, 1963), pp. 131–38.

himself. The language of revelation, therefore, must be understood entirely as paradoxical, even when it appears to conform to normal usage. Kierkegaard refers to the language of Christian revelation as the absolute paradox or the "absurd."

Many have misunderstood the expression and equated it with nonsense. Yet Kierkegaard clearly distinguishes the two.[36] The religious paradox for him does not go against reason; it uses contradictory expressions to draw attention to its attempt to go *beyond* rational expression, not to destroy the laws of reason.[37] The antipathy of many linguists for the paradoxical language of religion is partly due to the fact that much of it is no more than confused language.[38] Yet after all the confusion has been cleared up, religious language is still paradoxical. The question then remains: Can paradoxical language be meaningful? Some philosophers, even some linguistic analysts, would consider paradoxical

[36] *Samlede Vaerker*, X, p. 236; *Concluding Unscientific Postscript*, p. 504. See also, *Samlede Vaerker*, VI, p. 91, *Philosophical Fragments*, p. 127. In fragments of an unpublished article written in the early eighteen fifties, Kierkegaard notes explicitly that the term "absurd," as he uses it, "is not the absurd in the ordinary sense of the word," but rather "the negative criterion of what is higher than human reason and knowledge." (*Papirer*, ed. by P. A. Heiber, V. Kuhr, E. Torsting (Copenhagen, 1909–48, X⁶, B79). The distinction is drawn even more clearly in a Journal entry of 1850:

> The absurd, the paradox, is so composed that reason by itself can in no way turn it into nonsense and show it to be nonsense; no it is a sign, an enigma, a composite enigma, about which reason is forced to say: I cannot solve this, it cannot be understood, but this does not mean at all that it is nonsense. But of course if faith is discarded and this whole sphere ignored, reason will become presumptuous and will perhaps conclude: ergo, the paradox is nonsense. (Papirer X² A 354. Both this and the preceding passage are cited in Søe, *art. cit.*, p. 219–20).

[37] This is also the interpretation of Emmanuel Hirsch, *Kierkegaard Studien*, Gütersloh, 1930–33, Vol. 2, pp. 768ff., against Bishop Torsten Bohlin in *Kierkegaards tro och andra Kierkegaardstudier* (1944), pp. 78ff. Lønning takes a somewhat different position by rejecting the alternative and declaring the paradox determined by existence rather than by reason (*art. cit.*, p. 165). This interpretation is at any rate closer to Hirsch than to Bohlin.

[38] See Ronald Hepburn, *Christianity and Paradox* (London: C. A. Watts, 1958), p. 17.

language false and yet meaningful. Thus John Wisdom writes about contradictory statements in a somewhat different context:

> The curious thing is that their philosophical usefulness depends upon their paradoxicalness and thus upon their falsehood. They are false because they are needed when ordinary language fails.[39]

This is a curious restatement of Jaspers' cipher theory. One need not call a religious paradox a necessary but "self-contradictory" statement to question whether the linguistic oddness of religious speech still attains the basic purpose of thetic language, namely, to intend the real as such.

The question must be answered on the basis of the relation between religious paradoxical language and ordinary speech. It is obvious that the paradoxical can be understood only through the nonparadoxical, for its entire purpose is to draw attention to its difference. Yet the question is: Can paradoxical language meaningfully coexist with the ordinary language upon which it relies, without one corrupting the other? Some authors answer this question affirmatively by attempting to show that the paradoxical can be reduced to the nonparadoxical. This is what William Christian describes as the "mild version" of paradoxical meaning:

> The mild version is that paradoxical expressions are necessary to suggest the extraordinariness of what is being alluded to in religious discourse. But it might be added that, though such expressions are necessary vehicles for suggestions, it is also possible to explicate these suggestions in non-paradoxical ways and to mitigate the paradoxes.[40]

That religious propositions can be reduced to nonreligious ones may be true for propositions which fulfill an auxiliary function

---

[39] "Philosophical Perplexity" in *Philosophy and Psychoanalysis* (Oxford: Blackwell, 1953), p. 50. This text was brought to my attention through Ferré's *Language, Logic and God*, p. 46. Cf. also D. M. Baillie, *God Was in Christ*, p. 110.

[40] William Christian in *The Problem of Religious Knowledge*, p. 154.

but, if it could be done for all religious propositions, faith would consist of a few empty factual statements. I therefore posit that basic religious propositions cannot be reduced to ordinary (non-paradoxical) language even though they cannot be understood without reference to it.

But then another dilemma emerges. The paradox remains paradox only within a religious context. Yet the religious paradox, by its very nature, includes all reality: faith discovers a new dimension in all aspects of life. Thus a confrontation between the strictly religious and all other aspects is inevitable. If the two are correlated in objective language, religious propositions lose their specific meaning. But if we use religious speech, the language of the paradox is carried into an area where it can only create confusion.

Is there a way out of this predicament? I believe there is, and that it can be found in the dependence of paradoxical upon ordinary language. Religious langage is often proposed as cryptic speech about a *separate reality* hidden from the nonbeliever. This view is mistaken on two counts. First, religious man knows no "separate" reality, but rather a transcendent *dimension* in the one and only reality accessible to him. Secondly, religious language is by no means cryptic. Its meaning is wide open—although disconcerting—to nonreligious man. Its relation to ordinary speech is primarily negative: it shakes man's accepted view of reality, challenges the self-sufficiency of the finite and questions the definitiveness of its limits. It also asserts that the new dimension it uncovers cannot be brought directly into words. This means that religious language is dialectically related to ordinary language as its negation and its transcendence. Without ordinary language it would have no content whatever. It provides no new information about the world. As Bochenski remarked, the Scriptures and the Creeds contain not a single term which is not either taken from nonreligious language or defined by its terms.[41] Of course, this does not imply that the understanding of those meanings requires a precise understanding of what the terms mean

41 *The Logic of Religion*, p. 95.

in ordinary language. The relation between religious language and ordinary language is unilateral: the former depends on the latter, but the latter does not depend on the former. The religious paradox presupposes what it questions: the paradoxical needs the nonparadoxical, but the converse is not true.[42] Ordinary and scientific language remain independent of the odd language of religion. However comprehensive religious propositions may be, they never interfere with the ordinary or scientific expression of the objectively real. Consequently, the paradoxical language of religion can coexist with nonparadoxical language without contaminating it. Like water and oil, the two never mix. This is not to say that religious language is appropriate to every situation. To introduce religious statements when an analysis of the objectively real is called for confuses the issue, though not the language.

From this description of the relation between religious and ordinary language it should be clear why I hesitate to separate the former from the latter. Although religious speech is distinctive in its use of odd expressions, paradoxes, and "deeper" meanings, it is questionable whether a difference which *presupposes a total dependence* warrants assigning it to a different universe of discourse. I prefer to consider religious speech a subspecies of ordinary language in which modifiers constantly negate and sublate the direct meanings. It is unique in that it never merges with ordinary expression, although it always remains intrinsically dependent upon it. However one chooses to classify it, religious language is definitely not "other" in the sense in which French differs from English, as two closed systems. Religious language constantly moves into ordinary speech. At the same time, the difference between the two is more substantial than that between two tongues. This point may seem purely technical, but the negative and dialectical relation between religious and ordinary language is essential.

[42] Authors as divergent in their convictions as Paul Tillich and Antony Flew express the same idea when they insist that the symbolic must be based upon the nonsymbolic to become intelligible. See Flew, *God and Philosophy*, p. 37; Tillich, *Systematic Theology* (Chicago: University of Chicago Press, 1957), I, p. 238.

4. THE SYMBOLIC NATURE OF RELIGIOUS LANGUAGE

As basic as its odd or paradoxical character is a trait which religious language shares with poetry. It is *symbolic*. This fact (if not the term) was known to Greeks as well as to Hebrews and primitive Christians. Early reflection narrowed it down to what we would now call the *typological* interpretation of a text by which an event comes to mean more than its actual occurrence directly implied. Striking examples of such an interpretation may be found in Israel's rereading of its own history in Psalms 104 and 105 (the exodus out of Egypt), Sirach, Ch. 44–50 (the great deeds of Israel's ancestors), Wisdom, Ch. 11–12 (exodus and the war with the Chanaanites). Indeed, the religious historiography of Israel consisted to a great extent in reinterpreting events of the past in the light of new, religiously interpreted occurrences,[43] in the way in which the Midrashim, commentaries on the Scripture, brought constantly new "hidden" meanings of the sacred texts to light.

In the Hellenistic center of Alexandria the Hebrew symbolizing trend met with Greek theories of allegorical interpretation. Together they gave birth to a Christian hermeneutical consciousness. But long before they made interpretation into an art and a science, Christians had been reinterpreting events and Scriptures. To the early Christians the entire history of Israel and its sacred writings carried a *typological* meaning. Jesus declared himself to be the fulfillment of the Law and the Scriptures.[44] The primitive Church expanded this typological interpretation until all the events of Christ's life received a deeper sense, whereby they became both illuminative of the past and salvific for the future.[45]

[43] Gerhard von Rad, *Old Testament Theology*, tr. by D. M. G. Stalker (New York: Harper & Row, 1962), Vol. I, pp. 306–54.
[44] See, among numerous others, Mt. 5:17–19; Lk. 24:25–27.
[45] This appears clearly in the Synoptics, for instance in Luke's arrangement of the largest section of his narrative as a journey to Jerusalem.

In the Fourth Gospel even material details such as bread and fish, wine and water are given a deeper, "symbolic" significance which anticipate the meanings of Eucharist and baptism. In Paul's Epistles, Adam prefigures Christ, and Hagar and Sarah the Old and New Testaments. One of the most primitive passages of the New Testament, Peter's Pentecost speech in the Acts of the Apostles, is mainly a symbolic reinterpretation of history. In declaring the true sense of Scripture the "spiritual" one, the Alexandrian theologians, Clement and Origen, merely systematized what Jews and Greeks had been doing since time immemorial.[46]

Ambrose and Augustine did in the West what Clement, Origen, Basil, and Gregory did in the East. Even the more conservative school of Antioch, traditionally opposed to the somewhat adventurous exegesis of Alexandria, interpreted Scripture "religiously," that is, symbolically. The search for a spiritual meaning of the scriptural text continued all through the Middle Ages until it was temporarily suspended by the new philological awareness of the Renaissance humanists and the theological disputes about the literal meaning of scriptural texts between Catholics and Protestants. Nevertheless, the literalism of the sixteenth century was not to become the foundation of modern scriptural hermeneutics. For gradually the awareness grew that the "letter" of Scripture itself was symbolic.[47]

Until the eighteenth century, symbolism remained primarily a principle of *interpretation* of a *given* "revealed" language, even though Medieval writers used it creatively outside scriptural exegesis. Through the studies on the origin and structure of language by early German romantics, symbolism came to be fully discovered as a *creative principle* of all religious speech. Once

[46] On Origen's concept of hermeneutics, see Henri de Lubac, *Histoire et Esprit. L'intelligence des Écritures d'apres Origène* (Paris, 1950). Also, Jean Daniélou, *Origen,* tr. by Walter Mitchell (New York: Sheed & Ward, 1955).

[47] See the magistral work of Henri de Lubac, *Exégèse médiévale* (Paris, 1959), Vols. I–II; 1961, Vol. III.

again, Hamann's role was a prominent one.[48] Inspired by the typological interpretation of the Old Testament as given in the New, Hamann attempted a similar Christian reading of Greek culture. Thus in the *Memorabilia,* he cast Socrates as the proto-type of Christ. Also Peter the Great, Noah, and a number of other historical figures appear in symbolic roles, for Hamann was convinced that all religious interpretation of history must be symbolic. Nor are the references exclusively to Christ; the Holy Spirit and the true believer are prefigured as well.[49] Hamann created his "types" with disconcerting freedom. Yet his symbolism was mainly restricted to typology, and this could never be con-sidered the essential category of religious language.

Typology is a particular form of religious symbolism, the one of which Christians have been most conscious, but which is neither universal nor essential. Even in Scripture most symbolism is not of the typological variety. An example, characteristic of the Fourth Gospel, is the episode of the blind man. The all-pervasive Johannine symbolism of light and darkness colors the entire narrative. It starts with Jesus' answer to the disciples' ques-tion why the man was born blind:

> "He was born blind that God's power might be displayed in curing him. While daylight lasts we must carry on the work of him who sent me; night comes when no one can work. While I am in the world I am the light of the world." (Jn. 9:4–5)

> Jesus cures the man and the passage closes with the following confrontation between them:

> "Have you faith in the Son of Man?" The man answered, "Tell me who he is, sir, that I should put my faith in him."

> "You have seen him," said Jesus, "indeed it is he who is speaking to you."

---

[48] That he had given the problem of language a great deal of thought is evident from his critique of Herder's prize-winning essay, *Des Ritters von Rosenkreuz letzte Willensmeynung über den göttlichen und menschlichen Ursprung der Sprache* (1772).

[49] See *Memorabilia, passim* and O'Flaherty's Introduction, pp. 80–84, 207–8.

"Lord, I believe," he said, and bowed before him. Jesus said, "It is for judgment that I have come into the world—to give sight to the sightless and to make blind those who see." (Jn. 9:36–39)

Christ is presented in these events as the light of the world and the cure of the blind man is but a symbol of the Savior's scattering of the powers of darkness.

Only symbols (in the strict sense) can provide religious language with the two essential conditions posited at the beginning of the present section: the subjective involvement of the religious speaker and the transcendent nature of his referent. Because they have not passed through the entire process of objectivation, symbolic representations are more apt to communicate the involvement of the subject than rational discourse. Of course, all linguistic expression objectivates to some extent.[50] But a symbolic one retains more of the subjective state of the speaker than a purely conceptual. Everyone knows that poetry and novels carry feelings more adequately than discursive language. For that reason students of religion, however opposed in other respects, are generally agreed that the language of faith is a language of symbols.[51] Max Müller once wrote that the whole dictionary of religion consists of metaphors even though we may have long ceased to experience them as such. Unfortunately, the subjective quality of symbols has made some interpreters conclude that religious symbols have no real reference outside the particular subjective state which they symbolize. Thus we read in a recent study on religious knowledge:

A symbol does not stand for the invisible subject-matter of religion, but *means* a state of feeling . . . The true character and function of the symbol picture cannot be understood unless one remembers all the time that its function is to bestow meaning upon feeling-

[50] It is this observation which led Kierkegaard to his theory that in faith only indirect communication is possible.
[51] To mention only a few: Peter Munz, *Problems of Religious Knowledge* (London: S.C.M. Press, 1959), pp. 53–55. Paul Tillich, *Dynamics of Faith* (New York: Harper & Brothers, 1958), p. 45. Auguste Sabatier, *Outlines of the Philosophy of Religion* (New York: Harper & Brothers, 1957), p. 321.

states and that it stands thus in a meaningful relation to the feeling-states. If the symbol picture is considered *per se*, there is a constant temptation for the traditional theologian, as we have just seen, to regard it as the symbol of the invisible.[52]

To religious man the subjective nature of the religious symbol signifies the opposite: it is because of its reference to a trans-objective reality, not because of the absence of any referent, that religious language is symbolic.

Indeed, the ability of symbols to express a transcendent reality is the ultimate reason why religious man cannot dispense with them. Discursive language can convincingly show the insufficiency of the objectively real. It may even conceptualize to some extent symbolic expressions of the transcendent—if they are available. But discursive language alone is incapable of giving man's relation to the transcendent its ultimate articulation. Its concepts are too closely bound to the objective reality which they are primarily created to express. Their very adequacy in this respect is their greatest drawback for religious symbolization, since the transcendent cannot be adequately expressed. Symbolic representations are less misleading precisely because, in spite of their physical concreteness, they are less determinate in their meanings. A representation has no actual meaning at all, but only a *potential* one. To use images to convey meanings, then, is to be aware of their inadequacy. Strictly speaking, a representation *means* nothing or, if we extend the term meaning beyond its conceptual usage, it means *itself*, not anything beyond itself. At the same time, we may bestow a number of meanings upon representations. Since this meaning is known to be superimposed and consequently without pretenses of accuracy, symbols are more tractable for religious expression than concepts. To be sure, a similar superimposition of meaning can occur to concepts. But in that case the concept itself becomes symbolic and turns into a representation. This happens constantly once religion reaches the level of theological reflection. All speculations on the Holy Trinity, how-

[52] Peter Munz, *Problems of Religious Knowledge,* p. 62.

ever theoretical and abstract, are of this nature. The question even arises whether any religious concepts can be considered to be more than symbolic.

The question is a serious one, for if archaic man could assert and structure the real by means of symbols (in the narrow sense), modern man uses primarily rational concepts for that purpose. Symbolic language may be necessary, but is it still sufficient for the religious affirmation? Must the basic religious affirmation not be nonsymbolic? For years Paul Tillich pondered this question, so essential to his theory of the two stages of culture. His answer is that to satisfy the demands of the rational mind the primary reference to the transcendent must be non-symbolic. The first, nonsymbolic expression is the assertion that God is foundation of the real. Tillich formulates it in the phrase: God is the Supreme Being.[53] For Tillich, this primary affirmation merely asserts that God is "the ground of the onto-logical structure without being subject to this structure him-self."[54] *All* further statements about God must be symbolic as describing a reality which strictly conceptual language is not fit to describe. This includes all discourse, whether it be devotional, theological, or even philosophical, about the attributes of this Supreme Being. To the initial nonsymbolic assertion, God is Being, the second volume of the *Systematic Theology* added a second: The statement that everything we say about God is symbolic, is itself a nonsymbolic assertion.[55]

Yet it would seem to me that the dialectical nature of the religious affirmation does not allow any true statement about God in a single proposition. Thus divine reality cannot be asserted in the saying: God is the Supreme Being. The full assertion includes, as we shall see, a negation that God is not Being in the sense in which the creature is, and a reintegration of created being into the Divine Being. Must these further statements also be regarded as

[53] "The Religious Symbol" in *Religious Experience and Truth,* ed. by Sidney Hook (London: Oliver & Boyd, 1962), pp. 314–15. Also, *Systematic Theology,* I, pp. 235–41.
[54] *Systematic Theology,* I, p. 239.
[55] *Systematic Theology,* II, p. 9.

nonsymbolic? My answer would be that they are, but only to the extent that they affirm divine existence, not insofar as they define it beyond what is strictly necessary for a meaningful existential affirmation. This means in fact that no statement about God is *entirely* nonsymbolic, not even the primary ones, but that all discourse about God *contains* a primary, nonsymbolic dialectical affirmation. Without this man would be unable to connect divine transcendence with his world-affirmation—which means that he would not be able to affirm God at all. It would be an illusion, however, to think that by sheer power of negation one can escape the symbolic nature of God-talk.

The language of negative theology is as symbolic as that of a positive one. In declaring all divine names inadequate, negative theology conveys a symbolic message. Is the message of inadequacy conveyed *with* the representation (or the concept) not the very essence of the religious symbol? The total destruction of concept or image which distinguishes an apophatic theology from one of divine names has an eminently positive character. Tillich himself wrote that the inner attitude which is oriented to the symbol does not have the symbol itself in view but rather that which is.[56]

5. APPENDIX: THE SYMBOLISM OF RELIGIOUS ART

A few words must be said about a class of symbols which appears to straddle the fence between religion and art. I write "appears" because religious art symbols are essentially aesthetic. Still they are unique in that they express aesthetically what was originally a religious experience. Since this experience demands a

---

[56] "The Religious Symbol" in *Religious Experience and Truth*, p. 301. My interpretation seems confirmed by Johannes Hessen's statement: "Behind the negations of this apophatic theology stands a very *positive* feeling. While expressing itself in these negations it allows them to some extent to participate in its own positivity. All negations thereby take a turn towards the positive: they become signs for the intentions of religious feeling. Thus they gain a symbolic character." *Religionsphilosophie*, Vol. II (München, 1955), p. 187.

unique symbolic expression of its own, the problems of religious art are highly complex. Before venturing into them we must briefly return to the relation, similarity, and dissimilarity between the religious and the aesthetic experience.[57] The aesthetic and the religious experiences both result in a total awareness which elevates life as a whole above ordinary meaning.[58] Both create order out of chaos by integrating existence in an all-comprehensive synthesis. Both tend to be absolutist in their claims. Because of this close relationship Santayana declared art and religion basically identical. We shall have to reject this position as too simplistic. Nevertheless art and religion are intimately connected. At one time they were even indistinguishable. Primitive rites and archaic religious objects were also man's earliest artistic expressions. Art did not express an attitude independent of what we would now call religion. Indeed, it is not even correct to say that artistic achievements were *for the purpose* of expressing religious attitudes, for the terms art and religion held no separate meaning to archaic man. Art expressed life in its totality. It was "religious" in the sense that *all* life was, not in the sense that it expressed the religious *alone*. Professor Van der Leeuw's statement about the dance, the most primitive religious expression, holds for all the arts in an archaic society:

That the dance has religious meaning does not mean that it can express only religious feelings. On the contrary, all feelings, from the most solemn to the most frivolous, find their expression in the dance. The religious is not a particular sensation alongside other sensations, but the summation of them all. Thus the dance can also serve a purpose which we, too, would call religious.[59]

[57] This was first considered in Chapter 1, Section 3.

[58] "What binds art to religion is not its 'proximity to experience,' but its distance from experience . . . Only the fact that both construct their own different worlds out of the ground of all things, and that both religion and art seek to leave the boundaries of this world binds them by nature." Gerardus Van der Leeuw, *Sacred and Profane Beauty: the Holy in Art* (New York: Holt, Rinehart & Winston, 1963), p. 282.

[59] *Sacred and Profane Beauty*, p. 17.

For us life has been broken up into various compartments. Even
if we consider ourselves religious, our ordinary occupations have
become secularized. For archaic man such distinctions did not
exist. The term "religious primitive art" is a pleonasm insofar
as all primitive art is religious, and a malapropism insofar as it
is never exclusively religious.

The religious culture which usually follows upon this archaic
stage clearly draws the distinction between the sacred and the
profane. Yet life is still lived as an integrated totality of prayer,
work, and play. The attitudes of the various religions with respect
to art differ considerably, not only because of consciously adopted
policies but even more because of each faith's peculiar mode of
envisioning the infinite in the finite. It will be recalled that the
Greek religion showed in this respect an aesthetically remarkable
but religiously dangerous power of accommodation. Contrary to
the Greek sense of harmony, the Christian faith tends to absorb
the finite into the infinite and this is the reason why, according
to Schelling, it is unable to produce an aesthetic mythology. It has
symbolic actions by which the finite *passes into* the infinite, such
as the baptism of Christ, the rituals of the liturgy, the life of
the Church; it does not possess static symbols such as the
Greek gods, in which the finite *is* the infinite.[60]

At any rate, the ties between religious attitude and artistic
expression remain close even after the dispersion of the original
unity. Faith continues to express itself in liturgical action, stylized
according to aesthetic standards. The religious community prays
in song, walks in dance, speaks in poetry, and acts in dramatic
play. This is true for Christianity, Judaism, and Islam; it holds
equally true for the Oriental faiths. Even today's secular art
still moves constantly on common ground with religion. Religious
myths survive in literature. The heroes and villains on the stage

[60] Schelling, *Philosophie der Kunst,* in *Werke,* ed. by Manfred Schröter, Vol.
3, pp. 453–55. For the Greeks the world carried its meaning *in itself,* for
Christians it receives meaning only by referring to an infinite *outside* itself.
Yet although only the Greek mythology could produce absolute beauty,
Schelling nevertheless feels that the more ideal nature of Christianity could
lead to a perhaps less harmonious but deeper expression of the absolute.

and on the screen often retain the superhuman glow of demigods and devils, and frequently their messages are delivered by prophetic voices. Religious and mythical subjects remain favorite artistic subjects.

Although in a religious culture both religion and art "integrate" life, they do so in such different ways that the very possibility of a "religious" art would seem to be problematic. To begin with, the artist is able to control contrasting elements in an aesthetic harmony, but he does not resolve their conflict. The tragedy, to take a pertinent instance, brings resignation, not resolution, to the conflicting forces of life. Whether they can ultimately be resolved in a higher, all-compassing unity, is not for the artist to decide. He articulates feelings and brings a new *appearance* to reality, but he introduces no new reality. The artist brackets existence and devotes all his efforts to essence. As the English philosopher R. G. Collingwood once wrote, art *asserts* nothing. But religious faith obviously does. It claims to give a new meaning to experience by asserting a transcendent reality in which the conflicts of life become resolved. Does art become assertive when it aesthetically articulates an affirmation of faith? The question allows of no simple answer. Of course, the case is clear enough for a work of art which deals with a religious subject but does not intrinsically depend on a religious world view. Whether one is religious or not, is totally irrelevant for the creation or aesthetic enjoyment of such masterpieces as Veronese's "Supper at Levi's" (indeed that was the very objection of the Venetian Church authorities to it), or Rafael's "Disputation of the Blessed Sacrament" or Caracci's "Pietà." The religious topics here were merely occasions for the display of aesthetic qualities. Even such deeply religious works as the paintings of Duccio and Sassetta, or the fugues of Bach require no sharing of the artist's beliefs. The aesthetic form is strong to carry the whole work. But does the same hold true for a poetic expression of belief such as the concluding verses of T. S. Eliot's *Four Quartets?*

And all shall be well and
All manner of thing shall be well
When the tongues of flame are in-folded
Into the crowned knot of fire
And the fire and the rose are one.

The English philosopher Ronald Hepburn comments:

> The poet is not in such command of his material as we were
> tempted to think. His image is not self-authenticating. Its extreme
> beauty and integrating power must not lead the reader to imagine
> that its *extra*-poetic truth has been established, that the integrative
> power of the poetry is pragmatic proof of the truth of what it
> expresses. If God does not exist or if his nature is other than
> Christianity paints it, then the flame and the rose will not be
> one, and the most potent alchemy of images cannot make them
> one.[61]

Of course, not all religious poetry has the affirmative ring of
Eliot's verse. Nor does the poetic quality of a religious poem
reside in the religious assertion as such, but rather in its rhythm,
images, and symbols. Thus we may safely maintain that a full
enjoyment of the *Divina Commedia* does not require a sharing
of Dante's religious beliefs. The purity of his aesthetic sense has
converted every religious affirmation into a poetic one. There
are no *merely* didactic or religiously assertive statements in the
Commedia, and consequently every verse becomes aesthetically
self-sufficient. Art appears to be religious only if it intrinsically
depends upon an affirmation of faith, yet the affirmation itself
is never part of the aesthetic expression. Aesthetic belief differs
from religious belief even though the former may be directly
influenced by the latter. All art therefore remains primarily
aesthetic even if it happens to have religious sources.

If this were the whole truth, religious art would remain a
purely aesthetic concern, and there would be no reason to discuss

[61] "Poetry and Religious Beliefs" in *Metaphysical Beliefs,* ed. by Stephen
Toulmin (London: S.C.M. Press, 1957), p. 146.

it here. Yet the aesthetic and the religious expression never simply coexist: they affect one another. Thus we see that art constantly expands the expressive powers of religious symbolism. Aesthetic images and symbols are basically self-sufficient: they do not point beyond themselves. Religious symbols, on the other hand, indicate in their very structure the transcendent nature of the reality to which they refer. Yet the opposition is not an absolute separation, for aesthetic and religious symbols have an affinity for each other. In some experiences the two almost coincide. Thus in the feeling and articulation of the *sublime* the content overwhelms the expression so much that it eclipses the purely aesthetic form.[62] The intrinsic dynamism of the act breaks through the finite form to lose itself in a transcendent beyond. Undoubtedly, sublime art still remains aesthetic even if it climaxes in a mystical ecstasy. Nevertheless, an experience of this nature reveals a common border between the aesthetic and the religious.

Yet art and religious faith share more than a border. Despite the differences in symbolization, aesthetic images are constantly used to express religious experiences. The religious artist receives his basic symbols from faith, but he combines them into entirely new patterns. The aesthetic imagination enjoys a freedom which the less playful religious symbolizing activity lacks, but which it needs to rejuvenate its traditional symbols. Thus old religious meanings are brought to life through new aesthetic processes. The entire Christian iconography as well as the liturgy consist of aesthetic variations on religious symbols. The aesthetic imagination can take even greater liberties which are no longer acceptable within the cult, by placing the content of faith in a new, imaginary setting. This is what happened when the mystery plays moved from the sanctuary into the churchyard, when the Gospel narrations spawned apocryphal legends, when ecclesiastic chant gave birth to religious song. But the same aesthetic impulse also produced the *Divina Commedia, Paradise Lost,* the *Passions* of Bach and the *Messiah* of Handel. In all these cases the

---

[62] Libert Vander Kerken, *Religieus Gevroel en Aesthetisch Ervaren* (Antwerp, 1947), pp. 67, 91.

aesthetic symbolization is so closely connected with the religious one that we may speak of a "double symbolization." Moreover, religious artists depend on the iconographic principles of the tradition which they express. The prohibition of graven images in Judaism and Islam compelled the artists of those cultures to explore new avenues of symbolization.

Because faith *needs* the artistic expression, art ends up changing faith itself. Thus Grünewald's "Crucifixion" anticipated the spirit of the Reformation. Artists change the tradition which they express, not because they prefer to ignore the original message but because they consider it inadequately expressed in the art forms of the past. New forms of expression open new perspectives on the content of faith and inevitably lead to conflicts with religious authorities who tend to identify the content of faith with its traditional expression. Almost every innovation in religious art has been accompanied by cries of blasphemy.

I called the conflict inevitable, for religion is just as absolutistic as art: it has no desire to release its hold over what it considers to be *its own* expression. "Holy power no more allows itself to be ruled by art than art allows itself to be constrained by holy power."[63] Indeed, religious faiths regularly revolt against their own need to express the infinite in finite form. Iconoclastic movements are a regular religious phenomenon and, at least in some instances, they have achieved lasting effects. Judaism and Islam gradually managed to suppress all direct representations of the sacred. Christianity adopted more tolerant habits but not without violent interruptions, one of them as late as the sixteenth century. Moreover, the arts were allowed only for nonaesthetic purposes. The documents of the Council of Constantinople (869–70) which firmly re-established the cult of images after the iconoclastic outbursts of the Byzantine emperors, can hardly be considered a charter for the pursuit of aesthetic excellence:

Just as all men receive salvation from the syllables contained in the gospels, so also all men, learned and ignorant alike, receive their

[63] G. Van der Leeuw, *Sacred and Profane Beauty*, p. 268.

share of that boon through the channel of the colored images placed under their eyes. For that which language says and preaches by means of syllables, that writing says and preaches by means of colors.[64]

Nor did the presence of a number of worldly prelates and art Maecenases raise the aesthetic standards for religious art established by the Council of Trent: sacred images remain exclusively objects of veneration or instruction.[65] Not even an allusion to artistic quality! Étienne Gilson concludes from those documents that the value of religious art for the Church is determined entirely by its success or failure to achieve the ends of instructing and edifying.[66] Since there is no standard recipe for exciting piety in all men, regardless of age and education, the safest course is on the conservative side. Religious authorities tend to stay with the proven formula, however inferior its quality may be. Their attitude reveals the schizophrenia of every religious mind with respect to the artistic expressions of his faith. Any believer who has ever entered a beautiful church knows the problem. Shall he walk around as in a museum, or kneel down and be "instructed and edified" by the images?

Interestingly enough, religious faiths seem to make few bones about the aesthetic seduction of *literary* art. In the Council text quoted above, the word was posited as the principal analogate to which all religious art had to conform. Obviously literary expression is considered indispensable to an advanced faith. It is the one art form which religious man entirely trusts. Such poetic masterpieces as Job, the Psalms, the *Bhagavad-Ghita,* parts of the Koran, and most Christian mystical writings were unquestioningly regarded as authentic expressions of the sacred.[67] The

[64] Denzinger-Bannwart, *Enchiridion Symbolorum,* edition 31 (Barcelona, 1957), ※337.
[65] *Enchiridion Symbolorum* ※987.
[66] Étienne Gilson, *The Arts and the Beautiful* (New York: Charles Scribner's Sons, 1956), p. 106.
[67] Reverence for the revealing word also appears in such terms as the Latin *vates* (designating both the poet and the prophet) and the notion of *inspiration* (referring to the poet as possessed by the divine).

Christian Churches could, despite some initial reservations, live
much more comfortably with literature (even the nonrevealed)
than any other form of sacred art. Many poems were later
elevated to the status of cultic prayer. *Vexilla Regis, Pange
Lingua, Alma Redemptoris, Veni Sancte Spiritus,* and a number of
other hymns of the Roman liturgy originated as noncommissioned
poems of private religious persons. How do we explain this
preference for the word? It is, I submit, because of the thesis
proposed earlier in this chapter: all advanced religious symbols
are either linguistic or based upon language. Symbols of the
transcendent are by their very nature obscure. Language alone
can be clearly metaphorical, that is, can evoke a contextual
meaning beyond and through its literal one.[68] All arts are
symbolic, yet language alone can do justice to the religious concern for precise meanings.

Metaphorical language is, at least in its structure, *poetic.* This
is confirmed by the literary history of Christianity: early Christian
poetry developed out of the symbolic interpretation of the
Scriptures. Philo's allegorical method provided the Alexandrian
Fathers with an instrument to discover the *gnosis* of the Scripture
beyond its obvious meaning.[69] Origen gave the method a theoretical basis, by ascribing spiritual meaning to all of Scripture
even where no acceptable literal meaning could be found.[70]
The theory ultimately resulted in the four meanings of the

[68] On this broad use of the term metaphor, see Monroe Beardsly, *Aesthetics*
(New York: Harcourt, Brace, 1958), pp. 142–43.
[69] "It is true that the symbolic technique of early Christian literature grew
largely out of Judaism, and specifically from the sort of mystical interpretation of the Scripture which we find in Philo of Alexandria, the Jewish
scholar and philosopher of the first century of our era." Herbert Musurillo,
S.J., *Symbolism and the Christian Imagination* (Baltimore: Helicon Press,
1962), p. 5. One may consult H. A. Wolfson, *The Philosophy of the Church
Fathers,* Vol. I (Cambridge: Harvard University Press, 1956), pp. 24–72;
Henri de Lubac, *Histoire et esprit. L'intelligence de l'Écriture d'après
Origène* (Paris, 1950).
[70] *First Principles,* Bk. IV, 3–5. Migne, P.G. 11, 346–51. An example of
this is the story of Adam and Eve which is "offensive to the understanding"
if taken literally but is full of "rational meaning and secret significance" if
taken allegorically. *Contra Celsum,* Migne, P.G. 11, 1086.

Scripture first stated by John Cassian (370–435) and popularized in the fourteenth-century distichon *Littera gesta docet. Quid credas allegoria. Moralis quid agas. Quo tendas anagogia.*[71] For all their arid pedantry the early Christian exegetes were the ones who opened up the Christian imagination. Medieval art cannot be understood without knowledge of the metaphorical readings of the Bible; they became the foundation of a new *Ars Poetica.*[72]

I have illustrated my case through the example of Christianity. But the influence of religious symbolism on the development of poetry and, indirectly, of all the arts, is not a uniquely Christian phenomenon. Everywhere religious symbols and myths enrich the poetic imagination. In a predominantly religious culture, as our own was until recently, they provide its main content as well as its inspiring force. Some literary critics have concluded from this that all poetry is intrinsically religious. The best known representative of this position was Henri Bremond.[73] For Heidegger also, the poet is the one who "names the gods." He intercepts their signs and interprets them. "The poet stands between . . . the gods and the people. He is the one who has been cast out—out into that *Between,* between gods and men."[74] In naming the gods the poet reveals the essence of all things.

[71] John Cassian, *Collatio,* 14, 8, in Migne, P.L. 49, 962–65. Nicholas of Lyre, *Distichon,* in Migne, P.L. 113, 28. One should compare also Dante's letter to Can Grande della Scala and St. Thomas, *Quodlibet,* VII, a 15. All these texts may be found in English translation in William F. Lynch, *Christ and Apollo,* Appendix IV by John McCall (New York: Mentor-Omega Books, 1963), pp. 220–32.

[72] William F. Lynch. *op. cit.,* p. 188.

[73] The position is most clearly stated in *Prière et poésie (Prayer and Poetry),* tr. by Algar Thorold (London: Burns, Oates & Washburne, 1927). But the same idea permeates other writings of Bremond, specifically his masterly *Histoire littéraire du sentiment religieux en France.* Although Bremond distinguishes a "natural" from a "supernatural" religious experience, it is difficult to see how "poetic grace" differs from "supernatural grace." *Prayer and Poetry,* p. 75.

[74] *Erläuterungen zu Hölderlin's Dichtung* (Frankfurt: Vittorio Klostermann, 1963), p. 43. "Hölderlin and the Essence of Poetry," tr. by Douglas Scott, in *Existence and Being* (Chicago: Henry Regnery, 1949), p. 312.

He reunites man with the foundation of his existence by establishing Being.[75]

Religious language may be called poetic in the widest sense of the term to the extent that it is metaphorical and symbolic rather than discursive. Yet poetry is not *per se* religious. Its basic orientation is to enlighten the empirical world by making its visible and audible forms transparent of a deeper reality. Religious language may develop into full-fledged poetry, as it does in a number of sacred writings. But its main purpose is not so much to enlighten experience as to refer to a "beyond" of experience.

We must now return to the question which particular characteristics distinguish religious from nonreligious art. As was pointed out, a religious subject alone does not make a work of art religious. Not every portrait of Filippo Lippi's or Rafael's mistresses may be called religious simply because it represents a Madonna. The subject was often determined by the commission rather than by the artist's own inspiration. A great artist like Memling, who painted almost exclusively religious subjects, hardly produced any truly religious art. On the other hand, a Rouault depicting the alienated, unholy condition of modern man conveys a religious impression in his portraits of clowns. Nor can we say that art is religious when it is religiously inspiring. For what is religiously inspiring to one man may appear merely sensuous to another. A great deal here depends upon the context. I remember how I considered the music of some late Medieval Flemish songs profoundly religious until I learned that the pious lyrics were only second versions succeeding explicitly erotic originals. Often a work of art impresses us religiously when it is associated with the cult. Most listeners would describe Schumann's piano music as refinedly romantic. Played on an organ in church the same compositions will be considered religious. An organist I knew used to improvise on any tune that happened to come to his mind during the quiet moments of religious services. Yet the audience easily assimilated his music to the generally religious

[75] *Ibid.*, pp. 39–40, 38, *Existence and Being,* 306, 304, 310.

atmosphere of the occasion. In fact many people consider organ music always religious because they mainly hear it in church. Such an association theory would allow no particular style to be regarded as intrinsically religious, for various cultures use different images and different musical instruments for the cult. To an African native the music of drums may sound more religious than that of an organ, and pictures which we consider to be merely obscene may be religiously inspiring to others. The religious effect, then, cannot be regarded as an adequate criterion for distinguishing religious art. Neither is the intention of the artist. For intentions alone never determine the nature of art—even in the case of skilled artists. Must we conclude that no objective criteria exist? Not quite. But I surmise that no *universal* rules could determine a form of expression as exclusively religious.

The religious experience itself is too polychromatic to be restricted to a single style of expression. Faith is not a distinct unit in the prism of human feelings, but a total attitude comprehending many feelings, and varying from one culture to another. A Catholic Christian lives his religious attitude differently than a Moslem or a Polynesian native. Even a homogeneous religious culture at a particular stage of its development requires a variety of expressions. The liturgical moods from Christmas to Easter range from joy through sadness to triumph. Within the pictorial representations of the crucifixion during a short span of time, we encounter such divergent images as Grünewald's stark dramatization, Perugino's meditative resignedness, Velásquez's triumphal majesty, Rembrandt's mysterious searching. Clearly, the religious attitude is too complex to be uniformly symbolized: it is life itself in another dimension.

Yet one basic condition is that a genuine understanding of the religious experience must determine the aesthetic articulation. Such an understanding does not require that the artist be a deeply religious person. To one Blessed Fra Angelico we can oppose a number of worldly painters, such as that most sensitive interpreter of the religious soul, Perugino, whose piety by contemporary accounts seems to have been less than average. The artist must

be acquainted with the experience and able to articulate it
aesthetically. Few religious men meet the second requirement,
even though they may feel an insurmountable urge to express
their experience in verse or color. Ignatius of Loyola was as much
a mystic as John of the Cross, but his style is pallid and
lifeless next to that of the poet of the Carmel. The absence of
aesthetic articulation dooms to insignificance most of the rhetoric
by means of which one religious faction attempts to establish
its position over another. Only if the believer has *aesthetically*
transformed his passion can real art result from religious polemics,
as it did in Pascal's *Lettres provinciales* or in the songs of the
Dutch Calvinists in their rebellion against Catholic Spain.[76]

Assuming, then, that a religious experience is at the origin of
a work of art, which principles are unique to its aesthetic articulation? I can think of only one that always applies. Religious art
differs from other art in stressing the inadequacy of its form
with respect to the expressed content. The difficulty is that it must
do so while maintaining an aesthetic harmony between form and
content, without which the symbol would cease to be artistic
altogether. Religious artists attempt to attain this uneasy balance
in a number of ways. The transcendence of the content may
be conveyed by the *monumental* character of the form. In the

[76] A great deal of the religious "art" of the Catholic culture in the preceding three centuries falls under the verdict of Paul Claudel's severe judgment:
  The art subsequent to the Council of Trent . . . seems to have taken
  for its object, not the object of the Gothic art, the *representation* of the
  concrete facts and historical truths of the Faith before the eyes of the
  public like a great open Bible, but the *demonstration* with noise, pomp,
  and eloquence, and often with the most affecting pathos, of that space,
  vacant like a medallion, access to which is forbidden to our ceremoniously
  dismissed senses. And so we have saints indicating to us by expression
  and gesture what is invisible and inexpressible; we have all the riotous
  abundance of ornamentation, angels in a whir of wings upholding a
  picture blurred and concealed by religious ceremonies, statues moved as
  it were by a great wind from elsewhere. But before that elsewhere the
  imagination recoils in terror.
Letter to Alexandre Cingria in *Revue des Jeunes,* August 25, 1919, tr. by
J. F. Scanlan, in Jacques Maritain, *Art and Scholasticism* (New York:
Charles Scribner's Sons, 1962), Appendix Note 134, p. 160.

sheer mass of stone or marble the artist attempts to show the all-surpassing nature of the sacred. The pyramids of Giza and Teotihuacán, the statues of Abu-Simbel and the colossi of Ramses II, the temples of Luxor and Karnak speak of a superhuman, supernatural reality.[77]

Another device of religious artistic expression is the incompleteness of the form.[78] In the indeterminacy the viewer or listener feels that the content of what is proposed cannot be fully comprehended in the expressive form and, consequently, that the aesthetic integration must remain incomplete. Thus originates that feeling, unique to the religious art experience, that the religious consummation inherent to the aesthetic awareness[79] is not closed, but opens up a new dimension which can no longer be articulated. Aesthetic satisfaction yields to a desire to penetrate into a trans-aesthetic area. W. H. Auden describes this incompleteness of feeling as the reader experiences it at the end of *Billy Budd:*

> If when we finish reading *Billy Budd,* we are left with questions which we feel have been raised but not answered, if so to speak the equation has not come out to a finite number, as in a work of art it should, this is not due to any lack of talent on Melville's part, but to the insolubility of the religious paradox in aesthetic terms.[80]

Finally, there exists what we might call the particular *expressiveness* of religious art. The artist attempts to go beyond the empirical and to convey the positive otherness of the religious object by deliberately distorting its forms, or by evoking strange

[77] On the massive and monumental as religious art category, see Gerardus Van der Leeuw, *Sacred and Profane Beauty,* pp. 206–7. The author draws attention to the existence of the same monumentality in the music of Bruckner and Mahler.

[78] Again I refer to Libert Vander Kerken's remarkable *Religieus Gevoel en Aesthetisch Ervaren,* p. 109.

[79] Cf. John Dewey, *Art As Experience.* Capricorn Books (New York: G. P. Putman's Sons 1958), *passim.*

[80] *The Enchafèd Flood* (London: Faber & Faber, 1951), p. 119.

contrasts. Thus he accomplishes the difficult task of revealing a metempirical reality in and through an empirical image. There is nothing religious about a man hanging on a cross. By some other device, then, he must convey a surplus of meaning beyond that of a body in ultimate pain or, as it was often for Renaissance art, a body in its naked beauty. By changing the ordinary the artist attempts to evoke the extraordinary. He may elongate the figure as Van der Weyden and El Greco did.[81] Or he may distort it as Grünewald and Servaes did. Or he may contrast it with its environment by means of an unnatural light technique as Caravaggio and Rembrandt did.[82] Or he may eliminate all distracting details and place it against a golden background of divine light as the Byzantine painters did and the Italian primitives did. But none of these procedures is intrinsically religious. Western man tends to identify the religious with emaciated bodies, subdued colors, and slow rhythms. But the fleshy Buddhas of Japan and Ceylon are equally expressive. And so are the obsessive music which accompanies orgiastic rites in primitive religions and the colorful displays of the Indians in Central and South America. No technique, style, or representation is *per se* religious. The concept of religious art is valid but must forever remain relative.

[81] Whether this procedure was *intended* for religious purposes is questionable but unimportant. Whether it was successful in the case of El Greco has been debated.

[82] On the religious meaning of Caravaggio's use of *chiaroscuro,* cf. Walter Friedländer, *Caravaggio Studies* (Princeton: Princeton University Press, 1955), esp. Ch. 5.

Chapter 6
The Myth and Its Survival

1. THE MYTH AND ITS TRUTH

The relation between religious symbol and myth cannot be defined in a single statement. Yet by way of opening the discussion we might say that myths are verbally developed symbols or, as Bachofen once wrote, that the myth is the exegesis of the symbol.[1] Originally all symbols and today all religious symbols need the verbal interpretation of the myth. "Myth—or more properly, myth ritual—brings order, meaning and structure to the world of the religious symbol."[2] Without this interpretation the primitive symbol would never have developed into the clarity of aesthetic images, religious symbols, and philosophical ideas. For myth is the language of the symbol and originally it was the only language.[3] At the same time the symbol is the exegesis

[1] Johann Jacob Bachofen, *Versuch über die Gräbersymbolik der Alten* (Basel, 1859), p. 46.

[2] Thomas Altizer, "The Religious Meaning of Myth and Symbol" in *Truth, Myth and Symbol,* ed. by Thomas Altizer, William A. Beardslee, and J. Harvey Young (Englewood Cliffs, N.J.: Prentice-Hall, 1962), p. 90.

[3] The relation between myth and language has been a long standing subject of controversy. In his famous essay on the origin of speech Herder claimed that the myth gives birth to language, or at least determines the function of language. The thesis was assumed by Schelling who in his *Philosophy of Mythology* declared language a "paled mythology." *Einleitung in die Philosophie der Mythologie, Werke,* ed. by Manfred Schröter (München, 1959), Vol. 6, p. 59. For Max Müller, on the contrary, mythology was born out of

of the myth. What was still undifferentiated in the myth develops into a number of *particular* symbols structuring the various spheres of existence. There is a dialectical relation, then, between myth and symbol. The symbolic deed precedes the myth, yet the myth itself develops into specific symbols and thereby overcomes the ritual indetermination.

Let us consider now how the myth originally accompanies the rite. In her classic study on the social origins of Greek religion Dr. Jane Harrison bluntly asserted:

A *mythos* to the Greek was primarily just a thing spoken, uttered by the mouth. Its antithesis or better correlative is the thing done, enacted, the *ergon* or work.[4]

The original connection between word and deed has been preserved in religion: the mythos is the spoken accompaniment of the acted rite.

This brings us to a second point: the myth belongs in the center of religious action. Its function is not to "explain" (as one might conclude from its interpretive character), but to provide the plot of the *dromenon*, of the ritual action. An example of this is the myth of the Titans devouring Zagreus, invented to explain the central rite in the Dionysian orgies: the dismemberment of an animal endowed with sacred power.[5] Only

misinterpretations of language at a time when it was no longer correctly understood. "The Philosophy of Mythology" in *Introduction to the Science of Religion* (Oxford, 1873), pp. 353–55.

Cassirer decides the dispute by the observation that language and mythology determine each other. "They are two diverse shoots from the same parent stem, the same impulse of symbolic formulation, springing from the same basic mental activity." (*Language and Myth*, tr. by Susanne K. Langer, New York: Dover Publications, 1953, p. 88.) It is through language that the myth can develop as myth. At the same time, the development of the myth is the condition for the development of objective language.

[4] *Themis*, pp. 328.

[5] Martin P. Nilsson, *A History of Greek Religion*, tr. by F. J. Fielden (Oxford: Clarendon Press, 1949), p. 217. See also by the same author, *The Minoan-Mycenean Religion* (Lund, 1950), p. 581.

later did it become also the justification of the ritual. The intimate connection between myth and ritual action has been confirmed by a number of other scholars.[6] The myth mediates to consciousness what resides immediately in ritual activity, and thus initiates the process of reflection.

> The cult is man's active relation to his gods. In the cult the divine is not represented and portrayed indirectly; rather a direct influence is exerted upon it. It is therefore in the forms of this influence, in the forms of ritual, that the immanent prayers of the religious consciousness will, in general, be most clearly expressed. The mythical tale is itself for the most part only a reflection of the immediate relationship.[7]

The symbolic forms of ritual out of which the myth grows are much less developed than the symbols which the myth itself produces, even though they are truly symbolic. Symbols grow out of myths, then, as much as myths grow out of symbols. The myth is the mediating factor in the dialectic from primary symbols to fully conscious symbolism.

The myth introduces a new stage of consciousness: it makes reflective what before was only "lived." Yet this first and most basic awareness of inner life is not the reflection of science or philosophy or even of what we now call ordinary language. The myth does not fully objectivate. It still participates so much in the lived reality that its meaning must be felt rather than rationally understood. Although its forms are fully conscious, the form-giving roots are buried deep in subconscious soil. The interest which psychoanalysis has long taken in these subterranean roots is slowly beginning to yield some results. Freud already considered myths to reflect primitive social conditions or, perhaps, prehistorical events.[8] Yet he restricted their significance pretty

[6] For instance, K. Th. Preuss, *Der religiöse Gehalt der Mythen* (Tübingen, 1933); G. Van der Leeuw, *Religion in Essence and Manifestation*, p. 413.
[7] Ernst Cassirer, *Philosophy of Symbolic Forms*, tr. by Ralph Manheim (New Haven: Yale University Press, 1953), II, p. 219, also 38–39, 157.
[8] Particulary in *Totem and Taboo*.

much to that of dreams which reveal unconscious, repressed wishes.[9] Jung, on the contrary, attributed to myths a unique role in revealing a collective subconscious, the stock from which dreams themselves draw their substance. To him myths are clear articulations of the archetypes which direct the individuation process. Jung first made us aware of the incomparable psychic power of the myth. Whether they accept the theory of the collective unconscious or not, most analysts today regard the myth as the community's most powerful means to adapt the individual to life in a particular group with a particular culture. It fulfills a primary role in the process of psychic integration. A recent Neo-Freudian study of the role of the myth in ego psychology describes the educational impact of the myth:

> . . . each society tries to fashion the younger generation in consonance with the ideals and goals of the particular society. Through its mythology the society tends to induce a climate favorable to the realization of appropriate identifications. Every society interprets and reinterprets its history and its heroes in keeping with the need. What makes this technique so effective is the powerful, motive force of the childhood instinctual wish through the medium of the vicarious (unconscious) gratification which comes from identification with the hero and the myth.[10]

The insights of psychoanalysis have led to interesting interpretations of the ancient myths. Thus the legends of Perseus' encounter with the Medusa is seen to reflect the concern of a society, well on its way to becoming patriarchal, about the formidable challenge of the matriarchal powers, while the Oedipus cycle is thought to describe a world dominated by the mother (the Sphinx, the Erinyes) in which the first seeds of rebellion have been sown.[11]

[9] See *The Interpretation of Dreams,* tr. under direction of James Strachey (London: Hogarth Press, 1958), pp. 261–66.
[10] Jacob Arlow, "Ego Psychology and the Study of Mythology" in *Journal of the American Psychiatric Association* 9 (1961), p. 388.
[11] See Leon Balter, "The Mother as Source of Power. A Psychoanalytic Study of Three Greek Myths," in *The Psychoanalytic Quarterly* 38 (1969),

Psychoanalytic interpretations have mainly emphasized the myth's reference to the past, the sediment left by the prehistory of a group. But the myth's connection with the future is equally important. A hint of it may be found in Freud's thesis that the myth expresses repressed wishes. Yet more than a wish, the myth is a vision of what is to come. According to Ernst Bloch, myths primarily reveal man's ideals: in them he formulates what he hopes for. They do not so much retrieve man's past as they give access to his future.[12] But the kind of future which man dreams up in his myths differs considerably from Bloch's Marxist utopianism, as we shall see shortly.

Yet first a word should be said about another contemporary trend which has brought to light the unique character of the mythical consciousness. Under the influence of their founding father, Auguste Comte, nineteenth-century sociologists and ethnologists regarded the myth as a prescientific way of thinking, distinct from philosophy and science only by its lack of logical accuracy and scientific method. The thesis has long since been abandoned and is not worth refuting any more. Yet it has continued to lead a subterraneous existence among scientists and philosophers of positivist inclination, particularly in France. Thus Émile Bréhier in a famous article written in 1914 opposed the mythic to the philosophical as the illogical, contingent, arbitrary, uncritical, to the logical, necessary, coherent, and critical.[13] All such theories have been dealt a death blow by the French anthropologist Claude Lévi-Strauss, who first embraced their basic rationalist assumption that the myth is a way of thinking, but then went on to prove that it is just as logical and accurate as that of science, although it follows entirely different laws. In his

---

pp. 217–74. I have serious reservations about the first part of this article which identifies each of the discussed myths with a particular ontogenetic stage in the developing individual. The genesis of a society and its ideals differs essentially from the development of the individual: any similarity here must be considered coincidental.

[12] *Das Prinzip Hoffnung* (Frankfurt, 1967), pp. 61–62, 70, 110.

[13] "Philosophie et mythe" in *Revue de métaphysique et de morale,* 22 (1914), pp. 361–81.

Structural Anthropology he announces his basic principle with the defying clarity of a manifesto:

> The kind of logic which is used by mythical thought is as rigorous as that of modern science . . . In the same way we may be able to show that the same logical processes are put to use in myth as in science and that man has always been thinking equally well; the improvement lies, not in an alleged progress of man's consciousness, but in the discovery of new things to which it may apply its unchangeable abilities.[14]

The mythic way of thinking has never been "surpassed" by scientific logic for the simple reason that it is a different and permanent method of structuring experience. But this structure is as rigorous as a scientific one: it follows identical laws in a variety of contexts and is concerned with the logical (not an emotional or socio-institutional) problem of conceiving relations. The purpose of this logic, however, is a practical one: to solve the contradictions of social life by stating them clearly and by providing a logical model in which they may be overcome.[15] One recognizes the Marxist dialectical theory of consciousness grafted upon the sturdy tree of French rationalism. Does it reveal the essence of the myth?

Two major objections have been leveled against Lévi-Strauss' theory, one dealing with the logical nature of the myth, the other with its social purpose. That some structure underlies the fantastic appearance of the myth seems to be beyond doubt. But is logic the best way to describe it? So many other elements (emotional, ritual, poetic) are involved that an exclusively epistemic interpretation is bound to impoverish the myth beyond recogni-

---

[14] "The Structural Study of Myth" in *Structural Anthropology,* tr. by Claire Jacobson and Brooke G. Schoepf (New York: Basic Books, 1963), p. 230. Since then the author seems to have become increasingly aware of the difficulty of his task. From *The Raw and the Cooked,* tr. by John and Doreen Weightman (New York: Harper & Row, 1969), pp. 3, 5, 12, it appears that no mythic *ratiocinator universalis* will ever be forthcoming.
[15] *Structural Anthropology,* p. 229.

tion. To interpret the meaning of the Oedipus cycle as the inability of a culture which believes in the autochthonous nature of the human race, to explain that human beings are actually born from the union of man and woman, is somewhat far-fetched.[16] Although no one can refute such an interpretation, one is left with an impression of total artificiality. The very attempt to discover a thought structure which can be univocally applied to an infinite variety of cases, regardless of content and linguistic differences, seems to originate in a questionable formalism. An Anglo-Saxon critic takes the French anthropologist to task for his logical simplicity:

> Lévi-Strauss' method seems to impose a spurious uniformity on the material, spurious because order springs not from the encounter between investigator and data but from the categories of a closed system which cannot admit further possibilities.[17]

How are we ever to be sure that any isolated structural principle has a universal application when form and content are as intimately united as they are in the myth?

The objections against an exclusively social interpretation of the myth are equally formidable. All functions of the mind are united in this first articulated reflection: the logical and the practical, but also the religious and the artistic. To focus exclusively on the social function of the myth is to ignore the variety of its tasks. One aspect which remains conspicuously undeveloped in Lévi-Strauss' theory is the original connection

16 *Structural Anthropology,* pp. 213–18. See also Lévi-Strauss' "The Story of Asdiwal" in *The Structural Study of Myth and Totemism,* ed. by Edmund Leach (London: Tavistock Publications, 1967), pp. 1–43, which reduces a complex Tsimshian (North Pacific) myth to an expression of the problems involved in matrilateral cross-cousin marriages. For a critique of this ingenious piece of decodification, see Mary Douglas "The Meaning of Myth" in *The Structural Study of Myth and Totemism,* p. 63.

17 K. O. L. Burridge, "Lévi-Strauss and Myth" in *The Structural Study of Myth and Totemism,* p. 113. See also, in the same collection, Nur Yalman, "The Raw: The Cooked:: Nature: Culture," pp. 82–84.

with ritual. Its author has challenged rationalism on its own terrain by accepting its basic premise—the attempt toward rationality—and then showing that the mythopoeisis, far from being an imperfect anticipation of scientific thinking, is a unique and lasting activity of the mind. The main flaw of the theory lies in the acceptance of the rationalist limitation that the myth is *only* a way of thinking, added to the sociologistic prejudice that it serves *no other* purpose than to overcome social contradictions. Lévi-Strauss' detailed analyses have confirmed the fundamental thesis first enunciated by Schelling and fully developed by Cassirer: the myth is a unique form of reflection. Yet it is unique not only in displaying irreducible structures of thought, but above all in articulating a unique reflection. It is a different way of thinking *because* it is a different stage of the reflective consciousness. In the beautiful expression of Georges Gusdorf, the myth is "une pensée avant la réflexion, avant la médiation, encore inhérente à l'action instinctive."[18] There is a certain truth, then, in the myth for which critical reflection can never substitute because it possesses a unique value in itself. Whether this "truth" will be able to survive critical reflection is another problem, but one can certainly not be replaced by the other.

The mythical mentality does not distinguish the self from the world in a subject-object opposition. It unites both in a highly personalized vision.

Primitive man has only one mode of thought, one mode of expression, one part of speech—the personal. This does not mean (as is so often thought) that primitive man, in order to explain natural phenomena, imparts human characteristics to an inanimate world . . . The world appears to primitive man neither inanimate nor empty but redundant with life; and life has individuality, in man and beast and plant, and in every phenomenon which confronts man.[19]

[18] "Mythe et philosophie" in *Revue de métaphysique et de morale*, 52 (1951), p. 177.
[19] Henri Frankfort, *Before Philosophy* (Baltimore: Penguin Books, 1966), p. 14.

Natural phenomena are used to explain personal conditions, and social relations, in turn, explain the world of natural phenomena.[20] A mythical explanation is always a full emotional response to a problem which is never regarded as purely theoretical. What was written about the Greek myths applies to every myth:

> The mythical explanation . . . is more emotional than rational and works not by describing cause and effect, but by associating one kind of experience with another and suggesting a connection or similarity between them.[21]

Actually the mythical mind is familiar with the principle of causality. Yet, it does not attempt to isolate a single factor as condition of the entire process but connects all empirical data in a largely emotional association. Thus, as Cassirer wrote, anything can come from anything "because anything can stand in temporal or spatial contact with anything."[22] Still the term causality with its purely theoretical connotation is misleading. For the problems to which the myth responds are mainly existential situations which interrupt the smooth course of archaic man's exchange with nature. Birth, adolescence, marriage, and death confront him with realities which he must in some way justify to himself. They demand an active response which in turn requires reflection. Such a situation differs essentially from that of a scientific or philosophical problem. Contrary to the scientific mentality for the mythical mind, life after death is not as much a problem as death itself.[23] That a person goes on living once he is alive seems normal enough. That life comes to an end is what requires justification. The existential challenges to which the myth responds are genuine, and modern man deludes himself when he thinks he has overcome them through scientific answers. The scientific insight that organic bodies must eventually decay offers no answer

---

[20] Cassirer, *The Philosophy of Symbolic Forms,* II, p. 95.
[21] Maurice Bowra, *The Greek Experience* (New York: New American Library, 1959), p. 115.
[22] *The Philosophy of Symbolic Forms,* II, p. 46.
[23] See Cassirer, *The Philosphy of Symbolic Forms,* II, p. 37.

to the question why life is such that it should decay. Its being organic is only one more part of the problem. In the myth we move at the fringes of the weightiest metaphysical problems. Yet the myth itself is not metaphysical, for its primary orientation is not theoretical but existential-practical.

Against the prescientific interpretations of the past, social anthropologists, from Malinowski through Lévi-Strauss, have rightly emphasized the practical nature of myth.

> The point where myth enters in these subjects is not to be explained by any greater amount of curiosity or any more problematic character, but rather by emotional coloring and pragmatic importance . . . The subjects developed in these myths are clear enough in themselves: there is no need to "explain" them, and the myth does not even partially perform this function. What it actually does is to transform an emotionally overwhelming foreboding, behind which, even for a native, there lurks the idea of an inevitable and ruthless fatality.[24]

Unfortunately, both Malinowski and Lévi-Strauss limit the myth's practical impact exclusively, or mainly, to social relations. Its real scope is considerably wider. The myth sets up a model for existence in its entirety. It aims primarily at restoring the primeval wholeness which man has lost through reflection. Yet such a restoration requires that man first clearly formulate the disjunction which he must overcome. The mythical model, then, is one of separation as much as of unity. But the myth separates only to unite: it creates dramatic tension in words in order to discover a model solution for life.

The myth is not the first symbolic dramatization of existence. As we saw earlier, ritual precedes it in this dialectical expression of reality. The oldest myths merely translate ritual action into dramatic narrative. By narrating primeval events in succession, the mythical story interiorizes the stages of the ritual action and gives them a dramatic character. Temporality, then, is an essential feature of the myth. Indeed, the myth *is* man's first reflective

[24] Bronislaw Malinowski, *Magic, Science and Religion* (Garden City, N.Y.: Doubleday, 1954), p. 137.

awareness of time.[25] To have seen this is the redeeming grain of truth in Bréhier's rationalist study:

> Essential in the myth is that it is the story of a destiny, that it narrates a succession of events. An animist concept of the universe is not necessarily mythical. It is not, as long as one merely attributes a determinate and permanent function to each spirit; it becomes mythical only if each one of the spirits has a history. The myth must have then an essential relation to time.[26]

Cassirer, Eliade, and Lévi-Strauss specify this mythical time as being dialectical in nature. The myth posits time only to abolish it immediately.[27] It relates the present to a mythical past, yet the ultimate purpose of this relation is not to insert it into the succession of time but rather to overcome the flux of temporality altogether. For the mythical past is no ordinary moment of succession: it is the totality itself, the wholeness from which the present has become separated. It introduces stability by reducing a questionable situation to one which requires no further questioning.[28] The beginning itself needs no foundation: it is creative while all that follows is imitative. The mythical past abolishes the present as well as other temporal moments. Yet in another sense it provides its ultimate foundation. For it justifies the present structures of reality by giving them a timeless permanence. Connecting actions and events with the timeless acts of the beginning, man recaptures the initial creativity from which they originated. In paradigmatic gesture and myth he is reunited with the primeval

[25] If we consider temporality the essence of consciousness, as Husserl does in his *Lectures on Inner Time Consciousness,* we realize all the more the importance of myth in the development of consciousness as such.

[26] "Philosophie et mythe" in *Revue de métaphysique et de morale,* 22 (1914), p. 365.

[27] Claude Lévi-Strauss, *The Raw and the Cooked,* tr. by John and Doreen Weightman, p. 16.

[28] "For mythical time there is an absolute past which neither requires nor is susceptible of any further explanation . . . once this past is obtained, myth remains in it as in something permanent and unquestionable." Cassirer, *The Philosophy of Symbolic Forms,* II, p. 106.

events. Mircea Eliade emphasizes again and again that ritual gestures are never commemorative but always foundational.[29] The same holds true for the myth which accompanies the gesture. Because every myth relives the beginning, Malinowski appropriately termed it "a narrative resurrection of a primeval reality."[30]

The return to the origins regenerates the mythical past or, better, founds the present upon the archetypal beginning. It would be mistaken, then, to interpret the myth of the origins as a primitive substitute for a scientific theory of causality. Part of the foundational process undoubtedly consists in the theoretical justification of the present, and this aspect will later be replaced by causal explanations. But this "gnostic" element, which loses its significance in a postmythical age, remains subordinate to a more basic existential need for structures.

We now come to the most important problem of this section: How does the myth establish the sacred? The experience of the sacred precedes the myth, since it occurs first in the primeval rituals out of which the myth itself arises. Yet this experience becomes *reflective* only when man starts distinguishing the sacred *verbally* from the profane. This he does in the myth. Most primitive myths do not even mention the sacred. But in opposing the archetypal structure of the beginning to the pure temporality of the present, the myth in fact divides the real into a sacred and a profane sphere. For what we term sacred is originally nothing more than what is regarded as more truly real because it is *whole* and *self-founded,* while the profane is what happens *only* now and is therefore purely contingent.

This trait of isolation, this character of the egregious, is essential to every content of the mythical consciousness as such; . . . It is

[29] For one representative sample: "A sacrifice, for example, not only exactly reproduces the initial sacrifice revealed by a god, *ab origine,* at the beginning of time, it also takes place at that same primordial mythical moment . . . All sacrifices are performed at the same mythical instant of the beginning: through the paradox of rite, profane time and duration are suspended." *Cosmos and History* (New York: Harper & Brothers, 1959), p. 35.

[30] *Magic, Science and Religion,* p. 101.

this characteristic *transcendence* which links the contents of the mythical and the religious consciousness.[31]

The sacred is constituted when man considers one kind of reality so far superior that all others become real only to the extent that they participate in it. This sacred reality reconciles the conflicting elements of ordinary reality by integrating them all into a higher organic unity. The myth is the mind's first and most powerful instrument of existential integration. It is in the myth that we become aware of the tremendous power of the sacred to unite contraries.[32]

The mythical distinction in time also produces a distinction between a sacred and a profane space. Obviously man possesses space consciousness long before he starts telling myths: he could not operate without being aware of spatial relations. Yet it is in the myth, in close connection with the discovery of sacred time, that he becomes aware of space *as such*. His return from the chaos of a dispersed world to the primeval harmony is also a conscious exploration of space. For the original events are conceived as *centrally located* with respect to all that follows. Thus the world obtains a center as well as a beginning.

If the world is to be lived in, it must be founded—and no world can come to birth in the chaos of the homogeneity and relativity of profane space. The discovery or projection of a fixed point— the center—is equivalent to the creation of the world.[33]

---

31 Cassirer, *The Philosophy of Symbolic Forms,* II, p. 74.
32 At the root of the daring theological speculations of Pseudo-Dionysius, Eckhart and Cusa, Mircea Eliade finds the mythical *coincidentia oppositorum. Patterns in Comparative Religion* (New York: Sheed & Ward, 1958), pp. 419–20. One mythical theme sublating the contradictions of the real is that of the androgyne, an omnipresent verbalization of man's attempt, first ritually expressed, to overcome sexual separation and to return to primeval unity. Eliade, *The Two and the One* (New York: Harper & Row, 1965); also, Thomas J. J. Altizer, *Mircea Eliade and the Dialectic of the Sacred* (Philadelphia: Westminster Press, 1963), pp. 81–104.
33 Mircea Eliade, *The Sacred and the Profane,* p. 22.

Thus the return to the creative event also provides the necessary orientation in space. Obviously this mythical space has nothing in common with the geometrical space in which each point equals each other point. Indeed, it is the exact opposite, for the main function of the mythical space division is to break up the homogeneity. Yet the mythical space negates the immediacy of sense perception as radically as the mathematical concept of space ever does.

This appears clearly in the relativity of the mythical center. The foundation of the world is the foundation of the ordered, inhabited universe—the only one that matters—not of the entire physical universe. But this is an ever expanding event: whenever new territory is occupied the world is founded again. The center of the world itself becomes a movable concept. Every epiphany makes the space in which it occurs into the center of the world.[34] According to Henri Frankfort, the Egyptian temple at Heliopolis marked the primeval hill from which the sun god had created the world. Yet later the inner sanctum of every other sun temple was identified with the same hill. This must have been done in full awareness of the symbolic meaning, since even the most recent temples were claimed to have come into being before anything else existed.

To us this view is entirely unacceptable. In our continuous, homogeneous space the place of each locality is unambiguously fixed. We would insist that there must have been one single place where the first mound of dry land actually emerged from the chaotic waters. But the Egyptian would have considered such objections mere quibbles. Since the temples and the royal tombs were as sacred as the primeval hill and showed architectural forms which resembled the hill, they shared essentials. And it would be fatuous to argue whether one of these monuments could be called the primeval hill with more justification than the others.[35]

[34] *Ibid.*, pp. 20–65.
[35] "Myth and Reality" in *Before Philosophy*, ed. by H. Frankfort (Baltimore: Penguin Books, 1966), p. 31.

2. THE SURVIVAL OF THE MYTH

Can man continue to believe in the myth once he becomes aware of its existence as myth? Can the mythical consciousness survive rational reflection? The question is not a new one and the answers have long preceded our own era. In the past the myth was mostly dismissed as a random play of the imagination which could at the touch of an artist bloom into poetry. Whatever truth it contained was considered to be so poorly expressed that only a translation into another language could bring it out. Thus the myth was interpreted "allegorically," as a fabulation on great historical figures, or a personification of natural powers or moral principles.[36] The turning point came at the end of the eighteenth century with the German philosopher Johann Gottfried Herder, and the philologists Christian Gottlob Heyne and Gottfried Hermann, who considered the myth an essential mode of thinking in the infancy stage of a culture. Herder actually went further and regarded the myth as an indispensable factor in creating and preserving a national spirit. His influence inspired the young Hegel to call for "a new mythology."[37] Yet it is Schelling (although he had originally shared the evolutionary position of Heyne and Hermann) who established the idea that the myth is more than a relic of the age of innocence and ignorance.[38]

[36] The first theory is usually ascribed to the third-century Greek writer Euhemerus. How long his influence persisted throughout the ages may be seen in Frank E. Manuel, *The Eighteenth Century Confronts the Gods* (New York: Atheneum Publishers, 1967), pp. 85–125.

[37] In his early program for a system (1796 or 1797). My information on these highly confused beginnings of German scholarship on mythology comes mainly from Otto Pöggeler, "Hegel der Verfasser des ältesten Systemprogramms des Deutschen Idealismus" in *Hegel-Studien* (Beiheft 4, 1966), pp. 17–32.

[38] Schelling has basically two mature theories of myth: during his Jena period he considered the myth primarily as the content of art, while in his later years (in München and Berlin) he defended a religious interpretation of myth. We shall have an opportunity to discuss both of them. On the second, cf. K.-H. Volkmann-Schluck, *Mythos und Logos* (Berlin, 1969).

The historical battles around the interpretation of myth have not ended. Bultmann's theory of demythologization has poured fresh fuel on the fire. Once more we see two camps confronting each other: one claiming that the myth belongs to an earlier stage,[39] the other defending its living presence.[40] Even if one chooses the second alternative, some basic distinctions are needed to make the survival of the myth in modern culture at all credible. The archaic mentality, in which mythical reflection determines all spheres of consciousness and leaves no room for nonmythical ways of thinking, belongs definitively to the past. Originally the myth was at once religion, philosophy, science, and poetry—and, of course, none of these as we know them today. Paul Tillich who has most clearly perceived the difference between the two stages of myth describes this first "totalitarian" stage as follows:

> In the unbroken myth three elements are linked together: the religious, the scientific, and the truly mythical elements: the religious element as relatedness to the unconditioned transcendent, the scientific as relatedness to objective reality, the truly mythical as an objectification of the transcendent through the medium of intuitions and conceptions of reality.[41]

I have quoted the text in its entirety despite my reservations about the expression, "the truly mythical" (everything in the myth is mythical), because it pictures accurately the unbroken nature of the archaic myth. This nature changes basically when other reflective attitudes appear. At that moment the original myth becomes fragmented over a number of separate areas. Part of it continues to exist in all of them, but in a modified form.

Mythical thinking appears at the roots of all great constructions

[39] Most followers of Bultmann find themselves on that side. See for instance the important study of Chr. Hartlich and W. Sachs, *Der Ursprung des Mythosbegriffs in der modernen Bibelwissenschaft* (Tübingen, 1952).
[40] Paul Tillich is perhaps the most representative figure on this side.
[41] "The Religious Symbol" in *Religious Experience and Truth*, ed. by Sidney Hook, pp. 311–12.

of the mind. Spinoza's intuition that the real is one substance, Hegel's dialectical concept of being, Darwin's notion of evolution, Marx's vision of man as progressing from alienation to freedom, Freud's representation of the subconscious, were mythical intuitions before being philosophical or scientific theories. I do not mean that great scientific and philosophical theories intrinsically *depend* on myth for their truth. For they have been developed into self-supporting structures. Yet the presence of mythical elements is undeniable. They have been called *transcendence models* because, like myths, they transcend all available evidence, project the future and escape the present.[42]

As a rule rational man is very reluctant to accept the presence of mythical elements in his thinking. Like the adolescent who has just left his childhood, he is anxious to repudiate his recent past and to brand as false what a few generations back was his only truth. Yet the more he attempts to lock out the myth, the more he drives it underground where it will do its work subconsciously. Undetected it grows ever more powerful and, if not subjected to the control of reason, ever more dangerous.[43] This is particularly evident in interpretations of history, social assumptions, and individual ideals.[44] White Americans tend to interpret the history of their country as the gradual realization of a dream of social equality and intellectual freedom. Such an interpretation enables them to live with the past and to hope for the future. Yet it is a mythical model which selectively eliminates such inconvenient complexities as resident Indians, imported slaves

[42] John F. Hayward, "The Uses of Myth in an Age of Science" in *New Theology*, No. 7, ed. by Martin E. Marty and Dean G. Peerman (New York: Macmillan, 1970), p. 62.

[43] An example of a myth that went originally unrecognized and later eliminated reason altogether is the concept of the national state as it developed in Germany during the past 150 years. See Ernst Cassirer, *The Myth of the State* (New Haven: Yale University Press, 1946).

[44] Mircea Eliade has beautifully written of the unconscious working of half-forgotten myths in modern life and of the masks behind which they hide. For one instance, see *Images and Symbols*, p. 16.

and undesirable immigrants.[45] The myth may serve a useful function as a model, but if taken as history it leads inevitably to prejudice and repression. Another, more innocent but equally powerful myth is that of the frontier. The sacred space of the West is all things to all men: the land of the free, the test of virtue, the reward of vice. Of particular interest is its ritualized representation in the Western film. Admirers of this popular art genre easily discover the eternal mythical core underneath the modern imagery.

> Gods and demigods, passions and ideals, the fatality of events, the sadness and glory of death, the struggle of good and evil—all these themes of the Western myth constitute an ideal ground for a liaison and re-elaboration of the Olympian world, a refreshing symbiotic relationship of Hellenic thought and Yankee dynamism. The cowboy on horseback shapes into the fabulous Centaurus, guardian of a newly acquired legend; the woman—whose presence is biologically sought in the frontier town—becomes a sort of Minerva, dispensing wisdom, often moral principles, warm comfort, and unrelenting excitement and incitement . . . Above this epic looms the pathos of the fight between good and evil so dear to Anglo-Saxon hearts, a theme that finds its highest literary expression in Herman Melville's *Moby Dick*.[46]

Yet by far the most influential and, at least by its orthodox believers, least recognized modern myth is Marx's half-Promethean, half-Messianic vision of history. Here we have a model (the victorious proletariat), a total interpretation of existence (communism is a science as well as a philosophy and a system of art and morality), the transcendence of a higher reality (the man of the future), and a *coincidentia oppositorum* (all

---

[45] For an analysis of mythical elements in historical interpretation, cf. Gregor Sebba, "Symbol and Myth in Modern Rationalistic Societies" in *Truth, Myth and Symbol*, ed. by Thomas J. J. Altizer (Englewood Cliffs, N.J.: Prentice-Hall, 1962), pp. 157–60.

[46] George Fenin and William K. Everson, *The Western* (New York: Bonanza Books, 1962), pp. 6–7.

inequalities will be erased in a total harmony). Marx's description of the final stage of history reads like Isaiah's vision in which the lion will live with the lamb and the panther lie down with the kid.[47] It is its mythical more than its scientific core which has given Marxism such an unparalleled power.

In only one area of modern culture is the myth fully recognized and openly welcomed—the arts, and particularly the literary arts. The reason is obvious. As a narrative the myth found an appropriate place in literary language and later, through the different medium of successive images, in the film.[48] Yet a literary myth, however faithful to its ancient model, still differs from the original. While the unbroken myth was told for the highly practical purpose of allowing man to live his life with hope and dignity, the poetic myth, even when it retains the original meaning, is primarily intended for aesthetic enjoyment. The poetic myth is not restricted by the well-defined existential concerns of its archaic model and thus enjoys a much greater freedom of the imagination. Its author may not even accept the original meaning, as in the dramatic treatments of ancient myths by Sartre, Cocteau, and Anouilh, or he may ridicule it as Lucianus did. Even Aeschylus' pious attitude toward the old traditions did not prevent him from embellishing his original themes and making the aesthetic expression his central concern. The conscious culture of the artist differs substantially from the one that gave rise to the myths. Obvious as this seems to us, it mostly escaped our literary ancestors, whose lack of historical perspective and understanding of the myth led them to the strangest reinterpretations.[49]

[47] Isaiah 11:6.
[48] How literary devices have influenced the development of the early cinema appears in the instructive pages of the Soviet director Sergei Eisenstein, according to which D. W. Griffith, the father of the art, learned most of his technique (cutting, editing, flashback) in the novels of Charles Dickens. *Film Form* (New York: Meridian Books, 1959), p. 201.
[49] How classical mythology was treated during the Renaissance is documented in the interesting study of Jean Seznec, *The Survival of the Pagan Gods. The Mythological Tradition and Its Place in Renaissance Humanism*

The unique presence of the myth in literary art requires a much more extensive treatment than the scope of this study allows. Yet a few suggestions may at least illustrate the nature of the transformation. Some poems and tragedies attempt to recapture the sphere of wholeness of the original mythical theme. Such, I believe, was, in spite of the many adjustments which he made to contemporary situations, the essential aim of Vergil in the *Aeneid*. Such also were most of the classic Greek tragedies which still preserve the sequence of the ancient Dionysian rites.[50] Yet also a number of modern tragedies which no longer reflect in their structure the mythic origins still preserve the mythical content of Greek drama. The densely mythical *Eumenides* is re-created in T. S. Eliot's *The Family Reunion,* in which a modern Orestes, pursued by the furies after his wife's death, comes home for salvation and is redeemed after having gone through the ritual purifications of suffering and confession. The entire *Oresteia*

(New York: Harper & Row, 1961). The strange vagrancies of one mythic theme throughout centuries of plastic arts are told with charm and erudition in Erwin and Dora Panofsky, *Pandora's Box. The Changing Aspects of a Mythical Symbol* (New York: Harper & Row, 1965).

[50] Gilbert Murray, "Excursus on the Ritual Forms Preserved in Greek Tragedy" in *Themis* by Jane Harrison, pp. 341–44. The interpretations of Murray and Harrison are contradicted in two recent studies. Gerald F. Else, in *The Origin and Early Form of Greek Tragedy* (Cambridge: Harvard University Press, 1965), rejects Aristotle's statements associating the beginnings of tragedy with ritual worship of Dionysus. He is highly critical of Murray's Dionysiac-religious interpretation of Greek tragedy. Albin Lesky in *A History of Greek Literature* (New York: Thomas Y. Crowell, 1966) accepts Aristotle's statements in the *Poetics* as good historical evidence. He accepts Dionysiac influence on what he calls the "sub-structure" and the "pre-history" of the drama. "But however much in tragedy may be Dionysiac, one thing is generally not: that is the subject matter. 'Nothing to do with Dionysus' was a proverbial phrase among the ancients, and the various explanations offered of it show that the question exercised them also. Occasionally the birth of the god or attempts to oppose him (e.g., Lycurgus, Pentheus) provide the plot, but there is no evidence for a stage of development in which the content of tragedy was essentially Dionysiac. Thus the statements of Aristotle, while we do not reject them, leave us puzzled, and we have to supplement them with other information that can help us to understand the non-Dionysiac character of developed tragedy." (P. 227)

returns in Eugene O'Neill's *Mourning Becomes Electra* with the same fateful succession of punishment and revenge that once befell the house of Atreus.[51] The basic transformation began as soon as Greek tragedy ceased to be the ceremonial drama of Dionysus and turned into "play." At that moment the mythical drama lost its deepest reality.

Myth is employed to ennoble the reality of the hour, to disclose the deep meaning which it contains, and this is possible only because the myth is still considered just as "real" as in the days of the epic, in spite of its increasing tendency to assume the character of a special, a higher reality. Drama . . . removes itself from immediate contact with the reality of the present by severing its ties with the ritual situation. Simultaneously by becoming a play and an illusion, it robs the myth of its standing as a piece of reality.[52]

The transformation is most drastic in modern treatments of ancient myths, such as Goethe's *Prometheus*, Sartre's *The Flies*, or Melville's *Moby Dick*, in which a studious attempt to instill new meaning reduces the ancient myth to an allegory. Only great artists like Goethe and Melville can successfully perform such a blood transfusion. The case of Melville is particularly interesting, since he secularizes old Egyptian, Hebrew, and early Christian myths by remythologizing them.[53] Thus in *Moby Dick* Ahab is dismembered, dies, and descends to the nether world as Osiris did. But unlike Osiris he is not being revived as a savior of man. He relives Jonah's rebellion and fall, but not his salvation. Nor does his death prefigure the death and resurrection of Christ, as Jonah's did, for Ahab's whale does not

51 Doris V. Falk, *Eugene O'Neill and the Tragic Tension* (New Brunswick, N.J.: Rutgers University Press, 1958); Hugh Dickenson, *Myth in the Modern Stage* (Urbana: University of Illinois Press, 1969).
52 Bruno Snell, *The Discovery of the Mind*, tr. by T. G. Rosenmeyer (New York: Harper & Brothers, 1960), p. 97. The entire passage from p. 93 to p. 98 is relevant.
53 Bruce Franklin, *The Wake of the Gods* (Stanford, Calif.: Stanford University Press, 1966), pp. 50–57. Daniel Hoffman, *Form and Fable in American Fiction* (New York: Oxford University Press, 1961), p. 272.

return its victims. Moby Dick is still a myth, but it is no longer *religious* as its original material was, except perhaps in a negative sense.[54] More common in modern literature is the development of a theme that had remained obscure or ambiguous in the original myth, as the eschatological disintegration in Yeats's *Second Coming,* or the lost paradise in Alain-Fournier's *Le grand Meaulnes,* or the golden age in the poems of Vergil, Ovid, Dante, Ariosto, Tasso.[55]

Can we go further and declare all art mythological to the extent that it transcends the given space-time order? Some critics would say we can.[56] They might find support in Schelling's claim that the mythical gods first represent the absolute in visible form, which is the very object of all art.[57] For Schelling the myth is the poetry before poetry, the beacon in the dark succession of nature's cycles. Although the myth lacks the freedom of the aesthetic imagination, it offers the artist a subject already determined by the intrinsic necessity which characterizes great art. Such a view leads to a too-aesthetic interpretation of the myth. It is true that art plunges its roots in mythical soil and that the aesthetic intuition is nourished by the same sources of imagination as the myth. Yet Schelling oversimplified the problem by restricting the discussion to Greek mythology and classical art. The Greek myths as they have reached us, possess a unique aesthetic potential. Schelling himself considers beauty the chief quality of the Greek gods; when they are not moral or wise they are still aesthetic.[58] This poetic character of the gods is

[54] On the negative religious meaning of *Moby Dick,* see Gabriel Vahanian, "Fugitive from God" in *Wait Without Idols* (New York: George Braziller, 1964), pp. 72–92. Also, Lawrence Thompson, *Melville's Quarrel with God* (Princeton: Princeton University Press, 1952), pp. 147–243.

[55] Harry Levin, *The Myth of the Golden Age* (Bloomington: Indiana University Press, 1970).

[56] One who does is Richard Volney Chase, *Quest for Myth* (Baton Rouge: Louisiana State University Press, 1949), pp. 105ff.

[57] *Philosophie der Kunst* in *Werke,* Vol. 3, p. 425. This work and its ideas date from Schelling's middle period, which differs considerably from his final period.

[58] *Philosophie der Kunst,* p. 418.

typical of a particular mythology which achieved the aesthetic harmony of the finite and the infinite. It is, by Schelling's own admission, not true of other mythologies, such as the Hindu.[59]

3. THE RELIGIOUS SURVIVAL OF THE MYTH

Malinowski once wrote that all development of religious dogma occurs by means of the myth.[60] For the myth definitively establishes beliefs as well as rites and even moral practices. To religious man who is no longer aware of mythical elements in what he believes and practices, this position appears extreme. Yet a moment of reflection shows that all religious dogma has its roots in the symbolization process through which a particular faith took its original shape and this invariably contains mythical elements. It would, of course, be simplistic to equate highly rationalized theological theories with primitive myths. But the mythical element is retained throughout the development.[61] Myths may change profoundly in the evolutionary process. At the time when Christianity inherited and created its symbols, the mythical mentality no longer existed. Moreover, Judaism itself, throughout its long evolution, had already substantially expurgated its own myths. Yet, the myths survive, and in passing from one faith to another are incorporated into new structures of meaning.[62]

All this creates a serious problem for the modern believer who is unable to accept mythical elements without previously transforming them through his own reflective attitude. Many questions which to him are of primary importance cannot be answered within the myth. To ask if the fall was a historical event, how it could possibly affect others and whether God's

---

[59] *Philosophie der Kunst,* pp. 443–45.

[60] "Myth as a Dramatic Development of Dogma" in *Sex, Culture and Myth* (New York: Harcourt, Brace & World, 1962), pp. 245–55.

[61] Cf. Anselm Atkins, "If Theology Were Hypothetical," *Cross Currents,* 18 (1968), p. 337.

[62] Henry Duméry, *Philosophie de la religion* (Paris, 1957), Vol. II, pp. 161–66.

verdict afterwards was equitable, is not only to place oneself outside the mythical context but to change the original perspective. For the myth does not allow such critical questions. Myth and theological reflection exclude each other.[63] To "translate" the myth is to abandon a substantial part of its message. It also is to repeat the old error that the myth "prefigures" science, morality, and religion. On the other hand, to exempt the myth from critical questions is to deny that it can have any relevant meaning to the contemporary believer. What can the story of the fall still mean to the modern Christian once he comes to understand it as expressing a particular world view of which he is no longer capable? Full belief in the myth cannot survive the awareness that it is a myth. The believer's attitude is mostly ambiguous: he feels that the myth tells him something important, yet he seldom feels able to give the message a precise sense. Theological theories of myth attempt to clarify this meaning for contemporary faith. The variety of the answers indicates the complexity of the problem.

The first fact to recognize is that myth as such may not be considered the earliest expression of "religion." Cassirer is right: the myth as such is not religious at all. To become religious, it must undergo substantial changes. Nevertheless, the mythical consciousness results in the religious consciousness by an intrinsic dialectic. The myth is the birthplace of the gods: it initiates a movement toward transcendence which is completed and clarified in formal religion.[64] The negativity which distinguishes sacred reality from ordinary originates in the myth, but a reflective awareness of the sacred comes only after man has left the mythical mentality. The "other" reality of the myth remains essentially a part of nature, without achieving full transcendence. Only a further development can make it into the different realm of being to which man attributes the name *sacred*. Yet it is

[63] Gerhard Ebeling, *Word and Faith* (Philadelphia: Fortress Press, 1963), p. 353.
[64] Schelling, *Einleitung in die Philosophie der Mythologie*, in *Werke*, Vol. 6, p. 209.

the myth itself which initiates the dynamism that leads the mind beyond the mythical. In the religious consciousness alone are the gods fully separated from the men.

> The reflective consciousness elaborates the primitive experience of the sacred and thus gives rise to religion . . . For the primitive consciousness the relation between man and the deity is one of implication, of participation. The reflective consciousness takes its distance: it divinizes the gods and humanizes men. Henceforth man asserts his presence *before* God and this relation of exteriority corresponds here to an affirmation of divine transcendence.[65]

In the faith of Israel we see this religious demythologization process at work in the radical reinterpretation of Egyptian and Mesopotamian myths toward a clearer affirmation of divine transcendence. Natural phenomena and cultural achievements, to which the original sources ascribed divine attributes, are here devaluated to expressions of God's power. The faith of Israel has even been claimed to exclude myths in the strict sense (although not mythical elements) altogether.[66] We certainly notice here an unusually strong awareness of transcendence. Professor Frankfort attributes this to the Hebrews' constant exposure to the desert landscape.

> Wherever we find reverence for the phenomena of life and growth, we find preoccupation with the immanence of the divine and with the form of its manifestation. But in the stark solitude of the desert where nothing changes, nothing moves (except man at his own free will), where features in the landscape are only pointers,

---

[65] Georges Gusdorf, *Mythe et métaphysique* (Paris, 1953), p. 148.
[66] Hermann Gunkel, "Mythus und Mythologie im Alten Testament" in *Die Religion in Geschichte und Gegenwart; Handwörterbuch für Theologie und Religionswissenschaft,* ed. by H. Gunkel and L. Zscharnack (Tübingen, 4, 1930), s.v. John L. McKenzie, "Myth and the Old Testament" in *Myths and Realities: Studies in Biblical Theology* (Milwaukee: Bruce Publishing Co., 1963), pp. 198–99. To the contrary, the purely mythical interpretation of the first chapters of Genesis was recently revived by Edmund R. Leach, "Lévi-Strauss in the Garden of Eden" in *Transactions New York Academy of Sciences* (1961), series 2, pp. 386–96.

landmarks without significance in themselves—there we may expect the image of God to transcend concrete phenomena altogether.[67]

Jewish and Christian theologians will, of course, always refer to the privileged religious experience of Israel.[68] Although a "supernatural" causality falls by its very nature outside the scope of a philosophical discussion, it is indeed remarkable that in the Hebrew tradition the myth developed in a religious direction rather than, say, a scientific-philosophical one as it did for the Greeks. Undoubtedly, reflection upon the initial distinctions of the myth will sooner or later determine the sacred as transcendent. But the myth has many implications which may be developed in any order of succession. For the Greeks the notion of a transcendent God would emerge long after the more gnostic aspects of the myth—its implicit science and philosophy—had been successfully pursued. This explains why a philosopher as religious as Plato was never much concerned with the problem of God's transcendence or uniqueness.

Israel's growing awareness of divine transcendence was accompanied by an orientation toward historical time. Here again we might point to a nomadic life style in which the emphasis on the group rather than the soil favors a religion of events over one of cyclic returns. Sacred history means progression in time, and this is incompatible with endlessly returning patterns of sacred beginnings.[69] Still the transcendent, historical perspective of Israel did not exclude the mythical consciousness. For Israel's sacred history itself is encased in a mythic framework of time.[70] The historical events of Abraham's calling and

[67] *Before Philosophy*, p. 247.
[68] See, for instance, Avery Dulles, S.J., "Symbol, Myth and the Biblical Revelation" in *Theological Studies*, 27 (1966), pp. 15–16.
[69] For an account of the difference between the Hebrew historical time and mythical time, cf. Cornelius Loew, *Myth, Sacred History and Philosophy* (New York: Harcourt, Brace & World, 1967), pp. 106, 146.
[70] Even the interpretation of strictly historical events adopted mythic features. Thus the House of David came to be regarded as the permanent center of Israel's world. "In the long run, the ability of the Davidic dynasty

Israel's liberation are prefaced by the description of a mythical beginning in which all creatures lived in harmony with each other and man enjoyed the intimacy of Yahweh. The cult did not presentify this paradigmatic situation (as it did for the Babylonians). Yet it projected their return into a Messianic future, as appears in Isaiah's Messianic descriptions. The wedge of sacred history holds apart the golden age of the future from that of the past, thereby adding new power to the old mythical vision. Obviously, history here has not "replaced" the myth but intensified its dramatic character. Israel has converted history into *mythistory*.

The case of Christianity is still more complex. Although it places an even greater emphasis on historical uniqueness, it displays at the same time the renewed impact of the mythical mentality. It is unquestionably based upon a historical person, a few historical facts, and a historical community. The accuracy of much of the Gospel narratives may be contested. Yet their intent and substance is clearly historical. The purely "mythical" interpretations of the last century were all refuted during their authors' lifetime. The great initiator of mythical exegesis was the Hegelian David Friedrich Strauss, for whom the Gospel stories merely expressed the aspirations of the original Christian community.[71] Strauss's notion of myth was interesting insofar as he credited it with a unique truth, irreducible to philosophical concepts and physical facts. Yet the vagueness of his theory left it wide open to criticism. More specific were the authors of the *religionsgeschichtliche* school, such as Wilhelm Bousset and Richard Reitzenstein, who considered the Gospels reworked Greek myths. However, evidence soon indicated that the mythical elements in the New Testament were not predominantly Greek.

---

to maintain its continuity generation after generation led to a situation in which the David-Zion tradition functioned quasi-mythically in the sense that no new chapter of sacred history was expected. As the gods had established the institutional pattern of the Egyptian and Mesopotamian empires 'forever,' so Yahweh had established the Davidic dynasty 'forever.' Nothing really new needed to happen." Cornelius Loew, *op. cit.*, p. 131.

[71] *Leben Jesu kritisch bearbeitet* (Tübingen, 1835).

The *formgeschichtliche* school was able to trace a number of them back to Jewish apocalyptic literature and gnostic writings of various origins. Although the sweeping statements of Strauss's day are gone, the present concentration on myth, particularly in the interpretation of the Fourth Gospel, still tends to distort the basic perspective of the Christian faith. Jesus' first followers believed because of *facts*, their message consisted essentially in conveying what they considered to be *facts*, and they did not hesitate to stake their entire faith upon the historical nature of these *facts*. One may question how solid the factual basis of their belief was, but one cannot interpret this belief itself as mythically oriented.

On the other hand, Christianity is obviously full of mythical elements—more so, I believe, than the faith of Israel. The liturgical cycle, particularly as it is celebrated among Catholic Christians, has incorporated a great deal of the nature mythology of the Classic civilization. The communion rite relives the reality of the original act in the same intimate combination of rite and "myth" (in which the story accompanying the rite determines its significance). Some of the Gospel narratives (especially, the infancy stories of Matthew) are replete with mythical ingredients. Yet the mythic elements are always integrated with a historical context, to the point where it is impossible to discern one from the other. The attempt of *Form Criticism* to separate the facts from the myth has in the end proven to be futile. Nor is such a distinction essential to the believer. For the myths are all transformed by the historical intentionality which the founder himself bestowed upon the new faith.[72] The mythic element in Christianity was primarily a setting adopted and created for the purpose of receiving the *fact* Jesus.[73]

The myth substantially changes when it comes to serve an exclusively religious purpose. Within the archaic mentality the term

[72] Moreover, the myths inherited with the Hebrew legacy had already undergone a basic transformation by which they ceased to be pure myths when Christians adopted them.

[73] Henry Duméry has well described the relation between fact and myth in Christianity in his *Philosophie de la religion*, II, pp. 147–79.

"religious myth" has no definable meaning, yet once the myth is assumed within a religious perspective it becomes restricted to *one* of the many functions which it fulfilled in the primitive consciousness: to distinguish the sacred from the profane. The question, then, arises whether the myth is still needed after the sacred has been rationally defined. Why should religious faith retain the myth once it has outgrown the mythical mentality and is no longer able to grasp its original meaning? What may still be a vehicle of meaning at an early stage of religion becomes an obstacle at a mature stage of faith. Such are the facts on the basis of which in our time Rudolf Bultmann has raised his well-known questions.[74] Most myths present in the New Testament, he premises, have lost their meaning, since they are intrinsically dependent upon a world view excluded by the modern scientific attitude. They are not so much false as obsolete. Bultmann does not rule out the impact of myth on modern man, but myth exercises power only if it does not conflict with man's general view of the universe.

What is the solution? At times Bultmann suggests that we remove the mythical form from the true content; at other times, that we use literary criticism in order to *understand* the myth.[75] The two statements complement each other, for to interpret the myth is precisely to understand it as "man's self-understanding in the world in which he lives."[76] The myth requires its own suppression since its real purpose, "to speak of a transcendent power which controls the world and man," is "impeded and obscured by the terms in which it is expressed."[77] A demythized understanding of the Gospel will release the contemporary message

---

[74] Bultmann clearly formulated the problem in his now famous essay "New Testament and Mythology," republished in *Kerygma and Myth*, by Rudolf Bultmann and Five Critics, ed. by H. W. Bartsch, tr. by Reginald Fuller (New York: Harper & Row, 1961), pp. 1–44.

[75] For the first meaning, "New Testament and Mythology" in *Kerygma and Myth*, *passim;* for the second, p. 12.

[76] *Op. cit.*, p. 10.

[77] *Op. cit.*, p. 11. This "purpose" would certainly not apply to the myth in the archaic mentality, but it could still be true for the myth which "survives" within religion.

that man can attain an authentic existence only in total commitment. This message is not purely philosophical, for a true understanding of existence will reveal that authenticity is not available
in man's present state and must be revealed by an act of God.

But here the question returns: Is the act of God which enables
us to lead an authentic existence a mythical event? Bultmann
answers: It is mythical only for those who regard all God-talk
as mythical.[78] A number of critics wonder, however, whether a
message which, by Bultmann's own admission[79] first had to be
expressed in mythical language, can be adequately restated in
other language. An American theologian writes in Bultmann's
defense: If not all religious language is mythical it follows that
the religious character of the message may be preserved in the
restatement.[80] At some point the mythical must be inserted into
the literal. Such remarks are convincing enough, but do they provide a sufficient justification for a complete demythologization?
Undoubtedly, the literal affirmation is essential to the primary
religious statement, even at a primitive, highly mythical stage.
Once reflection becomes religious, it ceases to be purely mythical,
and, consequently, the myth if it survives at all must be made
subordinate to the new mental attitude. But that problem was
basically the same for, say, the primitive Christian community,
as it is for us. Nor do I believe that it is to be solved by trans-
lating the myth into some metaphysical language.

That the myth survives within the religious attitude should
alert us to the possibility that it might be indispensable. The survival in itself is surprising enough, for as soon as the reflective
awareness of the sacred as transcendent breaks through, the mythical mentality starts receding. The process continues, activated by
dynamic distinctions first established by the myth itself. The
negative impulse of the religious dialectic will relentlessly drive
the mind beyond the mythical. Cassirer, who strongly emphasizes the distinction between the religious and the mythical, de-

[78] *Op. cit.,* p. 43.
[79] *Op. cit.,* pp. 10–11.
[80] Schubert Ogden, "On Demythologizing" in *Pittsburgh Perspective* (1967),
p. 33.

scribes the decisive moment in which the myth "breaks" and the religious attitude emerges. When the dancer realizes that he is not the god whose nature he assumes, but only *represents* him, we have clearly left the purely mythical mentality.

> It is this separation that constitutes the actual beginning of the specifically religious consciousness . . . Religion takes the decisive step that is essentially alien to myth: in its use of sensuous images and signs it recognizes them as such—a means of expression which, though they reveal a determinate meaning, must necessarily remain inadequate to it, which "point" to this meaning but never wholly exhaust it.[81]

The original distinction between the sacred and the profane must inevitably result in a distinction between two realms of being, which the myth cannot fully express. All this seems to be so much grist for the demythologizer's mill.

Yet the problem is far more complex, for if the antimythical drive were ever to be completely successful, it would drain the life blood out of religion itself. Undoubtedly, some aspects of the myth cannot survive their recognition by the religious, philosophical or scientific mind. Thus, the concepts of space and time of the archaic myth, as well as its loose notion of causality, are incompatible with the scientific mentality. The religious mind finds the myth lacking in the radical negativity which transcendence requires. On all this, we must concede Bultmann's point. But is that all of the myth? Is it even its most essential trait? I think not. The myth possesses two qualities which make it irreplaceable for the religious symbolization process. One is a capacity to reflect, without objectivating the reality upon which it reflects. Earlier we saw that all religious symbols are reflective as well as nonobjective. We now may add that outside the myth such symbols cannot be formed and, once they exist, cannot be properly understood. This quality of the myth is but a result of its unique ability to reconcile and integrate opposed facets of existence.

[81] *The Philosophy of Symbolic Forms,* II, pp. 238–39.

The religious mind does the same, although in a different way. In one sense its scope is less ambitious than that of the mythical mind, since it grants the partial integrations of science, art, and philosophy a relative autonomy, reserving to itself only the *ultimate* one.[82] In another sense, however, the religious integration surpasses the mythical one, since it posits a reality beyond the ordinary realm of life and yet manages to bring man's entire existence within its compass by cult, prayer, and religious reflection. The only language available to express this kind of total integration is that of myth and poetry.

I add poetry, because poetic language also is able to overcome the subject-object opposition which separates the inner from the outer world and to reconcile the conflicting sides of existence in one dramatic vision. Yet *per se* the poet is not concerned with the *real* as such. Every poem illuminates reality, however playful and fantastic it may be, yet it always retains an aesthetic distance from reality. This makes it inadequate to be the principal carrier of religious meaning. For the religious mind is as much concerned with the real as it is unconcerned about the form quality of its expression. To be sure, a clearly conceived distinction between the real and the imaginary is itself of recent origin. Archaic poetry comprehends both in an undivided unity, but it is precisely in that respect that such poetry displays mythical qualities. Schelling therefore regarded the myth as the oldest poetry of mankind. At any rate, in an advanced cultural stage, poetry definitely no longer coincides with myth and may not be mythical at all. Religion, on the other hand, continues to need the symbolic expression which only the myth provides.

Still, this does not decide the issue; for granting that its symbols originate in myths only, one might wonder whether faith, once it is established, still needs the actual myths. My answer would be affirmative, at least in the case of a historical religion, because the myth introduces an indispensable awareness of time

[82] It should be well understood that the others are partial only if one accepts the religious integration. For someone who does not, science, philosophy or even art may provide the ultimate integration.

which the historical consciousness cannot provide. Faith reaches for a beginning and an end which fall entirely beyond the scope of history. Any attempt to integrate the beginning and the end with the rest of history is bound to be mythical. Moreover, as we shall see in the chapter on religious alienation, symbols such as those of fall and redemption are inherently temporal, yet inaccessible to history as the recording and analysis of human *phenomena*. In all such cases religious man has nowhere to turn but to the myth.

All this does not entirely dispose of Bultmann's problem, for he is troubled not so much by the presence of myth as by the *antiquated nature* of particular mythical expressions. Could we not remythologize religious faith and thus have new myths instead of outdated ones? Indeed, mythical renewal is a constantly ongoing process, whether religious man is aware of it or not. New myths emerge and old ones are remodeled. But mythical renewal cannot be commanded or controlled. A myth has no author: it grows out of the life of the community. No theologian or philosopher possesses the right or the ability to remodel myths on his own, apart from the religious community. Moreover, remythologizing is particularly hazardous when the old myth is part of a privileged, "revealed" founding tradition. I would ask with Helmut Thielecke: What man would be bold enough to attempt to produce an authoritative reinterpretation of the whole of the Bible?[83] If outmoded myths belong to the original authoritative expression, they must be retained. To eliminate or change them is to disconnect the link with the tradition.

> Foundations are given once for all; they cannot be replaced. Christianity, as a historical revelation, must always look back to its origins and develop in continuity with them. Scripture, even in its imagery, pertains to the patrimony which God has permanently entrusted to the Church . . .[84]

[83] "The Restatement of New Testament Mythology" in *Kerygma and Myth*, p. 163.
[84] Avery Dulles, S.J., "Symbol, Myth and the Biblical Revelation" in *Theological Studies*, 27 (1966), pp. 24–25.

This is theological language, but it is based upon philosophical wisdom.

How can man continue to believe in old myths after he has abandoned the mythical mentality? Admittedly, he cannot go on believing *in* the myth once he has recognized it as a myth and has thereby relativized its efficacy. Yet he can still believe *through* the myth. The myth does undergo a substantial change— in this I fully agree with Bultmann, Cassirer, and Tillich. It is no longer an unquestionable absolute, but it becomes an indispensable *means* for religious reflection. Paul Ricoeur has said that to modern man the myth *gives rise to thinking:* it constantly calls for a hermeneutics which "explains" it without ever exhausting it.[85] Thus the myth invites rational exegesis while fully retaining its transcendence over every single and all combined "interpretations." Its polyvalent richness continues to feed religious reflection.

In the religious consciousness man becomes reflectively aware of the symbolic meaning of the myth: he no longer takes it as reality itself but as its representation. The dichotomy, then, between meaning and reality in the interpretation of the myth did not emerge in recent times. It immediately followed the separation which the religious consciousness caused between the transcendent and its phenomenal expression. In the myth the two were still basically united. Once the distinction between the sacred and the profane which the myth first introduced develops into an awareness of absolute transcendence, all expression of it becomes relative. At that moment the mythical consciousness gives way to the religious, and a metaphorical meaning supersedes the literal one. Thus the dialectic initiated in the myth gradually abolishes the myth's immediate existence and integrates it into a different state of consciousness. The problem of modern man, then, is an ancient one. It did not start with Bultmann but with the birth of religion as a reflective, and therefore distinct, sphere of consciousness. We may feel it more acutely because of our

[85] *The Symbolism of Evil,* tr. by Emerson Buchanan (Boston: Beacon Press, 1967), pp. 349–50.

belief in the basic truth of a scientific world view, but the difficulty of adapting the closed yet unified world of the myth to the open universe of religion has preceded the modern mind by millennia.

Still we must make one final concession to Bultmann. For in one case rational explanation definitely must replace (and not merely reinterpret) the myth. Among other functions, the myth originally also satisfied man's intellectual curiosity. Most myths contain a *gnostic* element—the only one which Comte and later rationalists ever noticed—which at one time fulfilled the important task of making man intellectually alert. This function led man on to the discovery of science and philosophy, which subsequently replaced his archaic knowledge. Any attempt on the part of modern man to revive the cosmology or physics of the myth goes against the very grain of thinking. Fundamentalist interpretations of religious myths inevitably result in an outright rejection of the entire myth, for the spirit cannot suffer obscurantism for a long period of time. *Demythologization,* that is, according to Ricoeur's ingenious reading, the elimination of the ancient *logos* (the knowledge part) from the myth, is therefore necessary to preserve the deeper meaning of the mythic symbol itself. Demythologizing faith is a constant and necessary process, while demythizing is ultimately destructive of the particular nature of religious symbols.

Chapter 7
The Sacred Revealed

1. THE MANYFOLD REVELATION

We commonly associate the term revelation with a spoken or written message. Yet revelation is never primarily a word although it inevitably turns to words. Originally it is a *deed* or, in some instances, a historical *event* in which the transcendent discloses itself. Dance, rite, and sacrifice manifest a divine presence long before the gods start to speak. Revelation is the interior voice of all religious events, which, at first barely perceived as a mysterious whisper from a strange beyond, is heard ever more audibly until it clearly articulates a verbal message.[1] But the word never replaces the deed. Even those revelations, which because of the primary role of the word demand a response of "faith," originated as a succession of *events*. The Scriptures merely witness to those events and manifest their inner meaning. That revealing events must inevitably turn to the word to specify and explicate their meanings follows from their nature as religious symbols. The reader may recall here the law formulated in the previous chapter: All religious symbols either are verbal or need verbal interpretation. Christians have expressed this most forcefully by naming God-as-manifest the

[1] Rudolph Otto, somewhat one-sidedly, described this verbalization of the numinous as a rationalization process. See, e.g., *The Idea of the Holy*, pp. 134–35.

Word. Thus they defined their own faith but, at the same time, enunciated the deepest meaning of all revelation. For the Word is the instrument of God's self-manifestation. Paul Claudel dramatized the essence of revealing in his verses: "Le Verbe de Dieu est Celui en qui Dieu s'est fait à l'homme donnable. La parole créée est cela en qui toutes choses créées sont faites à l'homme donnables."[2] Unlike ordinary speech the revealing word never turns into an abstract, conceptual reflection *upon* reality; it retains the full reality of the content which it symbolizes.

> The word of God—is not "didache" (teaching), from beginning to end but proclamation in which the arrival of the thing proclaimed itself takes place. It is the mighty, creative *dabar* (word), of God to man, the way in which the reality which is being proclaimed discloses itself, and thereby and thus becomes present to us.[3]

Karl Rahner's description applies not only to the faith of Jews and Christians but to every religious revelation. In the *word* divine reality discloses itself to man: it is both the medium and the reality of God's communication.

Words, then, are indispensable to, but not restrictive of, revelation. The very faith which adores the Word declares that Word to be a person. Not until the seventeenth century did Christians fully identify God's revelation with Scripture, and this artificial construction was soon to be dismantled under the attacks of the Enlightenment. Nevertheless, the idea lingers on among Christians that revelation is Scripture. Such a conception misrepresents the belief of Jews, Moslems, and Christians, but it is even farther off the mark in the case of nonhistorical religions. The cycle of nature, the revolution of the heavens, an unusual appearance of man or animal, the inner experience

[2] "The Word of God is the One in whom God has made himself givable to man. The created word is that in which all created things have become givable to man." "La maison fermée" in *Cinq Grandes Odes* (Paris, 1948), p. 143.
[3] Karl Rahner, "The Word and the Eucharist," *Theological Investigations,* Vol. IV, p. 261.

induced by prayer, dance, or stimulants—they all reveal the Divine as do the *gesta Dei* to Jews and Christians. Nor is revelation necessarily a permanent phenomenon. What reveals today may not be revealing tomorrow. Frequently an object or person reveals only as long as its, or his, sacred character lasts, and returns afterward to "ordinary" existence. Their theophanies are transitory events, unpredictable and disconcerting. In other cases the revelatory power may be captured and contained within well-defined limits. Delphi was a specific place where one could "consult" the god and be reasonably sure of getting an answer. Similarly, the Roman haruspices knew under which precise rules the auguries would reveal the destiny of a future venture. Even more predictable, yet not less real, is the cyclic revelation of nature. Obviously all these "revelations" are not of the same nature. Many will withhold the name from the latter ones. Some distinctions, then, are needed.

I believe it was Max Scheler who first clearly opposed the *natural* revelation, in which the divine becomes manifest in things and events belonging to an order in principle accessible to everyone, to the *positive* revelation, in which its presence is revealed through words and persons. A transcendent reality conceived as a person can disclose itself only in a positive revelation.[4] The difference affects the revealed as well as the mode of revelation, for persons and words may manifest something of God's own nature (how much, we shall discuss later), while the natural revelation is restricted to the workings of God. A positive revelation somehow originates in a "free decision" of God.[5]

We may further distinguish the "manifestation" from the "revelation" of God in a positive religion. According to Wolfhart Pannenberg, no individual manifestation of God in the Bible may be called a revelation in the proper sense, because none reveals Yahweh *himself*. This excludes the proclamation of the law on Mount Sinai as well as the disclosure of the divine

---

[4] Max Scheler, *The Eternal in Man*, p. 161.
[5] This term will have to be defined and qualified carefully.

name in Exodus.[6] We must postpone discussion of this point until later. Although not every positive revelation reveals *through* history (as in the case of Israel), it always has some historical character, for a positive revelation occurs in definite words spoken or written by a specific person at a particular time. Nature, on the contrary, reveals constantly though perhaps not continuously.

A religion is not necessarily restricted to one type of revelation. Nathan Söderblom entitled his chapter on Mosaic faith in *The Living God,* "Religion as Revelation in History." Yet from the Psalms, Job, and Baruch, we learn that for the Hebrews nature also manifested the power of the Almighty. This is even more decidedly the case in Christianity, which in its earlier days was strongly influenced by the natural "revelations" of Hellenistic religions. Even in the New Testament we find next to a strong assertion of absolute novelty indications that the "Christian" revelation does not stand alone. Thus the Epistle to the Hebrews commences with a declaration that God has spoken to man in many ways. What is typical of Christian revelation is not that it is exclusively verbal but that the revelation of the Word has *subsumed* all other forms. The idea is not new.[7] Hamann claimed a double revelation for Christianity in nature and in Scripture. The former must be understood through the latter. Nature by itself yields only ciphers with cryptic meanings. Scripture provides the key to decipher their hidden mysteries.[8] Yet a historical revelation does more than decipher: it inevitably *transforms* the revelation of nature. Once

[6] *Revelation As History,* tr. by David Granskou (New York: Macmillan, 1968), pp. 9–15.

[7] Clement of Alexandria initiated a whole tradition of thought which attributed to Greek philosophy the role of a preparatory revelation. He calls it "the gift of God to the Greeks" (*Stromata,* I, 20, 1), "necessary for their justification" (*Stromata,* I, 28, 1), "given to the Greeks as a covenant of their own" (*Stromata,* VI, 67, 1). For relevant texts of the Alexandrian and Cappadocian Fathers, cf. René Latourelle, *Theology of Revelation* (New York: Alba House, 1966), pp. 107–32.

[8] Johann Georg Hamann, *Brocken* in *Sämtliche Werke,* ed. by Josef Nadler (Vienna, 1949–57), Vol. I, p. 308.

God reveals himself directly through words and events, nature loses its divine character and is reduced to a symbol. The cyclic and the historical may well be integrated, as happens in Catholicism, but they cannot coexist independently. A direct person-to-person revelation determines the impersonal, less articulate language of nature.[9] One characteristic which distinguishes a positive revelation from a "natural" one is its exclusiveness. Whoever has not heard the word remains an outsider to the divine sphere. The element of segregation, ever present in the religious attitude, appears here in the separation of those who *hear* from those who do not.[10]

As self-manifestation of the divine, all religion must be revealed. The transcendent cannot be forced to disclose itself. The mind remains forever incapable of conquering it. At the same time, to receive the transcendent the mind itself must be of a self-transcending nature. This results in a complex dialectic of active and passive religious attitudes. The transcending movement of the mind urges it to listen for a transcendent message.[11] Moreover, it must *constitute* that which it experiences as given. Nothing enters consciousness without being actively transformed into a conscious "object." Meaning originates only when "data" are *made* meaningful. On a mechanical level there may be

[9] On the difference between the mythological and the historical revelation, see Gerardus Van der Leeuw, *Religion in Essence and Manifestation*, pp. 573–75. Hans Urs von Balthasar is of the opinion that contemporary Christian theology has not been very successful in integrating the two forms of revelation. They are usually juxtaposed, even though this leads to contradictions in the concept of positive revelation. *Word and Revelation* (New York: Herder and Herder, 1964), p. 58.

[10] As so often, the atheist Feuerbach understood this more clearly than his believing contemporaries. "Faith has in its mind something peculiar to itself, it rests on a peculiar revelation of God, it has not come to its possessions in an ordinary way, that way which stands open to all men alike. What stands open to all is common and for that reason cannot form a special object of faith. That God is the creator, all men could know from Nature; but what this God is in person, can be known only by special grace, is the object of a special faith." *Das Wesen des Christentums* in *Sämtliche Werke*, VI, p. 298. *The Essence of Christianity*, p. 248.

[11] Karl Rahner, *Hörer des Wortes*, pp. 94–95; *Hearers of the Word*, p. 74.

reception without action. On the level of the mind such a passivity is impossible. To receive is still to grasp, to structure, to articulate. Locke's representation of the mind "as a blank sheet of paper" is an empiricist fiction inadequate to explain the most elementary act of perception. This active disposition of the mind predetermines the revelation, if one is to occur, to be illuminative rather than additive. Nothing can be "added" to the mind. We shall pursue this further, but first we must turn to the other, more obvious moment in the dialectic of revelation.

In the terminology used to describe the revelatory experience, passive traits unquestionably predominate. Tillich speaks of an event which "grasps the human mind," and in which "the ultimate becomes manifest in an ultimate concern, shaking and transforming the given situation."[12] For Buber the reality of revelation consists in "that we receive what we did not hitherto have and receive it in such a way that we know it has been given to us."[13] These lyrical descriptions are basically accurate, for revelation means to discover reality as *given*. Revelatory "knowledge" differs from ordinary knowledge as much by the method of perceiving as by its "object." When religious man claims that God has revealed himself, he means, rightly or wrongly, that he knows God through himself. Revelation, then, must be considered an essential correlate of the receptive attitude of faith. As the experience intensifies, the passivity increases. The masters of spiritual life leave us no doubt that religious awareness follows the direction opposite to that of logical reflection: instead of approaching ever greater spontaneity, it moves toward total receptiveness.[14]

However, the activity of the mind is never eliminated. Instead, it is in its entirety lifted onto a level of passivity where the mind experiences its acting as dependent. Religious man does not so much "receive" the revelation as he is *being received*

---

[12] *Dynamics of Faith*, pp. 78–79.

[13] *I and Thou*, tr. by Ronald G. Smith (New York: Charles Scribner's Sons, 1958), pp. 109–10.

[14] Ernst Cassirer, *Language and Myth*, p. 60.

in the revelation: both his activity and his passivity are sub-
mersed in an all-enveloping reality. Thus the constituting consciousness can still experience itself as constituted. The believer discovers divine speaking informing his speech, divine governance
directing his creations, divine mystery shining through his symbols.
This, I think, was the passivity which H. Richard Niebuhr had
in mind when he wrote:

> Revelation means the moment in our history through which we
> know ourselves to be known from beginning to end, in which we
> are apprehended by the knower . . . Revelation is the moment in
> which we find our judging selves to be judged not by ourselves or
> our neighbors but by one who knows the final secrets of the
> heart; revelation means the self-disclosure of the judge. Revelation
> means that we find ourselves to be valued rather valuing and that
> all our values are transvaluated by the activity of a universal
> value.[15]

2. THE GOD WHO REVEALS

An essential task of philosophy is to define the ultimate conditions of revelation. Yet this does not necessarily consist in a
transcendental deduction of the possibility of all revelation as
Fichte attempted in his early *Critique of All Revelation*. It may
assume the entire revelatory experience (whether its object be
real or illusory) and subject this experience to a philosophical
critique in order to discover its epistemic structure and ontological
foundation. To investigate the possibility of a revelation is not
our primary objective in the present chapter. Still, we cannot
simply bypass the fundamental question whether the *transcendent*
can truly be revealed. A good many philosophers would detect
a contradiction in the very concept. Buddhism and classical
forms of Hinduism denied the possibility of the absolute "revealing" itself in words, concepts, or events. But the difficulty

[15] *The Meaning of Revelation* (New York: Harper & Row, 1962), pp.
152–53. In a similar vein, Karl Rahner, *Revelation and Tradition*,
Quaestiones Disputatae, 17 (New York: Herder and Herder, 1966), p. 21.

appears also in the so-called faiths of revelation as Judaism, Islam, and Christianity. In Islam the problem emerged in the speculative question whether revelation itself is divine or created. The implication was that unless it is divine, we cannot fully claim that it reveals *God*. In the ninth century some rationalist theologians (among them the *Mu'tazila,* i.e., "withdrawers") claimed that God's speaking is an attribute of God which cannot be identified with God's essence. Although their position was defeated and condemned, the dilemma of created or uncreated revelation continued to haunt Islam.[16]

The problem in the final analysis is the same everywhere: How can the transcendent truly reveal itself without ceasing to be transcendent? A truly revelatory symbol would have to convey the very *reality* of the transcendent, but the process of communication would destroy its transcendence. Jaspers therefore drew the conclusion that a communication from the transcendent must be restricted to ciphers, that is, symbols which neither comprehend nor express their signified, as empirical symbols do, but merely refer to it. Ciphers possess no intrinsic meaning: their function consists entirely in pointing beyond themselves.

No cipher is more than a signpost or a light. No cipher is the last, the one and only. Each cipher is a phenomenon as well, a foreground, a language. Each requires us to realize its limitations, to feel what lies beyond it.[17]

Revelation, on the contrary, singles out certain symbols as divinely chosen and therefore revealing in a unique and unequaled way.

---

[16] The tenth-century divine Al-Maturidi attempted to compromise by identifying the word of God with his essence but its expression with creaturehood. See texts in *Islam*, ed. by John Alden Williams (New York: Washington Square Press, 1963), p. 168. The fourteenth-century Iraq theologian Hasan ibn Yusuf would resume the *Mu'tazila* position: "The meaning of His being a Speaker is that he makes Speech, not that He is one in whom Speech inheres." *Al-Babu-l-Hadi 'Ashar,* tr. by W. E. Miller (London: 1958), Creed #76.

[17] *Philosophical Faith and Revelation,* p. 134.

Consistent with the extreme expressions of negative theology, Jaspers denies that anything at all can be *revealed* about the transcendent, including even the existence of God. Instead, Jaspers advocates the use of ciphers which point to a transcendent dimension of existence without revealing it. Jaspers' theory raises a substantial objection against the Western concept of revelation while stating the philosophical principles of a religious alternative. Why should "revealing words" possess the once-for-all character which Christians and Jews ascribe to them? For a Buddhist or a Hindu of the classic period a revelation remains a relative affair, never definitive, which discloses more by what it leaves unsaid than by what it says. Nor is this religious alternative only found outside the Judeo-Christian tradition. All theologies of Neo-Platonic inspiration encounter similar problems in their efforts to break the transcendent silence.

Recently one philosopher has attempted to combine a negative theology with a Christian philosophy of revelation. For Henry Duméry, God transcends all categories of speech and must ultimately remain silent. Yet he is able to reveal insofar as he is at the origin of man's speaking. "God is beyond our grasp, our categories, but he appears through them. He is the high point of our aims, he is their soul."[18] Duméry's concept of revelation is at once more restrictive and more permissive than the traditional one. A revelation through nature is ruled out by definition: if revelation means speaking, it must occur through man since man alone knows verbal expression. Yet, how can one word be considered more divine in origin than another if man alone speaks and God remains entirely silent? Revealed language, Duméry fully admits, is entirely of human making and therefore relative. But this relativity does not exclude absolute significance or transcendent origin. For "revealed" language consists of those schemas and categories which allow the mind to return to its absolute origin. Not all speech, then, is alike, even though it is all human. Only a divine impulse can bring man to speak revealed language.

[18] *La foi n'est pas un cri* (2d ed.) (Paris, 1959), p. 225. Tr. in *Faith and Reflection*, ed. and introduced by Louis Dupré, p. 187.

The main difficulty of this interpretation consists in finding an adequate distinction between "revealed" language and any other religious language which would serve the henological return equally well. Until he provides this distinction, many will feel that Duméry's negative theology has not done full justice to the concept of revelation in the strict sense.

The main problem of a negative theology of revelation is not so much that God cannot speak (in the obvious sense this is unquestionably true), but that there is nothing to speak about. Even if a message were to originate in this empty freedom, it would not *reveal* the transcendent. One might object that God could attain his determination *in the very process* of speaking. But aside from the fact that such an evolution from *prius* to *posterius* in God will be hard to justify philosophically, the content of language cannot be entirely created in the act of speaking itself.[19]

Serious as the problems of an apophatic theology are, the alternatives are more consequential than many of its adversaries realize. Let us explore some of them now. First, a God who reveals *himself* must be a *revelatory God;* that is, his nature must both enable and force him to reveal. It is a gross anthropomorphism to claim that God is *free* to reveal or not to reveal himself, unless one carefully detaches all connotations of choice from the term "freedom." God can *truly* disclose himself only if he is necessarily, by his very nature, a revealing God. Unless the revelatory act expresses God's inner life, it does not reveal at all.[20] Among philosophers Hegel has been practically alone in accepting the full consequences of a divine self-revelation. Hegel admits that in some religions only man's *relation to* the transcendent is revealed while God himself remains hidden. Yet such a revelation inevitably raises further questions about the God who reveals. In Christianity (and many would add: in Judaism and Islam) God

[19] For a severe critique of negative theology, see Claude Bruaire, *L'affirmation de Dieu* (Paris, 1964), pp. 190–92, 242–44.
[20] Claude Bruaire, *Logique et religion chrétienne dans la philosophie de Hegel* (Paris: 1964), p. 25.

has revealed *himself*. In this case he becomes known as a revelatory God.

> [In the Christian religion] it is manifest what God is, that he is
> known as he is . . . Here the revealing manifestation is both
> determination and content, namely revelation, manifestation, being
> for consciousness.[21]

God reveals *because* he is the manifest one. It belongs to his very essence to turn self-possession into self-communication. Christian faith teaches that the Father's nature is *to be for* the Son, and the Son's *to be for* the Father. To reveal is *to be for another*. God then reveals himself as self-determination and self-division. This, according to Hegel, is the essential characteristic of Spirit. Spirit can be Spirit only in manifesting itself. "A Spirit which does not reveal is not Spirit."[22] In calling God Spirit, Christianity states explicitly what other faiths implied, namely, that God must be self-manifestation. Has Hegel merely read the conclusions of his own philosophical development of the concept of revelation into the Christian mystery of the Trinity? This may well be the case. Yet if it is, it is not done without methodic awareness. For the first principle of this development, that God is Spirit, is found in the revelation itself and its philosophical articulation is, in his opinion, required by the very nature of the revealed. Professor Kenneth Schmitz phrased it well: "Hegel sees in the Christian revelation the mandate and even the demand to go beyond that revelation in its given form."[23] Philosophy completes the revealing act and makes man reflectively aware of the total manifestation of God; it allows the infinite Spirit to permeate man's

[21] Hegel, *Vorlesungen über die Philosophie der Religion*, IV, p. 32.
[22] *Vorlesungen*, IV, p. 35. A comparison with Heidegger's revelation of Being imposes itself. Here also Being reveals necessarily by sending itself (*sich schickt*) to existence (*Dasein*). Language *is* the mission of Being. See William Richardson, "Heidegger and God—and Professor Jonas" in *Thought*, 18, pp. 35–36.
[23] "The Conceptualization of Religious Mystery" in *Proceedings International Hegel Symposium* (Milwaukee: Marquette University Press, 1971).

entire awareness.[24] In the Christian revelation, then, as completed in philosophy, God becomes totally known and the term "mystery" attains its full Pauline meaning: the transcendent which has become manifest. If there remains negativity in the highest mystery, it is not caused by God's hiding, but by the mind's reluctance to move beyond the imperfect rationality of the "understanding" or, perhaps, by negativity in the divine life itself.[25]

However one may judge Hegel's theory, one can hardly quarrel with the analytic proposition that a God who reveals is necessarily a revealing God, that is, an irresistible power to make itself known which is sufficiently determined to be known. Every religious attitude assumes that God is able to communicate with man. But is he able to manifest *himself* to man? If the answer is affirmative, revelation becomes a religious necessity. Yet the believer has always considered a positive revelation a free act of God. Does freedom not conflict with the necessity implicit in the notion of a revelatory God? If freedom is conceived exclusively in terms of choice, no act of God ought to be called free, for no act of God can be subject to the arbitrariness of choice. Yet neither does divine necessity result from need. For need and desire imply fulfillment outside oneself and the idea of God does not admit any extrinsic coercion. A free revelation may appear to be a choice determined by a preceding desire, because in man necessity can never be its own ground and therefore excludes freedom. Yet perfect self-determination must be free without choice.

Revelation, sooner or later, results in linguistic expression. But does language not imply a desire or a need of otherness incompatible with total self-possession? In a subtle study on the relation between desire and language in the affirmation of God, Claude

[24] James Collins, *The Emergence of Philosophy of Religion* (New Haven: Yale University Press, 1967), p. 337. How philosophy continues and fulfills the revealing act, Hegel explained most clearly in a passage written during the last year of his life in the *Vorlesungen über Beweise vom Dasein Gottes,* Appendix, ed. by Georg Lasson (Hamburg, 1966), p. 177.
[25] Whether the dialectic may be carried from the religious mind to God's own essence will be discussed in the next chapter.

Bruaire has attempted to answer this question. For him the revelation of God is not a transition from indecisive silence to the need and subsequent decision to speak. Far from being an imperfection, language is the fullness of self-possession.[26] Unity has content only when including multiplicity; simplicity when including relation; identity when including otherness. But God's intrinsic *necessity* to reveal himself does not reach beyond God's inner being to another than himself. It does imply relation and even otherness *within* God, but not necessarily outside him. Greek theologians taught long ago that the "logos endiatetos" precedes and conditions the "logos prosforikos." Only the former is intrinsically necessary. The "outgoing" word is necessary only in its origin. But since this necessity relates to a terminus which no longer is its own foundation and which is characterized by an *otherness*[27] of its own, it acquires a genuine contingency. We may not ascribe, then, to the ecthetic act the *intrinsic* necessity of the divine nature in which it originates. The revelation which man receives necessarily from God's revealing nature remains a contingent event. Considered in itself (rather than in its origin), it could have been different or not at all, as could the creature to which it is directed.

A second point on which Hegel is unquestionably right is that if God reveals, he must reveal something about *himself*. Even a faith in which God discloses no more than a relation to man hears a message *from* and *about* God. A revelation which would merely teach man how to pass through this world in authentic human style without determining his relation to the transcendent, as some secular theologians advocate, would not only be superfluous but is no revelation at all. In the revelation God must somehow communicate his own reality. This is more than a message about his reality, for the primary "content" is God himself. "Man receives, and he receives not a specific 'content' but a Presence, a Presence as power."[28] As Hegel wrote in a somewhat

[26] Claude Bruaire, *L'affirmation de Dieu,* pp. 246–47.
[27] This difficult term will have to be defined in the chapter on creation.
[28] Martin Buber, *I and Thou,* tr. by Ronald Gregor Smith (New York: Charles Scribner's Sons, 1958), p. 110.

different context, God's presence itself is the knowing of God (*ein Dasein das selbst das Wissen ist*).[29] The description is particularly appropriate for a faith which conceives the revealing Word as a living person: here God gives *himself* in his message. It is not sufficient, then, to define the revelation as a religious *experience*. A new experience may accompany the relation but does not constitute it. In fact, as Martin Buber remarked, the *meaning* of revelation always surpasses its experience. "This meaning can be received, but not experienced; it cannot be experienced but it can be done, and this is its purpose with us."[30]

After having defined the concept of revelation within manageable restrictions, we are now ready to tackle the initial question: How can the transcendent reveal itself and yet remain transcendent? In answering it we must take full account of the thesis, so heavily emphasized in negative theology, that all determination is finite and must therefore be negated. Hegel attempted to do this. For him God reveals himself not as determined but as the *movement* which both posits and abolishes all determinations.[31] The very act by which God differentiates and indifferentiates himself is also the act and content of the revelation. Two things are remarkable in this view. One, negation is essential to divine reality itself and should not be attributed exclusively to the inadequacy of the human mind facing the transcendent. Two, the mind actively participates in the divine movement toward the finite and back to the infinite. In the revelation man understands himself *in and through* God. To grasp one's relation to God requires therefore, at least implicitly, that God himself be revealed, for to see one's relation *to* God is to see it *in* God. A similar insight inspired the Greek Fathers to base the "economy" of salvation upon a "theology," that is, a revelation of God's inner life.

But does the dialectic of God's manifestation entirely coincide with the "theology" of his inner life? The answer to this specula-

---

[29] *Encyclopädie* (1830), 563.
[30] *I and Thou*, p. 110.
[31] *Vorlesungen*, IV, p. 35.

tive question determines whether divine revelation is exhaustive, as Hegel would hold, or whether the divine mystery remains ultimately inaccessible to the mind.[32] With most believers I would have serious reservations about a total revelation. For if the dialectic of manifestation coincides with the movement of God's own life, the latter falls entirely under the sway of an immanent logic. The formally revealed then becomes the autonomously intelligible. This implies, as Hegel knew, that faith cannot be man's final attitude with respect to the content of revelation: the definitive expression then must come from philosophy.[33]

To avoid this conclusion I see no alternative but to assume that God remains unspeakable after all has been said and that revelation ultimately manifests the impenetrable darkness of the divine mystery.[34] Abraham Heschel has drawn attention to the remarkable fact that perhaps the oldest instance of negative theology appears in a description of divine revelation. The story of God's manifestation to Elijah in 1 Kings 19:11–12 describes the Lord as being present not in the storm wind, the earthquake, or the fire, but in "the voice of silence" which followed the fire.[35] Revelation changes nothing about the fact, explained earlier, that all language about God must be symbolic. God as he is in

[32] Hegel does not stand alone with his concept of total revelation. Among contemporary theologians Thomas J. J. Altizer has advanced the bold claim that the dialectic of the sacred (as man experiences it) manifests the inner process of God and that man's present inability to perceive the sacred marks the real death of God. Others more optimistically believe that the religious dialectic continues beyond the present negation. But they also consider it an expression of God's inner life.

[33] Hegel never *substituted* philosophy for faith, as is often claimed, for his philosophy *presupposes* a revelation received in faith. Nevertheless it is philosophy and not faith which for Hegel ultimately determines the meaning of revelation. Taking its lead from the revealed, philosophy becomes entirely autonomous in the process of its development.

[34] The naïvely beautiful conclusion of the Fourth Gospel refers not only to the quantity of Jesus' deeds but to the unfathomable mystery of his existence to the eye of the believer: "There is much else that Jesus did. If it were all to be recorded in detail, I suppose the whole world would not hold the books that would be written." John 21:25.

[35] *God in Search of Man* (New York: Harper & Row, 1966), p. 186.

himself remains a *Deus absconditus* even though he reveals *himself*. For to reveal himself truly he must reveal himself *as transcendent*, that is, ultimately as beyond comprehension. "In being revealed [the transcendent] does not cease to remain concealed, since its secrecy pertains to its very essence; and when therefore it is revealed it is so precisely as that which is hidden."[86] All communication from God bears the mark of ultimate incommunicability. In that one sense it is true that revelation fully discloses only the *relation* between God and man, even though a revelation about the relation must be primarily about the one who initiated it. Nothing can reveal God totally as he is in himself.

3. FAITH, THE SOURCE OF REVELATION

The restrictions of the recipient affect the active constitution of the revelation as well as its passive reception. If the divine communication is to make sense at all, it must be actively integrated within a particular (and therefore limited) universe of discourse.[87] Since all human discourse is equipped to refer *di-*

---

[86] Paul Tillich, "Die Idee der Offenbarung" in *Zeitschrift für Theologie und Kirche*, 8, p. 406. The I Vatican Council which so strongly emphasized the cognitive aspect of faith, nevertheless declared: "Divine mysteries of their nature so excel the created intellect that even when they have been given in revelation and accepted by faith, that very faith still keeps them veiled in a sort of obscurity, as long as 'we are exiled from the Lord' in this mortal life." *Enchiridion Symbolorum*, Dz. �֍1796.

[87] Here at least John Locke understood that man's intake is determined by his cognitive equipment. His verdict on the communicability of private revelations applies even more directly to its primary reception. "Supposing God should discover to any one, supernaturally, a species of creatures inhabiting, for example, Jupiter or Saturn (for that it is possible there may be such, nobody can deny) which had six senses; and imprint on his mind the idea conveyed to theirs by that sixth sense: he could no more, by words, produce in the mind of other men those ideas imprinted by that sixth sense, than one of us could convey the idea of any color, by the sound of words, into a man who, having the other four senses perfect, had always totally wanted the fifth, of seeing." *An Essay Concerning Human Understanding*, Bk. 4, 18, 3.

rectly only to intra-mundane relations, the question arises how the transcendent can survive being expressed in the language of immanence. Hamann sought the answer in the ambiguous nature of revelatory symbols. Their appearance suggests a different content, but they do not yield this content directly. Faith alone can free the transcendent message from its immanent appearance.[38] Kierkegaard, influenced by Hamann, considered the paradox the medium by which revelation draws attention to the transcendent nature of its message and thus prevents it from being totally assimilated in the immanence of the subject. This position may seem surprising, since faith for Kierkegaard consists in inwardness. But it is precisely because the revealed object is not fully given and directly assimilable that the subject must turn into itself. Thus the inwardness of faith directly results from the transcendence of the revealed. By its paradoxical character revelation repels the understanding, drives the mind inward, and permanently maintains a dialectical tension between the revealed content and the interiority of the subject.[39]

Hamann and Kierkegaard are basically right. Faith alone provides the key to unlock the transcendent meaning of the revealed. It alone separates the transcendent content from the immanent appearances in which it resides. By themselves symbols, ideas, or events, however unusual, cannot point beyond the immanent universe to which they belong. Christians believe that Jesus was God. Yet any attempt to prove this on the basis of his deeds and words is doomed to failure. For the transcendent as such does not appear. What makes words and deeds surpass their intra-mundane appearance is the constitutive act of faith.[40] Faith alone transforms events into religious events and words into revelations. Only the eyes of the believer perceive the revealed

[38] See particularly his *Socratic Memorabilia,* ed. and tr. by James C. O'Flaherty (Baltimore: Johns Hopkins Press, 1967).

[39] *Samlede Vaerker,* X, p. 272. Unscientific Postscript, tr. by David Swenson and Walter Lowrie (Princeton: Princeton University Press, 1944), p. 540.

[40] The term faith is used here in the larger sense of an active religious attitude, not in the narrow, exclusively modern and Christian sense to which the first chapter restricted it.

as revealed. Words and events may appear unusual (Kierke-gaard would say "paradoxical"), but they do not appear divine. Faith receives them as such and thereby constitutes them as revealed. Prior to this constitution, words and events, however extraordinary, do not *reveal*. Faith and revelation are, therefore, religiously indissoluble.[41] This is particularly the case when the transcendent is revealed as a person. A person can never disclose himself objectively: to understand him in his uniqueness requires belief in him. Only in trust does one learn the "truth" about another person.[42] Faith is the only appropriate response to a God who reveals himself *personally*.

A revelation which demands faith can obviously not be a mere source of information. Yet in the past few centuries Catholic and "orthodox" Lutheran theologians came to regard revelation as a set of true propositions which the mind receives instead of dis-covering them by its own powers. The emphasis in such a view is all on authority. Its main qualities are clarity and certitude: a propositional revelation guarantees the accuracy of the wording (divinely inspired) as well as the reliability of the interpretations (for Catholics, the authority of the magisterium). Much to its credit modern theology has almost entirely rejected this view.[43] Knowledge cannot be *received*. Many theologians have therefore come to deny that revelation contains any truth. Such a position, however, must in the end be destructive of faith. Revelation may be more than "true" in the strictly cognitive sense to which Western usage now restricts that term, but some cognitive truth is a condition of its existence. Yet it is never a supernatural source of information on "objects" for which no natural sources

---

[41] This, in spite of his "liberal" bias, is a point which Auguste Sabatier had well understood in his *Outlines of a Philosophy of Religon*, tr. by T. A. Seed (New York: Harper & Brothers, 1957), pp. 32–33.

[42] See, e.g., Max Scheler, *The Nature of Sympathy*, tr. by Peter Heath (London: Routledge & Kegan Paul, 1954), pp. 147–61.

[43] It is hardly exaggerated to claim, as Ray Hart does, that no proposition would gain wider acceptance than the following one: "The content of revelation is not a body of propositions to be accepted as the condition of faith." *Unfinished Man and the Imagination* (New York: Herder and Herder, 1969), p. 80.

are available. How untenable such a view is appears as soon as
we raise the question: What enables man to *receive* information
on matters entirely beyond his comprehension?[44] Knowledge is
man's presence to himself. This presence to himself allows him
to illuminate all Being, but not to accept a totally unrelated
piece of information. The informational view faces the dilemma
that either the revealed is ultimately irrelevant to human existence, at least in its present condition, or that revelation teaches
truths which man could discover by himself. In the latter supposition, revelation, as Lessing saw very well, is no more than
the education of the human race to its own self-understanding.
As truths of faith develop into truths of reason, revelation, like
a good educator, would make itself superfluous.[45]

I submit that revelation contains no "information" in the ordinary sense at all. No one can learn from it how and when the
universe originated, whether history progresses or regresses, which
moral and cultural goals man should pursue at a given time.
The truth of the revelation—and every positive revelation claims
above all other things to be *true*—is the truth of a new *interpretation* of man's place in the universe. Rather than providing new
information, revelation opens up a new dimension in a reality
known through the mind's own activity. It is, in the words of H.
Richard Niebuhr, "a special occasion which provides us with an
image by means of which all the occasions of personal and common life become intelligible."[46] It unites the disparate moments
of existence into one meaningful totality. But this meaning cannot be expressed in purely conceptual terms. Nor is the new
dimension "added" to existence: it is present from the start and
revelation brings it to full awareness. That is its truth. Such a

[44] As Karl Rahner does in *Hörer des Wortes*, pp. 33–34, *Hearers of the
Word*, p. 19.
[45] Gothold Ephraim Lessing, *Die Erziehung des Menschengeschlechts*, in
Werke, ed. by Rob. Riemann (Leipzig, 1908), VI, pp. 201–19. *The Education of the Human Race* in *Lessing's Theological Writings*, tr. by Henry
Chadwick (Stanford, Calif.: Stanford University Press, 1967), pp. 82–98.
Kant would follow this thesis of the Enlightenment in his *Religion Within
the Limits of Reason Alone*.
[46] *The Meaning of Revelation*, p. 109.

definition may at first seem to reduce revelation to an immanent quality. But it does nothing of the sort, for the very definition of the transcendent implies that it cannot be *actively conquered*. Even though transcendence belongs to the core of existence, I can only await its self-manifestation. If I could explore it by my own powers, it would cease to be transcendent.

Still the fact remains that all "truth" must be actively articulated by the mind. This activity cannot be bypassed by revealed truth. Yet the essential givenness of the revealed does not interfere with man's cognitive activity. In its contact with the transcendent, existence itself is experienced as given, and speaking (which remains active) turns into listening. Listening itself is still an *act* which brings the act of speaking to completion. This view of revelational truth is not new. It was implied in the doctrine of divine illumination which was continuously asserted from the Alexandrian Fathers to the Cappadocians, to Augustine, to Thomas and Bonaventure. Meanwhile, even the speaking that is listening must use all the apparatus (logic, syntax, ideas) of ordinary speech. Without active articulation there can be no *truth,* even about the most passive experience. No revelation can bypass man's cognitive creativity. Hence, a profound insight is hidden in Feuerbach's remark that what comes from God to man, comes to man only from man in God.[47] To make sense at all, a revelation must be expressed in a particular language whereby it becomes tied to a particular set of symbols of man's own making.

Enough was said in an earlier chapter on the nature of religious symbols and on the creative process which produces them. Here we must merely investigate whether symbolic creativity does not preclude the passive reception which is said to characterize man's attitude toward revelation. Symbolic creativity is the single gate through which the transcendent must enter consciousness, for symbols alone can convey meanings which sufficiently surpass the empirical appearance to express a transcendent content. Yet

[47] *Das Wesen des Christentums* in *Sämtliche Werke,* VI, p. 250. *The Essence of Christianity,* p. 207.

symbolization itself occurs not merely, and perhaps not primarily, on the conscious level. This fact has inspired the most serious objections against a passively received revelation. What we experience as passive, it is said, may be no more than the subconscious activity of the mind. That subconscious powers are at work in the images and concepts of revelation is beyond doubt. As was pointed out in a recent study on the meaning of revelation, the mind is never a vacuum: it is stocked with the archetypal images of times past.[48] The Trinity, the virgin birth, the cult of the Mother are obviously more ancient than their appearance in Christian revelation. Yet religious man should have no difficulty admitting the effect of unconscious symbolization processes upon his understanding of revelation, since *per se* subconscious activity conflicts no more with receptivity than conscious activity. The real question is: Is the revelation *entirely* reducible to this activity? If it is, the claim of uniqueness, essential to historical faiths such as Islam, Christianity, and Judaism, is false. Yet it is not, and again for reasons which Professor Hart has pointed out. Type images are intrinsically undetermined: they mean nothing at all until they come to signify a specific event or object.[49] By themselves archetypes are neither religious nor revelatory; they merely provide the building stones which the mind uses in *constituting* the actual revelation. The existence of archetypal structures excludes a revelation only if one assumes that the process of constitution must occur entirely on a conscious level. But more insight into the epistemic activity of the mind should convince us that this is never the case. It is essential to a historical religion, then, not that it have no symbolic archetypes (it obviously does have them), but that they not be its sole foundation. Archetypal patterns lift the narration of revelatory events out of the ordinary cause-and-effect pattern and charge them with a paradigmatic meaning which ordinary occurrences do not possess. The exodus from Egypt and the forty years of nomadic life in the desert meant more to Israel than the birth of their nation: the events

48 Ray Hart, *Unfinished Man and the Imagination,* p. 297.
49 *Ibid.,* pp. 297–98.

bestowed meaning upon all subsequent life in Israel and definitively molded the Hebrews' religious attitude. They did so by imposing symbolic structures upon historical events. Nevertheless the events themselves are unique occurrences, not returning patterns. Sacred history is so full of mythic and symbolic models that we may call it "mythistory." Yet its content consists of new happenings and it is in this novelty that a historical faith detects the hand of God.

4. REVELATION AS HISTORY

So much interpretation goes into the presentation of "religious" events that we must raise the question whether revelation as history may still be called history. A first part of the answer is easy enough. History always interprets events. Facts remain meaningless until they are compared with previous occurrences and are linked to subsequent events.[50] A theological interpretation of events, then, does not *a priori* rule out their historical character, particularly if this interpretation was given by the men (Jesus, Moses, Mohammed) who initiated the events. But the difficulty reaches much deeper. Sacred history cannot be resolved into the sort of phenomenal continuity which seems to be essential to the scientific concept of history. Granted, the historian uses models, perhaps even myths, in his interpretation of events, but empirical evidence must be the ultimate criterion for their adoption or rejection. The types and interpretations of the sacred historian, on the contrary, can never be borne out by the facts, for they belong in the final analysis to a nonempirical realm. His way of telling a story is ultimately nonhistorical, not because it is interpretive (all history is), but because his interpretation can-

---

[50] Wolfhart Pannenberg rightly remarks: "The events of history speak their own language, the language of facts; however, this language is understandable only in the context of the traditions and expectations in which the given events occur." "Dogmatic Theses on the Doctrine of Revelation" in *Revelation As History*, p. 153.

not become more or less acceptable by additional evidence.[51] Most of the time there is no evidence or insufficient historical evidence to favor a religious interpretation above a nonreligious one. Professor Austin Farrer underscored this point in a lecture given toward the end of his life:

> Theological history [i.e., history as revelation] does not and cannot resolve its mythical diagrams into the succession or interplay of human acts; they must stand for a reality which is the continuous operation of the divine will . . . [Believers] unquestionably hold that God is an historical agent not pinned to a point of time, but able as out of another dimension to exert his power at every moment; and if sacred history does not show the hand of God it neither is nor mediates divine revelation.[52]

If history consists of a coherent interpretation on an *empirical basis* of observable events, revelatory history cannot be called history at all. Its interpretative models differ entirely from the ones which scientific history uses. Nor can sacred history claim a separate set of facts as its own, for facts alone are not sacred. The same historical science deals with all facts, the ones which theology declares "revelatory" as well as others; and it deals with all in the same way. The notion of revelation-history belongs in theology and nowhere else.

This does not mean that history as such is of no concern to the believer. It obviously is, since the believer must interpret his faith *within* the events of the past, not *à propos* of them. His-

---

[51] There are exceptions to this rule. The resurrection of Christ must be considered an essential fact. Theoretically it is conceivable that new historical evidence would confirm or weaken the establishment of this fact. This would have a direct impact upon sacred history as such. We might add that all miraculous facts are of this nature. They carry their own interpretation to the extent that if the mere *fact* is proven false, the entire religious interpretation of it collapses; if it is proven to be true, the presumption is strongly in favor of the religious interpretation.

[52] Austin Farrer, *Faith and Speculation* (New York: New York University Press, 1967), p. 93.

torical verification of some sort, then, becomes an essential ingredient in any faith which claims to rest upon historical revelation. Such historical research becomes abusive only when it takes itself as ultimate criterion for the interpretation of faith.[53] In what sense can history be said to be revealing for religious man? Not by attributing a hierophanic meaning to time, for, as Eliade has shown, all religions recognize a sacred time.[54] Nor by giving history a place in the religious attitude, for it does so inevitably once man starts attributing any meaning at all to history. At that moment every experience, including the religious one, attains a historical dimension.[55] But that is obviously not what the Hebrews meant in saying that God reveals himself through history. In a historical faith, such as that of Israel, history occupies a *privileged* revelatory position: it is more revealing than anything else.[56] But how? Once again, the revelatory quality of an event does not reside in the event alone but in the *interpreted* event. As a rule this interpretation itself is not immediately settled. It is an ongoing process in which the past is constantly reinterpreted. The first chapters of Genesis articulate Israel's vision of the beginning at a particular stage (or stages) of its history. Later reports in Ben Sirach 42:15–43, 35; Baruch 3:24–35; Job 37–40; Psalms 8 and 104; cover the same ground and

[53] This point is well developed in Louis Monden, S.J., *Faith: Can Man Still Believe* (New York: Sheed & Ward, 1970).

[54] *Images and Symbols,* p. 170.

[55] History-conscious man, whatever the nature of his revelation may be, cannot but agree with the words of Eliade: "There is no such thing as a pure 'religious' datum, outside of history. For there is no such thing as a human datum that is not at the same time a historical datum. Every religious experience is expressed and transmitted in a particular historical context." "History of Religions and a New Humanism" in *History of Religions* (Summer 1961), p. 6. As soon as man becomes aware of history the sacred takes on a historical dimension.

[56] To say this is not to say that believers in a historical revelation invented the historical science, as is often maintained. None of the Hebrew historians compares with Thucydides or Polybius. See James Barr, "Revelation Through History in the Old Testament and in Modern Theology" in *New Theology,* I, ed. by Martin Marty and Dan G. Peerman (New York: Macmillan, 1964).

reinterpret it according to new needs and insights. But at each stage of the process events are presented in such a way that they cannot be explained as the deeds of men only. Sacred historiography endows its facts with a mysterious quality which requires further investigation. The suggestion of something that cannot be explained by ordinary laws of history, it has been said, is what distinguishes the narratives of Genesis from those of Homer.

> The stories are not, like Homer's, simply narrated "reality." Doctrine and promise are incarnate in them and inseparable from them; for that very reason they are fraught with "background" and mysterious, containing a second, concealed meaning . . . and therefore they require subtle investigation and interpretation, they demand them.[57]

One other prefatory remark. A historical faith does not consider all events of equal status. Some are thought to express the divine will in a unique way. Are we to call such paradigmatic events revelatory? Not if revelation means *self-disclosure* of God. Paradigmatic events reveal God indirectly insofar as they refer to him as to their principal agent, but they do not manifest God himself. Originally the Hebrews seem to have conceived of no other revelation than the salvific interventions which led to the occupancy of the promised land. Later prophets as Ezekiel and Deutero-Isaiah turned from the past to the future and announced a full disclosure of the Lord in which history would come to an end. Primitive Christian faith shared those ideas: until the day of Judgment, Jesus would not directly reveal his divinity.[58] Paradoxically, then, in historical faiths a full revelation does not take

[57] Erich Auerbach, *Mimesis* (Princeton: Princeton University Press, 1953), p. 15.
[58] See, the important studies edited by Wolfhart Pannenberg under the title *Revelation As History,* particularly the "Introduction" by Pannenberg (esp. pp. 15–16), "The Concept of Revelation in Ancient Israel" by Rolf Rendtorff (p. 27), "The Understanding of Revelation Within the History of Primitive Christianity" (pp. 59, 111).

place *in* history but at the end of it. Only after the event does history become truly revealing.[59]

The Christian concept of revelation is usually opposed to the Hebrew one in that it includes all of history, not merely the history of one people.[60] Actually, every historical revelation must eventually involve all of history. The eschatological vision of the end which Israel developed during the last centuries before our era was to include all nations. Even earlier, the story of a universal creation had been added as a prelude to Israel's salvation history.[61] It is overly simplistic, then, to oppose Christian to Hebrew sacred history as the universal to the particular. Yet there is a difference, for in Christianity the idea of a universal salvation is not restricted to the beginning or the end. Christ is given a central place in world history whence he reaches out to the beginning and to the end. Endowing Christ with all the attributes of the *Chokma,* the Hebrew "Wisdom" (in Proverbs, Ben Sirach, the Book of Wisdom), Christian faith envisions him as transcending the restrictions of his particular place in history and participating in the work of creation.[62] Heir to the eschatological visions of Ezekiel and Daniel, Christ is expected to occupy the chair of the final Judge at the end of history.

Since salvation consists in God's self-communication, it ultimately coincides with revelation. If God reveals through history,

[59] "It is not so much the course of history as it is the end of history that is at one with the essence of God. But insofar as the end presupposes the course of history, because it is the perfection of it, then also the course of history belongs in essence to the revelation of God, for history receives its unity from its goals." Wolfhart Pannenberg, "Dogmatic Theses on the Doctrine of Revelation" in *Revelation As History,* pp. 132–33.

[60] See Karl Rahner, *Revelation and Tradition, Quaestiones Disputatae,* 17, p. 14.

[61] A well-known Midrash relates how God revealed the Torah not only to Israel but to all the nations, and how for one reason or another, all but Israel repudiated the offer. The legend shows that at least the original purpose of revelation was universal. *Hammer on the Rock. A Midrash Reader,* ed. by Nahum Glatzer (New York: Schocken Books, 1962), pp. 45–46. Commentary in Solomon Schechter, *Aspects of Rabbinic Theology* (New York: Schocken Books, 1961), pp. 130–33.

[62] See, e.g., Coloss. 1:13–20.

then, he must also save through history, even though his revelation involves judgment and condemnation of the faithless. The Incarnation determines all of history and the historical event as such becomes capable of transmitting transhistorical salvation. "Since the incarnation of Christ, the Christian is supposed to look for the interventions of God not only in the Cosmos . . . but also in historical events."[63] But a universal salvation history creates some peculiar problems. Faith saves *from* the world and frequently *against* the world. To be truly salvific, world history must ultimately be lifted out of its own course onto another plane where the opposition between the elect and "the world" will be fully revealed. The very notion of historical revelation implies an eschatological end. Here again we perceive the negative impact of religious transcendence: the transcendent can reveal itself in history only by abolishing it as history. How closely the idea of the *end* is connected with the concept of historical revelation appears if we compare it with a nonhistorical faith. In the latter the course of human events participates in the periodic alternation of nature (without necessarily following the same cycle). Far from requiring an end of history, its revelation would be abolished altogether by such an end. On the other hand, the eschatological view of history survives even in the secularized offsprings of Judaism and Christianity. The idea of progress, first substitute for development toward a transcendent terminus of history, is deeply rooted in religious eschatology. Only when the fullness of reality is expected at the end of history does progress make sense. Similarly, the Marxist projection of the communist society of the future cannot be fully understood without the anticipation of a transhistorical parousy.[64]

Also implied in the idea of historical revelation is the connection between God's revealing will and man's autonomous activity. History consists of the deeds of man. To reveal himself through history, then, God must manifest his presence in human actions. The difficulty of combining divine determination with human

[63] Mircea Eliade, *Images and Symbols*, p. 170.
[64] Mircea Eliade, *Cosmos and History* (New York: Harper & Brothers, 1959), pp. 152, 154.

freedom is not eased by juxtaposing revelation and human autonomy as codeterminants, for freedom cannot coexist with "other" determinations without being suppressed, and revelation loses its transcendent character if it is to "depend" on independent human decisions. Revelation through history must not be understood as a divine *choice* predetermining or complementing a human choice. In history man alone chooses, although God may be the ground of his choosing. If all of history is revelatory, as in Christianity, God must be everywhere at once—even in contradictory and morally unacceptable choices. The genealogy of Jesus according to Matthew includes Solomon—"his mother had been the wife of Uriah" (Mt. 1:6)—thus making David's adultery with Bathsheba an integral part of divine salvation. Further discussion of this problem must be postponed to the ninth chapter. Unless we are able to show there that freedom and divine determination are genuinely compatible, a historical revelation is impossible.

5. RELATIVITY AND PERMANENCE OF THE HISTORICAL REVELATION

In the meantime an equally difficult problem demands immediate attention: How can a message be historical without being subject to all the changes of history? A historical revelation is necessarily restricted by the symbolic idiom of a particular civilization. Its images and ideas are part of the same cultural totality as those literary creations which the believer does not regard as revealed. The writings of the New Testament share a number of conceptions and prejudices with the late Hellenistic culture in which they originated. Ideas about magic, slavery, and nationalism are not divided along the lines of Scriptural inspiration. Moreover, the events of revelation are with all other events woven into a single historical fabric. A revelation *through* history is necessarily subject to the laws of history. Believers in a historical faith are anxious enough to claim the first half of this statement but reluctant to admit the second. Yet, whatever stands in history becomes part of a changing process. The past takes on new meanings as it moves into the future. If we are fortunate enough to retrieve the original meaning of a historical message (no mean task, indeed), we must still integrate it within our own, different universe of discourse. Language develops as culture expands, and in developing it articulates the ongoing revision of values in man's axiological creativity. The revealed message does not escape this common fate of all historical expression. Most often the evolution happens so gradually that the believer is hardly aware how he is adapting old texts to new contexts. Yet at certain times the words of revelation seem to come from a strange past which has vanished forever. How can the religious consciousness survive this ordeal?

A positive revelation inevitably takes place at a particular moment of a cultural process which continues to develop afterward. Since man constantly re-creates himself and his world, no concrete statement concerning his situation in the world can be definitive. To the extent that a historical revelation contains such judgments—as it invariably does—it must be subject to change. Christians are usually startled when confronted with these inexorable consequences. If Christ was truly human in more than a biological sense, as his followers so strongly proclaim, he was bound by the cultural limitations of his time.[65] His message contained elements which would be developed long after him and other elements which later believers could no longer accept in their own world view. The price to pay for a historical revelation is some sort of contingency.

[65] This would seem to be clearly implied by the definitions of the Council of Chalcedon (*Enchiridion Symbolorum* No. 148). It is obviously not sufficient to take refuge from these consequences in his divine nature, for the whole problem is how the two must be synthesized. One does not have to be Arian or Monophysite to understand that a person can have only one consciousness. Nor does the hypostatic union imply that the Godman could grasp the fullness of divine nature. For an intelligent discussion of this problem see Gabriel Moran, *Theology of Revelation* (New York: Herder and Herder, 1966), pp. 68–71; also Avery Dulles, "The Theology of Revelation" in *Theological Studies*, 25 (1964), p. 47.

At the same time a revelation must possess a lasting quality which allows its central message to resist the flux of historical change. By itself the purely historical cannot convey a permanent message. If revelation became mere process, it would cease to be revelatory. H. Richard Niebuhr, after having conceded the relative nature of all that is historical, rightly concluded:

> Revelation if it be revelation of God, must offer men something more immovable than the pole star and something more precise than our measurements of the winds and currents of history can afford.[66]

Some theologians hope to escape the dilemma of stability and historicity by settling for a continuous message rather than a permanent one. But this compromise does not solve anything until it appears that continuity can exist without permanence.

How could events and words of a historical past ever be permanently decisive in establishing a relation to the transcendent? The full moment of the question was first perceived by Lessing. How, he wondered, could the acceptance of Jesus' resurrection as a historical fact ever lead one to conform his entire existence today to the claim that he is God? "What is the connection between my inability to raise any significant objection to the evidence of the former and my obligation to believe something against which my reason rebels?"[67] We may discard as an odd reminder of Lessing's own historical relativity the rationalist belief that every person would indeed be willing to stake everything on a revelation of the necessary truths of reason.[68] Yet the main question stands: How can the purely historical ever attain a transhistorical status? Or, how can the past remain permanently present? In spite of the strong historical awareness of our own age, I find little desire among current theologians

---

[66] *The Meaning of Revelation* (New York: Harper & Row, 1962), p. 54.
[67] Gothold Ephraim Lessing, *Werke*, ed. by Rob. Riemann, Vol. 6, p. 224. Tr. "On the Proof of the Spirit and the Power" by Henry Chadwick, in *Lessing's Theological Writings*, p. 54.
[68] Kierkegaard would say that every risk requires an act of faith: a commitment to a historical event is in that respect on a par with an irrefutable, "necessary truth."

to tackle this problem. Most of them are perfectly satisfied with "historical" or "Scriptural" theology, optimistically hoping that a better understanding of the past will somehow make the original revelation reverberate into the present. The position implies the remarkable contention that revelation will reach us as it reached the early community if only we study history, while it is precisely its past character which seems to make the message irrelevant or even unacceptable.[69] The underlying argument, I believe, is the easy analogy that, since the events and words of revelation at one time sparked off a new relation to the transcendent, there is no reason why they could not do so again if properly placed in their original context. But there is a reason! For the better we understand the past, the more we realize that it is not the present. Others, steeped in hermeneutics, promise less and deliver nothing. They are too busy showing the uniqueness of the events and the inevitable change of every subsequent reading of it to explain how throughout all these changes it can still remain identical.

What we need is a proof that a historical event can convey a lasting message to each subsequent generation. To provide such a proof is beyond the scope of this chapter, since it would imply a full clarification of all the ways in which the past can be present.[70] Yet restricting ourselves to religious symbols, we find that they always surpass the immediate present, insofar as they always point beyond their actual appearance. Unlike some other symbols, symbols of the transcendent are not tied to their historical form and expression. The awareness of the intrinsic inadequacy of expression, which is inherent to the religious symbol, gives it a unique flexibility. Thus the symbols of a historical

[69] See Gabriel Moran, *Theology of Revelation*, p. 53.
[70] Karl Rahner went to the roots of the problem: "Only when it can be demonstrated in a metaphysical anthropology that the foundation of man's spiritual existence in historical events (and hence the question about historical happenings) belong *a priori* to the nature of man and form part of his inescapable duties, do we find that a basis for the assumption of the proof of a specific historical fact and the difficulty of a rationalist and enlightened philosophy such as Lessing's can be basically resolved." *Hörer des Wortes*, p. 36. *Hearers of the Word*, p. 21.

revelation are able to adopt new meanings while maintaining a full continuity with their past.[71] Their religious intentionality enables them to transcend their historical context and to overcome the cultural restrictions of their origin.

Surely, to point out the tension between the noema of the religious symbol and its forms of expression is not to solve the entire historical problem. For one might think, with some theologians of the recent past, that the culturally antiquated form of the revelation can be detached from its lasting content. Such an endeavor, as a moment's reflection might have suggested, is wholly unsatisfactory. For one thing, it presupposes that man can lift himself sufficiently out of his historical condition to commit a perennial content to a historical form and subsequently translate it out of this form into a "universal" language. If this were the case, one wonders why the content was not formulated directly in its universal form. The historical embodiment, then, appears to be a mere detour. But if the original expression is historically determined, so is the later interpretation. A complete "demythologization"—which eliminates all historical determinations—is therefore intrinsically impossible.

A reflection on the nature of the symbol exposes even more the methodological error in all attempts to separate form from content. A symbol never consists of a disposable form wrapped around a permanent content. More than any other characteristic, the indissoluble unity of form and content is essential to the symbolization process. A change in form affects the content of the symbol. No one would question this for the work of art, but the reason is just as cogent for the religious symbol, for its function is precisely to open a *perspective* upon the transcendent reality and for this purpose the form cannot be an indif-

[71] Karl Jaspers is wrong in regarding the symbols of revelation as univocal and unambiguous, and therefore ultimately unsatisfactory as symbols of the transcendent. (*Philosophical Faith and Revelation*, pp. 104–14.) Revealed symbols are no more self-contained than other religious symbols. If they did not point beyond themselves, they would cease to be religious altogether. That a symbol is revealed does not mean that the transcendent reality is "contained" in it, but that religious man considers it a privileged, less inadequate way of speaking of the transcendent.

ferent matter. The Churches have, therefore, upheld in the face of major difficulties that also the revealed form must be preserved and that divine inspiration extends to the wording itself. Fundamentalists corrupt this profound insight by attributing to the original expression a magical and superhuman quality which conflicts with the nature of the symbol. The confusion results from the mistaken assumption that if the wording is revealed it cannot be human and must thus escape all historical relativity. Revelation, in this view, retains its divine quality only by freezing its symbols into immutable past facts. The role of the sacred writer is confined to that of an *amanuensis,* a secretary who contributes nothing but a pair of ears to perceive the inspired whisper and a hand to write it down.

Our purpose in defending the indissolubility of expression and meaning-content of revealed symbols is the exact opposite. Instead of eliminating all possibility of development, as the fundamentalist does, we extend the development to the entire symbol —form and content. The original expression must be preserved, but that is only half the work. It is not sufficient to let the façade stand and erect a new building behind it, as communities pressed for change and unable to justify it tend to do. (One recalls the farfetched "interpretations" of Catholic theologians during the antimodernist repression of the Holy Office.) The meaning must be preserved with the expression, yet in such a way that it fully incorporates the entire evolution from the moment of revelation to the present. To discover this meaning is the true task of hermeneutics. Beyond an up-to-date exegesis of the past as past, it must attempt to understand the past in the light of the present. The present introduces a new element which ought to be fully accepted if the past is to be understood as a living reality. Attempts to bypass the distance between past and present inevitably reduce the message to a dead letter and a purely historical event.[72]

[72] The hermeneutic task of understanding the past through the present does not consist exclusively, or even primarily, in an interpretation of words. Words are the illuminating side of events. Far from being the whole problem,

Still, reading the past in the light of the present is not without risk, for we bring to it a number of presuppositions. Which ones are legitimate? Which ones are biases of our time? Time alone will determine which principles of today will turn out to be prejudices tomorrow. But one rule would seem to provide at least a basic principle of discernment to prevent destructive innovations. The interpretation of the past through the present must fully acknowledge the tradition in between the two historical points.[73] Man never thinks alone: he always stands in a tradition, and his only possibility of attaining truth lies in fully recognizing this tradition. This is particularly true in the case of a historical revelation where the believer's faith attains the original events only through the various stages of interpretation. We have assumed the legitimacy of historical development. But is this assumption justified, particularly in view of the erratic and often irrational character which marks the process of religious traditions? Is a revelation able to transmit its transcendent message through subsequent interpretations which cannot reasonably be claimed to have been present, even "implicitly," in the original message? If historical faith originates in a clearly defined message, all later additions would seem to jeopardize the purity of the origin. The existence of a tradition, which has caused so much legitimate concern in theology, can be justified only by estab-

---

they provide most of the assistance for the solution. Gerhard Ebeling has aptly drawn attention to this extension from word to event. "The primary phenomenon in the realm of understanding is not understanding of language, but understanding *through* language. The word is not really the object of understanding—and thus the thing that poses the problem of understanding —the solution of which requires exposition and therefore also hermeneutics as the theory of understanding. Rather the word is what opens up and mediates understanding, i.e., brings something to understanding. The word itself has a hermeneutic function." *Word and Faith,* p. 318.

[73] In an enlightening study on the hermeneutical problem in theology Edward Schillebeeckx illustrates this principle: "Thanks to the distance in time between, for example, the Council of Trent and our present, we can understand the Council of Trent in the light of the present. Thanks to this distance which is filled by the continuity of tradition, we can make a distinction in our understanding between legitimate and illegitimate prejudgments." *God the Future of Man,* tr. by N. D. Smith (New York: Sheed & Ward, 1968), p. 27.

lishing the traditional character of the original revelation itself. If the events and writings of revelation had been delivered directly, without the intermediacy of interpretation, all later interpretations would be spurious, since they would always deviate from the original, uninterpreted message. Yet if the revealed events and words were interpreted from the very beginning, then revelation may be considered as traditional in its very nature. In the past, the Christian Churches usually posed the problem in the narrow terms of a dilemma between "Scripture" and "tradition." Catholics would uphold tradition, Protestants Scripture. But revelation is neither Scripture alone nor Scripture interpreted by a *subsequent* tradition. Underneath their violent polemics, the antagonists harmoniously agreed in misstating the problem. To its lasting credit, *Formgeschichte* has placed tradition *before* Scripture, thereby changing the terms of the problem to a point where pertinent discussion becomes possible. Scripture does not come first. Jews have always known that Israel existed as a religious society long before prophets and priests, sages and historians, interpreted its unique experience; and Christians were aware that the community of their earliest predecessors flourished long before Paul and Mark started writing. Yet *Formgeschichte* has made it unambiguously clear that the Scriptures were intended as *interpretations* for the instruction of the communities. Thus tradition and interpretation are established in the very heart of Scriptural revelation. Even Jewish theologians, with their profound respect for the Word of God, do not hesitate to refer to the Bible as a *midrash* of revelation, that is, a commentary upon the original mystery.[74] The new insight is not limited to Scripture; it goes back to the original events and words. For events become religious and, *a fortiori*, revelatory only in and through interpretation. By themselves they all belong to the one skein of history, the raw material of historical science, which is neither religious nor profane. The religious consciousness alone makes an event stand out as religious and even as revealing. This may be done during its very occurrence. One and the same intentionality made the

[74] Abraham Heschel, *God in Search of Man*, p. 185.

acts of Jesus' adult life both into historical facts and religious events. He himself *intended* (that is, interpreted) his acts religiously and thereby constituted them into revelations. Henry Duméry defined the original event of Christian revelation with great precision:

> The fact Jesus is nothing if not constituted by the subject Jesus, not only on the psycho-empirical level but also on the level of its profound spiritual meaning (where faith perceives the person of the Word). Once constituted, it carries a meaning. This meaning may be recaptured, literally reconstituted by other subjects.[75]

Yet there is more than reconstitution, for the religious event does not end at the moment of its occurrence. The great deeds of the liberation of Israel were not completed after Moses had finally looked down upon the promised land, or even after David had conquered and pacified the new country. Centuries of prophetic proclamation and sapiential reflection were to complete the *process of meaning* initiated by the exodus. They also belong to the revelation. Similarly, Jesus' message was not delivered after his final words were spoken on the Mountain in Galilee. The Christian revelation consisted as much in interpretations after the events—by the synoptics, by Paul who never witnessed any of them, by the theologian who authored the Fourth Gospel, and, before all, by the primitive Christian community. Even Jesus' words were not final, for they also required that unique process of meditation which lately we have come to call "proclamation." The religious intepretation of the revelation is for a major part *reinterpretation*. It was so from the beginning. Scripture is a privileged part of the tradition,[76] decisive in that it gives tradition a definitive turn, but not, as the term "inspiration" has all too often suggested, in that it starts the revelatory process or closes the tradition. Scripture emerges out of tradition, first by reflecting a particular stage of it, then by being selected

[75] Henry Duméry, *La foi n'est pas un cri,* 2d ed. (Paris, 1959), p. 253.
[76] Privileged more by the content and circumstances in which it took place than by the mode of expression.

(at a later stage) above other expressions of the religious community. The selection of canons in Israel and the Christian Church was as much an interpretive event as the writing itself. Why, for instance, are the Shepherd of Hermas and the Didache not canonical, while the Second Letter of Peter is, even though it may be later in date and not more "religious" in content? Nor was this choice settled after the first five centuries. For the Reformers reopened the whole problem by rejecting some of the previously accepted works, and in some cases, as for example the Epistle of James, mainly for doctrinal reasons. Further problems arose in the wake of nineteenth-century text criticism concerning the "revealed" character of later insertions in canonical writings. Even if all problems of authenticity could come to rest, we would still forever face the difficulty of understanding what was actually intended by the written word. As Newman suggested, the Bible does not carry with it its own interpretation.[77] Scripture in itself can be no more the sole norm of revelation than the initial events and words were. Scripture needs a tradition to be codified and canonized; it needs a further tradition to be understood and interpreted. Revelation, then, succeeds as much of Scripture as it precedes it.

Still, we notice a marked difference in that, subsequent to Scripture, interpretation tends to be *of Scripture* rather than of the original words and events themselves. Jewish, Christian, and Moslem beliefs today are determined by the particular way in which the Scriptures envision those words and events. All post-Scriptural tradition must somehow refer to some original, authoritative expression. That is where the real problem of Scripture and tradition originates. How far can the meaning of the Scriptures be stretched without losing its primitive intentionality? At which point does our interpretation introduce a new meaning instead of capturing anew the old one? That new meanings may be discovered has always been fully accepted by Jews and Christians. The lengthy rereadings of the creation story in Ben Sirach,

[77] *The Via Media of the Anglican Church*, Vol. I, *Collected Works* (London: Longmans, Green, 1874–1921), p. 245.

Baruch, and Job, the interpretations of Old Testament texts by Peter, Paul, and Matthew, leave no doubt on this issue. Even more radical was the discovery of the polyvalent nature of sacred texts in the Jewish and Christian schools of Alexandria. The allegorical interpretation was primarily a way of finding new meanings in old words. The efficacy of this particular approach is dubious, as appears in the polemics over the question whether the allegorical meaning was inspired or not. It avoids the problem by juxtaposing a new meaning to the old one, while the real question is whether the *same* meaning can develop.

No satisfactory answer has been given to this question. Older theories claimed that the development of interpretation consists in explicating what Scripture implicitly contained. Thus for John Henry Newman revelation is an "idea" of many facets which can be fully explored only from a variety of perspectives. "There is no one aspect deep enough to exhaust the contents of a real idea, no one term or proposition which will serve to define it."[78] According to Newman, the existentially rich ideas which determine a man's *Weltanschauung* have a life of their own and need to be developed in order to realize their full potential. They expand with the stages of civilization through which they pass. If revelation is such an idea—and history proves that it is—then it needs an authority to guide its growth lest it deviate from its transcendent source.[79] Development, then, is not an extrinsic addition but an essential requirement of the living idea. The singular merit of Newman's theory is to have stated clearly what is implied in the notion of historical revelation. Yet its limitation is that it unduly restricts development to notional

[78] *An Essay on the Development of Christian Doctrine* (London: Longmans, Green, 1949), p. 33.

[79] "If development must be, then, whereas Revelation is a heavenly gift, He who gave it virtually has not given it, unless He has also secured it from perversion and corruption, in all such development as comes upon it by the necessity of its nature or, in other words, that that intellectual action through successive generations, which is the organ of development, must, so far forth as it can claim to have been put in charge of the Revelation, be in its determinations infallible." *An Essay on Development of Christian Doctrine*, p. 85.

development. Thus revelation is seen as a set of principles which develops into a body of doctrine. Newman writes that Christian teaching from the first age was headed toward "those ecclesiastical dogmas, afterward recognized and defined with (as time went on) more or less determinate advance in the direction of them till at length that advance became so pronounced as to justify their definition and to bring it about."[80] For him, development, however new and unpredictable, basically occurs along the lines of notional explication.

But revelation does not develop primarily as an idea, since it never was primarily an idea, although ideas form a necessary part of its message. Newman, as so many Catholics and Anglicans in the past, one-sidedly emphasized the believer's *intellectual* assent to the revelation. His basic intellectualism is most clearly evident in what he considers to be the criteria of genuine development. Two of them, continuity of principles and logical sequence, are so obviously restricted to *doctrinal* development that Newman's theory could never be seriously considered outside the theory of the Catholic Church. The implicit premise that revelation is a doctrine was outrightly rejected by Schleiermacher and Kierkegaard and has seldom since reappeared in Protestant theology. For Catholics, Newman's theory marks a decisive step forward from the purely conceptual view, according to which development explicates what is logically implicit (as recently restated by Marin-Sola with a dialectical subtlety worthy of a better cause). At least in Newman one may speak of genuine evolution; in the others, one cannot. Newman may be an intellectualist, but he is not a rationalist. His concept of truth is less rigidly confined to a set of propositions than that of his theological contemporaries in the Catholic tradition.

The root of the difficulty is, as Leslie Dewart has perceived, in the concept of truth as adequation to a finished, pre-existing reality. Such a view allows no true development, for "any change in conceptual knowledge would imply a change in the mind's conformity to reality; therefore, a more adequate conformity

[80] *Ibid.,* p. 113.

would imply a previous falsity and, conversely, the truth of earlier concepts would preclude any substantial improvement in their adequation."[81] For Dewart, truth must be understood as man's self-achievement within the requirements of a given situation. Such a definition allows subsequent stages of history to bring out novel values which were not present in the previous ones. Continuity of a religious tradition does not consist in fidelity to a particular cultural expression, for the expression itself is but a process by which we render ourselves present to that-in-which-we-believe.

> This is not, therefore, the continuity of sameness, or the continuity of that which remains (substantially) unchanged in the midst of (accidental) change. Truth cannot remain the same . . . It is rather a *faithful* continuity, that is, a continuity like that of human existence itself which embodies and brings up to the present the progress of its career and the perfection of the original inspiration.[82]

Much as I agree with Dewart's critique of past theories of development I have serious reservations about his theory of truth as conceptualization of experience. Whatever the value of such a definition in other domains may be, the original symbolization of revealed truth expresses more than an experience. Its evolution cannot, therefore, be guided by experience alone, for the expression determined the experience as much as it was determined by it and was, at least partly, meant to surpass experience altogether. Development in such a case must maintain a close continuity with the expression as well as with the experience. Yet new symbolization undoubtedly does take place. To justify it, I would add to Dewart's principle that the new experience must be faithful to the old one, the requirement that the new symbols must be developed in continuity with the old ones. Concretely, the new ones should never replace or contradict the basic intentionality of the old ones. Here Newman's principles,

---

[81] *The Future of Belief* (New York: Herder and Herder, 1966), p. 109.
[82] Dewart, *op. cit.*, p. 117.

interpreted in a less intellectualistic way, would still prove very valuable.

However, such a purely restrictive principle still does not answer the question why evolution follows one direction rather than another. How does its intrinsic dynamism function? The answer falls far beyond the limits of this study and the competence of its author. Nevertheless, an adequate answer must stay clear of the intellectual fallacies of the past. Development of a revealed faith, then, can never be a logical explication, not even in Newman's much wider sense of a developing "idea." As I see it, the development of revelation consists in the ever ongoing reinterpretation of existence as it creates and re-creates its values in the light of a particular, historically determined vision of man's relation to the transcendent. Today theologians seem to have dropped the problem altogether, but eventually they will have to return to it in order to determine whether the novel interpretations which daily emerge out of the present theological confusion may still be called Jewish, Moslem, or Christian. Radical interpreters of the past, such as Spinoza, Lessing, and Strauss, displayed considerably more responsibility in first attempting to establish the basic meaning and authority of Scripture.

Part of today's confusion, particularly in the Catholic Church, stems from the breakdown of ancient authority structures which for centuries fulfilled the function of ultimate criteria of interpretation. The Catholic view of tradition, as Ebeling noticed, was primarily an answer to the hermeneutic question how Scripture may be further interpreted.[83] The infallibility of the Church was a mere consequence of the infallibility of Scripture. This appears clearly in the early Anglican tradition where the term infallibility is used for Scripture in a way which suggests that it is self-sufficient and needs no infallible body for its interpretation.[84] But Catholics became increasingly aware of the fact that

---

[83] Gerhard Ebeling, "Word of God and Hermeneutics" in *Word and Faith*, p. 305.

[84] The position is based on the sixth of the Thirty-Nine Articles: "Holy Scripture containeth all things necessary to salvation, so that whatever is

the hermeneutic problem does not stop at the ecclesiastical *magisterium*. Many of its declarations require an interpretation of their own: they cannot be understood without a great deal of information on the historical circumstances which provoked them. In some cases this information lies so deeply buried under a forgotten controversy that no amount of historical research enables us to determine its exact import. Does the statement of the Fourth Lateran Council that God created the world "from the very beginning of time"[85] define that the universe has existed only a finite number of years, or does it merely reject the Albigensian doctrine that the "creation" of the world was preceded by centuries of an uncreated (in their vocabulary meaning: unredeemed) existence? What is the meaning of the Fourth Constantinopolitan Council's condemnation of Photius' "error" that man possesses two souls, when for all we know he explicitly taught the opposite thesis?[86] It is of little avail to declare all such authoritative interventions infallibly true as long as we do not know what they mean.

But unless one assumes that the revelation is self-evident,[87] the solution to this problem must ultimately lie, as the Churches have always believed, with the religious community as a whole. There is a great divergence of opinion as to how the authority of the community ought to be exercised in matters of interpreta-

---

not read therein, nor may be proved thereby, is not to be required of any man, that it should be believed as an article of the Faith or be thought requisite or necessary to salvation." For documentation, see the entire chapter on "Tradition in Anglican Theology" in Günter Biemer, *Newman on Tradition,* tr. by Kevin Smyth (New York: Herder and Herder, 1966), esp. pp. 22–24.

[85] *Enchiridion Symbolorum,* Dz. ¥428.

[86] *Enchiridion Symbolorum,* Dz. ¥338.

[87] Early Protestants did just that, either by assuming that the text wherever it contained "necessary" truths was "plain" (e.g., William Chillingworth, *The Religion of Protestants a Safe Way to Salvation,* 1664, p. 52) or by postulating a direct assistance of the Holy Spirit to the faithful reader of Scripture.

tion, but all believers in a positive revelation accept that in some way this authority exists. Here again we encounter tradition as the first and last word on revelation. Professor Wilfred C. Smith refers to tradition as a structural element of all religion.

> Every religious person is the locus of interaction between the transcendent, which is presumably the same for every man, and the culminative tradition, which is different for every man. And every religious person is the active participant, whether little or big, in the dynamics of the tradition's development.[88]

One final question of great importance for the development of a religious tradition initiated by a historical revelation is whether such a tradition can ever envision the possibility of a new beginning. Must a historical faith restrict revelation to what it has codified and canonized in its Scriptures? Is the present and future dimension of revelation exclusively a reading of a past message? Has God spoken his last word once the religious community has decided upon its Scriptural canon? The orthodox forms of Islam, Judaism, and Christianity rule out any other than a continuous development, in which the sacred books provide a definitive norm and structure. The Scriptures may be further interpreted, but they allow no new revelatory events. In Christianity the eschatological events of Jesus' death, resurrection, and ascension are either the end of revelation history or they lose altogether the definitive meaning which tradition has bestowed upon them. From the future, Christians expect only the fulfillment of what Jesus announced and anticipated. The original event is not entirely past: it continues to be present in proclamation and worship.[89] Nevertheless, the revelation is closed insofar as no new revelatory events can be added to the original ones.[90] The same is not exactly true for Israel, which still expects the revelation of the Messiah. Yet until then its revelation is closed.

---

[88] *The Meaning and End of Religion* (New York: New American Library, 1963), p. 168.

[89] Gabriel Moran, *Theology of Revelation,* pp. 89–90, 115–30.

[90] To introduce novelty is, according to Newman, the very definition of heresy. *An Essay on the Development of Christian Doctrine,* p. 330.

Even original religious teachers like Rabbi Aqiba would claim no innovations upon Moses and the prophets.

Nevertheless the question of a new revelation is raised intermittently in historical faiths. Judaism had its Pseudo-Messiahs, Christianity its "third age" of Joachim da Fiore. More recently the problem emerged again in Kierkegaard's unpublished book on the claims of the visionary pastor Adler of Bornholm.[91] For Kierkegaard every revelation is a new beginning and finds no place in an order established upon a previous revelation. Even to question the definitive character of the old order is to place oneself outside it.

> The *extraordinarius* must leave the ranks. It is true that Christianity is built upon a revelation, but also it is limited by the definitive revelation it has received.[92]

The condemnations by the Catholic Church of Joachim da Fiore and the recent decree *Lamentabili* point in the same direction. Yet the question of a new revelation once again haunts the imagination of many Christians. Our contemporaries are not millenarian as their visionary ancestors. They do not expect new words or new events, but a new experience. Disheartened by bland secularity and anemic Churches, they long for the integral experience of archaic man. They use the words of the Christian and Jewish historical revelations, but their minds are set upon an entirely different theophany, one in which the communion with their fellow men and with nature would directly yield the illuminating awareness of transcendence. Although the holy as thus "revealed" is obviously not the personal God of Scripture, a widespread awareness of the anthropomorphic nature of the Biblical representation seems to enable them to overcome the basic discrepancy between the two "revelations." Nor does

---

[91] The manuscript was posthumously published in Kierkegaard's *Papirer*, ed. by P. A. Heiberg and V. Kuhr (Copenhagen, 1909ff.), VII, B235, and tr. into English under the title *On Authority and Revelation* by Walter Lowrie (New York: Harper & Row, 1966).

[92] Kierkegaard, *Papirer*, VII, B235. *On Authority and Revelation*, p. 92.

Kierkegaard's objection against introducing a new revelation into a community established upon an old one cause them too much concern, because the concept of religious community is as much subjected to critical investigation as that of Biblical interpretation. Many see no contradiction in calling themselves Christians while outrightly rejecting the restrictions which the Christian Churches traditionally imposed upon that name. The confusion itself testifies eloquently to the interconnectedness of revelation and tradition. The present revolt against tradition makes it all but impossible to decide how far the notion of revelation may be stretched. A criterion presupposes an authority and this requires a tradition.[93]

The philosopher is not qualified to take sides on this issue because the concept of Church is not a logical construction, but a complex, intrinsically religious reality on which he can reflect only *as it exists*. It is precisely the structuring of the religious community which is in full turmoil, even within the established Churches. Since the possibility of revelatory innovation depends on this structure, he must leave the subject to the developing religious reality.

[93] Frederick Sontag, *The Crisis of Faith* (Garden City, N.Y.: Doubleday, 1969), p. 79.

Chapter 8
The Name of God

The problem of God is not a metaphysical one. Metaphysics reaches the concept of transcendence; it does not attain the idea of God. This is the reason why we discuss it only after revelation, that is, the manifestation of the sacred in the religious act. One might even argue that the problem is not a primary one in philosophy of religion insofar as the idea of God appears only at a late stage in the religious consciousness. For millennia men have recognized a transcendent dimension in their lives without coming close to the complex notion of God. Yet in this chapter we do not hesitate to focus on that particular affirmation of religious transcendence because the idea of God includes all qualities which were previously attributed to the religious "object."

In describing this "object" we must keep in mind that it is not attained in a single assertion. Every religious affirmation must be followed by a negation. Thus far we have understood this to be an act negating ordinary reality. But our understanding of the "object" of the religious act shares the complexity of the act itself in which it appears. God can never be named by a simple name, such as Being, or power, etc. Religious men have always known but philosophers and theologians sometimes forget that divine names are as negative as they are positive and remain so throughout to the final affirmation. Yet to assert the dialectical nature of the divine name is not to declare God's Being dialectical. If he is, he can definitely not develop according to the laws of man's affirmation, for the dialectical nature of that affirmation is entirely determined by the *transcendence* of the affirmed. For man to affirm the divine is to assume that the simple affirmation must be followed by a negation which both denies its absolute truth and establishes its relative truth. But it would be meaningless to consider God as developing from a moment of untruth to a moment of truth. This principle may seem obvious, but no less a philosopher than Hegel transposes the restrictions of the God language upon God himself. Altizer's religious negation of God also originates in a direct application to God of the dialectic of faith.

As was pointed out, divine names appear in the religious consciousness long before they are attributed to a "God." Yet ultimately they all converge in him. In the following discussion we shall try to retrace the dialectic of attribution without pretending that this is the order of actual succession. Our objective is merely to show how the simple in this matter inevitably leads to the complex. In an earlier chapter we encountered the notion of *power* as one of the most elementary attributes of the religious "object." I expressed grave reservations about the older *dynamist* theory as it was initiated by James Frazer, but these reservations were all based upon the underlying assumption that the religious "object" can be *reduced to* power. Power remains the primary and most immediate manifestation of the sacred. Perceptive phenomenologists of recent years have preserved the idea of power as a fundamental characteristic.[1] According to Hegel, who also considered power the most elementary manifestation of God, power is characterized by subjectivity.[2] What is powerful has a

---

[1] Van der Leeuw reinterpreted animism and dynamism as permanent structures rather than successive stages in the affirmation of the religious "object." (*Religion in Essence and Manifestation*, p. 88) Mircea Eliade subordinates both to ontic richness. Whatever *is* supremely possesses *mana:* it is dynamic because it is transcendently *real*. (*Patterns in Comparative Religion* [New York: Sheed & Ward, 1958], p. 459) Eliade also calls each theophany a manifestation of power, a *cratophany*. Cf. also K. Goldammer, *De Formenwelt des Religiösen* (1960), p. 62.

[2] *Vorlesungen über die Philosophie der Religion*, III, p. 5. My intention in following Hegel's analysis of the religious notion of power is obviously not

will of its own by which it controls the nonpowerful. "It is with the appearance of subjectivity that God is for the first time posited as power."[3] Yet religious power at first is far from being *totally* subjective. Power is merely the inner core of what is, the inner substantiality which eclipses the particularities of each being. "Everything subsists by means of this power, or, in other words, it is itself the subsistence of everything, so that the freedom of a self-dependent existence is not as yet recognized."[4] Hegel ascribes this lack of differentiation between substantial power and individual existence to what he defines as "the religion of magic." It has little to do with magic but comprehends mostly what was later referred to as *mana,* a concept originally discovered among the Melanesians but later identified with a number of more or less related notions such as the American Indian *orenda, wakanda, manitu.* It is a power which, as we recall, reveals itself in physical force or any other form of excellence.[5] This power may be impersonal—even the king merely "embodies" it and passes it on to his successor[6]—or personal, in the sense that it is usually connected with belief in spirits.[7]

Related to *mana* is the Polynesian notion of *taboo,* the negative, prohibitive aspect of sacred power. Something is *taboo* because it is charged with extraordinary powers, as all matters directly connected with the king, with procreation, with certain periods of the year. What is potent is dangerous.[8]

In this original power-experience there is little awareness of subjective freedom. Nevertheless, power already implies a relation to otherness insofar as it negates the nonsubstantial, the powerless. Power thereby ceases to be a mere substantial founda-

---

to revive the outmoded categorization of various faiths which he connects with it.

[3] *Philsophie der Religon,* II, p. 152.

[4] *Philosophie der Religion,* II, p. 105; *Philosophy of Religion,* I, p. 317.

[5] R. H. Codrington, *The Melanesians* (London: Clarendon Press, 1891), p. 118.

[6] G. Van der Leeuw, *op. cit.,* pp. 115–16.

[7] M. Eliade, *Patterns in Comparative Religion,* p. 22. Eliade considers the distinction personal-impersonal unsatisfactory.

[8] Eliade, *op. cit.,* pp. 14–19; Van der Leeuw, *op. cit.,* pp. 46–48.

tion. The evolution toward the full assertion of power, then, is an evolution toward subjectivity. Subjectivity differs from substantiality in that it *determines itself* and in that it *asserts itself negatively* with respect to the other-than-the-subject. Subjective power dominates another which is truly independent but powerless. To assert itself fully, power requires true opposition. Only when nature has attained a certain degree of independence can divine power assert itself as *different*. Hegel finds this subjectivity emerging in the Hindu belief that the One is the substance of all things.[9] But full power requires at once true opposition and total dependence.

Once divine power has asserted itself as subject, nature, in which power had been originally revealed, loses its force. The Divine now appears as the *Lord* in whose hands nature becomes a mere plaything. Power itself is reduced to a mere attribute of the God who *exercises it*. God *is* what he *is*, and the creative display of his power only manifests his Being. Moreover, his creative act is no longer an expression of power alone. For the Lord rules his power in goodness and in wisdom. "The creation is not the effect of power as such, but of power that is wise."[10] While power was once the determining element, it now becomes one determination among others. Nevertheless, in the first manifestation of subjectivity it remains predominant. Thus for Hegel the God of Israel is totally subjective but his subjectivity remains abstract: it asserts itself as will, but refuses to determine this will. Yahweh dominates his creation, negating whatever is not in accordance with his will. The created world exists exclusively through his will and goodness. It has no being or meaning of its own.[11]

At this point the determination of holiness, which had been

9 *Vorlesungen*, II, p. 122.
10 *Vorlesungen*, III, p. 36.
11 *Vorlesungen*, III, p. 56. A Hegel commentator, Albert Chapelle, points out how this Hebrew idea of creation differs from the Christian in which the creating Logos becomes part of this world thereby giving it a positivity of its own: creation is no longer determined by the abstract negativity of the One. *Hegel et la religion* (Paris, 1967), Vol. II, pp. 118–19.

present from the beginning and had qualified the notion of power as a religious category, becomes predominant. When God reveals himself *as subject,* he reveals himself *as holy.*[12] Holiness pertains to the Divine, insofar as it is a self-determining subjectivity. Being an ultimate, irreducible quality it cannot be adequately defined. We may call it a value-category.[13] But the value of holiness is of a peculiar nature: it does not express what is valuable to me but what is valuable *in itself.*[14] It entirely precedes man's pursuit of it. Religious man can appreciate the holy only after the holy has first called him to do so. We might therefore say that its value is not one of self-realization but of total self-transcendence. The term "value" itself is appropriate only to the extent that religious man can never face the religious "object" without being involved with it. The word *God* never carries a purely objective meaning: it always expresses belief in a supreme value.[15] Even the question of God's existence cannot be raised independently of man's involvement. God never exists as a *fact.*[16]

1. THE AFFIRMATION OF BEING

A growing awareness of God's absolute priority as value and as power leads the religious consciousness to what was implicit in both these revelations: God is eminently *real.* Mircea Eliade has shown in a number of books how ontological richness is the

[12] *Vorlesungen,* III, p. 57.

[13] See Max Scheler, *On the Eternal in Man,* p. 169.

[14] Rudolf Otto, *The Idea of the Holy,* pp. 50–53.

[15] See Donald Evans, *The Logic of Self-Involvement* (Toronto: Ryerson Press, 1964). Schubert Ogden, "How Does God Function in Human Life" in *Christianity and Crisis,* May 1967, p. 107. Tillich expresses it very succinctly: "Man cannot speak of the gods in detachment. The moment he tries to do so he has lost the god and has established just one more object within the world of objects. Man can speak of the gods only on the basis of his relation to them." *Systematic Theology,* Vol. I, p. 238.

[16] Einen Gott den es *gibt,* gibt es nicht." Dietrich Bonhoeffer, *Akt und Sein* (München, 1956), p. 94.

primary, although not always the most obvious, characteristic of the religious "object."[17] The "sacred object" is the ultimate foundation of all reality.[18]

> Always it is given to man as one which is unconditionally superior to all others (including the *ego* to thinking) in capacity for sheer "being," and one on which man is therefore utterly dependent in his whole existence.[19]

It is in the logical articulation of this ontic quality that the religious attitude becomes reflective. In Christianity this step was taken when its philosophers identified Good with pure Being.

Although an old philosophical tradition concluded in this divine name, some eminent historians have argued that Western philosophy received more from religious insight than it invested in it.[20] The notion of Being had briefly occupied a primary position in the philosophy of Parmenides, but this was lost soon afterward. For Plato it was one Form among others, all-pervasive to the extent that other Forms participated in it, but not supreme.[21] Although Being is a primary principle in the philosophy of Aristotle, it refers to the nature or substance of a thing and its

[17] "The real in archaic ontology is primarily identified with a 'force,' a 'life,' a fertility, an abundance, but also with what is strange or singular—in other words with everything that exists most fully or displays an exceptional mode of existence. Sacredness is above all *real*." *Patterns in Comparative Religion,* p. 459.

[18] M. Eliade, "Methodological Remarks on the Study of Religious Symbolism" in *The History of Religions,* ed. by M. Eliade and Joseph M. Kitagawa, p. 88. On the identity of the sacred with Being in Hinduism and Buddhism. See Eliade, *The Two and the One,* tr. by J. M. Cohen (London: Harvill Press, 1965), pp. 50–51.

[19] *On the Eternal in Man,* p. 163.

[20] See Étienne Gilson, *Elements of Christian Philosophy* (New York: Doubleday, 1960), p. 132; Joseph Owens, *An Interpretation of Existence* (Milwaukee: Bruce Publishing Co., 1968), p. 132; Cornelia De Vogel, "'Ego sum qui sum' et sa signification pour une philosophie chrétienne," *Revue des Sciences Religieuses,* 35 (1961), pp. 346–54.

[21] *The Sophist,* pp. 351–55.

accident. There is no notion of Being as existence to add anything to *what* a thing is.[22] Plotinus, following the Platonic tradition, placed Being under the One, his own interpretation of Plato's Form of the Good. Yet, Christians understood the words of Exodus 3:14, "I am, I am," to mean that God was Being and subordinated their entire philosophy to that statement.[23] The notion that God is Being was born out of theological reflection. But Being also became the ultimate principle of explanation.

This, of course, created its problems. For if Being is universal, how can it be transcendent? Or, from God's point of view, if God is Infinite Being, how can he avoid being all Being? Infinite Being leaves no room for anything to be outside itself. How can Parmenides' dilemma, Being is and non-Being is not, fail to exclude everything but God? Infinite Being is absolute plenitude without emptiness—with no possibility of non-Being. Even the term "monism" does not apply to Infinite Being, for there is no terminus outside this Being to establish a numerical reference.[24] If the existence of the finite requires a vacuum, where must it turn, since infinite Being is totally saturated? Creation is defined as *productio ex nihilo sui et subjecti,* but how is *nihil* to be found in this infinite fullness? If there were no finite consciousness, the problem would not exist, for outside consciousness no being could assert itself as truly independent and God could be the one substance of Spinoza. But the existence of a fully autonomous (for itself) and yet finite consciousness requires a vacuum in Being, a nothingness. Thus the question arises: How can there

[22] Joseph Owens, *The Doctrine of Being in the Aristotelian Metaphysics* (Toronto: Pontifical Institute of Mediaeval Studies, 1963), pp. 471-72.
[23] "No Christian needs to draw from this statement any metaphysical conclusions, but if he does, he can draw only one, namely, that God is Being. On the other hand, the Christian God is the supreme principle and cause of the universe. If the Christian God is first, and if He is Being, then Being is first, and no Christian philosophy can posit anything above Being." Étienne Gilson, *Being and Some Philosophers* (Toronto: Pontifical Institute of Mediaeval Studies, 1952), p. 30.
[24] Maurice Blondel, *L'être et les êtres* (Paris, 1935), p. 201.

be nothingness, the basis of finite consciousness, if Infinite Being exists?

Christian philosophy has struggled with this problem for centuries. I am not altogether sure that it has solved it satisfactorily. Perhaps further reflection on the religious attitude which gave rise to the definition of God as Being may also shed new light on its further development. First let us look at the attempted solutions. Christian philosophers have always known that finite beings cannot be "added" to God. "In no sense are we allowed to say that, if we 'add' their perfection to that of their infinite Cause, we shall obtain a 'sum' of perfection which is greater than that of the divine perfection."[25] St. Thomas fully accepts the old adage: *Dantur plura entia, non datur plus entis.* Whatever existential perfection there is in a finite being is divine.

> Being is innermost in each thing and most fundamentally present within all things, since it is formal in respect of everything found in a thing . . . Hence it must be that God is in all things, and innermostly.[26]

Yet the question is *how* God can be the Being of all finite beings. Thomas rejects Amaury de Bène's position (condemned in 1210) that God is their act of existing. He finds it unacceptable because, paradoxically enough, more existing finite beings would add Being to God.

> If we say that God is purely and simply the act of existing, we need not fall into the mistake of those who assert that God is that universal existence whereby each thing formally exists. The act of existing is such that no addition can be made to it. Consequently, in virtue of its very purity it is the act of existing distinct from every act of existing.[27]

[25] Louis De Raeymaeker, *The Philosophy of Being* (St. Louis: B. Herder Book Co., 1957), p. 320.
[26] *Summa Theologiae,* I, 8, 1.
[27] *De Ente et Essentia,* ed. by M.-D. Roland (Gosselin, Le Saulchoir, 1926), pp. 37–38. Tr. as *On Being and Essence* by A. Maurer (Toronto: Pontifical Institute of Mediaeval Studies, 1949), p. 50.

Even William of Auvergne's more moderate interpretation that
God's Being is in all things as the soul is in the body is rejected.[28]
For if God were the common Being (*esse commune*) in which all
finite beings share, a specific difference would have to be added
to him in each instance.[29] Consequently, it is mistaken to conceive of Being as a common notion divisible into infinite and
finite Being. God's Being, though the very essence of Being, is
its *primary instance*. Common Being, on the contrary, is transcendental insofar as it is shared by all finite beings. "As transcendental it is not above all its instances. It does not transcend
to its primary instance, but transcends *from* it to all others.
Subsistent Being, accordingly, is not transcendental, but is the
cause of that Being."[30] God is Being, but he is not *a* being
(*habens esse*); he is subsistent Being (*esse purum*), but not
common Being (*esse commune*).[31]

There is, then, no common Being shared between God and
the finite beings: he *is* his own act of Being while they *possess*
Being in an essence which differs from the act of Being. Of
course, we must find some common ground, since we speak of
infinite *Being*. Scholastics here usually invoke the principle of
analogy. But as was pointed out in Chapter 5, the *analogia entis*
is not entirely free of problems either. It has perhaps caused more
controversy than the notion of subsistent Being which it must
explain. If God is not *a* being, he cannot be regarded as a mere

[28] *Summa Theologiae*, I–II, 110, 1 ad 2.
[29] "From the fact that it neither receives nor can receive addition we
can conclude that God is not common Being but proper Being; for his
Being is distinguished from all the rest by the fact that nothing can be
added to it." (*Summa Contra Gentiles*, I, 26. Tr. as *On the Truth of the
Catholic Faith* by Anton Pegis [Garden City, N.Y.: Doubleday, 1957],
p. 132.) "All existing things are contained under common Being, but not
God; rather, common Being is contained under his power . . ." (*In
Dionysii de Divinis Nominibus*, V, Lect. 2, n. 660. Tr. in *Elements of
Christian Philosophy* by Étienne Gilson, p. 306. In this and the preceding
quotation I have changed the capitalization for the sake of uniformity.)
[30] *An Elementary Christian Metaphysics* (Milwaukee: Bruce Publishing Co.,
1963), p. 117. Capitalization ours.
[31] The term *esse commune* really means *ens commune*, as Gilson explains in *Elements of Christian Philosophy*, p. 306, note 32.

analogatum in a proportionality, obtained by relating his Being to his nature as the Being of the finite being is related to its nature. Finite beings simply do not *possess* Being the way God *is* Being: no real proportionality exists between God's nature and his Being, since one *is* the other.[32] Moreover, in analogy we assume that we know what the Being is which is God's essence. But do we really? We know Being as it is common to all finite beings, but this has been explicitly ruled out in the case of God. So we really know only the finite side. Can one still speak of a true proportionality when there is so little common meaning between the two relations? In a way one can and one must, if one is to talk about God at all. For speech about God is symbolic, and all symbolism is based upon analogy. Religious symbolization is based upon the assumption that the finite can be used to make assertions about the infinite.

But apart from the difficulties which we encountered earlier, the analogy of Being does not explain how infinite Being can *coexist* with finite beings. By relating his Being to his essence as I relate finite being to its nature I give the impression that he is *a* being. No real proportion exists between God's nature and his Being, since one is the other. Moreover, I assume that I know what the Being is which is God's essence. But do I really? I know being as it is common to all finite existents, but that is explicitly ruled out in the case of God. Consequently, I know nothing of the first proposition—neither God's nature nor his Being. Whatever the merits of the theory of analogy may be—and we saw that it has many—it cannot serve as a means for defining the Being that is God. By analogy alone man produces a notion of God's Being after the likeness of his own being. A truly transcendent notion of God must combine the affirmation with a genuine negation.[33] Moreover, even if the analogy of Being could reach an adequate notion of Divine Being, it still would

[32] N. J. J. Balthasar, *Mon Moi dans l'Étre* (Louvain, 1946), p. 210.

[33] Kant was well aware of this fact, cf. *Vorlesungen über die philosophische Religionslehre,* ed. by K. H. L. Politz (Leipzig, 1817), pp. 86–88. Comments in James Collins, *The Emergence of Philosophy of Religion* (New Haven: Yale University Press, 1967), pp. 124–25.

require another theory to *relate* this infinite Being to finite beings.
The two cannot simply remain juxtaposed to one another, as they
are in the theory of analogy. For if finite being exists at all, it
must intrinsically *depend* upon infinite Being. How then does the
finite depend upon the infinite?

Traditionally philosophers have answered this question either
by a theory of participation or of causality or by a combination
of both. At first the notion of participation seems to be an unlikely candidate for clarifying the relation between finite and the
infinite Being. For in Plato, with whom the notion originated,
participation means that a common form is shared by a number
of beings. But, as we saw, infinite Being cannot be the common
form of finite beings. St. Thomas avoided the difficulty by transforming the participation theory which he inherited from Boethius, at least in his later years, by reducing it to a relation of
causality. Let us first consider the early interpretation in which
participation is not mixed with causality. Boethius had already
modified the original Platonic idea by formulating the entire
problem in terms of Being: "Everything that is, participates in
Being through the fact that it is (*eo participat quod est esse*)
. . . Hence that which is, participates in Being through its being."[34] Yet Boethius' Being (*esse*) was still a Neo-Platonic pure
Being which had nothing to do with actual finite existence.
Thomas would change all that by reading Being as the act of
existence which for him is the supreme perfection.[35] Now if the

---

[34] Boethius, *Quomodo Substantiae*, text and tr. by H. F. Stewart (Cambridge: Harvard University Press, 1962), p. 49. Translation slightly
modified. It is to be noted that Boethius stated the original problem in terms
of goodness: How can substances be good without being the substantial
good?

[35] *In Boetii De Hebdomadibus*, Lectio II. A detailed commentary on this
important text may be found in Cornelio Fabro, *Participation et causalité
selon St. Thomas d'Aquin* (Louvain, 1961), pp. 268–80. The idea that Being
is the supreme perfection is not fully established by St. Thomas until the
Summa Theologiaie (1265) and, most emphatically, in his late *De Anima*,
a. 6, ad 2. Yet already in the early commentary on Boethius he asserts the
primacy of Being. On the evolution of the term *Being* in Thomas, cf.
Louis De Raeymaeker, "De zin van het woord 'esse' by den H. Thomas van
Aquino," in *Tijdschrift voor Philosophie* (1946), pp. 407–34.

term participation is understood as a perfection being received by a pre-existing subject, it obviously does not apply to Being, since the receiving subject itself is a being. Yet, Professor Geiger has proposed the theory that the participation of Being in the early work of St. Thomas exclusively refers to the presence in an imperfect degree of a quality which elsewhere is realized in absolute fullness. Geiger opposes this sort of participation by similitude to the one by composition in which the essence receives a limited amount of existence according to its capacity, and asserts that only the former correctly expresses the relation between Infinite Being and finite beings.[36] The composition of the finite being is secondary; it follows from participation but does not constitute it.[37] Nor is it a determining element in the procession of beings from pure Being. The advantage of this entire structure would be that causality is no longer needed to describe the primary relation between infinite Being and finite beings.

Yet if one accepts the controversial thesis that participation without causality appears in the early work of Thomas,[38] he still has to explain how the imperfect presence of Being in the creature *depends* upon the perfect one in the Creator. Apparently Thomas himself felt this and returned to a causal explanation. In the composition theory of participation the need for a causal explanation is built in. For any being which does not possess

[36] L.-B. Geiger, *La participation dans la philosophie de St. Thomas* (Paris, 1942), pp. 27–28; Cornelio Fabro, who had devoted an earlier work to the same problem (*La nozione metafisica di partecipazione secondo S. Tomasso d'Aquino,* Brescia, 1939), strongly opposes this distinction in his recent study, *Participation et causalité selon S. Thomas d'Aquin* (Louvain, 1961), pp. 64ff. Fabro argues that finitude and composition must not be separated in transcendental participation. Although his arguments convinced me personally, I still state Geiger's position because it offers the only form of participation between finite being and Infinite Being which is not formally determined by causality and which thereby escapes the objections against a causal relation between God and creature.

[37] Geiger, *op. cit.,* p. 392.

[38] An early text like *Commentary on the Sentences of Peter Lombard,* I, Dist. 48, q. 1, a. 1 makes the thesis difficult enough to accept.

Being through its very essence is contingent and owes its existence to a Being which possesses it *necessarily,* that is, through its very essence. The act of existing, then, becomes an *effect* of the Pure Being and to create is "to *produce* the existence of things."[39]

My problem with causality is that if this notion is understood in any of its usual meanings, God's Being becomes separated from that of the creature. The "innermost" presence of God, then, to which St. Thomas referred, is now watered down to: "God is in all things by his essence, inasmuch as he is present to all as the cause of their Being."[40] Joseph Owens draws the logical conclusion from Thomas' argument when he reduces participation to causal action: "The participation of being, accordingly, means merely that the one nature of being makes all other things be through efficient causality."[41] The difficulty with a purely causal relation between Creator and creature is not only that religious man means more than causality when he refers to God's innermost presence; the problem is metaphysical as well. For if pure Being "causes" created being, then the two are separated as one thing is from another, and the unanswerable question reappears: How can Infinite Being avoid being *opposed* to the finite without becoming finite itself? An infinity which does not fully include the finite is finite itself, as Spinoza and Hegel well knew.

Scholastic philosophers were not entirely unaware of the difficulties surrounding the term causality, for they refer to God as the First Cause, thus distinguishing it from all other causes. Tillich would say: this qualifier transforms the category into a symbol, subjecting it to the complex movement of negation and

---

[39] *Summa Theologiae,* I, 45, 6.

[40] *Summa Theologiae,* I, 8, 3. Gilson's commentary does nothing to avert such a disappointing conclusion: "The reason that this presence of God to things as their cause can be called a presence by essence is that, as has been shown above, God is creator of the world by his essence and not separately through any divine Person. Thus, for God to be the cause of what is innermost in finite beings and to be present to them by essence are one and the same thing." *Elements,* p. 180.

[41] *An Elementary Christian Metaphysics,* p. 107.

transcendence.[42] But some symbols are appropriate while others are not. Among the latter are all symbols which can convey a religious meaning only by changing the original one beyond recognition. This is precisely what happens to the category of causality if it is to express a relation between infinite Being and finite being which takes place *within* the Infinite rather than outside of it. "God creates in Himself and from Himself, not from nothingness. Consequently I am in God more than in myself, because I am of God more than of myself."[43] Blondel is among the few who have fully recognized the problem. Next to God, he admits, there can be no vacuum. But God himself is plenitude. So where must creation take place in this "compact monism"? Reinterpreting the words of St. Paul about Christ, "Exinanivit semetipsum," Blondel responds:

> To create, God did not produce outside and beside himself a new *plenum*, for that would be absurd . . . It is less deceptive to start from the gracious intentions of a Creator who prepares, not in empty space, not in his substantial plenitude, but in his deep love a capacity of life, of beatitude, of a union for which he transforms himself for others.[44]

Infinite Being has to withdraw from its own fullness in order to open up a vacuum within itself in which finite beings could be created.[45] The descriptive metaphor shows a complete awareness of the problem but contributes little to solve it.

Scholasticism appears to offer few alternatives to a causal interpretation of causality. The most remarkable among them is Eckhart's theory of Being. Eckhart identifies God with Being and unhesitatingly declares all things divine in their Being. Yet Being for him is not existence: it is the ideal essence of each existent insofar as it is not a principle of limitation but of unique presence. We shall have an opportunity to discuss the theory further in the chapter on mysticism. It is more an expression of

---

[42] *Systematic Theology*, I, p. 238.
[43] N. J. J. Balthasar, *Mon Moi dans l'Être*, p. 213.
[44] *L'être et les êtres*, p. 311.
[45] *Op. cit.*, p. 208.

the mystical experience in Scholastic terminology than a coherent theory of Being. For what is Being without existence, particularly after we eliminate the limiting aspects of the essence? If a new philosophical insight is contained in this Neo-Platonic position, we can only say that Eckhart has not adequately articulated it.

The preceding discussion has concentrated on Scholastics not because they deserve more criticism than others, but because they alone have given serious attention to the relation of Being between God and the creature. Only two other names must be mentioned here: Tillich and Heidegger. The former ends up with the same conclusions as St. Thomas; the latter refuses to discuss the problem explicitly, yet sheds new light on the problem. Tillich is off to a promising start when he equates creation with participation. "In calling it [Being itself] creative, we point to the fact that everything participates in the infinite power of Being."[46] He avoids the usual pitfalls of participation—that God becomes the form or the Being of all things or that the participated Being is *received* in a pre-existing receptacle—by naming God the *power* of Being. Thus God is present in everything without becoming the form of everything, for as power he is above everything. But power of Being for Tillich is another way of saying *ground* of Being.[47] And ground of Being "oscillates between cause and substance and transcends both of them."[48] Yet the entire question is how the alternatives of *cause* and *substance* can be "transcended." One tends to reduce God to a being (finite); the other tends to obscure the autonomous existence of beings.

Heidegger struggles with the same problem, although he is extremely reluctant to be drawn into the philosophical debate of God. The god of metaphysics, for him, is the result of a misunderstanding and must be discarded with the misunderstanding itself. To answer the question *Why is there something rather than nothing?* by referring to a First Cause is to reveal the basic

---

[46] Paul Tillich, *Systematic Theology*, I, p. 237.

[47] *Op. cit.*, pp. 235–36.

[48] *Op. cit.*, p. 156. Commentary in Carl J. Armbruster, *The Vision of Paul Tillich* (New York: Sheed & Ward, 1967), pp. 137–38.

flaw of metaphysics: its inability to go beyond beings to Being itself. For by regarding the *ground* of all beings as their cause, I simply add another being to the series.[49] Even less appropriate is it to call God his own cause.

> This is the fitting name for the god in philosophy. To this god man can neither pray nor sacrifice. Before the *causa sui* man can neither fall to his knees in awe nor sing and dance. Accordingly, godless thinking that must give up the god of philosophy, god as *causa sui,* is perhaps nearer to the divine God.[50]

Philosophy, Heidegger writes in the *Letter on Humanism,* is incompetent to deal with God. Its task is to define the essence of man in the relation to the truth of Being. On the relation to God it can make neither positive nor negative assertions, although it is highly interested in it. However, philosophy does deal with the divine realm of Being. This realm directly concerns the religious mind, for man cannot relate to God at all unless he stands in a correct relation to the truth of Being.[51]

Most of Heidegger's assertions on the sacred nature of Being are found in his later commentaries on Hölderlin and Rilke. This is no coincidence, because, according to Heidegger, the poet alone is still able to "name the holy" and to show his fellow men the road to conversion.[52] Poets alone can make the *holy* appear.[53]

[49] *Einführung in die Metaphysik* (Tübingen, 1958), p. 5. *An Introduction to Metaphysics,* tr. by Ralph Manheim (Garden City, N.Y.: Doubleday, 1961), p. 6.
[50] "Identity and Difference" in *Essays in Metaphysics,* tr. by Kurt Leidecker (New York: Philosophical Library, 1960), p. 65.
[51] *Ueber den Humanismus* (Frankfurt, 1949), p. 36. *Letter on Humanism,* tr. by Edgar Lohner in *Philosophy in the Twentieth Century,* ed. by William Barrett and Henry Aiken (New York: Random House, 1962), p. 294.
[52] *Holzwege* (Frankfurt, 1957), p. 250. In *What Is Metaphysics?* Heidegger assigns to the poet the task to name the holy and to the philosopher to utter Being. *Was Ist Metaphysik?* (Frankfurt, 1955), p. 5; *What Is Metaphysics?* tr. by R. F. C. Hull and Alan Crick in *Existence and Being,* p. 391.
[53] "Heimkunft" in *Erläuterungen zu Hölderlins Dichtung,* pp. 26–27. Tr. as "Remembrance of the Poet" by Douglas Scott in *Existence and Being,* pp. 284–85.

But what is the *holy,* and how is it related to God? Heidegger
answers this question in deeply metaphorical language. "The
holy is not holy because it is divine, but the divine is divine
because it is holy."[54] Holiness is the essential attribute of Being,
the power that keeps the gods in the integrity of Being.[55] The
problem of God can be posed only when man has opened himself
to the holiness of Being.

> Only from the truth of Being can the essence of the holy be
> thought. Only from the essence of the holy, can the essence of
> divinity be thought. Only in the light of the essence of divinity
> can it be thought and said what the word "God" is to signify.[56]

This passage shows the identity of the *holy* and Being as well as
their distinction.

Can we define any closer the relation between God and Being?
At first one might think them identical. Being is transcendent,
holy, the source of all that is. God, on the other side, is described
in the commentaries on Hölderlin in terms which could equally
apply to Being.[57] The attributes of Being include the religious
predicates of light (*claritas*), highness (*serenitas*), and joy (*hi-
laritas*).[58] Heidegger's development of these attributes reads like
a religious hymn. "The serene preserves and holds everything
in tranquility and wholeness. The serene is fundamentally healing.
It is the holy."[59] Even human existence in which Being comes

[54] *Erläuterungen zu Hölderlin's Dichtung,* p. 58.
[55] William J. Richardson, *Heidegger. Through Phenomenology to Thought*
(The Hague, 1963), p. 444.
[56] *Brief über den Humanismus,* p. 36; tr. in *Philosophy in the Twentieth
Century,* p. 294.
[57] See, for instance, "Dichterisch wohnt der Mensch" in *Vorträge und
Aufsätze* (Pfullingen, 1959), p. 200; "Wie wenn am Feiertage . . ." in
Erläuterungen zu Hölderlin's Dichtung, pp. 61–71; in the same collection,
"Hölderlin und das Wesen der Dichtung," pp. 31–45, tr. as "Holderlin and
the Essence of Poetry" by Douglas Scott in *Existence and Being,* pp.
293–315.
[58] Scott translates it as "the serene," Richardson as "the gladsome."
[59] "Heimkunft" in *Erläuterungen zu Hölderlins Dichtung,* p. 18. "Remembrance of the Poet" in *Existence and Being,* p. 271.

to lighting participates in the divinity of Being.[60] The relevance
of the poet who "names the holy" and "intercepts the signs of
the gods" to the philosopher who studies Being, also would seem
to imply at least a partial identity of formal object. Some theologians have been sufficiently impressed by these connections to
identify Heidegger's Being with God. Heinrich Ott, for instance,
considers the philosopher's wonder at the Being of all beings
a vision of their createdness, and compares God's revelation to
the unveiling of Being.[61]

Yet, fundamental objections preclude a full identification of
God with Being. The *serenitas* which was used as an attribute of
Being is explicitly differentiated from God.[62] Also, the philosopher cannot deal with the problem of God, although he
studies Being.[63] Finally, in the *Letter on Humanism* Heidegger
calls God *a* being:

"Being" is neither God nor the basis of the world. Being is further
from all that is being and yet closer to man than every being, be
it a rock, an animal, a work of art, a machine, be it an angel or
God.[64]

[60] Heidegger translates the adjective *Deinos* which is attributed to man in
the first stasimon of Sophocles' *Antigone* as "awesome," "overpowering,"
"terrible," "violent"—all terms which are used by Rudolf Otto to describe
the *mysterium tremendum*. See *Einführung in die Metaphysik*, pp. 114–15;
An Introduction to Metaphysics, p. 126. Commentary in Richardson, p. 270.
[61] In *The Later Heidegger and Theology*, ed. by James M. Robinson (New
York: Harper & Row, 1963), pp. 38–42.
[62] "Heimkunft" in *Erläuterungen*, pp. 17, 19, 25–26; "Remembrance of
the Poet" in *Existence and Being*, pp. 271, 273, 283–84. It seems almost
impossible to unify the various usages of the term God in Heidegger under a
common denominator. Is it a general term for whatever "dwells in the
holy" expressing a plurality of attributes and meanings? Perhaps Guardini is
not too far wrong when he sees in it a modern form of polytheism.
[63] Cf. *supra*.
[64] *Ueber den Humanismus*, p. 14. *Letter on Humanism* in *Philosophy
in the Twentieth Century*, p. 282. This text is important only for what
it denies. Whether Heidegger really thinks that God could be a being

From a religious point of view the identification of God and Being would be equally objectionable, for God cannot simply be the ground of all beings in the sense in which Heidegger's Being is it.[65] Neither does Heidegger himself consider his thinking an adequate tool for theology.[66] Traditional religious thinking about God cannot be expressed in terms of his distinction between Being and beings. Nevertheless, friend and foe alike feel that the notion of Being in Heidegger's later work has strongly religious overtones. It has been claimed that religious believers alone could understand what he says about the revelation of Being, or even that the Bible is the ultimate source of Heidegger's insight.[67] To us this would only confirm the position enunciated in Chapter 3 that, *by itself,* even a religiously oriented philosophy of Being is unable to handle the idea of God adequately, although it makes an essential contribution to the philosophical discussion of this idea.

A philosophy of God must always move beyond a philosophy of Being. Being is only the first stage in man's dialectical attempt to name God. It is therefore of the utmost importance in the discussion of God as Being that we avoid using concepts which allow no further development. Spinoza failed to do this when he defined God as substance. The result was an infinity without transcendence and a finitude without autonomy. There is *per se* nothing wrong with defining God as the substance of all

---

is a matter of dispute. It seems rather unlikely in the light of the preceding passages. It also would create invincible theological problems. For as a being God would become an occasion for the experience of Being, which in Heidegger's philosophy would require that we grasp it against the backdrop of non-Being. This would make God contingent and finite. (Hans Jonas, "Heidegger and Theology" in *Review of Metaphysics,* XVIII (1964), pp. 207–33.

[65] See Arnold Come, "Advocatus Dei - Advocatus Hominis et Mundi" in *The Later Heidegger and Theology,* p. 128.

[66] In a 1960 meeting with theologians he submitted the analogy that his philosophy is related to Being as theology is related to God. James M. Robinson, "The German Discussion" in *The Later Heidegger and Theology,* p. 43.

[67] James M. Robinson, *op. cit.,* pp. 13, 39.

things, if this substantiality does not exclude genuine relations. Hegel achieved this by introducing an element of reflection, and therefore of negativity, into the substance. Substance to him is the fullness of power of a being, which relates itself negatively to the accidents in which that being manifests itself.[68] The determinate character of the accident negates the absolute power of the substance, but the substance in turn negates the independence of the accidents. For ultimately the determination of the accidents results from the substance and must return to its power.[69] In such a dynamic philosophy to describe God as the substance of the world is to say *eo ipso* that he is not the world.[70] It is because they lack a dynamic concept of substance that the classical philosophers of Being so radically rejected the idea of God as substance of the world. For them to refer to God as the substance of his creation would have indissolubly identified him with it. Their static position has prevented them from doing justice to the substantialist thesis. Even those philosophers who denied subsistence to finite beings did not simply identify God with the finite beings of which he is the substance. When Parmenides asserts that only Being *is* and that non-Being is not, he includes under the latter all determinate modes of Being.[71] Far from deifying finite beings, he denies that they possess any true reality at all. Nor did Spinoza or the monist Upanishads and Sankara ever assert that God is everything. They referred to him as the essential Being of which all particular forms are mere appearances. And this, as Hegel perceived, is an entirely different thing.

> When Brahma says: "I am the brilliance, the glitter in the metals, the Ganges among the rivers, life in the living, intelligence in the intelligent," he goes beyond the individual. Brahma does not say: "I am this metal, the rivers, the particular things of all kind as

[68] *Encyclopädie* (1830), ⚹151.
[69] Franz Grégoire, *Études hégéliennes* (Louvain, 1958), p. 228.
[70] Albert Chapelle, *Hegel et la religion* (Paris, 1963), Vol. I, p. 65, Note.
[71] Hegel, *Vorlesungen über die Philosophie der Religion*, II, p. 52.

they exist immediately." The brilliance is not the metal itself, but the universal, the substantial taken from the individual, but no longer the πᾶν, the all as sum of the individuals.[72]

A substantialist approach negates finite being without ever re-affirming it.[73] What is missing here is not negativity, for all the finite is denied, but the determination that the notion of substance points beyond itself. That God is the substance of all things is correct in what it affirms, namely that he is present to all things as their very Being. This insight is the very basis of a mystical view of the world.[74] But if philosophy posits Being unqualifiedly as an ultimate principle, such an assertion becomes religiously suspect. For religious man God is never exclusively determined as pure Being. Philosophers have prematurely halted the move-ment of the religious assertion by fixing it in the notion of Being. Other aspects of the Divine are equally essential, even though they cannot be "affirmed." Yet the religious experience is not a pure affirmation but a complex movement which negates as much as it affirms. This negation also affects the terminus of the experience.

Does that mean that religious man *experiences* God not as *Being,* as a recent study claimed?[75] I do not believe so, for religious man experiences God as eminently *real,* and the most adequate way to translate this in philosophical terms is still to call the referent of the religious assertion "Being." The term *presence* may be phenomenologically more descriptive, but it needs fur-

[72] *Vorlesungen,* I, p. 196. The citation comes from the *Bhagavad-Gita.*
[73] Hegel, *Vorlesungen über die Beweise vom Dasein Gottes,* pp. 121–30. Tr., III, p. 320.
[74] Teilhard de Chardin's basic intuition of a developing universe also presupposes this presence of God to all creatures: "As early as in St. Paul and St. John we read that to create, to fulfill and to purify the world is, for God, to unify it by uniting it organically with himself. How does he unify it? By partially immersing himself in things, by becoming 'element,' and then, from this point of vantage in the heart of matter, assuming the control and leadership of what we now call evolution." *The Phenomenon of Man,* pp. 293–94.
[75] Leslie Dewart, *The Future of Belief,* p. 175.

ther philosophical interpretation which I believe will eventually
lead us back to the notion of Being. Of course, we do not know
God as *he is in himself* (except the mere negation that God's
essence differs from his existence), but only as *he is present to us.*
But this truth is not adequately expressed as "We know only a
presence." If we are to know this presence as the presence *of God,*
we must somehow know *what* God is.[76] At this point Being re-
enters. Nor should we ascribe this philosophical interpretation to
a Hellenic slant in Christian thinking. For the *real* is the primary
characteristic of the sacred everywhere. It is rather as the result
of a religious affirmation that it became the ultimate philosophical
principle of Western philosophy.[77] That the philosophical interpretation of this vision was done within a Greek frame of thinking is true enough, but this occurred only after faith had radically
changed the trend of Greek philosophy.

Being is the first, most fundamental determination of the sacred
"object," but it is also the most comprehensive denotation of
the real. Everything *is* and in Being all things are one. If God
were conceived exclusively as Being, he would be no more than the
One in which infinite and finite merge. To be sure, in a theistic
philosophy of Being, subsistent Being and finite beings are clearly
distinguished. The question is, however, whether such a distinction is consistent with the basic affirmation. I think it is not,
as appears in the arguments for the existence of God. From the
existence of finite beings the argument concludes that infinite
Being also "exists." This statement is then qualified by the
further affirmation that in infinite Being existence coincides with
essence. But the *existence* which we "prove" either refers to the
act of Being as opposed to the essence—and then it belongs to

[76] In a memorable essay on "The Feeling of Presence" Joseph Maréchal
has shown how this religious feeling always refers to a reality beyond
the self. "The judgment of presence . . . presupposes the affirmation, which
logically precedes it, of the distinction between subject and object on the
one hand, and of their reality on the other." (*Studies in the Psychology of
the Mystics,* tr. by Algar Thorold, New York: Magic Books, 1964, p. 60.)
[77] With the clear exception of Parmenides for whom Being was obviously
the ultimate principle.

another *being* (which is necessarily finite)—or it refers to Being itself as we discover it in finite beings and then it is not distinct from these beings. The reason why the arguments were so popular among philosophers who defined God as pure Being is that they did not go beyond a positive affirmation of God. They do not bring out the essential negation which follows every affirmation of God, including the one of the most fundamental concept. A philosophy that defines God exclusively as Being either negates the finite altogether, as the systems of Parmenides and Spinoza do, or strikes an uneasy balance between the infinite and the finite as the traditional philosophies of Being do. No religious philosophy of Being has ever claimed that the notion of Being *alone* can do justice to the idea of God. But its basic philosophical principle does not allow it to integrate fully the dialectical qualifications which it is willing to make.

2. THE NEGATION OF BEING

This study started from the assumption that the sacred can maintain itself only by means of an opposition to a nonsacred, profane reality. The opposition between the sacred and the profane is found in every religious experience. But it is expressed in a number of ways, which vary according to the positive determinations of the religious "object." The elementary determination of *power* negatively relates to all nonsacred reality by its ability to do away with the profane. Hegel wrote: "Power as such is negativity, essentiality, but only *in relation to the other* which is negated by it."[78] Power retains its negative character even after it has been determined by wisdom and justice: God still dominates things even when he dominates them wisely.[79] Yet, it is only after religion has become fully reflective that this

---

[78] *Vorlesungen über die Philosophie der Religion,* II, p. 119.
[79] Interesting passages on this topic may be found in Hegel's *Vorlesungen,* Vol. III. On power as negativity in the Book of Job, pp. 74–76, in the Greek mysteries, pp. 178–81, in Roman religion, p. 234.

negativity can be understood as an intrinsic necessity.[80] In the preceding section we situated that reflection at the moment when religious man starts referring to God as the supreme reality which is the principle of all reality. At that point we also become aware of basic distinctions in the religious negation. Thus most religious people will consider Spinoza's negation of the subsistence of the finite inadequate because it lacks a further negation which Infinite Being performs *upon itself*. Only when the negation takes place *within* the Infinite can the existence of the finite as finite be reaffirmed. Otherwise the Infinite destroys the finite.

We shall now study the dialectical development of the notion of Being as it is affirmed of the religious "object." Various philosophers have recently discussed the dialectic of Being and nothingness: Hegel, Heidegger, Sartre. Although their approaches differ substantially, in all cases Being is posited as dialectically related to non-Being. In Hegel's *Logic* Being consists almost entirely of negative characteristics. It is the logical absolute which the mind knows after it has run the entire gamut of all the finite stages of knowledge. It has no content of its own, but it is totally determinable. It is everything and nothing. Being is necessarily connected with nothingness, for without *nothingness* philosophy could never proceed beyond the basic thesis of Parmenides' identity system that Being *is* and non-Being is not.[81] If Being alone is taken as ultimate principle, development is excluded and no further determination can ever be asserted.[82] Only by opposing Being to non-Being can reflection lead to further determinations.[83]

[80] Here, once more, the reader must be reminded that this "necessary development" occurs exclusively in man's philosphical *idea* of God. What happens in God the philosopher does not know, but he does know that religious man affirms God dialectically and once this affirmation reaches the reflective level of Being he understands the philosophical necessity of a dialectical affirmation.

[81] *Wissenschaft der Logik*, ed. by Georg Lasson (Hamburg, 1967), Vol. I, p. 69. See the excellent pages of Jaap Kruithof, *Het Uitgangspunt van Hegel's Ontologie* (Brugge, 1959), pp. 151–74.

[82] *Logik*, I, p. 80.

[83] In his *Philosophy of Religion* Hegel mediates the transition from Being into non-Being by *substance*. Substance is the *power* of Being.

A dialectical opposition, then, is important to philosophy. It is essential to religion. Without some kind of subsequent negation, the original affirmation of being is not religious at all. Religious positions vary regarding the nature of this negation. Some radically assert that the sacred alone *is* and that all other reality *is not* truly; others apply the religious dialectic to the divine Being itself and declare that since Being is a category taken from finite existents, God must be beyond Being. The first is usually referred to as monism and the second as negative theology. We shall have to say more about them in the chapter on mysticism. In between those two extreme forms are an almost unlimited number of qualified negations of Being, either in God or in the creature or in both. All these forms suppose that the finite does not exclude the infinite. Other world views reject this assumption and conceiving of the finite and infinite as mutually exclusive, give the priority to finitude, and rule out the infinite. This is precisely what occurs in atheism. The atheist negation shows a remarkable resemblance to the religious one. It originates in the same dialectic but follows an opposite course: from the awareness of the finite to the exclusion of the infinite.

Atheism, then, may have an important religious meaning, not only in its religious forms but in any form which makes the opposition between the Infinite and the finite explicit. Not religious at all is the practical atheism which, out of ignorance or of deliberate indifference, ignores even the possibility of such an opposition. It is for that reason excluded from our consideration.

First we must briefly discuss that strange phenomenon, called "religious" atheism. In Christianity it has probably never existed until today (with the possible exception of some Romantics, particularly William Blake). During the past decade a few theolo-

---

It was through his substantiality that God first revealed himself as Being. The idea of God as ground and power of all that is precedes the idea of God as Being. But if substance is the power of Being it is also that which carries Being into its own negation. (*Vorlesungen über die Philosophie der Religion*, II, p. 56) gians, impressed by the apparent incompatibility between the traditional idea of God and modern man's way of thinking, attempted to develop a god-less variety of the Christian religion. At least one of them, Thomas Altizer, tried to support his effort by a speculative theory of the Incarnation. By becoming man God initiated an immanentization process which reaches its completion in our own secular age. God now has become totally immanent in the world, which means that he has disappeared altogether.[84] Religious atheism is not unknown outside Christianity. An entire segment of Buddhism may be considered atheistic in its complete refusal of form and will. It also appears in the Samkhya school of Hinduism where the individual self is taken as the only absolute.[85] The intriguing aspect of this atheism is its religious origin. It expresses an essential movement of the religious consciousness which ordinarily is counterbalanced by a further dialectical movement. In religious atheism the dialectic comes to an end.[86] That is also its weakness. For atheism is unable to maintain itself as religious. The religious negation by its very nature requires a reaffirmation of both the finite and the Infinite. Without this new affirmation the negative attitude (in which the sacred reality is negatively present) will soon rid itself altogether of the need for talk about the Infinite. Religious atheism then degenerates into plain atheism. Nevertheless as long as the atheist

[84] A key statement is the following phrase: "Thus the radical Christian reverses the orthodox confession, affirming that 'God is Jesus,' rather than 'Jesus is God.' Before the Incarnation can be understood as a decisive and real event, it must be known as effecting a real change or movement in God himself: God becomes incarnate in the Word, and he becomes fully incarnate, thereby ceasing to exist or to be present in his primordial form." *The Gospel of Christian Atheism* (Philadelphia: Westminster Press, s.d.), p. 44.

[85] R. C. Zaehner, *Hinduism* (New York: Oxford University Press, 1969), pp. 73–75. Also Mircea Eliade, *Yoga, Immortality and Freedom*, tr. by Willard R. Trask (New York: Pantheon Books, 1958), Chapter I and Appendix I, 7.

[86] This becomes evident if we compare Altizer's understanding of the *kenosis* of Christ in the Incarnation with the original treatment of this idea in Phil. 2:5–7. In Altizer *kenosis* is final, a definitive downfall of the divine. In Paul it is followed by an upward movement of glorification.

"misses" the Infinite, he somehow retains the tension between the Infinite and the finite, and his attitude resembles in many respects that of the negative theologian.

Religious atheism basically differs from anti-theism, the aggressive negation of God, and from ordinary atheism, the consciousness of the absence of God.[87] The most common forms of anti-theism are scientism, axiological humanism, and dialectical materialism. Scientist anti-theism orginates in a positivist refusal to accept as true what cannot be verified by scientific methods. Believers tend to identify this attitude with Promethean pride. But just as often it is inspired by the humbly critical attitude of the scientist who considers religious dogma a threat to the requirements of reason. Scientist atheism originated when Epicurus and Lucretius refused to accept the world as it was supposed to have been made by the gods. It culminated in the eighteenth-century belief in the scientific omnipotence of man. In recent years this atheism has lost some of its uncritical enthusiasm for science as an absolute value in itself. But in lieu of that, it has gained a more solid theoretical foothold, for the work of the mind is no longer thought of as "discovering" the laws of "nature," but rather as imposing its own rationality upon a world which is only potentially intelligible. Not only the solutions but also the problems are the mind's own creation.[88] Once man came to realize that the power to control his environment resided entirely within himself, the need for a transcendent princi-

[87] This absence of God must not be understood as if the ordinary atheist somehow "missed" God, as the religious atheist does. He simply observes that there is no God.

[88] John Dewey precisely expressed the nature of the scientific revolution long ago: "Mind is no longer a spectator beholding the world from without and finding its highest satisfaction in the joy of self-sufficing contemplation. The mind is within the world as a part of the latter's own on-going process. It is marked off as mind by the fact that wherever it is found, changes take place in a directed way, so that movement in a definite one-way sense—from the doubtful and confused to the clear, resolved and settled—takes place." *The Quest for Certainty; A Study of the Relation of Knowledge and Action* (New York: G. P. Putnam's Sons, 1929), p. 291.

ple of order in the universe was no longer felt, while any interference of such a principle with man's own free experimentation
was considered to be a threat to the mind's creative power.[89]

The new emphasis on the mind's creativity in scientist atheism
connects it with the axiological humanism of more recent vintage.
Humanism refuses to give scientific inquiry a privileged position
among human values; each value must remain subordinate to
the total well-being of its human creator. Yet its atheism is no
less radical. According to Jean-Paul Sartre any predetermined
order of values and ideas such as the idea of God implies would
obstruct the autonomy of freedom. If God exists, man can no
longer create his own possibilities: he can only ratify what has
been established before him. God and authentic human freedom
are therefore incompatible.[90]

For dialectical materialism heaven is an escape from earthly
realities, a compensation for the miserable social-economic conditions of man's existence in this world. In religion man expresses
his alienation while protesting against it. Marx saw no purpose
in opposing religion as long as the situation which creates religion
persists.

> The abolition of religion as the illusory happiness of men, is a
> demand for their real happiness. The call to abandon their illusions

[89] Georges Van Riet, "Notre foi en Dieu" in *Collectanea Mechliniensia*
(1968), p. 192.

[90] *The Devil and the Good Lord,* tr. by Kitty Black (New York: Alfred
A. Knopf, 1960). *Existentialism and Humanism* (London: Methuen, 1948),
pp. 33–48. *Situations,* Vol. I (Paris, 1947), pp. 314ff. An attempt to
refute this position was made by Henry Duméry, *Foi et interrogation*
(Paris, 1953); the main passages are translated in *Faith and Reflection,*
ed. by Louis Dupré, pp. 6–27. Sartre's atheism has other foundations as
well. The idea of God is contradictory since it absolutizes the *en soi* of
reality and the non-Being of consciousness. *Being and Nothingness,* tr. by
Hazel Barnes (New York: Philosophical Library, 1956), pp. 90–91. For a
critique, see Wilfrid Desan, *The Tragic Finale* (New York: Harper &
Brothers, 1960), Chapter VIII. Also God is *the Other* whose constant
and intimate presence would eliminate the subjectivity which is the essence
of man. *Being and Nothingness,* pp. 290–91.

about their condition is the call to abandon a condition which requires illusions.[91]

At the same time no attempt to restore man's original dignity can be successful as long as the religious outlook is retained which reconciles man with his condition. Marx's own philosophy is actually more atheistic than anti-theistic, for anti-theism is still an "ideology," a mental attitude mistakenly detached from man's dialectical struggle with nature out of which it grew. Not religious beliefs but social conditions must be attacked. Nevertheless, Marxism as interpreted by most present day communist regimes usually takes an aggressive, anti-theistic position.

In all forms of anti-theism the infinite is considered the alienation of the finite, that which obstructs its full development. It revolts against a transcendent reality which is believed to prevent man from creating his own destiny. "Because absolute self-assertion and self-creation conflict with a God whose superabundance includes all freedom, thereby abrogating all human freedom, God must go. Modern atheism is the dethronement of God for the sake of the freedom of man. It is revolt."[92] Unbelief may be a speculative attitude; anti-theism is a revolutionary one, resulting from a heightened awareness of freedom.

In atheism the battle between the two principles has ended and the supremacy of the finite has become absolute. Yet an awareness of absence remains. This may take the form of nostalgia (as in Altizer's religious atheism), or of a tolerant confidence in the supremacy of the finite (as in the philosophy of Merleau-Ponty). Atheism, much more than anti-theism, expresses the nonreligious mood of our time. God is absent as he never was before. He is no longer missed in public life, and modern life can spare no time for him as a private luxury.

[91] Karl Marx—Friedrich Engels, *Historisch-Kritische Gesamtausgabe*, ed. by D. Rjazanov (Frankfurt, 1927), Vol. I, 1, p. 608. Tr. as *Contribution to the Critique of Hegel's Philosophy of Right* by T. B. Bottomore in *Karl Marx—Early Writings* (New York: McGraw-Hill, 1964), p. 44.
[92] Georg Siegmund, *God on Trial*, tr. by E. C. Briefs (New York: Desclee, 1967), p. 400.

The negativity of getting along without God is only incidental to the driving and positive intention to live humanly. It is a full-scale campaign for a more human life with the accompanying notion that relying on God for this was, and remains, a mistake.[93]

Modern man does not deny or "reduce" religious phenomena; he considers them as mere phenomena and brackets their reference to a transcendent reality.[94]

The most accomplished expression of this secularism is found in the writings of Maurice Merleau-Ponty. His denial of God lacks the belligerent character of Sartre's anti-theism, although it shares some of its premises. Merleau-Ponty even objects to having his philosophy called atheistic, because such emphasis on a negative corollary diverts attention from the main purpose. Atheism for him is still an "inverted act of faith."[95] The philosopher must not start with the denial of God but with the affirmation of man, the sole source of meaning. Man is contingent, but this contingency cannot be "explained" by founding it in some necessary Being. On the contrary, a necessary Being can only do away with contingency. For by linking it to necessity we make contingency itself necessary.[96] To accept something as contingent means to abandon all attempts to give it a foundation of necessity.

It is not our intention here to refute anti-theism or atheism since the purpose of this study is not to persuade but to explain religious attitudes. Yet atheism (henceforth we return to this

[93] Robert Johann, "Modern Atheism" (unpublished paper).
[94] Georges Van Riet, "Notre foi en Dieu" in *Collectanea Mechliniensia* (1968), p. 192.
[95] *Éloge de la philosophie* (Paris, 1953), p. 59. See W. Luypen, *Phenomenology and Atheism*, p. 294.
[96] *Éloge de la philosophie*, pp. 61–62. Luypen, *Phenomenology and Atheism*, p. 306. Luypen (p. 309) shows a basic ambiguity in Merleau's use of the term "contingency." What he requires is a mode of being in which the subject is not the product of processes and forces that act with necessity. But theological and metaphysical contingency merely signifies that "no being (*Seiendes*) whatsoever, precisely as being, has the ground or reason of its Being in itself." Necessity in the latter sense is not excluded by contingency in the former.

common term which includes anti-theism) holds a religious meaning which requires further explanation. It provides a dialectical counterpart to the essentially inadequate affirmation of the sacred. As man outgrows the gods that he had set up for himself, he inevitably confronts atheism. The gods die constantly; that is why the atheist is a steady companion of the believer, and, indeed, sometimes is the believer himself. If faith survives the confrontation the believer will forever be on his guard against idolatry. It is mostly in the experience of his own deficiency that man faces the transcendent. But here also he is most tempted to turn the transcendent into a substitute for values which he himself has been unable to secure. God's name then is used to patch up the holes in the fabric of culture which his own industry has not succeeded in closing. This kind of religiosity falls back upon an earlier, more primitive stage of religion when man was less conscious of his cultural autonomy. What was authentically religious at one time may no longer be authentic at a more developed stage of self-awareness. Clinging to older forms of religious expression without adapting them to one's present state of consciousness is regression. Once God becomes a necessary feature of the natural environment he loses his transcendence, and faith degenerates into idolatry. As Gabriel Vahanian so forcefully proclaims, theism cannot for long maintain the tension between God and the world: either one of them must be eliminated.

> The dilemma of the theist is that he takes God for granted and ends by building a tower of Babel. The dilemma of the atheist on the other hand, lies in that he eliminates God but cannot avoid him. It is the dilemma, furthermore, of the contemporary world. Being immanentist, modern man's view, so to speak, seeks to dig the pit of Babel.[97]

Nothing is lost by the present secularism, Vahanian maintains, since the religious expressions of the past have become imma-

[97] *Wait Without Idols* (New York: George Braziller, 1964), p. 223. Cf. also by the same author, "Le monde, la grâce, la liberté" in *Archivio di Filosofia* (1968), p. 153.

nentized to a point where the idea of God is no more than an
empty shell of transcendence.[98]

As long as the negation of the sacred in modern life remains
aware of itself as a negation, it fulfills an important dialectical
function. For the negative experience of God's absence stops the
religious mind from identifying the sacred with the ordinary world.
For our contemporaries the road toward the sacred seems to
start from the awareness of the secular. The feeling of absence
of the sacred, the despair about the secular quality of our existence
is undoubtedly religious in nature. Langdon Gilkey has pointed
out how in this epoch man notices his relation to the unconditioned as much by its absence as by its presence. We become
aware of the need for an ultimate meaning and instead find only
a void. "If however we find *nothing,* no foundational security
or meaning in existence, then that nothing itself, as the now
evident character of the horizon within which we exist, takes on
an ultimate or an unconditioned quality."[99] The purely negative
awareness of the absolute which originates in the sense of absence
performs the same negation of the self-sufficient finite which at
all times has been the main characteristic of the religious attitude. To be sure, the dialectical negation which *represents* the
absolute by the feeling of absence, is poorly expressed in the
nondialectical, flat assertion of atheism. But then the painful feeling of "missingness" is hard to admit, and many disguise their
fundamental frustration by flaunting an aggressively self-sufficient
atheism.[100]

Often "atheism" refers to a negative religious experience which
man finds too complex to describe but which is mainly characterized by the experience that God is no longer present.

[98] Cf. "Der Tod Gottes und der Christliche Glaube als Ikonoklasmus" in
*Theologie im Umbruch—Der Beitrag Amerikas zur gegenwartigen Theol-
ogie* (München, 1968), p. 200.
[99] *Naming the Whirlwind,* p. 310.
[100] This is the thesis of Geddes MacGregor's beautiful book, *The Sense of
Absence* (Philadelphia: J. B. Lippincott, 1968), p. 113. On the presence in
the absence, pp. 141, 18.

Men are frightened at the absence of God from the world, they feel that they can no longer realize the Divine, they are terrified at God's silence, at his withdrawal into his own inaccessibility. The world becomes profane and devoid of meaning, its laws are impersonally objective, even where man rather than nature, is involved. Men believe they must interpret this experience theoretically as atheism. Yet it is an authentic experience of the most profound existence.[101]

In the meantime atheism remains a nondialectical and therefore inadequate religious attitude. Secular theologians are wont to say that to modern man the secular must take the place of the sacred. If this means that the secular experience can now fulfill the function which the religious once fulfilled, it is patently false. The modern believer may learn from secular atheism, but he can never call it his own without ceasing to be religious. The awareness of the secular is not the same as the awareness of the secular *as profane*. Only the latter, negative awareness is religious. It can maintain itself as religious only by a constant reaffirmation of the sacred. Such a reaffirmation of the sacred does take place in the equally radical negation of so-called negative theology. The term "negative theology" covers two distinct modes of religious discourse: one, mystical; the other, speculative-theological. Both agree only in denying that any positive attributes can be predicated of God. In the mystical language this denial expresses the actual awareness of surpassing all intelligible determinations in the mind's approach to God. We shall postpone discussing it until the last chapter. The speculative denial follows from the consistent application of certain initial principles of God-talk. Persistent negations appear mostly in strictly monotheistic traditions where all attributes are profoundly distrusted lest they introduce multiplicity into God's unity. We notice this in the eleventh-century Moslem Avicenna as well as in the twelfth-century Jew Maimonides.

[101] Paul Tillich, "Wissenschaft als Konfession" in *Wort und Wahrheit*, 9 (1954), p. 812.

According to the Koran, God is one. Thus all particular properties can be no more than human ways of speaking about God. In the *Metaphysics of the Shifa* (VIII, 7), Avicenna attributes only existence to the necessary Being. The function of the predicate is merely to negate creaturely qualities or to relate the divine reality to the creatures. Thus to call God "one" is to say that he is not divided; "good," that there is no potency in him; "living," that he is at the origin of all that lives. Maimonides likewise rejects all attributes that are not purely negative or expressive of a divine activity with respect to the creature. In Aristotelian fashion he reasons that positive attributes would either define God's essence (which is impossible) or add something to that essence (which would ascribe to him accidents). It is not sufficient, he warns his adversaries, to change the terminology in order to solve the problem, for the determinations are in their very nature limited and imply multiplicity.[102] Even the four basic attributes found in the Bible, life, power, knowledge, and will, merge so completely in the divine substance as to become meaningless. Their distinctness is meaningful only for describing how God acts toward man, not for defining what he is in himself. Maimonides goes even further than Avicenna and excludes existence as a divine attribute, because, as he reads Aristotle, existence also must be an accident added to the substance. God *is* his Being: he does not possess the attribute of existence.[103] Even on the level of Being, then, there can be no similarity between God and the creature. Thus he eliminates the fundamental analogy which allowed the Scholastics, by means of a dialectic of negation and supereminence, to predicate ontological perfections of the Creator. Maimonides regards all such attempts as inconsistent.

When they ascribe to God essential attributes, these so-called essential attributes should not have any similarity to the attributes of other things, and should according to their own opinion not be

---

[102] *The Guide of the Perplexed,* tr. by M. Friedländer (London: Routledge & Kegan Paul, 1947), Bk. I, Ch. 51.
[103] *Ibid.,* Bk. I, Ch. 57.

included in one and the same definition just as there is no similarity between the essence of God and that of other beings. They do not follow this principle, for they hold that one definition may include them, and that nevertheless there is no similarity between them.[104]

Only in a negative sense can attributes be predicated of God without impairing the divine unity. Thus life, power, knowledge may be attributed to God insofar as he is not life-less, not powerless, not ignorant.

That negation is necessary in the affirmation of the transcendent is a principle on which all religious writers agree. The question is whether the negation is final or whether it leads to a new affirmation. This crucial issue has for centuries divided all theories about God-talk. The unmitigated negation has received its strongest support in the East. In some of the *Upanishads* and even more in their monist commentators (particularly Sankara), the absolute remains without any determination whatever. The main traditions of Islam, Judaism, and Christianity, on the contrary, integrate the *apophatic* theology as a movement into an overall affirmation. Thus for St. Thomas the *via remotionis* primarily purifies of all restrictive qualities those attributes which will be used for a higher affirmation.[105] I do not believe that Thomas' solution meets the objection of negative theology that no subsequent negation can ever overcome the inherent finitude of names which belong entirely to the human order of expression. But for the time being I prefer to concentrate on the difficulties of negative theology.

The major problem consists in the very attempt to assert a positive transcendence by means of negations alone. It is an illusion to think that terms like "absolute," "unity," "simplicity," which are reached at the end of the negating process, can subsist independently. Either they are positive attributes or they say nothing whatever about God and in that case they cannot be adequately distinguished from speculative atheism. Yet negative

[104] *Ibid.*, Bk. I, Ch. 56, p. 79.
[105] *Super I Lib. Sentent.* d. III; *De Potentia*, qu. 7, a. 5.

theology is almost never purely speculative: it mostly expresses a religious drive which remains primarily negative. That is why great mystics so often recur to it. If negative theology were entirely consistent, it would jeopardize the religious attitude itself. For man cannot relate to a God whom he can in no way conceive. What can he say to what is in all respects unknown? If religion is a dialogue between man and the transcendent, some manifestation of the transcendent is required. But a God beyond all determinations cannot initiate a dialogue. There is literally nothing to talk about. To speak to God man must in some way be able to speak meaningfully *about* him.[106] We may apply to God-talk what Kant said about man's capacity of being free: he *must,* therefore he *can.* Positive language about God finds its ultimate justification in the fact that man needs it to be religious at all.

3. THE INFINITE IN THE FINITE

The preceding conclusion is obviously dangerous. For how can any positive statement about God possibly be true, that is, related to the *real?* We cannot qualify the radical negation without jeopardizing divine transcendence. In matters concerning the absolute, compromises seldom produce solutions. Instead we must radicalize the negative movement inherent in the religious attitude. Negation becomes destructive of meaning only when it is artificially brought to an end. But religious man continues to negate. Philosophy should take its lead from his attitude. The problems of a discontinued negation clearly appear in Spinoza's philosophy. From the principle that every determination is a negation, Spinoza deduces that all determinations must be overcome in the absolute substance. But, as Hegel pointed out, Spinoza does not relativize the negating movement itself.[107] Thus the negation of all relativity from the substance ultimately precludes

---

[106] Cf. Claude Bruaire, *L'affirmation de Dieu,* pp. 185–89, 229–35.
[107] Hegel, *Logik,* ed. by Georg Lasson, Vol. II (Hamburg, 1966), p. 164.

the existence of any determination at all. To some extent Spinoza concedes this when he asserts the existence of one single substance. Yet full consistency would have required more: it would have eliminated *all* determination. Spinoza's attempts to give an acceptable status to the attributes of God and to deduce finite modes out of the infinite substance are doomed to be inconsistent.

In a different theory of negation this problem would have been avoided. To be sure, the relative cannot *coexist* with the absolute, but it can exist as dependent upon the absolute. This is precisely what happens when the negation includes its own negating impulse which is still relative. Spinoza discontinues the negative movement as soon as he reaches the notion of self-identity for the absolute. But a radical negativity relativizes itself and thus leaves open the possibility of self-movement in the absolute and of self-determination. Determinations obviously exist in the universe, and since there is no place outside the absolute, they must have originated within the absolute. Such determinations are not contradictory because they are not opposed to the absolute, or juxtaposed with it, but posited by it.

Only a radical negation allows the reflective believer to accept the existence of determinations in God and, consequently, the possibility of a revelation. Important conclusions follow from this, but only mystics seem to have drawn them. Since the relative exists through the absolute, the existence of relative determinations implies the existence of a *self-determining* absolute. If one defines God as the absolute (as religious man does), then one must also accept that all relative determinations have their origin in God and that God is a determining God. Eckhart wrote that in each creature God is born anew. Indeed, in each one he attains a new self-determination.

A further conclusion which follows from the acceptance of a simultaneous existence of the finite and the infinite is that they cannot remain extrinsic to one another. The divine is usually identified with the infinite and opposed to a finitude which is conceived as subsisting independently "outside" the divine. But finitude is essentially a relative concept: it cannot subsist by itself

alone, as Spinoza showed long ago. For to be finite is to be
limited and nothing can be limited only through itself.[108] The
finite implies a reference to the infinite: it is never self-explana-
tory and requires a connection with the infinite. As Austin Farrer
phrased it:

> The existence of no being would be a simple fact, the existence of
> the fullness of being equally a simple fact, and of simple facts no
> explanations can be asked . . . But the existence of one or more
> limited beings is not a simple fact. Why this limitation rather than
> that, or why any at all?[109]

To avoid false problems we should add that only absolute or
metaphysical finitude relates the finite to the infinite. Not every
limitation implies a comparison with the infinite. Every finitude
is relative but not every finite directly relates to the infinite. The
restrictedness of each individual or even of an entire species does
not need a transcendent interpretation. But to declare finite the
totality of empirical reality is to relate it to an infinity.

From a finite point of view infinity is the negation of limitation,
the limitless limit. In that sense the finite is opposed to the
infinite which it presupposes. Yet this opposition is not definitive,
for as Hegel pointed out, the finite is all that it is through the
infinite; it has its essence in the infinite.[110] Concretely, consciousness surpasses the opposition in the religious experience. Here
the *isolated* finitude is considered to be a defect or an evil from
which man must be liberated through his union with the infinite.
At this point infinity reveals itself as eminently positive and far
more than a negation of finitude. Its transcendence has a content

---

[108] Spinoza, *Short Treatise on God, Man and His Well Being,* in *Werke,*
ed. by C. Gebhardt (Heidelberg, 1925), Vol. I, p. 20. In the *Ethica,* I, 8,
Spinoza posits that the finite must be limited by a substance of the *same*
nature. But this is a further conclusion and a questionable one. For a
criticism, cf. Gerard Verbeke, "De menselijke beleving van de eindigheid"
in *Tijdschrift voor Philosophie* (Louvain, 1948), pp. 460–61.
[109] *Finite and Infinite* (London: Dacre Press, 1959), p. 15.
[110] *Vorlesungen über die Philosophie der Religion,* II, p. 50.

of its own which makes it into an "other." Lévinas is right in claiming: "La négativité est incapable de transcendance."[111] At the same time infinity implies the negation of the finite, for without this negation the finite and the infinite would be once again juxtaposed in a contradictory opposition.[112]

Such a juxtaposition is as impossible on the side of the infinite as on that of the finite. For an infinity which is merely *opposed* to finitude is limited by it and *eo ipso* ceases to be infinite. If there is finitude at all, it must be contained *within* infinity. The term *within* is obviously metaphorical, but it expresses well the literal truth that the infinite must retain the finite as otherness *of itself*.[113] The finite does not add to the infinite except through the otherness of the latter. It empties itself—makes the *nihil* out of which the creation originates—in order to allow for otherness. Finitude is the distinctness of the infinite. Hegel concluded from it that consciousness is the finite mode of the absolute.[114] Whether consciousness could exist without finitude is a difficult problem, but it is not ours at the moment. We know that finitude does exist and hence that it must have its function in and through infinity.

If the finite is *in* the infinite, and if God is defined as infinite, he must partake in the development of the finite. At the same time the autonomy of the finite must be respected. Few philosophers have combined those qualities without lapsing into some sort of divine predestinationism or without recurring to a merely extrinsic form of divine cooperation. One noteworthy attempt to make God immanent in the creature without sacrificing his transcendence is the philosophy of Whitehead. For Whitehead, God attains actuality only in and through the world.[115] Since God is

---

[111] *Totalité et Infini* (The Hague, 1961), p. 12.

[112] The defect of Lévinas' study is that after having posited the originality of the infinite and the autonomy of the finite, he makes no attempt to explain how finite and infinite can coexist. Exteriority cannot be a final category.

[113] Hegel, *Vorlesungen*, IV, p. 47.

[114] *Vorlesungen*, IV, p. 7.

[115] *Process and Reality* (New York: Macmillan, 1929), p. 521.

actualized in the creative process, he cannot be said to remain above it. He is the nontemporal actuality which provides every phase of the process with definiteness and limitation.[116] Each temporal actuality concretizes a number of potentialities (resulting from completed realities) in an actual synthesis according to self-given goals. But it is unable to do so without a regulative principle. This is provided by God. "He is that actual entity from which each temporal concrescence receives that initial aim from which its self-causation starts."[117]

In such a view the terms causality and creation cannot be unambiguously applied to God. Every creature causes itself, and so does God. Moreover, the potentialities out of which the creature concresces are as much required as conditioned by God's own nature. God is the primary condition for the existence of all novel entities, but he cannot be said to create by divine decree or to precede the creature's own creativity. Indeed, he himself is the "aboriginal instance" of the creative process which he conditions.[118] Insofar as God himself is driven from a simple, primordial nature toward a multiple, consequent nature, he is a creature of creativity. Whitehead skillfully avoids the idea of predetermination: the divine *conatus* is not a specific desire for any particular realization. God's creative act is "untrammeled by reference to any particular course of things . . . deflected neither by love nor by hatred of what in fact comes to pass."[119] No preconstituted particulars guide or attract divine love or desire. God is indifferent to the quality as well as to the preservation

---

[116] *Science in the Modern World*, p. 160; *Religion in the Making* (New York: Meridian Books, 1961), p. 91.

[117] *Process and Reality*, p. 374.

[118] *Process and Reality*, p. 344. Whitehead has expressed the interdependence of God and the creature in a set of paradoxes: "It is as true to say that, in comparison with the World, God is actual eminently as that, in comparison with God, the World is actual eminently. It is as true to say that the World is immanent in God, as that God is immanent in the World. It is as true to say that God creates the World, as that the World creates God. God and the World are the contrasted opposites in terms of which Creativity achieves its supreme task." *Process and Reality*, p. 528.

[119] *Process and Reality*, p. 522.

of what emerges out of the multiple appetitions of the existent. "The primordial appetitions . . . jointly constitute God's purpose."[120] God has no aims as the creatures do. His only purpose is the "evocation of intensities," the realization of each actual entity's highest possible intensity.[121]

Whitehead's theory justifies the essentially religious view that the creation must make a difference to God. The God of religion never adopts the detached attitude of Aristotle's Prime Mover toward the universe. If values exist on their own account, they must also exist for God. However, Whitehead uses language which religious man naturally distrusts. What is he to make of the "consequent" nature of God and similar expressions which appear at the end of *Process and Reality?* The implied idea of a finite God is repugnant to most believers. To defend it the American philosopher Charles Hartshorne spent his entire life fighting against "the idolatrous worship" of the infinite. Cosmic wholeness, not pure infinity, is the essential concept in the religious mind whether it be Christian, Jewish, or Moslem.[122] God includes the entire creation: the believer clearly regards him as a total reality. Speculatively this religious view is supported by the fact that a finite reality existing *outside* God would either add to the divine perfection or be utterly meaningless.[123]

Important consequences directly follow from such a *panentheist* position. If God is all-inclusive, he is subject to change and must partake in the creative novelty of an ever progressing reality. Only the actual is in God as actual; the possible *as potential.* The religious mind, accustomed to identifying the perfect with the permanent, may balk at such a conclusion. A God who grows by increasing actualization grows into ever greater perfection. Does such a process not imply a self-surpassing and therefore im-

---

[120] *Process and Reality,* p. 160.

[121] *Process and Reality,* p. 161. Cf. Ivor Leclerc, *Whitehead's Metaphysics* (London: George Allen & Unwin, 1965), pp. 204–5.

[122] *A Natural Theology for Our Time* (La Salle, Ill.: Open Court Publishing Co., 1967), pp. 7–8.

[123] *The Divine Relativity* (New Haven: Yale University Press, 1948), p. 19.

perfect God? Against this objection Hartshorne posits that supreme perfection does not require simultaneous actuality of all
possible values (which is a contradiction), nor does it exclude
the possibility of being surpassed by oneself but only by others.

Panentheism is not pantheism. The creatures retain their independence within God. This presupposes the existence of real
relations between God and all other beings. In this respect panentheism goes further than traditional theism which accepts the
existence of external relations on the part of the creatures, but
rejects all real relation from God to the creature. A real relation,
the theist argues, implies a dependence and this would introduce
imperfection in God. Such a view is clearly too simplistic. For
the more perfect a being is, the more it is able to relate to, and
even to depend on other beings. A man relates more than a
stone. On the other hand, if God is truly related to his creatures,
the absolute and the Divine no longer coincide. "The Absolute is
God with something left out of account. God is more than his
absolute character."[124] Yet how can God be absolute (and
absolute he must be) while at the same time being relative?
How can the relative coexist with the absolute? Hartshorne's
answer: In the way an object is contained in a subject. The
object exists within the subject without "relating" to it: the relating is all done by the subject. In the same way God's absolute
remains fully independent while requiring the relative realization
of an existence. As absolute Being God is without relations or
determinations. But absolute Being implies existence which is always *determinate*. Determination, Spinoza taught us, is negation,
but, even more, *relation*. To exist is to coexist. Thus the existence
of a divine relativity is implied by the absolute essence of God.

The absolute remains an essential characteristic of the Divine.
Divine relativity therefore must be conceived in such a way that
it does not exclude divine absoluteness. For if God were to
depend upon the creature as one creature depends upon another,
he would cease to be absolute. But God's dependence differs

[124] *The Divine Relativity*, p. 83.

from that of the creature in two respects. First, God's relativity itself is absolute; that is, it does not depend upon further relations. "Regardless of circumstances, of what happens anywhere or when, God will enjoy unrestricted cognitive relativity to all that coexists with him. By contrast, the extent of our human relativity is itself a relative matter, varying with circumstances."[125] Since no circumstances can ever change God's relatedness to his creation, he remains entirely stable and suffers from no subjective fluctuations. God relates to all aspects of the creature at once: he simultaneously penetrates and surrounds it. No new discoveries in existing states of affairs could possibly change God's view of the world or force him to review his position. All actuality with the totality of its relations is there. All novelty emerges out of the development from the potential to the actual. God's relativity then is an eminent one, or, as Hartshorne calls it, a surrelativity.

> To be relative in the eminent sense will (accordingly) be to enjoy relations to all that is, in all its aspects. Supreme dependence will thus reflect all influences—with infinite sensitivity registering relationship to the last and least item of events.[126]

The other unique quality of divine relativity is that God remains independent with respect to the particular nature of each and all creatures. He is not bound to any given creature. He is not predetermined to a specific universe, not even morally as Leibniz thought. It is in this respect particularly that panentheism differs from pantheism. For any universe is intrinsically compatible with the divine essence. Although God necessarily relates to a universe, he transcends it as the necessary transcends the contingent. "He is both this system and something independent of it."[127] The fact that God includes the entire creation then does not make the actually existing universe intrinsically necessary. Each universe remains open to alternatives and additions.

[125] *The Divine Relativity*, p. 82.
[126] *The Divine Relativity*, p. 76.
[127] *The Divine Relativity*, p. 90.

Far from excluding contingency from the world, then, panentheism introduces contingency in God himself. A Being that includes realities which could be different from what they are and which at each moment differ from what they were, must in some respect be contingent itself. That God exists is a *fact,* even though his existence follows necessarily from his essence. His actual existence inserts him in a web of contingent relations. Without a contingency which allows God to have real, reciprocal relations, no religion would be possible. For religion always assumes that God reacts and responds to man's initiative. To know us as we are and to reveal himself as he is, he must become involved in the contingent and ever-surprising play of creatures that have a mind of their own. Such an involvement cannot but be contingent. By contrast, if God were totally noncontingent, no real interaction with free beings would be possible and religion itself would be reduced to a meaningless cult of an irresponsive and unchangeable Absolute. To religious man it is essential that his speaking be heard and responded to. Guardini therefore concluded that the reality of God cannot be grasped with the categories of "absoluteness" only, but that we must add those of facticity.[128]

It is at this point that negative theology shows its full deficiency. A God who is merely above all determinations is not only silent; he is totally uninteresting. No believer can pray to an Absolute that "refuses to enter into any correlation in which he would be compromised by the homogeneity of relationship."[129] Obviously, God must be transcendent, absolute, and necessary. A God who would be only contingent would be no God at all. In his own essence God must be entirely necessary and independent of all relations which actually obtain. Yet God's essence remains an abstraction until we conceive of it as actually existent. At that moment he exposes himself to the contingent experience of a contingent world. His necessity must not be conceived in such a

[128] *Unterscheidung des Christlichen,* p. 332.
[129] Henry Duméry, *Philosophie de la religion,* I, p. 67, tr. in *Faith and Reflection,* ed. by Louis Dupré, p. 173.

way as to preclude those relations. The self-sufficiency of God must be provided for *within* his outgoing relativity.[130]

4. IS GOD OMNIPOTENT?

The immanence of God has far-reaching conclusions. The unity of God which is absolutized in negative theology excludes self-determination from the Divine. To conceive God as only *one* is to conceive him solely in the mode of self-containment, in which he jealously guards his lonely transcendence. But such a one-sided concept is not in keeping with the religious attitude which always presupposes a communication from God to the creature. Theology has traditionally been more concerned about preserving God's transcendence than about explaining this relation. Thus the creation becomes an *opus ad extra* which does not intimately (i.e., as he is in himself) involve God with the finite. Even the incarnation is presented as an *opus ad extra* which only in its terminus, but not in its origin, affects God's inner life. Yet to posit God at the origin of all that is, is to draw him most *intimately* into the finite. This holds true for creation as well as for redemption: the religious mind does not separate what belongs to the same order of salvation. The next three chapters will provide ample opportunities for developing this theme.

Meanwhile a more general problem demands immediate attention. How can a God who preserves the autonomy of the creature be called omnipotent? It is hard to find a theological topic on which more nonsense has been written. Peter Damian argued against the eleventh-century dialecticians that it was in God's power not only to make Rome cease to exist but even to make it cease from having existed. More recently and in a less obviously absurd way Descartes grounded all fundamental truths in a divine *decision*. No one would accept such an absolute idea

---

[130] Cf. Boyce Gibson, "Two Strands in Natural Theology" in *Process and Divinity,* ed. by William L. Reese and Eugene Freeman (La Salle, Ill.: Open Court Publishing Co., 1964), p. 471.

of omnipotence today, but some who reject it still ascribe it to their believing adversaries. For their benefit an American philosophy professor recently argued that since no being has the power to move a stone from the earth to the sun at a velocity exceeding the speed of light, God did not exist.[131] Theories so ill-conceived do not deserve to be refuted.

An adequate discussion of divine omnipotence ought to begin not with an abstract philosophical concept but with the notion as it developed out of the actual religious experience. There is no point in treating a notion so ambiguous as if it had a single, clearly defined meaning. The root of the concept lies in the experience of power which, as we saw, is from the beginning present in the concept of the sacred. Once the sacred becomes personalized it is conceived as an agent who can do things and do more than any other. This leads to the idea that God can do anything possible and, eventually, to the further idea that he is omnipotent.[132] Yet difficulties arise as soon as we subject this idea to rational reflection. St. Thomas candidly admitted:

> All confess that God is omnipotent; but it seems difficult to explain in what His omnipotence precisely consists. For there may be a doubt as to the precise meaning of the word "all" when we say that God can do all things. If, however, we consider the matter aright, since power is said in reference to possible things, this phrase God can do all things, is rightly understood to mean that God can do all things that are possible.[133]

But what is possible? To define it as "what is within divine power" is merely to state that God's omnipotence consists in doing what he can do. Instead, Thomas defines the possible as that which does not run afoul of the principle of contradiction.

[131] Paul Ziff, "About God" in *Religious Experience and Truth*, ed. by Sidney Hook, p. 202.
[132] Donald R. Dunbar, "On 'Omnipotence'" in *The New Scholasticism*, 42 (1968), p. 286.
[133] *Summa Theologiae*, I, 25, 3 c. Tr. in *Basic Writings*, ed. by Anton Pegis (New York: Random House, 1945), pp. 262–63.

But it is hard to predefine what is contradictory. After all, our idea of what is thus possible or impossible is based upon a limited knowledge of what actually exists and therefore mainly takes into account what is *compossible* with the existing structure of the world and the laws which *de facto* prevail in it.[134] But from the Creator's point of view absolute possibility looks different, since all that exists is assumed to be intrinsically dependent in its entirety.

The difficulty is aggravated when the idea of God's acting is translated into philosophical categories. Usually this is done in terms of causality, but an omnipotent cause is even harder to conceive than an omnipotent agent. If a creative "cause" would remain absolutely omnipotent, it would undo its own effects at every moment, for the autonomy of creatures is incompatible with a continued, unlimited omnipotence. This is particularly the case for free creatures. Freedom tolerates no absolute interference and weakens even at partial intervention. In view of this "paradox of omnipotence" a distinction has been proposed between a first order of omnipotence which consists in an unlimited power to act, and a second order omnipotence which merely determines what powers to act things shall have.[135] God, then, would be omnipotent in creating autonomous beings but not in controlling them after they have been created.

Yet even this distinction does not solve the problem. For if autonomy were to place the creature entirely beyond the sphere of divine power, the notion of omnipotence would lose practically all its meaning in the present state of affairs. To survive meaningfully, an omnipotent God must in some way be at the origin even of the autonomously acting creature *while it acts*. Indeed, the notion of omnipotent power expresses in the first place that all power we experience is limited. Religious man would add that it is dependent. But this dependence is obviously not of the same kind as the one by which an effect depends upon a cause.

[134] Paul Kuntz, "Omnipotence: Tradition and Revolt in Philosophical Theology" in *The New Scholasticism*, 42 (1968), p. 272.
[135] J. L. Mackie, "Evil and Omnipotence" in *Mind*, 64 (1955), p. 212.

It is at once more fundamental (a cause is always partial) and less determining. Although divine power fuels the entire activity of the creature, this activity remains nevertheless active of itself. It is not determined to go in a particular direction, as a cause is usually conceived. A cause is directed toward a particular effect, but this is not how divine power operates. "(God) is not tied to any base of operation that is exclusively his; he enters into the subjectivity of all the world's constituents."[136] Divine power fills and at the same time transcends each phase of finite action.

This general impact of divine power is still not sufficient to justify the notion of omnipotence. For we also attribute to an omnipotent God the power to achieve specific goals beyond, and sometimes even against, the self-determination of the creature. To the believer God is able to deflect events from their initiated course and even to halt that course altogether. If it were not for such specific interventions, the notion of omnipotent power might never have occurred to the religious mind. That things do what they usually do and that they do it according to their own intentionality is hardly a fact to attract attention to divine power. But beyond that the believer is aware of abnormal manifestations of power in which the ordinary scheme of things no longer obtains. We shall have to say more about this in discussing salvation as history. Yet we cannot at this point abandon the notion of omnipotence without looking for the minimal support which prevents it from lapsing immediately into contradictoriness.

Let us be clear, then, on one point: no occurrence, however transcendent in meaning, takes place without an intramundane context. A miracle out of the blue, entirely unconnected with all preceding and following events, would be a destructive and therefore ultimately contradictory interference. But that is not what happens in what religious man considers to be a direct act of God. C. S. Lewis once wrote:

> A miracle is emphatically not an event without cause or without results. Its cause is the activity of God: its results follow according

136 Austin Farrer, *Faith and Speculation,* p. 154.

to Natural Law. In the forward direction (i.e., during the time which follows its occurrence) it is interlocked with all nature just like any other event.[137]

I agree with the second part of this statement but would qualify the first, "Its cause is the activity of God." Events which religious man considers providential or even miraculous are interlocked on both sides. It is misleading to call divine activity "the cause" of an event. For each event, however extraordinary, takes its origin in another, an intramundane event or series of events. The transcendent does not interrupt the closed circuit of connected events. Religious man *interprets* certain occurrences as miraculous because they are disproportionate to what precedes them and take place in a religious setting. Yet such an interpretation is not logically inevitable. For the transcendent is never directly perceived. Even the most extraordinary events are on all sides attached to the world and whatever transcendent influence there may be must be channeled through an empirical context. Extraordinary events are as contextual as ordinary ones, although the context is a different one. Even if they occur in a religious setting, they are solidly anchored to this universe. The observer may always invoke hidden immanent sources of energy which boost a causality that in itself is insufficient.

The point of these remarks is not to reduce the extraordinary to the ordinary—without the extraordinary the idea of omnipotence would never have emerged—but to show that the transcendent can never be *juxtaposed* to the causal relations by means of which we connect events. Even where the normal connections would prove inadequate and man invokes a transcendent energy, he still thinks of this energy as reaching its effect through intramundane "causes" such as prayer, an act of faith, etc. In the Gospel narratives Jesus' miracles are presented as directly dependent upon the faith of the bystanders, to the point where Jesus can work no miracles where there is no faith. To speak of "divine causality," then, is always inappropriate.

[137] C. S. Lewis, *Miracles* (New York: Macmillan, 1966), p. 61.

A divine causality which would, even for a moment, brush *all* immanent causal contexts aside would destroy the very concept of nature and in the end, I suspect, that of causality as well.

Yet problems of causality are not the only ones which beset the notion of divine omnipotence. More difficult even is the question why God should want to "intervene" in the first place, and to intervene at some occasions rather than others. Does this not presuppose a blatantly anthropomorphic idea of the transcendent? At present I cannot hope to do more than draw attention to the problem. But in order to see the real problem we must avoid getting trapped in a false one. The question is not: Why should God be so inconsistent as to interfere with self-given laws? For what we call "laws" are abstractions of our own making in which with a certain amount of arbitrariness we symbolize what usually happens in a well-defined sector. Such a pragmatic device should make no claims of completeness, since it leaves out huge segments of an essentially united experience. A "complete" law would be as comprehensive as experience itself and would include the so-called spiritual as well as the physical. Since it would also include the religiously extraordinary, the inconsistency would vanish.

The real problem is more serious. Perhaps it could be formulated thus: How can God be such that he is able to enter into *dialogue* with his creation? For only in such a dialogue can he truly be said to *act*—the fundamental belief which is at the root of the notion of omnipotence. This question does not disappear after one reaches a more sophisticated view of the relation between the finite and the infinite. On the contrary, the single major credit of old-time theism is precisely to have brought out the dialectical nature of the relation between God and the creature. So far panentheism has been extremely short on this issue. Yet to most religious men the point is of capital importance. Unless they can talk to God and be assured that he can hear them and respond, they will dismiss the religious attitude as impossible or, at best, useless.

Rephrased in its simplest form the question becomes: How can God be a person vis-à-vis the creature? Of course, the simple answer here would be: Because he *is* a person. But that cannot be unqualifiedly true. If the divine is the absolute and the infinite which includes the relative and the finite, it cannot be expressed in the category of person. For the person is nothing if not relative.

Before discussing the problem we must recall that the sacred is not always personal and is never confined to the personal. According to Rudolf Otto the numinous experience is not primarily personal. The numen displays some traits which will allow it to develop into personal gods. But in the process of this development it inevitably loses some of its original meaning which goes far beyond the personal.[138] To be sure, experiencing the numinous is not yet being religious. The active response decisive for the religious attitude may still require the development toward a personal God. In fact religious men usually tend to personalize the sacred for the purposes of worship, even in religious faiths (such as Buddhism and Vedantic Hinduism) which speculatively recognize no personal god. But never is the sacred restricted to the personal. Even the Old Testament in which the idea of a personal God has been developed to an unusual degree, still reveals a tension between what Jaspers calls "silent, incomprehensible transcendence" and the God who speaks.[139] For Christians the personal aspect of the sacred culminates in the description of divine life in terms of interpersonal relations. Yet they also surpass the category of the personal, as we witness in the impersonal names given to the second person (Logos, Pneuma) and, even more, to the third person of the Holy Trinity. The beautiful hymn *Veni Sancte Spiritus* addresses the Spirit as light, rest, refreshing coolness.[140] The early development of the doctrine of the Holy Spirit often describes him in terms of

[138] *The Idea of the Holy,* p. 198.
[139] *Philosophical Faith and Revelation,* p. 143.
[140] "In labore requies, in aestu temperies, in fletu solatium. O lux beatissima reple cordis intima tuorum fidelium."

the Neo-Platonic ψυχή, the world-soul.[141] It is also well known how mystics of all faiths tend to surpass the personal often to the point where their statements become unacceptable to established theology.

Yet after those necessary qualifications we must still investigate whether the notion of a personal God has any philosophical standing at all. The term person as applied to God refers in the first place to his self-containment, his active otherness. It originates in the religious awareness that God must be "inside himself as I am inside myself," that his life is not ours.[142] The existence of a divine autonomy which is able to respond and to take initiatives appears to be essential to the very possibility of a religious attitude. To express this idea the notion of person comes immediately to mind, all the more since the divine is at the basis of the human person. God cannot be less than personal and he possesses some essential traits of the person.

Unfortunately, the personal appears to have some inherent limitations as well which make it questionable as a divine attribute. The most obvious one is individuality. If God is the absolute ground of all that is—the substance—then he can clearly not be one individual opposed to others. The individual is singular; the substance universal. What is merely finite can obviously not be absolute. Can the anthropomorphic limitation of the idea of person be overcome? Many philosophers feel that it cannot without draining the term of all definable meaning. Others consider individuality not inherent in the notion of person as such, but only in the particular conditions in which the human person exists.[143] Which features are essential to the personal as such? Self-containment to the extent that it excludes others conflicts with the substantial presence of God in the creature. "God is

[141] Tullio Gregory, *Anima Mundi* (Firenze, 1955), pp. 123–27. Cf. also such impersonal expressions as those of the prayer of the Greek Symeon: "Come treasure without name; come unutterable thing." *Hymns of Divine Love,* Migne, P.G. 120, 507.

[142] Austin Farrer, *Faith and Speculation,* pp. 49, 47.

[143] Jacques Maritain, *The Degrees of Knowledge,* tr. by Gerald Phelan (New York: Charles Scribner's Sons, 1959), pp. 231–34.

called a person, but he is a person not in finite separation but in an absolute and unconditioned participation in everything."[144] I would qualify the first part of this statement by Paul Tillich to read: ". . . not only in separation, but also . . ." Person implies openness as well as self-containment. The term *persona* means that a being has a face of his own, but also that he faces others. It is only through the communication with others that the person possesses himself. Applying this to God, Jean Daniélou concludes: "When it is said that God is personal, it seems that . . . what is meant above all is that it is possible to enter into communication, into communion with him."[145] Most philosophers who reject the notion of person do so on the basis of the person's alleged lack of communicability. They assume that the person is confined to the self, while God communicates his Being beyond selfhood.[146] But self-transcendence belongs to the essence of the person. To be a person means to be able to communicate freely.

Those remarks obviously do not clear the road for calling God a person. For if person implies *otherness,* one cannot *a priori* claim that God must be a person unless one also ascribes to God's essence the need of otherness. *If* the other exists, God must be both self-contained and giving. But *must* the other exist? God may be conceived without it, I should think, and hence also without personality. Only in the actual creation of persons can one say that God himself becomes personal in the usual sense which implies facing and being faced. Christians may object to this way of reasoning on the basis of the interpersonal relations which they posit in God independently of the creation. But of those relations the philosopher knows nothing through his own science. From the fact that there is a creation he may well conclude, if he is a believer, that the God in whom he believes is a self-expressing one and, consequently, that there must be intradivine relations. But their nature remains unknown. For the philosopher as such the personal nature of God is established

---

[144] *Systematic Theology,* I, pp. 243–44.

[145] Jean Daniélou, *God and the Ways of Knowing,* tr. by Walter Roberts (New York: Meridian Books, 1965), pp. 78–79.

[146] Cf., for instance, Leslie Dewart, *The Future of Belief,* p. 188.

through the personal nature of man. God becomes a person first when man recognizes him.

Even after all those precautions the notion of person must remain primarily symbolic. For divine communication differs so essentially from that of ordinary interpersonal exchange that many men prefer not to use the term. Karl Jaspers articulates their misgivings:

> Given to himself he knows not whence, man feels the urge to let Transcendence appear to him as a person. He finds a cipher for it: "God." But the cipher is inadequate, for even as the best that man knows in the world, as personality, Transcendence is still debased, so to speak, into his own kind of being.[147]

Jaspers is right; yet if his remark implies that to be authentically religious man must overcome the notion of person, he is wrong. For in the principal religious attitude with which Western man is acquainted—that of prayer—the transcendent cannot be addressed but in a personal way. Within this attitude the symbol of the person is necessary and irreplaceable.

[147] *Philosophical Faith and Revelation,* p. 141.

Chapter 9
The Mystery of Creation

1. THE RELIGIOUS ORIGIN OF THE IDEA OF CREATION AND ITS PHILOSOPHICAL DEVELOPMENT

That God is the creator of heaven and earth is neither a scientific theory nor a philosophical conclusion. Creation is primarily a religious symbol articulating man's experience of being dependent upon an absolute principle. It has been called the most fundamental religious category.[1] Yet it is hardly visible in Buddhism and in Hindu writings of the classical age.

Even where creation myths play an important part their primary subject is not the origin of the totality of what is (an idea too abstract to occupy the archaic mind) but the origin of the things that really matter. These are the institutions existing at the time of the myth rather than the past stages of development in the emergence of the real. The questions which the creation myth answers are limited by the interests of the culture in which they originate.[2] In Egypt the center of the entire cosmic order was the king: the principal mythical theme of Osiris and Horus deals with his divine origin more than with the birth of

[1] Johannes Hessen, *Religionsphilosophie* (München, 1955), II, p. 198.
[2] Robley E. Whitson, "The Concept of Origins," in *Thought,* 37 (1962), p. 247.

the universe.[3] Similarly, in reading *Enuma Elish* one learns considerably more about the social institutions of the Sumerian-Babylonian culture than about its cosmological views.[4] In some primitive creation myths as that of the Arikara Indians the world is already present at the beginning of creation.[5]

Even where the idea of creation fulfills a strictly religious function (as opposed to the functionally undifferentiated myth), it is seldom primary. Religion is mainly concerned with salvation. Now in some instances, as in the Babylonian epic *Enuma Elish,* salvation itself comes through the creation, that is, through the dissipation of the original chaos, annually renewed at the beginning of the year. In other instances, as in the faith of Israel, this is not the case, but the creation gradually imposes itself as a necessary prelude to God's mighty deeds of salvation. To accomplish such deeds God must be omnipotent; to be omnipotent he must be at the origin of all things. I therefore consider the idea of creation, wherever it is developed, fundamental, although not necessarily primary. I also suspect that it still occupies a similar position in the religious consciousness of modern Western man.

> Religious concern being with the actual will of God as it affects us, faith will affirm God's direction of nature before she comes to the ultimate mystery, the creation of all from nothing. But she has only to persevere in the same path in order to reach it . . . The will of God cannot be limited by anything pre-existent to his action; he must be the first, total and sufficient cause.[6]

[3] Rudolph Anthes, "Mythology in Ancient Egypt," in Samuel N. Kramer, *Mythologies of the Ancient World* (Garden City, N.Y.: Doubleday, 1961), pp. 68–85. John A. Wilson, *The Burden of Egypt. An Interpretation of Ancient Egyptian Culture* (Chicago: University of Chicago Press, 1951), pp. 58–60.

[4] Alexander Heidel, *The Babylonian Genesis* (Chicago: University of Chicago Press, 1963). Cornelius Loew, *Myth, Sacred History and Philosophy,* pp. 26–42.

[5] Cf. Robley E. Whitson, "The Concept of Origins," in *Thought,* 37 (1962), p. 249. I used the term "primitive" merely to distinguish this mythical expression from that of civilizations with developed agriculture and urban culture, as the Egyptian and Babylonian.

[6] Austin Farrer, *Faith and Speculation,* p. 80.

The latter half of this quote by Austin Farrer is misleading in that it again suggests a speculative origin. But the idea of creation was in no way conceived to answer the ultimate philosophical question: Why is there anything rather than nothing? Earlier we quoted Heidegger saying that its acceptance may be an obstacle to philosophical thinking if the believer considers it to be an explanatory interpretation. For to exclude the Creator from questioning is not to ask the ultimate question.[7]

A philosophical absolute even if called "God" always remains distinct from the God upon whom the believer asserts his total dependence in what to him is the *mystery* of creation. Creation is exclusively a religious concept which entered into philosophy through faith and which disappears as soon as philosophy is severed from its religious roots. Philosophy can do very well without it, because the philosophical question of the real is an entirely different one. Langdon Gilkey in his beautiful book on creation phrases this question:

> Is there any basic, fundamental, permanent substance, being, a set of principles which underlies [the changing things] and so which gives them all the reality they possess?[8]

This question differs from the scientific one, *how* a particular situation arose empirically, but even more from the religious one which does not primarily inquire about the nature of the Absolute but about man's relation to it and the conditions which make this relation possible.

The idea of creation was not seriously entertained at the beginning of our philosophical tradition. This in itself indicates that it is not a primary philosophical concern. The philosopher needs a principle to unite and justify the real in its totality. The Presocratics searched for it among the elements and proposed in succession, water, air, fire. Finally philosophy settled on the

[7] *Einführung in die Metaphysik*, p. 5. *An Introduction to Metaphysics*, tr. by Ralph Manheim, p. 6.

[8] *Maker of Heaven and Earth* (Garden City, N.Y.: Doubleday, 1965), p. 17.

notion of Being, the only one sufficiently comprehensive to cover all reality.[9] Naturally, the notion of Being generates the problem of becoming. We remember its origins in Parmenides and Heraclitus. If things *are* what they are, why do they change? Plato first reconciled becoming with Being by distinguishing the unchangeable realm of *what truly is* from *what only participates* in the supreme reality. This inevitably raised the further question how the second realm depends upon the first. In the *Timaeus* we witness the birth of that problem.

> We must, then, in my judgment, first make this distinction: what is that which is always real and has no becoming, and what is that which is always becoming and is never real? That which is apprehensible by thought with a rational account is the thing that is always unchangeably real; whereas that which is the object of belief together with unreasoning sensation is the thing that becomes and passes away, but never has real being. Again, all that becomes must needs become by the agency of some cause; for without a cause nothing can come to be.[10]

At this point the reader expects a rational explanation. Instead, Plato turns the whole discussion into a mythical cosmogony: a divine Demiurge has fashioned the world. The problem belongs to the realm of reason but, his procedure suggests, its solution surpasses rational inquiry. The myth of the Demiurge is clearly more than a literary device. Plato attached a unique truth value to the myth as such—a myth which in this case had already attained a specifically religious meaning. The religious invocation at the beginning (27c) sets the mood and this mood prevails during the entire narrative. The language throughout is that of pious reflection, rather than rational inquiry. For Timaeus the world is good and so is its maker: "the contrary supposition . . . cannot be spoken without blasphemy" (29a). Yet to call

[9] See, for instance, Étienne Gilson, *Being and Some Philosophers* (Toronto: Pontifical Institute of Mediaeval Studies, 1952), p. 6.
[10] 27d–28a. Tr. by Francis M. Cornford in *Plato's Timaeus* (Indianapolis: Bobbs-Merrill, 1959), p. 16.

Plato's myth religious is not to identify it with the great epics of creation of Genesis or *Enuma Elish*. For Plato maintains a critical attitude toward the myth even while fully respecting it. The myth may be profound but it is always uncritical and therefore likely to be mixed with untruth.

After Plato, creation disappears once more from philosophy (if that term applies to the myth of the Demiurge). In Aristotle there is no talk of a creating god. He outright repudiates "the theologians who generate the world from night."[11] The unmoved mover of the twelfth book of *Metaphysics* seems designed for the sole purpose of providing a rational explanation of the possibility of change. Plato's mythical creator is not even considered. The idea of a beginning change is rejected as equally unfit (1071b). Since the static Ideas are obviously a poor principle to explain actual change, Aristotle replaces them by an unmoved *mover* who, to avoid the unacceptable idea of a beginning or an end, must move from all eternity. Thus creation in time is excluded in principle. Nor does the self-contained nature of the unmoved mover allow any involvement with the lower regions. Even the thought of a world would blemish his infinite perfection.[12] Nevertheless, Aristotle does not hesitate to ascribe divine qualities to this detached mover and ultimately identifies him with god (*Met.*, 1072b). Obviously the introverted goodness of this Supreme Being is far above the outward-directed concerns of the God of Jews, Christians, and Moslems.[13] We may well wonder whether it deserves the sacred name at all. At any rate, in our Western tradition the idea of creation is decisively not of philosophical origin.

[11] *Metaphysics,* 1071b.

[12] "If it [i.e., divine thought] thinks, but this depends on something else, then . . . it cannot be the best substance . . . Evidently, then, it thinks of that which is most divine and precious, and it does not change; for change would be change for the worse and this would be already a movement." *Met.,* 1074b, tr. by W. D. Ross in *The Works of Aristotle* (Oxford: Clarendon Press, 1930).

[13] How much opposed the two views of God are is shown in Boyce Gibson, "The Two Strands in Natural Theology," in *Philosophy of Religion,* ed. by John E. Smith (New York: Macmillan, 1965), p. 65.

Nevertheless philosophy has had a profound impact upon the theological formulation and development of the idea. Later rationalizations of the creation concept prove this abundantly: its origin out of nothing (*ex nihilo*), the beginning in time, the unicity, goodness, and freedom of the Creator. The idea of a creation from nothing seems to appear first in the Jewish writer Philo (first century B.C.). Resisting for once his concordist inclinations, the Alexandrian theologian draws attention to the difference between the Creator of Genesis and the Demiurge of the *Timaeus*. Yahweh "also made things which before were not, not just handling material as a *demiurge,* an *artificer,* but being Himself its *creator*."[14] Yet the notion of creation *ex nihilo* appears nowhere in the Bible, least of all in the first chapters of Genesis to which Philo refers.[15] The problem simply did not arise. We might add that Philo's interpretation not only exaggerates the philosophical tenor of the Biblical concept of creation, but misunderstands Plato as well. For the "matter" out of which the Demiurge creates is clearly a metaphysical principle, not a pre-existing component. Plato here presents in mythical form what goes into the making of a world. To this, a metaphysical principle of permanence underlying the flux of change seems essential. But at no time does Plato intend to report a historical succession. The Genesis account itself mentions an original chaos— "the earth was a formless void"—but it would be equally in-

[14] *De Somniis,* 1, 13, 76. It was precisely this distinction which made the Septuagint translators choose the term κτιδτης rather than Δημιουργός· Erich Frank, *Philosophical Understanding and Religious Truth,* p. 74. In other passages Philo himself seems to adopt what he took for Plato's position. For instance, *De Mundi Opificio,* V 22.

[15] Catholics used to quote 2 Maccabees 7:28, in which the mother of the seven Jewish martyrs under the persecution of Antiochus Epiphanes exhorts her youngest son to face death with courage. "I implore you, my child, observe heaven and earth, consider all that is in them, and acknowledge that God made them out of what did not exist, and that mankind comes into being in the same way." Yet the point of the argument is not that God created things out of nothing, but rather that He who created a world which did not exist before, must certainly be able to restore life after it has died. The author is not concerned with the problem whether the world was produced out of nothing or out of formless matter.

appropriate to conclude from this to the existence of a pre-creational matter. The abstract idea of nothingness was insufficiently developed to admit of a distinction between utter chaos and nothingness. The chaos merely represents the initial, totally unstructured (and therefore unreal) state of things.

Nevertheless, if Philo and even more his Christian successors made so much out of a small point in a philosopher of excellent religious standing, we may be assured that more than a purely speculative dispute is at stake. Plato's text, I suspect, alerted Philo and the early Christian thinkers to the implications of their own religious position. Through the *Timaeus* they first realized that God's absolute sovereignty as affirmed in the Bible could not be maintained if the Creator was in need of pre-creational assistance. Yahweh's sovereignty was asserted not so much in the expressions of the creation account as in his absolute rule over Israel. It was now understood that any reality pre-existing God's creative act would put restrictions on his dominion.

At the same time Jews and Christians discovered an arsenal of positive ideas in Plato for elaborating their own theology of creation. The most fruitful was perhaps that of the creature as image of God. In the *Timaeus* the imitation of the sensible world had been combined with the idea of creation. Thus Plato provided the ideal tool for developing the meaning of Scripture that God created man to his image and likeness. Gregory of Nyssa and Augustine were to bring the idea to its perfect expression. To Gregory the likeness of God implies that man *imitates* God as a Platonic archetype.[16] In a more dynamic way man also *participates* in God by aspiring toward the divine in love and cognition. Gregory reconciled his ideal view of mankind with its lowly appearances by means of a theory of double creation; one purely

[16] J. T. Muckle, "The Doctrine of St. Gregory of Nyssa on Man as the Image of God" in *Mediaeval Studies,* VII (1945), p. 61. Already Origen and Gregory's brother Basil had conceived the "likeness" as a Platonic assimilation to God. Yet they had reserved the *homoiosis* to the redemption while the creation made man only into the image ($\epsilon i \kappa \omega \nu$) of God. Gregory abolished this distinction and regarded man as created directly to the likeness of God.

ideal and nonsensuous; the other in which God, foreknowing Adam's sin, provided man with an animal body and a sexual mode of reproduction in order to prevent the human race from dying out with the first man (as a result of sin) and to allow it to regain its original image of God through the process of time.[17] The theology of Gregory indicates the extent to which Plato's philosophy affected the Biblical idea of creation.

Yet Plato's thought was not the only spiritual force to challenge the Christian idea of creation. Gnosticism confronted Hellenistic Jews and Christians with a strictly religious alternative. Despite their variety all Gnostic systems agree on one basic point which neither Jews nor Christians could ever accept: the material creation was intrinsically evil and could not have originated from the same principle as the spirit. For Jews and Christians the same God was the maker of all things, "visible and invisible." Through the writings of Irenaeus, its most competent Christian antagonist, Gnosticism would have a negative but lasting impact on the development of the idea of creation. For Irenaeus "all . . . things, visible and invisible, are made by one God."[18] From this principle he deduces that the entire man (not merely the spirit) is made after the image and likeness of God.[19] The one concession Irenaeus is willing to make to Gnostic theology is a distinction between an original body-soul combination (the *plasma*) and the spirit (*pneuma*) which is received after man has grown to maturity.[20] Other Christian writers were willing to adopt more Gnostic elements. Thus, to Origen man is the image of God not in body and soul, but only according to the "interior man" renewed by spiritual perfection.[21] Origen seems to share

[17] *De Hominis Opificio* in Migne, P.G. 44, 203–10. One may consult Gerhart B. Ladner, "The Philosophical Anthropology of Saint Gregory of Nyssa" in *Dumbarton Oaks Papers*, 12 (1958) (Cambridge: Harvard University Press), pp. 59–94.

[18] *Adversus Haereses*, Bk. II, Ch. 30, 6. Migne, P.G. 7, 818. *Against Heresies*, tr. by John A. Keble (London, s.d.), p. 186.

[19] *Op. cit.*, Bk. V, Ch. 6, 1. Migne, P.G. 7, 1137. *Against Heresies*, p. 460.

[20] *Op. cit.*, Bk. IV, Ch. 38, 3. Migne, P.G. 7, 1108. *Against Heresies*, p. 438.

[21] *Contra Celsum*, VI, 63. Migne, P.G. 11, 1394–95.

the Gnostic belief that the body is a punishment for sins committed in a previous existence.[22]

The Gnosis made Christians aware of the antidualistic character of their own concept of creation. Of course, the idea of the integral goodness of creation did not originate in the confrontation with Gnosticism, no more than the creation *ex nihilo* or the concept of the image of God was due to the encounter with Plato. Our thesis here is that philosophical systems and different religious traditions played an important role in helping Christians (and to some extent also Jews) to articulate their own religious concept of creation. In fact the man who did most to make the essential goodness of creation universally accepted in the West was never much concerned with Gnosticism. Augustine's battles on this issue were all with Manichaeans. Still without the preceding confrontation with the Gnosis, Augustine would not have written:

> Every nature, therefore, is good . . . A nature is called evil only when it is corrupt.[23]
>
> All natures are good, seeing that the Author of absolutely all natures is supremely good. But because, unlike their Author they are not supremely and unchangeably good, the good in them can dwindle and it can grow.[24]

Of course, to affirm the absolute goodness of creation is to complicate the explanation of evil in the world. Hebrews and Christians reduced evil to a subordinate principle for which the Creator is not responsible, yet which does not escape his supreme power. This complex solution allowed them to maintain simultaneously God's absolute sovereignty and the goodness of

[22] *De Principiis*, Bk. I, Ch. 8. In the edition of Paul Koetschau (Leipzig, 1913), fragments 17[a] and 17[b].

[23] *De natura boni contra Manichaeos*, Migne, P.L. 42, 553.

[24] *Enchiridion de fide, spe et caritate*, 12, Migne, P.L. 40, 235, tr. by Edmund Hill, O.P. On the goodness of bodily natures also *De Civitate Dei*, Bk. XI, Ch. 4, Migne, P.L. 41, 352, and *Quaestiones ad Simplicianum*, I, 2, 8, Migne, P.L. 40, 116. Augustine's idyllic descriptions of Eden also support his antidualistic thesis: the world was good as it came from the hands of God—whatever evil there is comes from man.

his creation. To what extent both can be upheld will be discussed later.

First, we must still consider two other aspects of the idea of creation, which were developed under philosophical influence: God created freely and he created in time. Neo-Platonism is directly or indirectly responsible for the theological elaboration of both ideas. In *Enneads,* V, 1, 6, Plotinus raises the question whether finite beings could be said to emanate freely out of the absolute principle. The answer is negative since an assent or free decree would introduce movement into the Absolute, and thereby destroy its absolute unity. The "creatures," he concludes, are the necessary radiation of the eternal One.

> All that is fully achieved engenders: therefore, the eternally achieved engenders eternally an eternal being. At the same time the offspring is always minor.[25]

In the same declining line the eternal offspring will emanate a temporal one. Some early Christian theologians eagerly picked up this theory to use it as a foundation for the Trinitarian hypostases. But, the overall results were not considered successful by the Christian community. The doctrine of necessary emanation was almost universally repudiated as a theory of creation. Christians by and large felt that the Creator had to be totally independent of the creature, and they showed little patience with theologians whose explanation came too close to Plotinus' necessary generation. This is the main reason why John Scotus Eriugena's theological system (ninth century) was almost entirely rejected by the tradition. In spite of mounting philosophical criticism the traditional position has little changed over the centuries, as appears in the condemnations of Vatican I:

> If anyone . . . says that God did not create with a will free from all necessity, but that he created necessarily, just as he necessarily loves himself . . . let him be anathema.[26]

[25] *Enneads,* V, 1, 6.
[26] *Enchiridion Symbolorum,* �etc1805.

Since the concept of a free creation has some basic metaphysical implications, we must subject it to a rigorous philosophical critique.

To oppose divine freedom to divine necessity in the act of creation would appear to be a particularly uncritical way of speaking. For all divine activity is both free and necessary. Although the creative act is unique in that it results in a contingent reality, one cannot simply substitute arbitrariness for necessity and conclude that no compelling reasons occasioned the act. If God is necessary, so is his creative activity. Nothing seems more obvious. But then why have the sharpest religious minds in the Judeo-Christian-Moslem tradition chosen the narrow and crooked path of thinking that leads to a nonnecessary creation? Because the believer refused to jeopardize an important religious insight by easy philosophical solutions, even if this refusal required a temporary sacrifice of coherence. What is this insight which withstood the more obvious emanation theory?

The answer lies in the idea of absolute transcendence. Religious man in our tradition becomes uncomfortable whenever God and the creature are connected too closely. He prefers to maintain a proper distance between the two and is therefore reluctant to consider the creature a necessary product of God's immanent activity. "God creates the creature in freedom" means, according to Dietrich Bonhoeffer, that their connection is not conditioned by anything except freedom—which means that it is unconditioned.[27] Taking our lead from this interpretation we may perhaps find an acceptable philosophical sense in the concept of a free, nonnecessary creation.

An initial distinction must be made between freedom and contingency: the latter affects not the divine act but its created effect. To the religious mind the act results in an otherness which cannot be assimilated with its originating principle. Since divine creativity is totally unconditioned, the created effect can never claim any pre-existing necessity. Creation explodes in a void,

[27] Dietrich Bonhoeffer, *Creation and Fall,* tr. by John C. Fletcher (New York: Macmillan, 1959), p. 18.

scattering the ontologically novel to all sides. The term causality is wholly inappropriate to describe this event, for a cause is effective only within a chain of conditions, while the creative act excludes any necessity which links Creator to creature. One cannot omit one of the constituent factors of causality and still hope to preserve the basic concept. To be created means to originate in a vacuum of conditions. This, I take it, is the ultimate meaning of the paradoxical but deeply religious expression: *ex nihilo,* creation from nothing.[28] The void surrounding the creative act is remarkably similar to the gratuitousness which man in times of crisis and anxiety so clearly senses in the heart of existence itself. Why should anything exist at all? And why should things be as they are? Why should the grass be green and why is pain necessary? The very absurdity of these questions brings out the ultimate strangeness and frightening loneliness of finite being. Existentialist philosophy has made a great deal of this experience. To religious man it had been known for a long time: from the returning myriadic cycles of the Buddhist universe, through the interminable succession of Gnostic aeons, to the Christian feeling of fear before the infinite space of an ever-expanding universe. Pascal's exclamation *"Le silence éternel de ces espaces infinis m'effraie*[29] reveals more than philosophical wonder: it is the terror for the void around being. To the religious mind the strangeness of existence is not a source of philosophical reflection; it expresses man's deep-felt need for transcendent foundation.

[28] Of course, the expression also signifies the difference between God and the creature. The creature was no more made out of God's substance than out of any other pre-existing substance; hence it is said to be made out of nothing. According to Ramsey, *ex nihilo* must be understood as a qualifier which fundamentally transforms the ordinary usage of the model *creation.* "To talk of a 'creation *ex nihilo'* is not at all like talking of a painting from oils, a building from stone, a dress from brocade. In other words, it is *not* something which can be the subject of a plain straightforward assertion . . . We may put the point alternatively by saying that whereas creation *ex nihilo* seems on the face of it, and from its grammar, to be talking of a great occasion in the past, it is rather making a present claim about God." Ian Ramsey, *Religious Language,* pp. 84–85.

[29] *Pensées* in *Oeuvres,* ed. by Jacques Chevalier (Paris, 1950), 91.

Any world which is created—even "the best possible"—lacks intrinsic necessity. To accept createdness is to deprive oneself of the ultimate answer to the question: Why one thing rather than another? It is an admission of the absence of conditions for the presence of anything at all. At the same time it is a confession of total dependence. If God creates out of nothing, no thing can ever subsist apart from the creative act. To perceive the creature, then, is to perceive the creative event. The creature *is* the divine act in its otherness. Creating means creating of otherness, but since the creative act is unconditioned, the otherness can never move outside the act. This means that even the otherness of the Creator remains within Him. Nothing can be detached from the living act, for outside the act no conditions exist to support created being. The universe and all things in it are entirely superfluous; they hang in an absolute vacuum. Yet, the total dependence of all that is upon the unconditioned creative act converts the experience of nothingness into one of presence. To exist is to participate in an act of divine communication. This unique mixture of loneliness and presence is what believers attempt to express in the notion of a free, unnecessary creation.

Pantheism has been aware of the divine presence but has expressed it poorly. For to deny that I exist in order to assert all the more strongly that God is present, is not to appreciate the full force of this presence. If God's presence merely means that all other reality is an illusion, then he is not present enough to achieve autonomous selfhood. Pantheism is only a half-baked religious idea. To the religious mind God's creative act is always powerful enough to have "another" side. The creature is the total otherness of God within the total dependence upon God.

No answer to the question "Why did God create the world?" should begin with the words "in order to . . . ," for they would place a condition between God and the creature. The world as a whole contains no reason for its existence. We may ask what things *within* the world are for, but we cannot ask the same question about finite reality as such. If the universe was not created to fulfill any divine need, and if outside God there is nothing to need it, then no preconditioning rules for its creation can be laid down. To *require* an intrinsic finality of the creation beyond the one without which a being would contradict itself out of existence, is to postulate the intrinsic necessity characteristic of an emanationist universe. God may create necessarily, but this necessity does not carry over to the nature of his creatures. Between God and the creature there are no rules except those of intrinsic coherence. The absolutely unconditioned is "surrounded" by total emptiness. To demand from God's wisdom and goodness a best possible world, as Leibniz did, is to attribute to the world God's own necessary status and, consequently, to return to emanationism. God did not and could not create a replica of himself: he created "something other" that possesses no intrinsic necessity of its own.

The concept of divine freedom, Paul Tillich wrote, symbolizes the absence of any ground "compelling" God to do one thing rather than another.[30] But if the term "freedom" is taken in a nonsymbolic sense—as if it were the *condition* of a Being which, like the human agent, is not free to be free, (Sartre would say, is condemned to be free)—then it introduces a prior reality, incompatible with the idea of God. Therefore, God is neither bound nor free.

2. THE MYSTERY OF EVIL

The preceding remarks do not solve the basic philosophical problem of creation. For if God is not bound by the condition to create any particular good, he still may have to avoid the creation of all evil that is not inherent in the nature and coexistence of finite beings. Reduced to the necessity of creating the least possible evil, the thesis of the best possible world appears a more plausible hypothesis. How could a perfect creator ever cause any evil that could have been avoided within the context of a finite universe? How, even, could he create free agents who

[30] *Systematic Theology*, I, p. 248.

themselves will cause evil and thereby inflict suffering upon others, unless their absence would necessitate an even less perfect world? Not only the existence of earthquakes, black plague epidemics, and the children's crusade require a justification, but also the free deeds of Hitler and Genghis Khan. No issue has more profoundly disturbed believers of all times and more effectively blocked the road to belief in our time. To preclude false expectations the writer of these pages feels obliged to declare from the outset that he has no solution to offer to the problem of evil. He doubts, however, that it is a "problem," i.e., a set of data which can be combined in a coherent order. Problem or mystery, evil remains a shocking reality for which no amount of reflection softens the shock. The most we can hope for is to exonerate the Creator from the charge of willfully inflicting useless suffering, by exposing our total ignorance concerning what is needed and what is dispensable in the making of a universe. Only a clear awareness of the inherent weakness of his faculties will prepare the believer to confront the Medusa face of evil.

The few philosophers willing to come to the believer's rescue have mostly claimed either that evil is inevitable or that it is necessary for the existence of a greater good. Is evil inevitable? Let us break the question down into physical suffering and moral evil. Unquestionably, in the actual structure of reality, man's ability to suffer is the price he pays for a heightened sensitivity. For that reason we may perhaps consider it a perfection. But the need for a potential to suffer does not justify the creation of a world in which actual suffering affects such a substantial portion of human and, for all we know, animal existence. Could it have been avoided? Hume certainly thought that the same effect could have been obtained by a diminution of pleasure. Moreover, a spokesman of his *Dialogues* asks, why should the universe be so rigorously conducted by general laws, when temporary suspensions could avoid suffering?[31] His arguments continue to stimulate speculation. Why could an omnipotent God not have created

[31] *Dialogues Concerning Natural Religion*, ed. by Norman Kemp Smith (New York: Social Sciences Publishers, 1948), pp. 206–7.

a more harmonious universe, or at least why could he not miraculously intervene (as believers say he does occasionally) to prevent the more painful effects of its laws?[32] The preceding pages showed that in the believer's own conviction the present world structure was certainly not necessary. Even the assumption of a hypothetical necessity of suffering in a finite universe does not discharge the Creator of all responsibility. For then the whole argument turns into the question whether a structure which demanded so much suffering was worth its price. A number of men have answered this question negatively, and some have proven the seriousness of their denial by terminating their own lives. How can the creation of so much avoidable suffering be reconciled with the idea of an all-good Creator? Of course, God's goodness differs from man's goodness. But, as John Stuart Mill pointed out, there are limits to the usage of terms, beyond which they lose all intelligible sense.

> If in ascribing goodness to God I do not mean what I mean by goodness . . . what do I mean by calling it goodness? And what reason have I for venerating it? If I know nothing about what the attribute is, I cannot tell that it is a proper object of veneration. To say that God's goodness may be different in kind from man's goodness, what is it but saying, with a slight change of phraseology, that God may possibly not be good?[33]

The arguments are impressive enough. Yet I am not convinced that they represent the only possible or even the correct way of phrasing the question. Undoubtedly, any suffering which is no more than hypothetically necessary could have been avoided. Yet most people and, from all appearances, also most animals seem to regard life on the whole as good. In that global sense, at least, the universe seems worth its steep price. To propose that from this basic goodness all suffering be excised is to take a purely

[32] H. J. McCloskey, "God and Evil" in *The Philosophical Quarterly,* 10 (1960), pp. 103–4.
[33] *An Examination of Sir William Hamilton's Philosophy* (London: Longmans, Green, 1872), p. 128.

imaginary stab at the possible and the impossible. Long ago Bergson exposed the arbitrariness of such a discrimination between a good substance and its evil accidents.

> What, looked at from one side, appears as an infinite multiplicity of things, of which suffering is indeed one, may look from another side like an indivisible act, so that the elimination of one part would mean doing away with the whole. Now it will be suggested that the whole might have been different, and such that pain had no place in it; therefore that life, even if it is good could have been better. And the conclusion will be drawn that, if a principle really exists, and if that principle is love, it is not omnipotent and it is therefore not God. But that is just the question.[34]

Indeed it is, and as our discussion of the concept of omnipotence has shown, the possibilities here are not unlimited. All this is not to say that a world without suffering was impossible, but merely that we do not know whether it was or not.

A word should be said also about the analogous use of the term goodness. For the case is more complicated than Mill suggests. Anyone sufficiently aware of the meaning of transcendence will concede that our models must indeed be qualified to the point where we no longer know what the divine attribute is like in itself. The purpose of attributing human qualities to God is not to acquire additional knowledge—the believer fully accepts Mill's charge that he no longer exactly knows what he means—but to assert divine perfection. In doing this we have no other choice but to conceive it after our own patterns of perfection. Religious man is usually not deceived by the rules of his own language game. On the contrary, he is more aware of their restrictions than the philosopher is. Thus the Hebrews ascribed absolute perfection to Yahweh and at the same time referred to him as the "author of good and evil."[35] Admittedly, there is a point beyond which words become meaningless, but it is impossible to define

[34] *The Two Sources of Morality and Religion,* tr. by Ashley Andra and Cloudesley Brereton (Garden City, N.Y.: Doubleday, 1957), p. 261.
[35] See Ian Ramsey, *Religious Language,* p. 100.

a priori where it will be reached in naming divine perfections. When he calls the Creator "good," the believer means that God is the source of all known goodness, but he does not try to justify this goodness in the face of the evil which also exists. He merely connects human perfection to a transcendent origin. Whether such a speech be rationally justified or not, it is meaningful and contains no contradiction.

Let us now turn to the even more complex case of moral evil. The prosecution asks: Why did God create free beings whom he knew would do evil and inflict suffering upon others? Granting that freedom itself is a perfection, could he not have created men who would *freely* choose to do good? Must freedom necessarily imply the possibility of committing evil? Not according to the believer's own vision of eternal beatitude in which all participants are both free and unable to do evil! Even if freedom must imply the possibility of evil, God could still have prevented a great deal of the moral evil which now occurs. A slight difference in the mental make-up of Hitler might have saved us the second world war without sacrificing his freedom. Antony Flew logically argues that if an action can be both freely chosen and yet fully determined by caused causes, predetermination toward good and freedom are no longer incompatible. God then could have created men who would always as a matter of fact choose to do the right.[36] As long as miracles do not exclude freedom, some intervention of the Creator might have been expected at the critical moments of history.

Formidable as these charges are, they, and most of the usual replies to them, show a lack of appreciation for the full autonomy of human freedom. Whatever freedom may be in an afterlife of which we know nothing, in man's present state it is a force which *creates* its own values by means of choices among alternatives. Once it exists no God can stop its momentum. Now, such an autonomous freedom inevitably implies the possibility of choosing self-contraction and isolation rather than self-expansion and open-

[36] "Divine Omnipotence and Human Freedom," in *New Essays in Philosophical Theology,* ed. by A. Flew and A. MacIntyre, p. 160.

ness. Moral evil, as we shall see in the next chapter, consists in a desperate drive to be oneself against the whole of all reality while refusing to accept his basic givenness in this totality. The power to seclude oneself is implied in the nature of finite freedom. If freedom means autonomy, every free agent which is part of a larger whole can turn in upon himself rather than outward in communication with fellow creatures. The ability to create values includes the ability to pervert them.

> The creaturely freedom from which evils spring, with probability in particular cases and inevitability in the general case, is also an essential aspect of all goods, so that the price of a guaranteed absence of evil would be the equally guaranteed absence of good . . . Risk of evil and opportunity for good are two aspects of just one thing, multiple freedom; and that one thing is also the ground of all meaning and existence.[37]

Divine intervention can never eliminate the deficiencies of freedom. The separation of the waters of the Red Sea may be seen as an affliction of physical evil for the Egyptians or a miraculous escape from it for the Hebrews, but it did not affect the moral or immoral intentions of either party.[38] Freedom does not receive or sanction values: it invents them. Good and evil do not pre-exist to the moral choice as independent ideals: they are created in the process of exercising this choice. Nor are they absolutes. Evil consists in choosing a certain good while deliberately excluding a higher good. It therefore should be appropriately called a *degradation*. What at a lower level passes for good becomes inadequate once man reaches a higher level; to prefer it at that moment is to commit moral evil.[39] To preclude such a

[37] Charles Hartshorne, *A Natural Theology for Our Time* (La Salle, Ill.: Open Court Publishing Co., 1967), p. 81.
[38] Obviously in all this I do not take a position on the historical character of this event or of any particular miracle. On the impossibility of miraculous interventions to prevent moral evil, see Ninian Smart, "Omnipotence, Evil and Supermen," in *Philosophy*, 36 (1961), pp. 193–94.
[39] See Radoslaff A. Tsanoff, *The Nature of Evil* (New York: Macmillan, 1931), p. 397.

preference inevitably results in the abolishment of freedom itself. As Berdyaev wrote: "Evil presupposes freedom and there is no freedom without the freedom of evil, that is to say there is no freedom in a state of compulsory good."[40]

The implied possibility of committing evil offers in itself no justification for the creation of free agents. As in the case of physical evil we would still have to show that the good of free will outbalances the moral evil which it produces. No minor task indeed. Is freedom so worthy an end that it justifies all evil deeds perpetrated by man since the beginning of the human race? The answer to this question depends on one's estimate of freedom itself and such a value judgment is conditioned by the exercise of freedom. The very act of accepting or rejecting freedom as an ultimate value already presupposes its acceptance. It is impossible, then, to weigh freedom against the physical evil which it has inflicted, for the two belong to different scales of reality: one to that of creating being; the other to created being. Freedom is a self-sufficient end, not a means to the production of physical good. Therefore, to measure one in terms of the other is to apply the wrong yardstick. The appreciation of freedom must come exclusively from within freedom itself, not from its physical results. This leaves us in a circle with no exit. Must it be our last word on the subject? Perhaps some light may be cast on it from the second argument used for the justification of evil: evil is a necessary means for the attainment of good.

We ourselves have already used this argument in declaring physical evil a possible implication of every finite world, and moral evil a certain possibility of every finite freedom. We may omit the forms of physical necessity which various philosophers have invoked to justify the existence of physical evil. As we discovered during the discussion of the first argument, in doing this we totally ignore what is necessary for the physical existence of a universe differing from the one which we actually inhabit. Consequently, all claims in this area must remain ultimately

[40] *The Divine and the Human,* tr. by R. M. French (London: Geoffrey Bles, 1948), p. 92.

unverifiable. Slightly different but equally strange is the thesis, proposed by the Stoics, Augustine, Thomas, and others, that the presence of physical evil effects a more harmonious universe than its absence.[41] Remarkably enough, the argument is still being repeated today. Josiah Royce, for instance, refers to the bitter attractiveness of struggling for victory, the subtle pleasure derived from uncomfortable social occasions, the sweet delay in satisfying physical desires. He generalizes his conclusion:

> I insist that, in general, the only harmony that can exist in the realm of the spirit is the harmony that we possess when we thwart the present but more elemental impulse for the sake of the higher unity of experience; as when we rejoice in the endurance of the tragedies of life, because they show us the depth of life, or when we know that it is better to have loved and lost than never to have loved at all, or when we possess a virtue in the moment of victory over the tempter. And the reason why this is true lies in the fact that the more one's experience fulfills ideals, the more that experience presents to one, not of ignorance, but of triumphantly wealthy acquaintance with the facts of manifold, varied and tragic life full of tension and thereby of unity. Now this is an universal and not merely human law. It is not those innocent of evil who are fullest of the life of God, but those who in their own case have experienced the triumph over evil.[42]

This is well expressed and, as far as it goes, undeniably true. Without tension there can be neither intensive pleasure nor true depth; contrast is an essential condition of aesthetic harmony as well as of moral victory. Yet that is hardly the problem of evil as those experience it who are directly affected. Sophocles' *Antigone* is a great tragedy, but it gives little consolation to those who had their own brothers die in an actual fratricide or who

---

[41] *The City of God*, Bk. 11, Ch. 20–23. *Summa Contra Gentiles*, Bk. III, Ch. 71. For a discussion, see Nelson Pike, *God and Evil* (Englewood Cliffs, N.J.: Prentice-Hall, 1964), pp. 93–97.

[42] Josiah Royce, *Studies in Good and Evil* (New York: D. Appleton & Co., 1898), p. 23.

lost a sister through an actual suicide. Moreover, the tension connected with a struggle to the top or with a delayed satisfaction has little in common with the experience of watching one's child die with leukemia. There is no visible compensation at all to most of the evils that befall mankind. The harmony of tension and contrast exist mainly for those who observe evil at a distance —that is, aesthetically; to the victims, suffering appears unredeemingly ugly. Even when compensations follow, they appear seldom proportioned to the ills which conditioned them. The contrast theory appears to be a last-ditch attempt to save the idea of the best possible world: not only is evil inevitable, it is indispensable in achieving a harmonious universe. Witnessing the final moments of a young cancer patient immunized me permanently against its acceptance.

Yet the argument that evil serves a higher good makes a much stronger case in the moral order. We already perceived a hint of it in the quote from Royce. It might be formulated as follows. Physical hardship is indispensable for the achievement of some moral good, and since the moral order is higher than the physical, suffering is justified by the opportunity for virtue which it creates. Unquestionably, much heroism, benevolence, and charity would never have existed without the physical trials which occasioned them. Still, a great deal could be objected to in this way of reasoning. For if suffering provokes original virtues, it produces original vices as well. Cowardice, cruelty, and malevolence originate in the same ills which induce some to be courageous, kind, and benevolent.[43] Moreover, such an interpretation still leaves us with the useless suffering of the young, the insane, the animals. The deficiencies are so blatant that any attempt to justify the existence of evil as an occasion for virtue will provoke the indignation of the reflective person.

The mutilating of children whose parents are morally good, the natural deformities of disease, the hideous crimes which take

[43] For a more complete treatment of this ambiguity, see J. L. Mackie, "Evil and Omnipotence," in *Mind*, 64 (1955), pp. 206–8.

victims at random—these hardly function as warnings to repent, but rather as warnings to repair the course of nature by the application of intellectual law.[44]

To maintain the mass of human misery in order to create opportunities for practicing virtue would be such a poor calculation that most of us would select any other way for introducing virtue into the world. Why could the attraction of good not lead to the same moral effects? Indeed, if physical evil is really indispensable to moral progress, morality itself becomes a self-defeating process. For it obliges each man within his means to lessen the amount of physical evil in the world. It exhorts him to eradicate war, famine, disease. Yet think of the wonderful opportunities for the practice of virtue which would be lost if man were ever moral enough to be successful in this struggle!

> The theist's argument is seen to imply that war plus courage, plus the many other moral virtues war brings into play are better than peace and its virtues; that famine and its moral virtues are better than plenty; that disease and its moral virtues are better than health.[45]

The basic error of the moral indispensability thesis is exactly the same which we denounced in our discussion of the first argument: a lack of appreciation for the full autonomy of freedom. Freedom is an end in itself, not a means to attain certain pre-existing values. Positive values (which constitute the moral good), as well as their negative perversion (evil), are created exclusively in and through the exercise of freedom itself. The "good" is not a result of the proper use of freedom; it is the blossoming of freedom itself. Consequently, the attainment of those values does not depend upon the existence of any particular physical situation (say, suffering which necessitates heroism); any situation may invite

[44] James F. Ross, *Philosophical Theology* (Indianapolis: Bobbs-Merrill, 1969), p. 242.
[45] H. J. McCloskey, "God and Evil," in *The Philosophical Quarterly*, 10 (1960), p. 108.

freedom to create its values. The only condition for free creativity is the existence of freedom itself. This existence may be threatened, it is true, by unusual physical hardship or it may be stimulated into compensatory action. Yet neither one is *a priori* certain or predictable, for freedom leads its own life and, as Kant knew, accepts no absolute external law. Our discussion of the second argument for the justification of evil in the world (its indispensability) merely confirms the conclusions of the first: (1) of the necessity or contingency of physical evil in a finite universe man knows nothing, and all arguments for or against the possibility of a more perfect world must remain hypothetical; (2) moral evil neither requires nor allows any extrinsic justification since any curtailing of its exercise would jeopardize its autonomous nature. Whether this autonomy itself is a blessing or a curse is ultimately an unanswerable question, since the asking of the question already implies the full acceptance of the principle. Or, in different phrasing, the answer to the question depends exclusively on the free agent himself. Freedom provides its own evaluation.

One of the reasons why the believer is so disturbed by the objection of God's permissiveness toward the wicked is that all too often he shares the same basic view that an omnipotent God must in some way predetermine the course of all events, including the free ones. We have disposed of this view and will only consider here how it affects the problem of moral evil. As Whitehead pointed out, in a predetermined universe moral evil becomes an invincible problem for theology. "If the theory of complete determinism, by reason of the necessity of conformation with the nature of God, holds true, then the evil of the world is in conformity with the nature of God."[46] Yet complete determinism is a widespread view of creation among believers as well as unbelievers. In Exodus 9:12 we read that Yahweh had hardened Pharaoh's heart so that he would not listen to him, and in Isaiah 6:10, Yahweh orders his prophet to make the heart of his people sluggish, to dull their ears and close their eyes, lest they

[46] *Religion in the Making*, p. 92.

understand, hear, and see. The Qumran sect that left us the scrolls seems to have been totally predestinationist. John echoes Isaiah's words applying them to the majority of the Jewish people (Jn. 12:37–41) and Paul in the famous passage on predestination (Rom. 9:18) repeats that God makes men stubborn as he chooses. Except for the short-lived Pelagian heresy, divine predestination was never seriously questioned in Christianity, but over the centuries it was occasionally more strongly emphasized until it culminated in Calvin's theology. Yet Calvinists are by no means the only Christians to accept its basic principle. Jansenism with its small number of elect allows hardly any more *genuine* moral freedom, nor did Catholic theologians in the notorious seventeenth-century discussion of the problem. Bañez's distinction between an antecedent divine decree which first permits the free agent to commit evil and then, in a predetermining decree, refuses grace to prevent it, leaves the entire initiative with God. Molina's effort to save freedom by advocating a dual causality in which the finite agent operates as an equal partner by determining God's indeterminate motion adds only an absurdity. The problem was never solved, but it ended in an armistice imposed by the Pope after the Jesuit and Dominican adversaries started plucking each other's beards. A mature concept of moral freedom is still wanting in most discussions on grace and free will. Nor is the problem of freedom restricted to the Judeo-Christian tradition. In the Koran, Allah also "leads the wicked astray." Even the severest philosophical critics often unquestioningly accept these predestinationist schemes. Antony Flew, for instance, in a discussion of divine omnipotence and human freedom, suspects no alternatives within the theistic hypothesis but a strict predetermination in which the creature exercises no free choice in adopting good or evil and a divine arrangement of circumstances which induce some people to choose (freely) good and others evil, while a different arrangement would have triggered a different choice.[47]

All such interpretations assume that divine wisdom implies a

[47] *New Essays in Philosophical Theology*, p. 164.

foreknowledge allowing God to decide *beforehand* which particular evil he wants to occur and to affect either the will itself or circumstances which he knows to be irresistible for a particular will, in accordance with his decision. Apart from introducing actual succession in God, such a theory rules out freedom. Freedom is a creation in its own right; it is no real possibility—and therefore not present to God—until it acts. To prearrange the course of this creativity is to eliminate it altogether. Freedom has a life of its own, an independence which allows it to turn the best possible world into the worst actual one. Creation, we recall, means creation of otherness. In freedom this otherness acquires full autonomy, to the point where it can turn against its own origin. "In creationist metaphysics, all concrete reality is in principle creative . . . Reality is always in part self-created, *causa sui,* creativity being the supreme transcendental."[48]

Freedom directs the creative impulse of the entire creation; to interfere with it would be to replace creation by causality. This is true in all instances, even those which believers attribute to the order of redemption. Here also the "events" of historical faith must be seen as divine responses to human initiatives. To say that the sacrifice of Christ required executioners as a "necessary evil" is to re-enter the imbroglio of predestinationist thinking.[49] A God who first "chooses" his purposes and then realizes them "by means of man's free action" is always an anthropomorphic fantasy, destructive of human freedom. If man is truly free, the redemptive events of exodus and Incarnation cannot be regarded as predetermined any more than the evil which occasioned them. On all levels moral evil remains man's sad but exclusive privilege.

At this point the believer may want to call a halt to the argu-

---

[48] Charles Hartshorne, *A Natural Theology for Our Time,* p. 82.
[49] To escape the difficulty Maritain proposes the strange theory of an "indetermined" but statistically predictable evil act. No one had to kill Christ but God made sure that his coming occurred in a situation where the murder was all but inevitable. Such a solution justifies the divine plan by means of an indetermination characteristic of imperfect knowledge. It also introduces succession in God. *God and the Permission of Evil,* tr. by Joseph Evans (Milwaukee: Bruce Publishing Co., 1966), pp. 67–106.

ment and to claim that, since neither adversary won, no one lost. If evil is a mystery to him, it is an insoluble problem for the nonbeliever. The two parties might then settle the issue out of court, so to speak, by leaving the Creator out of it altogether. With or without a Creator, evil remains unexplained. Yet, the nonbeliever will not agree to such a settlement. For he still enjoys a distinct advantage in not having to accept, next to the intrinsic irrationality of evil itself, the idea of an all-good Creator at the origin of it. He may rest his case without doing violence to reason and attempting to square human misery with divine goodness. But from the believer, he feels, more is demanded than a simple confession of ignorance, since faith claims to provide an ultimate integration of all values in God. Moreover, throughout the centuries religious man has in fact constantly attempted to integrate the existence of evil within a total, ultimately harmonious world view. For instance, he has considered suffering a punishment for moral evil. He may now regard this answer as exceedingly simplistic, but that only forces him to search for a more complex integration. Nor can he simply dismiss the past tradition of his faith without casting grave doubts on its general ability to deliver what it promises. It is not sufficient, then, for the philosopher of religion to show the absence of compelling arguments against the logical compossibility of a good and omnipotent Creator with a wicked world as long as all positive religious explanations may still be meaningless. For if faith has nothing to offer but antiquated philosophy or if it admits its incapacity to integrate the existence of evil meaningfully in the religious world view, faith ceases to fulfill the function which it was designed to fulfill. Let us, then, reflect upon the religious response to the challenge of evil. Once again, this response seldom emerged as consciously religious; it usually originated in an earlier, mythical stage of consciousness.

There is no uniform "religious" answer to the question of evil. Various religions have attempted to cope with it in different ways. Some, as the Vedic writings indicate, reduce evil all the way to the creative act which broke up the original unity into the oppositions of light and dark, life and death. Evil then would result directly from the contradictory tensions which gave birth to the universe. It makes little sense in such a context to raise the question of responsibility for evil. The beautiful creation hymn of *Rig-Veda* 10, 129, gives us no indications about this responsibility. Neither does the story of the *Sathapatha-Brahmana,* according to which the first man, born from a golden egg, created both the gods and the devils. A different approach was taken in the dualistic religion of Zarathustra which was so preoccupied with the responsibility for evil that it structured its entire universe around the division between good and evil. Ahriman, the principle of evil, is coeternal with Ormazd, the principle of good. One cannot be reduced to the other. Thus the principle of good escapes all responsibility for evil, but only at the price of a reduced hegemony over creation. The two principles are abstractly juxtaposed and no real effort is made to relate them.

In the Babylonian epic *Enuma Elish* evil precedes the creation: it consists in the primordial chaos which dissolved in the creation. The Biblical story of Genesis has preserved some elements of this Babylonian myth. God's creative act is an overcoming of chaos, and evil consists in a return to it.[50] Yet the original myth is reinterpreted to conform to the idea that a good God has absolute power over a creation which is essentially good. Evil entered the world *after* the creation, as a *historical* fact. Within this basic reinterpretation, the yearly restoration of the cosmos by the king loses its redemptive meaning. If evil is no longer a return to the original disorder, salvation cannot be identified with the restoration of order.[51] The Hebrew myth allows the principle of

[50] Remnants of a pre-creational evil appear also in a number of allusions to the monstrous symbols of the chaos which Yahweh subdued. (See, for instance, Psalms 73:12–14, 89:10–15; Job 26:12; Isaiah 51:9–10.) Even the king's ritual restoration of the cosmos at periodic intervals out of the ever-returning chaos, as faint echoes in the so-called enthronement psalms (47, 93, 95, 100) and some of the Messianic literature (particularly Isaiah and Psalm 2).

[51] Obviously, when evil precedes the creation and is basically conquered by it, no justification of the creating god is needed, for he is the savior from, rather than the instigator of, evil. See also Paul Ricoeur, *The Symbolism of Evil,* p. 203.

evil a certain independence, yet it avoids the Zoroastric dualism by making this principle subordinate to God. Both the devil and sinful man are creatures whose evil power will in the end be defeated.[52] The Hebrew-Christian God is conceived as pairing innocence with ultimate control of evil. Consequently, a source had to be found which escaped divine responsibility without escaping divine power. The Hebrews articulated this principle in a number of ways, ranging from the almost purely mythical to the abstractly philosophical.

The story of the fall marks a first elaboration. By disobedience man brought evil into the world—not only suffering and hardship, but as Christians were to say later, concupiscence, that is, the inclination toward moral evil, as well.[53] This latter interpretation, inspired by Paul's speculation on the Biblical theme, may surpass the meaning of the original story but remains faithful to its primary intention to show that all evil came into the world through man's fault. How man could commit a fault without evil already being present in some way is a question which did not preoccupy the ancient narrator, although the serpent indicates that he was not totally unaware of it. Nor was he concerned about the functioning of a world based on struggle—in which some creatures necessarily afflict evil upon others—in a situation where

[52] Mircea Eliade shows how a number of Eastern European legends still waver between a monist and a dualistic world order: they recognize God as the supreme principle but seem reluctant to attribute the evil in the world to him. Thus God is told to have asked the devil to create the world. In other stories he is said to ignore the origin of the devil. *The Two and the One,* pp. 86–87.

[53] The Council of Orange read in the Genesis account that "the whole man, that is, body and soul, was changed for the worse." *Enchiridion Symbolorum,* Dz. ℀174. It is, of course, well known that the myth of the fall also exists in other traditions and with a different meaning. Thus the Orphics posit the origin of evil in a free act which was committed before the beginning of history. It is hard to tell whether man himself is held responsible for his evil situation, since in the extant versions of the myth the original fault is ascribed to a race of Titans of whom man is the degenerate offspring. The body was the place of exile as well as the instrument of expiation for the fallen spirit. Salvation consists in the deliverance from the body, mostly achieved through knowledge. Related to the Orphic myth are the various Gnostic myths.

struggle is eliminated. Undisturbed by such theoretical questions, the author considered his basic goal accomplished; the world which God created was good—man bears all responsibility for the introduction of evil.[54] The conclusion reduces all physical evil to moral evil and attributes the latter exclusively to the autonomy of the only creature which was able to follow an independent course.

According to the principles formulated in a previous chapter, one may take this myth on two levels: as an aetiological "explanation" of the presence of suffering (the Gnostic aspect), and as a total existential interpretation allowing man to live in the irrational presence of evil. The former aspect has long since lost all meaning to religious man. The Eden of the Yahwist narrator could never have existed in a world even remotely related to our own. Nor does the story offer any help in understanding the nature and purpose of physical suffering. Yet as interpretation of human existence, the myth remains important for the religious interpretation of evil within a universe created by a perfect God. In telling man how a free act of man has transformed a good world into a valley of tears and how in the end man's conversion may abolish evil or turn it into good, the myth enlightened the darkness of human existence and answered questions which every human being raises during the course of his existence. Its answer remains significant, even though it appears insufficient to the rational mind. The myth provides all the rationality which mythical man required, but not enough to satisfy rational man. It is, of course, impossible to translate its message into nonmythical language. Nevertheless, the myth, as we recall, must be *interpreted* in a post-mythical age. It is not as a substitute, then, but as an interpretation that I propose the following remarks. They

[54] On the meaning of the Genesis account of the fall, see Henricus Renckens, S.J., *Israel's Concept of the Beginning* (New York: Herder and Herder, 1964), pp. 157–67. Gerhard Von Rad, *Genesis. A Commentary*, tr. by John H. Marks (Philadelphia: Westminster Press, 1961), pp. 83–99. Walther Eichrodt, *Theology of the Old Testament*, tr. by John A. Baker (Philadelphia: Westminster Press, 1967), Vol. 2, pp. 400–8.

merely explore the horizons of experience which the myth of the fall has opened up.

Confronted with the hostility of the world, man is inevitably reminded of the multiple occasions in which his own free decisions created evil for others. He may even, as he does in the myth of the fall, causally connect all evil to that evil which he himself commits continually. Of course, such a connection is a typical instance of mythical causality in which "anything can produce anything" as long as the two are related. Is there any foundation for such a causal connection other than a mental association or, perhaps, the desire to integrate the disorderly with whatever plan of order happens to be available? Certainly, the causal presentation of the myth fails to distinguish evil caused by the free will from evil produced by the structure of the world, a basic distinction which the rational mind cannot overlook. Yet the connection between physical evil and moral responsibility is more than a casual one and fully deserves the reflection which men of all times have spent on it. My free acts and decisions are obviously not responsible for all or for most of what is wrong with the world. However, there is what Jean Nabert has called an impure causality by which evil is present to man as a possibility before he actually chooses it. The awareness of this presence evokes a new sense of responsibility reaching far beyond all actual evil deeds.[55] Prior to any actual decisions, man discovers in himself a complicity with nature which induces him to share the responsibility for whatever occurs in nature.[56] Of course, it would be absurd to hold man morally responsible for possible evil before its actual commitment. Nevertheless, the mind itself

---

[55] Jean Nabert, *Essai sur le mal* (Paris, 1955), pp. 55–57. This highly suggestive but philosophically elusive study exemplifies how one can interpret a myth while fully participating in it. The story of the fall is never directly discussed, yet Nabert's entire work presents a remarkable attempt to penetrate its meaning.

[56] "How could the causal action of the self ever become the accomplice of nature if in following its own penchant it had not encountered and accepted the movements and solicitations of the instinct? And if a self-love constantly nourished by the natural tendencies were not consubstantial with it?" Jean Nabert, *Essai sur le mal*, p. 57.

refuses to accept as *given* the moral will from which all decisions for good and evil flow. The sense of shared responsibility turns into moral guilt when man actualizes some of the possibilities of evil and thereby initiates the process in which moral evil *de facto* inflicts physical suffering upon other creatures. The *actual* sharing of evil makes him feel corresponsible for all physical evil, even that which he has suffered rather than afflicted. Jean Nabert describes this development in a page which is worth quoting in its entirety.

> Usually we discern no link between the forms in which the unjustifiable appears in the world and those decisions over the quality of which we exercise control. The free play of the laws of nature alone seems to account for a great number of ills. Nevertheless we are unable to dismiss the idea that every one of them stands in some direct or indirect, immediate or distant relation to the human will. How could we declare all those ills unjustifiable, if we had to reject this relation and if the laws of nature or of life, as they affect our senses in a wholly contingent way, provided a sufficient explanation? If this were the case he who suffers them would have to abandon surprise and revolt for acceptance and resignation, and the mind would be held responsible only for its actual decisions, not for a world structure which escapes its judgment. If all evil which we consider unjustifiable would not in some way involve the exercise of a spiritual causality, the word "unjustifiable" itself ought to be drained of all the mute protest which it contains. For the mind has no right to complain that our senses were not granted a natural finality or to be astonished that a blind nature strikes without discrimination. However, once it appears that nothing is unjustifiable without a confrontation with freedom, justification transcends the individual ego and it becomes more difficult to reassemble or even to conceive the conditions of its possibility.[57]

A great deal more is conveyed by the myth of the fall: the decline, implied in the symbol, from a higher level of freedom to a lower one; the solidarity of all men in the moral responsibility

[57] *Essai sur le mal,* p. 127 (my translation).

of the actual evil deed of one man—the basis of the entire concept of original sin. Yet we must postpone exploring these meanings until the next chapter, which deals with the notion of sin. Here we are concerned only with the presence of evil in a universe which our religious tradition attributes to a good Creator. The myth of the fall enabled man to accept suffering and imperfection. It symbolizes the responsibility which all men feel in the presence of evil. It also offers hope for the future. Yet it does not truly justify evil. The various stages of the narrative are connected by means of a mythical concept of causality which could not continue to satisfy men of a later age. Although the myth did not lose its essential meaning, it was no longer adequate alone to convey the full existential impact of this meaning.

The need for further reflection on the problem of evil did not start with modern man; it began right in the community which produced the myth of the fall. Out of this reflection came the Book of Job.[58] Job actually rejects personal responsibility for the evil fate which befalls him: his conscience is clear and against his friends he continues to proclaim his innocence. In the end he is resigned, but for reasons quite different from those of the Adamic story. God is transcendent, he learns, and, consequently, man is not in a position to question his decisions. "Job's basic experience is that God does not answer; that no authority, no tribunal, no umpire will hear his defense of himself and the truth against God. It is the experience of Transcendence."[59] Karl Jaspers' interpretation is correct as long as Job's confrontation with Yahweh is not interpreted as an act of rebellion but rather as an act of resignation under protest.

[58] In the last two centuries philosophers have increasingly turned to Job for solace in the scandal of evil. In his essay *On the Failure of All Philosophical Attempts in Theodicy* (1791) Kant first drew away from the Leibnizian style theodicy which attempted to explain evil through a philosophical reflection on the divine attributes, and instead meditated on the attitude of the religious man Job who suffers without understanding and yet preserves his faith. Other philosophers to interrogate Job were Kierkegaard, Jaspers, Jung.

[59] Karl Jaspers, *Philosophical Faith and Revelation*, p. 225.

In the story of Job, Israel first took a critical look at its original interpretation of evil. Job is not another myth; it is an allegorical reflection on the theology of the fall.[60] The author frankly states that not all evil must be attributed to man's sinfulness. Nevertheless, he maintains, man can continue to believe in God's goodness, although on different grounds. This answer is often interpreted to mean that God is above the law. Yet rather than referring to the inscrutable nature of divine justice, the poet points to the transcendence of creation. "Where wast thou when I laid the foundations of the earth?" The difficulty is not merely to understand divine goodness, but all God's attributes. As Charles Hartshorne pointed out, we know no more of what it takes to create a world as to be transcendently good.[61] The story of Job is a total affirmation of divine transcendence. Thus it becomes a religious expression in its own right rather than a rational or pseudo-rational reflection upon the myth of Genesis.[62]

Job proclaims that man is not on a level to understand the ways of God. His ultimate justification of evil consists in an appeal to divine transcendence. This answer adds an important correction to the myth of the fall, but it gives little positive meaning to the existence of evil. Indeed, it gives less meaning than the myth which declared it a deserved punishment. Only when it tells him what to do about evil can an interpretation fully satisfy religious man. Job is brought to look beyond the

60 We may note here that the allegory is always the first stage of reflection on the myth.

61 *A Natural Theology for Our Time*, pp. 117–18.

62 Rudolf Otto found the correct perspective for reading Job. "This chapter does not proclaim as Paul does (Rom. 9:20), the renunciation of, the realization of the impossibility of a 'theodicy'; rather, it aims at putting forward a real theodicy of its own, and a better one than that of Job's friends; a theodicy able to convict even a Job, and not only to convict him, but utterly to still every inward doubt that assailed his soul . . . In this last resort it relies on something quite different from anything that can be exhaustively rendered in rational concepts, namely on the sheer absolute wondrousness that transcends thought, on the *mysterium* presented in its pure, non-rational form." *The Idea of the Holy*, pp. 78–79.

myth, but some indication is needed to show that evil can be overcome and serve a purpose in the process of salvation. The myth assumed this possibility in presenting man's evil condition as a "fall" from an original state which can be regained. Eventually, this mythical assumption would be religiously justified in the idea of salvation through suffering. In Israel the idea was expressed in the vision of the suffering servant, in some passages of Jeremiah, and perhaps in the Second Book of Maccabees. In Christianity, it culminated in redemption through Jesus' blood.

The religious justification of evil is contained in the paradox; evil is there to *be overcome*. This is not a variation of the thesis, rejected earlier, that God *needs* evil to accomplish good. No, evil is recognized as totally irrational and serving no intrinsic purpose. However, once it is present, religious man manages to integrate it within an overall scheme of divine goodness. Such a religious "justification" of evil has nothing in common with the rational theodicies which we studied earlier in this chapter. Religious man does not pretend to explain the existence of evil, nor does he feel the need for an explanation once he has found a good use for existing evil. His attitude here, as in other matters, is more existential-practical than speculative. His main concern is what to do about evil, not to explain where it comes from. It is an illusion, then, to hope that religious "explanations" of evil will bridge the gap left by philosophy. Nevertheless, in a religious perspective, some of the arguments which we denounced as philosophically inadequate acquire a new meaning. Thus the theory that evil provides the contrast and struggle needed for a harmonious universe holds its place in the optimistic world view of the believer who considers every occurrence, however unfortunate in itself, a means to salvation. To the believer, "trial" is a profound religious category, based upon the certainty that suffering will come to an end and that the end will be an improvement over the beginning. The philosopher has no such certainty. Someone who reads Josiah Royce in a religious mood cannot but agree that, once evil exists, God must somehow overcome it and *once it is overcome,* it is a good. "The evil will is a conquered element *in* the good will, and is as such necessary to goodness."[63] But the philosopher Royce attributes the same divine necessity to all moments and thereby abolishes evil as such. That God must necessarily create goodness out of existing evil does not mean that he needs evil. Divine salvation requires no executioners, as Maritain assumes. A salvation through suffering, as the Christian faith—and in a different way, also the faith of Israel—proposes, results from a dialogue between contingent evil and divine response. The evil which requires—and, in the form of suffering, operates—salvation remains a purely contingent fact. God's necessity enters this contingency only by allowing it to overcome itself. Thus the curse turns into a blessing. But outside the religious vision there is no evidence that evil will ever change into good. It is—and remains—intrinsically irrational and destructive. Only after it has been redeemed in an order of divine salvation can one conclude with Berdyaev:

> The experience of evil cannot in itself enrich, if one surrenders to it. It is only that positive, radiant spiritual power which is brought out in the overcoming of evil, which is able to enrich. Light presupposes darkness, good presupposes evil, creative development presupposes not only "this" but also "the other."[64]

Such a statement is obvious to the religious mind; it is gratuitous to rational understanding alone.

3. IN THE BEGINNING . . .

Perhaps the most striking feature of creation theology is the concept of the beginning. In our religious tradition it has provoked more philosophical speculation than any other. Yet it is and remains, I believe, exclusively mythical. Several ideas discussed in

[63] *The Religious Aspect of Philosophy* (New York: Harper & Brothers, 1958), p. 456.
[64] *The Divine and the Human* (London: Geoffrey Bles, 1949), p. 92.

this chapter had a mythical origin. Yet as religious reflection progressed, the original vision somehow merged with rational exploration into a more or less harmonious theory. The same cannot be said about the temporal origin of creation. The idea basically resists rational reflection. There may be a place for rational speculation on the origins of the universe, but it has nothing to gain from the mythical representation.

With the idea of the beginning we come to the very heart of the creation myth and perhaps of mythical thinking itself. In the myth man sets up a primordial model in order to give meaning to his present reality. The success of his attempt depends entirely on his ability to establish an original time structure for the model-reality. The time of the beginning must be such that it envelops and founds the present. Mircea Eliade has indicated the connection very clearly:

> For religious man of the archaic cultures, every creation, every existence begins in time; *before a thing exists, its particular time could not exist.* Before the cosmos came into existence, there was no cosmic time. Before a particular vegetable species was created, the time that now causes it to grow, bear fruit, and die did not exist. It is for this reason that every creation is imagined as having taken place *at the beginning of time, in principio.*[65]

Time, then, requires a beginning, because all things have mythical models and these models can exist only in an original time. Without a beginning in time there could be no present reality. Paraphrasing this notion of the beginning into rational language, we might say that the real is not complete until we can place it in some permanent model—an idea which possibly inspired Plato, the greatest of all interpreters of myth, in his theory of the eternal forms.

Yet this mythical purpose was totally ignored by theological reflection. In Judaism and Christianity the idea of the beginning was taken to mean that the createdness of the world excludes an

[65] Mircea Eliade, *The Sacred and the Profane,* p. 76.

unlimited duration in time. It is difficult to exaggerate the amount of havoc which this idea has wrought in philosophy and theology. The creative beginning was commonly represented as a particular point in an infinite succession of moments. Thus an infinite time was thought to exist independently of the world and was mistakenly equated with divine eternity. One philosopher who spotted the flaw in this argument was Philo. To him time and cosmos belong together; one cannot exist before the other. Thus in his *Creation of the World* we read:

> Moses says also: "In the beginning God created the heaven and the earth," taking the beginning to be, not as some men think, that which is according to time; for before the world time had no existence, but was created either simultaneously with it, or after it; for since time is the interval of the motion of the heavens, there could not have been any such thing as motion before there was anything which could be moved; but it follows of necessity that it received existence subsequently or simultaneously. It therefore follows also of necessity, that time was created either at the same moment with the world, or later than it—and to venture to assert that it is older than the world is absolutely inconsistent with philosophy.[66]

We shall have to wait for Augustine to find a comparable clarity of conception.

One of the first great minds to investigate the Biblical concept of the beginning was Origen. However, he posed the problem from a divine point of view, which is the surest way to misstate it altogether. Ironically, the same consideration of God's nature which led most Christian philosophers to postulate a beginning in time, induced Origen to exclude it. If time had elapsed, he reasoned, during which the creation did not exist, God would have had no object over which to exercise his power and would not have been almighty during that period. Therefore, he con-

[66] *De Opificio Mundi*, VII, tr. by C. D. Yonge (London: Bohn Classical Library, 1854–55).

cluded, the universe must always have existed.[67] Origen himself finds it hard to understand "how during the whole of God's existence his creatures have existed also, and how these things, which we must undoubtedly believe to have been created and made by God have subsisted, if we may say so, without a beginning."[68] He solves the difficulty through the eternal life of God the Son in whom all things ideally pre-existed. But he jeopardizes his case again by assuming the *actual* existence of minds from all eternity which were later "created" into a body as punishment for a sin committed before the present world.[69] Throughout, God's duration is conceived as a protracted temporality which runs parallel with duration in man.

Neo-Platonic philosophy leads to more adequate concepts. The first major theological achievement under Plotinus' influence is Gregory of Nyssa's theory of time. For Gregory, the *diastema* (extension) of time is precisely what distinguishes the creature from the Creator who is above time and space.[70] Still, Gregory hesitates to equate temporality with finitude and posits a dual creation in which only the second involves time as a means to overcome the anticipated results of sin. Augustine, also under Neo-Platonic influence, clearly attributes time to movement. As such it is always distinct from eternity. Time belongs to the world of becoming, and cannot exist without change.

[67] *De Principiis,* Bk. 1, Ch. 2, 10. Migne, P.G. 11, 139. *On First Principles* (Koetschau's text), tr. by G. W. Butterworth (New York: Harper & Row, 1966), pp. 23–24.

[68] *Ibid.,* Bk. 1, Ch. 4, 4. Tr., p. 42.

[69] *De Principiis,* ed. by Paul Koetschau (Leipzig, 1913), Fragment 15, taken from Leontius Byzantinus *De Sectis,* Migne, P.G. 86, 1264–65. Tr., p. 67. This text has been taken from a quote in another author. Its authenticity is somewhat dubious. Koetschau's reconstruction has been called "a strange mosaic," which leaves the critics "very sceptical," by Gustave Bardy in *Recherches sur l'histoire du texte et des versions latines du De Principiis d'Origène* (Paris, 1923), pp. 140, 205.

[70] *Contra Eunomium,* Migne, P.G. 45, 365D–368B. My major source of information on Gregory's view of time is John Callahan, "Gregory of Nyssa and the Psychological View of Time," *Proceedings of the XIIth International Congress of Philosophy,* XI (Florence, 1960), pp. 59–66. Callahan accepts the Neo-Platonic influence without establishing to what extent Gregory profited directly from the works of Plotinus.

Now, since God, in whose eternity there is absolutely no change, is the Creator and Ruler of time, I do not see how we can say that He created the world after a space of time had elapsed unless we admit also that previously some creatures had existed whose movements would mark the course of time . . . Undoubtedly, then, the world was made not in time but together with time. For what is made in time is made after one period of time and before another, namely, after a past and before a future time. But there could have been no past time, since there was nothing created by whose movements and change time could be measured.[71]

The beginning of time, then, coincides with the beginning of the universe, but it bears no relation to God's eternity.

Augustine's separation of time from God's duration solves only half the problem. The question still stands. Assuming that the universe and time are simultaneous, do they have a beginning or are they unlimited? Augustine bases his answer upon a literal interpretation of the Genesis story. The text clearly implies, he thinks, that time itself had a beginning. "Though himself eternal and without beginning, he (God) caused time to have a beginning."[72] This conclusion had been anticipated by most of the Hebrew and Christian tradition. For the Greeks, on the contrary, the world approached the changelessness of divine eternity by its own cyclic movement. Within these world cycles the concept of an absolute beginning has no place.[73] The Judeo-Christian

[71] *De Civitate Dei*, Bk. 11, Ch. 6, tr. by Gerald Walsh, *et alii* (New York: Doubleday, 1958), p. 212. In the next book Augustine wavers a moment in his conclusion. If the angels were not created in time, do they not become coeternal with the Creator? But the doubt vanishes, and he decides that if the angels introduced movement in succession, "time came into being along with them." (*De Civitate Dei*, Bk. 12, Ch. 15)

[72] *Ibid.*, Bk. 12, Ch. 14.

[73] In his work *On Generation and Corruption*, Bk. 2, Ch. 10, 336[b], Aristotle writes: "Not all things can possess 'being,' since they are too far removed from the 'originative source.' God therefore adopted the remaining alternative and fulfilled the perfection of the universe by making coming-to-be uninterrupted: for the greatest possible coherence would thus be secured to existence, because that 'coming-to-be should itself come-to-be perpetually,' is the closest approximation to eternal being." Tr. by H. H. Joachim in

notion of a beginning of time clearly asserted, against the Greeks, that God and the world belonged to two entirely different planes of reality. After Augustine, it was considered to be part of the revealed deposit of faith that the creation had not always existed.

Nevertheless, as we saw, the "beginning" of the myth responded to an entirely different question. It established a model-time which is never truly past. The newer reading—that time had a beginning—was strongly suggested by the equation of divine creativity with causality. Since a cause precedes its effect, it followed that a created world must have a beginning. Earlier in this chapter we questioned the appositeness of the notion of cause for describing a creation which takes place in a condition-less void. The religious necessity of assuming a beginning for the universe seems to depend exclusively upon this causal view of creation. The entire Western tradition, from Augustine on, con-sidered it essential, but the reasons are not compelling and are counteracted by other religious traditions which attach no im-portance to the beginning. Even in the Christian tradition the authoritative affirmations concerning "the beginning" did not originate in disputes over the finitude or infinity of the time of creation. The first major pronouncement that God has created the world "from the very beginning of time,"[74] was made by the Fourth Lateran Council in 1215. It was primarily intended to refute the Albigensian claim that the world had been "created" (that is, transformed from the evil thing it was originally into something good) after a long period of time. Against this dualistic doctrine the Council declared that both the material and spiritual universe had been created in *simul* (simultaneously, by the same God), *ab initio temporis* (not after having existed for a long time), *de nihilo* (not out of something that already existed). The word "beginning" here is used only to negate any pre-exist-

---

The Works of Aristotle, tr. under the editorship of W. D. Ross, Vol. 2 (Oxford: Clarendon Press, 1930), p. 336b. On the difference between the cyclical theory of the Greeks and the Christian concept of time, Langdon Gilkey, *Maker of Heaven and Earth,* pp. 295–309.
[74] *Enchiridion Symbolorum,* Dz. ☩428.

ence of the world to the creation. The question of finitude or infinity of time did not come up, even though we may be assured that the Council Fathers, as everyone else in the Christian world, took the finitude of time for granted. The question whether an infinity of time is compatible with a created universe was first officially raised in Vatican Council I. To answer it the Fathers unearthed the old Lateran text (of which the context had long been forgotten) and used it to prove that according to venerable tradition the world must indeed have had a beginning.[75] Obviously, such a declaration, based upon an incomplete exegesis and intended to solve a misstated problem, provides little new insight to the philosopher. He remains puzzled by the unanimity of a tradition, built on such a weak basis. Yet philosophy itself is unable to support either view by cogent proofs. Great minds, such as Thomas Aquinas and Kant, tried the arguments on both sides and found them eminently refutable.[76]

[75] *Enchiridion Symbolorum*, Dz. ⁜1783.
[76] The arguments of Thomas show an amazing grasp of the complexity of the problem. For instance, the common assumption that the cause must precede the effect, is easily dismissed: such a procedure is necessary only in things that produce by way of motion where the effect requires the completion of the motion, not in things which act instantaneously as the production of sun rays by the sun. (*Summa Contra Gentiles*, Bk. 2, Ch. 38, 9) Noteworthy also is Thomas' refutation of the argument that a finite time would always have a "before" and thereby become infinite. "The *before* that we speak of as preceding time implies nothing temporal in reality, but only in our imagination. Indeed, when we say that time *exists after not existing,* we mean that there was no time at all prior to this designated *now*." (*Op. cit.,* Bk. 2, Ch. 36, 7. Tr. as *On the Truth of the Catholic Faith,* II, *Creation,* by James F. Anderson, Garden City, N.Y.: Doubleday, 1956, p. 108) With similar flourish Thomas confronts the argument that to an eternal God all moments are alike and no priority can be given to one moment rather than another in beginning to create the world. God's duration has no parts. Consequently, no reason is required in the Creator as to why a creature should be brought to existence "in this designated part of that duration rather than at some other or preceding point: all moments of time are simultaneously present to God's eternity." (*Op. cit.,* Bk. 2, Ch. 35, 6. Anderson, p. 104) Thomas concludes the discussion with a weak argument of convenience which merely shows that he considers the notion of an infinite world time contrary to the dogma of his faith. A finite world, he claims, more clearly reveals its intrinsic contingency and its total dependence upon God.

Chapter 10
Religious Alienation

1. THE VARIOUS FACES OF ALIENATION

Salvation is not meaningful until man has become aware of the wretchedness of his condition. It implies that life is not good enough to be accepted as it is. To awaken the feeling of insufficiency, then, is the first task of faith. William Ernest Hocking once wrote:

> Religion is often described as the healing of an alienation which has opened between man and his world: this is true; but we may not forget that it is religion which has brought about that alienation. Religion is the healing of a breach which religion itself has made.[1]

The concept and experience, then, of alienation are part of the religious attitude itself. Yet they exist also outside this attitude. Religion adds a unique trait which distinguishes the religious consciousness of alienation from any other: man is a stranger to himself *because he is estranged from the sacred*. However, the religious consciousness does not build in a vacuum: it integrates all human experience. Its dialectical negation incorporates all negative experiences affecting human existence. Faith amplifies their awareness and reinterprets their meaning to fit its own requirements. I suspect that it is primarily his strong feeling of

[1] *The Meaning of God in Human Experience*, p. 238.

alienation which, despite an increasing secularization, keeps contemporary man intrigued by the religious interpretation of existence.

Before entering into our subject we must be aware of the disproportionate emphasis which the individualizing drive of our culture has placed upon this concept. Christianity itself, both as shaper and as product of the Western mind, reflects this emphasis. The term itself rose to prominence only in the past century and remained pretty much confined to the philosophies of Hegel and Marx. In our own century it gained two new connotations, one psychological, the other existential-philosophical. We shall discuss them in succession and then compare them with the universal religious meaning which, although essentially different, has been so substantially affected by them that it can no longer be understood without the secular meanings.

The term owes its present currency to a passage in the *Phenomenology of Mind* where Hegel describes the state in which the mind is no longer able to recognize its cultural creations as its own.[2] In addition the mind desires to flee into another world, the beyond of faith. The description which illustrates this cultural-religious definition of alienation is mainly social and political.[3]

Yet without Feuerbach and Marx the term would never have become as widespread as it is. Taking the term from Hegel, both gave it entirely new meanings. According to Feuerbach's *Essence of Christianity* the true alienation is man's projection of a God to whom he ascribes qualities which rightfully belong to the human race itself. Later Feuerbach was to include in this religious aliena-

[2] *Phänomenologie des Geistes,* ed. by Johannes Hoffmeister (Hamburg, 1952), p. 347; *The Phenomenology of Mind,* by J. B. Baillie, p. 509.
[3] Hegel found the term *Entfremdung* in Goethe's translation of Diderot's *Le neveu de Rameau.* But this passage does not explain all the political connotations. There appears to be some indirect influence of Rousseau, although the term *Entfremdung* was never used to translate Rousseau's *alienation.* Cf. Friedrich Müller, *Entfremdung* (Berlin, 1970), Conrad Boey, *L'aliénation dans la Phénoménologie de l'Esprit* (Paris, 1970), and my own "Hegel's Concept of Alienation and Marx's Reinterpretation of It" in *Hegelstudien* (1972).

tion of man all speculative philosophy, particularly Hegel's: what faith refers to as God, Hegel terms "Spirit."

Hegel's Absolute Spirit is nothing but the abstract, alienated, so-called finite spirit, just as the essence of theology is nothing but abstract, finite being.[4]

Marx's concept of social alienation initially owed more to Feuerbach than to Hegel. Later the situation was reversed. Yet, whether dialoguing with Feuerbach or with Hegel, Marx always emphasized that the roots of man's alienation lie in his social-economic conditions. According to the Paris *Manuscripts* of 1844, alienation is that *particular form* of objectivation which separates man from the product of his work and, consequently, from his productive activity itself which is synthesized in the product. Industrial labor in a capitalist society debases man instead of humanizing him, as work should do: it is forced upon the worker by the bare need to survive. At the same time industrial capitalism deprives the productive impulse of its native ability to surpass individual needs toward true universality. Instead of becoming more universal, man returns to a primitive, isolated state. His fellow man becomes either a means or a competitor.

Alienation, then, displays a triple aspect: man is estranged from his producing activity, from the product of this activity, from his fellow man. All three are institutionalized in private property. Although private property is not the cause but the effect of alienated labor, once it exists it becomes the most powerful means to perpetuate alienation. Marx therefore calls it "the sensuous expression of alienated human life." Gradually Marx became more and more convinced that private property itself is based upon the division of labor, and that the causal connection between the two determines the stages of social development.[5]

[4] *Vorläufige Thesen zur Reform der Philosophie, Sämtliche Werke,* Vol. II, ed. by G. W. Bolin and F. Jodl (Stuttgart, 1959), p. 226.
[5] *Karl Marx-Friedrich Engels Historisch-Kritische Gesamtausgabe,* ed. by D. Rjazanov (Frankfurt, 1927), Vol. I[5], p. 11, *German Ideology,* tr. by R. Pascal (New York: International Publishers, 1947), p. 9. The in-

Although Marx's critique directly attacks the ills of nineteenth-century capitalism, his indictment goes far beyond his own society. The term *fetishism,* which appears more frequently in Marx's later work, refers to a general attitude in which commodities become ends rather than means. This fundamental alienation remains, even today when the work hours are shorter, the wages are higher, and automation has eliminated a great deal of the stultifying assembly line labor.[6] Herbert Marcuse calls *progressive* alienation the state of soporific euphoria in which contemporary capitalist society manipulates the needs of its members in order to let them satisfy only those which will deprive them of all desire to go beyond the present object-oriented system. Thus art is debased to a consumer's item, science to a technical tool, and philosophy to a rational justification of the present state of affairs as well as a prohibition to move beyond it.[7]

But is it merely the social-economic system which is responsible for man's alienation? Even Marxist writers, despite their commitment to a social-economic interpretation of history, begin to question whether the cause of the acquisitive mentality lies entirely in the capitalist system.[8] More and more, alienation has come to be considered as a state of mind. Erich Fromm defines alienation as "a mode of experience in which the person experiences himself as an alien."[9] This does not imply that alienation is an exclusively individual phenomenon, for there may be an intimate connection between such a state of mind and a particular state of society which promotes it. Nevertheless any interpretation of the alienated person must ultimately raise a psychological question: What leads

terested reader may consult: Louis Dupré, *The Philosophical Foundations of Marxism* (New York: Harcourt, Brace & World, 1966), pp. 120–37, 149–59.
[6] For a description of the alienation created by an advanced technical society, see Jiri Cerny, "Zum Begriff der Entfremdung: Der unvollkommene-entfremdete Mensch in marxistischer Sicht" in *Disputation zwischen Christen und Marxisten* (München, 1966), p. 116.
[7] *One-Dimensional Man* (Boston: Beacon Press, 1968), pp. 123–99.
[8] See, for instance, Miklos Almasi, "Alienation and Socialism" in *Marxism and Alienation,* ed. by Herbert Aptheker (New York: Humanities Press, 1965), p. 136.
[9] *The Sane Society* (New York: Fawcett Publications, 1968), p. 111.

man to adopt social-economic structures which prevent him from developing his full human potential? Attitudes are undoubtedly perpetuated and reinforced by these structures, but originally the attitudes created the structures. Marx has little to say about this process, even though in his early work he vaguely ascribed the ills of society to man's "egoistic needs." What are these needs? How did they grow? Hobbes's *Leviathan* with its pessimistic view of the vanity and avarice of human nature is in this respect much more enlightening. To be sure, a psychological interpretation can retain a Marxist framework. Thus Erich Fromm considers alienation the result of a "hoarding mentality" which leads to the erection of a possessive society and is in turn reinforced by it. To overcome the state of alienation we need to modify the social structures as well as to change our ideals. This may be complicated, but it is not impossible.

However, the question is whether the roots of alienation are not buried in the subconscious soil of man's drive toward *civilization itself* rather than in the urge toward a possessive society. Any developed culture imposes heavy, largely unconscious demands upon the individual, which must inevitably result in a great deal of frustration. In *Civilization and Its Discontents* Freud attempted to show how heavily cultural progress taxes the individual by keeping a constant check on his aggressive and sexual instincts. The complexity of Western culture has made the burden all but intolerable. "The price of progress in civilization is paid in forfeiting happiness."[10]

Does cultural development offer an adequate explanation for the existence of the alienated mind? Many philosophers think not. Camus, for instance, considered man's estrangement from himself an essential part of his existence. He therefore repudiated the optimism of the revolutionary who hopes to change man by changing his conditions, and instead became a rebel against an unchangeable fate. For Camus, neither revolution nor therapy can cure a disease which is *man himself*. Other existential philosophers

[10] *Civilization and Its Discontents,* tr. by James Strachey (New York: W. W. Norton, 1962), p. 81.

have reached similar conclusions. Gabriel Marcel, after having emphasized the alienating conditions of modern society, still defines alienation as an *ontological* problem.

> By alienation I mean the fact that man seems to have become more and more a stranger to himself, to his own essence—to the point of calling this essence into question.[11]

Anguish, frustration, social pressure are but expressions of man's existential condition. Beyond the feeling of alienation is its reality. No one has shown this more clearly than Heidegger. In *Being and Time* man is estranged from himself by falling from an authentic existence into a reduced, thinglike state of Being.

> When existence [*Dasein*], tranquillized and "understanding" everything, thus compares itself with everything, it drifts along towards an alienation [*Entfremdung*] in which its own-most potentiality-for-Being is hidden from it. Falling Being-in-the-world is not only tempting and tranquillizing: it is at the same time alienating. This alienation closes off from existence its authenticity and possibility, even if only the possibility of genuinely foundering. It does not, however, surrender existence to an entity which existence itself *is* not, but forces it into its inauthenticity—into a possible kind of Being *of itself* . . . This "movement" of existence in its own Being, we call its "downward plunge" [*Absturz*]. Existence plunges out of itself into itself, into the groundlessness and nullity of inauthentic everydayness. But this plunge remains hidden from existence by the way things have been publicly interpreted as a way of ascending and living concretely.[12]

That alienation is a "fall" into inauthenticity implies that it is a transitory state of Being. Nevertheless it is not a contingent event limited to particular epochs of history or particular persons.

[11] *Problematic Man,* tr. by Brian Thompson (New York: Herder and Herder, 1967), p. 18.
[12] *Sein und Zeit* (Tübingen, 1960), p. 178. *Being and Time,* tr. by Edward Robinson and John Macquarrie (New York: Harper & Row, 1962), pp. 222–23. I changed the term *Dasein* into *existence.*

Neither primitive nor civilized man is exempt from it. The lapse into everydayness is a permanent feature of existence. Every individual is distracted by the world of beings from his task of becoming himself.[13] As soon as man begins to view the world as an interesting multitude of phenomena, he becomes forgetful of the Being which human existence is there to illuminate. His curiosity may display great intellectual acumen and his action high efficiency, but his self is fragmented and his existence diminishes. He "falls," not outside the self, but into an inauthentic self.

Alienated existence never fully recognizes itself as such. Indeed, the more alienated man is, the more he feels at home in the world and at peace with himself. A return to authenticity, according to Heidegger, is possible only through the feeling of anguish which brings man's entire existence in the world into question.[14] In anguish the familiar becomes "strange" and anguished man no longer feels "at home" in his world. Anguish reveals the nothingness which surrounds existence, and thus also reveals Being, the core of existence. Being can be understood only against nothingness.

Only in the clear night of dread's nothingness is Being as such revealed in all its original overtness: that it "is" and is not nothing . . . The essence of Nothing as original nihilation lies in this: that it alone brings existence face to face with Being as such. Only on the basis of the original manifestness of Nothing can our human existence advance towards and enter into Being.[15]

---

[13] Heidegger, *Kant und das Problem der Metaphysik* (Bonn, 1929), p. 224.
[14] *Sein und Zeit*, p. 187. *Being and Time*, p. 234.
[15] *Was Ist Metaphysik?* 7th ed. (Frankfurt, 1955), p. 34. *What Is Metaphysics?*, tr. by R. F. C. Hull and Alan Crick in *Existence and Being* (Chicago: Henry Regnery, 1949), p. 369. I changed *what-is* into the more common *Being*. See also *op. cit.*, pp. 33–34; tr., p. 366. It is well known that Heidegger found the idea first expressed in Kierkegaard's *Concept of Dread: Samlede Vaerker,* ed. by A. B. Drachman, J. S. Heiberg, H. O. Lange (Copenhagen, 1964), VI, pp. 135–37. *The Concept of Dread,* tr. by Walter Lowrie (Princeton: Princeton University Press, 1944), pp. 37–40. Comments in Louis Dupré. *Kierkegaard as Theologian* (New York: Sheed & Ward, 1963), pp. 54–56.

Paradoxically, anguish returns existence to its aboriginal state, and thereby overcomes alienation.

Of course, all this presupposes that anguish is more than a pathological phenomenon. It comes with existence itself. It is man's existential awareness of the nonbeing inherent in his being, of "finitude experienced as his own finitude."[16] Psychic or cultural conditions may intensify this emotion to the point where it disturbs the normal development of the individual. But it is inherent in the experience of freedom itself. For the feeling of freedom reveals the nothingness out of which man creates as well as the nothingness which he *can* create. In our age man has tested his power to control life and his capacity to destroy it altogether: that is why he is more anguished. Anguish is seldom experienced over a prolonged period of time. Yet even after it has ceased to be active, anguish does not disappear without leaving a trace. A continued uneasiness prevents man from settling down comfortably in an everyday existence. Thus what we take to be the essence of alienation turns out to be only a symptom of our ontological self-estrangement.

2. RELIGIOUS ALIENATION

Religious alienation always refers to an ontological estrangement, yet, the two are by no means identical. By itself the experience of alienation is neither religious nor conducive to the adoption of a religious attitude. To face one's estranged condition is not *per se* a religious act. On the contrary, the literature from Dostoevski to Kafka and Camus shows those most keenly aware of human alienation also to be most strongly inclined to reject the religious meaning of existence. Nevertheless, the situation

[16] Paul Tillich, *The Courage To Be* (New Haven: Yale University Press, 1960), p. 35. On the distinction between psychic and existential anguish, *ibid*, p. 64; also Franz Neumann, *The Democratic and the Authoritarian State*, ed. and with a preface by Herbert Marcuse (Chicago: The Free Press of Glencoe, 1957), pp. 275–76. For a good psychological description of anguish, see Juliette Boutonier, *L'angoisse* (Paris, 1949).

from which religious man must be "saved" appears as an alienated existence. Yet there is an important addition: the religious consciousness considers itself estranged from a transcendent principle which lies beyond existence. Moreover, it causally connects to this primordial alienation the experiences of suffering and death which for others remain unquestioned facts of life or are regarded as mere *symptoms* of an ontological alienation.

The characteristic difference of religious alienation appears clearly if we compare the "fall" in the various systems of the Gnosis to Heidegger's *Geworfenheit* and *Verfallenheit* with which they display an obvious similarity.[17] In the Gnostic writings the fall is a fall from a sphere of reality which transcends man altogether; it is not a fall from the authentic self as it is in Heidegger. The expression "alien life" which occurs frequently in Mandaean literature refers to the transcendent origin of the soul fallen into a body which it inhabits as a stranger. The theory accounts both for man's greatness and for his degradation. The more the soul feels alien in this world, the more it is at home in the true life.

Anguish and homesickness are a part of the stranger's lot. The stranger who does not know the ways of the foreign land wanders about lost; if he learns its ways too well, he forgets that he is a stranger and gets lost in a different sense by succumbing to the lure of the alien world and becoming estranged from his own origin . . . In his alienation from himself the distress has gone, but this very fact is the culmination of the stranger's tragedy.[18]

The *feeling* of alienation is the first step on the way to salvation. While created existence is the supreme evil, estrangement from this existence is the highest good.[19] The ancient dualism of good and evil, light and darkness permeates Gnostic theology. Yet

[17] On this comparison, cf. Hans Jonas, *The Gnostic Religion* (Boston: Beacon Press, 1963), pp. 320–40.
[18] Hans Jonas, *The Gnostic Religion* (Boston: Beacon Press, 1963), pp. 49–50.
[19] Serge Hutin, *Les Gnostiques* (Paris, 1963), p. 21.

the dualism here is caused by a deliberate decision. Gnostic interpretations differ on the nature of this fall into bodily existence. It may have been a conversion toward *libido* by which the soul comes under the influence of the stars, or a descent into a lower region ending in a narcissistic union, or an inordinate passion for the primeval, celestial Father resulting in an abortive being. But in all versions the material world is the outcome of a process of degeneration, initiated by a guilty act. The guilt has become inherent in terrestrial existence itself.

While in the Gnosis the fall occurs before the creation and is in fact the event which gives birth to the creation, in the Judeo-Christian tradition it happens afterward. Here applies the term *sin* in the strict sense, that is, a deliberate breach with the divine in man's present condition. Precisely because of the emphasis on the deliberate nature of the act, the moral aspect of this religious alienation has always been stressed. Yet other facets appear around this core, particularly the connection with suffering and death. Israel suffers defeat *because* the first man was disobedient. Here as always the religious view covers the whole of existence even while focusing on one aspect. We shall concentrate mostly on our tradition, which identifies religious alienation with sin and moral perversion. But we must keep in mind that the alienated situation is by no means always conceived as a diseased relation resulting from a human decision. I mentioned the Gnosis, but the great Oriental religions are even farther removed from our concept of sin. In Buddhism man is estranged from his true self by *samsara,* the cycle of suffering, death and rebirth. Redemption consists in taking off the mask, including the individual personality (in Latin *persona* means mask), which hides true reality. Salvation is the state in which all becoming and opposition is overcome, even the consciousness of salvation itself.

Buddhism borrowed the concept of *samsara* from the Hindu tradition, even though this tradition was originally (in the *Veda* and even more of the *Upanishads*) not world-denying. Yet in the latest of the *Upanishads* we find the *samsara doctrine* most force-

fully stated in a well-known description, according to which existence itself is part of the flux from which man must be saved:

> Foul-smelling, insubstantial, is this body, a compact mass of skin
> and bones, sinews, marrow, flesh and semen, blood, mucus, tears
> and rheum, urine and faeces, bile and phlegm: what point is there
> in satisfying one's desires in that? Assailed is the body by desire
> and anger, greed and delusion, fear, depression and envy, separation
> from what one wants and close association with what one does
> not want, hunger and thirst, old age and death, disease, sorrow
> and the like: what point is there in satisfying one's desires in that?

The author considers subsequently the great conquerors and
kings, the divine spirits and the wonders of nature. He concludes:

> Of such is the round of coming to be and passing away (*samsara*).
> What point is there in satisfying one's desires in that? For once
> a man has tasted of them he is seen to come back to earth ever
> and again. Save me I pray thee: in this round of existence I am
> like a frog in a well without issue.[20]

Even the sacred task of doing one's duty (*dharma*) is part of
man's alienated condition, for the dharma is part of his being in
the world from which redemption must be sought. In the final
state of salvation there is neither righteousness nor unrighteous-
ness.[21]

Whether religious alienation be interpreted through the notion
of sin or through some other religious symbol, its basis remains
always a profound dissatisfaction with a life which implies suffering and death as well as moral imperfection. The awareness of
inadequacy is essential to the religious consciousness as such. In
the Hebrew tradition the awareness of alienation is most no-
table in those Psalms which deal with penance and exile, in the
Lamentations and some passages of the Prophets (particularly
Jeremiah). Christian writers who most strongly expressed it were

[20] *Maitri*, I, 3–4, in *Hindu Scriptures*, tr. by R. C. Zaehner (New York:
E. P. Dutton, 1966), pp. 219–20.
[21] R. C. Zaehner, *Hinduism*, pp. 63–64.

Paul, Augustine, Luther and Kierkegaard. The direct connection between sin, suffering, and death, briefly indicated in Genesis is elaborated by Paul (Romans, 1 Corinthians) and Augustine (particularly the twenty-second book of *The City of God*). In line with the modern mentality Luther emphasized the aspect of consciousness: man must be *aware* of his wretched condition in order to be redeemed.[22] Since this consciousness of man's wretchedness before God is intrinsically religious, it must be *revealed*.

More even than Luther, Kierkegaard stressed the religious need of the negative awareness of sin. Only through negation can a genuine, that is, a dialectical relation with God be established.[23] Consciousness of sin is considered to be a permanent feature of the religious attitude.

> This negativity is not a transitory stage in the religious experience, it is inherent to religion as such. All the positive elements in man's relationship with God will be constantly wrapped up in the negative.[24]

Even though religious alienation must be revealed according to Kierkegaard,[25] such a revelation becomes meaningful only if it is supported by negative human experiences, such as the collision between autonomous freedom and the opacity of fate (in *Repetition*), or the breakdown of ethical categories (in *Fear and Trembling*). The consciousness of sin always takes its content

[22] For instance, the eighteenth of the Heidelberg *Theses* reads: "It is certain that man must completely despair of himself in order to become fit to obtain the grace of Christ." *Martin Luther. Selections from His Writings,* ed. by John Dillenberger, tr. by Karlfried Froehlich (Garden City, N.Y.: Doubleday, 1961), p. 502.

[23] *Papirer,* ed. by P. A. Heiberg, V. Kuhr, and E. Torsting (Copenhagen, 1909–48), IX A 32, 242. Precisely because this condition was lacking, Kierkegaard did not consider the Greek attitude toward the gods as fully religious.

[24] *Samlede Vaerker* (3d ed.) X, p. 198; *Concluding Unscientific Postscript,* tr. by David Swenson and Walter Lowrie (Princeton: Princeton University Press, 1944), pp. 514–15.

[25] *Papirer,* VII A 192.

from some common experience of alienation. Thus in Kierkegaard's *Sickness Unto Death* sin in presented as despair, a unique
mixture of existential inauthenticity, religious perversion, and
permanent commitment to moral evil. Despair is a free act in
which man at once rejects his given self and chooses an impossible self. Insofar as it is a refusal of one's *given* condition, all
despair is ultimately religious.

> That self which he despairingly wills to be is a self which he is not
> (for to will to be that self which one truly is, is indeed the opposite
> of despair); what he really wills is to tear himself away from the
> Power which constituted it.[26]

The refusal may not be fully conscious: it may proceed from a
hidden fear to assert oneself. Even when it is conscious, it may
not understand itself, as when someone who has lost his possessions thinks that he despairs about them rather than about a
self which depends upon thinghood. At times, however, a man
recognizes the true nature of despair, that it is despair *of God*. In
that case we call it sin. Sin is despair allowed to run its full
course.[27]

Kierkegaard identifies the refusal to be authentic (corresponding to the existential of alienation) with the religious category of
sin. Moreover he declares moral and religious *perversion* to be
the root of all alienation, and even identifies despair with suffering and, as the title of his study indicates, with death.[28] The
connection is not arbitrary, for all those elements actually appear in the religious consciousness of alienation. Yet despair is

[26] *Samlede Vaerker* (3d ed.) XV, p. 79; *Sickness Unto Death,* tr. by
Walter Lowrie (Princeton: Princeton University Press, 1967), p. 153.
The refusal to accept one's true self may be an unwillingness "to submit
to the necessary in oneself, to what may be called one's limit." (S.V. XV,
p. 94; *Sickness,* p. 169) Or it may consist in a lack of faith in the given
possibilities of freedom. (S.V. XV, p. 95; *Sickness,* p. 171)
[27] *Samlede Vaerker,* XV, p. 134; *Sickness Unto Death,* p. 212.
[28] The reference to Jesus' words in John 11:4: "This sickness [of the
dying Lazarus] is not unto death" indicates that despair is a disease that
leads to "real" death.

too narrow a category to accommodate all the aspects of sinfulness without being stretched beyond recognition.

In *The Concept of Dread,* Kierkegaard declares that sin is an intrinsically religious category, which can be understood only *within* the religious experience.[29] The philosopher, then, has no alternative but to turn to the direct expressions of the religious consciousness and to reflect upon their intrinsic meaning, however primitive and irrational they may be.[30]

The Christian asserts the intrinsically religious character of "sin" in his belief that sin must be "revealed" to man. Yet the term "revelation" here must be taken in its most comprehensive sense so as to include the primitive symbols of evil which precede a clear awareness of revelation. In his *Symbolism of Evil,* Ricoeur has shown how the primordial symbols precede even the myths of evil which are already interpretations of far more archaic elements.[31]

Most striking in the pre-mythical symbols of evil is that, de-

---

[29] *Samlede Vaerker* (3d ed.), VI, p. 114; *The Concept of Dread,* tr. by Walter Lowrie (Princeton: Princeton University Press, 1967), p. 14. In the *Philosophical Fragments* Kierkegaard implies that left to himself alone, man is unable to recognize the true nature of his negative relation to God. *Samlede Vaerker* (3d ed.), VI, p. 46; *Philosophical Fragments,* tr. by David Swenson, rev. by Howard V. Hong (Princeton: Princeton University Press, 1962), p. 58.

[30] To be sure, the philosopher may also investigate man's ability to commit moral evil. Paul Ricoeur has done this in his remarkable study, *Fallible Man,* tr. by Charles Kelbley (Chicago: Henry Regnery, 1965). But moral evil is not yet sin, for sin requires an additional awareness of transcendence. Even in his study of moral evil the philosopher cannot go beyond the possibility of what is intrinsically irrational. He merely explains the weakness which drives man toward the unintelligible.

[31] Ricoeur does not clearly distinguish between the moral and the religious meaning of evil. And indeed, in the stage of consciousness where the primitive symbols and the myths originate, such a distinction does not yet exist. On that level everything is religious without being *only* religious. But in more developed stages of the moral consciousness the religious symbols of sinfulness provide little help for the understanding of moral evil. At a certain point morality goes its own way, independent of the religious consciousness. The opposite is not true, for the religious consciousness always retains its comprehensive character: even in our days, to religious man moral evil is *sin.*

spite their primitive character, they are already potentially religious. This clearly appears in their ability to transcend the crudeness of their forms. Even the primitive notion of defilement, unintentionally contracted, possesses a high symbolic potential, as appears in its capacity to survive on a higher, ethico-religious level. The symbol still speaks to us as it did to our ancestors millennia ago. We become aware of this in reading those passages of the Bible and of the Greek dramas in which the ancient language of defilement is preserved. We continue to find meaning in the darkly irrational symbol of evil that spreads as a stain and soils bystander as well as criminal. We continue to be fascinated by the visions of Aeschylus, Sophocles, and Shakespeare. By its primitive connection with vengeance the symbol of defilement prepares the idea that all violations *ought* to be punished. Crude as such a physical idea of retribution appears to us, it was an important attempt to create moral order and to bestow meaning upon that least rational of all human experiences, suffering. Equally important, as Paul Ricoeur shows, was the function of the defilement symbol in defining the transcendent. Behind the negation is a vision of primordial integrity which through vengeance restores the original order.

> In fearing defilement man fears the negativity of the transcendent; the transcendent is that before which man cannot stand; no one can see God—at least the god of taboos and interdicts—without dying. It is from this, from this wrath and this terror, this deadly power of retribution, that the sacred gets its character of separateness.[32]

Still the full meaning of sin is not reached until the symbol comes to refer to a *personal* relation. *Sin* originates in a *dialogue* with the sacred in which the word of God reveals itself as a holy *will*. Evil then no longer consists in the contraction of a physical stain, but in the violation, through ritual fault or ethical transgression, of a personal bond. As the internal *disposition* becomes more

[32] Paul Ricoeur, *The Symbolism of Evil,* tr. by Emerson Buchanan (Boston: Beacon Press, 1969), p. 33.

important than the physical deed, sin loses its purely objective character. It now becomes a diminished selfhood: an awareness that the self is *intrinsically* guilty. Consciousness of sin leads always to feelings of guilt. But at a certain point the emphasis seems to shift from God to the self. While one is sinful *before God, one is guilty primarily before oneself.* "The 'thou' that is summoned becomes the 'I' that accuses itself."[33] In responding to the divine call the self discovers itself as a center of decision. This gives new depth to the awareness of sin and marks a critical stage in the development of the religious consciousness. For if the consciousness of sin is reduced to moral guilt, the bond with the transcendent is severed altogether. Guilt depends upon the verdict of the self's evaluation of itself. It does not necessarily include a reference to a higher tribunal.

Yet guilt tends to extend beyond the responsible individual. Among civilized people as well as among primitives it retains a transindividual meaning. This became evident once again in our secular times when, at the end of the war, the concentration camps were opened and the Nazi crimes were exposed in all their horror. Evil was commonly experienced as a communal power which had taken a firm possession of man and was only gradually loosening its grip. Those who were responsible for the atrocities were members of our own community. The feeling of guilt led to years of soul searching in Germany, but shame and remorse spread all over the Western world. In the Hexateuch the solidarity of guilt is conveyed by penalties which in reprisal for one man's sin strike an entire family as after Abimelech took Sarah (Gen. 20:18), or even the entire people as when Achan illegally appropriated some of the booty (Jos. 7:11). It may also affect the future community. In Jeremiah 7:24–28, Yahweh reproaches the Israelites for all the disobedience of their ancestors. Hosea prophesies God's vengeance over Israel for all its past crimes, starting with Jacob supplanting his brother Esau in their mother's womb (Hos. 12:4). Ezekiel's realistic parable of the harlotry of Ohola and Oholiba concludes in a universal condemna-

[33] Ricoeur, *op. cit.,* p. 103.

tion of Israel for its innumerable infidelities to the covenant (Ezek. 23). The idea of solidarity in sin persists in the post-exilic writings, as appears in the highly personal Psalm 51: "In guilt was I born and in sin my mother conceived me." Sin extends beyond the individual act in space and time. Yet it remains a personal act of rebellion. The myths of sin attempt to reconcile these opposite aspects.

3. ADAM AND HIS INTERPRETERS

Ricoeur has shown how the myths of evil contribute a unique element in that they *dramatize* a universal condition in a concrete story. Thus in the Biblical myth Adam is the man who introduces evil into a good world by a personal decision. Until the eighteenth century few interpreters questioned the literal truth of the story of the fall. Although the criteria for distinguishing the mythical from the nonmythical way of thinking were lacking, reflection upon the myth led to new and original insights. Later the myth was recognized as a different way of thinking. Superior as this position appears, it often resulted in an unenlightened dismissal of the myth as a *pre-rational* form of consciousness, to be "replaced" by rational thought. The obsolete character of the gnostic elements in the myth itself strongly favored demythizing. Only in recent times did the myth come to be recognized as a unique symbolic articulation essentially different from rational thought.

Let us now consider some of the creative interpretations of the first kind, specifically the ones that led to the notion of "original sin." This notion first appears in Paul.[34] In the Epistle to the

[34] André-Marie Dubarle, *The Biblical Doctrine of Original Sin*, pp. 93–120. Remarkably enough, not a single clear reference to Adam's fall appears in the Hebrew canonical books. In the Book of Sirach (25:24) it is mentioned as a cause of death, although in other places the author ascribes death to the earthy origin of man. The Book of Wisdom (2:24) contains a doubtful allusion to death as connected with the devil's seduction. In neither case is there any question of an inherited guilt.

Romans (5:12–20) the solidarity implied in the Adamic myth is interpreted as a participation of all men in the *sin* of one.

> It was through one man that sin entered the world, and through sin death, and thus death pervaded the whole human race, inasmuch as all men sinned. (5:12)
>
> For as through the disobedience of the one man the many were made sinners, so through the obedience of the one man the many will be made righteous. (5:19)

Paul does not yet envision this participation as an inherited guilt, but rather as an original sin which is reactualized in each subsequent sin. It is in that sense also that the Greek Fathers almost unanimously interpreted the text. Some even rejected the notion of an inherited punishment. Thus Theodoretus writes: "Not through the sin of the first parent but through his own, does each man receive the fate of death."[35] Adam initiated sin; he did not cause it. At most his fall was said to have "occasioned" later sinning through the concupiscence which it introduced.

Yet there is unquestionably another aspect present in Paul's commentary which a mere "imitation" theory fails to account for. Every myth presupposes a bond between the model which it proposes and those to whom the model is proposed. In the myth of Adam this solidarity was formalized in the Semitic category which since H. Wheeler Robinson has become known under the name "corporate personality." Its main feature is that one individual comes to represent the entire community.[36] Thus the defeat of Israel's army in Joshua 7 is attributed to Achan's crime: he stands not only for himself, but also for his family and tribe

---

35 *Interpretatio Ep. Rom.*, in Migne, P.G. 82, p. 100A. I owe my information on the Greek Fathers to an unpublished manuscript *De Peccato Origininali* by Roger Leys.

36 "The Hebrew Conception of Corporate Personality" in *Zeitschrif fur die alttestamentische Wissenschaft.* Beiheft. 66 (1936), pp. 49–61. The article was later published separately as *Corporate Personality in Ancient Israel* (Philadelphia: Fortress Press, 1964). See also by the same author, *The Religious Ideas of the Old Testament* (London, 1943), and *Redemption and Revelation in the Old Testament* (London, 1944).

and even for the entire people of Israel. An individual may represent others by physical descendance, or by being the first in doing something (Jubal in Genesis 4 is called the father of all who play the lyre and the flute), or by having juridical authority over others.[37] In the text of Romans 5, Adam may have been considered either as the father of the human race, or as the first sinner, or as the one who was considered juridically responsible for all men to come. The Western tradition has restricted the connection to the bond of physical descendance.[38] Augustine became its main protagonist because a physical link with Adam would provide irrefutable evidence against the Pelagian position that each man was born innocent. The suggestion of Romans 7:23 that the law of the bodily members conflicts with the law of reason enabled him to identify the "original sin" with the concupiscence manifested and transmitted in the desire of the sexual act. This concupiscence theory was to determine all Western interpretations of the Adamic myth of the fall until Anselm of Canterbury. It was revived by Luther and the Protestant confessions. Yet Luther, more consistent than Augustine, concluded from the persistence of concupiscence after conversion that man remains sinful even in his justification—*simul justus, simul peccator.*[39]

Anselm transferred the original sin from the presence of concupiscence to the absence of original justice. Attempts to define this state finally resulted in Thomas' theory of submission of the body to the soul, and of the soul to reason.[40] Deprived of original justice and at the mercy of a consequent concupiscence, man was no longer in a position to attain his ultimate end. The Anselmian-Thomist idea found its way into the definitions of the Council of Trent according to which Adam "immediately lost the justice and

[37] On the various applications of the idea of corporate personality, see Jan De Fraine, *Adam and the Family of Man* (Staten Island: Alba House, 1965), pp. 49–122.
[38] Precedents for this were not lacking among the Greek Fathers. Origen in his Commentary on Romans 5 considered all men to be "in the loins of Adam" when he was exiled from Eden. Migne, P.G. 14, 1009.
[39] *Disputatio de Homine* in *Werke Ausgewählt*, 39, 1, 176 (15, 26ff.).
[40] *Summa Theologiae*, I, 95, 1.

holiness in which he was constituted"[41] after he sinned, and transmitted his sinfulness (not only his punishment) to the entire human race "by propagation, not by imitation."[42] So much for solidarity.

Another facet of the Adamic myth was the exile from Eden. The "change for the worse"[43] was an essential part of the myth which attempted to reconcile the belief that God is good with the fact that man is inclined toward evil, suffers, and dies. The grim reality of the present was therefore projected against the ideal state of paradisiacal existence. Not too much was made of this somewhat incoherent dream of the happiness that is supposed to accompany innocence until Augustine interpreted the utopia of what could have been as a detailed historical description of what was.[44] Augustine's purpose was no longer that of the myth, namely, to justify *what is* (the miserable state of an existence which nevertheless was created good), but rather to explain *what no longer is,* that is, to strike a death blow at Pelagian optimism by a detailed inventory of what was lost by sin.[45] His description was formalized in the Catholic doctrine of the "praeternatural gifts." If Augustine in his theory of physical descendance had rationalized (and thereby deformed) the *model* aspect of the myth, he now did the same with the *ideal* element of the myth by giving it a strictly historical interpretation, which was obviously absent from its original purpose. The confusions to which those rationalizations led are too numerous to mention, but they all stem from a total inability to recognize the myth as myth.

[41] *Enchiridion Symbolorum,* Dz. ✗788.

[42] Dz. ✗790. A remote but distinct Augustinian echo is heard in the word "propagation." Moreover, the Council studiously avoided condemning the "concupiscence theory."

[43] The expression is found in the fifteenth Council of Carthage, the second Council of Orange of 529 (Dz. ✗174), and the Council of Trent (Dz. ✗788).

[44] Henricus Renckens, *Israel's Concept of the Beginning* (New York: Herder and Herder, 1964), p. 160.

[45] Augustine's most plastic descriptions may be found in *De Civitate Dei,* 14, 26 and 14, 17.

Since the eighteenth century, philosophers (Kant, Schelling, Hegel) and theologians (Schleiermacher, Kierkegaard) have been aware of the nonhistorical character of the Biblical narrative. Thus Kant intelligently concludes his interpretation of the fall:

> The foregoing agrees well with that manner of presentation which the Scriptures use, whereby the origin of evil in the human race is depicted as having a [temporal] *beginning,* this beginning being presented in a narrative, wherein what in its essence must be considered as primary (without regard to the element of time) appears as coming first in time.[46]

Unfortunately, Kant one-sidedly emphasized the moral aspects of the myth. What he reads in the myth is that man, if he is to be truly responsible for his acts, must assume responsibility also for his evil disposition.[47] Yet the disposition toward evil is obviously rooted in human nature itself, since all members of the human race share it. The myth, then, reconciles the two opposite principles of free act and innate disposition by ascribing the latter to an evil act committed at the beginning of history. The mythical expression enables man to refer to the past that for which he finds no rational ground in the present. Of course, such a reference does not justify the origin of evil. But evil has no ground outside itself. By moving ever further back into the history of the race to an act which had neither precedents nor preceding propensity, the myth suggests that man has always been inclined toward evil and yet that he must take full responsibility both for the inclination and the act. The story of Adam does not "explain"—its point is precisely that evil cannot be explained—but it *describes* the origin of evil. For Kant Adam is Everyman. The discrepancy between the situation of the first man and our own is merely apparent.

[46] *Religion Within the Limits of Reason Alone,* tr. by Theodore M. Greene and Hoyt H. Hudson (New York: Harper & Brothers, 1960), pp. 36–37.
[47] This argument will later be resumed by Jean Nabert, *Essai sur le mal,* pp. 41–66.

With us sin is represented as resulting from an already innate wickedness in our nature. This propensity, however, signifies no more than this, that if we wish to address ourselves to the explanation of evil in terms of its *beginning in time,* we must search for the causes of each deliberate transgression in a previous period of our lives, far back to that period wherein the use of reason had not yet developed, and thus back to a propensity to evil (as a natural ground) which is therefore called innate—the source of evil.[48]

Kant keenly perceived one facet of the Adamic myth: it is not history but a *model* for man in his attempts to cope with evil. However, he almost totally overlooked the element of ontological solidarity whereby the deed of one member could affect all others. This latter element, so important in the understanding of the Christian tradition, would be developed by Kierkegaard. But before discussing Kierkegaard's theory we must turn to two of his sources: Schleiermacher and Hegel.

Like Kant, Schleiermacher was aware of the nonhistorical character of the Adamic myth which he considered "an ancient attempt to make good the lack of a historical account of the beginnings of the human race."[49] But to him the Biblical narrative also discloses a unique religious meaning.[50] Sin always originates in a personal decision, yet its roots reach far beyond man's personal, conscious life.

The sinful self-assertiveness of sense, proceeding as it does from its earlier development, has a more remote source than the individual's own life.[51]

The myth of the fall, as Schleiermacher reads it, links the religious consciousness of one generation to the preceding. The first men were different because they were *first* and thus "were in a

[48] *Op. cit.,* pp. 37–38.
[49] *Der Christliche Glaube* in *Sämtliche Werke,* p. 366; *The Christian Faith,* ed. by H. R. Mackintosh and J. S. Stewart (New York: Harper & Row, 1963), Vol. I, p. 250.
[50] In this respect he is strongly at odds with Augustine and some of the Protestant confessions. See, *op. cit.,* pp. 373–74; *Christian Faith,* pp. 254–55.
[51] *Der Christliche Glaube,* p. 410; *The Christian Faith,* p. 280.

position to influence the development of the God-consciousness in the next generation."[52] Yet their position was not unique, for "the actual sin of the earlier [generation] is always the originating original sin for the later."[53] Original sin, then, is only one moment in a process which connects my own sinfulness with that of all previous generations. If that moment is severed from the actual, personal sin, it turns into the contradictory concept of inherited guilt.

> Original sin is not guilt until it breaks forth in actual sins . . . Original sin is purely a thing received only in the degree in which the individual is not yet spontaneously active, and it ceases to be such in the degree in which that activity is developed. Up to that point, and in that measure, it is rightly termed *originated*, as having its cause outside the individual.[54]

Just as absurd as the notion of inherited guilt, is a theory of legal imputation according to which God declares Adam's descendants coresponsible for the first sin. Only by actively embracing his negative inheritance does man convert his originated sin into an originating sin. Nor would Adam's resistance to the temptation have secured his descendants a perpetual state of moral peace. For Schleiermacher cannot believe that the destiny of the entire human race would have been contingent upon a single decision of an inexperienced individual.[55]

In the preceding interpretation sin has a corporate character as well as an individual. The individual is ontologically linked to all other members of the human race—an element which was notoriously absent from Kant's theory.[56] Yet for Schleiermacher

[52] *Op. cit.*, p. 369; *The Christian Faith*, p. 252.
[53] *Op. cit.*, p. 446; *The Christian Faith*, p. 304.
[54] *Op. cit.*, p. 419; *The Christian Faith*, p. 286.
[55] *Op. cit.*, p. 442; *The Christian Faith*, p. 301.
[56] It is precisely in virtue of this connection, in fact, that the individual is the representative of the whole race in this regard, for the sinfulness of each points to the sinfulness of all alike in space and time and also goes to condition that totality both around him and after him. *Op. cit.*, p. 422; *The Christian Faith*, p. 288.

as for Kant the myth remains exclusively a *model* of the sinfulness of man.[57] He barely distinguishes the situation of man *before* and *after* the fall and thereby reduces the historical and dramatic impact of the story.

4. THE FALL WITHOUT SIN

Hegel would develop the historical, dramatic element of the myth, but largely at the expense of its religious meaning. For him the fall is the story of man's breakthrough toward reflective freedom. The loss of innocence which this process inevitably involves is a spiritual necessity. To become moral, man must experience evil as well as good.[58] Hegel bases his gnostic interpretation upon the nature of the Biblical prohibition: Yahweh forbade Adam to eat from the tree of *knowledge* of good and evil. Knowledge could not have meant the power to discern between good and evil, since the very prohibition already implied the existence of such a discernment. It must have referred to a cognitive awareness which man would acquire only by experience.[59] Whatever the merit of Hegel's exegesis may be, there are undeniably gnostic elements in the myth which earlier commentators had conveniently ignored. Yahweh himself admits that the fruit of knowledge has given man some sort of divine status: "See the man has become like one of us, with his knowledge of good and evil." (Gen. 3:22)[60] Hegel has exploited those gnostic elements in his view

[57] "We can use the story, as the early theologians did, in illustration of the universal process of the rise of sin as something always and everywhere the same, and it is in this illustrative quality that, for us, the universal significance of the narrative resides." P. 444; *The Christian Faith*, p. 303.
[58] *Vorlesungen über die Philosophie der Religion,* II, p. 31.
[59] Hegel is not alone with this interpretation of the tree. Respectable exegetes as Reuss and Gunkel also read some idea of cultural progress or awakening to full adulthood in the text.
[60] Yet the process of divinization would not be completed until man had also acquired immortality by eating from the tree of life. Although the trees of knowledge and of life seem to be distinct in the story of Genesis (God drives the man out of Eden lest "he stretch his hand out next and pick from the

of Adam's sin as a transition to freedom and to true wisdom. Even the innate knowledge which the myth attributes to Adam does not conflict with the progress theory: primitive man and the sleepwalker also possess some connatural acquaintance of their environment as a remnant of the original identity between man and nature. True knowledge, however, requires distance, reflection, and separation from nature.[61]

Precisely because it removes man from his sheltered identity with nature, the first step toward freedom places man in a state of separation which cannot be his ultimate goal. The paradox of the myth, as Hegel understands it, is that God's creation reaches its fulfillment first when man asserts his independence and that this assertion at the same time negates the very dependence of his createdness. "The act which completes God-given independence is also a defiance of God-imposed dependence."[62] As a negative act, man's assertion of independence is evil and punishable, but the punishment itself is no more than what the full realization of finite freedom implies: effort, suffering, death.

For Hegel, the fall is not a *contingent,* historical event that might not have taken place at all. Innocence and fall are necessary moments of man's progress toward freedom and truth. Together with contingency, Hegel also seems to rule out the historical nature of the fall. "Divine history has neither past nor future."[63] Hegel does not exclude temporal succession in the transition from "innocence" to culture, but only temporal contingency. However, an attack upon historical contingency eliminates the *dramatic* element of the myth and must ultimately be

---

tree of life also, and eat some and live forever." Gen. 3:22), they are still sufficiently confused (the tree of life stood "in the middle of the garden" and so did the tree of knowledge) to betray their original identity. And indeed, in the Babylonian myths the forbidden fruit is the fruit of immortality.
[61] *Vorlesungen,* II, pp. 33–35.
[62] Emil Fackenheim, *The Religous Dimension in Hegel's Thought* (Bloomington: Indiana University Press, 1968), p. 131. Cf. *Vorlesungen,* III, p. 86; *Lectures on the Philosophy of Religon,* tr. by Speirs and Sanderson, II, p. 201.
[63] *Vorlesungen,* II, p. 27.

fatal to the myth itself. It may only survive as an *ordinary,* that is, a nondramatic religious symbol, "a representation which is very profound; not a contingent history, but the eternal, necessary history of man, here expressed in an external mythical fashion."[64] In this interpretation the myth has been reduced to a shell. A gnostic theory as the one implied in Hegel's interpretation in the *Philosophy of Religion* admits of no dramatic freedom. If drama is an essential characteristic of myth, all gnostic interpretations of history are antimythical. Yet has the gnosis not given us a wealth of myths? It has indeed. But the gnosis uses its myths in an *allegorical* way, that is, as static symbols not as genuine dramatizations of human freedom. Even those "gnostic" theologies which were developed within a tradition that fully accepted the myth of the fall display this "de-dramatization."

Origen writing under gnostic influences placed the fall outside the reach of human freedom in a prehuman realm of pure minds. Existence in the body is a state of punishment for that mysterious, pre-existential event.[65] Similarly, for John Scotus Eriugena, who wrote under Greek influence, the real fall occurred before the

[64] *Vorlesungen,* II, p. 30. I am not entirely sure that I have done full justice to Hegel's thought. For in the *Philosophy of History* which dates from the same period as the *Philosophy of Religion* on which this interpretation is based, historical contingency is admitted. Hegel there distinguishes the exteriorization of culture which is a necessary event, from the alienation of the fall which is contingent.

[65] "Some sinned deeply and became daemons, others less and became angels; others still less and became archangels; and thus each in turn received the reward for his individual sin. But there remained some souls who had not sinned so greatly as to become daemons, nor on the other hand so very lightly as to become angels. God therefore made the present world and bound the soul to the body as a punishment." *De Principiis.* Migne, P.G. 86, 1264–1265. *On First Principles,* tr. by G. W. Butterworth (New York: Harper & Row, 1966), p. 67. On Origen's gnosticism, see Eugène de Faye, *Origène, sa vie, son oeuvre, sa pensée* (Paris, 1923), pp. 100ff. Until Origen's posthumous condemnation at the Council of Constantinople his theory was accepted by a number of theologians, including such luminaries of the Western Church as St. Jerome. I should add that Origen seems to have given an allegorical interpretation to the story of Adam's fall. This, of course, brings him very close to an understanding of the myth *as myth.* See *Contra Celsum,* P.G. 11, 1086.

"historical" event in the Garden of Eden took place. It consisted in a deliberate lapse of the soul from its purely ideal state in God's mind. At no moment of history was man truly innocent. Adam's act of disobedience reported in Genesis merely gave expression to an already existing evil will.[66] History itself must be considered an effect of this pre-temporal sin; yet it also provides man with the means to return to his divine origin.[67]

The gnostic interpretations of Origen and Scotus Eriugena ultimately destroy the myth as myth. They accept the "event" of the fall, but they place it before the present creation, entirely out of man's reach. Since history begins after the fall, the myth does not dramatize his present condition. Sin, then, is the very heart of existence. Origen and Scotus' explanation why man's present state is unsatisfactory leaves no room for models and provides no ideals to pursue. It proposes redemption through insight into *what is necessary*. In such a context the concept of *sin* is drastically altered, for when sin becomes an inevitable situation it ceases to be a free moral decision.

To restore this freedom was Kierkegaard's major concern in his criticism of Hegel. For Hegel, sin follows with logical necessity upon innocence. But if sin "comes into existence" it cannot be a logical necessity, Kierkegaard argues, for the necessary does

---

[66] *De Divisione Naturae*, Migne, P.L. 122, 838.

[67] "God provided this [variety of species and multiplicity of parts] in order that at least after his fall from the spiritual into the corporeal, from the eternal into the temporal, from the incorruptible into the transitory, from the highest into the lowest, from the spiritual man into the animal, from the simple nature into the division of sexes, from angelical dignity and procreation to the animallike, despicable, and corrupt generation in the body, man might through his punishment come to recognize his miserable condition and, longing for his previous dignity, might lay down his pride and request his return to his past state by henceforth observing the laws which he had transgressed." *Op. cit.*, p. 540. In this description we hear more than an echo from Gregory of Nyssa's idea that man's historical existence in space and time offers, simultaneously with the punishment, the means of salvation. Yet Gregory does not place the fall before man's present existence in the body, and that saves his interpretation from being gnostic. See *De Hominis Opificio*, Migne, P.G. 44, 189.

not truly "come into existence": in one form or another it always is.[68] Kierkegaard's concern is not with a literal exegesis of the text—his own is no more literal than Hegel's—but the preservation of freedom in the concept of sin.

This freedom he also considers to be jeopardized in the early Protestant confessions. In assuming that Adam's fall has *substantially* changed the human condition, the confessions in fact take away the common ground between the first sin and all later ones.[69] If a totally corrupt nature *predetermines* man to evil, his situation radically differs from Adam's who *freely* made the step from innocence to sin. If Adam's sin was the *cause* of the others, no common term applies to both. To restore each man's full responsibility, Kierkegaard places the first sin back into the human race. In one respect only, the first sin was different: it introduced sinfulness into a sinless world, thereby effecting a qualitative change in the human situation.[70] In assuming that the deed of one man affects all others, Kierkegaard strongly asserts the ontological unity of the human race. "Man is an individual and as such is at once himself and the whole race, in such wise that the whole race has part in the individual and the individual has part in the whole race."[71] Yet this union never

[68] *Samlede Vaerker,* 3d ed., VI, p. 69. *Philosophical Fragments,* tr. by David Swenson, rev. by Howard V. Hong (Princeton: Princeton University Press, 1962), p. 69. Nor can innocence be the *logical* antecedent of sinfulness, for an innocence which must be logically "mediated" by transgression requires its own annulment. True innocence cannot be overcome by itself, but only by something different. "Innocence is something which is annulled by transcendency, precisely because innocence is a *something* . . . and for this reason also when innocence is annulled by a transcendency, something quite different comes out of it, whereas mediacy is just immediacy." *Samlede Vaerker,* 3d ed., VI, p. 132. *The Concept of Dread,* tr. by Walter Lowrie (Princeton: Princeton University Press, 1967), p. 34.

[69] *Samlede Vaerker,* VI, p. 123; *The Concept of Dread,* p. 25.

[70] *Samlede Vaerker,* VI, p. 128: *op. cit.,* p. 30. "By the first sin sinfulness came into Adam. It would not occur to anybody to say of any subsequent man that by his first sin sinfulness came into the world, and yet it comes through him in like manner (i.e., in a manner which is not essentially different) into the world."

[71] *Samlede Vaerker,* VI, p. 124; *op. cit.,* p. 26.

eliminates responsibility; it merely circumscribes the situation within which freedom operates.

Yet at the same time, Kierkegaard attempts to maintain the Augustinian concupiscence theory by declaring sensuality sinful after the fall. Sinfulness is already active in man while he is still innocent, insofar as he is drawn to favor the sensuous over the spiritual part of his nature. This inclination toward an inauthentic assertion of freedom is the "original sin."[72] But at this point all the difficulties of freedom and necessity return.

Could man's sensuous nature have remained in perfect harmony with his spiritual aspirations? Kierkegaard's description of the state of innocence presents it as a situation in which the synthesis of the sensuous and the spiritual has not yet been posited.[73] Once more we face Hegel's thesis that man must leave innocence in order to become fully human. The interpretation is indirectly confirmed by a passage of *The Sickness Unto Death* according to which a refusal to "posit" oneself is the most basic form of despair. Kierkegaard obviously did not intend innocence to be taken for imperfection—it was the very thesis he attacked—but his own description leaves us little choice but to consider it as such.

The implications of Kierkegaard's position emerge more clearly in some of his followers, particularly Paul Tillich. Tillich is eager enough to give the dramatic element of the myth its due: he also criticizes Hegel for not having taken seriously "the self-con-

[72] "Original sin must have the dialectical ambiguity *out of which guilt breaks forth* in the qualitative leap." (My italics.) *Samlede Vaerker,* VI, p. 145. *Op. cit.,* p. 47. Strangely enough, in some diary entries written after *The Concept of Dread,* Kierkegaard refers to original sin as guilt before God (*Papirer* X², A 481). He justifies this innovation by the idea that God sees in each individual the entire race which in Adam has become guilty (*Papirer* X², A 473; X², A 421). These statements cannot be reconciled with Kierkegaard's earlier position and seem to indicate that it no longer satisfied him.

[73] Kierkegaard's answer is restricted to one statement: "Supposing Adam had not sinned, then the sexual [considered the extreme expression of the sensuous] would never have been posited as a propensity." *Samlede Vaerker,* VI, pp. 168–69; *op. cit.,* p. 71.

tradicting power of human freedom and the demonic implications of history."[74] Yet in his own interpretation the fall symbolizes a transition *inherent in freedom as such* rather than an event that happened "once upon a time." The only difference from Hegel is that the transition to sin here is caused by a necessary leap, rather than by a dialectical move in a logical system.[75] Once more the state of innocence is not a perfection but merely an absence of actuality. Freedom must assert itself and it can do so only by contradicting itself, for a finite freedom is inevitably restricted in the realization of its unlimited aspirations by its own destiny as well as by "nature" and the freedom of others. This self-contradiction may be called an *event,* not because it "happened" at one time in the past, but because it is the necessary condition which precedes every happening in space and time. Man "exists" only after he has started contradicting himself.

Again, sin becomes a necessity, resulting from man's need to assert his freedom. For Tillich even more than for Hegel "the notion of a moment in time in which man and nature were changed from good to evil is absurd."[76] The fall merely symbolizes the tragic aspect of created freedom which can never be as real as it wants to be. Yet the dramatization of destiny through self-entanglement hardly accounts for the myth's emphasis on the evil consequences of sin. If sinfulness coincides with freedom, every man is in the same situation, and no man's sin can restrict the freedom of others.[77]

The persistent recurrence of theories which place the fall before the actual beginning of history suggests that there may be other symbolizations of it than the Adamic myth. Students of

[74] *Systematic Theology* (Chicago: University of Chicago Press, 1967), II, p. 30.

[75] *Ibid.,* p. 23.

[76] *Ibid.,* p. 41.

[77] Tillich's concept of a necessary fall coinciding with the creation has been criticized from various angles. See, e.g., Reinhold Niebuhr, "The Biblical Thought and Ontological Speculation in Tillich's Theology" in *The Theology of Paul Tillich,* ed. by Charles W. Kegley and Robert W. Bretall (New York: Macmillan, 1952), pp. 216–17. Also George H. Tavard, *Paul Tillich and the Christian Message* (London: Burns & Oates, 1962), p. 41.

comparative religion such as Ernst Benz[78] and Mircea Eliade[79] have shown to what extent this is the case. We find some vestiges of them in Origen, Maximus Confessor, Gregory of Nyssa, and Scotus Eriugena—for whom the loss of the original harmony is accompanied by sexual differentiation. Of course, as Christian writers they had to combine this pre-existential "fall" with the "historical" fall of Adam, either by anticipating the consequences of Adam's fall (Gregory of Nyssa) or by placing Adam himself in a prehistorical existence (Origen, Scotus Eriugena). But the two myths really have little in common. This appears clearly in the romantic theologian Franz von Baader, who neatly juxtaposes the loss of wholeness with the loss of innocence without attempting to integrate them. For Baader the detachment of Eve from Adam's rib was the first fall.[80]

The myths of the pre-existential fall symbolize the same dissatisfaction of man with his present condition which we find in Genesis. Life is experienced as broken and estranged from what Eliade calls "something *powerful,* something utterly *other* than [man] himself."[81] Like the Biblical story those myths enable man to live with a fragmented present by giving him hope for a future, unified existence. Less emphasis is placed on man's responsibility but the element of succession is stressed just as much: the world has come into existence *by a loss* of the original unity.[82] Similar myths appear to be at work in the great religions of the Orient. Thus we understand the Hindu view that life itself is a burden chaining man to a cycle of death and rebirth from which the soul can be liberated only by a return to a primordial unity. The same ideal of undifferentiated unity appears in Taoism, while in Buddhism the self is to be liberated from its personal

---

[78] *Adam. Der Mythus des Urmenschen* (München, 1955). In all the excerpts of this anthology, the loss of wholeness (which includes the union with God) is connected with sexual differentiation.

[79] *The Two and the One,* tr. by J. M. Cohen (New York: Harper & Row, 1965).

[80] Ernst Benz, *op. cit.,* pp. 224–27.

[81] *The Two and the One,* p. 122.

[82] *Ibid.*

existence to return to an uncreated state of oneness. Even secular references to the fall imply a primordial harmony which was broken by division.[83] Thus Sartre writes: "My original fall is the existence of the other."[84]

Having stressed the notion of sin because of its importance in the Judeo-Christian tradition, we must not lose sight of the fact that religious alienation is more comprehensive than sin. Salvation is not restricted to a restoration from sin: it also appears in faiths which do not ascribe sinfulness to man's fall. The universal religious concept here is alienation. Sin, and particularly sin through a free act, is only a specific instance of it. Wherever it exists we also find *expiation*.

5. EXPIATION

Of all religious concepts expiation may well be the most widely misunderstood, not only by outsiders but also by believers and even by theologians. Christians and Jews, to whom I shall restrict my observations, frequently believe that divine justice demands, in reparation for sins, the death of the sinner. Hence the substitution theory according to which one dies for the sins of all. To be sure, expiatory sacrifices in Israel were characterized by a more intense application of blood. Yet the connection between blood and death as penal substitution is by no means the determining one in the expiation rites of the Bible.[85] Blood is the carrier of life, according to Leviticus 17:11: "The life of the flesh is in the blood." Precisely because the symbol of life

[83] See Thomas J. J. Altizer, *Mircea Eliade and the Dialectic of the Sacred* (Philadelphia: Westminster Press, 1963), pp. 84–86.

[84] *Being and Nothingness,* p. 263.

[85] I owe most of my information on this subject to an unpublished series of lectures on expiation delivered by Stanislas Lyonnet, S.J., at the Biblical Institute in Rome, and to the articles of A. Metzinger, "Die Substitutionstheorie und das Alttestamentliche Opfer mit besonderer Berucksichtigung von *Lev.,* 17, 11" in *Biblica,* 21 (1940), pp. 159–87, 247–72, 353–77, and of A. Médebielle, "Expiation" in *Supplement au Dictionnaire de la Bible* (Paris, 1938), Vol. III, pp. 2–262.

was reserved to God the Hebrews were not allowed to drink it.[86] In a sacrificial immolation man surrenders life as a symbol of his own total dedication to God. That death accompanies this surrender appears accidental to the rite. "The death is vital to the sacrifice, because it sets free the blood, which is the life. But the victim is, in a true sense operative, not as dead but as alive 'as it had been slain': not as νεκρόν but ὡς ἐσφαγομένον."[87] Substitution occurs in the oblation of the *life* of the victim. Death inflicted as punishment for a crime was not regarded as a sacrifice in Israel.[88] The expiatory function of the blood, then, is not to placate God by the death of the victim but to reconcile him by means of the offering of life.[89] The penal substitution theory did exist in ancient Near Eastern religions,[90] and infiltrated Israel's expiation rites.[91] In the expiation rites of the Day of Atonement it appears, when the high priest heaps all the sins of Israel on the head of the scapegoat. Substitution is partially supported by the tendency of the religious mind to connect sin, suffering, and death. However, this connection precedes the idea of a personal God, and, consequently, cannot be reduced to a purely juridical, contractual interpretation.[92]

[86] Genesis 9:4; Deuteronomy 12:23.

[87] F. C. N. Hicks, *The Fullness of Sacrifice: An Essay in Reconciliation* (London: Macmillan, 1930), p. 18.

[88] Moreover, if the victim's immolation had been a symbol of penal execution, its flesh could not have been considered holy nor would its blood and fat have been offered upon the altar. W. Robertson Smith, *Lectures on the Religion of the Semites*, p. 389.

[89] A totemist such as W. Robertson Smith regards the effusion of the blood as a means to re-establish the physical bond of kinship between the worshiper and his god. Thus at the covenant sacrifice on Mount Sinai the blood was applied both to the people and to the altar (Exodus 24:4ff.). *Op. cit.*, pp. 348, 314–16, 400. Although a totemic interpretation is inadequate for understanding the expiatory rites of Israel, the similarity between Smith's interpretation of the blood rites and the one which is here advocated is worth noting.

[90] See Édouard Paul Dhorme, *Les religions de Babylone et d'Assyrie* (Paris, 1910), p. 229.

[91] Perhaps in the wake of the tallion law which required a life for a life and an eye for an eye. Exodus 21:23; Leviticus 24:17–18; Deuteronomy 19:21.

[92] See Hubert and Mauss, *op. cit.*, p. 74.

At any rate, in Israel the substitutional meaning of expiation was of later origin and always remained of secondary importance.

The primary meaning of the giving of life is also preserved in the New Testament texts which deal with the sacrifice of Christ.[93] The propitiatory aspect of his death is strongly emphasized, as might be expected in a religion in which the relation to the transcendent is characterized by negativity. The less man feels originally one with the sacred, the greater need he experiences for *at-one-ment*. An unfortunate side effect of the Christian emphasis on propitiation was the idea of penal substitution which, although by no means inherent in it, often accompanies it. In Christianity the idea did not become a full theology of redemption until St. Anselm.[94] According to him, man is unable to give satisfaction for his sin because of the infinite dignity of the God whom he has offended. Therefore only a God-man can fully expiate man's sin by a gratuitous and undeserved death.[95] St. Thomas considerably mitigated this juridicism in his *Compendium Theologiae* by distinguishing satisfaction for sin from reparation of original justice: only the latter required a

[93] The main passage on the redemption by blood is Romans 3:24-25: "All are justified by God's free grace alone, through his act of liberation in the person of Christ Jesus. For God designed him to be the means of expiating sin by his sacrificial death, effective through faith. God meant by this to demonstrate his justice." The literal translation of verse 25 reads: "in Christ Jesus whom God put forward as a propitiatory through faith by his blood." The term "propitiatory" (*hilasterion*) refers to the throne of mercy which on the Day of Atonement was sprinkled with blood. The true meaning then would be, as C. H. Dodd suggests, that God has given Christ as "a means by which guilt is annulled." (*Moffatt Commentary. Romans, sub loco*) Nor does the term "justice" at the end favor a substitution theory, for the justice here mentioned is not one to claim revenge but the *justifying* attitude of a God who remains faithful to his covenant. (E. Tobac, *Le problème de la justification dans S. Paul,* Louvain, 1928, pp. 125-30. Also, Stanislas Lyonnet, "De 'justitia Dei' in Epistola ad Romanos" in *Verbum Domini,* 25, 1947, pp. 23-34; Vincent Taylor, *The Atonement in the New Testament Teaching,* London: Epworth Press, 1958, p. 133.)

[94] According to Gustaf Aulén under the influence of the Latin idea of penance, *Christus Victor,* p. 98.

[95] *Cur Deus Homo. Opera Omnia,* ed. by F. S. Schmitt, O.S.B. (Edinburgh, 1946), Vol. II, pp. 68-91.

God-man and it did not require his death.[96] The Nominalism of the late Middle Ages re-emphasized the juridical elements of the substitution theory and influenced Luther and Calvin's adoption of it.[97]

Although death or destruction was never a primary factor in the expiation rites of our religious tradition, we still must face the fact that expiation in Christianity did occur through Jesus' actual suffering and death. Why should suffering and death possess a redemptive quality? The question far exceeds what a rational explanation can hope to clarify. Although not all religious men connect suffering with redemption,[98] the existence of such a connection is one of the most primitive beliefs of the human race, of which we find vestiges everywhere. In a creation hymn of the *Rig-Veda,* the self-sacrifice of the primal Being, the Purusha, gives birth to all creation and will be repeated in all later sacrifices.[99] A similar connection of death and salvific creation is found in *Enuma Elish* when the victorious Marduk forms the world out of Tiamat's body.[100] According to Hubert and Mauss, the conviction that life comes out of suffering and death underlies a number of Greek myths of heroes such as Perseus, Theseus, Hercules. The loser in these struggles often

[96] *Compendium Theologiae,* Ch. 198–200. A modern version of the Thomist doctrine may be found in Émile Mersch, S.J., *The Theology of the Mystical Body,* tr. by Cyril Vollert (St. Louis: B. Herder Book Co., 1951), pp. 247–62.

[97] Luther, *Commentarium in Galatas,* Weimar, 1883ff., Vol. 40, Abteilung, I, pp. 432–52. Calvin, *Institutio Christianae Religionis* in *Corpus Reformatorum* (Brunsvigae c.a. Schwetschka, 1864), Vol. 30, col. 527–28.

[98] Nicholas Berdyaev finds it clearly present only among Christians and (with qualifications) Jews. *The Destiny of Man* (New York: Harper & Brothers, 1960), pp. 117–22.

[99] R. C. Zaehner, *Hinduism* (New York: Oxford University Press, 1969), p. 44. A translation of the hymn may be found in *Hindu Scriptures,* sel., tr. by R. C. Zaehner (New York: E. P. Dutton, 1966), pp. 8–9. Obviously this Vedic hymn has none of the pessimism of the latest *Upanishads* which equate coming-into-being with evil. On the contrary, here as so often in archaic religion, redemption consists in the renewal of creation.

[100] The German Bible scholar Hermann Gunkel saw the same belief present in the Genesis creation story. *Schöpfung und Chaos in Urzeit und Endzeit.*

turns out to be the real victor.[101] Thus the death of a god
became his main title to glory. The sacrificial bull became the
god Dionysus *as a result* of his life-giving death. Others have
shown how these themes of the *agon* and the *pathos* of a god
made their way from the oldest Greek rituals into Greek tragedy.[102] The idea of an *agon* resulting in a passion permeates the
New Testament and the Christian Easter liturgy. Jesus' mission is
presented as a battle with the powers of evil and a healing of
those who were "oppressed by the devil" (Acts 10:38). The
sequence *Victimae Paschali* describes the Easter event as a
struggle between life and death in which the king of life triumphs
over death by submitting to it: "Mors et vita duello conflixere
mirando: dux vitae mortuus, regnat vivus." Similarly the Easter
vigil concludes with the darkness of death producing the light
of life.[103] In an Easter procession hymn of the Orthodox
Church Jesus' descent into hell symbolizes the basic belief that
salvation originates in death: "Christ is risen from the dead,
trampling down death by death, and bestowing life upon those
in the tomb."

Poets and writers have at all times attempted to symbolize
the mystery of redemptive suffering.[104] To philosophers, suffering

[101] Hubert and Mauss, *op. cit.*, pp. 112, 121. The authors point to
similar themes in Nordic mythology.

[102] Gilbert Murray, "Ritual Forms in Greek Tragedy" in *Themis* by Jane
Harrison, pp. 343–46.

[103] The *Exultet* sings: "Nox sicut dies illuminabitur: et nox illuminatio mea
in deliciis meis."

[104] Among the more recent attempts is Mauriac's *The Lamb* (Paris, 1954),
which expresses the need for having Christ's sacrifice repeated by Christlike
figures. They are psychologically and even physically destroyed by those
whom they redeem. The same theme appears in Bernanos' work, where
all redemption is achieved through the dark night of living souls. (See particularly *Dialogues of the Carmelites* and *The Diary of a Country Priest*,
where salvation is the result of total psychic destruction.) In Péguy's *The
Mystery of the Charity of Joan of Arc*, Joan's exclusion from the community of saints as a heretic, and her death at the stake, save the country.
Similar strands may be found in Melville's *Billy Budd*, in Faulkner's *A
Fable*, in Kazantzakis' *The Greek Passion*, and most impressively in Dostoevski's *The Idiot*. Cf. F. W. Dillistone, *The Novelist and the Passion
Story* (New York: Sheed & Ward, 1960), pp. 26–40.

has always been a dark mystery, as we saw in the previous chapter. It should not surprise us, then, that they have not advanced very far beyond a mythic symbolization of redemption through suffering, such as Plato's famous description of the just man who suffers injustice, is scourged, blinded, and crucified, yet who thereby assures the victory of good over evil.[105]

[105] *Republic*, II, 361e. Whitehead did make an attempt to rationalize what man dimly perceives through the myth in his description of the consequent nature of God, where each actuality passes into a further stage of God's expanding nature. "The sense of worth beyond itself is immediately enjoyed as an overpowering element in the individual self-attainment. It is in this way that the immediacy of sorrow and pain is transformed into an element of triumph. This is the notion of redemption through suffering, which haunts the world." (*Process and Reality*, p. 531.) If this is meant to be an explanation, the best one can say is that it begs the question.

Chapter 11
Salvation: the Consummate Life

1. GRACE AND FAITH

In most religious faiths salvation appears as a central idea.[1] It is so exclusively religious as to defy any translation into nonreligious language. Even such secularized versions of the idea as Marxism, manage to preserve a great deal of its original content.[2] The connotation of healing presupposes the existence of a state of sickness and estrangement from one's true being.[3] Yet this healing is conceived in as many different ways as the alienation which it overcomes. Christians envision it as a relation that is restored. But in some *Upanishads* liberation is achieved by surpassing temporality and abandoning determinateness. Similarly, for the

[1] I write "most" because there is little evidence of it in some archaic cultures. But then religion itself remains implicit in primitive society. More amazing is that there is no indication of it among Assyrians and Babylonians who could at best expect a neutral attitude on the part of the gods and whose general pessimism seems to have been enhanced by the fear of a dismal afterlife in the land of no return. Cf. S. G. F. Brandon, *Man and His Destiny in the Great Religions* (Toronto: University of Toronto Press, 1962), pp. 94–105. A somewhat similar situation seems to have existed among the Phoenicians. Cf. G. Contenau, *La civilisation phénicienne* (Paris, 1926).

[2] Cf. Jean-Yves Calvez, *La pensée de Karl Marx* (Paris, 1956), pp. 596–602.

[3] "In this sense healing means reuniting that which is estranged, giving a center to what is split, overcoming the split between God and man, man and his world, man and himself." Paul Tillich, *Systematic Theology*, II, p. 166.

Buddhist the state of Nirvana is an emptiness without support, a wisdom without content, an awakening without consciousness.[4] Rather than being converted in salvation, the Buddhist dissolves in it. Different again is the concept of liberation in the Samkhya-Yoga tradition, where the soul isolates itself from all things in order to reach the timeless essence of the individual self.

It is beyond our scope and competence to pursue the study of those and other particular forms of salvation, although some aspects of them will have to be explored in the next chapter. Here I shall discuss salvation mainly from the viewpoint of Christianity and Judaism. In doing so I make, as I did in the previous two chapters, a selective decision which is open to criticisms. But if I am to show the *concrete* dialectic of the religious affirmation in a general study, I must limit myself to one specific instance. The fact that this instance is predominant in the Western world supports the choice but makes the maintenance of a critical perspective all the more imperative.

The modern churchgoer tends to identify salvation with forgiveness of sins. Although this is an essential part of salvation in the Christian faith, it is by no means the entire concept. Indeed, to consider the supersession of evil as its primary function falsifies the perspective altogether. For the idea of salvation may well precede that of sin in the religious consciousness. Still we shall first consider how salvation liberates a freedom which has become trammeled in its own estrangement. By being reintegrated with the sacred, man also restores the harmony with himself and the rest of creation. Christians have traditionally referred to this integration by the elusive idea of *atonement*.

In most Christian theologies the idea of atonement has been philosophically discredited by the anthropomorphic assumption that someone must "atone" in some other man's place. In itself

---

[4] A famous Mahayana text reads: "Nirvana is the realm of self-realization attained by noble wisdom, which is free from the discrimination of eternality and annihilation, existence and non-existence." *The Lankavatara Sutra,* tr. by D. T. Suzuki (London, 1956). Cf. also Edward Conze, *Buddhism,* pp. 35–40; D. T. Suzuki, *On Indian Mahayana Buddhism* (New York: Harper & Row, 1968), p. 39.

the idea of mediation is perfectly acceptable. But the notion that the function must be fulfilled by a being *between* God and man is as spurious as it is widespread. We find it among Christians, Jews, and Moslems. Yet, clearly man can be reconciled with God only through God. On the other hand, God need not be reconciled to man. Consequently, there is no use for a "third" reality. At the same time the idea of *mediation* is profoundly religious and particularly significant in Christianity. Schleiermacher once wrote: "The religion of Christ is that the idea of redemption and mediation is the center of religion."[5]

Yet atonement is not the whole of salvation. According to St. Anselm the saving event of Christ's incarnation would have taken place even if man had not sinned. God entered the world to reveal himself to man; since man was *de facto* estranged from him, the revelation implied a redemption.[6] Although this theory fails to account for the negative aspect inherent in man's relation to God, it conveys that salvation, beyond restoring lost innocence, is the self-communication of God and the supreme fulfillment of human existence. It is the *fascinans* aspect—the attractiveness—of the sacred. The negative terms in which religious man mostly describes salvation refer to an eminently positive experience of partaking of the divine in a *regeneration,* a rebirth to another dimension of existence.

Salvation reintegrates man with the primordial wholeness of life. Its symbols of life, harmony, joy, and light are frequently taken from the cycle of nature. This has many an outside observer misled into thinking that the two are identical, while in fact salvation transforms the original meaning of the cycle.[7]

---

[5] *On Religion,* p. 264. Schleiermacher understood that God alone can reconcile man to the divine presence. In his early works Schleiermacher presents Christ as only one of the many divine mediations. In *Die Weihnachtsfeier* (1806) and *Der Christliche Glaube* (1821) Christ's mediation is described as unique.

[6] *Cur Deus Homo.* Migne, P.L. 158, 359–432. For an updated version of Anselm's theory, see Herbert Richardson, *Toward an American Theology* (New York: Harper & Row, 1967), pp. 127–30.

[7] That the cycle of seasons may have "occasioned" the rise of the notion of salvation, does not justify applying the concept of causality to it, since salvation is generically different.

This is most obvious in the Catholic cult. Catholics like all Christians have based their faith upon a unique *historical* event in which all salvation was synthesized. Yet under the influence of the ancient agricultural religions, they also adopted the seasonal cycles. However, the liturgical cycles fulfill the subordinate and primarily subjective function of incorporating the objective event of salvation into the individual and communal life of the Christian. Their return makes the instant of the Incarnation into a permanent present. Thus salvation becomes an ongoing process although it was entirely present at a particular point of history.

This process results in a *state* of being saved which is unique to religious man and to which Christians today usually refer by the term *grace*. But the connotations of this term are not sufficient to convey the full meaning of the state of salvation.[8] A number of concepts converge in the Christian idea of being saved. First there is the Old Testamentic belief that God reveals himself through special acts in history: God adopts Israel and guides it to its special destiny. In the New Testament the adoption is extended to all men. Salvation now consists in a divine transformation, a *theopoiesis* of the entire man. This ontological transformation had psychological effects, such as the restoration of original innocence. But while those were not ignored by the Greek Fathers, they were not one-sidedly emphasized as in the Latin Church. The entire idea of predestination, born out of the Pelagian controversies, corrupted much of what was good in the conception of grace as freedom and would lead to centuries of inane disputes over grossly anthropomorphic ideas.[9]

The Christian vision was further narrowed down by the Scholastics' unfortunate attempts to classify grace somewhere in the Aristotelian category of accident. What was originally conceived as a gratuitous state of being, came to be regarded as a

[8] Henri de Lubac suggests that χάρις should be combined with μυστήριον to render the full meaning of the Christian supernatural. *Surnaturel* (Paris, 1946), p. 325.

[9] Our development of the Christian idea of grace owes much to Henry Duméry, *Philosophie de la religion*, Vol. 2, pp. 155–265.

gratuitous "addition" to human nature.[10] This would lead to a juxtaposition of natural and supernatural life in which the latter was a mere extension of the former. "Nature" then became gradually a profane concept without the religious content necessary to make grace a meaningful "gift."[11] Fortunately, mystical theologians continued to consider grace as an intrinsic rather than an added transcendence. In Eckhart the distinction between the two orders disappears entirely in the uncreated Being of the soul, which is divine as well as human. According to Ruusbroec also, God operates *directly* in the soul through his Trinitarian nature. Even after the Council of Trent had rejected Luther's relational views of grace and advocated one of "immanence," mystically oriented theologians continued to speak of an indwelling of *God himself,* rather than a created grace, in the soul.[12]

The entire history of Christian theology could be written in terms of the emphasis which one or another of the aspects of grace received. In Catholic theology since the late Middle Ages the notion of gratuitousness has predominated. In Lutheran theology the accent was on justification and forgiveness of sin. The ideas of liberation and restored freedom permeate all the predestination theologies from Augustine to Calvin. The primary idea of divinization seems to be best preserved among Orthodox theologians thanks to their uninterrupted contact with the Greek Fathers.

[10] Abelard, *Expositio in Epistolam Pauli ad Romanos,* Migne, P.L. 178, 928. Also Peter Lombard, *In Epistolam ad Romanos,* P.L. 191, 1361.
[11] In Thomas nature is still open to the supernatural in a way which makes it religious and self-transcending: man has only one end and that is religious. It is only in the theologies of Molina, Bañez, Jansenius, and some of the theologians of the Protestant orthodoxy that the two concepts are totally severed. Cf. Duméry, *Philosophie de la religion,* I, pp. 227–41.
[12] The Flemish theologians Leonardus Lessius (*De Perfectionibus Moribusque Divinis,* Antwerp, 1626) and Cornelius a Lapide (*Commentarium in Oseam,* Antwerp, 1625) speak, in Ruusbroec's tradition, of the substantial inhabitation of the Holy Spirit. The same language is used by the seventeenth-century Patrologists Petavius and Thomasinus, and the late nineteenth-century dogmatic theologians Scheeben and de Regnon. On this whole development one may consult the suggestive pages of Peter Fransen, *Divine Grace and Man* (New York: New American Library, 1965), pp. 122–35.

The state of salvation is attained through the totality of religion: revelation, sacred rites, sacraments, direct experience. Yet in the case of modern man all of these are determined through, and sometimes replaced by, faith. Faith is not merely a believing acceptance of events of the past: it also includes hope for the future and love in the present. In the following sections we shall have the opportunity to discuss hope and love as religious attitudes. Faith itself was treated in the first chapters. Here I shall only discuss briefly its relation to salvation. The existence of a connection is in itself enough of a problem. How could a believing acceptance of objective facts ever be redemptive? Karl Jaspers' harsh words voice the opinion of many outsiders:

A reconciliation by faith in the objective process of salvation—by the belief that the sacrificial death and resurrection of Christ has redeemed me—is philosophically incomprehensible if meant as the "justification by faith alone" of St. Paul and Luther. Failing utterly to understand, we can only marvel at the fact that men can speak in that vein. Not even as a cipher can I find any approach to such "justification." How can it be meritorious to believe in something laid down in a creed, in statements about an objective occurrence?[13]

Yet no believer will recognize his own attitude in the one described by Jaspers. Faith is not what "justifies" or saves in itself: it is an instrument of salvation, not a magical reality. Schleiermacher refers to it as a receptive organ.[14] It is a conversion by which the mind comes to stand in an entirely new relation to the sacred and to share in its reality. Christians consider faith the adoption of the attitude of Jesus toward the Father. Some participation in his attitude is what gives faith its saving quality.[15]

---

[13] *Philosophical Faith and Revelation*, p. 243.
[14] *Der Christliche Glaube*, II, p. 202. *The Christian Faith*, p. 504.
[15] "Christ cannot live in us without His relation to His Father being formed in us also and making us sharers in His sonship." Schleiermacher, *Der Christliche Glaube*, II, p. 194. *The Christian Faith*, p. 499.

Faith then opens a new perspective. Yet the conversion of consciousness which enables the mind to receive the divine life must itself be a gift. The Christian Churches have therefore always emphasized that faith is part of the salvation process itself, rather than an autonomous decision of man. The Council of Orange decreed against the Semi-Pelagians:

> He is an adversary of the apostolic teaching who says that the increase of faith as well as the beginning of faith and the very desire of faith—by which we believe in Him who justifies the unjustified, and by which we come to the regeneration of sacred baptism—inheres in us naturally and not by gift of grace.[16]

More than others, Protestant Christians have emphasized the gratuitous character of faith. Man does not receive God but is being received by God. That this attitude is connected with the redeeming *events* and *words* of Christ's life is inevitable in a historical religion. But it does not imply, as Jaspers suggests, that faith consists in a mere acceptance of objective information. Moreover, faith is not entirely directed toward the events of the past. A historical faith is equally concerned with the events of the future and even with the present course of history. If God reveals himself through history, he also saves through history. Faith then becomes trust on the basis of past words and events that God's governance in the present prepares his full revelation in the future. To the extent that faith is expectation of the future, believers usually refer to it as hope. But if God saves through history, all events become to some extent salvific. This creates enormous problems which we shall now consider.

2. HISTORY AND HOPE

Through history salvation may come to an entire nation, as it did for Israel, or to individuals of all nations, as it did for the

[16] *Enchiridion Symbolorum*, Dz. ✗178.

primitive Christian community. In the former case sacred history is also national history; in the latter, salvation history moves along with profane history without coinciding with it. Christian theologians, unlike the prophets of Israel, cannot interpret the development of history. The victory or defeat of one camp over another is never a decisive sign of the ultimate success or failure of the Christian faith. As Karl Löwith puts it in his illuminating theology of history: "The most we can say about their connection, is that for the believer also profane history may have a sign character, more or less as world catastrophes symbolically prefigure the last judgment."[17] Such at least was the initial state of affairs.

Yet further reflection upon the historical foundations of their faith would soon stimulate Christians into renewed speculation on history. If the coming of Christ marked a decisive progress over the past, it was easy to believe that all real progress of history would consist in the furtherance of the Christian faith. Thus a new theology of history was born. After a brief association with the Roman Empire (in Eusebius), the invasions of the barbarians obliged Christians to separate the "progress" of their faith from that of any earthly cause and to attempt a deeper synthesis with history. The well-known result was Augustine's *City of God*. History once more seemed detached from salvation or reduced to a subordinate, symbolic function.

> One part of the earthly city became an image of the heavenly city, not having any significance of its own, but signifying another city, and therefore serving, or "being in bondage." For it was founded, not for its own sake but to prefigure another city . . . In the earthly city, then, we find two things, its own obvious presence, and its symbolic presentation of the heavenly city.[18]

[17] Karl Löwith, *Weltgeschichte und Heilsgeschehen*, Stuttgart, 1953, p. 166. This statement does not appear in the original English version, *Meaning in History: The Theological Implications of the Philosophy of History* (Chicago: University of Chicago Press, 1955).
[18] *De Civitate Dei*, XV, 2. *The City of God*, tr. by Marcus Dodds (New York: Modern Library, 1950).

Yet Augustine was not willing to let the earthly city escape God's ruling governance. Providence must at critical moments actively intervene in the course of events in the earthly city. The final verdict lies beyond history, yet God cannot let the wicked prevail.[19] Nor does Augustine abandon the Christian idea of progress. But unlike his predecessors, Eusebius, Jerome, and Ambrose, he detaches the progress of salvation from *particular* historical developments. The truly "progressive" events were completed with the revelation. The present time is for sowing the good seed of the Gospel, but the harvest will not come until the apocalyptic end of history.

However, history would cease to be secular (with occasional divine interventions) if the City of God could take over the rule of the earthly city. This possibility materialized during the Middle Ages, when the Church ruled *de facto* the entire civilized world. Since the Church was under direct governance of God, all of history henceforth would be under the sway of God's direct power.[20] A growing awareness of human autonomy culminating in the Enlightenment and the philosophy of Kant would eventually cause an insurmountable tension between this universal divine dominance and human initiative.

The very notion of progress which Christianity had spawned and cultivated proved the most retractive element to integrate into a synthesis of the two. Indeed, it ended up becoming the battle cry of the forces which rejected the belief in God's governance altogether. Progress and Providence became alternatives, one standing for autonomous human development, the other for divine guidance of history. The two were not reconciled until Hegel in his theory of the Absolute Spirit once again posited that salvation comes through history and coincides with the progress of freedom. His synthesis of the divine and the human, which he

[19] *De Civitate Dei*, I, 8.
[20] Bossuet's *Discours sur l'histoire universelle* gave a classical expression to this view after the *res publica christiana* which had produced it was already in full decline.

took to be the outcome of modern Protestantism, definitely over-
came the opposition between human self-realization and religious
salvation.[21]

Hegel's synthesis was impressive. But it wrought its own un-
doing, for if man's progress in history is his ultimate salvation,
the idea of a divine redemption becomes ultimately superfluous.
The philosopher may still feel the need to retain the link with
the religious representation which gave birth to the modern
consciousness. To the man of action such memories of the past
hold little meaning. If man alone works his salvation, Hegel's
left-wing disciples were soon to conclude, all talk about God
withdraws attention from the main agent and can only slow down
true progress. Thus the new humanism, much against Hegel's
original intention, dispensed with the idea of God altogether. In
Marx's philosophy atheism is a precondition for efficient historical
action.

Obviously religious man had to reject such an interpretation.
But even if no left-wing Hegelians had ever deformed Hegel's
original message, there was enough in it to alarm Christians.
For if God is entirely immanent in history, he also must take
the blame for all its crimes. Unless we accept moral evil to be
necessary for man's salvation, God's salvific designs must in some
respect be separated from man's choices. Most believers therefore prefer to leave God out of the ordinary course of events
altogether and fall back upon Augustine's eschatological dualism.
Thus the notion of a divine guidance of history is once again
abandoned in favor of that of a special Providence which interferes only at special occasions.

[21] "The infinite autonomy of modern moral self-hood, far from challenging
religious truth, on the contrary refers to it, as *its* truth, and since it may be
described as the highest and most concrete self-assertation of autonomous
Reason in modern life, the Hegelian philosophy may be described as an
attempt to reconcile a Reason which asserts itself *against* the reality which
is, with a religious truth which *already* is." Emil Fackenheim, *The Religious
Dimension in Hegel's Thought* (Bloomington: Indiana University Press,
1967), p. 67.

How could modern man discover divine guidance in this domain of his own from which he purposely has excluded God? In such a world he can feel only complete desertion and utter remoteness from God. The forces that are active here are entirely independent of religion—they are openly opposed to God. To see with modern philosophers an immediate manifestation of divine Providence in the political and social history of mankind means to reduce God to a political ruler, to turn society and its order into "visible Gods." Providence is a religious idea; it does not signify God's interest in political parties or social agents, but rather his concern about the ethico-religious individual and the secret of his soul. Only in the spiritual sphere is it appropriate to speak of Providence.[22]

One cannot but sympathize with the refusal to make God responsible for all the crimes of our time, including the ones staged for the sole purpose of eradicating the belief in God. On the other hand, a salvation scheme in which God takes certain events entirely for his own account and leaves others completely to man, is plainly arbitrary and unable to withstand the critique of philosophy. If Providence predisposes some events, it affects all events, for all are interrelated.

Salvation history allows neither an unqualified attribution to God of all human events nor a selective exclusion of some. In one respect Hegel was unquestionably right: since man's free will, with all its potential for good and evil, is the culminating point of a divine creation, the entire course of history may be said to express a divine will. Yet to the believer history means more than the total realization of human freedom. Through it God operates man's salvation, in a way which sets certain events apart from others. In Chapter 7 we discussed the distinctness of so-called revelatory events. The case of the salvific event is more complex, for it both distinguishes *and unites*. Like divine creativity it permeates the entire historical process; like revelation it distinguishes certain historical events from others.

[22] Erich Frank, *Philosophical Understanding and Religious Truth*, pp. 129–30.

At first it may appear that only some events are strictly salvific. Thus, to the Christian the Incarnation stands out above all others as *unique* and unequaled. The historian will raise no difficulty against such a discrimination, since events differ in import. The storming of the Bastille was obviously more important, although probably shorter in duration than the hunting party which Louis XVI noted in the last entry of his diary. Nor does the selection of certain events as salvific *per se* conflict with the human autonomy which rules all of history. The Incarnation does not rend the fabric of human history. The story of Christ can be smoothly inserted in the course of events described as a footnote in a study of Judea under the Roman Empire. A man called Jesus pretended to be the Messiah expected in Israel; he was crucified in Jerusalem; later his followers claimed that he rose from the dead and adored him as a god. The web of historical connections remains intact. Only for the believer certain events acquire a new significance. All "salvific" events of the Christian faith can be and have been described in the non-committal language of secular history. Even proven miracles are linked in an uninterrupted chain of events. They may fit in a different context, not in a different world. To see them as expressions of a special governance, the believer needs the eyes of faith.

Yet those events which have been recognized as "salvific" affect all others insofar as they open up a new perspective on the entire course of history. Thus if a decisive act of atonement is admitted into history, it becomes a permanent feature of it. Pascal drew a necessary conclusion from the Christian faith in his mysterious saying: "Jesus will be in agony until the end of the world."[23] If the transcendent takes on a temporal character, it cannot but transform all of history and bring "all times equally close to God."[24] Henceforth salvation must operate

[23] *Pensées,* 553.
[24] The expression is Leopold von Ranke's who clearly had something else in mind when he used it.

through all of history. However, such a religious insight does not provide a norm for the interpretation of history. Nor does it allow the believer to find order where previously was chaos. Undoubtedly, to the religious mind salvation determines the ultimate meaning of history—to all of it. And Péguy's words about the Roman legionaries marching for Christ apply to all armies— C'est pour toi qu'ils ont marché.

But to equate salvation through history with historical progress is to confuse two different levels of reality and to immanentize once again the transcendent in the very act which constitutes it. The birth of Christ offers no guarantee to the Christian that subsequent human affairs have been handled more deftly or even more morally. Whether history progresses or regresses is an interesting subject for speculation. But, even to the Christian, faith can in no way be helpful to decide the case. The identification of salvation with progress has merely confused the issue.[25]

Nor does the Christian gain new historical insight by his belief in a final, apocalyptic revelation. For whether history continues indefinitely or whether it grinds abruptly to a halt, in neither case does the transcendent take the place of the immanent. History proceeds by means of natural causes and this is also the way it will terminate, if it is to terminate at all. The possibility that in a distant future the transcendent will coincide with the immanent is excluded by the very meaning of the terms. Yet this seems to be precisely what some adherents of the so-called theology of hope expect.

Resuming a line of thought initiated by Hegel but prematurely interrupted by his secularist followers, theologians of hope look for salvation in the future of history. In his monumental work, *Das Prinzip Hoffnung,* Ernst Bloch, the philosophical prophet of

[25] Nonetheless all philosophies of progress from Voltaire to Marx have been based upon unadmitted and strongly repudiated religious postulates. Such is the thesis of Löwith's entire work. It is confirmed by Jan Nota, *Phenomenology and History* (Chicago: Loyola University Press, 1967), pp. 54–89, although Professor Nota himself does accept the Christian revelation as a factor of historical progress.

the movement, envisions the transcendent as a becoming of man's future.[26] Bloch's position, although inspired by Marx, by no means returns to the secularism of Marx. It marks a genuine attempt, anticipated by Feuerbach, to integrate the divine with the human. Nor does he equate the divine with man's present condition: only the beyond of a never-completed future holds the divinity of man. To Bloch transcendence is no idle word, for man cannot conceive of his own potential in terms of what he is or of what he may rationally expect to be. Only religious symbols enable him to project his future infinity. Even Feuerbach's attempt to translate the religious dimension in terms of this life lost most of the original meaning in the process. "The *res infinita* of the religious ideal cannot be reduced to the *res finita* bourgeois as conceived by Feurerbach."[27] Only the Messianic language of the prophets reveals the utopia of man's hidden possibilities.[28]

Clearly a transcendence confined to the future of man cannot satisfy the believer. God is no more the future than he is merely the past or the present. Yet after having expressed those reservations about a future convergence of immanence and transcendence, I cannot but agree that the Jewish and Christian believer always expects his salvation in the future. To justify this trust and to free the notion of transcendence from the spatial metaphors in which it had become fixed, Christian theologians were right

[26] In a speech to Viennese students he describes the kingdom of the Son of Man "not merely as something 'above' but also as something before us." "Der Mensch als Möglichkeit" in *Forum. Oestreichische Monatsblatter für Kulturelle Freiheit*, 13 (1965), p. 361. Tr. in *Cross Currents*, 18 (1968), p. 283. The qualifiers "not merely" and "also" do not appear in *Das Prinzip Hoffnung*.

[27] *Das Prinzip Hoffnung* (Frankfurt, 1967), p. 1518.

[28] Still Bloch's atheism is as fundamental as that of Feuerbach and Marx. For in his view any other than a purely humanistic interpretation of the Messianic kingdom assumes that the divine is already with us and thereby diminishes its utopian power. "Without atheism there is no place for Messianism" (p. 1413). Salvation, then, consists exclusively in man's self-realization. I have criticized Bloch's position in a contribution, "Hope and Transcendence," to The God Experience: Essays in Hope, ed. by Joseph P. Whelan, S.J. (New York: Newman Press, 1971).

to draw once more attention to the salvific meaning of history as such. If God becomes involved in history, its development (I avoid the term progress) must mean more to him than a meaningless parenthesis within an unchanging eternity: its course must have a divine significance. In a historical faith all events contribute directly to the advent of salvation.

Nor is this advent restricted to an eschatological ending of history. Various cults such as Zoroastrianism, the religion of the ancient Celts, and a number of gnostic sects included eschatologies in which the divine ultimately triumphs over evil. Yet the development of history played no role in them. To the Gnostics, for instance, divine reality is timeless. Even if a historical Savior appears, as in Christian Gnosticism, his real being must remain above true temporality, for time belongs to the lapsed world and consequently can have no part in salvation.[29] In Judaism and Christianity, on the contrary, the temporal itself brings salvation. Because of the new meaning which all of history receives from the presence of certain salvific events, Jews and Christians are religiously concerned about actual historical situations. Their faith does not allow them to watch time go by in detached contemplation. Even the contemplative feels an obligation to "redeem the time" and to engage in historical action. Yet frequently this leads them to expect salvation from history, as if the future held the fulfillment of their religious aspirations—a misconception which some contemporary theologians have enthusiastically endorsed. However much the believer operates his salvation *through* history, he never attains its fulfillment *in* history, neither in the present nor in the future. He may redeem history, sanctify it, and bestow an eternal meaning upon its events, but he can never integrate divine transcendence with historical immanence.

[29] We still hear some remote echoes of this theory in such an orthodox Christian writer as Gregory of Nyssa, who considered the *diastema* of time exclusively a result of sin. The difference here is, however, that although time for him results from the lapsed condition of man, it also fulfills a function in his recovery.

The opposition between the two dimensions of existence remains unchanged, even though autonomous striving opens up into another dimension.

3. LOVE: SALVATION AS PRAXIS

Even in historical faiths salvation is never a mere event, but also *a way,* that is, a particular mode of conduct which leads to, and in some respects already anticipates, the beatific life. Christians have traditionally referred to their way by the term "love." Before investigating how they understand this comprehensive, not exclusively religious term, we must discuss the belief, widespread among Christians today, that love is the essence of all religion. Clearly, such an opinion finds little support in archaic religion. The old-time critics Lucretius and Hume may have been closer to the truth in claiming that religion originates in fear. To be sure, religious fear belongs in an emotional class of its own,[30] but originally the religious attitude was closer to ordinary fear than to love. Nor does fear ever disappear from the religious attitude.

In civilized religion we find hardly more justification for identifying religion with love. Buddhism displays an infinite respect for life, yet the individual as such is never an object of divine love. In the Hinayana tradition the individual self is broken down into a number of elements which alone are real. In Mahayana Buddhism only the absolute Whole is real and the self is not. Instead of love for the individual, Buddhism preaches compassion for all beings still in the grip of illusion. An attitude that results in the annihilation of the individual, rather than in the creation or cultivation of individual values, should not be called love. The Buddhist himself would be the first to object to having his ideal described as love. In the

[30] Otto knew this; Lucretius and Hume did not. Cf. *The Idea of the Holy,* p. 132.

Dhammapada we read: "From love comes sorrow; from love comes fear. Whosoever is free from love, for him there is no sorrow: whence should come fear to him."[31]

In the *Upanishads* we find references to love, as in the following passage from the *Brihadaranyaka:*

> Mark well, it is not for the love (kama) of a husband that a husband is dearly loved. Rather it is for the love of the Self that a husband is dearly loved. Mark well, it is not for the love of a wife that a wife is dearly loved. Rather it is for the love of the Self that a wife is dearly loved . . . Mark well, it is not for the love of the All that the All is dearly loved. Rather it is for the love of the Self that the All is dearly loved.[32]

Yet the Self which in this passage appears as the ultimate principle of love is obviously not the spiritual principle of individuality, but the universal unity out of which all individuals (including the gods) arise. The Hindu mystic to an unusual degree identifies with the entire cosmos. But individual existence as such has no positive quality: it is the source of evil.[33]

---

[31] Cited and translated in Ananda K. Coomaraswamy, *Buddha and the Gospel of Buddhism* (New York: Harper & Row, 1964), p. 92. It is true enough that some sort of personal cult (which included affective attachment) of the Buddhas and Bodhisattvas developed in Buddhism almost from the beginning. But although this development is emotionally understandable enough, to the extent that it denies the extinction of the Buddha in the Nirvana, it deviates from orthodox doctrine. See Edward Conze, *Buddhism: Its Essence and Development* (New York: Harper & Brothers, 1951), pp. 152–53.

[32] *Brihadaranyaka,* II, 4, 5, in *Hindu Scriptures,* tr. by R. C. Zaehner, p. 45.

[33] Of course, the term "Hinduism" comprehends such different things that no general statement is possible on this or any other matter. One undoubtedly finds personal love expressed in poetry such as that of the Tamil devotees of Shiva, or the beautiful verses of the fifteenth-century mystic Kabir:

Kabir says: "O my loving friend! I have got for my gift the Deathless One."

This day is dear to me above all other days, for to-day the Beloved Lord is a guest in my house;

My chamber and my courtyard are beautiful with His presence;

My longings sing His Name, and they are become lost in His great

The religious vision always unifies and integrates. For the believer in a personal God, this drive toward union easily develops into a union of love. Israel's strong affirmation of one personal God combined with the Western emphasis upon the individualization process created an ideal climate for the development of an intimate personal relation.[34] Yet this is one particular form of the religious attitude, not *the* religious attitude. Moreover, a personal relation to an eternal *Thou* is not necessarily a relation of love. Buber himself refused to interpret the dialogue between God and man as a participation of love. Aspects of love emerge in most faiths. For some individuals they may determine the entire religious attitude. But most men would consider the term "love" inappropriate to describe the relation between God and man. Total identification appears to be a uniquely Christian phenomenon. Even then the term love is to be given an entirely new meaning.

Christians have always been aware of the special nature of religious love. But in recent times they have started comparing this love with other forms of affection. According to Anders Nygren, Christian love, *agape,* is distinguished by its transcendent origin. Thus love should become the center of the Christian

---

beauty: I wash His feet, and I look upon His Face and I lay before Him as an offering my body, my mind, and all that I have.

What a day of gladness is that day in which my Beloved, who is my treasure, comes to my house. All evils fly from my heart when I see my Lord.

My love has touched Him; my heart is longing for the Name which is Truth.

Thus sings Kabir, the servant of all servants.

(Rabindranath Tagore, *One Hundred Poems of Kabir,* quoted from *North Indian Saints,* Madras, n.d., pp. 27–28)

[34] Nowhere does this appear more clearly than in Martin Buber's description of the I-Thou encounter as a religious experience.

"In every sphere in its own way . . . we look out towards the fringe of the eternal *Thou;* in each we are aware of a breath from the eternal *Thou;* in each Thou we address the eternal *Thou.* Every sphere is compassed in the eternal *Thou* but it is not compassed in them. Through every sphere shines our present." (*I and Thou,* p. 101) It is by no means an accident that Judaism gave birth to the love mysticism of the Spanish *Cabala* and of such men as Rabbi Juda the Chasid. Cf. Gershom G. Scholem, *Major Trends in Jewish Mysticism* (New York: Schocken Books, 1946), Lectures III and IV.

faith, because for the Christian, God himself *is* love.[35] Love has
been a powerful "religious motif" in other faiths, but mostly
in the form of a desiring and purely human *eros* unknown to
the gods. *Agape* descends from heaven toward man; *eros* originates
in man alone and, if it enters the religious attitude, ascends to
heaven.[36]

Denis de Rougemont brought out another aspect of the same
distinction. He defines *eros* as an inexhaustible drive toward
infinite perfection which, in order to maintain its upward momentum, refuses all finite objects. Beyond the concrete reality of the
earthly beloved, *eros* soars into its own infinity. Christian *agape*
on the contrary finds the infinite love of God in the finite reality
of the person.

> Eros had treated a fellow-creature as but an illusory excuse and
> occasion for taking fire; and forthwith this creature had had to be
> given up, for the intention was ever to burn more fiercely, to
> burn to death! Individual beings were but so many defects and
> eclipsings of the one and only Being; and as such none was sus-
> ceptible of being really loved. Salvation lay *hereafter,* and a
> religious-minded person forsook the creatures from which his god
> had turned away. But the Christian God has not forsaken us. He

[35] "To the religious question, now stated in theocentric terms, what is
God? Christianity replies with the Johannine formula: God is agape. And
to the ethical question, What is the Good, the "Good-in-itself"? the answer
is similar: The Good is agape, and the ethical demand finds summary
expression in the Commandment of Love, the commandment to love God
and my neighbor." *Agape and Eros,* tr. by Philip S. Watson, pp. 47–48.
[36] "Religion is fellowship with God. But two different conceptions are
possible of the way in which this fellowship is brought about. It can either
be thought of as achieved by the raising up of the human to the Divine—
and that is the contention of egocentric religion, of Eros; or else it is
held to be established by the gracious condescension of the Divine to
man—and that is the contention of theocentric religion, of Agape." *Agape
and Eros,* pp. 206–7. Aside from a few occasional remarks Nygren
pays but scant attention to the love of God for his people described in the
Old Testament. He proposes the Christian idea as totally new. I think, on the
contrary, that Jesus considered his own religion of love very much in
continuity with the Law and the Prophets, to which he constantly refers.
See, e.g., Lk. 10:25–28.

alone, among all gods known to us, has not turned away. Quite the contrary, 'He first loved us'—loved us as we are and with our limitations.[37]

This is the love for the person already *present* which gave birth to the concept of neighbor, that is, *he who happens to be there* regardless of his personal qualities. Neighborly love climaxes in love for the enemy, the supreme challenge to human affection. It is, as Kierkegaard defines it, the love for the man one encounters rather than for the man one prefers.[38] Such a love has its roots in the faith in a divine Providence which has placed the neighbor on my path.[39] It reverses the "natural" attitude in which the self and its preferences come first.

Nevertheless, one distorts the nature of Christian love by distinguishing eros and agape in such a way that they exclude each other.[40] For nondesiring love is not the exclusive privilege of religiously motivated Christians.[41] Some passages of Plotinus would, despite Nygren's protest, come closer to *agape* than to *eros*. On the other hand, entire sections of the New Testament,

---

[37] *Love in the Western World*, tr. by Montgomery Belgion (New York: Fawcett Books, 1966), p. 71.

[38] "Self-love and passionate preferences are essentially the same; but love of one's neighbor—that is genuine love. To love the beloved, asks Christianity—is that loving, and adds, 'Do not the pagans do likewise?' . . . Love of one's neighbor, on the other hand, is self-renouncing love, and self-renunciation casts out all preferential love just as it casts out all self-love—otherwise self-renunciation would also make distinctions and would nourish preference for preference." Søren Kierkegaard, *Samlede Vaerker* (3d ed.) (Copenhagen, 1963), pp. 57, 59. *Works of Love*, tr. by Howard and Edna Hong (New York: Harper & Row, 1962), pp. 66–67.

[39] See Romano Guardini, *Willie und Wahrheit* (Mainz, 1933), pp. 164–66.

[40] We might also observe that a classification of love as eros and agape is not sufficiently comprehensive. Recent writers have felt the need for widening the spectrum. Thus C. S. Lewis adds affection and friendship, while Paul Tillich distinguishes eros as the drive toward value, from libido as pure desire. C. S. Lewis, *The Four Loves* (London: Geoffrey Bles, 1960). Paul Tillich, *Love, Power and Justice* (New York: Oxford University Press, 1954).

[41] Martin d'Arcy, *The Mind and Heart of Love* (New York: Meridian Books, 1964), p. 48.

even in the so-called Gospel of love, advocate a desiring love of God. Such Christian mystics of love as Bernard of Clairvaux and William of Saint-Thierry move easily from desiring love to giving love.[42] True, the fact that man is *primarily* self-centered, according to Bernard, results from an unnatural, "sinful" attitude. But self-love is inherent in even the most disinterested human love.[43] The same movement by which God loves himself is also the one by which man, created in God's image, loves both God and himself. Gilson aptly describes creaturely love as "an essentially interested participation in an essentially disinterested love."[44] Even interested love partakes of divine love.[45] Thus St. Thomas could claim that the creature naturally loves its Creator more than itself, for to love its own good is to love even more that of which that good is merely an effect and an image.[46] Since according to Christian doctrine man is closer to God than he is to himself or any other being, even the most ecstatic love was never entirely separated from desire.

[42] St. Bernard distinguishes four degrees of love: love for one's self, love of God for one's own sake, love of God for his and one's own sake, purely disinterested love of God. *De diligendo Deo*, Migne, P.L. 182, 987–92: *On the Love of God*, tr. by Terence L. Connolly, S.J. (New York: Spiritual Book Associates, 1937), Ch. VIII–X, pp. 37–46.

Pierre Rousselot has accused Bernard of inconsistency in his theory of divine love: for him love must either be "physical" (seeking its own good) or ecstatic (severing all ties with the self) and Bernard seems to mix both kinds. "Pour l'histoire de l'amour au moyen âge" in *Beitrage Baeumker*, VI, 6 (Münster, 1908), pp. 1–5. This criticism which anticipates Nygren's absolute distinction between *eros* and *agape*, has been thoroughly refuted by Étienne Gilson. How could a finite being live without desiring satisfaction of its finite needs? "To love God we must live, and to live we must love ourselves." *The Spirit of Medieval Philosophy* (New York: Charles Scribner's Sons, 1940), p. 292.

[43] Étienne Gilson, *The Mystical Theology of St. Bernard*, tr. by A. H. C. Downes (New York: Sheed & Ward, 1940), p. 87. The entire fourth chapter deals with the topic.

[44] Étienne Gilson, *The Spirit of Medieval Philosophy*, p. 279.

[45] "To say that if man of necessity loves himself he cannot love God with disinterested love, is to forget that to love God with distinterested love is man's true way of loving himself." *Ibid.*, p. 288. In the same spirit William of Saint-Thierry wrote "Et haec est hominis perfectio, similitudo Dei." *Epistola ad Fratres de Monte Dei*, II, 3, 16.

[46] *Summa Theologiae*, I, 60, 5 ad 1. Gilson's exegesis in *op. cit.*, p. 286.

Nonetheless, love is not by its very nature religious; it becomes so only by actively striving to surpass its "desiring" tendencies. Moreover, even when love is a fundamental religious motif (as it may have been for the Greeks), it is not the essence of the religious attitude unless God reveals himself as love. The novel element of Christianity was not the commandment of love, which was well established in the Jewish tradition, but the fact that God himself is identified with love.[47] God here is no longer the unmoved mover who κινεῖ ὡς ἐρώμενον; his very nature is declared to be movement, self-communication, creativity. If God is love, then love itself is the highest—not the beloved object.[48] Through his participation in grace the Christian believes to share the divine movement of *Being-in-love*. Here the life-giving, determining element is love itself, not what it attains or achieves.

When love comes ontologically first, no prior norms can instruct man as to what object is worthy of his love. It is love itself that makes the object lovable, not what precedes it. The Christian must therefore love the man who happens to be near him, and in doing so, he *eo ipso* loves his God. One cannot be separated from the other as a condition, a result, or even a motive.[49] If God is love and if all creatures are the objects of this love, then

[47] One can hardly maintain that what the Hebrews had recited for centuries before Christ is a Christian innovation. The Golden Rule is clearly stated in Lev. 19:18, and explained both positively and negatively ("Whatever is hateful to you, do not do to your neighbor.") by Rabbis Hillel and Akiba. The identity of God and love is stated verbatim in I Jn. 4:16, but was already present in Jesus' precept to love one's enemies in order to be children of the heavenly Father (Mt. 5:44) and was implied in a number of passages in the Synoptics and Paul which present love as the fulfillment of the religious attitude (e.g., Lk. 10:25–37, Mk. 12:28–34, Rom. 13:8–10, Gal. 5:14–15, I Cor. 13).

[48] This would seem to give a more Christian tinge to courtly love than De Rougemont was willing to admit.

[49] "Where the whole 'transcendental' depth of interpersonal human love is realized and represented, the neighbor himself must really be loved and must be the formal object of the love and its motive." Karl Rahner, "Ueber die Einheit von Nächsten—und Gottesliebe" in *Schriften zur Theologie*, VI (Einsiedeln, 1966), p. 285. "The Unity of Love of God and Love of Neighbor" in *The Theology Digest*, 15 (1967), 89.

man encounters in each one of them the living presence of the divine. Thus man's love for God's creatures *is* ontologically identical with his love for God. They are as lovable as the divine love itself which they manifest. This, I take it, is the meaning of the disconcerting statement in I Jn. 4:11–12: "If a man says, 'I love God,' while hating his brother, he is a liar. If he does not love the brother whom he has seen, it cannot be that he loves God whom he has not seen."

At the same time, if what the Christian loves in his fellow man is the divine ground of his being, Christian love must always surpass feeling. True love is never a sentimental matter. It contains a volitional moment by which the lover *gives* himself to the beloved. Feelings, however altruistic, remain self-enclosed. Their center is the self and their subject is less interested in letting the beloved be himself than in drawing him into its own circle. Feelings may be passionate, affective, or benevolent, but they do not primarily *intend* the other as other. Even the expressions of affective feelings remain self-centered: caresses expect a response, gifts tend to appropriate affection. "The very granting of affection remains the *possession* of the one who grants it."[50] As love grows deeper, the importance of *giving* goes up, while that of *feeling* declines. This is precisely what Christian love demands.

The Christian is asked to recognize in the very selfhood of the other a transcendent dimension which by its very nature lies beyond the reach of experience. To love God in man is to place the essence of the act of love beyond feeling. Of course, even in religious love a human subject cannot but *feel* its way to the other, but the feelings no longer determine the act of loving. As Martin Buber wrote: "Feelings are 'entertained': love comes to pass. Feelings dwell in man; but man dwells in his love."[51] Religious love may follow its course even where barriers of feeling separate man from his fellow man. It originates in and moves toward a reality which is not "given" in the empirical order.

[50] Libert Vander Kerken. S.J., *Loneliness and Love* (New York: Sheed & W. d, 1966), pp. 51, 65.
[51] *I and Thou*, p. 14.

Beyond the actual appearance of the other, it aims at the invisible core of his personality which is at once object of divine election and center of infinite possibilities. Thus religious man continues to love after he becomes aware of the imperfections of those who are his fellow men by choice or by necessity.

Similarly, religious love subsumes other forms of love under its own intentionality.

It is independent of the other qualities of love and is able to unite with them, to judge them, and to transform them. Love as *agape* is a creation of the Spiritual Presence which conquers the ambiguities of all other kinds of love.[52]

It may be less passionate but incites more sacrificial action.[53]

This expansive, giving love is far removed from the anemic feelings of benevolence and sympathy which Nietzsche passes off for Christian charity.[54] Whether the benevolence or sympathy which Nietzsche describes results from the weakling's denial of life or not,[55] it is not Christian love. The etymologies of "sym-

[52] Paul Tillich, *Systematic Theology*, Vol. III, p. 137.

[53] Libert Vander Kerken notes that it is mostly love for one's neighbor which enables man to practice heroic unselfishness and to lay down his life for others. *Op. cit.*, p. 94.

[54] In a well-known passage of *Zarathustra* the Christian is said to run to his neighbor only because he runs away from a self which he neither trusts nor loves. (*Thus Spoke Zarathustra*, tr. by Marianne Cowan, Chicago: Henry Regnery, 1957, pp. 65–66) Full living requires appropriation, suppression, exploitation. (*Beyond Good and Evil*, tr. by Helen Zimmern in *The Philosophy of Nietzsche*, New York: Random House, 1954, pp. 577–78) The religion of love originated out of the "resentment" of this aristocratic code of conduct by those too weak to follow it. (*Genealogy of Morals*, tr. by Horace B. Samuel in *The Philosophy of Nietzsche*, pp. 647–50)

[55] Max Scheler admitted this in *Das Ressentiment im Aufbau der Moralen* (1915), republished in *Vom Umsturz der Werte*, Bern, Francke, 1955, pp. 33–148. *Ressentiment*, tr. by William W. Holdheim (New York: The Free Press of Glencoe, 1961), esp. pp. 122ff. Later he qualified his admission by restricting it to the social exploitation of the feelings of sympathy and their equation with the roots of love. See *Wesen und Formen der Sympathie* (1922) (Frankfurt, 1948), p. 116–17. *The Nature of Sympathy*, tr. by Peter Heath (London: Routledge & Kegan Paul, 1954), pp. 99–100.

pathy" and "compassion" refer to reactive experiences, while love is primary and indeed provides the only acceptable basis for all passive sympathy experiences.[56] Love wells up out of fullness of life and of self-possession, not out of morbid sympathy for weakness. It loves the suffering neighbor not because of his weakness but *despite* it.

Christian love does not remain indifferent to the nature of social structures, nor can it remain inactive in the presence of injustices. At the same time a love directed primarily at the divine core of man cannot be defined in terms of empirical objectives, nor can it provide a rule of thumb for resolving social conflicts. Rather does it relativize those conflicts by placing every man beyond them in a realm of peace where enemies become brothers. The Christian is a hypocrite if he neglects to work toward the same brotherhood in the visible world. Yet he is not discouraged if his efforts remain unsuccessful, because he knows that the primary reality is interior.

Today Jesus is often presented as a social reformer but the facts conflict with such a view. What Scheler wrote about him may be unpopular among contemporary Christians, but it remains true:

> He accepts the emperor's rule, the social distinction between master and slave, and all those natural instincts which cause *hostility* between man in public and private life . . . The forces and laws which rule the evolution of life and the formation and development of political and social communities, even wars between nations, class struggle, and the passions they entail—all those are taken for granted by Jesus as permanent factors of existence.[57]

This detachment from the immediate situation does not relegate Christian love to otherworldly resignation. But it refuses to be confined to any or all empirical solutions. It is revolutionary in

[56] "The only thing that makes pity *bearable* is the love it betrays." *Wesen und Formen der Sympathie*, p. 167. *The nature of Sympathy*, p. 143. See also *Vom Umsturz der Werte*, pp. 97–98. *Ressentiment*, p. 116.
[57] *Vom Umsturz der Werte*, pp. 91–92. *Ressentiment*, p. 108.

that it is never satisfied, and utopian in that it never despairs. Christian love must forever remain an ideal, because even the most heroic achievements cannot adequately respond to a transcendent call. At the same time its unlimited trust in the fellow man is founded upon the real fact that the other is himself a creature of divine love.

Salvation resides not only in the individual, but also and primarily in the community. In all religions the community is a center of sacred life. Yet Christianity *identifies* man's attainment of the divine with his attachment to a community universally conceived and concretely symbolized in a Church. Christian love, as Royce expressed it, is "a love of the unity of its (mankind's) own life upon its own divine level, and a love of individuals in so far as they can be raised to communion with this spiritual community itself."[58] Every man is called to be a member of the sacred community and can partake in salvation only through his attachment to the community. Nor is the individual submerged in the totality, for the sacred group consists of an *articulated* totality which does not abolish the individual, but allows him to surpass himself in the community.

The communal aspect of religion and particularly of Christianity has impressed a number of philosophers and sociologists. It has even been argued that religion alone can expand the community into true universality: without a transcendent head which reaches all the members and allows each one to respond to all others, no universal community is possible.[59] But I wonder whether a transcendent principle ever creates a truly *universal* community. Religious groups, and Christianity is no exception, find it necessary to segregate those who have already responded

[58] Josiah Royce, *The Problem of Christianity* (Chicago: Henry Regnery, 1968), p. 357.
[59] John Macmurray, *Persons in Relation* (New York: Harper & Row, 1961), p. 163. Robert Johann, *The Pragmatic Meaning of God* (Milwaukee: Marquette University Press, 1966), pp. 42–62. An obvious objection of fact seems to militate against this position: a secular community can be universalized without the idea of God. Marxists, for instance, whose social ideas are undoubtedly universal, admit at most that the community needs a transcendent principle in the relative sense of an indefinitely open future.

to the divine calling. Thus the Church is born as a *particular* community, separate from others. How can this be reconciled with the idea of universal love? Some deny that it can at all. According to Feuerbach, Christian faith, dividing men into believers and unbelievers, destroys what Christian love builds up. Faith restricts Christian love to love for Christians. "The Christian must therefore love only Christians—others only as possible Christians; he must only love what faith hallows and blesses."[60] The history of religious persecutions amply proves that the accusation is not entirely trumped up. Is a rigidly organized community, set up *beside* other societies, ultimately compatible with the idea of universal Christian love? To symbolize the transcendent nature of the community of man, faith needs some social expression of its own which allows its believers to anticipate the universal kingdom. But as soon as this community becomes a closed society competing with others, the universality is lost.[61] The sacred in all its forms opposes and integrates: it can never *coexist*.

The same idea is equally essential to the understanding of universal love itself. All profound love is exclusive. Can love survive without preference?[62] The very universality of Christian love poses a threat to the spontaneity which is the trademark of genuine affection. Are Christians not diluting the experience of love by universalizing it? The answer is undoubtedly affirmative as long as the universal religious love is simply *juxtaposed* to other forms of love. The best one may hope for is an uneasy truce between two things which are obviously not fit to coexist.

[60] *Das Wesen des Christentums* in *Sämtliche Werke,* VI, ed. by W. Bolin and F. Jodl, p. 305. *The Essence of Christianity,* tr. by George Eliot, p. 254.
[61] In judging the early Christian communities which eventually gave rise to the Medieval Church we must keep in mind that their closedness was not so much the result of exclusiveness as of pressure from without.
[62] Undoubtedly Christians have over the years created structures of priorities which enable most of them to live quite comfortably with "universal love." Perhaps too comfortably, for one wonders what is left of the original idea when, on the sole basis of political loyalties, they exhort their armies in the name of God to exterminate as many as possible of their fellow men who happen to stand at the opposite side of a political fence.

Yet true religion is never an "additional" reality: it is the depth, the ultimate dimension *of what is there*. Christian love then neither competes with, nor replaces human love, but gives it a new depth and a further expansion. Charity is not love at all unless it consecrates every human affection.

If openness toward a human Thou belongs to the essence of being human, and if religion is the transcendent depth of *what is,* then love can be religious only when it is truly human. Faith may expand and enlarge human love, but can never replace it by a love of its own making.[63] The Christian identification of religion with love originates from the awareness that love is the heart of life and that, consequently, it must also be the center of all religious activity. Precisely the fact that the disposition to love is essential to the structure of the human mind makes me believe that love will more and more become a central feature of *every* religious attitude. Although it must remain unproven, my belief finds some confirmation in the trend which several faiths appear to follow. I think specifically of Buber, of Gandhi and a number of contemporary Hindu writers, of the mystical trends in Islam. Is it unwarranted to suspect, therefore, that in an indefinite future all religion will be: "You shall love the Lord, your God, with all your heart, and with all your soul, and with all your strength" (Deut. 6:5), "You shall love your neighbor as yourself" (Lev. 19:18), "For God is love" (I Jn. 4:9)?

[63] I am happy to have Rahner on my side for this important point. "Man does not first meet God where he thematically represents the concept of God as a reality 'next to' others. God is given as the subjective and the objective transcendental ground of experience in the original act prior to thematic consideration. He stands as the whence and whither of an act that is objectively aimed at the world and therefore is loving communication with a worldly Thou (or its refusal)." "The Unity of Love of God and Love of Neighbor," *Theology Digest,* 15, 92.

Chapter 12
The Mystical Vision

I have reserved the discussion of the mystical experience for the final chapter, because I consider it a salvational, i.e., total, experience more than a subspecies of religious knowledge. In adopting this view I avoid a number of problems which arise from a purely cognitive interpretation. Mystics often use metaphysical language for expressing their experiences, yet they use it in a most disconcerting way. To interpret their utterances as straightforward ontological propositions is to run into insurmountable difficulties. Most of those difficulties vanish if the emotive import of statements that may at first appear to have only cognitive purport be taken into consideration.

There are other advantages in considering mysticism an aspect of salvation. Not the least of them is that it returns the mystical experience to the mainstream of religious life. The term "mystical" is now usually restricted to exceptional and strictly private states of ecstasy. But it permeates the entire religious experience; indeed, it is that experience itself in its purest form. To be sure, the mass of religious people never reach the passive states of contemplation. But all of them have occasionally experienced the unique joys and sorrows of their faith. The communal feeling which fills the participants at the end of a Passover meal, the inexplicable joy of Christmas night or Easter morning, the silent peace of a private visit to a church—all these experiences are fully continuous with the passive forms of contemplation. The drive toward mystical union is the vital principle of all religious life. Without it religion withers away in sterile ritualism or arid moralism. This mystical power is at work in all true prayer. Whoever prays is on his way toward total union. Few ever reach the end of the journey, but that is no reason to sever the beginning from the end. Nor is this experience essentially private. As far as I can ascertain, never during the entire Patristic period in which the term "mystical" gained acceptance among Christians did it refer to a private, exceptional experience. When it came to mean "experience," it referred to the experience of the entire Christian community. Even today the Eastern Orthodox look upon the mystical state as a normal feature in the life of the spiritual community.

Neither was the subjective connotation which we so easily attach to the term "mystical" present in the beginning. For the Greeks the *mystikos* was someone initiated in the mystery cults. Early Christians gave the word a different, but not a more subjective, meaning. For Clement of Alexandria, a "mystical" interpretation of the Scriptures was one in which the text of the Old Testament yielded a new, hitherto hidden meaning, when read in the light of Christian redemption.[1] Hence "mystical" came to denote all that was sacred to the Christian, particularly the sacramental reality. As Christ is hidden in the Scripture, so is he hidden in the Eucharistic bread and wine.[2] Origen gave the Biblical meaning a slight but decisive twist by applying it to the direct, experimental way of knowing God through the Scripture.

[1] *Stromata* 5–6. Migne, P.G. 9, 64A.
[2] Louis Bouyier summarizes the early Christian development as follows: "For the Greek Fathers the word mystical was used to describe first of all the divine reality which Christ brought to us, which the Gospel has revealed, and which gives its profound and definitive meaning to all the Scriptures. Moreover, mystical is applied to all knowledge of divine things to which we accede through Christ, and then, by derivation, to those things themselves. Finally the word, evolving always in the same direction, comes to describe the spiritual reality of worship 'in spirit and truth,' as opposed to the vanity of an exterior religion which has not been quickened to new life by the coming of the savior." "Mysticism" in *Mystery and Mysticism* (New York: Philosophical Library, 1956), pp. 127–28.

The scriptural connection will disappear later but is still present in Pseudo-Dionysius, the author mainly responsible for the modern usage of the word.

1. NONRELIGIOUS MYSTICISM

Are all forms of mysticism genuinely religious? Many authors simplify the answer to this question by declaring authentic mysticism to be religious and declaring nonreligious states of ecstasy inauthentic. But I find it hard to justify such radical distinctions for experiences that have so much in common. Obviously a mind-expanding experience of nature differs considerably from John of the Cross's third night of the soul. But is the difference sufficient to warrant a disqualification of the former as mystical? Essential as distinctions are in these matters, it is hazardous to draw them too rigidly. A comparison of William James's description of his experiment with nitrous oxide to the religious mystical experience, strongly suggests that the two experiences are at least related.

> Looking back on my own experiences, they all converge toward a kind of insight to which I cannot help ascribing some metaphysical significance. The key note of it is invariably a reconciliation. It is as if the opposites of the world, whose contradictoriness and conflict make all our difficulties and troubles, were melted into unity. Not only do they, as contrasted species, belong to one and the same genus, but one of the species, the nobler and better one, is itself the genus and so soaks up and absorbs its opposite into itself.[3]

Despite their great resemblance to religious states Zaehner relegates such drug-induced experiences, along with the more permanent, pathological forms of mind expansion in which "the opposites are reconciled and the peace that passes all understanding

[3] *The Varieties of Religious Experience* (New York: Crowell-Collier, 1961), pp. 305–6.

rules supreme,"[4] to the scrapheap of inauthentic mysticism. However, I do not see how psychology or philosophy can deny those phenomena the name which we give to similar extraordinary states in the religious consciousness. Philosophy must base its analysis upon the actual experience, not upon its alleged origin. Thus to oppose mysticism as a supernatural gift of God to mysticism as a natural acquisition of man, is not very helpful for philosophical classification. Every experience to the extent that it is *experienced* is "natural." The philosopher and the psychologist, must be satisfied to understand and evaluate mystical phenomena as *phenomena,* that is, as they appear to consciousness, regardless of their origin. Both in natural mysticism and in religious mysticism we observe an expansion of the self toward a transcending reality, a feeling of presence to all reality and an overcoming of previously existing oppositions. In both, the mind is in direct contact with what Bergson called the creative impulse of life itself.[5]

Nevertheless, the difficulty of setting up adequate distinctions does not dispense the philosopher from defining his subject matter sufficiently to make it meaningful, particularly today when there is a tendency to call every heightened perception mystical. Thus someone may present an outstanding folk singer as a "mystic" without feeling in the least obliged to define the term.[6] Indeed, the term "mysticism" has become so overworked that one hesitates to write about it at all. This was clearly brought home to me when, after the introductory lecture of a course on the Mystical Experience, a disappointed undergraduate confided that he had not realized I would be talking about "religion." To avoid some of the vagueness without prematurely closing doors, I propose the following description which will have to be considerably

---

[4] Quoted by R. C. Zaehner, *Mysticism Sacred and Profane* (New York: Oxford University Press, 1967), p. 93 from *Adventures Into the Unconscious* (London: Christopher Johnson, 1954), p. 4.

[5] *The Two Sources of Morality and Religion,* tr. by R. Ashley Audra and Cloudesly Brereton (Garden City, N.Y.: Doubleday, 1956), p. 220.

[6] Cf. Steven Goldberg, "Bob Dylan and the Poetry of Salvation," in *Saturday Review* (May 30, 1970), pp. 43–44.

refined as we enter deeper into our subject. In all forms of mysticism the self expands beyond its ordinary boundaries and is passively united with a reality which transcends its normal state. The expanding experience is accompanied by one of "integration" in which all oppositions both within the self and between the self and its environment are harmoniously overcome. It must be noted that these characteristics are not uniformly realized in the various forms of mysticism. Whether the higher reality preserves some transcendence with respect to the finite self *during the mystical union* is of capital importance, for this, I believe, determines the religious or nonreligious character of the mystical experience. I shall refer to the latter by the conventional term *natural mysticism,* without, however, opposing the term to a "supernaturally" induced mysticism. What causes the mystical state plays no part in our considerations.

Today a great deal of discussion is devoted to the nature of drug-induced mysticism. Dubious as the alloy of psychedelic visions may be, the philosopher must not determine the quality of the state on the basis of what brought it on, but exclusively on its own nature. From information I could gather on the subject (today's students provide an overflowing source of practical experience), it would appear that chemical "trips" may lead to some sort of religious illuminations. The experimenters whom I consulted agreed that the nature of the drug-induced experiences largely depends on the disposition which the subject brings to it. If this is true, they do not belong exclusively to natural mysticism. However, such states do share with natural mysticism a sudden, noncontextual character which, except sometimes for the initial stage (the "awakening" or "conversion"), appears to be rare in the slow and painstaking development of religious mysticism. Apart from his general aptitude and disposition the subject seems to have no other than a purely physical control over the mind-expanding experiences of LSD and mescaline. Once the proper psychic environment has been created and the chemicals are absorbed in the bloodstream, the process develops automatically. Also, the quality of the experience itself appears generally closer to that of natural mysticism *unless* the subject is religiously motivated. However, the religious potential of chemically induced ecstasies does not imply that they are of the same quality as the highest religious experience. If we may judge the tree by its fruit, mysticism which depends exclusively on drugs appears to have little positive effect upon the creative, moral, and religious abilities of the person. Genuine religious mystics would call it illusionary as they did with some of their own visions, because of their overall negative effect. Ignatius of Loyola, who experienced both kinds, advised the initiates into spiritual life to judge the experience according to the effect it had on their progress on the road to perfection. To me at least it is obvious that what requires no spiritual effort on the part of the mystic, and after prolonged use causes a serious unbalance in the personality structure, cannot be of the same caliber as the supreme achievements of spiritual giants resulting in outbursts of genuine creativity. Nevertheless, drugs apparently have been used by authentic mystics to assist them in a concentration which they might have achieved independently. But in that case the chemical element does not determine the quality of the experience. This, I should think, applies also to those communal religious services in which the members of the group partake of hallucinogenic fruits as an essential part of the cult.

For our purpose the distinction between "natural" and religious mysticism is sufficient. Descriptions of natural mysticism may be found in James's *Varieties of Religious Experience,* Zaehner's *Mysticism,* and Starbuck's *The Psychology of Religion.* Characteristic is the mind's power to break through its usual limits and to become part of a larger totality. The self merges with its environment and communicates its selfhood to its surroundings or, perhaps more correctly, comes to participate in a new, common selfhood. The animistic appearance of all things and the loss of previously existing oppositions in an unprecedented unity are perhaps the most striking features of this experience. These features closely connect natural mysticism with the aesthetic experience. In the aesthetic attitude the self attains a similar although usually less intensively felt union with the object of its contemplation. The mind reaches a state of harmony with the world in which it is able to recognize itself in objects filled with subjectivity.

All forms of mysticism are related to the aesthetic experience but one form of natural mysticism seems to coincide altogether with a particular aesthetic contemplation. In his classic *Essai sur les fondements de la connaissance mystique,* E. Récéjac describes how the mind gradually slides into it from an ordinary aesthetic experience:

> If the mind penetrates deeply into the facts of aesthetics, it will find more and more, that those facts are based upon an ideal identity between the mind itself and things. At a certain point the harmony becomes so complete and the finality so close that it gives an actual emotion. The beautiful then becomes the sublime, brief apparition, by which the soul is caught up into the true mystical state, and touches the Absolute. It is scarcely possible to persist in this aesthetic perception without feeling lifted up by it above things and above ourselves, in an ontological vision which closely resembles the Absolute of the Mystics.[7]

Obviously, not all true artists experience mystical states, no more than all natural mysticism leads to artistic expression. On the contrary, the total merging of consciousness with its surrounding world does not seem to be conducive to artistic articulation. More resistance on the part of the object may well lead to more significant expression. Although such experiences belong undoubtedly to the aesthetic realm, I see no reason to withhold from them the predicate "mystical," because there is no adequate way of generically separating them from religious ecstasies.

Yet, natural mysticism is not limited to the outward expansion of the self, commonly reached via aesthetic feelings. Mysticism develops in two directions: outward and inward. Rudolf Otto calls one the mysticism of unifying vision, and the other the mysticism of introspection.[8] Both ways appear in the East as well

[7] Paris, 1897, p. 74. My attention was drawn to this passage by Evelyn Underhill, *Mysticism* (New York: E. P. Dutton, 1961), p. 21.

[8] *Mysticism East and West,* tr. by Bertha Bracey and Richenda Payne (New York: Macmillan, 1970), pp. 57–72.

as in the West. Although clearly distinct, they must not be separated too strictly. For the unifying vision requires an attitude of recollection while the method of introspection leads to a unifying self. Let us now briefly consider the second way—the intuition of the self. The mind has an ordinary cognition of itself through reflection upon its acts. Yet, as Jacques Maritain points out, the self knows its existence only indirectly and its essence not at all. It is aware only of its operations and its psychic states, not of subjectivity itself.

> Doubtless, the more my attention comes to bear upon the existential experience of my soul, the more shall I tend to neglect the diversity of objects and of operations the reflexive grasp of which is nevertheless the very condition for such an experience. Yet it remains true that as long as we go in the direction of nature, the experiential folding back of which I speak, however powerful it may be in certain "interior" souls, leaves the soul prisoner of mobility and multiplicity, of the fugitive luxuriance of phenomena and of operations which emerge in us from the darkness of the unconscious.[9]

By an ascetic self-concentration the mind can stop reflecting upon its operations, purify itself from all images, and come directly face to face with the being of its own selfhood. In doing so it attains at the same time an entirely new awareness of Being as such and even of its sources. The experience may lead to a genuine metaphysical reflection. It has not escaped the attention of philosophers. In a memorable passage Schelling describes the beginning of this journey into the self:

> This presentation of ourselves to ourselves is the most truly personal experience, upon which depends everything that we know of the suprasensual world. This presentation shows us for the first time what real existence is, while all other things only appear to be . . .

[9] Jacques Maritain, "The Natural Mystical Experience" in *Redeeming the Ti e*, tr. by Harry L. Binsse (London: Geoffrey Bles, The Centenary Pr ss, 1946), p. 239. Maritain's interpretation is based upon Ambroise Gardeil, *La structure de l'âme et l'expérience mystique* (Paris, 1927).

This intellectual presentation occurs when we cease to be our own object, when, withdrawing into ourselves, the perceiving image merges in the self-perceived.[10]

The awareness of the self's own being may be religious, although it need not be so.[11] What makes it religious rather than natural? Nothing more than nuances in the experience, but those nuances are basic for a correct understanding of the act. In both cases the mind reaches the innermost self and the absolute in *one* and the same act. Yet in the religious experience the attainment of the absolute through the self is accompanied by a negative movement which *simultaneously* opposes the absolute to the self. This movement is of a most complex nature. For the opposition occurs *within* the self—not outside it. The religious absolute, then, is still discovered *as a self,* not as a nonself; and the opposition is one between an absolute Self and an ordinary self. The inadequacy of ordinary language to cope with those distinctions has led to a great deal of confusion. For the mystic describes his experience exclusively in terms of the self, a term which others are bound to understand as referring to the finite self. Those semantic problems, added to the difficulties connected with understanding a distant culture, make it almost impossible for a Westerner to evaluate properly Eastern descriptions of introspective mystical experiences. The absence of the words by which we refer to a transcendent, personal God must not be interpreted to signify the absence of a religious attitude. Rather than for "religious" words we should search for signs of an internal opposition *within* the experience. If no negative withdrawing moment is detected in the movement from the finite self to the absolute, the experience may be considered as nonreligious. However, this will occur very rarely in those authors of East and West whom the tradition has come to consider as mystics. The same rule also applies to the more expansive kind of mysti-

[10] *Philosophical Letters on Dogmatism and Criticism.*
[11] For Maritain it is always natural, but mainly because he opposes the term "natural" to "supernatural"—a distinction which I reject in this context.

cism: the religious experience begins with the withdrawal.[12] What distinguishes natural mysticism, then, from religious, is the absence of a *complete* dialectical movement. Natural mysticism usually displays the *coincidentia oppositorum,* so characteristic of the highest religious experience. But it does not maintain or constitute oppositions—as the religious attitude invariably does—it merely dissolves the existing ones.[13]

Before entering upon the discussion of religious mysticism we must clearly bear in mind that varieties in this area do not result primarily from theological distinctions (on the nature of God) but from intrinsic differences in the experience itself.[14] All too often it is still believed that religious mysticism is all of one kind and consequently that the distinctive categories are purely theological. This thesis conflicts with the facts. That theological beliefs may play an important role is true; that they determine the quality and even the authenticity of religious mysticism is false. The basic lines are drawn according to the nature of the experience, not according to theological distinctions. This explains why they are not conceptually rigid. Frequently mystics cross them and move into new territory. The tripartite division into monist, henological, and unitive forms of mysticism which I have adopted here, seldom becomes an absolute demarcation line. In many aspects Sankara, Eckhart, and John of the Cross agree entirely. Nor is the purpose of those distinctions to exalt one form of mysticism as more "authentic" than the others. If our analysis reveals certain preferences, they must be attributed not to greater

[12] In this respect I entirely agree with Professor R. C. Zaehner, *Mysticism Sacred and Profane,* p. 99. However, I would not limit the mystical to the religious as he does.

[13] One peculiar case in which the integrational movement is not obvious while the negation is, is that of Samkhya mysticism, which we will discuss below.

[14] I would thus have to qualify Otto Karrer's thesis that "pantheism" and theism originate in the same basic religious experience. The "basic" one may be the same, but not the specific one. Cf. *Das Religiöse in der Menschheit und das Christentum* (Freiburg, 1934), pp. 143ff.

authenticity, but to a greater inner complexity which allows the mystic to reach a more harmonious relation with the world in which he lives and which requires his active involvement.

2. MONIST MYSTICISM

I have based the discussion of what Zaehner calls monist mysticism mainly upon Hindu mystics who seem to have realized it in its purest form. However, nothing would be more misleading than to categorize Indian mysticism *as such* as monistic. The Hindu faith is not a tight system: it is a religious world of infinite variety.

In spite of its rather crude polytheism the *Rig-Veda* (1500–1000 B.C.) seems to contain the seeds of later monism. The famous creation hymn emphasizes that all beings derive from "the one thing." "That One breathed, windless, by its own energy: nought else existed then."[15] Everything appears to be returning to this divine, all-comprehensive unity. Yet while in the *Veda* the One is still conceived in material terms, it becomes spiritualized in the *Upanishads* (800–500 B.C.). Old religious terms as "Brahman" and "Maya" here receive entirely new meanings. Along with the spiritualization process grows the desire to be liberated from the world of appearances which separates the human spirit from its true reality. The central idea is expressed in the well-known words of the first *Upanishad,* the *Chandogya,* "tat tvam asi," "that thou art." In the self the mind discovers the Absolute—*atman is Brahman.* A mythical father, Uddalaka, exposes this sacred doctrine to his son, Svetaketu:

> As bees, dear boy, make honey by collecting the juices of many trees and reduce the juice to a unity, yet [those juices] cannot perceive any distinction there [so that any of them might know:] "I am the juice of this tree," or "I am the juice of that tree," [so

[15] *Hindu Scriptures,* sel. and tr. by R. C. Zaehner (New York: E. P. Dutton, 1966), p. 12.

too], my dearest boy, all these creatures, once they have merged in o Being do not know that they have merged into Being . . . This finest essence,—the whole universe has it as its Self: that is the Real: That is the Self: That *you* are, Svetaketu.[16]

Later mystics in the monist tradition will invoke this text to support their position. The words reveal the ambiguity of all monist mysticism. Do they imply a full identity of the finite self and the ultimate principle? I do not believe so, for *atman* may mean *selfhood as such,* referring to a deeper, hidden, universal Self rather than to the individual self. The personal self, then, would be only the occasion for meeting in its own depth the universal self, that is, *Atman.*[17] In a religious interpretation the self may be considered divine only as long as the divine is not restricted to the individual self. When Sankara, the eighth-century radical monist, declares *Atman* alone to be real, he refers to a deeper universal self, not to the principle of individuality. Religiously such a proposition is fully convertible: the only true reality is *Atman*. But that *atman* (the individual self) is divine, is not convertible.

How transcendence and immanence of Brahman alternate is clearly visible in another *Upanishad, Svetasvatara.* The following assertion of God's transcendence precedes the identification of mind, matter, maya with Brahman, "the one reality."

What is here conjoined together, perishable and imperishable, manifest and unmanifest, all this doth the Lord sustain; but for lack of mastery the self is bound, its [very] nature to enjoy experience. But once it knows [its] God from all its fetters is it freed.[18]

Similarly the affirmation that the self which is in everything "like butter in cream" is Brahman (1, 16), is preceded by the state-

---

16 *Chandogya,* 6, 9. *Op. cit.,* p. 109.
17 See John A. Hutchinson, *Paths of Faith* (New York: McGraw-Hill, 1968), p. 76.
18 *Svetasvatara* 1, 8, in *Hindu Scriptures,* p. 204.

ment that the Self is *within* the self (1, 15)—it is not simply the self. Brahman is *within* all persons as the Inner Self facing in all directions (2, 16). He is the Being of all beings who has assumed "the forms of all creatures, remaining hidden in them" (3, 7). Although he fills the universe, he does not share its form and limitations (3, 10). The third personal pronoun is used constantly, not to present God as a person, but as the root of being-a-person. Prabhavananda interprets *Svetasvatara* 3, 1: "The one absolute, *impersonal Existence,* together with his inscrutable Maya, appears as the divine Lord, *the personal God,* endowed with many glories."[19]

Of course, if the finite is nonbeing in the absolute sense, and if *maya* is understood as sheer illusion (as Sankara understands it), then the finite has no true reality status left. Whether such a monism can still be religious will be considered later. But in the meantime we must be aware of the other meaning which *maya* has in the *Upanishads.* Zaehner translates *Svetasvatara* 4, 9, 10:

All this does he who is possessed of creative power (*maya*) emit from that [same syllable]; and by the same creative power (*maya*) the other is there in constrained. Creative power (*maya*) is Nature, this must be known, and He who possesses it (*mayin*) is the Mighty Lord.[20]

Even the term *a-sat* (nonbeing) as applied to the world in *Brihadaranyaka* 1, 3, 28 ("From the unreal lead me to the real") is not absolutely negative, but negative only *in relation to* the absolute.[21]

In one *Upanishad,* however, the short *Mandukya,* the distinction between Brahman and all true reality seems to be abolished. Zaehner interprets it as a rigid monism that leaves nothing but the One which is a perfect and absolute blank: "Brahman is no

[19] Italics mine. A less interpretive translation reads: "He is the One who, spreading wide his net, rules with his sovereign powers." R. C. Zaehner, *Hindu Scriptures,* p. 207.
[20] *Hindu Scriptures,* p. 211.
[21] For a similar interpretation, cf. Sidney Spencer, *Mysticism in World Religion* (Baltimore: Penguin Books, 1963), p. 24.

longer the identical substrate of all things since that would contradict the monist position, nor *is* it all things, for there cannot be plurality in the One; for the One is just itself and all else is pure illusion."[22] The liberation process consists in eliminating all opposition, even the minimum necessary for consciousness. Not in waking or in sleeping can the mind find its true Self, but only in a state beyond sleep. Prabhavananda translates the *Mandukya* description of this state in modern terms:

> [It] is not subjective experience, nor objective experience, nor experience intermediate between these two, nor is it a negative condition which is neither consciousness nor unconsciousness. It is not the knowledge of the senses, nor is it relative knowledge, nor yet inferential knowledge. Beyond the senses, beyond the understanding, beyond all expression . . . it is pure unitary consciousness wherein awareness of the world and of multiplicity is completely obliterated. It is ineffable peace. It is the supreme Good. It is One without a second. It is the Self. Know it alone.[23]

It is not clear what an experience beyond the dreamless sleep, with neither subjective nor objective knowledge, should mean. The *Mandukya* seems to advocate a state of absolute unconsciousness as the only way to liberate the self from the illusion of the oppositions which the One has created within itself.

Yet usually the suppression of consciousness in favor of a totally unified reality is restricted to the *individual* consciousness. Even extreme monists as Sankara continue to distinguish three aspects in the One, namely being, awareness and bliss (*sac-cid-ananda*). Furthermore the very training of the mind which is required to reach this state of absolute repose indicates that we are dealing with a conscious process, the outcome of which ought to be a state of consciousness.

I therefore feel that enough opposition remains between the finite self and the true Self to consider even such extreme monism religious. For to negate the reality of the finite is not the same as

22 *Mysticism*, p. 164.
23 *The Upanishads*, p. 51.

to declare everything divine. To deny the reality of what appears is, on the contrary, to say that it has no place in the true reality. But in some way it must exist as appearance or illusion. If this be heresy, the name for it is not pantheism but substantialism. For what is missing is certainly not a negation of the finite. This negation opposes it to the infinite. Even if the infinite, then, is declared to be the only true reality, it remains transcendent. The concept of the absolutely One may not be adequate, but one cannot dismiss it as nonreligious. For as long as a dialectical negation takes place, mysticism retains a transcendent terminus. The process of religious negation is a very complex one and few mystics have been able to express it adequately. Christian mystics like Eckhart and Angelus Silesius also struggle with the problem.[24] Even John of the Cross uses language that could be interpreted in a monist sense. Much depends upon speculative clarifications of the concept of God which, as I have shown earlier, are the outcome of a long and gradual process. Perfection in expressing the divine is largely a matter of degree, since no concept is entirely adequate. Our judgment should rather be based upon the living experience which reveals itself through the inadequate concepts. By these standards most monist mysticism must be regarded as clearly religious. For it describes the movement of the mind toward a transcendent terminus, in such a way that the transcendent *remains* opposed to the finite.[25]

However, the basic options are not a matter of expression or even of philosophical speculation but of different religious attitudes. In the *Bhagavad-Gita,* for instance, God is referred to in personal terms. Yet it would be mistaken to interpret this as a speculative distinction. Aside from literary grounds (in an epic the poet has little choice but to present his hero as a person), the difference has a practical-religious origin. It is easier to concen-

[24] Zaehner, *Mysticism,* p. 205.
[25] I therefore cannot accept Zaehner's thesis that "monist" mysticism is a bridge between "theistic" mysticism (which alone he considers fully religious) and nature mysticism. The distinction between monist and theistic mysticism is by no means as basic as the one between religious and nonreligious mysticism. *Op. cit.,* pp. 140–41.

trate on God's manifestation, God as principle of the soul (*purusha*) and of nature (*prakrit*), than on God's own essence, the One. The author of the *Gita* left the speculative problems of the relation between the One and its manifestations to posterity to solve. In one respect God is identical with his manifestations, in another respect he transcends them.[26] In sum, there appears to be little ground for assuming that the speculative position differs much from the monism of the Vedanta. A passage like the following (one out of many) hardly gives the impression of being based upon a *theory* of a personal God.

> I am the taste in the waters, O son of Kunti. I am the light in the moon and the sun; I am the sacred syllable (*Om*) in all the Bedas, the sound in ether and the manhood in men. I am the pure fragrance in earth and the brilliance in fire; I am the life in all beings and the austerity in ascetics.[27]

Even Ramanuja's speculative opposition to Sankara's extreme monism, had a religious rather than a philosophical origin. For Ramanuja the highest religious union cannot be obtained when

[26] An English translator comments: "The Divine Reality is a state of oneness, It is a transcendent creative power, and It is the essential ground, the indwelling spirit of all that is." Eliot Deutsch, Introduction in *The Bhagavad-Gita*, tr. by Eliot Deutsch (New York: Holt, Rinehart & Winston, 1968), p. 174.

[27] *The Bhagavad-Gita*, 6, 8–9, tr. by Eliot Deutsch, p. 73. Obviously my short remarks make no pretense of solving the complicated problem of the personal God in the *Bhagavad-Gita*. All I maintain is that whatever is personal in the concept of God has a religious, not a speculative, origin. This thesis was confirmed by the more expert opinion of Patrick Olivelle in an article, "The Concept of God in *Bhagavad-Gita*," *International Philosophical Quarterly*, 4 (1964), pp. 514–40, where we read: ". . . the *Gita* has two streams of thought, one philosophical and borrowed for the greater part from the Upanishads, and the other religious, which is more original. Philosophically it asserts the undifferentiated absolute Brahman, but this does not serve in the least for its religious aspirations. Thus it may be that the *Gita* in its religious trend conceives of the Brahman as the state of perfect equilibrium which it more or less identifies with the Upanishadic Brahman, and offers it as the state to which men should aspire. Yet this state can be reached by devotion to the Personal God, thus placing this Brahman below God, and God Himself as its abode." (P. 519)

God is conceived as the attributeless substance of all things (*nirguna Brahman*) but only when he is worshiped and loved as a person with attributes (*saguna Brahman*). To assume an immediate identity with the Absolute prevents any real *relation to* God. One cannot pray to one's Self. This and not philosophy is the main reason why God is more personal and the world more real for him than for Sankara.

Most of the characteristics and problems of monist mysticism also appear in Buddhism. The practices of ascetism and mental concentration in the *Hinayana* branches are comparable to those of Hinduism during the classical period. They are distinct perhaps because of the emphasis on emotional peace and because of a radically antimetaphysical attitude which rejects personal consciousness as a pure illusion. At the same time Buddhist mystics of the *Mahayana* branches display a more dynamic attitude than Vedanta mystics. Buddhists distinguish eight different stages (*Dhyanas*) in the exercises by which the ultimate state of peace is to be achieved. On the lower level, they range from mere concentration of the senses to simple vision of the intellect and total equanimity of emotions. The higher states include perceptive void (unlimited space), emptiness of consciousness, total absence of feelings and emotions.[28] If the practices are successful, the individual self will be temporarily eliminated. But salvation will not come until the subject enters the state of *Nirvana* in which individual consciousness permanently disappears.

The method of concentration, which was only one among several practices in the Old Wisdom of Hinayana Buddhism, would become predominant in the Yogacara school (founded A.D. 400). In this school the absolute is explicitly described in terms of a state of *consciousness*. Salvation consists in the lasting awareness of the pure, totally deobjectivated self.

By ruthless withdrawal from each and every object, in the introversion of trance, one could hope to move towards such a result. In

[28] Cf. Edward Conze, *Buddhism: Its Essence and Development* (New York: Harper & Brothers, 1959), pp. 99–101.

any condition in which my personality might normally find itself, the subject is always associated with some object. If, on the other hand, there is, in the absence of an object standing up against the subject, no such admixture of any relation to an object, then I could be said to have realized my *inmost self* in its purity. Salvation could then be said to consist in a revulsion from all objective and external accretions to that inmost self itself, which is realized when it can stand alone, without an object or the thought of one.[29]

Yoga exercises go back in origin to Hindu practices which had received a metaphysical foundation in the *Samkhya School.* Unlike most contemporary Hindu philosophy, the *Samkhya* adopted a dualistic vision of reality which conceived the soul (*purusha*) in a strictly individual way and opposed it to nature (*prakriti*). The purpose of the exercises is to liberate the individual self from its contamination with nature. Obviously Yoga is a different thing to different people. While for *Samkhya-Yoga* it was a means for achieving the isolation of the self, monist schools of Hinduism and Buddhism used it to eliminate the individual self. There are other differences: the metaphysical *Samkhya* is atheist (*an-is-vara*), while the practically oriented *Yoga-Sutra* is theist (*as-isvara-yoga*).

Yet in all cases does the Yogin pursue an *empty self,* whether it be personal or impersonal. How emptiness can be a state of salvation is difficult to understand for the outsider. It has been pointed out that the Buddhist *sunyata* (state of selflessness) is more than the absence of what is not present, or the extinction of what was present. For absence and extinction are still relative, while the *sunyata* is an absolute. D. T. Suzuki describes it in the following way:

It is Absolute Emptiness transcending all forms of mutual relationship, of subject and object, birth and death, God and the world, something and nothing, yes and no, affirmation and negation. In Buddhist Emptiness there is no time, no space, no becoming, no-

[29] Edward Conze, *Buddhism,* pp. 166–67.

thing-ness; it is what makes all these things possible; it is a zero full of infinite possibilities, it is a void of inexhaustible contents. Pure experience is the mind seeing itself as reflected in itself, it is an act of self-identification, a state of suchness. This is possible only when the mind is sunyata itself . . .[30]

This description might have been written by a mystic of the Neo-Platonic tradition. Clearly, the empty self is highly positive, indeed so positive that it transcends all known reality. The truth revealed in this negative theology is not scientific or philosophical but exclusively religious. Buddhists, particularly those of the old schools, fully realize that to the supreme mystical truth ordinary categories of knowledge do not apply. Yet they consider this transcendent truth to be the ultimate one which in the end will destroy all others. Thus they declare false even their own sacred doctrines, including the four basic truths which the Buddha preached in Benares.[31] The self here is the absolute envisioned as, and approached through, selfhood. It is as far above the finite self as God in traditional theism is conceived to be above the word. Yet while one religious idea has been developed by means of objective, speculative concepts, the other has grown directly out of the subjective-mystical experience. The problems remain basically the same. The traditional theist must justify the objectivation of the absolute, the Buddhist its subjectivity. Buddhists have attempted to acquit themselves of this task by various theories, some of which are emanationist and some psychological.[32] Yet, we must not forget that in an essentially mystical system the

[30] D. T. Suzuki, *On Indian Mahayana Buddhism* (New York: Harper & Row, 1968), p. 270.

[31] Cf. E. Conze, *Buddhism*, p. 133. D. T. Suzuki, *On Indian Mahayana Buddhism,* p. 231.

[32] Thus, they claim, the absolute self creates a relative self in order to see itself reflected in it; the process of reflection is completed when the finite self returns to the absolute. The *Abbidharma* takes a different approach. Here the individual self is dismissed as a psychological illusion, resulting from the mind's inclination to give a substantial substratum to various acts of perception, feeling, desire, etc. This extreme empiricism (not even surpassed by Hume) will satisfy few speculative minds, and even less justify the acceptance of a transcendent self.

ultimate justification must come from the experience itself. The entire position of the mystic is precisely that speculation by itself does not lead to the absolute. Westerners should not judge the value of Eastern mysticism by its theology of "God," but by its unsurpassed achievements in the spiritual life. These are its truth on the basis of which it wants to be evaluated. Most Buddhists and a number of Hindu mystics take little interest in speculations on the nature of God. We must not forget this when trying to determine the quality of their mysticism.

To be sure, the problem of God can never be dismissed from the discussion. It poses particularly thorny questions in the case of a professed atheism (as in the *Samkhya School* and in some forms of Buddhism). Still the determining factor is not whether the *concept* of God is present, but whether the mind in transcending itself establishes a relation to what surpasses it altogether. The Buddhist may be profoundly religious without worrying about the existence or nonexistence of a personal God, Creator, Providence, and most of the questions that form the content of the Christian faith. His faith is easily compatible, and has frequently been connected, with polytheism. Indeed, it is more sympathetic to polytheism or even to what the theist would call atheism, than to monotheism. But it is and remains religious because of the unique way in which the mind transcends itself.

Most disturbing to Westerners in the spiritual writings of the East is the subjective terminology. As a rule we do not consider the term *self* appropriate to denote the religious Absolute. But the Eastern mystic might answer that the term "Self" (*Atman*) is most appropriate to refer to the final stage of a process of introspection. What matters religiously is not which approach we take to the absolute, but whether the absolute is clearly differentiated from ordinary reality. Most monist mystics unambiguously assert this distinction.

The question remains whether the absolute Self can ever be confined to the individual, as is the case in *Samkhya-Yoga.* If the individual self were merely *opposed* to nature and to other selves, it could not be a religious absolute, for that must ultimately *integrate* the real. Opposition never terminates the religious dialectic. An isolated self can therefore not be called divine. Yet is isolation the last word in *Samkhya?* Not according to Mircea Eliade, who insists that the reality of nature is a relative one, destined to disappear after the self turns into itself.

> For Samkhya and Yoga, the world is *real* (not illusory—as it is, for example, for Vedanta). Nevertheless, if the world *exists* and *endures,* it is because of the "ignorance" of spirit; the innumerable forms of the cosmos, as well as their processes of manifestation and development, exist only in the measure to which the Self (*purusa*) is ignorant of itself and, by reason of this metaphysical ignorance, suffers and is enslaved. At the precise moment when the last Self shall have found its freedom, the creation in its totality will be reabsorbed into the primordial substance.[33]

According to this reading the Self integrates, as in all monist mysticism, by reducing the different aspects of reality to a single one, "the undifferentiated completeness of precreation, the primordial unity."[34] This leaves a number of metaphysical questions unanswered. But metaphysics in our sense is the last thing the Yogin is concerned with. What is most important from a religious point of view is whether he brings the religious dialectic to its conclusion.[35]

The relation between God's immanence and his transcendence is not only a problem for Eastern mystics. To every mystic the Absolute is the only *true* reality. Even when the term *true* is not taken in an ontologically exclusive sense, some negation of the finite follows. Thus the world is declared either illusory or unimportant, and the difficult question arises how the finite may be reasserted. Yet without a true *opposition* between the finite and

[33] *Yoga: Immortality and Freedom,* tr. by Willard R. Trask (New York: Pantheon Books, 1958), p. 9.
[34] Eliade, *Yoga,* p. 98.
[35] Without being religious Yoga may still be a method by which the mind overcomes its natural boundaries and reaches a new harmony with the world. Mysticism requires self-transcendence but not necessarily the total integration that comes with a religious attitude.

the infinite, the religious attitude cannot maintain itself. That is why even an extreme monist like Sankara somehow distinguishes the absolute from the universe, albeit at the price of speculative consistency.

The basic affirmation of the monist mystic is profoundly religious: the Absolute is transcendent. But this transcendence is so exclusively asserted that in the process the finite, the dialectical counterpart which alone made the Absolute transcendent, almost disappears. I say "almost" because the finite is preserved at least as an illusion—but an illusion which is constantly on the mystic's mind. Now an affirmation of divine transcendence always opposes God's simplicity to the world of multiplicity. For the monist the One Absolute is so exclusively real that it leaves no room for multiplicity in the realm of the real. If monism were entirely consistent, it would cease to be religious, for God would then become the universal, abstract unity of all that is.[36] It also would exclude self-consciousness. To the extent that it is conscious, it is imperfect. The objection was raised by Indra himself at the end of the *Chandogya Upanishad*. After the god has learned about the saint who attains the supreme state of *Moksha* from Prajapati he objects:

> Such a man has no present knowledge of himself (atman) [so that he could say] "This I am," nor for that matter [has he knowledge of] things around him. He becomes as one annihilated. I see nothing enjoyable in that.[37]

Prajapati's reply is somewhat short on logical consistency: the liberation from the bodily self will give the self the entire world and the fulfillment of all its desires.

Total liberation may be a mere ideal or a *Grenzbegriff* (a limit-concept). But that does not eliminate the difficulty. For the more it approaches the supreme beatitude the less the mind retains the states of consciousness which it values most highly.

[36] See G. W. F. Hegel, *Philosophie der Religion,* IV, p. 57. Comments in Albert Chapelle, *Hegel et la religion,* II, pp. 64–65.
[37] *Chandogya* 8.11. Zaehner translation.

Conspicuously lacking is a relation from mind to mind and from heart to heart. Only an extreme dissatisfaction with the mind *as it is* could induce a man to consider beatific a state which dispenses with what normally man considers his most satisfactory experience: the loving dialogue with the other. Many will refuse to follow this path toward salvation, particularly in our culture which so highly esteems what is here rejected. One of them was Martin Buber:

> These are the loftiest peaks of the language of It. The sublime strength of their disregard must be respected, and in the very glance of respect recognized as what is, at most, to be experienced, but not to be lived . . . Nor does he (the Buddha) lead the united being further to that supreme saying of the *Thou* that is made possible for it. His innermost decision seems to rest on the extinction of the ability of say *Thou*.[38]

One must not give undue weight to the extreme expressions of the Vedanta. No mystic is ever a consistent monist. "Monist mysticism" is a trend more than a reality. Yet the difficulties inherent in the ideal which inspired this trend must be pointed out in a philosophical critique. This critique may help us to understand why many have preferred not to continue on this road to the Absolute, even among the disciples of monist teachers (such as the eleventh-century Hindu sage Ramanuja, raised in the Sankara tradition). The qualified monist position which we shall discuss next is inspired by the same relentless drive toward an absolute that is one and transcends all determinations. Yet at the same time it admits multiplicity as fully and permanently real.

3. NEGATIVE THEOLOGY

The basic principles of negative theology have been so widely adopted by mystics in the West that the term has become almost

---

[38] *I and Thou* (2d ed.), tr. by Ronald G. Smith (New York: Charles Scribner's Sons, 1958), pp. 90, 92.

convertible with mystical theology. Like the monist mystic the negative theologian negates any common bond between God and the finite. Yet instead of denying the reality of the finite, he denies of God all predicates that can be attributed to finite beings. No positive name can be given to the ultimate, undivided principle.

In accordance with our usual procedure we shall concentrate primarily on the Christian tradition. Yet negative theology appears just as much in other religions, particularly Islam. In the West the henological type of mysticism[39] goes back to Plotinus. Like the Oriental mystics by whom he may have been influenced, Plotinus situates the Absolute beyond the multiplicity of all ideas. The knowledge of it is by nature ecstatic and can be attained only in the unity which the mind possesses in itself before moving outward into determinations. God is present in that innermost part of the soul where it proceeds from the One and is one itself.

Awareness of the One comes to us neither by knowing nor by the pure thought which discovers the other intelligible things, but by a presence transcending knowledge. When the soul knows something, it loses its unity; it cannot remain sinply one because knowledge implies discursive reason and discursive reason implies multiplicity . . . Having freed itself from all externals, the soul must turn totally inward; not allowing itself to be wrested back towards the outer, it must forget everything, the subjective first and, finally, the objective. It must not even know that it is itself that is applying itself to contemplation of the One.[40]

Unity must not be understood as a positive attribute of God. It expresses no objective determination, but is a sign of the Absolute or, more correctly, a sign of the mind's relation to the

---

[39] Etymologically the term *henological* does not basically differ from *monist* but its actual usage is restricted to a Neoplatonic, negative theology. Since we are speaking of a *type* of mysticism rather than a particular current of thought, the term henological seems preferable to Neoplatonic.
[40] *Enneads*, VI, 9 (4, 7), tr. by Elmer O'Brien in *The Essential Plotinus* (New York, 1964).

Absolute. The term "One" does not in any way bring us closer to knowing *what* God is.[41] In itself unity is still a determination of quantity, and thus belongs to the intelligible order. But this order is immediately negated, for the absolute "One" admits no other points of comparison and thereby ceases to be quantitative. Still the affirmation of the One is more than a thought-destroying process, for it posits the Absolute as ultimate end of all affirmations and expresses the mind's need to move beyond the multiplicity of the intelligible order. This ecstatic nature distinguishes Plotinus' mysticism clearly from the impassibility which characterizes most Hindu and Buddhist mysticism. Rudolf Otto calls Plotinus a "hot" mystic because of the strong emotional and "erotic" drive in his experience, while Sankara is essentially a "cool" mystic. The distinction applies, with some qualifications, to all the mystics discussed in this section.[42] Only in transcending itself does the mind discover its own essence. According to Karl Jaspers such mysticism expresses the most fundamental drive of the mind.

> The strength of unity brings me from distraction to myself. I want to be one with myself. The binding forces of my life grow in the same measure as my links with the source of unity. Unity for me is the one Transcendence as well as myself.[43]

The henological negation of all determinations in God is total. It includes Being and even the common ground between God and the intelligible order which would result from *producing* being. The Absolute allows the relative to posit itself as a being. "To create for the One is to make autoposition possible and participation impossible."[44] The One, then, is the source of all beings without sharing any determination with them. "From God

---

[41] *Enneads,* V, 3, 14.
[42] Rudolf Otto, *Mysticism in East and West,* pp. 169, 181.
[43] *Philosophical Truth and Revelation,* p. 137.
[44] Henry Duméry, *Le problème de Dieu,* p. 98.

to the intelligible there is no transmission of essences but only a derivation of energy."[45] Negative theology appeals to the mystic, because it has its roots in a heightened awareness of divine transcendence. It is not merely negative, for it strongly asserts that God is so totally and exclusively *himself* that his reality can be adequately expressed only by himself.

Still, negative theology would have little appeal to the mystic if it could not express the presence of God. Philosophers commonly assume that a heavy emphasis upon transcendence *eo ipso* excludes immanence.[46] But it is precisely the strong awareness of the immanence of the divine light which drives the mystic beyond all categories of intelligibility into the dark of total incomprehension. The more God is experienced the more the soul goes beyond itself. The intensity of the awareness leads to the ultimacy of negation. Even in Plotinus the most distinctive feature of the One is its *immanence* in the many. It is precisely the emphasis on God's immanent presence which made Plotinus' philosophy so attractive to mystical theology. By an inward movement of mental concentration and asceticism the mystic attempts to make his entire consciousness coincide with the One of which he experiences the active presence. The union, if ever reached, consists in an awareness of total identity, far beyond what the term "vision" conveys. Plotinus finds no adequate words to communicate the experience.

> It is so very difficult to describe this vision, for how can we represent as different from us what seemed, while we were contemplating it, not other than ourselves but perfect atoneness with us? . . . The vision, in any case, did not imply duality; the man who saw was identical with what he saw. Hence he did not "see" it but rather was "oned" with it.[47]

45 Henry Duméry, *op. cit.,* p. 105.
46 Thus Léon Brunschvicg questions whether Augustine's divine illumination theory can be reconciled with his notion of total transcendence. Léon Brunschvicg, *La vraie et la fausse conversion* (Paris, 1951), p. 128.
47 *Enneads,* VI, 9, 10–11. Tr. by Elmer O'Brien in *The Essential Plotinus.*

Plotinus' mystical theology reached Christianity mainly through Pseudo-Dionysius.[48] Dionysius' influence on Christian mysticism was enormous. His *Divine Names* and *Symbolic Theology* leave no doubt that he also accepted a positive theology in a preparatory function. Yet mystical theology proper repudiates all names of God. The *Mystical Theology* shows how God is hidden behind anything the mind can conceive, including Being, in a total dark of consciousness.

> In the earnest exercise of mystical contemplation abandon all sensation and all intellection and all objects or sensed or seen and all being and all nonbeing and in unknowing, as much as may be, be one with the beyond being and knowing.[49]

God is even beyond divinity and beyond contradiction.[50] To reach God the mind likewise must attain a state "beyond illuminations and voices and words from heaven" and enter the "dark of unknowing" to meet "the transcendent Dark." "Into this Dark beyond all light, we pray to come and, unseeing and unknowing to see and to know Him that is beyond seeing and beyond knowing precisely by not seeing, by not knowing."[51] God, then, dwells in total "unknowing and unbeing."

Dionysius was not the first spiritual writer to use strong negations: we find them in Gregory of Nyssa's *Commentary on the Song of Songs* as well as in the desert father Evagrius.[52] But no one negated more persistently and more influentially. Dionysius became the leading theologian of the Eastern Churches. Yet his

[48] Whether he was a mystic himself is a disputed question. See Jan Vanneste, S.J., *Le mystère de Dieu: Essai sur la structure rationelle de la doctrine mystique du Pseudo-Denys l'Aréopagite* (Paris, 1959).

[49] *The Mystical Theology*, Migne, P.G. 3, 997. Tr. by Elmer O'Brien in *Varieties of Mystical Experience* (New York: Holt, Rinehart & Winston, 1964), p. 79.

[50] *Ibidem*, Migne, P.G. 3, 1048.

[51] P.G. 3, 1025, *Varieties of Mystical Experience*, p. 84.

[52] We assume that Pseudo-Dionysius lived after the fifth century. But this is not certain.

impact reached far beyond the Greek-Christian world. All Rhine-
land mysticism was basically Dionysian. So was the mysticism of
the Low Countries and England. He even left his impact on
mystical writers of a different tradition, such as John of the Cross
and Teresa of Ávila.

The most impressive Dionysian theologian is the late thirteenth-
century Dominican Johannes Eckhart, who strangely combines
Dionysian thought with Thomist philosophy. Due to a terminology
mainly taken from a philosophy of Being, his mystical theology
has provoked constant controversy up to our own time. It now
appears well enough established, however, that Eckhart gave his
Thomist terms entirely novel meanings.[53] In the *Opus Tripartitum* he simply declares, Being is God ("Esse est Deus . . .
Deus igitur et Esse idem.").[54] This thesis seems to place Eckhart
immediately outside the Dionysian tradition. But Being for him
is not the highest intelligible: it is an unnamable mystical reality
which refers simultaneously to God and to the secret ground of
the creature.[55] This *esse absconditum* is not the Thomist *actus
existendi* but the act by which God is immanent in himself and
in his creature. Eckhart's Being is beyond the One of Plotinus,
for the One is only the cognitive aspect of the divine Being, its
first manifestation before proceeding internally into divine persons and externally into the creation.[56] God's Being is the unnamable *I am who I am* of Exodus 3:14, a "reality" which
refuses to be named in any category of intelligibility. Thus Eckhart denies being from God when being refers to the individual
existence of the creature. "God is something that must transcend
being. Anything which has being, date or location does not belong

---

[53] See Vladimir Lossky's masterly study *Théologie négative et connaissance
de Dieu chez Maître Eckhart, Études de philosophie médiévale*, 48 (Paris,
1960), p. 27.
[54] *Opus Tripartitum.*
[55] Lossky, p. 37.
[56] This interpretation clearly differs from Plotinus' according to which
the One is not knowable. Cf. B. Spaapen, "Bij de zevende eeuwfeestviering
van Eckharts geboorte" in *Ons Geestelijk Erf*, 36 (1962), p. 255.

to God, for he is above them all."[57] Again in the same sermon: "Great authorities say that God is pure being but he is as high above being as the highest angel is above a fly and I say that it would be as incorrect for me to call God a being as it would be to call the sun pale or dark."[58] At the same time he claims that a stone which has Being would be better than the Godhead without Being if this could be imagined.[59] But for Eckhart *Being* is a religious more than a metaphysical notion. It is primarily an expression of value referring to that which brings salvation from the instability of *becoming*. Being is the terminus of an experience of total identity and simplicity.[60]

God differs so radically from his creature that one cannot speak meaningfully about him in positive concepts. Nor is it sufficient to purify these concepts from their finite determinations and then predicate them *per eminentiam,* for concepts themselves are inherently creature-like.[61] The dissimilarity is due not to a lack of creature-like reality on God's part but to the absence of any true reality on the part of the creature. "To see God is to know that

[57] Sermon *Quasi stella matutina*. (All the German sermons have been published in Vol. I of the *Deutsche Werke,* ed. by J. Quint, Stuttgart, 1958. I shall refer to them by the first words of the Latin motto which introduces each sermon.) Tr. by Raymond Bernard Blakney, *Meister Eckhart* (New York: Harper & Brothers, 1957), p. 218. Henceforth I shall refer to this translation as Blakney.

[58] *Quasi stella matutina*, Blakney, p. 219 (corrected).

[59] *In occisione gladii*, Blakney, p. 172.

[60] "In speaking of this experience Eckhart departs often enough from a mere definition of Being. He can, indeed, entirely forget it. He is then no longer in the sphere of Being: he is purely and absolutely in the sphere of 'wonder' (as he himself calls it), in the region of a purely numinous and non-rational valuation. When on these heights he still uses the word 'Esse' and 'collatio esse,' this esse has become in very fact a sheer 'wonder,' which is completely incomprehensible and fantastic to the ontologist and the metaphysician, but quite familiar to the theologian." Rudolf Otto, *Mysticism East and West,* p. 45. Cf. also pp. 34, 36. The expression "non-rational valuation" may be exaggerated, but the emphasis is not.

[61] As Lossky describes it: "We must also cut that thread, renounce the eminence which presupposes the resemblance between effects and cause and reject the similarity in order to ascend to God, attracted by grace, to the total dissimilarity of the First Cause." *Op. cit.,* p. 199.

all creatures are as nothing."[62] This does not mean that the creature is an illusion as the monist would claim, but rather that there is a basic equivocity between God and the specific being of the creature, that is, its existence. "Where the creature ends, there God begins to be."[63]

At the same time, the creature is identical with God, for its true Being *is* God. Eckhart never attempts to harmonize the two opposite aspects, as Thomas does in his doctrine of analogy. He envisions the relation at once as more intimate and more remote. In its essence the creature is identical with God; in its existence it has nothing in common with God. God then is totally immanent in the creature while totally transcending it. Eckhart leaves the dialectical antinomies standing as he experiences them in the religious experience. To analogy he prefers antinomy, as being a more direct expression of the mystical experience.[64] If we speak of analogy in Eckhart it must be to refer simultaneously to two irreducible aspects of the same opposition.[65]

Eckhart has elaborated on this relation of total distinctness and total identity between God and the creature in a famous passage of his commentary on *The Book of Wisdom*. The difference with Thomas is obvious despite the Thomist terminology. Eckhart here gives two series of arguments to show the opposition and the

[62] *Scitote quia prope est,* Blakney, p. 131. Compare also *Omne datum optimum,* Blakney, p. 185, and *Elisabeth impletum est tempus,* Blakney, p. 153.

[63] *In hoc apparuit caritas,* Blakney, p. 127. Rudolf Otto gives the exact distinction: "They (the creatures) must exist somehow in order that this judgment of their non-existence may be cast in their faces. They 'are' not, does not mean that they have no empirical existence, no physical reality. They cannot be non-existent in this empirical sense, for they could not then be 'pure nothing.'" *Mysticism,* p. 111.

[64] Alois Dempf in *Meister Eckhart* (Freiburg, 1960), pp. 98, 101, on the contrary considers Eckhart's theory a beautiful example of the *analogia entis* and of Eckhart's dependence upon St. Thomas. The distinction between an analogical concept of being and a dialectical one was first used by Coreth on Thomas and Hegel, and later applied to a comparison between Thomas and Eckhart by H. Hof in his study *Scintilla Animae* (Lund, 1952).

[65] See Lossky, *op. cit.,* p. 287.

identity between God and the creature. In the first series he proves that they are totally opposed: God's very indistinctness distinguishes him from the distinctness of the creature. The second series shows that God and the creature must be one in the creative act. The argument on distinctness is now reversed: the distinctness of beings does not oppose them to their *Being,* the indistinct creative act on which all distinctness depends.[66]

In his *Commentary on Exodus*[67] Eckhart states the antinomies in an even more formally dialectical way. The thesis states that nothing can be more dissimilar than the finite and the infinite. According to the antithesis, the creature's dependence in Being requires a more intimate resemblance between God and created being than could ever exist between two creatures. In the synthesis Eckhart repeats the argument of the *Wisdom Commentary*. If God is distinct through his indistinctness, he must be dissimilar through his similarity. The more the creature resembles the Creator, the more the gap between them widens, for the plurality of forms which makes the creature resemble its Creator is totally absent from the divine Being. Nevertheless, all created forms display a deep similarity with God in whom they somehow pre-exist without multiplicity.

First we must turn to what for Eckhart is the primary manifestation of God's Being, namely his Oneness. In the *Book of Divine Comfort* Eckhart refers to God as "that pure One which has been purified of multiplicity and division."[68] To reach God the soul must overcome the fragmentation of time and space.[69] The oneness of God is a gradual manifestation in which the soul first sees the creatures in the One, then the One in the creatures and ultimately only the One. Rudolf Otto has described the religious dialectic of the One from predominant presence to negation.

[66] *Archives d'histoire doctrinale et littéraire du Moyen Âge,* Vol. IV, p. 253.
[67] *Lateinische Werke,* II, pp. 103–8.
[68] *Deutsche Werke,* V, Tr. I, Blakney, p. 61.
[69] *Scitote quia prope est,* Blakney, p. 131.

What first began as a mere form of the many appears now as the *real* above the many. Only a step further is necessary for it to appear in contrast and opposition to the many. If it is One it can no longer be many. The many, at first identical with the One, comes into conflict with it, and disappears. Thereby the meaning of unity and of oneness changes. At first, Unity, being one, was a fact in the sense of a (mystical) synthesis or multiplicity, which though not reproducible by any of our rational categories was nevertheless a synthesis. But out of this synthetic unity, out of this one in the sense of united, grows a unity as One and Aloneness. That is, in other words, out of the united comes the One only, out of the All-One the Alone.[70]

I have quoted this text in full because it so clearly indicates the qualities as well as the limitations of Eckhart's mysticism and, for that matter, of all negative theology. No return to multiplicity takes place. Integration occurs only by identifying the many with the One. Although the finite is not eliminated as in monist mysticism, neither is it fully restored as in love mysticism. Yet Eckhart's Oneness is not a static identity. It is a living, ever ongoing process of self-identification in which the One *reveals* itself to itself. Indeed the One (as opposed to Being) becomes the principle of differentiation, of the Trinitarian procession and of the creation. The One *reveals* Being as principle from which all reality proceeds and into which all reality returns. While Being was all purity and admitted no names, the One is all plenitude and permits us to name God. As One, God manifests himself and the Father is the first principle of this manifestation, the self-generation.[71] At times Eckhart opposes the One to the Father.[72] But this apparent inconsistency can be explained by the fact that the One refers to the divine Being *as it is to reveal itself,* while the Father refers to the One as the procession, that is the self-manifestation in the Word, has already started. For

---

[70] Otto, *Mysticism East and West,* pp. 70–71.
[71] See B. Spaapen, *art. cit.,* p. 258. Also Lossky, *op. cit.,* p. 113.
[72] E.g., in a text from the sermon *Intravit Jesus* which will be quoted later.

the entire nature of the Father is to be *to the Son*. Manifestation implies multiplicity. But this multiplicity is *within* God's unity. The Trinity is the *self*-manifestation of God: as such it is not opposed to the One.[73]

The One reveals itself in the Word: this is the Son, in essence totally identical with the Father.

> He is the Father's Word. In this Word, God expresses himself together with all the divine Being, all that God is, as only he can know it. And he knows it as it is, because he is perfect in knowledge and power. Therefore he is also perfect in self-expression. When he utters his Word, he expresses himself and everything else in a second Person, to whom he gives his own nature. He speaks, and all intelligent spirits, re-echoing the Word, repeat his idea, just as rays shining from the sun bear the sun in themselves. So each intelligent spirit is a word in itself; even though it is not like God's Word in all respects, it has received the power to become a likeness of the Word of God, full of grace. And thus the Father has completely expressed his Word, as it really is, with all that is in him.[74]

This remarkable text describes not only the birth of the Son but in him of the entire creation. Unlike the Word the creatures move outside the circle of God's unity. Yet insofar as they are outside the One they are not fully real, and insofar as they possess true Being they exist *in the Word* as the One's self-manifestation. Their Being is their eternal existence in the Word. Their being is created and separated from their true reality.

Eckhart distinguishes two stages in the relation between the Word and the creation. In the first which he bases on the text *In principio erat Verbum,* the Son is not distinct from the Father. He is the omnipotent word through which God calls all things

---

[73] See Raphael Ochslin, "Der Eine und der Dreieinige in den deutschen Predigten" in *Meister Eckhart der Prediger. Festschrift zum Eckhart-Gedenkjahr,* ed. by Udo M. Nix and Raphael Ochslin (Freiburg, 1962), pp. 149–66.

[74] *Intravit Jesus in Templum,* Blakney, pp. 159–60.

into existence. In the second stage, *Verbum erat apud Deum,* the Son is considered distinct from the Father and *as such,* that is, as God's manifestation, he is the exemplar of the entire creation. In the first stage God gives the creature a created *existence* by efficient causality. In the second stage the Word is the prototype of the creature's internal and uncreated *essence.* The true Being of the creature is its essence, its *ens cognitivum.* This Being is timeless and has never left its divine origin. All creatures coexist from all eternity in God and their essence forever remains there. To know a creature, then, is to participate in the Word in which this ideal essence is grounded, and, ultimately, to share in the divine One which the Word itself expresses.[75] This is the deepest meaning of the "intellectualism" that makes Eckhart write: "Where, then, is God in his temple? In intelligence? Yes. Intellect is the temple of God and nowhere does he shine more holy than there."[76] Obviously Eckhart's *intellectus* is not discursive reason; it rather is the overcoming of reason in an intuitive awareness of the one, divine reality, which is infused rather than acquired. Every word expresses implicitly the eternal Word of God, for without its divine exemplarity there could be no speaking at all. At the same time each word is ultimately directed to the absolute silence in which the Word itself has its unspoken origin and its ultimate aim. Human understanding, then, is in the final analysis the presence of God to the soul— eternal, uncreated, and unintelligible.

It is on this ontological unity of the soul with God that Eckhart's mystical doctrine is based.

There is something in the soul so closely akin to God that it is already one with him and need never be united to him . . . If one

[75] By now it must be obvious that Eckhart tags a Neoplatonic meaning to the Thomist term *esse.* The word refers to the ideal, the noetic presence of God rather than to any existential reality. The result remains ambiguous. As Lossky writes: "When he seeks the God *Esse* of St. Thomas in the *abditum mentis* of St. Augustine, Eckhart betrays both theologians by uniting them on a mystical plane and, at the same time, attempting to express this union in terms of speculative theology." (P. 32)
[76] *Quasi stella matutina,* Blakney, p. 220.

were wholly this, he would be both uncreated and unlike any creature.[77]

God's Being is my life, but if it is so, then what is God's must be mine and what is mine God's. God's is-ness is my is-ness, and neither more nor less.[78]

In its *esse primum,* that is, in its essence, the creature is a living idea of God and is identical with him. This essential Being is God himself insofar as he is present to the expression of himself in the Word. The Being of the created universe may be called eternal insofar as *in* God the world can have no temporality.[79] The Father begets the Son in an eternal *now.* That *now* is preserved in the essence of all creatures. The *now* of creation and the *now* of God's self-expression are identical, for the creature is in the Son and the Son in the creature. "It is the real now-moment . . . in which the Father begets his only begotten Son and the soul is reborn in God."[80] The rebirth of the soul consists in its becoming aware of its divine essence. There is no break, then, between creation and grace, for whenever the rebirth of the soul in God occurs "it is the soul giving birth to the only begotten Son."[81] More specifically, when the soul becomes conscious of its own essence, the One expresses itself in the Word. So, to say that the Son is born in me, is to say that I am reborn as the Son.

[77] *Qui audit me,* Blakney, p. 205.
[78] *Justi autem in perpetuum,* Blakney, p. 180. Eckhart waters down these unambiguous expressions in his Defense to the Inquisition. In Chapter IX he interprets them to mean "that all the being of a just man, to the extent that he is just, is from the Being of God—but analogically." Quotations from the *Rechtfertigungsschrift* are taken from Blakney's translation based upon the Latin edition by Augustus Daniels (Münster, 1923), Blakney, p. 295.
[79] The confusion between *essential* and *existential* Being led to John XXII's condemnation of Eckhart's thesis that the world is eternal. Yet Eckhart had clearly distinguished the *esse absolutum* from the *esse formaliter inhaerens creaturae.*
[80] *In diebus suis,* Blakney, p. 214.
[81] *In diebus suis,* Blakney, p. 212.

The Father ceaselessly begets his Son in the soul exactly as he does in eternity and not otherwise. He must do so whether he will or not. The Father ceaselessly begets his Son and, what is more, he begets me as his Son—the selfsame Son. Indeed, I assert that he begets me not only as his Son but as himself and himself as myself, begetting me in his own nature, his own Being. At that inmost source, I spring from the Holy Spirit and there is one life, one Being, one action. All God's works are one and therefore he begets me as he does his Son and without distinction.[82]

The Father expresses himself in the Son in the core of his Being, but "the core of God is also my core, and the core of my soul the core of God's."[83]

One might well wonder whether anything more than an act of cognition is required to lift man above the created world. To some extent, the intellect in Eckhart possesses a self-transcending nature. But by itself the intellect would see only dimly what it sees clearly in mystical knowledge when the divine light "elevates the intellect to what it cannot see naturally." It would be mistaken, then, to consider Eckhart's mysticism one of nature rather than of grace. Yet grace itself is not an "accident" as in Thomistic theology, but rather an essential return to the self's true Being, its *esse primum*. And this return is primarily cognitive. Here again Eckhart would disagree with Thomas.[84]

Eckhart's intellectual interpretation does not mean, however, that the mystical conversion consists in objective knowledge. It demands a continuous negation, on all levels including the intellectual, of created being—a true "decreation."[85] Eckhart presents this transcending of creaturehood as a pursuit of evangelical poverty and humility. But what he has in mind is obviously

---

[82] *Justi autem in perpetuum,* Blakney, p. 181.
[83] *In hoc apparuit,* Blakney, p. 126. In the *Defense* this is weakened down to the following: "Wherever God is the Father and the unbegotten begetter, there is the begotten Son too. Therefore, since God is in me, surely God the Father begets the Son in me." Blakney, p. 267.
[84] Lossky, *op. cit.,* p. 195, note 88.
[85] Eckhart already uses this term which has become known through Simone Weil. See *In diebus suis,* Blakney, p. 214.

more radical. "If one wants to be truly poor, he must be as free from his creature will as when he had not yet been born."[86] His poverty is not merely a privation of possessions or even of self-will, it is a total emptying of the mind. The true mystic will have to give up even the idea of God.

> He shall be quit and empty of all knowledge, so that no knowledge of God exists in him . . . Therefore we say that a man ought to be empty of his own knowledge, as he was when he did not exist, and let God achieve what he will and be as untrammeled by humanness as he was when he came from God.[87]

But even such absolute mental poverty is only a step toward a higher goal: to leave one's created existence altogether. The soul should bring itself to a state where it is no longer a receptacle of God but where God becomes his own receptacle. Eckhart expresses this most forcefully in the sermon on poverty from which I have already quoted.

> If it is the case that a man is emptied of things, creatures, himself and God, and if still God could find a place in him to act, then we say: as long as that place exists, this man is not poor with the most intimate poverty. For God does not intend that man shall have a place reserved for *him* to work in, since true poverty of spirit requires that man shall be emptied of God and all his works, so that if God wants to act in the soul, he himself must be the place in which he acts—and that he would like to do. For if God once found a person as poor as this, he would take the responsibility of his own action and would himself be the *scene* of action, for God is one who acts within himself. It is here, in this poverty, that man regains the eternal being that once he was, now is, and evermore shall be.[88]

When the soul is totally possessed by God, God no longer exists *for it,* but the soul itself becomes a divine presence. Nor does

[86] *Beati pauperes spiritu,* Blakney, p. 228.

[87] *Beati pauperes spiritu,* Blakney, p. 229.

[88] *Beati pauperes spiritu,* Blakney, pp. 230–31.

God live "in" the soul, since the soul is being "lived by" God. The final state of union, then, is one of total Godlessness, for the soul has lost the power to objectivate what it has become.[89]

What is reached, then, at the end of the decreation process is an Absolute which is at the same time the essence of the self. Self-renunciation is more than a means to an end: it is the negative side of the Absolute. To come face to face with the uncreated self is to shed one's creaturehood. Only when the self coincides with the Absolute is the true nature of the soul revealed. The soul discovers its essence in the act in which God knows himself.[90]

Eckhart places no limits on the mystical union: beyond the Trinity, indeed beyond the Oneness of God (insofar as that is still an intelligible principle) the soul is accepted in the Godhead where there are no more distinctions. In a famous passage Eckhart reports his inner voyage from God to the Godhead:

> When I existed in the core, the soil, the river, the source of the Godhead, no one asked me where I was going or what I was doing. There was no one there to ask me, but the moment I emerged, the world of creatures began to shout: "God" . . . Thus creatures speak of God—but why do they not mention the Godhead? Because there is only unity in the Godhead and there is nothing to talk about. God acts. The Godhead does not. It has nothing to do and there is nothing going on in it. It never is on the lookout for something to do. The difference between God and the Godhead is the difference between action and nonaction.[91]

This text eloquently states that the mystic returns to the apophatic Being in which God's self-manifesting movement originated. The inner road of the soul leads to the heart of the Godhead. At the end of that road lies the inmost part of the soul, the little castle, in which the soul is divine and divine without any personal or interpersonal determinations.

[89] Cf. Otto, *Mysticism*, p. 150.
[90] Michel Henry, *L'essence de la manifestation* (Paris, 1963), p. 410.
[91] *Nolite timere*, Blakney, pp. 225–26.

If God is to steal into it [the little castle] it [the adventure] will
cost him all his divine names and personlike properties; he would
have to forgo all these if he is to gain entrance. Except as he is
the onefold One, without ways or properties—neither the Father
nor the Holy Spirit in this [personal] sense, yet something that is
neither this nor that—See!—it is only as he is One and onefold
that he may enter into that One which I have called the Little
Castle of the soul.[92]

The highest knowledge of God is, then, ultimately, a knowledge
"through God"[93] as well as a knowledge through "the highest
power of the soul."[94] In one of his sermons Eckhart says: "The
eye by which I see God is the same as the eye by which God sees
me. My eye and God's are one and the same—one in seeing, one
in knowing, and one in loving."[95] This divine knowledge of the
soul is nondiscursive and nontemporal, "unconscious of yesterday
or the day before, and of tomorrow and the day after, for in
eternity there is no yesterday nor any tomorrow, but only
Now."[96]

Nevertheless, Eckhart considers the symbolic knowledge of God
(he calls it the "cognition of the evening") useful in preparing
the soul for the pure knowledge without images (the "cognition
of the morning"). In the former the creatures are known in
their distinctness, in the latter they are known in God "without
distinction, without representative images and without resemblance
to anything, in the unity which is God himself."[97] One may well
wonder how the world could be an image of God for Eckhart
after his strong declarations of the disparity between God and

---

[92] *Intravit Jesus in quoddam castellum,* Blakney, p. 211.
[93] See *Intravit Jesus in templum,* Blakney, p. 160.
[94] *Elisabeth impletum est tempus,* Blakney, p. 153. See also *Consideravit semitas,* Blakney, p. 161.
[95] *Qui audit me, non confundetur,* Blakney, p. 206. Hegel refers to this text in his *Philosophy of Religion* to support his own position on the presence of the divine Spirit in the human mind. *Vorlesungen über die Philosophie der Religion,* I, p. 257. Commentary in A. Chapelle, *Hegel et la religion,* II, pp. 12–14.
[96] *Elisabeth impletum est,* Blakney, p. 153.
[97] From a text quoted in Michel Henry, *op. cit.,* p. 412.

the creature. Its only function appears to be to start the soul on its inner search, not to provide meaningful images. Yet Eckhart considers it indispensable. "If the soul could have known God without the world, the world would never have been created. The world therefore was made for the soul's sake, so that the soul's eye might be practiced and strengthened to bear the divine light."[98] All negative theology redeems and reintegrates the finite, although not as finite. This last restriction distinguishes it from the mysticism of love. A strong negation of the finite is essential to all forms of mysticism. To be united with the absolute the soul must take its distance from the relative. For that reason the basic thought of all schools of mysticism shows a great affinity with speculative trends of negative theology. Yet the mystical negation itself varies so much that further distinctions are essential. It is the negation which determines whether the relation between the soul and the absolute is one of love or of identity.

4. LOVE MYSTICISM

The title of this section refers only to a specific difference, not to the entire essence of a mystical tradition: there is a great deal more to love mysticism than love. Moreover, it comprehends such heterogeneous groups as Moslem sufis, early Franciscans, Flemish laymen, Spanish saints of the Baroque, and French Jesuits of the seventeenth and eighteenth centuries. Yet to all of them the union with God is a state of love. With the negative theologians they ultimately declare God beyond predication and the soul in need of total abnegation. But they differ on the ultimate status of the finite. They reassert the independence of the finite in a way which allows them to value it for its own sake and to assume an active role in the affairs of the world. Paradoxically they achieve this complex balance by means of a second more radical negation by which they overcome the human viewpoint itself and adopt a divine attitude toward the creation—which is entirely

[98] *Consideravit semitas,* Blakney, p. 161.

positive. According to John of the Cross, the most articulate interpreter of this type of mysticism, first all finite determinations are declared incommensurate to the divine reality. But then, the mystic abandons the right to judge the finite on his own terms. Instead of declaring that the finite does not truly exist as finite, he asserts that it depends even in its finitude upon the infinite. After denying his own determinations in God, he adopts God's own viewpoint with respect to the finite. To George Morel, a French commentator of John of the Cross, the radical negation of the finite is an attempt to grasp the divine as it is itself; it therefore culminates in a divine reaffirmation of the finite.

> Only in this perspective does the apophasis receive its full meaning. Until then the notion of infinity, for instance, appears under the mode of negation and relativity: God is not this or that as the contingent realities are. As long as man attempts to define God from the spatial and the temporal, the very concept of difference still posits a relation.[99]

This second negation has excluded the relational viewpoint itself. God and the creature must not even be compared.

> Although it is true that all creatures have, as theologians say, a certain relation to God, and bear a divine impress . . . yet there is no essential resemblance or connection between them and God.[100]

The creature then may be reaffirmed in its distinctness as God creates it. In himself, beyond the relation of the creature to Him, God is not *opposed* to anything. The sacred now entirely takes over the profane and retains its opposition to it only as a conquered moment within itself.[101] Thus divine transcendence ceases to mean negation of the creature, and instead becomes its eleva-

[99] *Le sens de l'existence d'après S. Jean de la Croix* (Paris, 1960), Vol. II, p. 167.
[100] John of the Cross, *The Ascent of Mount Carmel*, II, 8, 3, tr. by E. Allison Peers (Garden City, N.Y.: Doubleday, 1958). Henceforth I shall refer to this work as *Ascent*.
[101] Morel, *op. cit.*, p. 172.

tion. Transcendence is no longer found *above* creation but *in* creation. The creature is *in* God and God is *in* the creature. It is *as creature* and not only as uncreated essence that the creature manifests transcendence: God is the ultimate dimension of the finite reality, the inaccessible in the accessible. Unlike negative theology, the mysticism of love refuses to consider God's transcendence to the creature as ultimate. In spite of its radical denial of creaturely determinations, negative theology never negates the creaturely standpoint. As a result its religious reassertion of the finite is also weaker. For in spiritual life certainly the rule holds that one possesses as much as one is willing to lose. Only the mystic who has lost the whole world will gain it back. Francis' universal love, Ignatius' efficiency, Teresa of Avila's humanity were made possible only by their renouncement of creaturely desire and even creaturely knowledge. It is precisely this complex and demanding character which makes love mysticism the most human form of mysticism, accessible only to men of heroic religious virtue. To have produced it so abundantly is one of the glories of the Christian faith.

How can the creature first be totally renounced and then continue to survive in God? Rather then answering this question speculatively, mystical writers describe the actual purification of the soul which leads to total negation, and the subsequent reintegration which overcomes it. Yet they are clearly aware of the complexity of the movement. At the end of the first book of the *Ascent of Mount Carmel* in which he deals with the abnegation of the creatures, St. John of the Cross already anticipates their readmission:

> Desire to have pleasure in nothing.
> In order to arrive at possessing everything,
> Desire to possess nothing.
> In order to arrive at being everything,
> Desire to be nothing.
> In order to arrive at knowing everything,
> Desire to know nothing.[102]

[102] *Ascent*, I, 13, 11.

We shall now follow this dialectic from the initial negation to the final union with God and, in God, with all of creation. Traditionally, Christian mysticism has expressed the development in its three stages of purgation, illumination, and union.[103] Yet the three stages are not definitive phases of a rectilinear development in time: they are cyclic occurrences in the rhythmic movement of spiritual life. In Ignatius' *Spiritual Exercises,* for instance, where the division is rather clearly marked,[104] we find illuminative elements in the first week (which is purgative), while the deepest purgation takes place in the third week (which is considered to be mostly illuminative). John of the Cross, on the other hand, presents the entire process of mystical life as a gradual purification of the soul, although he clearly discusses also the other "ways." Only the first of the three nights in the *Ascent of Mount Carmel* and the first part of the *Dark Night of the Soul* correspond to the purgative way in the strict sense. In the second night, which St. John describes as the stage of faith "as dark as night to the understanding,"[105] imagination and understanding are illuminated as well as purified. The third night of "purgative contemplation which causes passively in the soul the negation of itself,"[106] belongs entirely to the unitive state. I basically follow John of the Cross's dialectic of love mysticism in the *Ascent* and the *Dark Night.*

(a) *The Way of Purgation*

St. John describes the first night as "the privation of every kind of pleasure which belongs to the desire."[107] Detachment from desire, not physical asceticism, is what matters. With most

---

[103] The expression first appears in Pseudo-Dionysius, but the idea goes back to the Alexandrian Fathers. See Ernest Larkin, "Ways" in *New Catholic Encyclopedia.*

[104] For a dissenting judgment see Gaston Fessard, *La dialectique des Exercices Spirituelles de Saint Ignace* (Paris, 1956).

[105] *Ascent,* I, 2, 1.

[106] *The Dark Night of the Soul,* tr. by E. Allison Peers (Garden City, N.Y.: Doubleday, 1959), I, Prologue, 1.

[107] *Ascent,* I, 3, 1.

spiritual writers John warns against excessive mortification of the body and insists instead on detachment with respect to the "thoughts and conceptions" of the creatures, and even to the "images of the creatures in memory."[108] Detachment is a universal requirement of spiritual life. Yet it has little appeal to modern man who tends to identify abnegation with a morbid psychic attitude or with a cultural heritage of contempt for the body. The critique of the past may be correct but the idea that a spiritual life can be had without denial is shallow and false. The absolute is by its very nature basically incommensurable to the relative, however much it may be present in it. In order to be initiated into the new life the spiritual candidate must begin by leaving his relative world behind. This process is painful but it should not be conceived exclusively in negative terms.[109] Initially, however, love of God is experienced as incompatible with the desire of the creature.[110] The purgation process empties the soul of a diminished reality in order to allow it to discover its deeper existence. Christian mystics here often quote the words of Paul: "When that which is perfect comes,

[108] *Ascent*, I, 9, 6. The Catholic Church has institutionalized spiritual detachment in the vows through which the religious person abandons the right over his possessions, his body, and his will.

[109] Teilhard de Chardin describes it entirely in positive terms. "For those in whose eyes God has become the supreme reality in the universe, there can logically be no more stable and more profound happiness than to feel this reality painfully taking the place of their own being—insofar as that being has been faithful in shaping and developing itself." Letter to Marguerite Teilhard on November 13, 1918, in *Pierre Teilhard de Chardin—Maurice Blondel Correspondence*, ed. by Henri de Lubac, tr. by William Whitman (New York: Herder and Herder, 1967, p. 118).

[110] Yet the renouncement of the creature in spiritual purgation does not exclude the creature from playing a role in preparing the soul to religious life. George Morel draws attention to the exact words in which John of the Cross phrases his negation: "Since . . . no created things can bear any proportion to the Being of God, it follows that nothing that is imagined in their likeness can serve as *proximate* means to union with him." (*Ascent*, II, 12, 4. Cf. also I, 6, 1.) But, he adds, these images may serve as "remote means" which the soul commonly uses to reach the divine union. (*Ascent*, II, 12, 5.) This preparatory function is, however, as transitory as it is in Pseudo-Dionysius and Eckhart.

then that which is imperfect, and that which is in part are cast away." (I Cor. 13:10) The fourteenth-century *Theologia Germanica* comments:

> For in what measure we put off the creature, in the same measure are we able to receive the Creator; neither more nor less. For if mine eye is to see anything, it must be purified, or become purified from all other things; for if heat and light are to enter, cold and darkness must needs depart; it cannot be otherwise.[111]

The soul must purify itself, then, of the *desire* of the creature, but the motive, spiritual writers insist, must be the union in love.[112] Not pleasure, then, but desire, that is, the self-centered aspect of pleasure, must be renounced. Even the renunciation of desire must not be self-centered as, for instance, the drive to attain a higher state of perfection would be. Nor must the purification aim at the attainment of a future good. Its sole purpose is to express its *present* love of God. This presupposes that the soul has already gone through a spiritual awakening or conversion."[113] To the mystics the renunciation of the self and the creatures is an inevitable expression of love. In his revelation to Catherine of Genoa, Christ says: "To whomsoever understood the least spark of my love all other love would seem false, as in truth it is."[114]

[111] *Theologia Germanica,* tr. by Susanne Winkworth (New York: Pantheon Books, 1949), p. 114.

[112] As John of the Cross expresses it: "Every pleasure if it be not purely for the honor and love of God, must be renounced and completely rejected for the love of Jesus Christ." *Ascent,* I, 13, 4.

[113] Striking cases were those of Paul, Augustine, Pascal. Cf. in Evelyn Underhill's perceptive study, *Mysticism,* Part II, Ch. II, "The Awakening of the Self" (New York: E. P. Dutton, 1961). But mostly it is the outcome of a process that starts with ordinary prayer and gradually blooms open into a habitual state of prayer. On this gradual preparation, see Joseph Maréchal, *Studies in the Psychology of the Mystics,* tr. by Algar Thorold (Albany: Magi Books, 1964), pp. 155–62.

[114] *The Treatise on Purgatory* and *The Dialogue,* tr. by Charlotte Balfour and Helen Douglas-Irvine (New York: Sheed & Ward, 1946), p. 94. Compare this with St. John of the Cross's words: "in order to conquer all the desires and to deny itself the pleasures which it has in everything . . .

Christians have traditionally made the connection between the love of God and the purgation of the soul in the notion of imitation of Christ.[115] St. John's first counsel to attain purity is: "Let him have an habitual desire to imitate Christ in everything that he does, conforming himself to his life."[116] This raises the difficult question what Christ precisely means to the Christian mystic. Comparing such disparate writers as Eckhart, John of the Cross, Ruusbroec, Suso, and Teresa, one feels immediately that there is no single answer. Eckhart surpasses not only the humanity of Christ but even the Trinity in the highest stage of contemplation. Within love mysticism itself there is considerable disagreement. For Teresa the humanity of Christ is the object of unitive contemplation, while for John of the Cross the soul remains alone with God at the end. Nevertheless, all mystics of love have one thing in common: Christ is not merely an ideal of unitive love of God, but he is also the *object* of that love. Moreover, he is model and beloved *at once*. The imitation of Christ is primarily an *act of love*. The Christian attempts to be united with God by adopting the attitude of the man in whom he believes God to be personally present.[117] It is a desire to be united with the divine nature, not a need to follow a model of moral virtue, which inspires him to imitate Christ. Or, in the paradoxical words of Kierkegaard, it is as God that Christ is my model, not as man.[118] Christ is a model only to the extent that one believes in his divinity. To imitate Christ *becomes* a virtue to the Christian mystic even though the matter of imitation be morally neutral. Thus the soul finds in the fact that Christ actually under-

---

(the soul) would need to experience another and a greater enkindling by another and a better love, which is that of its Spouse." *Ascent*, I, 14, 2.
[115] The masters of spiritual life often mention the imitation in the second, illuminative stage (for instance, the second week of Ignatius' *Exercises*). But it belongs just as much to the first.
[116] *Ascent*, I, 13, 3.
[117] This theocentric aspect of the imitation is strongly emphasized by the best spiritual writers. Cf., for instance, the remarkable pages in Jean-Baptiste Saint Jure, *L'homme spirituel* (Paris, 1691), pp. 45–92.
[118] *Papirer*, X² A208. Elsewhere he notes that Christ is more than my model: as God he is primarily my savior. *Papirer*, X¹ A132.

went suffering, a sufficient motive to prefer hardship to pleasure, though one is morally not preferable to the other. To an outsider this looks ethically suspect. Yet, the code of conduct which the mystic follows has nothing in common with an ethics based upon human nature—a *sequere naturam*—but is rather an attempt to break through the boundaries of nature into another dimension. Only the gratuitous, loving imitation can accomplish the purgation which this breakthrough requires. Here, obviously, and not in masochistic perversion, lies the explanation of Francis' delight in pain and of Teresa's prayer to die or to suffer. Similarly in his *Exercises* Ignatius exhorts his followers to embrace the "third degree of humility":

> Whenever the praise and glory of the Divine Majesty would be equally served, in order to imitate and be in reality more like Christ our Lord, I desire and choose poverty with Christ poor, rather than riches; insults with Christ loaded with them, rather than honors; I desire to be accounted as worthless and a fool for Christ, rather than to be esteemed as wise and prudent in this world.[119]

And John of the Cross summarizes the entire purgative attitude in the following rule:

> Strive always to prefer, not that which is easiest, but that which is most difficult;
> Not that which is most delectable, but that which is most unpleasing;
> Not that which gives most pleasure, but rather that which gives least;
> Not that which is restful, but that which is wearisome;
> Not that which is consolation, but rather that which is disconsolateness;
> Not that which is greatest, but that which is least;
> Not that which is loftiest and most precious, but that which is lowest and most despised;

[119] *The Spiritual Exercises*, tr. by Louis Puhl (Westminster, Md.: Newman Press, 1954), p. 69.

Not that which is a desire for anything, but that which is a desire
for nothing;
Strive to go about seeking not the best of temporal things, but the
worst;
Strive thus to desire to enter into complete detachment and emptiness and poverty with respect to everything that is in the world, for
Christ's sake.[120]

Remarkably enough, this drive to convert suffering and contempt
into positive values is found primarily in Christian mysticism. In
spite of the emphasis on abnegation of desire, the Hindu and
Buddhist attitudes toward suffering reflect resignation rather than
preference. Apparently because of his active recognition of and
deep involvement with the created world, the Christian needs
this counterbalance to maintain his upward attitude.

Nevertheless, the active purification, however intensive, remains
essentially insufficient for mystical progress. A *passive* night is
required in which God purges the senses of the many impurities
which no mortification can ever eliminate. One such impurity is
attachment to the pleasure of divine love, which diverts the
soul from the Beloved himself.[121] In the first book of the
Dark Night of the Soul John describes this passive purgation,
"bitter and terrible to sense":

When they are going about these spiritual exercises with the
greatest delight and pleasure, and when they believe that the sun
of divine favor is shining most brightly upon them, God turns all
this light of theirs into darkness, and shuts against them the door
and the source of the sweet spiritual water which they were tasting
in God whensoever and for as long as they desired . . . And
thus he leaves them so completely in the dark that they know not
whither to go with their sensible imagination and meditation.[122]

This passive night is quite distinct from the spiritual aridity resulting from a remaining attachment, in that the soul remains

[120] *Ascent*, I, 13, 6.
[121] *Dark Night*, I, 1, 3.
[122] *Dark Night*, I, 8, 3.

centered upon God without receiving any consolation from the creatures. While the mind is being spiritualized it is no longer able to fulfill its previous tasks and is not yet ready to take on its new functions. The mystics use their strongest expressions for this final purification. Catherine of Genoa's entire treatise on purgatory was modeled after this mystical state of total desolation. John of the Cross also refers to the passive purification as death and purgatory.

(b) *The Way of Illumination*

In the rhythm of spiritual life the purgation of the senses is followed by the perception of a new, transcendent reality. Some consider the overwhelming awareness of divine presence which characterizes this mystical stage as *the* fundamental mystical phenomenon.[123] Yet many who experience the presence of God cannot be called mystics if the term is to preserve any distinctive quality. Moreover, nonreligious mystics also know the feeling of a mysterious presence.

Let us first attempt to distinguish a religious feeling of presence from a nonreligious one. A mystical awareness of presence undoubtedly exists outside the religious sphere, particularly in artistic temperaments.[124] How do we distinguish one from the other? Once more, by the *negative* character of the religious illumination. It was this negativity which inspired John of the Cross to refer to the divine illumination as the *night* of the understanding. The light which the soul receives in faith affects the understanding like darkness, "for it overwhelms greater things and does away with small things, even as the light of the sun overwhelms all other lights whatsoever, so that when it shines and disables our visual faculty they appear not to be light at all."[125] The metaphors of light and darkness which entered the

[123] Maréchal, *Studies in the Psychology of the Mystics*, p. 102.
[124] Evelyn Underhill, *Mysticism*, pp. 234–36. Some of the examples cited in James's *Varieties of Religious Experience* would seem to belong to a cosmic rather than to a religious experience.
[125] *Ascent*, II, 3, 1.

mystical language through Pseudo-Dionysius are omnipresent in the spiritual writings of the West. Julian of Norwich refers to the illumination of faith as "our light in our night."[126] And Tauler emphasizes the darkness of this light "which by its blinding clearness appears dark to human and even to angels' understanding, just as the resplendent orb of the sun appears dark to the weak eye."[127] Divine illumination sheds no light on ordinary matters and even blots out his previous knowledge as ignorance. "Not only does it give no information and knowledge, John of the Cross writes, but . . . it deprives us of all other information and knowledge."[128] The usual ways of understanding have to be suspended, "If the window (of the mind) is in any way stained or misty, the sun's ray will be unable to illumine it and transform it into its own light."[129] One might well call this stage a purgation of the mind (which it is) were it not for the profound transformation which takes place in the cognitive powers.

The illumination may occur on several levels: sense perception, imagination, understanding. What the illumination of the senses involves may be gathered from the various exercises which Ignatius describes as "applications of the senses." Although they are obviously not intended for mystics only,[130] I doubt whether they hold much meaning for a beginner in spiritual life. In the fifth contemplation on the Incarnation and the Nativity after suggesting that one must see the persons and hear their words, Ignatius tells the exercitant "to smell the infinite fragrance and taste the infinite sweetness of the divinity" and "to apply the sense of touch, for example, by embracing and kissing the place

---

[126] *The Revelations of Divine Love of Julian of Norwich*, tr. by James Walsh, S.J. (London: Burns & Oates, 1961), p. 206.

[127] *Signposts to Perfection. A Selection from the Sermons of Johannes Tauler*, ed. and tr. by Elizabeth Strakosch (St. Louis: B. Herder Book Co., 1958), p. 132.

[128] *Ascent*, II, 3, 4.

[129] *Ascent*, II, 5, 6.

[130] He explicitly prescribes the "use of the five senses" for the uneducated. *Exercises*, 18.

where the persons stand or are seated."[131] To the outsider such a simplicity may seem childish; to the spiritual man it is deeply illuminating.

Nevertheless John of the Cross warns against deception in this type of illumination. The initiate is tempted to stay with it, which would prevent him from making further progress.

Things that are experienced by the senses derogate from faith, since faith as we have said transcends every sense. And thus the soul withdraws itself from the means of union with God when it closes not its eyes to all these things of sense. Secondly, if they be not rejected, they are a hindrance to the spirit, for the soul rests in them and its spirit soars not to the invisible.[132]

John is equally apprehensive of the imagination. Eventually all images must be discarded, for they fulfill no function in the final state of union. However, images are indispensable to the beginner and John himself warns against prematurely abandoning the exercise of "meditation" (which he defines as "a discursive action wrought by means of images").[133] Until the soul is ready for the prayer of quiet in which all discursive acts are replaced by a total awareness of God's presence, the "imaginary" presence to the object of the meditation is necessary.[134]

The words "night" and "darkness'" apply particularly to the illumination of the understanding. For here the mind becomes fully aware of the inadequacy of its own powers.

In this active night of the mind (more than in the senses or the imagination) the person may have the vehement and more or less

---

[131] *Exercises*, 124, 125. Perhaps even more advanced is the contemplation on hell which seems to have originated out of a passively purified sensibility.
[132] *Ascent*, II, 11, 7.
[133] *Ascent*, II, 12, 3.
[134] *Ascent*, II, 13, 4. A beautiful example is the *Meditationes Vitae Christi*, formerly attributed to St. Bonaventure. In the *Spiritual Exercises*, Ignatius advises the soul at Jesus' nativity to become "a poor little unworthy slave and as though present look upon them (the persons in the mystery), contemplate them and serve them in their needs with all possible homage and reverence." Second week, second contemplation.

lasting impression of falling into a void. Representations seem to recede more and more toward the horizon until they merge with nothing. Thought without apparent support may lapse into anxiety or dizziness according to the mystics. Then arrives the critical moment in which one is tempted to believe that the finite is only the finite, that the movement toward the Absolute is no more than the expression of a dream.[135]

This moment of self-negation is the turning point toward the *passive* illumination which John of the Cross calls "pure and dark contemplation."[136] The chapters of the *Dark Night of the Soul* dealing with this high form of contemplation contain the most sublime descriptions of the pain of being purified which is at the same time the joy of being illuminated.

Yet the "dark contemplation" is preceded by other passively infused and incontrollable cognitive states to which John of the Cross refers as visions, revelations, voices, and spiritual feelings.[137] We shall only consider the first three and call them all visions. Their passive character provides no direct evidence of their divine origin, even to the mystic.[138] In his remarkable *Studies in the Psychology of the Mystics* Joseph Maréchal calls numerous visions of the imagination "pseudo-hallucinatory or even completely hallucinatory."[139] But if a hallucination consists in a perception which is not occasioned by the corresponding sense stimulus, all "visions" may be regarded as hallucinatory. The visionary sees or hears what others, in the same physical environment, do not see or hear. From a perceptional point of view such visions are deceptive in the sense that the subject considers to receive under ordinary physical conditions

[135] George Morel, *Le sens de l'existence d'après St. Jean de la Croix*, II, p. 92.
[136] *Dark Night*, II, 3, 3.
[137] *Ascent*, II, 10, 4.
[138] John cautions against them: "Even as the five outward senses represent the images and species of these objects to the inward senses, even so, supernaturally, as we say, without using the outward senses, both God and the devil can represent the same images and species, and much more beautiful and perfect ones." (*Ascent*, II, 16, 3)
[139] *Studies*, p. 169.

what has in fact an entirely different origin. Nonhallucinatory are only those visions in which the subject remains aware throughout of the nonsensitive origin of his images.

Yet the question of the psychological status of mystical visions must be clearly distinguished from that of their religious truth or falsity. A hallucinatory vision may well be religiously authentic and thereby differ essentially from a nonreligious hallucination. If the latter takes on religious appearances (as often happens with schizophrenics) it still remains a religious illusion. The case becomes particularly complex in those noncontextual, semihallucinatory experiences in which the subject suddenly becomes aware of a mysterious presence. Are they religious or nonreligious? What appears to be the same feeling has been interpreted in either sense.[140] I suspect that in such a case only the subsequent interpretation of the subject determines an essentially ambiguous and indeterminate experience. However, this is not to say that the experience of presence is always neutral or, even less, that it is always an illusion. A mystical experience of presence which occurs *within* a definite religious context and after a certain religious preparation, may be hallucinatory, but it is religious.

The feeling of presence permeates the entire mystical life and can be authentically religious on each level of consciousness. It is commonly assumed that, since the physical sense of presence depends upon actual sensations, such sensations are a *conditio sine qua non* for the awareness of presence. But, as Maréchal has proven, the experience of presence does not *intrinsically* depend upon those sensations. It is a primary experience depending upon conditions that are *normally* fulfilled by sense perception. But if those conditions could be fulfilled in a different way, such as a direct impact upon the imagination or an intellectual intuition, the ordinary stimuli of perception could be dispensed with.

[140] An interesting example of the complexity may be found in a description by the Danish writer Johannes Anker-Larsen who compares his sudden experience of a strange presence to that of a child that is taken by the hand in the dark. Cf. *The Protestant Mystics,* ed. by W. H. Auden and Anne Freemantle (New York: 1966), p. 310.

Religious experiences of presence accompanied by actual visions (in the larger sense of the term) of sense or imagination may be "hallucinatory," but they are not pathological "deviations" of perception. For they may not be perceptions at all. Primary is the sense of presence; the perception plays a subordinate, conditional role.

Of course, this still leaves open the problem of the content of those visions. Even if they have a transcendent origin, some immanent source must provide the *material* for the supernatural message. William James faced this problem long ago and suggested as a possible source "the abode of everything that is latent and the reservoir of everything that passes unrecorded or unobserved."[141] Thus inactive memories, hidden passions, and all the subconscious elements which become active in dreams would provide the images and symbols of mystical visions. A similar theory was developed, without James's methodological moderation, by H. Delacroix.[142] Delacroix explains the entire experience, including its appearance of "coming from without," by subconscious forces. James holds his interpretation within the limits of the psychic mechanism, without engaging in causal explanations. Unfortunately, James's theory of the subconscious is insufficiently developed. Jung's theory of archetypes, despite its airiness of argumentation, is the only attempt to explain the birth of religious symbols out of the structure of the subconscious.[143] Yet, images and symbols are not mystical visions: they merely provide the material out of which visions are made. But they remain indeterminate until the mystical presence informs them into a specific religious meaning.

141 *The Varieties of Religious Experience,* p. 375.
142 *Études sur l'histoire et la psychologie des grands mystiques chrétiens* (Paris, 1908).
143 A theory of mystical symbols was already initiated in Récéjac's *Essai sur les fondements de la connaissance mystique* (Paris, 1896), according to which symbols are constantly being formed and abandoned in the will's ascent to the absolute. The problem with this theory is that it restricts the symbolization process to the conscious level while the fundamental formation of symbols takes place in the subconscious.

At the same time imaginary and sensory visions have a physical distinctness of their own which hides as much as it reveals, the transcendent presence. A considerable hermeneutic problem originates when the mystic starts interpreting what was only a sign of the invisible. Mystics of the past have been aware of the problem and recommend extreme caution. According to John of the Cross "the language of God" is so far removed from human understanding that we can never be sure of the meaning of private prophecy and revelation.[144] The difficulty concerns not so much the status of visions while they are actually being experienced (although here also plenty of illusions are possible), but their subsequent translation into ordinary discourse. In such a verbal articulation the mind actively intervenes and severs the ties by which a vision was held in a total religious situation. To support the "truth" of a vision it is not sufficient to refer to the original experience, for truth is in discourse, not in the experience itself. Since ordinary discourse cannot be adapted to the unique visionary experience, the translation process will almost inevitably distort the original meaning. Of course, this difficulty affects all language about mystical experiences. But trustworthiness becomes a unique problem when the sensible nature of the vision precludes any direct conformity with its transcendent referent. This is the reason why the masters of spiritual life are more cautious with visions than with other mystical experiences.[145] The outsider, on the contrary, is all too often inclined to identify mystical illumination with hallucinatory visions or, worse, with the physiological phenomena which accompany them. Visions are imperfect stages of mystical illumination, the main function of which is to carry the soul from the active into the passive.

Entirely different is the passive illumination to which John of the Cross refers as "dark contemplation" and which lacks the distinct physical features of visions. Here we notice two characteristics: a negative simplicity and, what Spanish mystics have called, an intellectual quality. The term "intellectual" refers to

[144] *Ascent*, II, 19, 1 and 10.
[145] St. John of the Cross considers them only a remote means of union. Cf. *Ascent*, II, 24, 8.

the absence of sensory elements, not to any form of active comprehension. Tauler's description of the highest contemplation brings out both these characteristics:

> It is the mysterious darkness wherein is concealed the limitless Good. To such an extent are we admitted and absorbed into something that is one, simple, divine, illimitable, that we seem no longer distinguishable from it . . . This obscurity is a light to which no created intelligence can arrive by its own nature.[146]

Yet the most articulate analysis of the highest state of contemplation is to be found in Chapters IV–VIII of the second book of *The Dark Night of the Soul*. John of the Cross refers to it as "an inflowing of God into the soul."[147] The mind reaches a height of awareness in which the normal powers of cognition are no longer operative.[148] The term "night" is appropriate, not only because this illumination means utter darkness for the active powers of the mind, but also because it is affliction and torment. The pain results from "the direct assault of the divine Light" upon the soul. In this light, which both blinds and burns, the soul faces its innate impurity and basic incompatibility with God. At the same time it is being consumed "in a cruel, spiritual death, even as if it had been swallowed by a beast and felt itself being devoured in the darkness of its belly."[149]

It is in the darkness and emptiness of this passive contemplation that the highest illumination takes place. St. John of the Cross gives us some idea of this experience in a passage of the *Ascent* where he deals with "visions of spiritual substances" which cannot be seen clearly in this life but which "can be felt in the

---

146 *Signposts to Perfection, A Selection from the Sermons of Johann Tauler,* tr. by Elizabeth Strakosch, p. 132. Both the state described and the images of this description remind us of Pseudo-Dionysius' "ray of divine darkness."
147 *Dark Night,* II, 5, 1.
148 See St. John of the Cross's laborious attempts to explain this passive activity of the mind Thomistically as direct cognition by the passive intellect without any cooperation of the agent intellect, in *Cantico,* 38, 9.
149 *Dark Night,* II, 6, 1. John further compares this state to the pains of hell (II, 6, 2) and of purgatory (II, 12, 1 and II, 7, 7).

substance of the soul."[150] Spiritual writers often refer to this by the paradoxical name of "intellectual visions." A clear instance of such a "vision" is the illumination which Ignatius received near Manresa and which he described in his spiritual biography:

> As he sat there the eyes of his understanding began to open. Without having any vision he understood—knew—many matters both spiritual and pertaining to the realm of letters and that with such clearness that they seemed utterly new to him. There is no possibility of setting out in detail everything he then understood. The most that he can say is that he was given so great an enlightening of his mind that, if one were to put together all the helps he has received from God and all the things he has ever learned, they would not be the equal of what he received in that single illumination. He was left with his understanding so enlightened that he seemed to be another man with another mind than the one that was his before.[151]

The so-called "intellectual vision" here turns out to be neither vision nor intellectual. St. John of the Cross calls it the knowledge of naked truths.[152]

It no longer relates to "particular matters," but directly pertains to the union between the soul and God.[153] The illumination takes place in the "substance" of the mind, rather than in any of its specific functions. Tauler describes it in his First Sermon of the Second Sunday after Epiphany: "The spirit is transported high above all the faculties into a void of immense

---

[150] *Ascent*, II, 24, 4.

[151] *Acta Patris Ignatii Scripta a P. Ludovico Gonzalez da Camara*, in *Fontes Narrativi de S. Ignatio de Loyola*, Vol. I, Rome, 1943, pp. 404–5. Tr. by Elmer O'Brien in *Varieties of Mystical Experience*, pp. 246–47.

[152] "This kind of vision or, *to speak more properly, of knowledge of naked truths, . . .* is not like seeing bodily things with the understanding; it consists rather in comprehending and seeing with the understanding the truths of God, whether of things that are, that have been or that will be." (*Ascent*, II, 26, 2. Italics mine.)

[153] *Ascent*, II, 26, 5. Cf. Fr. Gabriel de Ste. Marie Madeline, "Le problème de la contemplation unitive" in *Ephemerides Carmeliticae*, I (1947), 13.

solitude whereof no mortal can speak."[154] Mystics in this state
are able to continue their normal activities and even to increase
them because of a greater power of concentration. What Elmer
O'Brien writes about St. Ignatius applies to a number of other
mystics.

> Unlike the majority of mystics, who when they have the experience
> of God are so invaded that they can experience nothing else,
> Ignatius was able to carry out the most absorbing and distracting
> occupations. He could do so because the experience was limited
> to the substance of his being. There was no ligature of the
> faculties.[155]

The term "intellectual" is not entirely appropriate for a unified
experience which is no more "knowing" than "loving," and which,
as the fourteenth-century English mystic Walter Hilton wrote, consists in "the enlightening of the understanding joined to the joys
of his love."[156] Clearly the "intellectual vision" is the purest
form of the religious experience as such in which the mind
concentrates entirely on the single awareness of its own unity.
To speak of infused knowledge is misleading, for there is no
evidence that mystics in this state know *more* than before. They
use the word knowledge often enough and some have even
maintained that they learned more in one moment of illumination
than in an entire lifetime. Yet those words refer not to an
increase in the ability of comprehension but to a new *dimension*
of consciousness in which what they knew previously, takes on a
different meaning. From the constant usage of such terms as
"indeterminate knowledge" and "night" we may safely conclude
that no new ideas are being infused. Rather does the total
transformation of consciousness have unique repercussions upon

[154] *Signposts to Perfection.*
[155] *The Varieties of Mystical Experience*, p. 253.
[156] *The Ladder of Perfection, Scala Perfectionis*, Bk. I, Ch. 9, tr. by Leo
Sherley-Price (London: Penguin Books, 1957) p. 8. John of the Cross also
writes that the highest vision can neither be seen nor understood but only
"felt in the substance of the soul, with the sweetest touches and unions, all
of which belong to spiritual feelings." *Ascent*, II, 24, 4.

the cognitive power of the mind. With Maritain we might name this "practical knowledge," that is, a connaturality of the mind with that which is directly present to it.[157]

Still the term "intellectual" is not altogether gratuitous. For aside from its nonsensuous character the highest mystical illumination possesses a permanence comparable to that of an intellectual insight, which is absent from the transitory visions of the imagination. This must not be understood as if the flow of divine light were always even. But the intermittent intensive illuminations do not entirely disappear in the subsequent period as imaginary visions do. They are retained in some sort of habitual state of enlightenment, compared by St. Teresa to the awareness of a person's presence which continues after the shutters of a bright room have been closed. In her own case Teresa testifies that "however numerous were her trials and business worries, the essential part of her soul seemed never to move from that dwelling-place."[158] And in the *Relations:* "I seem to have always present the intellectual vision of the three divine persons and of the humanity of Christ."[159]

Yet no new "knowledge" is infused. The descriptions of intellectual visions are even less articulate than those of the visions of the imagination. The reader recalls Ignatius' illumination near Manresa. In another entry of his diary the same saint notes a "vision" of the Trinity:

During the Mass, I knew, I sensed or saw—God only knows—that in speaking to the Father, in seeing that He was a Person of the most Holy Trinity, I was moved to love the Trinity entirely, the more so because the other Persons were in It entirely.[160]

[157] Jacques Maritain, *The Degrees of Knowledge,* tr. by Gerald Phelan, p. 449; cf. also 338–39.
[158] *Castillo Interior o las Moradas,* in *Obras de Santa Teresa de Jesús,* ed. by P. Silverio de Santa Teresa, Vol. 4, Burgos, 1917, p. 190. *Inner Castle,* The Seventh Mansions, Ch. I, p. 211.
[159] *Relacion,* VI, in *Obras de Santa Teresa de Jesús,* Vol. 2, p. 40.
[160] *Ephemeris S.P. Ignatii,* in *Monumenta Historica Societatis Jesu,* Vol. 63, Rome, 1934, pp. 102–3. The entire section from February through March 1544 (pp. 86–132) is full of similar descriptions of visions.

No one will learn much trinitarian theology from this "insight." The intellectual vision seems to consist primarily in an increased awareness of God's presence: the soul perceives both itself and all other creatures as existing in God. The more sensorious visions serve a preparatory function by presentifying God to those faculties of which the mind is most conscious in the feeling of presence. In the "intellectual" intuition the mind directly knows its being in God.

Nevertheless certain mystics have unquestionably used the mystical illumination as a source of knowledge. To some extent the intellectual vision invites a gnostic exploration insofar as it is not only of God but also of the entire creation including, as John of the Cross would say, of "corporeal substances." One spiritual writer who one-sidedly emphasized the illumination aspect of the mystical state was Jacob Boehme. With him the awareness common to all mystics turned into a conceptual, rationalized system of the entire creation. Yet seldom does mystical insight become philosophy as it did in the case of a few theosophic writers. This is fortunate enough, for spiritual gifts are no guarantee of dialectical power or, for that matter, of theological accuracy. When Jacob Boehme writes about the *Mysterium Magnum* of his illumination that it is "nothing else than the hiddenness of the Deity together with the Being of all beings, from which one mysterium proceeds after another, and each mysterium is the mirror and model of the other,"[161] he expresses a genuine mystical insight. But once he starts interpreting this union of God and creation in philosophical concepts, experience stops and theology begins. Most mystics tend to look with suspicion upon this sort of systematic interpretation, because it takes the cognitive element out of its context in order to give it an independent function. For them the mystical experience is primarily one of union and, if the mystic believes in a personal God, frequently of love.

[161] *Sex Puncta Mystica*, tr. by John Rolleston Earle in *Six Theosophic Points* (Ann Arbor: The University of Michigan Press, 1958), p. 136.

(c) *The Union with God*

The structure of the three "ways" proved somewhat inadequate with respect to purgation which continues through all three stages. We now may add that the distinction between illumination and union is equally vague. Mystical illumination is only the awareness of mystical union. This is particularly the case for "intellectual" visions. The reason why John of the Cross advised the spiritual candidate not to adopt the same negative attitude toward those visions as toward the imaginary ones is that "they are a part of the union towards which we are leading the soul."[162] But particularly St. Teresa of Ávila emphasizes that intellectual visions belong to the unitive state. In the *Interior Castle* she describes the light of the mystical union as "an intellectual vision in which by a representation of the truth in a particular way, the Most Holy Trinity reveals itself, in all three Persons."[163] Teresa distinguishes those visions of the permanent union of spiritual marriage from the imaginary ones in that they take place in the substance of the soul without affecting the normal function of the faculties:

There is the greatest difference between all the other visions we have mentioned and those belonging to this Mansion . . . for this secret union takes place in the deepest center of the soul, which must be where God himself dwells, and I do not think there is any need of a door by which to enter it. I say there is no need of a door because all that has so far been described seems to have come through the medium of the senses and faculties . . . But what passes in the union of the Spiritual Marriage is very different. The Lord appears in the center of the soul, not through an imaginary but through an intellectual vision.[164]

[162] *Ascent*, II, 26, 10.
[163] *Castillo Interior*, in *Obras*, Vol. 4, p. 182; *Interior Castle*, The Seventh Mansions, Ch. I, p. 209.
[164] *Ibidem*, p. 186; *Interior Castle*, The Seventh Mansions, Ch. II, p. 213.

The mystical union completes that integration which I described in the first chapter as the ultimate aim of all religious experience. In it the self is lifted out of its lonely isolation and renews the primeval oneness in which all reality was in harmony with itself. It thus overcomes the fundamental "alienation" of existence: to be separated from the rest of creation. The oneness does not abolish the creaturely differences. But in and through the variety the mystic perceives the same glowing, all-pervading presence of God, the inner reality which invites all creatures to enter confidently into each other's intimacy. All beings are one again, as we always knew they were, and God is with us everywhere. No part of the creation remains strange when all express that God is the Being of all that is. Contingency no longer means detachment and otherness implies no more absence. All being is consecrated through the divine presence. The mystic sees "how God dwells in all creatures" and "how God works and labors in all creatures."[165] At that moment man's ultimate dream is being fulfilled and the words of the poet become true:

> And all shall be well and
> All manner of thing shall be well
> When the tongues of flame are in-folded
> Into the crowned knot of fire
> And the fire and the rose are one.[166]

[165] Ignatius, "Contemplation to Attain the Love of God" in *Spiritual Exercises.*
[166] T. S. Eliot, *Four Quartets.*

Index